MARCHING
WITH
THE TIGERS

MARCHING
WITH
THE TIGERS

The History of
THE ROYAL LEICESTERSHIRE REGIMENT
1955–1975

MICHAEL GOLDSCHMIDT

Pen & Sword
MILITARY

First published in Great Britain in 2009 by
PEN & SWORD MILITARY
an imprint of
Pen & Sword Books Limited
47 Church Street
Barnsley
South Yorkshire
S70 2AS

ISBN 978 1 84884 035 5

A CIP catalogue record for this book
is available from the British Library

Typeset in Sabon by S L Menzies-Earl

Printed and bound in England
by CPI

Pen & Sword Books Ltd incorporates the imprints of
Pen & Sword Aviation, Pen & Sword Maritime,
Pen & Sword Military,Wharncliffe Local History, Pen & Sword Select,
Pen & Sword Military Classics and Leo Cooper.

For a complete list of Pen & Sword titles please contact:
PEN & SWORD BOOKS LIMITED
47 Church Street, Barnsley, South Yorkshire, S70 2AS, England.
E-mail: enquiries@pen-and-sword.co.uk
Website: www.pen-and-sword.co.uk

Contents

Maps

Foreword

Many of us may have thought that Brigadier W E Underhill's history of The Royal Leicestershire Regiment, which covered the period 1928 to 1956, would be the concluding volume. At that latter date, The Royal Leicestershire Regiment consisted of a regular 1st Battalion on active service in Cyprus, a Regimental Depot at Glen Parva and two territorial units, the 5th Battalion (TA) and Q/438 (The Royal Leicestershire Regiment) LAA Battery RA (TA), in Leicester. It was very much the County's Regiment with a strong feeling of 'family' about it. In the event, the Regiment's life continued significantly after 1956.

Colonel Michael Goldschmidt now recounts the history of the final operations, activities and achievements of the Regiment's units. I am most grateful to him for writing this book on the Regiment's behalf. He also records The Royal Leicestershire Regiment's absorption into The Royal Anglian Regiment, itself created by the amalgamation of the county regiments of East Anglia and the East Midlands.

Despite the organizational changes, members of The Royal Leicestershire Regiment continued the traditions and example of their predecessors, serving in their different roles at home and abroad with admirable loyalty, skill and devotion. They integrated with dignity into The Royal Anglian Regiment. This, the final chapter of our Regiment's long history, is one of which its members can be proud.

I would also like to thank the many friends of the Regiment who have generously sponsored the publication of this book.

Now, with the new Regimental Museum, the Regimental Chapel and Royal Tigers' Wood, this History book stands as a lasting testimony to The Royal Leicestershire Regiment.

A J G Pollard
Major General
President, The Royal Tigers' Association
Leicester, November 2008

Sponsors
The following organizations and individuals sponsored the publication of *Marching with The Tigers*:

Captain R J Allen
Alliance and Leicester plc
Anonymous donor
Chetwode Samworth Charitable Trust
The family of Brigadier Alan Cowan
David Laing Foundation

Draper Property Ltd
Garfield Weston Foundation
J Hadfield Esq.
R C M D Heggs Esq.
Maud Elkington Charitable Trust
J H M Pinder Esq.

Preface

A Regiment, great in history, bears, so far, a resemblance
to the Immortal Gods, as to be old in power and glory
– yet to have always the freshness of youth.

A W Kingslake

Having written this History, I recognize that The Royal Leicesters were not a 'run of the mill' Line Regiment. I have sought to portray 'ordinary men doing extraordinary things in extraordinary places extraordinarily well', a sentiment which tracks well with the theme of the Museum in Leicester where the Regiment's heritage is graphically displayed.

Much of what I have documented relates to events between fifty and thirty years ago; memories fade and key documents are not easily found. The main sources used have been Regimental Digests and War Diaries, newspaper reports, citations, and *The Green Tiger* and *Castle* journals. I have also been greatly assisted by those who have recorded earlier deeds of the Regiment and into whose books I have regularly delved, notably Brigadier W E Underhill's *The Royal Leicestershire Regiment – A History of the Years 1928 to 1956* (1958), Colonel H C Wylly's *History of the 1st and 2nd Battalions The Leicestershire Regiment in the Great War* (1928), and Lieutenant Colonel E A H Webb's *A History of the Services of The 17th (The Leicestershire) Regiment 1688-1912* (revised 1912).

Several authors have generously let me use information from their books, especially Michael Barthrop's history of The Royal Anglian Regiment 1964-74, *Crater to the Creggan* (1976), Michael Dewar's *Brush Fire Wars* (1990), Matthew Richardson's *The Tigers* (2000) and *Fighting Tigers* (2002), and Derek Easton's *A Tiger and a Fusilier* (2001). Details from these books have informed my narrative.

The following officers have given of their time to proofread specific chapters: Bob Allen, David Carter, Bill Dawson, Christopher Keeble, Tony Pollard, Richard Robinson, Martin Romilly, Geoffrey Simpson, Anthony Swallow, Richard Wilkes and Paul Young. A number of them and others have carried out research for me on various topics. Terry Holloway lent me his notebooks and maps from his time as a company commander in Borneo and as Battalion 2IC in Aden, and some files from his time as Commanding Officer. Tony Cowan has done some important research about his father's time in command and I was given access to transcripts of Alan Cowan's autobiographical audiotapes. The staff at RHQ The Royal Anglian Regiment and at the HQ at Leicester (which holds much of The Royal Leicesters' Regimental records) have been very responsive to my requests and inquiries; again Anthony Swallow's knowledge and help has been invaluable. The RHQs of The Princess of Wales's Royal Regiment, The Royal Regiment of Fusiliers and The Sherwood Foresters have likewise assisted.

Various museums and other offices have been immensely helpful. I thank the staff of the libraries of the National Army Museum, the Joint Services Command & Staff College at the Defence Academy and the Scottish Rugby Union; The National Archives, Leicester Museums and Galleries (for their coloured photography) and the Dean and Chapter of Leicester Cathedral; and the Regimental Museums of The Royal Anglian Regiment at Duxford, The Royal Corps of Signals at Blandford, The Lancashire Fusiliers at Bury and The Manchester Regiment; the Services Personnel & Veterans Agency, the Historical Disclosures section of the Army Personnel Centre; and the *Leicester Mercury*.

The assistance given by Robin Jenkins and his staff at the Record Office for Leicestershire, Leicester & Rutland, and the work of Suzannah Angelo-Sparling (who produced the coloured photographs of the capbadges and the button) and of Dr Robin Thomas, the regimental medallist, have been invaluable. Many people have responded to the hundreds of emails and many letters I have sent, requesting information and photographs. They have provided data, photographs and maps, and I am grateful for their input, interest and encouragement. Many of their contributions appear as anecdotes in the narrative, as pictures or in the maps.

At the outset I was asked by the President of The Royal Tigers' Association to 'include in this final volume any part of the History of the Regiment that previous volumes have omitted'. I have endeavoured to do this, putting in the appendices much information which I do not believe has been published in this form before. At Appendix A I have listed the Honours and Awards earned by members of the Regiment both during and – perhaps unusually for a Regimental History – after their military service. This is because those who served in the Regiment underwent grounding, not just for their military career but for their wider contribution to the public good. That recognition of all their accolades merits being recorded in this History.

I would like to thank Pen & Sword for their encouragement, help and guidance and for the maps, and finally and most especially my wife Margaret, who has helped edit this book and provided so much patience and wise counsel throughout.

M K G

Battle Honours

Those emblazoned on the Queen's Colour are shown in bold.

Namur, 1695 – Louisburg – **Martinique, 1762** – Havannah – **Ghuznee, 1839** – Khelat – **Afghanistan, 1839** – Sevastopol – Ali Masjid – **Afghanistan, 1878-79** – **Defence of Ladysmith** – **South Africa, 1899-1902** – Maryang-San – **Korea 1951-52**.

Those emblazoned on the Regimental Colour are shown in bold.

Aisne, 1914, '18 – La Bassée, 1914 – Armentières, 1914 – Festubert 1914, '15 – **Neuve Chapelle** – Aubers – Hooge, 1915 – **Somme, 1916, '18** – Bazentin – Flers-Courcelette – Morval – Le Transloy – **Ypres, 1917** – Polygon Wood – **Cambrai, 1917, '18** – St Quentin – Lys – Bailleul – Kemmel – Scherpenberg – Albert, 1918 – Bapaume, 1918 – Hindenburg Line – Epehy – **St Quentin Canal** – Beaurevoir – Selle – Sambre – **France and Flanders, 1914-18** – Megiddo – Sharon – Damascus – **Palestine, 1918** – Tigris, 1916 – Kut-el-Amara, 1917 – Baghdad – **Mesopotamia, 1915-18**.

Norway, 1940 – Antwerp-Turnhout Canal – **Scheldt** – Zetten – **North-West Europe, 1944-45** – Jebel Mazar – Syria, 1941 – **Sidi Barrani** – Tobruk, 1941 – Montaigne Farm – **North Africa, 1940-41, '43** – **Salerno** – Calabritto – **Gothic Line** – Monte Gridolfo – Monte Colombo – **Italy, 1943-45** – **Crete** – Heraklion – Kampar – **Malaya, 1941-42** – **Chindits, 1944**.

Family Tree of Leicestershire's Infantry – 1935–2008

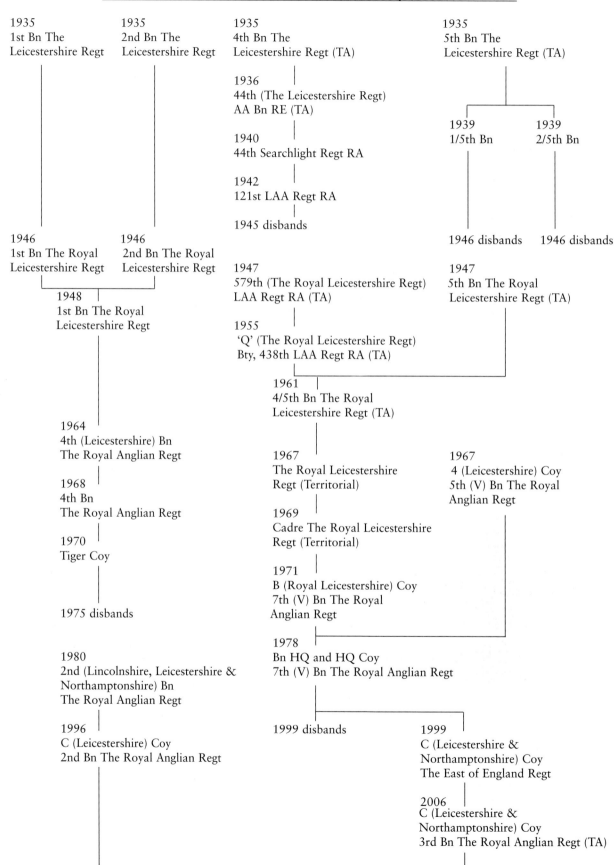

1935
1st Bn The
Leicestershire Regt

1935
2nd Bn The
Leicestershire Regt

1935
4th Bn The
Leicestershire Regt (TA)

1935
5th Bn The
Leicestershire Regt (TA)

1936
44th (The Leicestershire Regt)
AA Bn RE (TA)

1940
44th Searchlight Regt RA

1942
121st LAA Regt RA

1945 disbands

1939
1/5th Bn

1939
2/5th Bn

1946 disbands

1946 disbands

1946
1st Bn The Royal
Leicestershire Regt

1946
2nd Bn The Royal
Leicestershire Regt

1947
579th (The Royal Leicestershire Regt)
LAA Regt RA (TA)

1947
5th Bn The Royal
Leicestershire Regt (TA)

1948
1st Bn The Royal
Leicestershire Regt

1955
'Q' (The Royal Leicestershire Regt)
Bty, 438th LAA Regt RA (TA)

1961
4/5th Bn The Royal
Leicestershire Regt (TA)

1964
4th (Leicestershire) Bn
The Royal Anglian Regt

1967
The Royal Leicestershire
Regt (Territorial)

1967
4 (Leicestershire) Coy
5th (V) Bn The Royal
Anglian Regt

1968
4th Bn
The Royal Anglian Regt

1969
Cadre The Royal Leicestershire
Regt (Territorial)

1970
Tiger Coy

1971
B (Royal Leicestershire) Coy
7th (V) Bn The Royal
Anglian Regt

1975 disbands

1978
Bn HQ and HQ Coy
7th (V) Bn The Royal Anglian Regt

1980
2nd (Lincolnshire, Leicestershire &
Northamptonshire) Bn
The Royal Anglian Regt

1999 disbands

1999
C (Leicestershire &
Northamptonshire) Coy
The East of England Regt

1996
C (Leicestershire) Coy
2nd Bn The Royal Anglian Regt

2006
C (Leicestershire &
Northamptonshire) Coy
3rd Bn The Royal Anglian Regt (TA)

Colonels-in-Chief and Colonels during the years covered by this volume of the History

HM Queen Elizabeth The Queen Mother
Colonel-in-Chief The Royal Anglian Regiment, 1964-2002.
Trustees R Anglian Regt

HRH The Duchess of Gloucester
Deputy Colonel-in-Chief, 1964-2002.
D R C Carter

Lieutenant General Sir Colin Callander KCB KBE MC
Colonel The Royal Leicestershire Regiment, 1954-63.
Trustees R Leicestershire Regt

Major General Sir Douglas Kendrew KCMG CB CBE DSO
Colonel The Royal Leicestershire Regiment, 1963-64
Deputy Colonel The Royal Anglian Regiment, 1964-65.
Mrs R F Abel Smith

Major General J M K Spurling CB CBE DSO
Deputy Colonel The Royal Anglian Regiment (Leicestershire and Rutland), 1965-71.
Mrs A E F Cowan

Colonel M St G Pallot
Deputy Colonel The Royal Anglian Regiment (Leicestershire and Rutland), 1971-77.
D M Pallot

Chapter 1

1st Battalion: Cyprus
1955-58

After a six-month tour of duty in Khartoum in the Sudan as the last British battalion to be stationed in that country, 1st Battalion The Royal Leicestershire Regiment left there on 10 October 1955 – as did the Egyptian Army. There were few regrets from either the Sudanese or from the Battalion as it moved from the frying pan of the Sudan into the fire of Cyprus. It was gratifying to learn subsequently from a long-serving British church missionary that Sayed Abd el Rahman, one of the two great religious leaders in the Sudan (and the posthumous son of the Mahdi), at a party to bid farewell to the Battalion, had said, 'The Sudanese have never been made conscious of an occupying Army. The Royal Leicestershire Regiment is the last regiment and they have well maintained the best traditions of the British Army.' In 1923, 2nd Battalion The Leicestershire Regiment had served in Khartoum, taking part in the suppression of the mutiny of Sudanese troops in 1924, and returning to England in 1925 – after having been abroad continuously since 1906. By coincidence the 2nd Battalion had also been one of the last infantry battalions to leave India after Partition in 1947.

Earlier in 1955, the 1st Battalion had received news of the transfer to Cyprus with considerable joy: life on an isle set in the blue Mediterranean within 50 miles of Turkey and easy reach of Greece, Lebanon, Palestine and Syria, appeared idyllic. Cyprus is an island of some 3,600 square miles. It is 140 miles from the south-west corner to the north-east tip (the 'Pan Handle') and 60 miles from north to south. Covered in pine forests, the Troodos Mountains (rising to 5,600 feet) cover much of the west of the Island, and the Kyrenia Mountains (rising to 3,350 feet) run in a spine west to east parallel with and about 3 miles from the north coast.

Quick preliminary reports received stated that prices were low, quarters adequate and that amenities were plentiful. It was true that some trouble on the island had begun in the previous year, but with the move of GHQ Middle East Land Forces (MELF) from Egypt in 1954, Cyprus was becoming the new strategic base to serve Britain's needs in the Eastern Mediterranean, both within NATO and CENTO, and as a national staging post to its interests in the Middle and Far East. Troop levels were gradually increasing, and all would shortly be well. A good accompanied posting was the general opinion, and the sooner it came to be, the better.

At that time, in military terms Cyprus was a District, commanded by a brigadier, whose

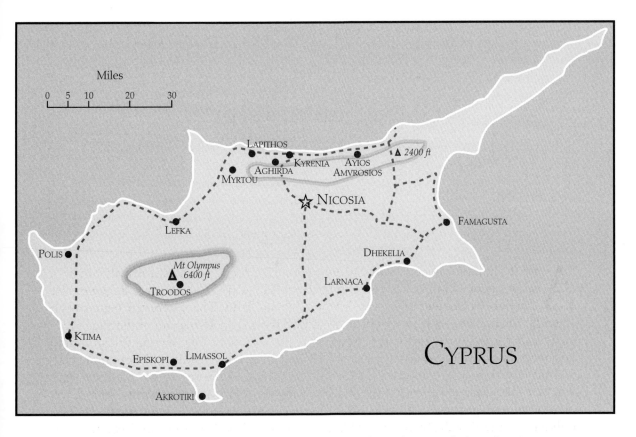

Miles

CYPRUS

forces comprised: a field regiment Royal Artillery in the infantry role based at Famagusta in the east, and an infantry battalion in each of Nicosia – the capital – and Larnaca on the south-east coast; a field engineer regiment; Brigade Troops; and a hospital at Dhekelia. 3 Commando Brigade arrived from Malta in September 1954, to be followed later in the year by the Headquarters of 50 and 51 Independent Infantry Brigades (Indep Inf Bdes). The RAF's Air HQ Cyprus Levant was established in Nicosia, and there were a number of RAF elements on Cyprus: at Nicosia Airport with troop-carrying and liaison helicopters, in the south at Akrotiri where a major airbase began to be constructed, and on Mount Olympus where there were radar and electronic listening stations.

Geographically, Cyprus is in the north-eastern end of the Mediterranean, at the crossroads of Europe, Asia and Africa. It enjoys more than 300 days of sunshine each year. Historically, throughout the centuries Cyprus had been the centre of clashes between the great maritime powers of the Eastern Mediterranean. It had been a British possession in the twelfth century, and from 1572 for some 300 years was a part of the Turkish Ottoman Empire. In 1821, Greece had gained its independence from the Ottoman Empire, and the idea was first spawned of a 'Greater Greece', with Cyprus aspiring to establish Union with Greece (or Enosis). In 1878, the Sultan of Turkey assigned the island to be occupied and administered by Britain and, when in 1914 Britain found herself at war with Turkey, Cyprus was formally declared a part of the British Empire, becoming a Crown Colony in 1925. The Greek Cypriots (of the Greek Orthodox religion) outnumbered the Turkish Cypriots (of the Muslim religion) by five to one, and there was also a large number of miscellaneous minorities: Britons, Armenians, Jews, and various others who had sought peaceful refuge from Europe and the Middle East. The education and religion of the Greek section of the population was controlled largely by the Greek Orthodox Church, which was in turn controlled from Greece. The position of the Greek Orthodox Primate in Cyprus had in the previous century evolved into that of an Ethnarch, with political as well as religious responsibilities, a situation that was to have far-reaching consequences by the middle of the twentieth century. The island, therefore, was torn by the conflicting claims and aspirations of Greece and Turkey. In the aftermath of the Second World War the Greek Cypriots, like the citizens of other countries of the British Empire, sought to achieve 'self-determination', whilst Britain, anxious to maintain her military base there, was ready to consider limited 'self-rule' and to set up a Constitutional Assembly to rule the island, provided arrangements could be reached by all parties. Attempts to reach agreement had failed in 1947 and 1948.

In a further effort to force their claims on Britain, in 1954, under the leadership of Archbishop Makarios, the Ethnarch, Enosis began to gain momentum and his supporters demanded the withdrawal of British interests from the island. In parallel and led by retired Greek Army Colonel George Grivas, an organization of Greeks and Greek Cypriots calling itself EOKA (*Ethniki Organosis Kypriou Agonistou*: 'National Organisation of Cypriot Fighters') was setting up an army of guerillas in the mountains of Cyprus. That autumn relations between Britain and Egypt deteriorated to such an extent that the former began to evacuate troops from the Suez Canal Zone and to redeploy them to Cyprus. This move was viewed by the Greek Cypriots as provocative and it coincided with the UN General Assembly refusing to debate the Cyprus issue. Accordingly, EOKA began its campaign of terrorism in April 1955. In turn Dr Fazil Kutchuk formed the Kibris Turktur Party ('Cyprus is Turkish'). Other clandestine organizations, such as Akel (the Greek Cypriot Progressive 'Communist' Party of Cyprus) and Vulkan (Turkish Nationalists), had appeared in reply and were active to further their own interests, in varying degrees.

EOKA was never a large organization. It seldom numbered more than a few hundred, but it exerted a strong influence on the Greek Cypriot population. It operated in two ways: small groups stirred up trouble in urban areas, coordinating riots, distributing propaganda, murdering and intimidating; large armed gangs attacked rural police stations (to acquire weapons) and ambushed Security Force vehicle and foot patrols in the hills and mountains (particularly the Troodos and the Kyrenia Mountains) where their own guerrilla camps were located. During the summer of 1955, EOKA carried out a series of offensive actions as a consequence of which in July the Governor, Sir Robert Armitage KCMG MBE (a career diplomat), introduced new anti-terrorist laws, similar to the Section 18B detention laws enacted in 1940. These laws allowed the Security Forces to arrest suspected members of EOKA without warrant and to detain them indefinitely without trial. In early October, Field Marshal Sir John Harding GCB CBE DSO MC was appointed Governor and Commander-in-Chief of Cyprus, with George Sinclair CMG OBE as Deputy Governor & Political Adviser, and Cyprus District was upgraded to a major general's command. Harding's arrival coincided with that of four more infantry battalions, including 1st Battalion The Royal Leicestershire Regiment, which was commanded by Lieutenant Colonel J E D (Derek) Watson DSO[1].

On 16 October 1955, after a five-day Red Sea and Mediterranean cruise from Port Sudan, the Battalion (less A Company which remained behind in Sudan for a few weeks)

Arrival at Famagusta. *Trustees R Leicestershire Regt*

disembarked from the SS *Charlton Star* at Famagusta. For years that ship had plied along the coast of East Africa carrying native troops, so it was a relief for all to escape from the thoroughly inadequate conditions and amenities on board. On the dockside the Battalion was greeted by Major General A H G (Abdy) Ricketts CBE DSO, GOC Cyprus District[2], Brigadier J A R Robertson DSO OBE, Commander (Comd) 51 Indep Inf Bde, and the Band of 2nd Battalion The Royal Inniskilling Fusiliers (2 RIF). The Battalion was then transported off to Golden Sands Camp, a tented camp 3 miles south of Famagusta. The men were naturally pleased to be reunited with their families who had moved from the Sudan to Famagusta in advance of the main body.

On arrival in Cyprus senior appointments were held as follows:

CO:	Lieutenant Colonel J E D Watson DSO	OC B Coy:	Major I G Jessop MC[6]
		CSM B Coy:	WO2 Marshall
2IC:	Major A W D Nicholls MC[3]	OC C Coy:	Major R J H Pacy
Adjt:	Major J P N Creagh	CSM C Coy:	WO2 W J Pound MM[7]
RSM:	WO1 T J Marston	OC Sp Coy:	Major J H Marriott MC[8]
QM:	Captain (QM) E H Scanlon	CSM Sp Coy:	WO2 R A Crisell
		OC HQ Coy:	Major D P Carey
RQMS:	WO2 R A Ross MM[4]	CSM HQ Coy:	WO2 P O'Sullivan
OC A Coy:	Major S A Smith MBE[5]	Bandmaster:	WO1 D K Walker ARCM
CSM A Coy:	WO2 H D Benham	Drum Major:	CSgt W Bradburn

Although Support Company nominally possessed two 17-pdr towed anti-tank guns, Vickers .303" MMGs and six 3" mortars, none of these weapons were deployed operationally during the tour. Support Company along with A, B and C Companies (and from February 1956, D Company) was organized as a rifle company for Internal Security (IS) duties. In the rifle companies there were one Regular and two National Service platoon commanders. Rifle platoons' weapons were the Lee Enfield .303" rifle and similar calibre Bren LMG, the 9mm Sten gun and the 2" mortar; the 3.5" rocket launcher was usually left in the armoury; the .38" revolver was also used as a personal protection weapon. Communication was provided by the WS19, 62 (both HF), 31 and 88 (both VHF) radio sets, and dispatch riders on motorcycles. The number of WS19 sets was well over the normal infantry battalion establishment and formed the mainstay of the radio communications network. Mechanical transport comprised ½-ton Land Rover and Austin Champ 'jeeps', 1-ton and 3-ton Bedford trucks, and on occasion Ferret scout cars. How they longed still to be equipped with the three Daimler armoured cars the Anti-Tank Platoon had had in the Sudan for riot-control purposes, which would have been invaluable for mobile patrols in Cyprus.

Dress on operations was a variant of Parade Dress, with 1938 Pattern webbing belt and pouches, and on occasion a steel helmet. Parade Dress was blue beret, Khaki Drill (KD) shorts and jacket, with the sleeves rolled up, 2" web belt (1938 Pattern), boots and ankle puttees with green hosetops, and garter tabs in red, pearl grey and black. Variations for officers were Service Dress (SD) cap with a bronze capbadge, cloth belt or Sam Browne belt if appropriate, regimental lanyard (red, pearl grey and black), medal ribbons, garter tabs and Fox's puttees, which were a light shade of khaki. The regimental buckle was worn with the web belt by officers, WOs and SNCOs in all forms of dress except on operations. A regimental stable belt was worn by officers in shirt sleeve order or KD when not on parade with troops. In hot weather in barracks, working dress for soldiers was often just shorts, boots with socks rolled down. All KD was washed and starched by the dhobi wallah, and *in extremis* there was an express service – the flying dhobi. In the winter months and in the Kyrenia Mountains, all ranks wore the worsted battledress (BD). Mess Dress for officers was white monkey jacket, black tie, No. 1 Dress trousers and pearl grey cummerbund. There was also a less formal version called 'Red Sea Rig', as in the previous sentence but without the monkey jacket.

Along with the rest of the British Army, a large proportion of the Battalion's subalterns, junior NCOs and private soldiers were National Service men, on two-year engagements. Thus there was a continual turnover of personnel. The steady flow of new drafts from the Depot, arriving after ten weeks' recruit training, had rapidly to undergo continuation training in Cyprus before being capable of successfully integrating into their role as riflemen.

The Battalion was fortunate that, from its time in Waziristan in 1939 and the 2nd Battalion's time in Palestine in 1938-39, many of its field officers and senior NCOs had experience of counter-insurgency and internal security (IS) operations, and operating in mountainous terrain and hot climates. Indeed two of the company commanders (Marriott and Dalglish), during what was to be a thirty-month tour of duty in Cyprus, had been awarded the MC as junior officers in the similar environment of Palestine fifteen years earlier. Moreover, most of the company commanders, warrant officers (WOs) and SNCOs had fought in the Second World War and in Korea. The regular element was both the glue and the backbone of the Battalion and, consequently, in Cyprus the Battalion was extremely well led; despite the continuous introduction of inexperienced young men and the repatriation of those who had completed their two years' Colour Service or three years' Regular Service, it performed with commendable expertise in a very happy atmosphere. At that stage the Battalion strength was some 850 all ranks and capbadges.

On landing in Cyprus the Battalion found itself on an island of strain, tension and uncertainty. Families, who mainly lived in civilian hirings in Varosha, were discouraged to leave their quarters except for essential shopping and the Battalion was confined to its camp when off-duty. The Army's role in Cyprus was threefold: to 'maintain law and order; protect lives and property; and to establish stability'. Into that the Battalion rapidly fitted.

Having hardly moved into Golden Sands Camp, on 22 October, Support Company under Major J L (John) Marriott MC and one platoon of B Company moved to the north of the island to be under command of 45 Commando Royal Marines (45 Cdo RM). The remainder of the Battalion was employed in enforcing a night curfew in Famagusta. Astride and north of the spine of the Kyrenia Mountains (of which the peaks rise to over 3,000 feet), Support Company HQ and two platoons went to Ayios Amvrosios, two platoons under Lieutenant C W (Bill) Byham to Kyrenia, and one platoon to Aghirda, all located in police stations. That same day, in direct response to two very serious incidents on 21 October (the blowing up of a police station in Limassol and the shooting of an RAF officer in Famagusta), the Governor banned all celebratory processions and firework displays announced for 28 October, the fifteenth anniversary of OXI Day – OXI Day was the commemoration of Greece's refusal to capitulate to the Italian Army in 1940, when the Italian Minister in Athens had given an ultimatum to the Prime Minister of Greece, demanding the unconditional surrender of Greece. His answer had been 'Oxi', which means 'No' in Greek. In 1955, the Governor also banned celebrations of Turkish Republic Day on 29 October (the thirty-second anniversary of the founding of the Republic of Turkey in 1923), despite the fact that the Turkish Community in Cyprus had to date shown the greatest restraint while under considerable provocation.

The town of Famagusta was placed under curfew from 1700 hours to 0500 hours nightly for ten days, and the Battalion was actively engaged in manning roadblocks and patrolling during the hours of darkness. On 29 October, in Famagusta, 2 RIF used for the first time Ack-Pack, a vehicle which sprayed green dye, thus enabling the Security Forces to identify those involved in illegal demonstrations long after they had dispersed. This equipment was used by the Royal Leicesters in the following months. 2 RIF was at the time commanded by Lieutenant Colonel I H (Ian) Freeland DSO of The Royal Norfolk Regiment, who in 1971, when a lieutenant general, was to become the third Colonel The Royal Anglian Regiment (and have a decisive effect on Leicestershire's infantry – see Chapter 8).

On 28 October, the balance of 1st Royal Leicesters deployed for a week to the north of the island on Operation *Fox Hunter*, working with 45 Cdo RM in the search of a large area for EOKA camps and ammunition dumps. It was the first of what were to be many examples of Inter-Service cooperation: the infantry platoons searched the foothills immediately to the seaward side of some of the mountain peaks, leaving the Commandos with grappling irons to scale and search the sheer faces. That day too, the Mortar Platoon of the Battalion under Lieutenant Bill Byham was deployed to assist in quelling a riot in the prison at Kyrenia Castle (the Castle was reputed to have been where King Richard the

Lionheart spent his honeymoon with Queen Berengaria en route to the Crusades in 1191). On 7 November, the Security Forces' senior command structure was further strengthened with Brigadier G H Baker CB CMG CBE MC being appointed Director of Operations.

A further large and more permanent deployment took place on 10 November, when the Battalion left Famagusta and moved north to relieve 45 Cdo RM in various locations along the northern coast of Cyprus, a deployment which was to last for some three months. As this move was declared a temporary measure, rear details remained at Golden Sands Camp, where A Company under Major S A (Stuart) Smith MBE, which had been the rearguard at Khartoum, soon arrived to join them. In the north the Battalion was widely dispersed: Battalion HQ and B Company under Major I G (Ian) Jessop MC were at Aghirda, a delightful camp in the pines at 1,100 feet in the Kyrenia Mountains, whilst companies, platoons and sections were scattered far and wide in the hills and along the northern coast; C Company under Major R J H (Dick) Pacy was in Myrtou and Lapithos; and Support Company was in Kyrenia and Ayios Amvrosios. The distances between detached sections, platoons and companies from their headquarters, combined with the rugged terrain, created communication problems and the Signals Platoon swiftly became adept at transmitting with the WS19 HF sets in Morse code. Indeed those sets were very old and difficult to maintain; some even had the dials and switches annotated in Russian! It was recorded that 'Whilst in the Kyrenia area, the Battalion's task was very similar to the one carried out by the 2nd Battalion in Samaria in the winter of 1938/39: mountaineering by day and night!!' On 14 November, the platoons in Kyrenia were sent to augment the guards of the Category 18B detainees who were rioting at the top-security prison at Kyrenia Castle. During the next few weeks the Battalion was visited by Major General Abdy Ricketts, the GOC, and it assisted in the move of the Category 18B detainees from Kyrenia Castle to the new detention camp west of Nicosia, C Company providing roadblocks in the Kyrenia area, and B Company picquetting the pass between Kyrenia and Aghirda. Elements of Support Company were then billeted in the Castle – in the recently vacated prison cells!

On the political front, on 17 November, the Governor announced a comprehensive economic and social development plan for Cyprus, aimed at appeasing the majority of citizens seeking Enosis: an improved standard of living and full employment; agricultural irrigation schemes and access to electric power resources for all communities; updating the road network; introducing forest management programmes; and modernization of port facilities at Famagusta.

Two weeks earlier, the unveiling and dedication of a memorial to The British Battalion took place in Singapore on 6 November 1955. The British Battalion had been formed in December 1941 in Malaya during the retreat from Penang in the face of the Japanese invasion. 1st Battalion The Leicestershire Regiment and 2nd Battalion The East Surrey Regiment had suffered such heavy casualties that the remnants of the two Battalions were amalgamated into The British Battalion, under the command of Lieutenant Colonel C E (Esmond) Morrison MC[9], with Major R G G (Dick) Harvey as second in command, both of The Leicesters and subsequently awarded the DSO for their gallant and distinguished services there. Morrison was additionally Mentioned in Dispatches as a prisoner of war. It is widely considered that the character played by Alec Guinness in David Lean's 1957

Oscar-winning film *Bridge on the River Kwai* was based on Morrison. The RSM of 1st Leicesters and of The British Battalion, WO1 J T (John) Meredith, was awarded the DCM for his conduct in that campaign.

In 1946, the Cathedral Hall of St Andrew's Cathedral, Singapore, was built as a general Memorial to all who lost their lives in the Second World War. The Leicestershire Regiment (as it then was) and The East Surrey Regiment had given generous donations in the hope that the memory of the formation of The British Battalion would be perpetuated. On 6 November 1955, that hope was realized when the Bishop of Singapore dedicated a tablet to The British Battalion during the Remembrance Sunday service in the presence of senior representatives of the three Services and of public life in Singapore. After speaking of the trials of the campaign which led to the formation of that Battalion, the Bishop stressed

The British Battalion memorial at Singapore Cathedral. *P A A Rapp*

the unity which existed between the British and Malayans – whether Malay, Chinese, Tamil or Eurasian – in the common adversities of the dark days of 1942, and called for the revival of such a spirit again. Major R L ('Polly') Perkins asked the Governor, Sir Robert Black KCMG OBE, to unveil the Memorial, which the Bishop then dedicated with the words:

> O God our Father, who didst give Thy Son to die on the Cross for the sins of the world; we dedicate this plaque in Thy Name and in honoured memory of those that died in the cause of humanity; beseeching Thee that, as Thou hast also called us to Thy Service, we may be worthy of our calling; through Jesus Christ our Lord, who livest and reignest with God, world without end. Amen.

Meanwhile, back in Cyprus, on 21 November a patrol of Support Company in Kalogrea was stoned by some locals, in which action Lance Corporal F H (Frank) Rogers suffered a serious fracture of the skull and a civil policeman was also wounded. On 26 November, in response to what he called a 'total breakdown in law and order' in Cyprus, the Governor declared a State of Emergency: guards were doubled and sentries posted at all government facilities and British schools; the death penalty was extended to cover all forms of lethal weapons and explosives-related convictions; it became a criminal offence to incite a riot; public assemblies were not permitted; paramilitary uniforms and Greek flags were banned; church bells – currently used by nationalists for signalling the arrival of military patrols in rural locations – were to remain silent; communities could be collectively punished by a curfew or a fine when atrocities occurred in their vicinity; deportation of suspects was permitted, as was censorship; military personnel were to carry loaded side arms at all times when out of barracks, including off-duty; and the Security Forces were issued with an eight-point 'Orders for Opening Fire' card, their rules of engagement. That Vice-Regal

Proclamation did not seem to have noticeably altered the Battalion's sense of proportion for on the very next day the officers of Battalion HQ and B Company found time to give a small party for local residents and officials at their Aghirda base, and the Regimental Band played in the evening.

During this period companies were employed in supporting the civil police and maintaining law and order in their respective villages, whilst detachments garrisoned rural police stations holding arms. On 4 December, around midnight, the camp of Support Company (now commanded by Major G E ('Jimmy') Smart) at Ayios Amvrosios came under attack by six terrorists using automatic and single-shot weapons, and home-made bombs; Corporal Clark and Craftsman Worth were both wounded. In addition, there began for all the ceaseless programme of patrols, roadblocks, cordons and searches, which was to continue for so long. Day after day and night after night, in fair weather and foul, troops were out combing village and plain, farmhouse and hill. On 8 December, acting on intelligence that Colonel Grivas was planning to site arms dumps on clerical property, Operation *Black Beard* – a large-scale search of twenty-four Greek Orthodox monasteries – was carried out by six battalions over a wide area of central and eastern Cyprus. The Royal Leicesters searched four of the monasteries, and a quantity of military equipment and weapons and explosives were recovered. As an example of the sensitivity displayed in the military operations, RAChD padres were on hand to ensure that no unintentional acts of desecration or disrespect occurred. The following week the Battalion embarked on a three-week operation searching the Mavronoros Forest area, which on 22 December led to the find near Kalogrea of a hideout containing 300 rounds of .300" ammunition, unfilled home-made bombs and sticks of gelignite. In that village on 30 December a house was searched by B Company and a .300" rifle found, which led to the arrest of two men. On 14 December, as part of an island-wide Operation *Lobster Pot* to round up and detain known Communists (members of the recently proscribed Akel Party), elements provided by the Battalion took into custody nineteen such men. A month later, after masked terrorists had stolen a number of shotguns from private houses, an island-wide collection of shotguns was carried out, and over two days the Battalion collected some 550. Thenceforth it was illegal for any civilian to possess a firearm.

Generally speaking, the search was for an enemy whose identity was unknown, who wore no uniform, who struck in cowardly fashion only when his target was off guard and then vanished into the midst of a population who, from fear or sympathy, never knew, heard or saw anything of him. Initially the troops welcomed this change from the normal routine of training they had experienced in the Sudan. Their normal kindliness and good humour made them reluctant to suspect the casual villager, the seemingly harmless passer-by. It was foreign to their British nature to be harsh, rough and ill-mannered to those who might well be innocent; but, as the days passed and the total of casualties throughout the island mounted, a perceptible change could be seen. Inevitably the turn of the Battalion came: a village riot, an arms hoard found, a detachment attacked and in Famagusta on 18 December, Lieutenant J C (Charles) Wrighton of A Company was shot by a terrorist and badly wounded in the leg. The following day in the Kyrenia area Lance Corporal H G (Harry) Hill of B Company was reported 'missing', and in May 1956 'missing presumed killed' when EOKA claimed to have hanged him as a reprisal for the hanging of Michael Karalous. Hill's body was not found until ten months later. Now it was personal, and noticeably the Battalion sat up and settled even more seriously to the job in hand. On 19 December, on a visit to the Battalion at Aghirda and Kyrenia, the Governor told the men, 'Use your skill, energy and determination to live up to the great name of your Regiment. Be ready, be alert, never relax. The lives of other men are in your keeping – never fail them.' During this three-month deployment away from Famagusta, married men were able to return to their families for forty-eight hours once a fortnight.

In his New Year 1956 broadcast, the Governor reiterated that any future political and constitutional solution would have to satisfy the needs of both the Greek and the Turkish communities on the island, as well as the strategic interests of Britain and NATO. He also warned Colonel Grivas that EOKA would soon be rendered impotent. In order to counter EOKA's growing use of young women as couriers, the Security Forces started to deploy WRAC and WRMP soldiers at all checkpoints so as to subject Cypriot women to the same physical searches as men. At a higher level, with the worst of the Mau Mau campaign in Kenya over, there were more troops to spare for operations in Cyprus and three more battalions arrived. This led to a general redeployment on the island. Having handed over its northern area of operations (AOR) to 1st Battalion The Wiltshire Regiment, the Battalion again regrouped as an entity in Famagusta at the end of January. As part of 51 Indep Inf Bde, the Battalion's new AOR covered the contiguous towns of Famagusta and Varosha, twenty-five villages and 250 square miles of the surrounding rural area. It was 25 road miles from Karaolos Camp to the westernmost village. The land was generally flat, never rising above 200 feet; citrus groves, vineyards and grain fields abounded, and there were some small forests.

On its return from deployment on the north coast, the Battalion moved into Karaolos Camp, a rambling collection of Nissen huts and tents a mile or so north of Famagusta, and some 300 yards from the sea. The camp was split into two halves, the Battalion sharing the available space with 40th Field Regiment Royal Artillery (40 Fd Regt RA), who, though gunners by trade, were performing infantry security duties in the rural areas to the north and north-west of Famagusta, and into whose AOR the Battalion was frequently tasked to provide support. Famagusta was an ancient Turkish walled town whose history dated back to pre-Crusade days. The old town and docks lay within the city walls and it was to seaborne trade that Famagusta had owed its early prosperity. In more recent years a new town of Varosha had grown up just to the south of the old town to accommodate the expanding, predominantly Greek Cypriot population. This new township, still dependent upon the harbour for its prosperity, had a population of some 40,000 people. New buildings and industries had sprung up rapidly, the main expansion resulting from the development of a large orange and citrus export trade. Varosha and its environs were surrounded by immense orange groves, delightful to the eye but providing perfect cover and refuge for the unlawful.

Quartered in a camp designed to hold a unit two-thirds of its strength, it was as well that the main strength of the Battalion was committed outside. One company garrisoned police stations in rural areas (at Athna, Dherinia and Vatili) and carried out rural patrols, one company provided immediate day-and-night riot squads in the town of Varosha and patrols within the town area, whilst a third company stood by in reserve for any and every task. One further company was detached at Golden Sands Camp to guard administrative units and a leave camp, and to patrol the southern section of Varosha. In this pattern, a

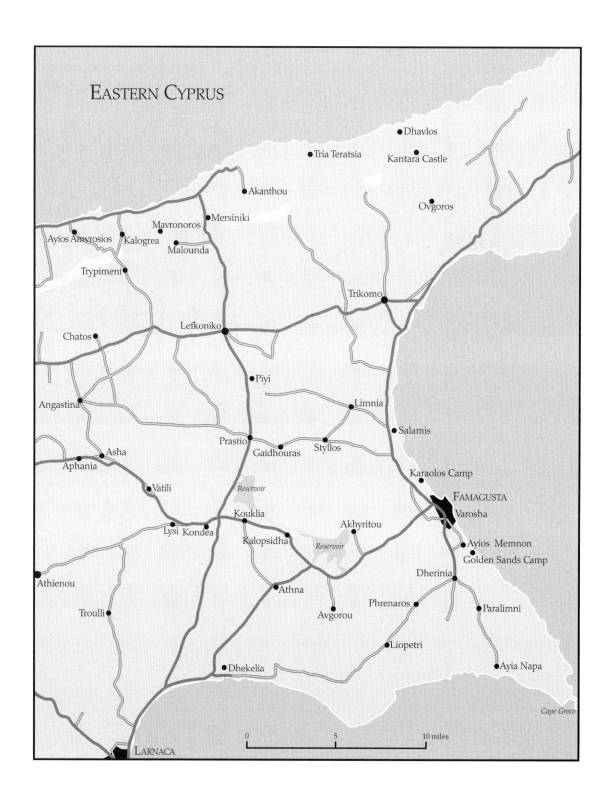

EASTERN CYPRUS

Dhavlos

Tria Teratsia

Kantara Castle

Ovgoros

Akanthou

Mavronoros   Mersiniki

Ayios Amvrosios   Kalogrea

Malounda

Trypimeni

Trikomo

Lefkoniko

Chatos

Piyi

Angastina

Limnia

Salamis

Prastio   Styllos

Asha   Gaidhouras

Aphania

Karaolos Camp

Vatili

Reservoir

FAMAGUSTA

Kouklia   Varosha

Lysi Kondea   Akhyritou

Kalopsidha   Ayios Memnon

Reservoir   Golden Sands Camp

Athienou   Dherinia

Athna   Phrenaros   Paralimni

Troulli   Avgorou

Liopetri

Dhekelia   Ayia Napa

Cape Greco

0   5   10 miles

LARNACA

24

Vatili Police Station. *Trustees R Leicestershire Regt*

subaltern's life was described as a merry round of IS Platoon, Greyhound Platoon (move at forty-five minutes' notice), town patrols by night (1800 till midnight), rural patrols by day and night, with the odd snap roadblock (0530-1000 or 1730-2200) and, when the Adjutant could catch him, a tour as Orderly Officer! From time to time, the Battalion was also required on a roster involving all major units on the island to provide for a fortnight the guard to the Governor at Government House in Nicosia. The first such task fell to the Mortar Platoon under Lieutenant Bill Byham on 22 March. All companies shared the innumerable internal and external calls that the situation invariably made upon them. Quickly settling in, the Battalion set about the process of converting each camp or detachment into home and commenced the slow, difficult and frustrating task of subduing the enemy within its area. To make the operations, duty and training plot simpler, on 1 February, a new D Company was formed under Captain J T (John) Dudley, significantly expanded and comprising the former Training Cadre element plus three rifle platoons. So the Battalion then had available five fighting companies.

The process of patrol, cordon and search, dispersal, raid and ambush went on day and night, week after week. Companies rotated on the various duties and discovered two new enemies to combat: boredom and fatigue. A target for assassination whenever out of camp, and only permitted to go out on duty or when under armed guard, the Battalion found itself virtually confined within its own wire on the infrequent occasions when not on duty.

25

Married families in quarters were a favourite target for EOKA's bombs, and social gatherings and outdoor jaunts became unhealthy pastimes. The families other than on essential activities lived behind their shutters, watching and listening, and sometimes nervous, but never demanding to be returned to safer climes. Under such conditions it would be pardonable to suppose that morale would be low, that the irritating pinpricks of IS duty, the allegations of theft, the attitude of the population, the seeming incomprehension of the British newspapers, would, on top of the deaths and casualties received, provoke the men of the Battalion to violence and anger.

The contrary was evident and morale was never higher. There was never any shortage of volunteers for any dangerous task, and, although individual tempers might run high for short periods over the death of a friend, in the main typical British control of emotion was always evident. The only dissatisfaction ever voiced was over the lack of action or against over-insurance. The soldiers, instead of a life of static guards or of 'confined to camp', wished to get out and find the enemy and bring him to fight. As the summer of 1956 wore on, a new problem on the island appeared, that of inter-racial enmity between Greek Cypriot and Turkish Cypriot. In many places over the island, Turks and Greeks lived in separate villages, but the vast majority lived cheek by jowl. It was inevitable that sooner or later the death of one would be blamed upon the other and, though initially the Turks exercised admirable restraint on a number of occasions, by May this enmity had become a very real threat to peace. There was no doubt, also, that amongst the numerous shootings of both Greeks and Turks many cases had no connection whatsoever with EOKA but were merely private feuds.

The arrival of the Battalion in Cyprus in 1955 had coincided with an increase in the number of acts of terrorist violence. During that winter and early spring 1956 the Battalion, in common with the Security Forces all over the island, appeared to make little or no headway, mainly because they were tied down with static guards in town and urban areas, which suited EOKA as it allowed their guerillas more freedom of action in the hills. True, there were successes here and there, but there was no marked progress, no lessening of the number of attacks. For five days on Operation *Plum Duff* in early January, elements of 1st Battalion The Royal Leicestershire Regiment, The Life Guards and two other infantry battalions searched the north-eastern coastal area of Dhavlos and Kantara. To indicate the developing Tri-Service nature of operations, the Royal Navy's 6th Frigate Squadron from Malta patrolled off the coast and remained thereafter to assist in anti-gun-running patrols. On 12 January, the first Turkish member of the Cyprus Police was murdered, an act which brought into action the Turkish Cypriot paramilitary organization Vulkan. During politically-inspired disturbances by schoolchildren which led to unrest followed by a riot in Varosha on 7 February, a Greek schoolmaster ringleader was shot by a battalion marksman. To quell the situation the Battalion occupied schools for a week, during which time men of 2nd Lieutenant A D (David) Barlow's 2 Platoon of A Company found weapons in the boys' Pan Cyprian Gymnasium school.

Late spring, however, saw considerable progress; it became evident that captures, plus the coastal blockade by ships of the RN, were rendering EOKA short of weapons and ammunition. Captured documents increasingly revealed disobedience of orders and faint-heartedness amongst the terrorist ranks, and, most heartening of all, information from the public began to come in under anonymous cover. During these months, all over the island, the Security Forces had been tightening their grip. Frequent patrolling, guards, searches and restrictive civil controls were all producing an accumulative effect, designed to hamper EOKA and sway public opinion against their methods. The Battalion had, in Famagusta and Varosha, one of the largest and most troublesome urban areas, the latter well known for its Communist outlook and pro-EOKA sympathies. There, too, it was evident that progress was being made but, despite successes, most regrettably the Battalion was suffering casualties. During February, Private R (Ronnie) Shilton of A Company was reported 'missing' and in May 1956 'missing presumed killed' when EOKA claimed to have hanged him (and Lance Corporal Hill, missing since December 1955) as a reprisal for the state-sanctioned execution of terrorists Michael Karalous and Andreas Demetriou. Shilton's body was not found until twelve months later. In Famagusta, on 27 February, Private G W (George) Sheffield of C Company was killed in a road traffic accident whilst on vehicle patrol, and on 9 March, Private M T H (Malcolm) Rowley, of the MT Platoon of HQ Company, was accidentally killed by misdirected friendly fire after a terrorist grenade incident, an action in which three other soldiers were injured by bomb splinters.

Throughout this time in negotiations with the Governor, Archbishop Makarios and his Ethnarchy Council failed to respond meaningfully and cooperatively to the Governor's political and constitutional initiatives. Among other things Makarios insisted that a full amnesty be granted both to convicted and to detained terrorists, and failed to condemn the violence; furthermore there was a marked increase in serious terrorist incidents. Consequently, on 7 March, Makarios was arrested and dispatched into exile to the Seychelles Islands. On Operation *Holiday*, in support of the civil police on 17 March, the bulk of the Battalion cordoned the village of Angastina, during which operation four wanted men were captured and detained. On Operation *Clamp* on 25 March – Cyprus' so called 'Independence Day' – in anticipation of unrest following the arrest of Archbishop Makarios, the Battalion imposed a 24-hour curfew on Famagusta and Varosha, which was the first of what were to be many over the following two years. Two days later Lieutenant S J M (Jim) Walker of D Company and Private R N (Ronnie) Bowman of the MT Platoon, while travelling in a ¼-ton jeep on patrol in Phrenaros, were killed in an ambush by close-range shotgun fire. The Battalion – whose dander was understandably up – was immediately deployed to cordon and search the village, where every male inhabitant was arrested and interrogated. The Drums Platoon under 2nd Lieutenant A J G (Tony) Pollard had the task of keeping the villagers penned in the detention cage. Tracker dogs led searchers to a house in which four fully clothed men were found in bed; they and sixteen others were arrested; six shotguns, a large quantity of home-made Molotov cocktails, plus grenades and ammunition were also recovered. The Governor imposed a £1,500 collective fine on the residents of Phrenaros in retribution for the ambush (£1,500 would be some £24,000 at 2008's prices). The success of the follow-up operation did little to assuage the sadness at the loss of these two fine men.

In Varosha, on 5 April, two men of D Company suffered minor splinter wounds in a bomb attack, and a man of B Company was similarly wounded on 17 April. On 11 April, while commanding a four-lorry convoy, Sergeant A F (Allen) Pinner of B Company was killed by shotgun fire in an ambush in Kalopsidha, as a consequence of which the Battalion began a three-day cordon and search of that village. The Governor imposed a £1,000 collective fine on the residents of the village and it was duly collected. In late April, D Company was deployed to cut down orange groves and demolish walls used as cover by terrorists in recent attacks, and subsequently was involved in the cordon and search of Aphania following communal violence between the Turkish and Greek elements in that village. A large number of home-made bombs with detonators fitted were found in haystacks. WO2 R A (Ronald) Crisell, CSM Support Company, was killed on 17 May when, a few yards from his house in Varosha, a bomb was thrown at the 3-ton truck in which he was a passenger; Corporal Osmond was wounded in the same attack.

The pace of military operations did not totally adversely affect Regimental life and routine. From early May, the Battalion had a permanent booking of thirty-five places at the Golden Sands Leave Camp. On 14 May, the Annual Administrative Inspection was conducted by Brigade staff, who sensibly confined themselves to checking the Quartermaster's stores and documentation in offices at each level. The RN Minesweeper HMS *Hickleton* was affiliated to the Battalion and, to break the routine, soldiers joined her and other RN ships on blockade-imposing tasks or runs ashore in Beirut. The Regimental Band under Bandmaster Desmond Walker had frequently performed for the various detached locations while the Battalion was in the north of Cyprus, and then became regularly engaged in recording programmes for the Cyprus Broadcasting Service. It played at the Famagusta dockside at the arrival and departure of units, performed at non-Teeth Arm Corps events, and provided a dance band at the Harbour Club in Kyrenia. On 27 April, it also provided the music at the Jimmy Edwards CSE Show at the new open-air theatre at Karaolos Camp. On the way to the show the cast's vehicle had a bomb thrown at it – presumably by a terrorist! Despite most of the cast's pretty young dancers and singers being really very scared, they gallantly ensured that 'the show went on'.

Preparations were made for Famagusta Garrison's Queen's Birthday Parade. En route back to Golden Sands Camp from the Dress Rehearsal on 30 May, a 3-ton truck carrying men of C Company (now commanded by Major K P P (Ken) Goldschmidt) was ambushed by terrorists throwing explosive and petrol bombs. Privates J T (John) Attenborough and K M (Kenneth) Hebb were killed at the scene, and Private J T (John) Argyle died of his wounds in hospital two days later. Seventeen others were injured, some very seriously, and many were evacuated by helicopter to the British Military Hospital in Nicosia. The most grievously wounded was Lance Corporal M (Maurice) Harrison, about whom a short time later the senior surgeon of that hospital wrote:

> He sustained severe multiple bomb wounds to his chest, abdomen, buttocks and thighs, with a compound fracture of the right femur, and severe petrol burns of knees, hands, arms and face. He has undergone several operations and numerous transfusions, suffering much pain and discomfort. In eighteen years of war surgery I have never before seen such ghastly wounds borne with such sustained fortitude; his courage has been an example and an inspiration to staff and patients alike, and his constant cheerfulness in adversity worthy of the highest tradition of the Army.

A fighting Tiger, indeed.

As a consequence of that terrorist attack on 30 May, four full companies of the Battalion (reinforced by sailors from two RN minesweepers) were immediately involved in imposing a curfew on Varosha for three days. Extensive searches of orange groves were carried out and the stone walls around them razed to the ground to remove cover for ambushes. The Governor imposed a £40,000 collective fine on the residents of Varosha in retribution for

Searching an orange grove. *Trustees R Leicestershire Regt*

the ambush. During the searches, arms, ammunition and explosives were found. The Queen's Birthday Parade went ahead, the 1st Battalion's representation being only the RSM and the Regimental Band. For his conduct at the scene of the attack on 30 May in which, despite wounds to arm and leg, Private T M (Trevor) Jervis of the MT Platoon drove the burning truck to the nearest fire point, he was awarded a Mention in Dispatches (MID). After a steady force build-up, by mid-May fifteen Battalion equivalents were stationed in Cyprus for deployment on IS operations.

On 4 June, after the burial in Famagusta of a Turkish Cypriot policeman who had been murdered by terrorists, a demonstration by a large crowd of Turks led to fire-bomb damage to Greek Cypriot property, all available troops of the Battalion were deployed there for several hours to quell the disturbance, and platoons picquetted the Sea Gate and Land Gate the following day. Dealing with inter-communal riots there and consequently imposing curfews had their lighter sides. The Turks were required to stay in the Old City, but many worked outside it and were ordered to return home. Marching in military ranks and saluting the Security Forces as they entered the Old City, their demeanour would turn to consternation when they realized that a roadblock had been inadvertently sited between the local Turkish brothel and its clients, and the angry young (and rather less young) women would berate the 'spoil-sport' platoon commander.

29

Officers of 1st R Leicesters 29 June 1956 (see Appendix P for names). *Trustees R Leicestershire Regt*

On 12 June, at Paralimni, Lance Corporal T P Williams of C Company was shot at while collecting fresh water at the Police Station, and Corporal W R (William) Holden of B Company was shot and killed by a revolver while out of bounds attending a Greek Cypriot cinema.

Royal Tigers' Weekend was held a month early that year, and for four days 40 Fd Regt RA graciously took over all the Battalion's operational duties (less the rural police stations). This enabled all ranks to play a full part in the programme of activities, which ranged from rifle shooting and sports competitions, to prizes being awarded to the company judged best at IS Drills (A Company – Major Stuart Smith), Police Station duties (D Company – Major P E B (Peter) Badger) and the Smartest Lines (Support Company – Major 'Jimmy' Smart), a farewell parade for the Commanding Officer, and a Drumhead Service. On 29 June – some twenty-six years after being commissioned into the Regiment in 1930 – Lieutenant Colonel Derek Watson handed over command, and a fond farewell was extended to him and his wife Barbara. He was replaced on promotion from 2IC by Lieutenant Colonel A W D ('Spike') Nicholls MC, who in turn was replaced as 2IC by Major M St G (Mike) Pallot on 4 September.

On the wider political front, Lord Radcliffe was appointed by the British Government to be Cyprus' Constitutional Commissioner, charged with formulating a set of recommendations to be implemented in a violence-free environment. Elsewhere in the Middle East the newly proclaimed President of Egypt, Colonel Abdel Nasser, seized the Suez Canal by nationalizing the Anglo-French Suez Canal Company. This was to have very serious repercussions within a few months. On 12 July, for a week, the Battalion was visited by a journalist from each of the *Leicester Mercury*, the *Leicester Mail* and the *Leicester Advertiser*, who produced pages of articles and local-boy stories in their respective publications. They much appreciated their visit to the Battalion and their feelings were reciprocated. An extract from their 'thank you' letter read 'We came in search of a story. Two thousand miles from Granby Street to the land of Grandpa Grivas and his bandits. Twelve hours by air from Filbert Street to Famagusta.'

A similar pattern and intensity of duties continued throughout the summer and autumn of 1956. In early July B Company (now commanded by Major J P N (Pat) Creagh) was deployed 120 miles west to Lefka to assist in fighting a forest fire. The Governor visited the Battalion on 27 July. He toured many elements in barracks that day, formally addressing the troops as he went, the main themes of his message being: 'Do not relax security measures during the present lull, practise marksmanship, endeavour to understand completely the importance of the Turks in the "Cyprus problem", and keep physically fit and well-disciplined.' On 3 August, B Company road-blocked the Dherinia, Nicosia and Salamis roads; and two days later it cordoned and curfewed Limnia, while D Company cordoned Akhyritou to support police in arresting two suspects. Overall, therefore, by early August the Battalion had taken part in two curfews of Varosha and one of the Old City of Famagusta; twelve villages had been curfewed, cordoned and searched, some more than once, and on one occasion at Paralimni every male out of the 4,500 overall population had been fingerprinted. And Battalion casualties, both killed and wounded, had been suffered at the hands of a stealthy and treacherous enemy.

That same week, in response to the deteriorating situation in Egypt, all Regular Release in British Forces worldwide was postponed for the duration of what became to be known as the Suez Crisis. In Cyprus, 3 Cdo Bde RM was replaced by 3 Infantry Brigade, and two battalions of the Parachute Regiment were also withdrawn to train for what was to become two months later the Suez Landings; they were replaced on the ground in Cyprus by two infantry battalions and two Artillery regiments in the infantry role. For the Royal Leicesters, operations in the Famagusta Sector continued unabated, despite Colonel Grivas' offer of a 'suspension of operations of all forces under his authority', a posture that collapsed by the end of that month and was subsequently viewed as a ruse during which EOKA reorganized. On 10 August, two rifle sections assisted the Police at Lysi, finding a secret cache of pamphlets and an EOKA flag, and detaining two suspects. This success led directly to a much larger deployment when, from 14 to 17 August, C Company cordoned Lysi. It was reinforced by large elements of HQ Company. 'Every available man' was required, so it really was 'scraping the bottom of the barrel' – a phrase implying no disrespect to those affected – as the list of indispensables in all departments was slashed and many men normally in reserved occupations found themselves once again performing riflemen's tasks. This invaluable source of additional combat power was nicknamed 'Scraping the Barrel'. This operation at Lysi was particularly successful as one of the largest quantities of terrorist arms ever found in Cyprus was unearthed, along with some very significant documents, which many referred to as the 'Grivas Diaries', indisputably linking the then-exiled Archbishop Makarios with the EOKA campaign.

On cordon operations, A Company (now commanded by Major P G (Peter) Bligh) deployed on 17 August to Prastio, and on 26 August to Limnia. Three days later, B Company was dispatched to apprehend terrorists suspected of hiding in a cave at Trypimeni, the snatch party deploying by RAF helicopter. In contrast to offensive operations, on 23 August, for a fortnight, Lieutenant J R A (John) Wilkes and the Machine Gun and Anti-Tank Platoons of Support Company mounted the Guard at Government

House in Nicosia. Private G A (George) Bott of D Company was killed in a road traffic accident on 31 August in Nicosia whilst on detachment to Cyprus District Signal Regiment. Despite the pace of operations, at platoon, company and battalion level, sport again began to be played, including football and basketball, and unit-level cricket against Army and RN teams.

By the end of August, Cyprus was well on the way to providing the forward mounting base for Operation *Musketeer*, the combined and joint Anglo-French Task Force of some 80,000 servicemen which was to become the Suez Landings. At this time the pattern of relentless IS duties was alleviated by the use of elements of the Battalion, including the stevedoring Band, to assist in unloading shipping in Famagusta Harbour and across the nearby beaches, and performing other logistic tasks in support of the build-up of force levels during the Suez Crisis. One such task involved C Company offloading 500 tons of petrol for the French Air Force, where they had the greatest difficulty in making the French obey the signs '*Défense de fumer*'. Indeed some of the Frenchmen, still seemingly oblivious to the ambient fumes, then proceeded to use some of the spilt fuel in a rock pool to cook shellfish in their steel helmets. '*Sacré bleu!*' Another task involved the Signals Platoon providing 'ship-to-shore' communications for merchant ships anchored outside the Harbour as Z-Craft lighters unloaded. One signaller, sunbathing beside his radio set on the bridge, became so embedded that the ship up-anchored and sailed without putting him ashore.

In spite of the strain which anti-terrorist operations imposed upon the restraint and discipline of every individual soldier, all ranks continued to maintain high regimental traditions. On 5 September 1956, the Colonel of The Regiment[10] visited the Battalion after it had been on operations for some eleven months. His busy programme included addressing as many as could be formed up for a battalion parade and culminated in a guest night at which the Governor was also a guest. As a cover plan to keep secret the Governor's movements, an invitation to the dinner was sent to two pre-briefed officers of 40 Fd Regt RA – they were fallen out at the last minute when the names of the Governor and his ADC were revealed. On his return to England, Sir Colin Callander was able to report that he had 'found the 1st Battalion The Royal Leicestershire Regiment in good form in every way. The Battalion was a unit of which the Regiment could be proud. Whatever the future might hold, it could be relied upon to do its duty well.' As an example of how priorities were revealed, the entry for 16 September in the Adjutant's Regimental Digest read, 'Battalion Cricket XI drew with the Royal Navy. Two bombs thrown in Famagusta at 2025 hours.'

Later that month the British Government announced the setting up of a Constitutional Commission under Lord Radcliffe, to make recommendations as to the form of a new constitution for Cyprus. This was to be based on the principle of liberal democracy and to confer a wide measure of responsible 'self-government' while guaranteeing protection to the special interests of the various communities, religions and races of the island.

The Regimental Band continued a busy round of engagements, which included playing during several weeks at Cyprus District's Families Leave Camp at Troodos, and a Massed Bands concert in Karaolos Camp with the bands of the 1st Battalions of the Middlesex and South Staffordshire Regiments, an All Ranks dance in the Black Swan amphitheatre, and Beating Retreat for the garrison children.

Privates Nicholson and Stocker, newly trained as dog handlers, returned to the Battalion at the end of September, thus providing its integral tracker dog team, which was first deployed on 7 October in the follow-up to the fatal ambush of two RAF vehicles near Paralimni. The following day during Operation *Sparrow Hawk* in the Kyrenia Mountains, British troops found the body of Lance Corporal Harry Hill. He had been buried for some time, along with his Sten gun which had been used by EOKA in several murders. He had gone missing ten months before. On 13 October, whilst driving his vehicle, Private D A (Derrick) Morris of the MT Platoon died as a result of another soldier's negligent discharge of a rifle.

The tracker dog team was in action again on 14 October as part of the Brigade's Operation *Plain Fair* in which the Battalion's task was to cordon and search Avgorou. It concluded five days later, the same day as Major General D A ('Joe') Kendrew CBE DSO[11] took over as GOC Cyprus District and the new post of Director of Operations. This most distinguished of Royal Leicesters officers was very soon to revolutionize the manner in which the campaign in Cyprus was conducted, with mounting success.

Unlike in 1955 when celebrations had been banned, 28 October 1956 was permitted by the Governor to be commemorated by the Greek Cypriots as OXI Day. Two companies of the Battalion were deployed into Famagusta to deter any disturbances.

On 31 October the Battalion provided a Guard of Honour and the Regimental Band played at the Famagusta dockside at the departure of the outgoing GOC, Major General Abdy Ricketts. As if that was not a sufficiently momentous occasion, concurrent with its Armed Forces' involvement in operations in Cyprus, that same day the British Government issued an ultimatum to Egypt requiring it to withdraw its troops from the Suez Canal by 5 November or an Anglo-French Force would reoccupy the Canal Zone by force – effectively turning the Suez Crisis into armed conflict. RAF aircraft also bombed targets in Egypt, which led to troops in Cyprus – and the Royal Leicesters in Famagusta – taking air-raid precautions in case of Egyptian retaliation: digging air-raid trenches, building anti-aircraft sentry posts and constructing blast walls around vulnerable points. Cyprus and Malta were mounting bases for the allied operations, which culminated in a British and French airborne and seaborne assault of Egypt on 5 November, with a ceasefire effected thirty-six hours later. Further regrouping and redeployment on Cyprus took place with B Company, which for a period of two hours had been preparing to deploy to Egypt for duty as the Assault Force's stevedores, relieving 40 Fd Regt RA manning police stations at Chatos and Lefkonico.

Despite the distractions of the Suez Campaign, there was no diminution of EOKA's campaign in Cyprus: bombs were thrown, including in Famagusta dockyards, an RAF man was killed when two RAF vehicles were ambushed in Paralimni, guard was mounted on the electricity booster station; and search operations of various numbers of troops committed continued to be mounted in response to intelligence. To all of this the Battalion responded as required and still had resources to participate at the Remembrance Day Service in St George's Garrison Church. On 12 November, making room for 1st Battalion The Duke of Wellington's Regiment (1 DWR), which also took over Dherinia police station, A Company was moved from Golden Sands Camp to close up with the remainder of the Battalion and squash into Karaolos Camp. In early December, two suspects were apprehended at Lysi by the Civil Police in Operation *Saint Barbara*, which involved Bn Tac HQ with C and D Companies; a week later Tac HQ with A and B Companies cordoned and imposed a curfew on the village.

Subsequently deployments returned to the previous roster: one company running and guarding Golden Sands Camp and some Key Points (KPs); one responsible for patrolling Famagusta and Varosha; and one responsible for the 'Rural Area' – some 200 square miles of the south-eastern corner of Cyprus – furnishing bases at the more-important police stations, and carrying out vehicle and foot patrols by day and night. The other two companies provided the Reserve Company, guards at other KPs and fatigue parties. All operations were designed to keep the initiative, restrict freedom of movement and make EOKA operations more difficult. Search operations, in which the Civil Police and at least the Reserve Company were invariably involved (and often reinforced by a heterogeneous 'Scraping the Barrel'), were more stage-managed events – usually based on intelligence, launched in the early hours of the morning in order that darkness would conceal the approach and could last anything from six to seventy-two hours.

Such things proceeded up to the New Year, the political scene being spiced up by the announcement of Lord Radcliffe's constitutional proposals for Cyprus on 20 December, which he stressed could only come into effect in a society free of terrorism. His proposals included that Cyprus should remain a Crown Colony and have a single-chamber Legislative Council of thirty representatives. Legislation should not conflict with either religion or culture, and there should be no discrimination based on ethnic background, birth, language or education. These proposals led immediately to some unrest in Famagusta, carried out mostly by children incited by their elders. One Cypriot civilian was shot and wounded by B Company's Bomb Squad under the command of 2nd Lieutenant A S (Tony) Moore. D Company celebrated its Christmas on due date, while it was not until the end of the month that the rest of the Battalion, having handed over all its IS responsibilities in Famagusta to 40 Fd Regt RA from 31 December for four days, could celebrate it appropriately. Morale in all companies remained buoyantly high. Wherever they were deployed, company canteens were established, with such predictable names as the Getsum Inn and the Dive Inn.

In early 1957 senior appointments were held as follows:

CO:	Lieutenant Colonel A W D Nicholls MC	OC C Coy:	Major K P P Goldschmidt
		CSM C Coy:	WO2 G Seagrave
2IC:	Major M St G Pallot	OC D Coy:	Major P E B Badger
Adjt:	Captain T Holloway	CSM D Coy:	WO2 P O'Sullivan
RSM:	WO1 T J Marston	OC Sp Coy:	Major G E Smart
QM:	Major (QM) E H Scanlon	CSM Sp Coy:	WO2 T Ward
RQMS:	WO2 R A Ross MM	OC HQ Coy:	Major A C V Sheppard
OC A Coy:	Major P G Bligh	CSM HQ Coy:	WO2 R Coulson
CSM A Coy:	WO2 H D Benham	Bandmaster:	WO1 D K Walker ARCM
OC B Coy:	Major J P N Creagh	Drum Major:	CSgt W Bradburn
CSM B Coy:	WO2 S Sears		

The year began with the pleasing news that Sergeant Kelly of B Company was awarded the Commander-in-Chief's Certificate in recognition of his work whilst with the Battalion in Cyprus. The routine of operations continued apace for the next few months and, for the Battalion, with some considerable success. At Liopetri on 4 January, a patrol of D Company led by Corporal Hoares captured a terrorist, in the pannier of whose bicycle were found three pipe bombs and 150 shotgun cartridges. On 10 January, D Company cordoned and searched Kalopsidha and C Company escorted Civil Police on a house raid in Vatili, where Photis Stavris, the gang leader of the local 'Red Soil' area, was arrested. On 31 January, Bn Tac HQ, with A, C, and D Companies cordoned and searched a large area south of Gaidhouras; eight suspect terrorists including a gang leader were arrested. The following day C Company reinforced 40 Fd Regt RA in a cordon and search of Trikomo, an operation in which twenty-four suspects were arrested.

February was another busy month, with several notable occurrences. On 3 February during the funeral of a Turkish Cypriot policeman (killed by an EOKA bomb the previous week) the Turkish crowd surged out of the Old City of Famagusta into the Greek Quarter of Varosha. The Battalion assisted the Police in restoring law and order but not before one Greek Cypriot had been killed, several injured and some shops damaged. While D Company was involved in imposing a curfew of the Old City and Varosha, Corporal Booth's patrol found seventeen bombs belonging to Vulkan, the Turkish Cypriot paramilitary organization. The next night, Corporal Bennett's patrol found two primed EOKA bombs and a large quantity of leaflets by the municipal market. The area was evacuated and the bombs were blown up *in situ*; the whole operation went very well except that the officer in tactical control, Major Peter Badger, failed to warn his wife, who lived in a nearby hiring, of the impending explosion! On 7 February, at Prastio in the Troodos Mountains, Security Forces found the body of Private Ronnie Shilton, who had been missing since February 1956 (and presumed killed by EOKA in May 1956 in retaliation to the state-sanctioned executions of terrorists Michael Karalous and Andreas Demetriou). On 10 February, Corporal N (Norman) James and three men of C Company, on patrol near

Pte Deacon, Cpl James, Ptes Scott and Young. *Trustees R Leicestershire Regt*

Lysi at dusk, were searching a sheep pen when they were fired upon by several gunmen. In the ensuing twenty-minute firefight one terrorist was shot dead and five surrendered, and three shotguns and a quantity of cartridges recovered. For his leadership in this event, Corporal James was subsequently awarded an MID.

On 14 February, C Company searched an area west of Ayios Memnon, to be followed a week later by the Battalion, with three other battalions, searching a large area on the north coast near Malounda, the most notable feature being a night march over the mountains to establish the cordon. In the subsequent search a soldier of D Company found a bomb, 'the age of which' – so it was recorded – 'seemed to offer some evidence that Archimedes did visit Cyprus!' The following day the Company was involved in another cordon in the Piyi area, and six known terrorists were captured. On 28 February, a patrol of A Company, led by Corporal Brian Moore, was carrying out a routine search of an orange grove near Athna when a man was seen running out of the grove into a nearby house. Suspecting him to be a sentry, the patrol rapidly followed up and without firing a shot captured seven terrorists, one of whom had a £5,000 bounty on his head. For the Battalion to account for thirteen terrorists in a fortnight was an excellent effort and a very great encouragement. It went some way to compensate for Shilton's death. By mid-February the Army's force levels in Cyprus had increased to twenty battalion equivalents, of which four were RA regiments in the infantry role.

It needs to be appreciated the degree to which over the previous fifty years rugby had meant so much to the Regiment. A short article in *The Green Tiger* in 1955 had ruefully observed:

In the years before the Second World War we tried very hard, without success, to win the Army Cup once more.[12] Even though we failed, we can be sure that the toughening effect of those endeavours was a source of strength to the Regiment on the many battlefields of World War II. It is only for this reason that we deplore the fact that the winning of the Army Cup has now passed beyond the reach of the 'teeth arm' to the hands of those whose immediate task in battle is not to close with the enemy.

During those early busy months of 1957, the Battalion's Rugby XV excelled. When winter approached it had begun training in earnest without the benefit of an inter-company competition. All their matches were played away because – it was said – the rock on which the Battalion's rugby pitch was sited was too big to move! Organized by Major Ken Goldschmidt (one of a number of fine sportsmen who joined the Regiment in the 1930s)[13] and captained by Lieutenant John Wilkes, it was reputed to be the Battalion's best rugby XV since the Second World War; it reached the semi-finals of the Cyprus Cup, losing to 1 DWR, whose team that day included three internationals and two Rugby League players. 2nd Lieutenant Tony Pollard and Bandsman Matthews were selected to play for the Army Cyprus against the RAF Cyprus.

Despite conflicts with operational duties, the Battalion also fielded strong football, hockey and basketball teams in various competitions, while inter-platoon small-bore rifle shooting and other sports competitions were also fitted in.

On the other side of the world, on 2 March 1957, the Singapore Memorial at Changi was unveiled by the Governor, Sir Robert Black. On a stone panel at the foot of the great pylon in the centre of the Memorial are inscribed the words:

1939-1945
ON THE WALLS OF THIS MEMORIAL ARE RECORDED
THE NAMES OF 24,000 SOLDIERS AND
AIRMEN OF MANY RACES UNITED IN SERVICE TO THE
BRITISH CROWN WHO GAVE THEIR LIVES IN MALAYA
AND NEIGHBOURING LANDS AND SEAS AND IN THE AIR
OVER SOUTHERN AND EASTERN ASIA AND THE PACIFIC
BUT TO WHOM THE FORTUNE OF WAR
DENIED THE CUSTOMARY RITES
ACCORDED TO THEIR COMRADES IN DEATH
THEY DIED FOR ALL FREE MEN

The long roll of 194 Leicestershire Regiment names – all from 1st Battalion in 1941-2 – is displayed on the fifth face from the east end of the Memorial and spreads over three columns. On the occasion of the unveiling Major 'Polly' Perkins laid two wreaths, one from All Ranks of the Regiment and one from the Royal Tigers' Association.

Meanwhile back in Cyprus, on 14 March, in Karaolos Camp the RSM hoisted the new Regimental Flag, the main colour of which was red (in place of the former white) – see plate section. On a wider scheme of things, since the time Major General Kendrew had been appointed Director of Operations in October 1956, some sixty-nine EOKA terrorists had been killed in Cyprus and sixteen terrorist gangs reduced to five in the four months November 1956-February 1957. The Royal Leicesters had clearly played an important part in eroding EOKA's ability to mount sustained acts of terrorism. Colonel Grivas had lost most of his senior officers, few mountain gangs remained in the field, and he was having extreme difficulty in the command and control of his urban groups. Almost certainly as a direct result of the Security Forces' operational successes, on 14 March, Grivas announced: 'EOKA ... in order to facilitate the resumption of negotiations between Britain and the real representative of the Cypriot people, Archbishop Makarios, hereby declares itself willing to order a suspension of operations as soon as Archbishop Makarios is released.' Mindful that this was only an offer to suspend operations and not to end violence, nevertheless on 28 March the British Government announced that Makarios would be released the following day from exile in the Seychelles, but that he was not allowed to enter Cyprus.

The release announcement was greeted with rejoicing by the Greek Cypriot community, and in Varosha young men paraded with Greek flags and shouted nationalist slogans. On 29 March, the demonstrations in Famagusta began early and three of the Battalion's companies provided baton and roadblock parties. A curfew of all people under twenty-seven years of age and of all nationalities was imposed at 1800 hours, and no incidents occurred. Over the following weeks, because the suspension of EOKA operations seemed to be holding, the GOC lifted some restrictions on the carriage of arms by Service personnel off-duty and on their movement off-duty in the towns; and on 12 April, virtually all restrictions for them and their families were lifted. Thus Famagusta and Varosha became open to those off-duty, to the advantage of the troops, their families and the shopkeepers, and the Families Beach Centre on Hippocrates Street became progressively more used as the weather hotted up. And as the summer approached, men and their families off-duty were able to explore many parts of the island. The Governor repealed some of the Emergency

37

Powers legislation, reducing the level of bounties placed on the heads of wanted terrorists and discontinuing communal fines.

Security Force operations continued. Avghorou, a small village 8 miles south-west of Famagusta and on the junction of tracks leading from several other infamous villages, had long been suspected of harbouring terrorists and their weaponry, and the previous November a vehicle patrol of D Company, led by 2nd Lieutenant W H V ('Ben') Elliott, had been ambushed nearby. (Elliott was subsequently informed by a contact in Ayia Napa that the ambush had been carried out by Gregoris Afxeniou, one of Grivas's gang leaders. Afxentiou was killed by a patrol of 1 DWR in the Troodos Mountains in March 1957. On completion of his National Service in August 1957, Elliott taught for two years at the English School in Nicosia, located close to Government House. By then a civilian teacher, whenever Field Marshal Harding's two helicopters took off, Elliott's Greek Cypriot and Turkish Cypriot pupils rushed to the classroom windows and shook their fists at the Governor; and on another occasion, Elliott was cycling 200 yards from the explosion which narrowly missed Major General 'Joe' Kendrew travelling in a convoy – a shaken Kendrew declined the brandy offered by the unrecognized former subaltern!)

The EOKA terrorist Michael Rossides was captured by the Security Forces on 23 March. He was subsequently found guilty of Private Shilton's murder and sentenced to death in June 1957, but ultimately avoided execution. Acting on information provided by Rossides, following a cross-country night approach march on 3 April led by 2nd Lieutenant Tony Pollard and 11 Platoon D Company, Bn Tac HQ and three companies cordoned and searched Avghorou, and arrested four terrorists. During the three-day operation it was necessary to deal with the village menfolk being kept in the screening cage and their women being let out of their curfewed houses to feed them, which led to a near riot as the men threw the offered bread back at their wives. All these challenges were handled with amazing calm and resilience by the soldiers. Still there on 8 April, patrolling the area to prevent the movement of arms, D Company found two 3.7" anti-aircraft shells, nine bombs, two pistols and assorted ammunition in a cornfield. On 12 April, B Company, acting on information provided by one of those arrested on 3 April, found at the village an arms cache containing eleven shotguns, a rifle and a quantity of ammunition, explosives and bombs, and a duplicating machine (used by leafleteers). The attrition of EOKA increased. But these successes were marred most regrettably on 19 April when Private J (John) Pegg of HQ Company died and Private Langham of A Company was injured in a collision with a French military vehicle in Lysi.

As if counter-terrorists operations were not sufficiently engaging, the Royal Leicesters (one of the few battalions on 2½-year accompanied tours) also had a strategic role in the Middle East. That was activated on 11 April when, as a consequence of King Hussein of Jordan dismissing his pro-Communist Government, the Battalion was placed at 72-hours Notice to Move to Mafraq in Jordan to assist if necessary in the evacuation of British nationals. It was stood down a few days later, but over the following weeks it carried out several land-based air movement exercises, *Skylark I-V*. Other duties continued unabated, and from 18 April to 2 May, a composite group of forty-four all ranks of Support and A Companies under Lieutenant J H (John) Rees and 2nd Lieutenant P N (Peter) Graham provided the Guard to the Governor at Government House. 2nd Lieutenant A P G (Anthony) Brown was appointed ADC to Major General 'Joe' Kendrew in Nicosia.

On 27 May, the Governor paid a visit to the Battalion, during which he watched Support Company carrying out range practice with the new Belgian-designed FN 7.62mm self-loading rifle (SLR), which would over the next several years replace the elderly bolt-action .303" Lee-Enfield and was to remain the Army's rifle for the next thirty years. Three days later, Bn Tac HQ and three companies cordoned Lysi for twenty hours in a move to control its population in the event of over-exuberance on the occasion of a memorial service for Gregoris Afxentiou, a terrorist leader who had been killed by the Security Forces three months before.

This period of reduced threat and lower intensity of operations by the Security Forces in general enabled much more military training to take place. In the Battalion, companies carried out battle shooting at Troulli and Cape Greco training areas. The Battalion's Pistol Team, under Major J L (John) Bromhead RAPC, won the Overseas Series of the Army Rifle Association (ARA)'s Non-Central Duke of Connaught Trophy competition, with Major D P (David) Carey winning the individual event. Sport at company and battalion level was vigorously engaged in and much enjoyed. Over three days in early June, the Battalion Athletics Meeting was held and despite little prior training having been undertaken, many good performances were recorded. A full season of cricket was played and the Battalion XI, captained by 2nd Lieutenant Nick Héroys, won twenty out of its twenty-three fixtures. Under CSM 'Jimmy' Jenks MM[14], two water polo teams were raised, the senior one being the first during the Cyprus Emergency to play a match against any Greek Cypriot side in any sport.

On 13 June, the Garrison's Queen's Birthday Parade was held in Famagusta in considerably more benign conditions than had prevailed the previous year. Major Peter Bligh of A Company commanded the Battalion's detachment and the Colours were on parade. On the operational side, on 29 June, under the command of Bn Tac HQ, C Company and a Battery of 29 Fd Regt RA (which had recently replaced 40 Fd Regt RA in Karaolos Camp) cordoned Piyi where three suspected terrorists were detained and a small amount of ammunition found. Royal Tigers' Weekend was celebrated at the beginning of July with the customary round of All Ranks Dance, Officers' Cocktail Party and Warrant Officers' & Sergeants' Mess Hindoostan Ball. The weekend culminated with a Drumhead Service, after which the Battalion marched past Major General 'Joe' Kendrew, the GOC and Director of Operations. Separately, at Wayne's Keep Military Cemetery in Nicosia, wreaths were laid on the graves of those of the Battalion who had been killed in the preceding twenty-one months.

During that summer, the task of one company at a time being deployed at Golden Sands Camp was a much more welcomed assignment. The Camp was situated on the sandy coast 3 miles south of Famagusta, and the company accommodation was sandwiched between the RASC Lines and a leave camp, frequented by families and by male and female soldiers. When not guarding the camp and carrying out operational patrols in the rural area of Paralimni and Leopetri, the men were involved in running the leave camp (including providing dance partners at the Friday night dances). July began with the pleasing announcement that the wearing of the General Service Medal (with 'Cyprus' clasp) was authorized for those who had served in Cyprus for a period of 120 days from 1 April 1955.

The Defence White Paper in April 1957 announced the future shape and smaller size of

Golden Sands Camp. *A J G Pollard*

Britain's Armed Forces, that National Service was to be phased out with the final call-up during 1960, and that in the Army the number of Teeth Arm units would be reduced. It was not until 24 July that the detail of the fundamental reorganization of the Infantry of the Line was promulgated, amalgamating some regiments and grouping all into fourteen brigades and The Parachute Regiment. The resultant smaller Midland Brigade[15] was to comprise The Royal Warwickshire Regiment (Royal Warwicks), The Royal Leicestershire Regiment and The Sherwood Foresters (Foresters), with a single Brigade Depot. The subsequent decision for it to be Glen Parva Barracks, Leicester, was met with great joy. It was pleasing too that the first Representative Colonel of the new Brigade was to be Field Marshal The Viscount Montgomery of Alamein KG GCB DSO, Colonel The Royal Warwickshire Regiment, and the Brigade Colonel was to be Colonel G E P (Teddy) Hutchins DSO[16]. In the Midland Brigade, all lieutenant colonels and majors were to be placed for purposes of promotion on a common Brigade list; Regular Other Ranks would serve where possible with the Regiment of their choice, but promotion of the more senior would be on a Brigade basis. It was sad to learn that, in these changes, The Royal Leicesters' former close ally, The Royal Lincolnshire Regiment, was to be amalgamated with The Northamptonshire Regiment and join The East Anglian Brigade, thus ending many happy years with the Midland county regiments. The Royal Leicesters, for their part, were mightily relieved that their Regiment survived, and that they would continue always to be cheered into battle, and on the playing fields, with the cry 'Come on the Tigers!'

Meanwhile in Cyprus, the suspension of hostilities by EOKA continued, while political wrangling on the future of Cyprus persisted in Greece (where Archbishop Makarios – still denied entry to Cyprus – was based most of the time), Turkey, Britain and the United Nations in New York. In contrast to the wishes of the Greek Cypriot Community, Dr Fazil

Kutchuk, who led the Turkish Cypriots, was proposing that not self-determination but partition was the only real answer. In response to the improving general security situation, the Governor repealed more elements of the Emergency Regulations. Yet at the tactical level the Battalion continued its extensive and repetitive roster of guards and duties, while remaining poised to deploy on larger operations whenever called upon. On occasion sizable elements stood by at short notice to keep the peace on the anniversary of the Turks' capture of Famagusta in 1571, and when memorial services were held in the home villages of dead terrorists. Despite the normal round of garrison duties continuing, the Battalion found time to hold its own Rifle Meeting on 6 and 7 September, with Support Company winning the Inter-Company Shield. At the end of the month, for a week, most of the Battalion (less Support Company and part of HQ remaining at Karaolos Camp) was involved either in organizing and administering, or in competing in, the Cyprus District Rifle Meeting at Dhekelia. As a result of those competitions (in which the Battalion team came fourth out of the twenty-nine Major Units), Major John Bromhead and Staff Sergeant Bidwell REME were

Connaught Trophy Team 1957 (see Appendix P for names). *Trustees R Leicestershire Regt*

selected for the Army Cyprus Team. In addition, for the second year running, the Battalion Pistol Team, again under John Bromhead, won the Overseas Series of the ARA's Non-Central Duke of Connaught Trophy competition, scoring 97 points more than in the previous year's success. The Battalion's team of twelve riflemen and two LMG pairs, led by Lieutenants John Rees, J C D (John) Heggs and W H (Bill) Morris, came second in the Non-Central Middle East Battle Trophy match, comprising a 5-mile cross-country march carrying 26lb of equipment and a battle shoot immediately afterwards.

In mid-October, as a result of bomb attacks against both the Cyprus Broadcasting Station at Nicosia and at RAF Nicosia, the Battalion was once again called upon to guard the Famagusta electricity booster station. On 21 October, it was announced that on 1 December the Governorship of Cyprus would be transferred to Sir Hugh Foot GCMG KCVO OBE, a former Colonial Secretary of Cyprus, who also had wide experience of civil strife and terrorism in Palestine before the Second World War. The iron fist of a senior military man was to be replaced by a more conciliatory colonial servant. This news of the supersession of such a fine and inspiring soldier as Field Marshal Harding,[17] who had done so much to return Cyprus to normality, was a precursor to the sadness experienced by the Battalion when on 24 October Sergeant T (Thomas) Phillips of D Company died as a result of injuries sustained when he fell from the back of a moving vehicle on the ranges in Karaolos Camp.

Military preparations were then put in place in anticipation of OXI Day on 28 October, for which, unlike the previous years, Greek flags were permitted to be displayed for all twenty-four hours of that day. Helpfully, due to the alertness of a rural patrol mounted by the Royal Horse Guards, the EOKA operation order for OXI Day right across the island was captured. This enabled appropriate countermeasures to be mounted, which for the Battalion involved intensified patrolling in Famagusta/Varosha and the rural area to prevent slogans being daubed on walls and subversive banners being displayed. A, C and Support Companies were poised to counter disturbances in Famagusta/Varosha, and B and D Companies were deployed to Paralimni and Vatili respectively. B Company under Major Pat Creagh at Paralimni bore the brunt of EOKA's ire that day, where initially a priest using a loudspeaker from within his church exhorted the crowds outside. Thus roused, the crowds spilled into the streets and for several hours stone throwing was countered by baton charges and tear gas, with the area returning to normal only by mid-afternoon. D Company under Major A V C (Alan) Sheppard removed banners in several villages and a roadblock at Athna, and broke up a post-church procession at Vatili. In Varosha itself companies deployed to control matters around Ayios Nicolaos Church, where loudspeakers relayed the nationalistic messages of the day to the 'congregation' both inside and outside the building. The appearance of EOKA banners necessitated the use of some 'minimum force' baton charges ably led by Lieutenant John Wilkes to effect the arrest of the most vociferous. In total contrast, Turkish flags were permitted to be flown on 29 October for the Turkish Cypriot celebration of Turkish Independence Day, and no trouble occurred at all.

On 29 October, Field Marshal Harding paid his farewell visit to Famagusta Garrison, for which the Battalion – as the longest-serving major unit on the island – provided the Guard of Honour, commanded by Major D R (Duggie) Dalglish MC[18], who had recently taken over Support Company. That there was only five days' warning of the event in which to prepare soldiers who were long accustomed to IS duties, rather than ceremonial, taxed those involved and most especially the RSM. In time-honoured fashion it was 'alright on the day', despite the fact that one of the helicopters of the Governor's party landed on the wrong 'H' at Karaolos Camp and covered the Band and Drums and the Guard of Honour in a cloud of dust! At the conclusion of his inspection the Governor said:

> I feel greatly honoured that your Regiment, whom I know so well, has mounted a Guard of Honour for me. The bearing and turnout was quite first class and up to the high standards you have always set. I would like to thank every officer and man on parade for the honour they have paid me and I would like to wish every one of them the very best of luck in the future.

There then followed a major military competition for which the Battalion had been quietly and proficiently preparing for several months, despite the pressures of operational duties. This was 51 Indep Bde's Assault-at-Arms, in which every Rifle and Support Company weapon was fired. The MT Platoon under Lieutenant R A (Bob) Ross MM, the Drums Platoon's Stretcher Bearers under Sergeant A Holland and the Signals Platoon under Regimental Signals Officer (RSO) Lieutenant P P (Paul) Young, all had to prove themselves in competition, coming first, second and third respectively against the other units – the only part of the Battalion that was not actively tested in the field being the Orderly Room. That the 1st Battalion defeated all the other major units in Eastern Cyprus was of immense credit and pride, an achievement which in a Special Order of the Day on 4 November, the Commanding Officer described as giving him 'more pleasure than anything else that has occurred since I took command'.

Life as the RSO was not always filled with congratulations, particularly as the Commanding Officer was naturally a stickler for radio procedure and the use of appointment titles (for example, he as CO being 'Sunray' and the RMP being 'Watchdog'). On a different occasion, the CO was passing 'Four Mile Point' crossroads west of Famagusta when he saw and reported on the Battalion radio net that there were too many 'Watchdogs' around. The Rear Link operator consequently asked Brigade HQ why there were so many 'wash tubs lying around'. The mistranslation led Brigade HQ on a merry dance, for which Paul Young took the blame.

The Assault-at-Arms competition was followed, ten days later, by the Battalion being tasked to provide a company for a month at a time to man a camp at Mersiniki at 900 feet on the Lefkoniko Pass in the Kyrenia Mountains. Support Company deployed first, and among other things was responsible for setting up and guarding a police station at Akanthou 600 feet up on the north side of the range. Life in that terrain was extremely cold and challenging during the winter months. This new company-sized permanent detachment necessitated a reorganization of the operational duties roster into: IS Company (Famagusta/Varosha), Rural Company, Patrol & Fatigue Company, Golden Sands Company and Mersiniki Company. From 22 November, for a fortnight, a composite group of forty-four All Ranks from various companies under Lieutenant W J G (Bill) Brown and 2nd Lieutenant T B F (Tom) Hiney provided the Guard to the Governor at Government House in Nicosia, and it was reported as one of the best ever known there. These changes to the pattern of deployments did not prevent the Officers vs. Sergeants Annual Shooting Match being held, being narrowly won that year by the former.

Operations continued at a steady but lower ebb with, for example, for a week in early December, elements of Support and B Companies with 29 Fd Regt RA, some deploying by Sycamore helicopter, cordoning and searching Tria Teratsia for four EOKA terrorists. In contrast, under the command of Major John Dudley of Headquarter Company, the Battalion provided the 100-strong Guard of Honour at Nicosia on 3 December to welcome the new Governor, Sir Hugh Foot, who consequently wrote a very laudatory letter to the Commanding Officer.

The arrival of the new Governor was an important watershed in the political and military situation in Cyprus. In a parallel with the suspension of hostilities announced in April, Colonel Grivas had dedicated the spring and summer of 1957 to rebuilding an energetic and revitalized EOKA. Additional specialist training had taken place, a new 'youth' wing established, the Valiant Youth of EOKA ('ANE'), and Greek Cypriot villages were encouraged to prepare defensive measures should Turkish Cypriots attack. ANE militants had begun to appear on OXI Day and by late November the EOKA suspension of hostilities seemed over. Sir Hugh Foot announced at the outset that he had an open mind regarding Cyprus's future, yet for the time being he continued to prevent Archbishop Makarios from returning to Cyprus as the Ethnarch – his return being a key Greek Cypriot requirement for progress and their first hope for an indication of conciliation. EOKA illegally announced a general strike for 9 December to coincide with the start of the key Cyprus debate in the UN General Assembly in New York. Most shops and schools remained closed and in Famagusta/Varosha, in support of the Police Mobile Reserve, the IS Company was heavily committed with platoons involved over several hours in open fighting with stone-throwing and slogan-shouting youths in procession; there were many arrests and combatants on both sides were hurt. The same day at the Police Station at Akanthou, B Company's 6 Platoon under 2nd Lieutenant J W (John) Mansfield was besieged and stoned, but unharmed. For several more days the Battalion's companies were stood to at varying degrees of notice to deal with potentially troublesome Famagusta and Varosha. On 15 December, tension further rose after a member of the RMP killed a Greek Cypriot woman when firing over the heads of a rock-throwing crowd. However, news from New York that the UN General Assembly had rejected the Greek resolution was met by a stunned Greek Cypriot silence.

Meanwhile, acting on intelligence, in the early hours of 18 December, on Operation *Safety Pin* in conjunction with a Civil Police snatch party, two platoons of A Company under 2nd Lieutenants Tom Hiney and Peter Graham cordoned Styllos, a village 6 miles from Karaolos Camp, in search of EOKA terrorists. At the 'safe house', one was arrested in bed and one shot dead breaking out of the cordon, but the terrorist leader Pavlos Pavlakis escaped. Further searches of the house, assisted by a team of experts from the IS Training School, led to the discovery of documents, letters and leaflets, EOKA literature which the Police subsequently regarded as the best find since the Grivas diaries in Lysi fourteen months earlier. Sergeant Brown and Private Warnock then found three pistols and a quantity of shotgun cartridges.

The successful conclusion of this operation coincided with the start of some three weeks of the heaviest rains experienced in Cyprus's history, which severely affected the Christmas celebrations and sports fixtures over this period. B Company was on detachment at Mersiniki, and 2nd Lieutenant D R (David) Nevile with 4 Platoon were deployed at the

Police Station at Ovgoros. Seeking to ameliorate matters in what was considered a particularly 'bad' area, Nevile asked the Battalion Intelligence Officer, 2nd Lieutenant F A H (Anthony) Swallow, to produce a banner, wishing the villagers a Happy Christmas. Duly delivered on Christmas Eve, the banner's message – looking very smart in Greek script painted in silver on a black background – turned out to have been misspelt. But it amused the locals immensely and had the beneficial effect in that a delegation from the village provided the soldiers with some special cakes on Christmas Day, the very first fraternization by them with the Security Forces.

With B Company detached at Mersiniki and D Company at Golden Sands Camp, for the rest of the Battalion the Christmas stand-down period was from 23 to 27 December, with 29 Fd Regt RA taking over the IS duties – the role being reversed for the Gunners' 'Christmas' over New Year. A familiar series of seasonal events was held in Karaolos Camp.

Early in 1958 senior appointments were held as follows:

CO:	Lieutenant Colonel A W D Nicholls MC	OC C Coy:	Major K P P Goldschmidt
		CSM C Coy:	WO2 G Seagrave
2IC:	Major M St G Pallot	OC D Coy:	Major A C V Sheppard
Adjt:	Captain T Holloway	CSM D Coy:	WO2 N H P Jenks MM
RSM:	WO1 T J Marston	OC Sp Coy:	Major D R Dalglish MC
QM:	Major (QM) E H Scanlon	CSM Sp Coy:	WO2 T Ward
RQMS:	WO2 P O'Sullivan	OC HQ Coy:	Captain J T Dudley
OC A Coy:	Captain D Wale	CSM HQ Coy:	WO2 A G Pugh
CSM A Coy:	WO2 W Reynolds	Bandmaster:	WO1 D K Walker ARCM
OC B Coy:	Major J P N Creagh	Drum Major:	Sgt A Holland
CSM B Coy:	WO2 C Sanderson		

Despite the tempo of IS operations during the cooler months, time was found for a range of sport to be played and to a very high standard at Battalion level and below. Organized by Major Duggie Dalglish (another of the fine sportsmen who joined the Regiment in the 1930s and who had played for Hampshire in 1937), captained by 2nd Lieutenant D R (David) Trentham and with nine officers in the side, the Battalion Rugby Team won the Area Cup for the second year running. This put them into the Cyprus Semi-Finals, which it lost due to serious injuries to six players and the rock-hard ground significantly degrading the number of available key players. The Football Team, led by Colour Sergeant C Murray, had a good season, as did the Hockey (with Lieutenant John Rees and Sergeant Castleton playing for the Army Cyprus), the Basketball and the Cross-Country (with 2nd Lieutenant Tom Hiney and Private Perkins running for Army Cyprus). Inter-Company SLR and Small-Bore shooting competitions were held and a Battalion Rifle Meeting in April shortly before the end of the tour, in which B Company's victory was a very satisfactory conclusion to Major Pat Creagh's two-year tenure of command. Overall in the 1957/58 Sports Season, 'Green Tigers' were awarded in six sports to forty-four men.

On the Inter-Service scene, temporarily detaching his ships from anti-gun-running patrols off the coast, Captain J S Dalglish CVO RN – Major Duggie Dalglish's elder brother – brought a hockey team from his Minesweeper Squadron to play the Battalion, a liaison

1st R Leicesters' Rugby Team 1957/58 (see Appendix P for names). *Trustees R Leicestershire Regt*

which led to soldiers and sailors exchanging places on operations to see how the other worked. It was Captain Dalglish who suggested to his younger brother that an affiliation between the Regiment and HMS *Tiger* be formally established when the ship was completed later that year. This affiliation is described in Chapter 13.

While the Governor continued to seek for a political solution, Greek Cypriot unrest broke out between Communist and Nationalist factions (which did not help the ENOSIS cause). For the first time, elements of the Turkish Cypriot community began to protest at the Governor's perceived pro-Greek stance as he had released a number of detainees, and they started to demand partition. In Famagusta this initially manifested itself with serious trouble on 28 January. Three companies of the Battalion were deployed to prevent the Turks from spilling out of the Old City into the mainly-Greek Varosha district. In the ensuing confrontation, some Turkish youths on the rampart walls hurled rocks and stones onto the soldiers below and injured among others Major Mike Pallot, the acting CO. Two Turkish rioters were shot dead and two wounded. A curfew was then imposed overnight and the following day the presence of the three companies helped to prevent any trouble during the Turks' funerals. On three separate occasions in February and March, companies were deployed to turn away coachloads of crowds and prevent disturbances during dead EOKA leaders' memorial services; at Lysi on 2 March it was recorded that 'Extremely good communications were established to the Commanding Officer's house by Major Pat Creagh, using a civilian telephone box!' Indeed, so often had that village been 'visited' by the Battalion over the previous twenty-eight months, that more than one company commander laid claim to the title 'Uncrowned King of Lysi'. It was also about this time that the Battalion was very pleased to receive the news of the awards of CB to Major General 'Joe' Kendrew, the GOC and Director of Operations, and MIDs for Major Peter Badger, 2nd Lieutenant Tony Pollard, both formerly of D Company, and Corporal Norman James of C Company.

Meanwhile in Burma, on 9 February 1958, the Rangoon Memorial was unveiled by General Sir Francis Festing GCB KBE DSO, C-in-C FARELF. On the stone frieze high inside the central rotunda of the Memorial are inscribed the words:

1939-1945
HERE ARE RECORDED
THE NAMES OF TWENTY-SEVEN THOUSAND SOLDIERS OF MANY RACES
UNITED IN SERVICE TO THE BRITISH CROWN
WHO GAVE THEIR LIVES IN BURMA AND ASSAM
BUT TO WHOM THE FORTUNE OF WAR DENIED
THE CUSTOMARY RITES ACCORDED TO THEIR COMRADES IN DEATH
THEY DIED FOR ALL FREE MEN

In the South Court of the Memorial are the names of fifty-five men of the 2nd and 7th Battalions The Leicestershire Regiment, who died in the 2nd Chindit Expedition in Burma in 1944. Surrounding the Memorial are 7,000 graves.

The Regiment was very greatly honoured on that day in February 1958 by The Royal Garhwal Rifles of the Indian Army which arranged for a wreath to be laid on the Regiment's behalf in memory of the eighty officers and men of The Leicesters who laid down their lives in the Burma and Assam campaign. From 1914 to 1916 the 2nd Leicesters had formed the third battalion of the Garhwal Brigade in France and had fought side by side with two battalions of 39th Garhwal Rifles at such famous actions as La Bassée, Neuve Chapelle and Festubert. An unofficial affiliation flourished for many years, and the Royal Leicesters remained grateful for what that fine Regiment had done for it.

In his address General Festing said:

This Memorial presents a picture of a simple truth – that of a multitude of men, of many Races and widely differing Faiths, who gave their lives in a common cause. Of that cause Field Marshal Slim has written:

'A spiritual foundation, belief in a cause, there must be. We had this. We fought for the clean, the decent, the free things of life, for the right to live our lives in our own way, as others could live theirs, to worship God in what Faith we chose, to be free in body and mind, and for our children to be free. We fought only because the powers of evil had attacked these things. No matter what the Religion or Race of any man in the Fourteenth Army, he *must* feel this, feel that he had indeed a worthy cause, and that, if he did not defend it, life would not be worth living for him or his children. They died for all free men.

It is these six words, carved in five languages in the centre of this Memorial, that I now have the honour and privilege to unveil.

Major Ian Hamilton laid a wreath that day on behalf of the Royal Tigers' Association.

Meanwhile, in Cyprus, early in March, Colonel Grivas urged the boycott of British goods and services, and announced that shops were not to serve the British. Apart from NAAFI staff occasionally going on strike, this 'economic blockade' actually disadvantaged the Greek Cypriot community rather more than the British. It swiftly led to the Governor enacting legislation to ban the nationalist youth movement ANE, whose members had been used to distribute EOKA propaganda and, beginning to make its presence felt more, was increasingly involved in intimidating shopkeepers in Famagusta and elsewhere. In mid-March, many small arson attacks on fire stations and explosions at water pumping stations took place around the island, perpetrated by EOKA activists. The Battalion henceforth provided a guard at the Kato Varosha pumping station. Because of these terrorist low-level activities, on 25 March the Security Forces were deployed in strategic places in anticipation of further disturbances on Greek Independence Day (1821), which across the island passed off peacefully, a situation which contrasted markedly with 1 April, the third anniversary of the start of the EOKA uprising, in anticipation of which all Security Force leave was cancelled. Again, pre-emptive deployment by the Battalion in its area prevented attacks on property it guarded, but did not stop bombs exploding at six other locations in the Famagusta area, and a limpet mine causing damage to a ship in the harbour. Across the island in the first fortnight of April some fifty bombs were detonated.

Despite the heightened security situation, the Governor attended the Battalion's farewell Beating Retreat and Officers' Cocktail Party on 12 April, and a week later the Warrant Officers and Sergeants held a farewell ball at Golden Sands Camp. In the meantime a Police Special Branch interpreter died of wounds after being shot while off-duty in Varosha on 14 April, EOKA claiming that he had been a brutal interrogator. The follow-up operation found bombs and explosives in a cinema which were too dangerous to move. Consequently they were destroyed *in situ* which in turn destroyed the cinema and damaged adjoining Greek Cypriot property. Sadly, on 19 April, Private R K Pountney of the Drums Platoon, who had joined the Battalion eleven weeks before, was drowned off Golden Sands; his was the Battalion's seventeenth and last death in Cyprus.

So the tempo heightened during the Battalion's final weeks on the island, as in response to the increase in the marked upturn in terrorist activity and an EOKA leaflet announcing that Britons would again be the targets of EOKA gunmen, the restrictions on Security Forces' movements, which had been lifted in April 1957, were reimposed. The Families Beach Centre on Hippocrates Street was again protected by the Battalion, whose troops were also involved in guarding the new Vatili police station as it was being built. The last major operational event in which the Battalion was involved followed the murder on 4 May of two RMP NCOs in Varosha when it assisted in rounding up 400 Greek Cypriot youths. Two days later the Battalion handed over all its IS duties and control of the Famagusta Battalion's AOR passed to 1st Battalion The Royal Ulster Rifles (1 RUR). It was but nineteen years since this Battalion handed over an operational role and a camp to 1 RUR. The previous volume of the Regimental History recounts that in 1939, on the North-West Frontier of India, 'On a terribly cold and rainy day, the 29th April, the Battalion was relieved at Razani by the Royal Ulster Rifles.' And so best Royal Leicesters' wishes were again extended to the men from Ulster. As a handover tailpiece, the Signals Platoon discovered that it had one WS19 radio 'buckshee', which seemed to 1 RUR nearly as bad as having one missing. As they were reluctant to accept it, it was handed to the grateful Middlesex Regiment!

Final preparations for departure were made, including a Thanksgiving Service at St George's Garrison Church and a Memorial Service at Wayne's Keep Military Cemetery at Nicosia, where wreaths were laid on the graves of fifteen of those who had died in Cyprus and had been buried there with full military honours – two of the dead, Private Malcolm Rowley and Lieutenant Jim Walker, had been flown home to England for burial; in November 1957, the family of the latter dedicated a stained-glass window in his home church at Charlton Marshall in Dorset. It was to be another forty-five years, in 2003, before a memorial for all seventeen was to be dedicated in the Regimental Chapel in Leicester Cathedral (see Chapter 12).

It was particularly gratifying for the Commanding Officer to receive a letter from the Commissioner Famagusta which said:

> On the eve of your departure from the Island, I would like to express my warmest thanks to all ranks of your Regiment for the loyal support given to me and the District Administration during the Regiment's stay in Famagusta District. The sense of discipline and responsibility of the officers and men in the face of extreme provocation during the worst period of the Emergency are worthy of the highest praise. Thank you again. May God bless you and your Regiment.

In addition, Major General 'Joe' Kendrew paid a farewell visit and with most of the Battalion on parade he made a brief and congratulatory speech, saying goodbye to all ranks.

On 13 May 1958, in a convoy of 10-ton lorries, the Battalion left Karaolos Camp for the last time, to embark at Famagusta Harbour on HMS *Devonshire*. Among the party of distinguished visitors who came aboard to say farewell was Major General 'Joe' Kendrew, whose presence in Cyprus as GOC and Director of Operations had always been a source of great pride and reassurance.

Battalion life had been an unusual mix of operations, normal military camp life and sport. Those in its senior positions had seen enough of *la vie militaire* in peace and war to know that training, sport and family life were all essential adjuncts to the type of military operations in which the Battalion was involved. They loved their families, the Regiment and sport, and knew that life had to be as normal as possible in order to keep up with the operational tempo. After two and a half years of active service and one of the longest tours of any battalion during the Cyprus Emergency, so ended another proud chapter in the history of the Regiment. Counter-terrorist and IS operations are demanding on soldiers, both physically and mentally, and call for diplomacy as well as fighting qualities, and a special kind of wariness and cunning. In that campaign, the young National Service officers and men of the Battalion in particular had played such a valuable part, and seventeen men of the Battalion had died during the tour. By unusual coincidence, four of the National Service subalterns who served in Cyprus (David Barlow, 'Ben' Elliott, P R (Robin) Starkey and G M (Malcolm) Stonestreet) plus Tom Hiney, a Regular officer, subsequently became priests in the Church of England.

Later in 1958, the Battalion was very pleased that its contribution to the success of operations in Cyprus had been recognized by several awards: the OBE to the Commanding

Officer, Lieutenant Colonel 'Spike' Nicholls, the MBE to RSM Tommy Marston, and an MID to Major Mike Pallot, the Second-in-Command, plus Commander-in-Chief's Certificates to HQ Company's Colour Sergeant J (John) Pearce of the MT Platoon and Sergeant J (Joe) Parren of the Medical Section.

Of note also is that, while the 1st Battalion was performing with such distinction in Cyprus, some officers and SNCOs of the Regiment were serving widely on secondment throughout the British Commonwealth, with the Aden Levies, Barbados Local Forces, the Federation of Malaya Military Forces, the Gold Coast Regiment, the Hong Kong Volunteers, the King's African Rifles and the Nigeria Regiment.

The Battalion left the Island in a state of renewed turmoil and an upturn in violence – with the Greek Cypriot community demanding self-rule and the Turkish Cypriot community demanding partition. On the basis of the Zurich and London Agreements, Archbishop Makarios was permitted to return to Cyprus from exile in 1959, Colonel Grivas declared a permanent EOKA ceasefire and left for Greece, and a political and constitutional settlement was reached between Britain, Greece, Turkey and the Greek Cypriots and the Turkish Cypriots. The settlement explicitly denied 'enosis' – the union with Greece sought by EOKA. A guarantee was also given by Turkey and Greece – both members of NATO – that neither would annex Cyprus. In August 1960, Cyprus became an independent republic within the British Commonwealth, with a Greek Cypriot President – initially Archbishop Makarios – and a Turkish Cypriot Vice-President – initially Dr Fazil Kutchuk. Britain retains two Sovereign Base Areas (around Dhekelia in the east and Episkopi/Akrotiri in the south) and other installations from which to exercise its strategic objectives in the Middle East.

In 1974 when the Right-Wing Greek officers of the Cypriot National Guard overthrew the recently re-elected Archbishop Makarios, the Turkish Army invaded Northern Cyprus on a 'peacekeeping operation to protect "its" Turkish minority'. This Turkish invasion brought Turkey and Greece into conflict. The Turkish Army occupied the northern third of the Island, forcing over 140,000 of the northern Greek Cypriot population to flee to the south of the Island, backfilling them with Turkish Cypriots from the southern part and later with very large numbers of Turks from Mainland Turkey. Since that time the Island has effectively been partitioned into two separate states, with a UN Buffer Zone (the 'Green Line') policed by UN troops separating the two sectors. In the east the Green Line winds its way through what was the 1st Battalion's 1956-58 AOR, with only Dherinia, Phrenaros, Avgorou and land to the south being in the Greek Sector, the remainder being 'Turkish'. Unforeseen by the original 1956 Greek Cypriot strategy, the unintended political outcome was exactly the opposite of 'Enosis with Greece'; it was the Turkish Cypriot Northern Cyprus being in 'enosis' (or whatever the Turkish word might be) with Turkey!

In 1983, in order to consolidate the *de facto* situation, the Turkish Cypriots declared the independence of the Turkish sector of the Island, the self-styled 'Turkish Republic of Northern Cyprus', recognised only by Turkey. It covers 38 per cent of the Island and contains some 250,000 people. In 2004 the UN drew up a plan for reunification on the basis of a loose federation. The Turks in the north voted for it, the Greeks in the south voted against. That year the 'Greek' Republic of Cyprus became a member of the

European Union, the Council of Europe, the World Trade Organisation, and the Organisation on Security & Cooperation in Europe. In 2008 the leaders of the two communities started talks in September to find a 'mutually acceptable solution to the Cyprus problem which will safeguard the interests of the Greek Cypriots and the Turkish Cypriots'. The most fundamental differences relate to the property rights of the Greek Cypriots who were forced to leave the north by the Turkish intervention of 1974.

To mark the 50th anniversary of the ending of the Cyprus Emergency, The British Memorial is to be erected in Cyprus in the old British cemetery at Kyrenia, to be unveiled on Remembrance Day 2009. On it will be inscribed the names of the 371 British servicemen – twenty-eight members of the Royal Navy and Royal Marines, 274 British Army, and sixty-nine Royal Air Force – who died there on active service 1955–1959. Wayne's Keep Cemetery near Nicosia – where many of the Servicemen (including The Royal Leicesters') are buried – has not been chosen as the site for the Memorial as Wayne's Keep is now in the UN Buffer Zone which lies between the Republic of Cyprus in the south and the Turkish Republic of Northern Cyprus in the north, and consequently public accessibility to it is very difficult.

Notes

1 Derek Watson had been awarded the DSO while commanding 4th KAR in Burma in 1944.
2 1st R Leicesters had served under Abdy Ricketts in 29 Brit Inf Bde in Korea 1951-52.
3 'Spike' Nicholls had been awarded the MC as a company commander in 2nd Leicesters, near Heraklion in Crete, in 1941.
4 Bob Ross had been awarded the MM while a Sergeant serving in 7th Leicesters on the 2nd Chindit Expedition in Burma in 1944.
5 Stuart Smith, then of The Royal Fusiliers, had been appointed MBE for work as a Captain IO of HQ 17 Ind Inf Bde and GSO3 (Air) of HQ 8 Ind Div in Italy in 1944-45.
6 Ian Jessop had been awarded the MC as a platoon commander in 1/5th Leicesters in Norway in 1940.
7 Bill Pound had been awarded the MM for action as a Private in 6th Para in Greece in 1945.
8 John Marriott had been awarded the MC as Intelligence Officer in 2nd Leicesters in Palestine in 1939.
9 Esmond Morrison had been awarded the MC serving as Staff Captain HQ 18 Inf Bde in France in Jan 1918.
10 Lieutenant General Sir Colin Callander KCB KBE MC, Colonel The Royal Leicestershire Regiment 1954-63. See Appendix N.
11 'Joe' Kendrew was to become Colonel The Royal Leicestershire Regiment 1963-64. See Appendix N.
12 1st Leicesters won the Army Rugby Cup in 1908, 1911 and 1912 (and were runners-up in 1910). 2nd Leicesters were runners-up in 1932 and 1933, and were semi-finalists on three other occasions in the 1930s.
13 Ken Goldschmidt had played for Hampshire when they won the County Championship in 1936 and had been a Barbarian.
14 'Jimmy' Jenks had been awarded the MM as a platoon sergeant in 1st R Leicesters in Korea in 1951.
15 In 1948, largely for administrative convenience, infantry county regiments had been grouped into territorial brigades, The Midland Brigade comprising The Royal Warwickshire Regiment, The Royal Lincolnshire Regiment, The Royal Leicestershire Regiment and The Sherwood Foresters. Its HQ was at Budbrooke Barracks, Warwick.
16 Teddy Hutchins had been awarded the DSO as CO of 1st R Leicesters in Korea in 1951-52. In 1961, he was to become Marshal of the City of London.
17 A former Somerset Light Infantry officer, on departure from Cyprus FM Sir John Harding GCB CBE DSO MC was created Baron Harding of South Petherton.
18 Duggie Dalglish had been awarded the MC as a platoon commander in 2nd Leicesters in Palestine in 1940.

Chapter 2

1st Battalion: Plymouth and Münster 1958-62

Plymouth: May 1958 to March 1959

At the end of February 1958, the Battalion Advance Party under Major M St G (Mike) Pallot, the Second-in-Command, had left Cyprus and after their leave assembled at the new posting, Seaton Barracks, at Crownhill 3 miles inland from Plymouth, a barracks built in 1938 which had been little used by regular soldiers since 1945. A great deal had to be done to the premises before they could be considered ready to be used by a peacetime Regular battalion. One untypical instance was the difficulty in persuading the local farmer that, convenient though it might have been to him, it was no longer acceptable for him to drive a herd of cows through the main gate and past the Main Guardroom twice a day!

It was at this time that Major O J (John) Mirylees MC rejoined the Battalion after secondment to the Federation of Malaya Military Forces, during which he had been awarded the MC for his conduct of a night ambush of communist terrorists at Siputeh near Ipoh, Perak, in October 1956. The *London Gazette* citation dated 28 May 1957 read: 'For vigorous leadership and gallantry in action in the Malayan jungle whilst in command of B Company 3rd Battalion The Malay Regiment.

Major John Mirylees MC. *O J Mirylees*

Although severely wounded and in great pain he continued to conduct an operation for over an hour until this action was completed.'

The Band had splendidly entertained the passengers on HMT *Devonshire* on its journey through the Mediterranean, and it was not until that ship had been played out of Gibraltar that the musicians could put away their instruments. The Main Body of the Battalion was in good spirits as it arrived from Cyprus at Liverpool on 23 May. There it was met by among others the Lord Mayor of Leicester, Alderman Sidney Brown TD[1], the Colonel of The Regiment, Lieutenant General Sir Colin Callander KCB KBE MC, and the Midland Brigade

Colonel, Colonel G E P (Teddy) Hutchins DSO.[2] The Battalion (less Support Company's baggage party) went straight on six weeks' leave, reassembling on 7 July. A Company under Captain Derek Wale returned in late June to deploy to Penhale in Cornwall to provide the sponsor headquarters for TA units' summer training.

Compared with Cyprus, the Battalion had a different Order of Battle and a lower Established Strength. D Company was disbanded as a rifle company and replaced by a small Training Company. The Anti-Tank Platoon, now equipped with the 120mm MOBAT towed recoilless anti-tank gun, was reformed in Support Company, which also comprised the MMG Platoon, equipped with Vickers .303" MMGs, and the Mortar Platoon, with six 3" mortars. The rifle company platoon weapons were the Lee Enfield .303" rifle and similar calibre Bren LMG, the .38" Sten gun, the 2" mortar and the 3.5" rocket launcher. The .38" revolver was the personal weapon of many officers. Communication was provided by the WS19, 62, 88 and B47, and dispatch riders on motorcycles (upon which on field training exercises several senior ranks appeared although it was not known whether they had passed their test). Mechanical transport comprised ½-ton Land Rover and Austin Champ 'jeeps', and 1-ton and 3-ton trucks.

The Battalion was part of 2 Infantry Brigade (2 Inf Bde) under Brigadier G H Lea DSO MBE, the other battalions being 1st Battalion The Northamptonshire Regiment (1 Northamptons) and initially 1st Battalion The Rifle Brigade. For operations it was part of 1st Infantry Division (1 Inf Div) of Southern Command; for administration it was commanded by HQ South-West District. The Battalion's arrival had already been heralded in the area by the opening in June of a new public house, The Tiger, near Seaton Barracks.

On arrival at Plymouth senior appointments were held as follows:

CO:	Lieutenant Colonel A W D Nicholls OBE MC	OC C Coy:	Major O J Mirylees MC
		CSM C Coy:	WO2 G Seagrave
2IC:	Major M St G Pallot	OC Sp Coy:	Major K P P Goldschmidt
Adjt:	Captain T Holloway	CSM Sp Coy:	WO2 T Ward
RSM:	WO1 T J Marston	OC Trg Coy:	Captain G A Havilland MC[3]
QM:	Major (QM) E H Scanlon	CSM Trg Coy:	WO2 N H P Jenks MM
RQMS:	WO2 P O'Sullivan	OC HQ Coy:	Major J T Dudley
OC A Coy:	Major A C V Sheppard	CSM HQ Coy:	WO2 A G Pugh
CSM A Coy:	WO2 W Reynolds	Bandmaster:	WO1 D K Walker ARCM
OC B Coy:	Captain W J G Brown	Drum Major:	Sgt A Holland
CSM B Coy:	WO2 C Sanderson		

It was a pleasant change from Cyprus for the soldiers now to be able to relax off-duty, to sample the local night life and public houses, and to make the occasional weekend round trip to Leicestershire. The important activity of training for new individual roles in conventional war (and its attendant infantry deployment in Field Service Marching Order (FSMO) over battledress) continued throughout the remainder of the summer but, disappointingly and in marked contrast to Cyprus, it was hampered by the continuous wet weather – heavy, chilling rain. The local Dartmoor area had many rifle and field-firing ranges, and manoeuvre areas, so good training facilities were close at hand and available.

During the summer the volume of The Regimental History previous to this one was published, edited by Brigadier W E Underhill OBE[4] and printed by the synonymous firm

Underhill (Plymouth) Limited. Covering the years 1928-55, it was very well received both by the Regiment and by a wider readership. Of note is the letter – dated 4 June 1958 and reproduced in full at Appendix H – which the Editor of *The Green Tiger* received from Brigadier B E Fergusson DSO OBE. Bernard Fergusson had been Commander 16th Infantry Brigade in which 2nd Battalion The Leicestershire Regiment had served with such distinction in the Second Chindit Expedition in Burma in 1944. He was a very shrewd judge and a distinguished public servant[5].

In what was to affect many units of the Regiment, in July 1958 the Colonel of The Regiment made an announcement of further organizational change, which would result in the formation of The Forester Brigade. He said:

Before the last War, each Regular Regiment had one regular battalion serving at home, and another overseas. Since the War, only one regular battalion has remained, and as a result there has been much cross-posting from one Regiment to another. The three regular battalions in our Brigade will in future be more closely linked, and this has presented a good opportunity to change the title of The Midland Brigade to one that would better reflect the ancient roots of the three Regiments comprising the Brigade. The Royal Warwickshire Regiment was founded 283 years ago, The Royal Leicestershire Regiment 270 years ago, and The Sherwood Foresters had their origin in The Nottinghamshire Regiment founded 217 years ago.

In olden days, the Midland land of England was historically forest land, the greatest forest country in England. The forests of Arden, Charnwood and Sherwood covered our present four regimental counties of Warwickshire, Leicestershire, Nottinghamshire and Derbyshire. The Colonels of the three Regiments decided to establish our historic connections with these great forests and chose the title 'The Forester Brigade' to be a good and inspiring name for a new Brigade, whose Regiments must be so closely linked together. Each Regiment will retain its individual name and identity, but Glen Parva Barracks, South Wigston, has been chosen as the Brigade Depot. All regular recruits from all three Regiments will be trained there, after the other two Depots close down in a few years' time. A Brigade capbadge and buttons have been designed and will contain something from each regimental badge. The Royal Tiger will be on the new badge.

This announcement was greeted with a certain sadness, combined with relief that the Regiment was not going to be amalgamated.

Within six months the design for the new silver-and-gilt Brigade capbadge had been approved by HM The Queen, containing as it did something from the existing badges of the three regiments (see plate section). The Maltese Cross of The Sherwood Foresters, charged in the centre with the 'Antelope within the Garter' of The Royal Warwickshire Regiment. Underneath in a 'scroll proper' is the title 'Forester Brigade', with branches of oak on each side, the whole surmounted by the 'Royal Tiger' of The Royal Leicestershire Regiment. Other aspects of the reorganization were finalized over the ensuing months, including: a green backing would be worn to the Brigade capbadge and rank badges; battalions would continue to fly their regimental flags and the Brigade Flag (comprising the Brigade badge on a green background) would be flown at the Depot; the Royal Leicesters' Regimental Headquarters would remain at Glen Parva Barracks; the Regimental

Association and the Regimental Magazine, *The Green Tiger*, would continue unchanged; each regiment would loan its best 'Depot Silver' to the new Depot, included among which was the old 2nd Leicesters' Officers' Mess centrepiece.

Glen Parva Barracks was chosen as the Brigade Depot because, despite its eighty-year age, it had superior training facilities, sports grounds, married quarters, availability and accessibility of amenities outside barracks, and a central position in the Brigade area.

Meanwhile Battalion life continued apace. Individual training led to platoon and company exercises. B Company spent three days marching back from Penhale. At the end of August B Company was involved in making a War Office training film on 'Escape and Evasion', just before the whole Battalion was placed at four days' notice to move on Operation *Dimension* under 2 Inf Bde, together with 1 Northamptons and 1st Battalion The South Wales Borderers (1 SWB). After preparing air move staff tables, weighing equipment and inoculating All Ranks, the operation was eventually stood down in late October. This 'practice' was not wasted – indeed any training seldom is – when in November another air movement exercise, *Sputnik*, utilizing Yelverton airstrip, was carried out and culminated in a battalion field training exercise, the first time it had deployed as an entity since Iserlohn in 1954. On the exercise, of special notoriety, Lance Corporal Evans, a bugler, earned distinction by sounding 'Company Commanders' instead of 'Company Guides' to report to the RSM!

At the end of November the Battalion was informed that it would move to Germany to be part of the British Army on the Rhine (BAOR) in April 1959, to replace 1st Battalion The Royal Northumberland Fusiliers. This news was still being digested when the Brigade Commander carried out the Administrative Inspection on 11 December. Having previously won the Inter-Company Drill Shield, HQ Company under Major John Dudley was the lead company on parade that day. The Battalion was on very fine form, and – having been selected to trial the new uniforms of No. 2 Dress, the new parade dress replacing Battle Dress and No. 1 Dress (Blues) – inspired perhaps at the prospect of new uniforms in the future. The inspection overall earned high praise, which was a most fitting and deserved result for Lieutenant Colonel 'Spike' Nicholls in his final month in command. It was with a heavy heart that a fond farewell was given to him and his wife Mary at Christmas.

Early in 1959, on return from a conventional Christmas break and the new Commanding Officer's reconnaissance to Germany, Lieutenant Colonel Mike Pallot addressed the Battalion, leaving it in no doubt about what he expected of it on its arrival in Germany, namely 'to make quite certain that we are going to be the best British battalion in Germany in 1959'. He also made clear his views on training, administration, discipline and competitions, and these provided a spur to renewed activity in the New Year.

Normal peacetime soldiering was continuing, of which battalion-level sport played a prominent part and was embarked upon on the softer and greener fields of England. Within the barracks area there were good sports facilities, including two gymnasia, several rugby and football pitches, and hockey on the square. Constrained by the soggy summer, the cricketers, led by Major Duggie Dalglish, played matches against local sides, and RN and Army units, with several players representing the United Services CC in Plymouth. An Inter-Company Novices Boxing competition was won by B Company and the Battalion team got through several rounds of the South-West District Inter-Unit competition. At football, under the direction of Captain T (Terry) Holloway, two strong teams represented the Battalion, playing in local Service and civilian leagues. The 1st XI, led by WO2 T Ward, won thirteen out of eighteen matches, with Private O'Connor playing many games for Plymouth Argyle Reserves, and Lance Corporal Alcock being on Coventry City's books – this 'professionalism' being one of the benefits of having National Servicemen. Rugby continued its search for the pre-war eminence that had been kick-started in Cyprus. The Battalion fielded two XVs on numerous occasions, but serious successes eluded them after the Advance Party to Germany departed in the New Year. Nevertheless, the 1st XV reached the Sixth Round of the Army Cup, and in a 'friendly' drew with its Brigade neighbours, 1 SWB, the UK Finalists of the Army Cup. The very best players were selected for Devonport Services, Captain R T (Roger) Bogg becoming an Army trialist and Lieutenant John Heggs playing for Devon both on the wing and in the second row. Despite the gladiators being needed by other sports teams, the Hockey XI under WO2 Charles Sanderson fulfilled a busy fixture list, which included matches on most Saturday and Wednesday afternoons. In contrast to Famagusta's rubbish dumps, the Cross-Country Team under Captain Bill Brown enjoyed the Plymouth countryside. In small-bore shooting, over 150 men took part in the twice-weekly training sessions, and Support Company, led by individual winner, Sergeant K (Ken) Colclough, won the Inter-Company Competition. Over this period 'Green Tigers' were awarded to eighteen players in three sports.

As the Army thinned down, the manning of the Battalion was not adversely affected by premature retirement of Other Ranks or of officers – many majors retiring with a redundancy payment which was universally known as a 'golden bowler' (hat). Looking ahead there were obvious and appealing advantages of an All-Regular Army, but these were not to manifest themselves until the mid-1960s. The phasing out of National Service began inevitably to reduce the throughput of the various skills and talents the individuals brought. Furthermore, recruiting of Regular private soldiers continued to be a problem. The Royal Leicesters were better than most infantry regiments with its throughput of Junior Leaders. But, due to very full employment in a diversity of industries in Leicester, the Regiment was consistently below its monthly target for recruiting Regulars. Hopes for improvement of recruiting and retention for the Army were increased with the publication of the Griggs Report. Among its many recommendations were improvements in Living and Service conditions, including Pay and Allowances, to take effect from 1 April 1959. They encompassed Disturbance Allowance, Boarding School Allowance, increases in pensions and gratuities, and an automatic review at least biannually. It also led to ORs' dining halls being equipped with cutlery, so that individuals did not have to carry their own KFS. All this was aimed at making a soldier's life much more comparable with that of a civilian.

The Band which, with the Corps of Drums, spent six weeks in Leicestershire during the 1958 summer, seeking to drum up recruits, appeared on national television in the 'Top Town' Competition when Plymouth were defeated by Brighton.

It was around this time that officers arrived from other Midland Brigade regiments, notably Majors R G M (Rodney) Green MC[6] and P J (Peter) Heath from The Sherwood Foresters, and Lieutenant R H (Dick) Robinson transferred in from the Royal Lincolns. Lieutenants Tony Pollard and Anthony Swallow, former National Service officers, rejoined as Regulars.

The short tour of duty at Plymouth drew rapidly to a close, happy for most, except for the MMG Platoon which had to disband to conform to infantry battalion orders of battle in BAOR. So ended many decades of the use of this weapon in the Regiment's Regular battalion, Lieutenant John Heggs being the Platoon's last commander.

In preparation for the departure from Seaton Barracks, the customary farewell events were held including an Officers' Mess Cocktail Party, attended by among others the Lord Mayor of Leicester, Alderman Sidney Brown.

Münster: March 1959 to July 1962

After a break of five years, in March 1959 the Battalion once more found itself in West Germany (officially the Federal Republic of Germany (FRG)) as part of the British Army on the Rhine (BAOR). A country of some 96,000 square miles, West Germany had a population of about 45 million, of whom 49 per cent were Catholic and 45 per cent Protestant, and had its capital in Bonn. The Battalion was based at Münster, in Westphalia, in the former British Zone of Occupation, in a country reconstructing well politically and militarily after the Second World War, and having since 1955 been a member of NATO.

After the steep hills and running streams of Plymouth, the flat countryside of Münsterland presented a striking contrast. Westphalia was a highly agricultural district, interlaced with canals and rivers. Münster itself was an old cathedral city about the size of Derby and, having been badly damaged during the Second World War, had been extensively rebuilt in pleasing style.

Being a university town and strongly Catholic, the entertainment offered was inclined to be staid, offering little 'night life' worthy of the name, though eating houses were plentiful and good. There was an excellent theatre in a modernistic design. A large hall (like London's Olympia) provided light relief for such events as ice shows, displays and show jumping. For the sightseer there were museums, the university buildings themselves and a large zoo; and also there was a splendid fifteenth-century cathedral. There was one Army Kinema Corporation (AKC) cinema in the town and a large NAAFI shop selling clothing, electrical appliances and the normal range of goods. A second NAAFI shop was situated conveniently near the married quarters some 2 miles out of town.

Münster was an old garrison town and to the local inhabitants the soldier was a familiar sight, though not always a welcome one, regardless of the soldier's nationality. The various barracks in 1959 were mainly outside the town. Buller Barracks, where the Battalion was based, was shared with other units, on a large camp built since the Second World War and widely spaced over what had been the site of a wartime aerodrome. The buildings were concrete, single-storey, flat-roofed, 'pre-fab' style blocks; soldiers' barrack rooms ranged from four to eight men in size, all centrally heated. The barracks contained a large NAAFI club and a WVS room, the NAAFI having been recently rebuilt to incorporate a 'call-order' system, whereby a soldier could order a grill and watch it being cooked on the counter in a few seconds. The WOs' & Sgts' Mess was situated furthest from the main gates and it was reported that the Battalion Orderly Sergeants found it necessary to retain a good supply of foot powder. The distances between the various departments probably contributed to the purchase of a large number of private cars.

Playing fields were situated within the barracks and consisted of three football pitches, one rugby pitch and a large square for hockey. The sports programme promised to be full with keen competition from the Brigade Group's 1st Battalion The Loyal Regiment (1

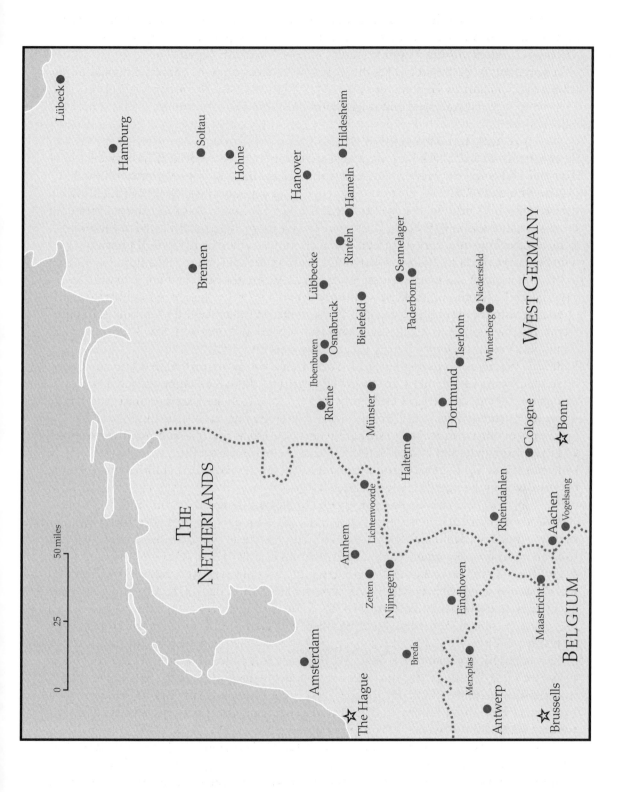

Loyals), 1st Battalion The Seaforth Highlanders (1 Seaforths), 2nd Royal Tank Regiment (2 RTR), 10th Royal Hussars, and old friend 40th Field Regiment RA, which had been in the same brigade in the Iserlohn area in 1952-4, and latterly in Cyprus. Its 38 (Seringapatan) Battery was to be the Battalion's close support battery throughout the BAOR tour.

Another programme, which promised to be full, was that of training. It was somewhat more restricted in scope than experienced five years previously at Iserlohn because in 1955 the German Army had reformed and was training vigorously and extensively. Yet exercises from subunit level upwards still abounded, and training areas near and far provided busy days and nights for all. An ominous sign, too, was the issue of winter combat clothing.

Married quarters became more and more plentiful and most families were housed within four months. The quarters themselves were pleasantly situated in a village some 2 miles out of the city and conveniently near the barracks and shops. The houses were, on the whole, fairly large and well equipped, many with large gardens and all with central heating, which relied on large coke-fed boilers in the cellar. Stoking these monster boilers provided much useful evening and weekend exercise for the heads of family. Woe betide the 'married pad' who let the boiler go out, especially in the winter!

The Battalion reorganized onto a BAOR infantry Order of Battle. It comprised three rifle companies, Support Company (with the Mortar Platoon with six 3" mortars, the Anti-Tank Platoon equipped with the 120mm MOBAT recoilless towed anti-tank gun, and the Assault Pioneer Platoon) and Headquarter Company. Due to severe undermanning and the need to have fully-manned Rifle and Support Companies, C Company became the Cadre Company, whose role included continuation training of drafts from the Depot – the first of which, sixty strong, arrived in mid-April. It was indicative of what was to become a serious problem that *The Green Tiger* in its Autumn 1959 edition contained a flier headed 'Please help to recruit Tigers', exhorting all to encourage men to join the Royal Leicesters. Recruiting sufficient soldier ranks was to become vital in the post-National Service era.

The rifle company platoon weapons were the Belgian-designed FN 7.62mm self-loading rifle (SLR) and similar calibre Bren LMG, the .38" Sten gun, the 2" mortar and the 3.5" rocket launcher. The .38" revolver was the personal weapon of many officers. Communication was provided by C42, B47, A41, and WS62 and 88 radio sets, and dispatch riders on motorcycles. All elements of the Battalion were vehicle mounted for mechanized warfare. Vehicles comprised ½-ton Land Rover and Austin Champ 'jeeps', and 1-ton and 3-ton trucks. With regard to field clothing, the men wore Battle Dress (supplemented by parkas during cold weather) and were still equipped with 1938 Pattern webbing equipment.

The Battalion was part of 6 Infantry Brigade Group (6 Inf Bde Gp), initially under Brigadier J F Worsley OBE MC, the other major units being 10th Hussars and 1 Seaforths. 6 Inf Bde Gp was part of 2nd Infantry Division, under Major General W G Stirling CB CBE DSO, whose HQ was at Lübbecke. 2 Inf Div was part of I (British) Corps, under Lieutenant General Sir Michael West KCB DSO, whose HQ was at Bielefeld. In its turn I (British) Corps was part of NATO's Northern Army Group (NORTHAG) whose HQ was collocated with HQ BAOR at Rheindahlen.

On arrival at Münster, senior appointments in the Battalion were held as follows:

CO:	Lieutenant Colonel M St G Pallot	CSM B Coy:	WO2 L E Loader
		OC C Coy:	Major P J Heath Foresters
2IC:	Major K P P Goldschmidt	CSM C Coy:	WO2 N H P Jenks MM
Adjt:	Captain G A Havilland MC	OC Sp Coy:	Major A C V Sheppard
RSM:	WO1 T J Marston MBE	CSM Sp Coy:	WO2 T Ward
QM:	Captain (QM) E Pratt N Staffs	OC HQ Coy:	Major J T Dudley
RQMS:	WO2 P O'Sullivan	CSM HQ Coy:	WO2 A G Pugh
OC A Coy:	Captain R T Bogg	Bandmaster:	WO1 D K Walker ARCM
CSM A Coy:	WO2 W Reynolds	Drum Major:	CSgt A Holland
OC B Coy:	Major M W McD Cairns		

The role of an infantry battalion in BAOR at that time probably demanded higher standards of training, endurance and resilience than had ever before been required in peacetime. So it was reassuring for the Commanding Officer to receive a signal from the Corps Commander: 'Very glad to welcome you and all ranks of The Royal Leicestershire Regiment. Hope you enjoy yourselves.' The Battalion set out to make an immediate mark in BAOR and in late March Battalion HQ deployed for two days on its own Command Post Exercise (CPX), *Tiger I*, to test its operational functioning. The Shooting Team moved out to Sennelager to prepare for the Brigade Group Rifle Meeting in May, and on 1 April the Rugby 7-a-Side Team, under Captain Roger Bogg, won the Brigade Group Tournament.

In April, well short of the allotted month to settle in, the Battalion set about the exacting task of learning its part in the higher-speed armoured and nuclear battles which were anticipated in any war against the Warsaw Pact Forces on the North German Plain. A vastly greater degree of mobility was required; flexibility was essential and, in consequence, junior commanders had to learn to accept far greater responsibility than in the past. The Battalion began to learn to fight a series of engagements in which the press of events and width of dispersion compelled the Commanding Officer and his company commanders to exercise their command entirely by radio. In the first forty-eight hours of an encounter battle the Battalion was required certainly to reconnoitre, and probably move between two or even three widespread localities. These were the circumstances which dominated training. The BAOR had to be ready to fight the hottest of all wars, and to fight it with the men and material stationed in-theatre. After a few demanding months, the Battalion proved well able to play its part to the full, but it was not achieved without considerable effort from all ranks. It became commonplace for Battalion and Company Group Headquarters to return exhausted to barracks after rigorous training in the field on CPXs, practising and testing the various echelons.

Pressure of training in no way curtailed the normal summer activities. In May, the Shooting Team under Major John Bromhead distinguished itself at the Brigade Group Meeting, winning two team matches and being second in four, and having three individual winners. This was an early taste of what was in store at the Rhine Army Meeting in June, where the team came a very creditable seventh out of the seventeen major units, and outstandingly won the SMG Match, fired with the new 9mm Sterling SMG. This was particularly gratifying as it was the first occasion on which the Regiment had ever won a BAOR shield. The team was Major John Bromhead, Captain G A (Geoff) Havilland MC,

Winners of BAOR SMG Shield. *Trustees R Leicestershire Regt*

2nd Lieutenant J R E (Berty) Bowes and Sergeant Alec Kerr. John Bromhead was selected as a member of the BAOR Rifle VIII.

The Battalion Shooting Team then competed for the very first time at the Army Meeting at Bisley, unfortunately without John Bromhead who, as Paymaster, could not be spared. Private Barnaby reached the 'Army 100', while 2nd Lieutenant Berty Bowes, Corporal Tilley and Lance Corporal Durman reached the Second Stage of the Army Championship. The team came fourth in the Coronation Cup and was twenty-seventh out of thirty-eight in the Major Units Championship. That was a pleasing performance and it was confidently expected that the team's strong nucleus would be built upon in subsequent years.

In May, Support Company won the Inter-Company Athletics Shield. The following month, at the Brigade Group Meeting, the Battalion Team, under Major M W McD (Monty) Cairns and Captain Bill Brown, won four team events and four individual events. So within three months of arrival in Germany the Battalion's competitiveness won early esteem from the rest of the Brigade Group. Considerable impact had been made earlier when on 2 May the Band and Drums beat retreat in the presence of a large number of distinguished and local guests. The standard of the parade and the music was considered by many to be one of the highest ever achieved by the Band and Drums. This was a fitting tribute to the unstinting efforts of the Bandmaster, WO1 Desmond Walker[7], whose final big event that was. In July, after nearly seven years, he was to hand over the baton to WO1 J E (Edgar) Battye. Immediately following the march-off on 2 May, both the Officers' and WOs' & Sgts' Messes each held a reception to mark their arrival in the Garrison. A bowl of cocktails mixed by the RSM and Sergeant A Hill, the WOs' & Sgts' Mess caterer, was long remembered as a 'kick with a punch in it'!

On 13 June, the Queen's Birthday Parade was held, at which the salute was taken by the Brigade Commander. All Ranks wore No. 1 Dress. The SLR was carried on a major parade for the first time, and likewise the Colours since the Second World War and Korean battle honours added. The long hours of rehearsals were rewarded by an extremely good parade, which engendered a sense of pride and satisfaction shared by all who took part. Royal Tigers' Weekend was celebrated on 26-28 June with the customary round of Band Concert and Supper, Potted Sports, and WOs' & Sgts' Mess Hindoostan Ball. The weekend was to have culminated with a Drumhead Service but, just after the opening prayers by the Padre, Revd D M Ryle RAChD, the heavens opened and the Service was abandoned. That weekend was the last one spent in barracks for six weeks as the majority of the Battalion was away on training throughout July and early August; indeed Support Company left that day for Rifle Shooting Classification at Sennelager.

Training for the new role was the proper and predictable focus of the first summer. In May, the Mortar and Anti-Tank Platoons live fired at Hohne, and the Assault Pioneers under Sergeant L ('Pablo') Grant carried out a valuable four weeks' training at Hameln with the affiliated 2 Field Squadron (Fd Sqn) RE. In addition to Battalion-organized exercises (usually named numerically in the *Tiger* series), on 15-19 June Bn HQ and four rifle Company HQs took part in the Corps CPX *New Harpoon*, and earned a name for itself for successfully completing many rapid moves. One soldier described the feature of the exercise as the 'complete non-existence of any opportunities to sleep'! During it the Commanding Officer was stopped by a frantic soldier who appeared to be talking about rations. It was soon discovered the soldier had seen some Russians! As a general observation about long exercises, keeping awake was a real problem, especially for drivers, navigators and watchkeepers. How they longed to be 'nuked' and consequently forced to stand down for a few hours before being reinstated in the exercise play.

Later in June, the Signal Platoon provided the British detachment at the NATO Guard of Honour for General Edelman at JHQ Rheindahlen, commemorating the tenth anniversary of the formation of the NATO Alliance. The Guard had to modify the 'Present Arms' drill to suit the new rifle and gave an excellent display alongside the French, Belgium, Canadian and German detachments.

In early July, HQ Company carried out its Annual Range Classification at Haltern; and A and B Companies deployed to Rheine and Haltern respectively for two weeks' field training, including initial infantry/tank cooperation with the affiliated B Squadron 10th Royal Hussars. From 14 to 17 July, elements of the Battalion took part in 2 Inf Div's Admin CPX *Blind Mouse*, the returning soldiers reporting 'sudden moves, sleepless nights and stinking farmyards'!

In all phases of training, there were frequent references to 'Dazzle Warnings' – the Immediate Action (IA) drill for which was to lie flat on the ground facing the anticipated dazzle, the flash of a nuclear explosion. In mid-July the Battalion deployed to Sennelager, living in a tented camp for three weeks and conducting field firing on mechanical ranges. This phase of training culminated in the rifle platoons competing for the Pinder Cup,[8] a field-firing competition, won by 6 Platoon under 2nd Lieutenant D M A (David) Needham and Sergeant H (Harry) Rankin. The Inter-Section Competition for the Creagh Cup[9] was won by Corporal A ('Alex') Alexander's Section in B Company.

There was then a month spent back in barracks. For four days most of the officers were involved in the Brigade Study Period and Telephone Battle, Exercise *Proud Warrior*, at Hameln. Over a weekend in early September, the Bishop of Leicester, the Rt Revd Ralph Williams DD MA, visited the Battalion and a Battalion Church Parade was held. The following week, Major Monty Cairns of B Company organized a particularly effective and realistic demonstration of IS riot dispersal as one of a series of training stands on Exercise *Proving Flight*, for the benefit of Army Staff College candidates. During the first half of September, inter-company hockey, rugby and football competitions were held.

In mid-September, the whole Battalion deployed to Soltau for four weeks' training, which included more infantry/tank cooperation with 10th Royal Hussars, and three battalion-level exercises. *Tiger V* practised movement, deployment and night attack; on *Tiger VI* the Battalion Group (including 38 Fd Bty RA and 1 Troop, 2 Fd Sqn RE) practised the 'Watch and Ward' counter-penetration role; and *Tiger VII* practised the occupation of defensive positions and the withdrawal. On 8 October, the Battalion conducted a long move to a Brigade Assembly Area for Divisional Field Training Exercise (FTX) *Phoenix*, in the Hildesheim area. The Exercise was arduous and protracted, with hard frosts each night, and proved a very satisfying climax to the first and very busy training season in BAOR. All ranks felt that the congratulations of the Brigade Commander had been well earned, and the GOC awarded an 'Exercise MID' to Lieutenant David Nevile and his radio operator Private Francis for a special Observation Post (OP) duty they performed. After the many absences during the summer, the Battalion's return to Münster in the middle of October seemed like the end of a campaign.

The services of the Band and Drums were much in demand during that year. Among other engagements they played at the ground of the Münster Football Team, which was at the time high in the Bundesliga. They were received with thunderous applause which, according to the Bandmaster, was 'more than the players got'! During the summer they deployed to England for six weeks, undertaking a series of engagements around the country – which are recorded in Chapter 4. The Band also deployed in the lead-up to Exercise *Phoenix*, performing twice while the Battalion was in the Assembly Area at Walperode, and much to the enjoyment too of the local German population.

The idea of starting a regimental affiliation with HMS *Tiger* had been first broached by Captain J S Dalglish CVO RN to his brother, Major Duggie Dalglish, when the ship was being completed in 1958. The manner in which this was taken forward in October 1959 and subsequently is described in Chapter 13.

From October to December, the Battalion undertook a period of cadre training of all types, and 'interior economy' in preparation for the Annual Administrative Inspection. The condition in which the barracks had been taken over on arrival in March had been far below the standard the Battalion was accustomed to present for inspection. During those winter months, in addition to completing the audits and other administrative checks that had been impractical while in the field, every barrack building was repainted throughout. The customary attention was also given to kit checking, marking and laying out for inspection, with time-honoured precision. A concentrated drive on soldiers' education merely added interest to organizational feats.

Company Shooting teams and the Battalion Rugby and Football teams began training in earnest. At the Battalion Rifle Meeting held at Sennelager at the end of October, the SLR for the first time was used for all rifle competitions. Private Farley of B Company was Rifle

Champion, and Headquarters 1 (under Major John Dudley) won the Inter-Company Musketry Shield. It was a valuable and enjoyable event held in brilliant autumn sunshine, during which Colonel B L (Basil) Gunnell OBE MC[10], now Brigade Colonel The Forester Brigade, paid a visit. He subsequently did much to relieve the critical shortage of both officers and other ranks which had burdened the Battalion so heavily the previous year. Eleven men were awarded 'Green Tigers' for Shooting.

Elsewhere on the sporting front, Private Lampell of HQ Company won the BAOR Table Tennis singles championship, and with Private Thomas of HQ Company won the doubles. Cricket was not much played at unit level that summer, though four members of the Battalion played regularly for the 2nd Inf Div team. At the Brigade Group's Cricket & Tennis Week, Captain E (Ted) Pratt and Lieutenant Tony Moore were runners-up in the Tennis men's doubles.

The voice of the Battalion was heard across Europe when the Garrison Church Service on Remembrance Sunday was broadcast on the Allied Forces Network radio service.

On the whole, Christmas was rather quieter than in some years, but all the traditional customs were observed. Although the normal attitude of the local population was one of reserve towards all troops, a number of German families invited the soldiers to spend Christmas with them. Notwithstanding the language difficulties, hosts and guests thoroughly enjoyed each others' company.

The well-earned holiday passed quickly and, before even the New Year, all elements of the Battalion were once more upon the square going through the drill parade in preparation for the coming Annual Administrative Inspection. Unfortunately, the daily practices proved to be wasted as heavy snow fell just over a week later, and lay until after the day of the inspection itself. The new Brigade Group Commander, Brigadier R M P Carver CB CBE DSO MC, another very perceptive senior officer and heading for the very top of the Armed Forces[11], was clearly impressed. In the formal report of his inspection, he wrote:

> The general standard of administration in the Battalion is so high that I consider that a formal parade and inspection of dress should suffice for the next annual inspection … Neither the officer nor the other rank situation of the Battalion is satisfactory, but this is beyond the control of the Battalion. The former should improve during the year, and there is some hope of the latter improving when recruiting for The Forester Brigade is handled on a brigade basis. Until then the Battalion can only remain administratively efficient at the expense of its operational strength.

At the beginning of 1960, senior appointments in the Battalion were held as follows:

CO:	Lieutenant Colonel M St G Pallot	OC B Coy:	Captain W J G Brown
		CSM B Coy:	WO2 L E Loader
2IC:	Major S A Smith MBE	OC C Coy:	Lieutenant J C D Heggs
Adjt:	Captain P P Young	CSM C Coy:	WO2 N H P Jenks MM
RSM:	WO1 T J Marston MBE	OC Sp Coy:	Major J T Dudley
QM:	Captain (QM) E Pratt N Staffs	CSM Sp Coy:	WO2 T Ward
		OC HQ Coy:	Major W G St S Brogan
RQMS:	WO2 P O'Sullivan	CSM HQ Coy:	WO2 A G Pugh
OC A Coy:	Captain R T Bogg	Bandmaster:	WO1 J E Battye ARCM
CSM A Coy:	WO2 W Reynolds	Drum Major:	CSgt A Holland

Band and Drums at Rosenmontag Festival. *Trustees R Leicestershire Regt*

In the early months of the year, various parties from the companies enjoyed a week's skiing at Winterberg Winter Warfare Training Centre in the Sauerland in North Rhine-Westphalia. The Band and Drums put on a dramatic display of British martial music when they marched in procession through Münster during the 'Rosenmontag' Festival, two days before Ash Wednesday. HQ Company's team under Sergeant 'Pablo' Grant reached the Final of the Brigade Group's Minor Units Small-Bore Shooting Competition. The Battalion Football Team, organized by Captain Ted Pratt and led by Private Maile, reached the Semi-Final of the BAOR Cup and was the 2 Inf Div champion. Corporal Wood and Privates Wilson and M Allen played for BAOR. Eleven men were awarded 'Green Tigers'. The Rugby Team, led variously by Captain Roger Bogg and Lieutenant Tony Pollard, had a mixed season, with many gallant individuals. Four played regularly for the 2 Inf Div side, Lieutenant John Heggs had a BAOR trial, and Lance Corporal H (Bert) Godwin played for the Army. The team won the Brigade Group's 15-a-Side and again the 7-a-Side Rugby. Six men were awarded 'Green Tigers'.

It was about this time that Sergeant E G T (Ted) Gibbons left after six years as Officers' Mess Sergeant, his loyalty and hard work throughout that long period unlikely to be surpassed. It was as a guest that he entered the Mess for the last time and during that visit was presented by the Commanding Officer with an inscribed silver cigarette box.

Faced by a second year in BAOR, the Battalion was encouraged by the reflection that 'the second time round must be easier' and that the knowledge and skills strenuously gained in 1959 would ease the road for 1960. The chill winds of March found the Battalion completing its individual training and making frequent sallies out of barracks in order to practise the deployment drills which the summer exercises would require. In mid-March,

66

for three weeks the Battalion operated at Vogelsang in the Eifel, a Belgian training area 40 miles south-west of Cologne, in the delightful surroundings of coniferous forests, to carry out section, platoon and company training with and without tanks. This was the Battalion's second visit there, the previous one having been in May 1947. The barracks had been built in 1936 as a training establishment for future leaders of the Nazi Party. The vast, imposing array of grey stone buildings had somewhat sinister echoes of Vogelsang's past.

On return, in mid-April, Bn HQ and skeleton Coy HQs took part in the Bde Gp CPX *King's Castle*. The highlight of that month was the four-day visit by the Colonel of The Regiment and a City of Leicester civic party, among whom were the Lord Mayor of Leicester, Alderman Bertram Powell, and one of his predecessors in office, Colonel A (Alfred) Halkyard CB MC TD DL[12]. Although the Lord Mayor of Leicester had attended the Presentation of Colours at Iserlohn in 1954, this 1960 visit was the first since the Council of the City of Leicester's 1959 decision that as far as was possible the Lord Mayor would visit the 1st Battalion annually wherever it was in the world. During this particular visit to Münster, the Mayoral programme included Beating Retreat by the Band and Drums, a Church Parade, a Regimental Guest Night and the Lord Mayor addressing the Battalion. It was yet another occasion cementing the relations between the City and County and its Regiment.

From 4 to 5 May, Major W G St S (Bill) Brogan, Lieutenant B N (Neil) Crumbie and thirty soldiers (a battalion football team, twelve members of the Signal Platoon and two drivers) visited Lichtenvoorde, near Arnhem in the Netherlands, as guests of the citizens, to mark the fifteenth anniversary of the liberation of the town by Allied Forces in 1945. The busy thirty-six hours began with a solemn Commemoration Service, parade and wreath-laying. Each soldier had been given a posy of flowers to lay on the grave of an individual Allied serviceman buried there. Then singly or in pairs, the officers and soldiers were taken to a Dutch home where they were entertained magnificently throughout their stay.

The second day was the day of celebration. The Battalion detachment won the Liberation Day Relay Race, and was presented with souvenir medals and the biggest loaf of bread any of them had ever seen: 4' long, 12" high, 9" wide – the loaf being the wartime Resistance custom of using bread as a symbol of freedom. A Liberation ceremony then took place, followed by the Battalion team playing Lichtenvoorde Football Club, a Dutch Second Division side, watched by 4,000 people. After the luncheon came a tight programme of sporting events. The Battalion detachment did well in athletics events and the tug-of-war. That evening the Freedom of the Town was extended to it.

Memories very forcibly brought home to each of the party two never-to-be-forgotten facts: first, the extent to which the host town, and others like it, suffered during the Second World War (in Lichtenvoorde in 1960 over 50 per cent of the population was under twenty-one years of age); secondly, the enormous depth of gratitude and goodwill which was still felt by the Dutch towards the Allied armies, and in particular towards the British Army and the British people.

Back at Münster, Major A W (Alex) Haycock of the Royal Warwicks, with a draft of eighty-seven men ineligible to join 1 R Warwick in Hong Kong, joined the Battalion. The private soldiers were dispersed among the rifle companies and with this timely injection of junior manpower, after fourteen months as a Cadre Company, C Company was reformed with Alex Haycock as OC. A month later the Battalion deployed to Soltau for three weeks' company group and infantry/tank training with B Sqn 10th Royal Hussars. In addition to celebrating the Queen's Birthday with a short parade, two battalion-level FTXs were carried out: from 16 to 18 June, *First Fling* practised harbour drills, road moves, attack, night attack, defensive positions and night withdrawal; and from 22 to 23 June, *Second Shot*, with B Sqn 10th Royal Hussars, Bty Comd and OP parties of 38 Fd Bty RA, Fd Tp RE, and Collecting Section of Field Ambulance RAMC, practised daylight attack and withdrawal, and involved exercise casualty evacuation (Casevac) to the Regimental Aid Post (RAP). Visits to the Battalion were carried out by the Divisional and Brigade Group Commanders.

On 25 June, the Battalion moved to Sennelager for three weeks' field firing. On 9 July, 2nd Lieutenants David Needham and J M (John) Osborne,and Lance Corporal B (Brian) Newman were tragically killed in a road traffic accident, thus robbing the Battalion of three fine young men. On 15 July, the Battalion returned to Münster, with the principal focus on preparing for Royal Tigers' Weekend and the Rebadging Parade to be held six weeks later. Sports team training also began. These preparations were interrupted by a number of other commitments. Elements of Bn HQ, with A and B Echelons complete, took part in the annual five-day Divisional Admin Exercise, *Blind Mouse III*. The new Comd 1 (BR) Corps, Lieutenant General Sir Charles Jones KCB KBE MC, visited on 26 July, followed a week later by the Permanent under Secretary of State for War, the Hon. Hugh Fraser MBE MP. And for ten days the Battalion hosted cadets from Nottingham High School, Loughborough Grammar School and the Leicestershire & Rutland ACF – a visit to the Regular Army which the teenagers were still talking about many months later.

At the end of July, the Battalion Athletics meeting was won by Support Company. Private Brian Punter won three events, and Private George Ferrance and Lieutenant Tony Pollard two each. A month later, the Battalion team led by Captain J F S (John) Agar won the Brigade Group Meeting, with Tony Pollard and Corporal Wood breaking its discus record.

A Royal Tigers' Weekend long remembered began on 25 August 1960. It was notable not only for the Rebadging Parade, which was its central feature, but for the many, serving and retired, from all branches of the Regiment and The Forester Brigade who came to join in the full programme of events.

On that opening day, the Corporals' Club ran a splendid social and dance. The following evening there was Beating Retreat. Under the direction of Bandmaster Edgar Battye and Drum Major A ('Dutch') Holland, the Band and Drums gave a performance that they have seldom bettered. Beneath the rays of the sinking sun, in ideal still conditions, they moved with a rhythm and precision that excited the admiration of a substantial and enthusiastic audience. This was followed by a large and hugely successful cocktail party in the Officers' Mess, and an equally notable dinner in the WOs' & Sgts' Mess. At the latter event, WO1 L (Tim) Russell from the Depot at Leicester presented from his Mess a silver tiger to the 1st Battalion's Mess.

On Saturday 27 August, the Rebadging Parade took place at Buller Barracks, Münster – a most appropriate spectacle as the culmination of the relatively few number of hours of preparation which were able to be fitted into the busy BAOR training programme. 1st Battalion The Royal Leicestershire Regiment, under command of Lieutenant Colonel M St G Pallot, changed its familiar and well-loved Royal Tiger capbadge to that of the newly formed Forester Brigade (see plate section). The following paragraphs – précised from *The*

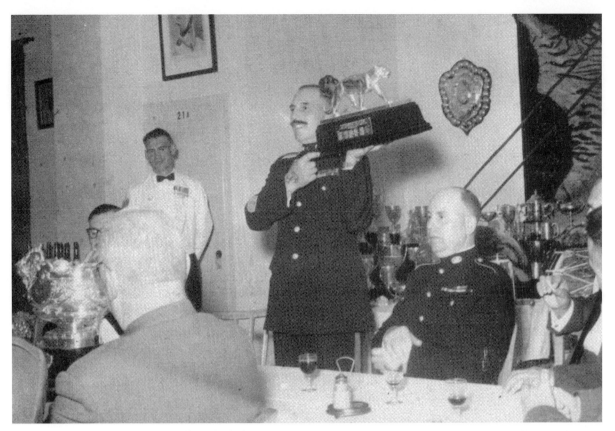

RSMs Marston and Russell with the Depot tiger. *Trustees R Leicestershire Regt*

Green Tiger – record some part of the passing of the Royal Tiger capbadge:

On the morning of 27 August driving rain from grey skies made it necessary to cancel the parade, an eventuality which caused amongst All Ranks a shocked silence of bitter disappointment that could be felt. That Parade meant so much to each man of the Battalion and to each member of the Regiment. There is an excitement connected with all big parades that mounts, and increases, as preparations proceed; that excitement was present, but there was also present something more, something that could be seen, or sensed, in each Tiger waiting to march on, or waiting to watch, that Parade. It could most nearly be described as a wish, and a determination, that that Parade, the last occasion on which the 1st Battalion would wear the Royal Tiger capbadge, should take place, and that it should be carried out as perfectly as possible. It seemed that, in that way only, could those present say farewell to the badge worn so long and so well by their predecessors, and only in that way, too, could those serving use this last opportunity of adding their quota to its honoured reputation gained by the efforts of so many over the years. The parade had to take place; the 'Royal Tiger' could not be replaced unhonoured and unsung. It was therefore with bated breath that all watched as, shortly before mid-day, magically and providentially the skies cleared, the sun shone on the rain-soaked square. 'Cancel the cancellation. Postpone the lunch.' The order to proceed was given. Within minutes, discarded uniforms were being put on, brushes and dusters waved, corridors rang to the rush of feet. Early guests were redirected from the Officers' Mess to the Square – the parade was on.

The parade was attended by senior BAOR and Forester Brigade officers and civilian representatives of the Garrison and by serving and retired members of the Regiment who were visiting for the occasion. In the unavoidable absence of the Colonel of The Regiment, the salute was taken by Major General D A ('Joe') Kendrew CB CBE DSO, the Director of Infantry. The parade troops comprised four Guards of sixty men wearing No. 1 Dress. The Colours were borne by Lieutenants Tony Moore and Tony Pollard. The Battalion marched past in Column of Companies and the Battalion then re-formed line. Then five Colour Sergeants marched on with the Forester Brigade capbadges. The badges were blessed by the Very Rev R J F (Richard) Mayston CBE MA[13], Provost of Leicester Cathedral, and then distributed to the ranks of the Companies who stood bare-headed awaiting them. To the strains of *Auld Lang Syne*, the Battalion rebadged – out came the 'Royal Tiger', the badge so proudly worn, so well-loved and familiar to countless thousands of Tigers during the 135 years as its symbol. A moment, moving and poignant, during which memory ran back over the years to the thousands who served, lived and died wearing the badge now to be discarded – and then, in went the new badge. The Parade then formed a hollow square, and was addressed by General Kendrew.' In his address he said:

First, I would like to congratulate all ranks on a magnificent parade. It was not a straight-forward manoeuvre and I consider your standard was quite first class. I would also like to congratulate the Band and Drums on the Beating Retreat last night. But I would add that this is the standard that I had expected, and I would have been disappointed if you had not risen to the occasion.

Secondly, I would like you to know how sorry our Colonel was that he could not be with you today. He did ask me to convey to all of you his very best wishes and wish you all good luck on this memorable day in the life of our Regiment.

In the long history of the British Army there have always been changes both in weapons and tactics. These of necessity cause the shape and structure of the Army to vary. Only by these changes can an Army remain virile, active and capable of carrying out the Queen's business. During the last fifty years both your fathers and you have seen considerable changes in our Army. New weapons and even a new service, the Royal Air Force, have been created. All I need say to you is that we now possess a balanced Army with nuclear weapons, a streamlined Army capable of rapid movement and deployment backed by a sound logistic system. Because of all this, our Teeth Arms and especially The Royal Regiment of Artillery, The Royal Armoured Corps and the Infantry of the Line, have had to change their size and shape.

For ourselves we no longer have two regular battalions and our own Depot. But we have formed a closer partnership with our nearest county regiments – The Royal Warwickshire Regiment and The Sherwood Foresters. By this close association we have formed The Forester Brigade. Now we share one Depot, and we have a similar uniform, buttons and a common promotion list. We also have one capbadge. This badge, we as a Regiment take today. It incorporates something from each of the Regiments, and by forming this Forester Brigade and wearing this badge we accept the change that has now taken place in the Infantry of the Line.

Today within our Regiment are officers and men from all three Regiments, and we parade together strengthened by this unity. May this close association grow stronger and richer; and I have no doubt whatsoever that by this acceptance of the Brigade system, and the change within the Infantry, we as a Regiment will be more resilient and better able to uphold and enhance the magnificent traditions of our three great Regiments now wearing this cap badge.

And then the Parade marched off.

In the evening the Hindoostan Ball was held in the WOs' & Sgts' Mess. The heights to which the Ball rose continued to surprise all every year, but on that occasion the Mess surpassed itself. The Garrison Gymnasium, taken over by the Mess for the evening, was completely transformed with colour and light. It was said that 'the woods and farms surrounding Münster had clearly suffered grievous inroads to provide the decorations and buffet!'

On Sunday 28 August, the Battalion paraded for Church Service in the Garrison Church of All Saints. The address was given by the Very Revd Richard Mayston, who also dedicated the stained-glass window presented to the church by the 1st Battalion. The window bears the crest of The Royal Leicestershire Regiment. It is the work of a local German artist and depicts Saint Martin (Bishop of Tours in the fourth century, a Patron Saint of France and also the Patron Saint of Leicester Cathedral) sharing his cloak with a beggar. It was to be in 2008, after the British Army left Münster, that plans were set in train to move the window to Leicester Cathedral.

The weekend closed on Monday evening with the Tigers' Supper and Concert. The cooks provided a magnificent spread, the PRI organized the provision of the requisite amount of beer and the Jazz Group of the Band provided the musical entertainment.

With the end of National Service coming ever closer, recruiting remained the Regiment's greatest problem. If it was to continue to take its rightful place in the Order of Battle of the British Army, then it needed rapidly and consistently to attract and retain sufficient junior officers and soldiers on Regular terms of service. The forecast was critical as it was estimated that at the present level of take-up, when conscription ended a year later and the last National Serviceman was demobilized, there would be only 250 Regular soldiers serving. Within the Battalion, the RSM

St Martin stained-glass window, Münster, Germany.
Trustees R Leicestershire Regt

vigorously encouraged National Servicemen to sign on. Back in Leicestershire, heralded with a fanfare of Press interest, Colonel (Retd) David Shaw DSO MC, a former Royal Inniskilling Fusilier, joined RHQ as the person responsible for Recruiting. He was determined that infantrymen from Leicestershire and Rutland – with those counties' unusually high level of employment – could be adequately represented in The Forester Brigade. It was not the unemployed joining as a last resort that were sought, but intelligent

71

young men, because individual qualities were required for the more complicated equipment and conduct of modern warfare. Most unfortunately for the Regiment, six months later he left the post on promotion in the Army recruiting organization.

Moving on to the BAOR autumn training season, in the first week of September, Exercise *Skeleton Key II*, a Divisional-level CPX held in the Hildesheim area, was unlike any other BAOR exercise in that the Battalion players did not move once! This was followed by a week's confinement to barracks on an undisclosed BAOR duty, and then most officers, plus the Signal and MT Platoons, were involved for a week as umpires on a NATO FTX, *Hold Fast*. Meanwhile, the remainder of the Battalion moved to Rheinsehlen Camp at Soltau for the final field training of the season. Five days were spent on company and company group training with A Sqn The Queen's Own Hussars (QOH). Then followed a Bn-level FTX, *Third Trek*, on which for the first time ever radios (the VHF six-channel A40 sets) were issued down to section level. From 3 to 7 October, two Bde-organized FTXs, *Brass Band* and *Steel Drum*, pitted the Battalion against 1 Loyals. These in turn were followed from 8 to 13 October by a Bde-level FTX, *King's Move*, in the Rinteln area, practising the Brigade Group in its operational role. The weather was atrocious throughout, the armour being 'sent home early', leaving the battlefield to the infantry. Most sad to record, on that exercise, Private R C (Clive) McMurragh died when struck by a passing lorry, and in a separate accident Private M (Melvyn) Wright was severely injured when a Centurion tank reversed into his jeep.

There then followed the so-called 'Winter Quarters', the cadre training period (which lasted into March), and preparation for the annual round of administrative inspections small and great, and as much sport as the weather would allow. Winter sport was again experienced by a large number of soldiers attending two-week military skiing courses at Winterberg. The Battalion Rifle Meeting was eagerly awaited in early November because, due to pressure of other activities, there had been no open-range competition shooting that year and no Battalion Team had entered the BAOR or Bisley championships. Lieutenant Berty Bowes won the Individual Rifle, Lieutenant Bill Morris and Sergeant 'Pablo' Grant the LMG, and C Company the Inter-Company Shield.

Three hundred and eighty all ranks paraded for Remembrance Sunday on 13 November. In October and November, a total of 198 recruits were posted in from the Depot, the last large National Service drafts, but which contained too few Regulars. The GOC 2 Inf Div carried out his Annual Administrative Inspection on 13 December, which – as recommended in the previous year's inspection report – comprised merely a parade of the Battalion wearing No. 1 Dress. After one wit had the nerve to ask the Bandmaster to play the 'Skater's Waltz', the snow and ice on the Square were vanquished by salt and the vigorous use of brooms.

The traditional round of Christmas activities was held in the barracks and various messes. Early in the New Year 1961, news was received that some groups of National Servicemen would be released earlier then expected and that the Battalion was unlikely to leave BAOR until July 1962. January also witnessed the departure of RSM Tommy Marston MBE. After nearly twenty-eight years' service and almost all with the 2nd and 1st Battalions, seldom if ever had his consistent record of devoted and loyal service been matched. He was given the honour of being dined out in the Officers' Mess. For the last six months of his service he was stationed at RHQ at Glen Parva Barracks, assisting

Colonel David Shaw in recruiting. He was succeeded as RSM by WO1 H D (David) Benham.

January 1961 furthermore saw the first of the numerous driving and maintenance cadres for those due to drive the new-issue 1-ton Humber armoured trucks (nicknamed 'the Pig' on account of the shape of its bonnet) as Armoured Personnel Carriers (APCs). The Inter-Section competition for the Creagh Cup was won by Corporal May's Section in B Company. A series of five officers' training days were held in January and February. On 14 March, the first Bn CPX of the season was held, *Sea Dog*, followed by a Bde Gp CPX, *Concert Grand*. Drummer Smith died in his sleep on 18 March and was buried in the British Military Cemetery at Hanover. *The Green Tiger* for the first time carried an advertisement from Carrington & Co Ltd, London's Regent Street jewellers, featuring a Forester Brigade diamond badge brooch.

On the sports front, the Battalion Football Team, organized by Captain Ted Pratt and led by Private M Allen, had an exceptional season. It had almost reached the pinnacle when, a few days before the final of the BAOR Cup, three National Servicemen (including the 'professional' goalkeeper) were demobilized early. In the Final the Argylls won 2-0. During the season seventy-two goals were scored in eleven matches. The Rugby Team, led by Captain Roger Bogg, also had a very successful season, winning the Brigade Group and Divisional Cups, but in the BAOR Semi-Final lost to the Welsh Guards. It again won the Brigade Group 7-a-Sides but was beaten in the Semi-Final of the BAOR Sevens. Perhaps the highlight of the 15-a-Side season, in addition to scoring 440 points against 117, was the match against 1 SWB. Whilst warming up on the pitch, the Battalion's prop, Corporal Bert Godwin, of Coventry and England[14], wore his England shirt, similar to the regimental white one but with the rose instead of XVII on it. Of course he changed back into the regimental shirt for the match! It had the desired effect and that was the only time the Royal Leicesters ever beat the 24th Foot.

In Cross-Country Running, the leading runner was Pte Hobbs of A Coy, and C Coy was the Champion Company. The Hockey Team had limited success, many of its key players being in the higher-priority Rugby and Football Teams; the Small-Bore Shooting Team won the Brigade Group Major Units League. All-in-all, 'Green Tigers' were awarded to forty-four participants in six sports.

The principal focus of the Battalion in the New Year was the preparation for the reorganization of the Battalion and the issue of the new APCs, down to section level. These APCs were to give the Battalion the ability to achieve the same mobility as its supporting armour and artillery. Consequently, training developed a new dimension, map reading was done at 25mph instead of 3mph and orders were given out over the radio as a matter of course, thereby rapidly increasing the speed of battle procedure at all levels within the Battalion Group. At the same time, everybody was issued with the 1958 pattern web equipment (which did not require cleaning with blanco and was due to be used by the Army in all theatres (less jungle) for the next twenty-five or so years) and olive-drab combat clothing, the field dress to replace battledress; and so was the new Parade Dress, No. 2 Dress.

On 10 April, Support Company was effectively disbanded. Each of the rifle companies gained a Support Platoon of a Mortar Section of two 3" mortars and an Anti-Tank Section of two 120mm MOBATs, and also their own slice of signallers and drivers from the Signals

Humber APC. *Trustees R Leicestershire Regt*

and MT Platoons. The Band and Drums, the Assault Pioneers and the Weapon Training Staff joined HQ Company. At that time senior appointments were held as follows:

CO:	Lieutenant Colonel M St G Pallot	OC B Coy:	Major J P N Creagh
		CSM B Coy:	WO2 G L Newbitt
2IC:	Major S A Smith MBE	OC C Coy:	Major A H Haycock
Adjt:	Captain R T Bogg		R Warwick
RSM:	WO1 H D Benham	CSM C Coy:	WO2 R C Gascoigne
QM:	Captain (QM) E Pratt N Staffs	OC HQ Coy:	Major J T Dudley
RQMS:	WO2 P O'Sullivan	CSM HQ Coy:	WO2 L E Loader
OC A Coy:	Captain P P Young	Bandmaster:	WO1 J E Battye ARCM
CSM A Coy:	WO2 W Reynolds	Drum Major:	CSgt A Holland

On 7 April, the RSO, Lieutenant P N (Peter) Graham, and twenty men of his Signal Platoon, wearing No. 1 Dress, provided the British Contingent at the five-nation parade at JHQ Rheindahlen, to celebrate the twelfth anniversary of the formation of NATO. The salute was taken by General Sir James Cassels and Air Marshal J Grundy RAF, the Joint Commanders.

The highlight of April was the four-day visit by the Colonel of The Regiment and a City of Leicester civic party led by the Lord Mayor of Leicester, Councillor Mrs Dorothy Russell. During this visit to Münster, the Mayoral programme included a Regimental Guest Night, visits to platoons training and some married quarters, lunch with the Oberburgermeister of Münster, the WOs' & Sgts' Mess Ball, and a Church Parade. The visit was yet another occasion cementing the relations between the City and County and its Regiment.

On 10 May 1961 in Greece, the Athens Memorial, commemorating the soldiers of the

Armies of the Commonwealth who fell in operations in Greece, Crete, the Dodecanese Islands and Yugoslavia in 1939-45, and who have no known grave, was unveiled by Field Marshal HRH The Duke of Gloucester KG, in the presence of HM The King of the Hellenes. It stands in the Phaleron War Cemetery near Athens, the principal burial ground of Commonwealth casualties of the Greek Civil War 1944-1945, wherein lie the graves of five men of The Leicestershire Regiment.

In a setting of brilliant and spectacular colour, the short Dedication Service, which was conducted by the Chaplain General, assisted by leading representatives of the Roman Catholic, Greek Orthodox and Muslim faiths, was very moving in its simplicity. The Athens Memorial (see plate section) consists of a great white marble Arch behind which stand eight panels inscribed with the names, ranks and units of the 3,000 missing. Between these panels is an altar-like monolith, the Stone of Remembrance, carved with the words 'Their Name Liveth for Evermore' – a symbol acceptable to all peoples of all religious faiths. On Panel 5 are commemorated the names of sixty men of The Leicestershire Regiment, all but one of them of the 2nd Battalion who fell during the battle for Crete in May 1941.

Meanwhile in Germany, on 15 May, the Brigade Group Rifle Meeting was held, at which the Battalion Team, led by Major John Bromhead, literally swept the board. Pte Davies of C Company won the Rifle and Young Soldier matches. A week later the Battalion (less the Athletics Team, in training) deployed to Sennelager for three weeks as the Range Battalion for the BAOR Rifle Meeting. The Battalion Team had seven in the BAOR 100 on the rifle and, although inspired by the Band playing on each day of the Meeting, as a team it came a disappointing eleventh out of twenty-two. Nevertheless accolades were received from as senior a person as the C-in-C BAOR at the manner in which the Meeting was organized. Led by Captain Bill Morris, the Team then competed in the Army Meeting at Bisley in July, achieving little success but gaining much experience.

Shortly after the Queen's Birthday Parade, the Recruiting Team led by Captain B N (Neil) Crumbie and comprising WO2 'Jimmy' Jenks MM, Sergeant Barlow and five men, assisted by the Band and Drums, set out for a tour of Leicestershire on 15 June, with the target of recruiting 100 men by Christmas. At that time, the Battalion was receiving only five or six Regular private soldiers a month, vastly insufficient to balance the outflow of the National Service drafts. The Recruiting Team's activities are covered in detail in Chapter 4.

From 18 June for a fortnight, a 36-man platoon under 2nd Lieutenant R J G (Jack) Knowles and Sergeant J P (Patrick) Kelly were attached to 1st Battalion The Royal Danish Lifeguards in Copenhagen. Included in a very busy and satisfying programme of field training and ceremonial, they had the honour of being inspected by HM King Frederick IX of Denmark at a parade to mark the 303rd Anniversary of the founding of Denmark's senior regiment.

The previous month the Battalion Athletics Meeting was held, which was notable for Lance Corporal Fielden and Private George Ferrance each winning two events, and A Company becoming Champion Company. Six weeks later, at the Brigade Group Meeting, Lance Corporal Wycherley and Private Johnson broke the Brigade javelin record. The Team had equal points with 'the other Tigers', 1st Battalion The York & Lancaster Regiment (1 Y & L), who won by dint of seven individual winners to six. Fifteen athletes were awarded 'Green Tigers'.

Royal Tigers' Weekend was held a week later than usual, at the conclusion of which Mike Pallot handed over command, and a fond farewell was extended to him and his wife Joan. In his departure message to the Battalion he wrote:

> I wish to thank All Ranks for the very splendid way they have worked during the last 2½ years during which I have been in command. The Battalion has done extremely well in all fields and has maintained the high traditions of our Regiment. We have been successful because of the willing and cheerful way in which All Ranks have tackled the many varied tasks we have been set, and I personally could not have asked for a finer set of Officers and Men to command. I am indeed grateful to each one of you.

He was succeeded as Commanding Officer by Lieutenant Colonel P E B (Peter) Badger, whom the Battalion was delighted to welcome back with his wife Joan.

On 5 July, the Advance Party set out for Sennelager where the Battalion was based under canvas for three weeks, field firing and learning to manoeuvre tactically in the APCs. On return to Münster, the Battalion was heavily involved in the Garrison Fête in aid of the Army Benevolent Fund. In August, the Battalion deployed to Vogelsang for a week's infantry/tank training with the QOH and 38 Fd Bty RA.

On 15 September, the *London Gazette* published the award of the MC to Captain T B F (Tom) Hiney for his actions on 27/28 April 1961 when a company commander in 2nd Battalion The Ghana Regiment of Infantry, on United Nations duty in The Congo. The citation describes the ambush of his Company about 50 miles from Port Francqui (now called Ilebo, in central Zaire) on a dark night on a narrow road with thick bush either side:

Capt Tom Hiney MC. *T B F Hiney*

> In spite of intense rifle, machine gun and mortar fire, in an action which lasted for an hour his Company fought its way through the ambush which dominated 180 yards of road. He commanded his men with coolness and gallantry, encouraging them by voice and example. He personally removed road blocks and attacked an enemy automatic post with grenades. But for his fortitude, competence and level-headed leadership, there would have been considerable loss of life and passage through the ambush would not have been possible.

Hiney's Company was at the time proceeding to Port Franqui with which military communications had suddenly been lost. Information was subsequently received that the Battalion's B Company (of which Lieutenant A P G (Anthony) Brown was the Second-in-Command) had been overrun there by a large force of the Congolese National Army, and almost all, including Anthony Brown, had been killed.

Starting at the beginning of September and lasting some six weeks, the Battalion was almost continually on exercise in the field. B Company acted as enemy to A and C Companies on Exercise *Iron Ration*, followed by A and B Companies deploying on Exercise *Wooden Horse*, during which Sergeant S (Sam) Small and Privates Gamble and Pratt were badly injured when their APC crashed. Then several officers took part in 2 Inf Div CPX *Sharpener*. In October, the Battalion was involved in the Bde Gp FTX, *Magic Flute*. Officers were employed as umpires between 1 Y & L and 1st Battalion The King's Shropshire Light Infantry (1 KSLI); and B Company was attached to the QOH in an independent role. This required considerable regrouping of the Battalion prior to concentrating for the 'biggest, bestest, BAOR battle' for years, the one-week 1 (BR) Corps FTX, *Spearpoint*, the first time that the Battalion had deployed with its APCs on such a large-scale exercise. Having its own organic transportation at the tactical level enabled it to stay in contact with the enemy for longer before withdrawing. At company level it was also logistically much more sustainable as cooking was based on each vehicle and it was no longer necessary to rely upon the CQMSs' hayboxes for hot food. And so after little sleep, much movement, order, counter-order but never disorder, *Spearpoint* was a fitting end to the third season's training in BAOR.

There then followed 'Winter Quarters 1961/62': the cadre training period, the various administrative inspections and however much sport the seasonal conditions would allow.

On Remembrance Sunday 400 all ranks attended the Battalion service, and a few days later came the first notification that the Battalion would be leaving BAOR in June 1962, destination and role as yet unknown.

From early December onwards, winter warfare and skiing was again undertaken by a large number of soldiers. 2nd Lieutenants B D (David) Hickman and D E A (David) Michael spent the season as ski instructors, the latter having joined the Battalion three months previously, on the day after coming 3rd in the Army Under-21 Pentathlon Championships. Two officers and ten soldiers went on each of the five two-week Army skiing courses at Winterberg. Additionally, most platoons attended one-week winter warfare courses at 'Tiger Base' nearby at Niedersfeld, run by Battalion instructors, to train every man how to live, fight and move in the snow. In the hills and forest it was a very pleasant change from flat Münsterland. The Band even ventured there and gave a concert for the 450 inhabitants who filled the village hall to hear such numbers as 'Berliner Luft' and 'Happy Wanderer', an event which enhanced the already excellent relations between Tiger and Niedersfelder.

Brigadier Mike Carver, Comd 6 Inf Bde Gp, carried out his Annual Administrative Inspection on 14 December. Due to heavy rain the formal parade was adversely affected, but it still comprised a drive past by all the fighting vehicles, whose glistening paintwork and serviceability was shown off to best effect. After he and his staff had inspected many departments, at the conclusion of a long day it was felt that he was well pleased with what he had seen.

The traditional round of Christmas activities were held in the barracks and various messes during the five-day stand-down. The celebrations that year included a Christmas party for children from two orphanages in Münster, the presents being paid for by donations from the soldiers. The Commanding Officer on the drums and the 2IC on the piano made several appearances when the Jazz Band performed at various functions.

Major John Parsons MBE **leads B Company.** *Trustees R Leicestershire Regt*

At the beginning of 1962 senior appointments were held as follows:

CO:	Lieutenant Colonel P E B Badger	OC B Coy:	Major A J Parsons MBE[15]
		CSM B Coy:	WO2 D G Grove
2IC:	Major P G Bligh	OC C Coy:	Captain J L Wilson
Adjt:	Captain R T Bogg	CSM C Coy:	WO2 W Bradburn
RSM:	WO1 H D Benham	OC HQ Coy:	Major J L Blackburn-Kane
QM:	Major (QM) G H Greaves		
RQMS:	WO2 P O'Sullivan	CSM HQ Coy:	WO2 L E Loader
OC A Coy:	Major R W F Penny R Warwick	Bandmaster:	WO1 J E Battye ARCM
CSM A Coy:	WO2 A L Clark	Drum Major:	Sgt R Osmund

The Battalion routine altered with the arrival of the five-day working week, all of Saturday now being available for shopping – which pleased the wives!

The Rugby Team, led by Captain Roger Bogg, had another good season, which included a two-match tour to Berlin in November and an exhausting seven-match tour to Leicester in March (the latter unfortunately without Roger Bogg, the Adjutant, who had to remain in Germany). Of the twenty-three matches played in Germany, twenty were won and three lost, all to Welsh teams, including eternal rivals 1 SWB in the Army Cup. Nevertheless, the team won the Brigade Group 7-a-Side Competition for the third successive year, Captain John Heggs had a BAOR trial, and during the season the team scored 471 points against 110.

The Football Team had a complete rebuild from the previous season. It was trained by Colour Sergeant Ward and led by Private Cobley. As perhaps an omen of a new Brigade rivalry which was to emerge eighteen months later, the team defeated 1st Battalion The 2nd East Anglian Regiment 10-0 in the third round, en route to the semi-final of the BAOR Cup. Its other highlights were a tour to Berlin in December and victory in the Münster Garrison League, runners-up in the 2 Div Inf Championships and a six-match tour in Leicestershire in May, where it lost but one match. The Hockey Team, led by Major J L (John) Blackburne-Kane (a former Army player) had a resurgence of interest, skill and fortune that season, but narrowly lost in the fourth round of the Army Cup. In Small-Bore Competition Shooting, the Battalion Team, led by sharpshooter Colour Sergeant Ken Colclough, won the Brigade Group Major Unit Championship, and HQ Company won the Minor Units Cup.

At the end of January the Battalion was notified that it would be moving to Watchet in Somerset in June. This was greeted with pleasure, though at that stage there appeared to be some doubt about what its role would be. It was also tinged with sadness because the Battalion would be much depleted as it was to leave behind in Germany some 250 deferred National Servicemen, the majority to join 1st Royal Warwicks.

In early February, four Royal Warwick subalterns joined 1st Royal Leicesters, to be gainfully employed until the 1st Royal Warwicks arrived in BAOR from Hong Kong. Helpfully, the number of Regular soldiers joining the Battalion was increasing, as a direct result of the success of the Recruiting Team in Leicestershire.

The last months in BAOR were by no means confined to move preparations and the Battalion played a full part in the early months of Rhine Army's training cycle. Battalion-level CPXs, appropriately named *Swan Song I* and *II*, were followed by the Brigade Group CPX *Golden Eagle*. April was an exceptionally busy month, among other things witnessing the culmination of a fortnight's annual field-firing period at Sennelager, during which the Battalion Rifle Meeting was held. Private W (Bill) McKenzie was the champion rifle shot, the Commanding Officer won the SMG, and A Company under Major R W F (Dick) Penny won the Inter-Company Shield. Six weeks later at the Brigade Group Rifle Meeting, the Battalion Team, shorn of several of its best shots who were on the Advance Party, was Runner-Up to 1 KSLI; 2nd Lieutenant David Michael was second in the Rifle.

April also saw the hosting for ten days of CCF contingents from Oakham School and Victoria College, a visit by the new GOC 2 Inf Div, Major General M A H Butler CBE DSO MC, and 2nd Lieutenant G A (Graham) Barrett leading a group to Norway on adventure training for three weeks. This was the first major such undertaking of this relatively new Army activity, following Lieutenant J C D (John) Heggs's four-man team's participation in similar training in the summer of 1960.

On 30 April, a detachment from the Battalion paid a second visit to the Netherlands town of Lichtenvoorde for two days, this time to take part in the celebrations to mark the 25th Wedding Anniversary of their Queen and Prince Bernhard. After a short church service and a march through the town, the Battalion's Football team drew 1-1 with Lichtenvoorde Football Club, a Dutch Second Division side. Later, after potted sports, the Band and Drums beat retreat under floodlights in front of 3,000 people. In the evening, several dances were held in the town, and each soldier was accommodated in a private home. Once again the citizens provided the warmest of welcomes and generous hospitality.

A three-day visit by Colonel of The Regiment started on 11 May. On the Battalion Parade, he presented to Major John Parsons, OC B Company, the Champion Company

Flag. In his address he congratulated the Battalion on its achievements in BAOR, wished good fortune to the National Servicemen shortly to leave, and the new All-Regular Battalion in its future. After being entertained in the Corporals' and the WOs' & Sgts' Messes, the highlight was Beating Retreat by the Band and Drums, which was attended by many Divisional guests. This was followed by a magnificent cocktail party and supper in the Officers' Mess. The WOs' & Sgts' Mess farewell party had been held a week earlier.

The following week, Brigadier Mike Carver, the Brigade Group Commander, paid his farewell visit to the Battalion. Formed up in hollow square, he told it that the advent of new radios and APCs, together with hard training inspired by the leadership of successive commanding officers, had transformed the Battalion from a Heavy Regiment of Foot to a lightly armoured, swift-moving battalion. Not for a long time would it be able to work in a brigade group with all its supporting arms as it had done over the last three years. He thanked it for all it had achieved for 6 Infantry Brigade Group, where the Battalion's reputation stood high and had helped to enhance the Brigade Group's good name in BAOR. He wished the Battalion well and especially the National Servicemen who had rendered such splendid service.

On 21 May, the Advance Party left for Watchet, and the Band and Drums for leave and a tour of Leicestershire. Four days later the Commanding Officer addressed all the National Servicemen (whose demobilization had been deferred for six months) before their dispersal: three officers and 155 men to 1 R Warwick at Hameln, and ninety men, who had requested to spend their last six months in Münster rather than Hameln, to 1 KSLI. Many had played vital roles both operationally and at sport within the Battalion. For the savagely depleted Royal Leicesters, the residual duties fell heavily on the remaining few, as final preparations were made for the handover to 1st Battalion The Cheshire Regiment whose Advance Party arrived on 10 June.

As almost the last act of any consequence, from 25 to 28 June, the Battalion team, led by 2nd Lieutenant Graham Barrett, took part in the Handorf Marches, near Münster. An annual event organized by the Royal Netherlands Air Force, it sought to promote goodwill and friendship among the Armed Forces of the different nations which were stationed in the local area. Teams of ten were required to march 15 kilometres on four successive nights. At its conclusion the Royal Leicesters were judged the best marching team. Competitive to the very end, it was a nice note on which to finish that chapter of its history, which finally ended on 3 July when the Band of 15th/19th The King's Royal Hussars played the Battalion's last buses out of Buller Barracks en route to Gütersloh, and on by air to Lyneham and dispersal on leave.

So ended a three-year tour in which the 1st Battalion had played its full part in the military and sporting life of 6 Infantry Brigade Group, 2nd Infantry Division, I (BR) Corps and BAOR. The observations of outsiders indicated that this was a quietly efficient unit carrying out whatever it was asked to do cheerfully, and without fuss or bother. Perhaps it was the people of Münster – military and civilian – who were sadder to see the Battalion depart than the Battalion was to depart for the UK. That departure marked the end of another era, as thereafter no National Servicemen served in the 1st Royal Leicesters, which became an All-Regular Battalion.

Of note also is that, while the 1st Battalion was in Plymouth and Münster, some officers and SNCOs of the Regiment were serving widely on secondment throughout the British Commonwealth, with the Aden Levies, Barbados Local Forces, the Federation of Malaya Military Forces, the Ghana Military Forces, the King's African Rifles, the Nigeria Regiment, and the Sultan of Muscat's Armed Forces. Additionally, four of its officers had at various times been serving with battalions of the Foresters, and two with the Royal Warwicks.

Notes

1 Sidney Brown had been OC HQ Coy 2/5th Leicesters in 1940 at Dunkirk, where he was taken prisoner by the German Army.
2 See Chapter 1, Note 16.
3 Geoff Havilland had been awarded the MC as a platoon commander in 1st R Leicesters in Korea in 1951.
4 Bill Underhill had commanded 7th Leicesters 1940-42 and had been appointed OBE in Feb 1945 for his work as a brigadier in command of 102 Reinforcement Group on the L of C in North-West Europe in 1944.
5 A former Black Watch officer, after retiring from the Army in 1958, Bernard Fergusson became Governor-General of New Zealand (as had his father, grandfather and father-in-law before him), and was later created Baron Ballantrae of Auchairne and of the Bay of Islands KT GCMG GCVO DSO OBE DCL LLD.
6 Rodney Green had been awarded the MC while serving as a platoon commander in 2nd Foresters in France in 1940.
7 Desmond Walker proceeded to Director of Music (DoM) Forester Brigade Music School; in 1962 he was commissioned and was DoM successively of the Band of the RTR 1962-63, the RASC/RCT 1963-69 and the Welsh Guards 1969 until his death in 1971.
8 Presented by Brigadier H S Pinder CBE MC, CO 1st Leicesters 1935-39, Colonel The Royal Leicestershire Regiment 1948-54. See Appendix N.
9 Donated by Lieutenant Colonel P H Creagh DSO. An Irishman who applied to join The Leinster Regiment, he was commissioned into The Leicestershire Regiment in 1902. He was awarded the DSO as Adjutant of 1/7th Manchesters at Gallipoli in 1915, and was CO 2nd Leicesters in Germany, Catterick and Londonderry in 1929-33.
10 Basil Gunnell was awarded the MC while serving as a platoon commander in 2nd R Warwick at Wormhoudt near Dunkirk in 1940. He served in 1st R Leicesters in Hong Kong, Korea and Iserlohn, and was appointed OBE in 1958 after commanding 1st R Warwick.
11 A former RTR officer, Mike Carver was later Chief of the General Staff 1971-73, Chief of Defence Staff 1973-76 and created Field Marshal Baron Carver of Shackleford GCB CBE DSO MC.
12 Lord Mayor of Leicester 1956-57, Alfred Halkyard had been awarded the MC serving in 4th Leicesters (TF) in France in 1918, had commanded 4th Leicesters (TA) 1930-36 and been appointed CB in 1956.
13 Revd Richard Mayston RAChD had served as chaplain of 2nd Leicesters 1937-39.
14 Bert Godwin had been capped twice for England in 1959, gained a further nine caps from 1963 to 1967, and toured South Africa with the British Lions in 1962.
15 John Parsons had been awarded the MBE as Adjutant of 1st R Leicesters in Korea 1951-52.

Chapter 3

1st Battalion: Watchet, Hong Kong and Borneo 1962-64

Watchet: May 1962 to March 1963

It had been in January 1962 that the Battalion had first learned that it was to be posted to Watchet in Somerset. The Advance Party under Major P G (Peter) Bligh, the Second-in-Command, had left West Germany in May 1962 and after leave had assembled at Doniford Camp, Watchet, near Minehead. The camp had been built some thirty years before and essentially comprised single-storey wooden huts and Nissen huts. The Advance Party rapidly set to to get the camp and the married quarters ready to receive the Main Body of what for the first time since 1939 was now an All-Regular Battalion.

On its arrival at Watchet senior appointments were held as follows:

CO:	Lieutenant Colonel P E B Badger	CSM A Coy:	WO2 A L Clark
		OC B Coy:	Major A J Parsons MBE
2IC:	Major P G Bligh	CSM B Coy:	WO2 D G Grove
Adjt:	Captain W H Morris	OC C Coy:	Captain C T Marshall
RSM:	WO1 H D Benham	OC HQ Coy:	Major J L Blackburn-Kane
QM:	Major G H Greaves	CSM HQ Coy:	WO2 W Bradburn
RQMS:	WO2 P O'Sullivan	Bandmaster:	WO1 J E Battye ARCM
OC A Coy:	Captain J L Wilson	Drum Major:	Sergeant R Osmund

Compared with Germany, the Battalion had a similar Order of Battle but was significantly below Established Strength. Due to the extraordinary energy and success of the Recruiting Team operating in Leicestershire under Captain John Heggs and WO2 'Jimmy' Jenks (which is covered in more detail in Chapter 4), it gradually increased its soldier strength to compensate for the departure of the 250 National Servicemen left in Germany. The Battalion comprised Headquarter Company and three rifle companies (A and B Companies with a Support Platoon of two 3" mortars and two 120mm MOBAT recoilless towed anti-tank guns). For the next seven months C Company – some fifteen men strong – was a Cadre Company, running cadres and continuation training for the ever-increasing number of recruits from the Depot. The Rifle Platoons' weapons were the 7.62mm self-loading rifle

(SLR) and similar calibre Bren LMG, the 9mm Sterling SMG, the 2" mortar and the 3.5" rocket launcher. The 9mm pistol replaced the .38" revolver. Communication was provided by C42, A41, A40 (all VHF) and the WS62 (HF) radio sets. Mechanical transport comprised ½-ton Land Rover 'jeeps', and 1-ton and 3-ton trucks. The Battalion was part of 2 Infantry Brigade (2 Inf Bde) at Plymouth under Brigadier K R S Trevor DSO OBE, which also included 1st Battalion The Devonshire and Dorset Regiment (1 D and D). 2 Inf Bde was part of 43rd (Wessex) Division/District, under command of Southern Command.

The Battalion was part of the Army's UK Strategic Reserve. Glad to be in England again, it settled in swiftly to the myriad of tasks, the principal one being training for its operational role as the first Seaborne Infantry Battalion in the UK, to which end a close affiliation was rapidly established both with 18 Company RASC (Amphibious) equipped with DUKW amphibious vehicles, and with the Royal Marines. By early August, Ratcliffe College CCF had been hosted for its summer camp (how pleasing for all it was to see the cadets wearing the Royal Leicestershire Regiment capbadge), a Battalion church service had been held to 'dedicate its work and life at Watchet to the glory of God', the Commanders of 43 (Wx) Div/Dist and 2 Inf Bde had paid their first visits, and A and B Companies had deployed for two weeks to Plasterdown and Okehampton to act as sponsor units for CCF contingents on summer camp. The Band and Drums were quickly into their stride and had beaten retreat at Plasterdown for the cadets and at the Watchet Flower Show, where some Officers' Mess silver was also on display, and the Cricket Team had belatedly begun its season against local sides. Sadly, Private Graham Hughes had died falling accidentally from a cliff at Watchet.

By mid-August, the Battalion had featured in the local Press when the Commanding Officer apologized to the Watchet Urban Council and the Williton Rural Council for incidents of bad behaviour by some of his soldiers while in town, assured them that the offenders would be punished and that there would be no more acts of misdemeanour in the town. Such an apology seems to have been something quite new in those parts and apparently was the first time in the long history of Doniford Camp that a commanding officer had showed such courtesy to the councils – 'Usually they argue with us!' On the operational front, one company in rotation was at seventy-two hours Notice To Move (NTM) to reinforce 1 D and D as the *Spearhead* Battalion over a period of six weeks. Lieutenant H T (Terry) Hutley led a team of twenty-four as the Arena Party at Plymouth Army Week, and while there his whole platoon passed the RM cliff-climbing test, an achievement that led to these 'experts' giving demonstrations whenever a high-ranking officer visited Watchet, of which there were many. The Football Team began its season with a match against Williton, and a number of soldiers took part as extras in the filming on the Quantock Hills of the Tony Richardson film *Tom Jones*, starring Albert Finney (and Sergeant Albert Glover, and others!).

On 23 August, the Signals Platoon under Lieutenant Tony Pollard set out on a two-day Exercise *Sea View* combining communications with watermanship to and at the island of Fairholm in the Bristol Channel, from which due to bad weather they escaped some forty-eight hours late. At the month's end a series of exercises with 18 Coy RASC (Amph) were planned over the next six months, to be named *Cormorant 1-5*, and a team of RM Commandos spent a week instructing a cadre of officers and NCOs in watermanship with assault canoes and in cliff-climbing. At the end of August, the Battalion strength was 448 All Ranks (including the Band and Drums which were sixty in number).

Beach assault at Fremington. *Trustees R Leicestershire Regt*

On 1 September, back from a three-week tour of the Midlands, the Band and Drums beat retreat in the camp for some 300 guests as the Battalion welcomed them to Watchet, the fine display in a perfect setting being followed by official entertainment in the three messes. A Company then went on Exercise *Cormorant 1*, night-marching 27 miles to Fremington, and carrying out a seaborne assault from DUKWs, to be followed by B Company on *Cormorant 2*, which marched a little bit further and then assaulted over the beach near Barnstable. On 14 September, Private A J H (Albert) Hurcombe died as the result of a cliff fall on Lundy Island.

A week later, A Company under Captain John Wilson set out for Leicestershire for a two-week KAPE tour ('Keeping the Army in the Public Eye'), to increase the Army's profile in the county and to supplement the work of the Recruiting Team. It started with a flourish with Beating Retreat by the Band and Drums in Leicester's Victoria Park in the presence of the Lord Mayor of Leicester and the Colonel of The Regiment. A Company, based with the 4/5th Battalion at Ulverscroft Road, spent four days in each of Coalville, Loughborough and Melton Mowbray. Next, B Company under Major John Parsons 'worked' Hinckley, Oakham, Lutterworth and the City of Leicester for three weeks. At the start of this period, accompanied by an ITV camera crew, Captains Jeremy North and Tom Hiney, plus eight soldiers, set out to march from Watchet some 25 miles a day for six days; a civic party welcomed them into Hinckley 169 miles later.

During October, Lance Corporal R W (Ronald) Spavins and Private J E Howsin tragically died in separate motorcycle accidents. The Colonel of The Regiment paid his first visit to Watchet at the end of the month, followed soon after by the GOC-in-C Southern Command, Lieutenant General Sir Robert Bray KCB CBE DSO, who watched various aspects of cliff-climbing and cadre training. During those several months the soldiers regularly trained climbing up and down 200' cliffs on ropes and canoeing in Watchet Harbour, before scrambling up nets on the harbour walls. And the Mortar and Anti-Tank Platoons took part in a Support Weapons Concentration at Okehampton in November.

Then came a major change. Following the War Office's consideration of the Bower Report, it was announced in Parliament on 14 November that, as part of the reorganization of the Infantry of the Line into ten brigades of four battalions and three of three, The Forester Brigade was to disband and its component regiments were to join other brigades to make them four-regiment ones. The Royal Warwickshires were to join The Fusilier Brigade and become The Royal Warwickshire Fusiliers, The Sherwood Foresters were to join The Mercian Brigade, and The Royal Leicestershire Regiment was to join The East Anglian Brigade. Depot The Forester Brigade at Glen Parva Barracks was to close in May 1963, recruits for the Royal Leicesters thereafter being trained at Depot The East Anglian Brigade at Bury St Edmunds in Suffolk. The other battalions of the existing East Anglian Brigade were:

1st Battalion 1st East Anglian Regiment (Royal Norfolk and Suffolk)
1st Battalion 2nd East Anglian Regiment (Duchess of Gloucester's Own Royal Lincolnshire and Northamptonshire)
1st Battalion 3rd East Anglian Regiment (16th/44th Foot)

The Colonel of The Regiment immediately announced:

I have been assured by the War Office that the transfer of our Regiment to The East Anglian Brigade will have no effect on our long association with the county of Leicestershire and the city of Leicester, and there is no desire and intention to weaken this link. This is very good news because our roots run very deep in the county and city, and at the present time over eighty per cent of the regular soldiers serving with our 1st Battalion come from Leicestershire.

The Regimental Headquarters of our Regiment and the Regimental Museum will remain in Leicester, and the Territorial battalion (4/5th Bn The Royal Leicestershire Regiment) will still be stationed in the county and city. For the future we will get a great welcome and find many friends in our new Brigade. We must be thankful, in these days of change, that these recent Infantry reorganisations have left us with our regular and territorial battalions in being and our close association with the county of Leicestershire and the city of Leicester, as strong as ever.

In a written reply in the House of Commons to a question by Mr John Farr, MP for the Harborough Division, the Secretary of State for Defence said:

Arrangements for the dispersal of this Brigade have already been put in hand. Adaptations have to be made to the Depots of the three Brigades which are receiving a regiment from The Forester Brigade, and dispersal will be completed by the autumn of 1963. In paying tribute to the loyal way in which this decision has been accepted, I wish to make it clear that the only reason that the choice fell on The Forester Brigade was that its dispersal could be effected with the least disturbance to the Infantry as a whole. The efficiency of the Brigade has been of a high order and I much regret that its existence is to end.

Gratifying though it may have been to learn of the appreciation in which the efficiency of The Forester Brigade was held in high places, nevertheless there was great disappointment at the prospective dissolution of the Brigade, the closure of the Depot at

Glen Parva which had been the Regiment's home for nigh on eighty-two years, and the dispersal of the Brigade's regiments with which such bonding and friendship had been built up over the years. But at least 1st Battalion The Royal Leicestershire Regiment was to live on in name and spirit.

And so life in the 1st Battalion at Watchet continued almost unaltered, with the focus on training for its seaborne role and enjoying peacetime soldiering in England. That calm existence was shattered in mid-December as a direct result of an Indonesian-inspired uprising against the Sultan of Brunei on the Indonesian Island of Kalimantan, normally referred to as Borneo. To quell that uprising, a force of British and Gurkha troops rapidly deployed from Singapore, to be followed by others. Consequently, additional British reserves were needed in the Far East. That unrest in Brunei soon widened to 'military and political stand-off' between Indonesia and the countries which were soon to form the Federation of Malaysia, a state of confrontation and occasional armed conflict which was to last for four years, and in which the Royal Leicesters were to become engaged on operations in September 1963 (described later in this chapter). At a similar time, although hardly noticed by soldiers stationed in England and destined for imminent deployment to the Far East, was a change of regime in Yemen in Southern Arabia, a new republic that abutted the Aden Protectorates and the British Crown Colony of Aden. This was an area known regimentally only by those who had served in the Aden Protectorate Levies (APL), two of whose battalions had been commanded by Royal Leicesters officers in the late 1950s and to where the Battalion would be deployed on operations in 1965 (described in Chapter 5).

Meanwhile in England, on 10 December 1962, the Battalion was placed at ten days NTM, with no destination or role specified. Three days later it was placed at three days NTM. Those on courses and leave were recalled and vehicles despatched to collect essential stores. Five C42 VHF radios that had been sought for four months arrived within twenty-four hours! Kit and equipment was packed and stowed ready for an air move, cholera and yellow fever vaccinations applied, and documents put in order. The emplaning strength was 392 all ranks, with a Rear Party of ninety, including the Band and other ineligibles. The Battalion not having been called forward by 17 December, it was decided that the original Christmas plans would be effected. By 20 December the Battalion had been put at a slightly more relaxed NTM of five days. So the children's Christmas Party was held, followed by a carol service in the Gym (surrounded by air cargo boxes, and at which 'the singing of carols was cheering and very loud – "Nowell" being sung better than either Padre had ever heard'). After Christmas dinner for the soldiers that evening, the Battalion proceeded on leave, reassembling at Watchet on 28 December.

Thoughts of warmer climes were dispelled by the blizzard that struck the West Country on 29 December. Every road in and out of Watchet became impassable, and road and rail movement throughout the south of England was severely curtailed for over a week. Several members of the Battalion skied into barracks.

On New Year's Day 1963, the Battalion became involved in Military Aid to the Civil Community (MACC). A party led by the Commanding Officer took food to an isolated pig farm on the Quantock Hills moor, carrying stock feed over a mile from the roadhead. Soldiers helped railwaymen dig out a snowbound train in a cutting at Doniford. A group of seventy all ranks spent four days in Bristol helping to clear snow from railway sidings;

another party went to Watchet Harbour to clear lines so that a ship's cargo could be put on rail. After a week the weather returned to normal, which coincided with the Battalion being formally warned for unaccompanied overseas service of six to nine months from early March.

By mid-January all cadres, already adversely affected by the disruption of the snow, were abandoned with the impending move and reorganization of the Battalion, C Company being built up to combat strength with the transfer in of a platoon from each of A and B Companies. On 29 January, all emplaning personnel proceeded on two weeks' embarkation leave, and two days later the Training Advance Party of three officers, three sergeants and three corporals emplaned for Singapore to undergo a six-week course at the Jungle Warfare School at Kota Tinggi, Johore, in Malaya. In order to achieve an emplaning strength of 450 (twenty-eight officers and 422 soldiers), twenty-five reinforcements were requested from 1st Battalion 3rd East Anglian Regiment (1/3 E Anglian), an early test of flexible posting within The East Anglian Brigade.

The Battalion's sports teams, competing for the first time without National Servicemen and having made encouraging starts to their seasons, quite apart from weather disruptions, had their aspirations nipped in the bud 'at half-time' with the operational deployment. Forty-four people played for the Rugby 1st XV which generally found that local rugby was tougher than Inter-Unit. The Football Team, under Captain Bill Morris, were finalists in the 43 (Wx) Div/Dist Competition. The Basketball Team, captained by WO2 D G (David) Grove, won the Div/Dist Competition. The Boxing Team won the Div/Dist Unit Novices. The Hockey Team played purposefully in military and civilian competitions. The Small-Bore Shooting Team, captained by Major A E R (Ted) Ross, as well as competing in a civilian league, was well placed in the Div/Dist League when 'time' had to be called on its England season.

Shortly before the Battalion's departure from Watchet, the Colonel of The Regiment paid a farewell visit. Accompanied by the Regimental Secretary, Lieutenant Colonel (Retd) P G Upcher DSO DL[1], that visit was to be Lieutenant General Sir Colin Callander's last in that appointment. All ranks had always been so appreciative and inspired by his interest during such occasions during the nine years of his Colonelcy, which spanned a most difficult time with many important changes taking place.

On 19 February, the Advance Party of thirty-five all ranks emplaned for Singapore, to join up with the Training Advance Party. News of that destination was received with considerable anticipation and excitement, as the Battalion was expecting to be stationed at Fort George (Bukit Terendak) 150 miles north of Singapore, in modern air-conditioned buildings with 'open plan' kitchens in a spacious camp hewn out of a rubber plantation nestling against a hill, with an IS role in Singapore. By 20 February, the Battalion's destination had been changed from Malaya to Hong Kong, to take over the IS duties of 2/7th Gurkhas, who were being transferred to Brunei. Such were the vagaries of the Military Movements system and strategic airlift over long distances and in combination with Cunard Eagle and Cathay Pacific Britannia aircraft, that the second Main Body flight actually arrived in Hong Kong ninety minutes before the Advance Party!

The Rear Party remaining at Watchet numbered 186 all ranks, initially under Major John Blackburn-Kane. Of those, forty were the Band, twenty detached on various activities, while most of the others were men who under existing rules were either too young or had insufficient remaining service to deploy to the Far East. Over the next few months the youngsters came of age and were posted out to Hong Kong, and the Band proceeded there in April for five months. The Rear Party strength was then about thirty-five at Watchet, a figure at which it remained until on 1 October reinforcements were 'cut off' from deployment overseas; thereafter it began to fill up with recruits from the Depot and with older soldiers returning from Extra-Regimental Employment (ERE).

Hong Kong: March to September 1963

On arrival in Hong Kong on 8 March 1963, senior appointments were held as follows:

CO:	Lieutenant Colonel P E B Badger	CSM B Coy:	WO2 D G Grove
		OC C Coy:	Captain C T Marshall
2IC:	Major P G Bligh	CSM C Coy:	WO2 P M Collins
Adjt:	Captain W H Morris	OC HQ Coy:	Major A E R Ross
RSM:	WO1 H D Benham	CSM HQ Coy:	WO2 W Bradburn
QM:	Major G H Greaves	OC Rear Party:	Major J L Blackburn-Kane
RQMS:	WO2 P O'Sullivan	Adjt Rear Party:	Capt A S Moore
OC A Coy:	Major T Holloway	Bandmaster:	WO1 J E Battye ARCM
CSM A Coy:	WO2 K Colclough	Drum Major:	Sgt T Roberts
OC B Coy:	Major A J Parsons MBE		

The Battalion, with a strength of 430 all ranks, was stationed on the mainland in the New Territories. The three rifle companies were at Sai Kung Camp, and Bn HQ and HQ Coy at Erskine Camp, 10 and 6 miles respectively from the bright lights of Kowloon. The camps comprised mainly corrugated-iron Nissen huts, divided by monsoon drains – which claimed many victims on return from a night out. Rather primitive, neither camp was intended as permanent accommodation for an infantry battalion, indeed the former was remembered by some from twelve years before when it had been a tented battle camp from which the Battalion had carried out final training before deploying to Korea. Both were within easy reach of training areas and well situated overlooking the sea, which was easy to reach from reasonably accessible beaches. Being able to swim was a particularly important feature as the Colony was experiencing one of the hottest and driest times on record, and the permanent garrison sweated away in Kowloon. A serious shortage of water afflicted the whole Colony, a situation that was not alleviated for the Battalion until the first decent rains in mid-June, restrictions only finally being lifted for the Colony in mid-July. Although it was administered by HQ Hong Kong & Kowloon Garrison (under the command of Brigadier W P L Lawson MC), operationally the Battalion was part of 48 Gurkha Infantry Brigade Group (48 Bde Gp), which also included 1st Battalion The Queen's Surreys (1 Queens Surreys) and 34 Field Regiment RA. 48 Bde Gp was subordinate to HQ British Forces Hong Kong (BFHK), commanded by Lieutenant General R W Craddock CB CBE DSO.

Dress on training and operations was Olive Green (OG) trousers, jacket and floppy hat, with the jungle 1944 Pattern webbing belt and pouches, and steel helmet for riots. Parade Dress was blue beret, starched OG shorts and jacket, with the sleeves rolled up, 2" web belt (1938 Pattern), boots and ankle puttees with green hosetops, and garter tabs in red, pearl

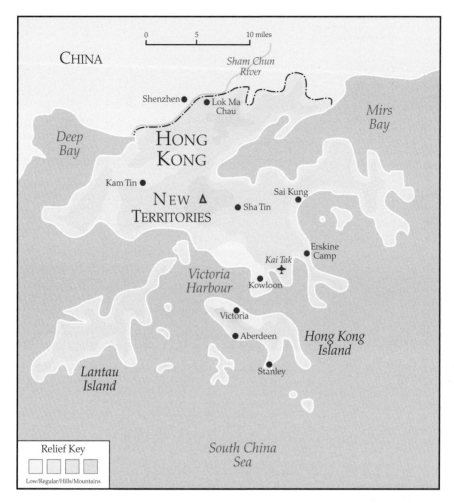

grey and black. The Band and Drums and the Colour Party wore white No. 3 Dress on ceremonial occasions. The Regimental buckle was worn with the web belt by officers, WOs and SNCOs in all forms of dress except on training and operations. A Regimental stable belt was worn by officers in shirt sleeve order or OG when not on parade with troops. In barracks, working dress for soldiers was often just shorts and boots, with socks rolled down. Mess Dress for officers was white monkey jacket, black tie, No. 1 dress trousers and pearl grey cummerbund. There was also a less formal version called 'Red Sea Rig', the same as Mess Dress but without the monkey jacket.

The rifle platoon weapons were the 7.62mm SLR and similar calibre Bren LMG, the 9mm Sterling SMG, and the 3.5" rocket launcher. Communication was provided by C42, A41, and A40 radios (all VHF). Mechanical transport comprised ½- and ¾-ton Land Rover 'jeeps', and 1-ton and 3-ton lorries.

The Battalion's operational role was to reinforce 34 Regt RA in Kowloon City in the event of civil unrest developing, to which end a number of briefings, recces and exercises were completed to bring it up to speed as soon as practicable. This culminated in Exercise *Lion Rock III* with the Gunners on 28 March. In addition, on 15 March the Battalion took over the twelve-man task at the observation post (OP) of the Lok Ma Chau police station overlooking the Chinese Border, platoons manning it for a week at a time in rotation.

Looking north into China from Lok Ma Chau OP. *T Holloway*

The Battalion was also required to provide a small Honour Guard in Korea. Seven men from C Company, under Lieutenant David Michael and Sergeant J T (John) Morris MM[2], set out by air on 7 April to form part of the 8th United States Army Honour Guard, stationed at HQ United Nations (UN) Forces in Seoul.

The Honour Guard was an eclectic group, comprising platoons furnished by USA, South Korea and the UN. The UN Platoon comprised four sections: Ethiopian, Thai, Turkish and British (found by 1st Royal Leicesters). There were two distinct duties to perform: ceremonial, and guard duty. Ceremonial required the troops to act as a guard of honour for any visiting general or person whose rank was accorded such privilege, and to parade daily for the firing of the 1800 hours gun at the Yongsan compound at Seoul.

The other main duty was to provide part of the guard at the Military Armistice Commission meetings at Panmunjom, 30 miles north of Seoul. This duty could come at any time, once a month or twice a week. Either side could call a meeting. The two sides sat at a table down the centre of which ran along the 38th Parallel – the demarcation line which split South from North Korea. The 'Blues' were represented by ROK (Republic of Korea), USA and UN members; the Communist 'Reds' by DPRK (Democratic Peoples' Republic of Korea), and Chinese members.

The Quonset huts that formed the buildings of the compound were painted blue for the UN side and green for the North Korean side. There was a dovecote on the North Korean side of the dividing line and the doves were trained not to land on any blue building – a move that caused much amusement to the 'Blues' as it meant that the birds only delivered their droppings on the North Koreans! Apart from these time-consuming military duties, a battlefield tour was made to Hill 235 (Gloster Hill), overlooking the Imjin River, the site of a fierce battle in April 1951 during the Korean War. A visit was also made to the UN War Cemetery at Pusan, where the graves of forty-eight of the fifty-three men of 1st Royal

Leicesters killed in Korea in 1951-52 are buried and were being tended with dedicated care and attention.

At the conclusion of this unusual detached duty, the Section returned to the Battalion in Hong Kong on 9 July, having made many friends with the Americans, and its commanders both receiving US 'citations'.

Meanwhile, back in April, the Battalion was concentrating on acclimatization and fitness training, while operational IS training (especially riot control), allied to sport and social events, became the order of the day. At the Officers' Mess's first dinner night, it was noticed that the combined length of service of the three longest-serving officers (Majors John Bromhead and George Greaves, and Captain Bob Ross) totalled a staggering ninety-eight years.

On 22 April, the sea freight arrived, most importantly including pikes for the Colours, swords for the officers, drums and tiger skins for the Drums, and the instruments of the Band. So at last those elements could set to to rehearse with full equipment for the Queen's Birthday Parade four days later. On 26 April, the Battalion paraded with four guards of sixty, all smartly dressed in starched OG, plus the Colour Party in white No. 3 Dress (see plate section). They put on a magnificent display marching at the head of the column along streets lined with enormous and noisy numbers of Chinese, proceeding through Kowloon and past HE The Governor, Sir Robert Black GCMG OBE, on the saluting base. He subsequently referred to the precision of their march past as 'parade ground arrogance'. Three days later Comd BFHK visited the Battalion.

On 1 May, the Battalion officially became part of The East Anglian Brigade. However, due to a delay in receipt of the soldiers' capbadges, it was not until 13 May that all ranks quietly replaced their capbadges of The Forester Brigade with those of their new brigade (see plate section) – an occurrence that was not even mentioned in *The Green Tiger*. The East Anglian Brigade badge was the Castle and Key of Gibraltar placed above a scroll 'East Anglia', set upon an eight-pointed star, the former granted to the antecedents of the Suffolks, Essex and Northamptons for their part in the Great Siege of Gibraltar 1779-83, and the star borne on the old badges of the Royal Lincolns and Bedfords. So, for the first time in 138 years, 1st Battalion The Royal Leicestershire Regiment did not have the Tiger emblem in its capbadge, but they were still Royal Leicesters by name and Tigers by nickname and spirit. The Royal Tiger superimposed with 'Hindoostan' continued to be worn as a collar badge in parade uniform. Most significantly, the Colonel of The Regiment had deflected any blandishments that the Regiment should become the 4th East Anglian Regiment. He argued successfully that, since the Royal Leicesters – unlike the predecessors of the three East Anglian Regiments – had not had to amalgamate in the late 1950s, there was no necessity to change its name as it joined an existing brigade, but it was sensible to wait until a Large Regiment was formed.

It is important to realize that for several years the Army Council had been considering how best to provide an organization for the sixty Regular battalions of infantry which was flexible enough – with 'minimum disturbance' – to be varied in number between fifty and seventy depending on the Nation's strategic needs. While the creation of the Territorial Brigades (e.g. The East Anglian Brigade and The Fusilier Brigade) was an important first step, the Army Council were of the view that Large Regiments should be allowed to develop by 'co-operative evolution', but that progress must be made in order to prevent the total extinction of any regiment should any further cuts in numbers of battalions be required at short notice. When other brigades failed to prepare properly for such an eventuality, in 1968 The York & Lancaster Regiment and The Cameronians had to disband. The viability of the Large Regiment concept was the organization of a regiment into that number of battalions necessary to ensure that, if and when cuts in the number of battalions were applied, the large regiment would still be capable of continuing to function efficiently as such. The Army Council stressed that 'the adoption of the Large Regiment concept will in no way make the Regiments concerned more liable in the event of making reductions.' Despite their relative seniority in the Infantry as the 17th Foot, the Royal Leicesters in 1963 then faced the possibility of extinction in any further cuts as they were the junior of the four regiments of The East Anglian Brigade, the others being the 9th, 10th and 16th Foot. The Colonel of their Regiment wrote to his colleagues on the East Anglian Brigade's Council of Colonels: 'I do not think that we can ever produce a true regimental spirit in our Brigade until we form a Large Regiment of four battalions.' As soon as the Royal Leicesters had joined the Brigade in May 1963, the Commanding Officer flew back from Hong Kong to a meeting chaired by the Brigade Colonel at which the Commanding Officers of all four Regular battalions recommended to the Council of Colonels that the Brigade should convert to a Large Regiment as soon as was practicable, subject to certain conditions, such as the maintenance of the county connections and that other brigades should also convert. In the event, only six out of the thirteen Brigades did so – until all infantry regiments (less the Foot Guards) were forced to do so in the first decade of the twenty-first century. So, from May 1963 over the ensuing year, preparatory work for the East Anglian Infantry's new shape was put in train.

In England that month, the final Royal Tigers' Weekend at Glen Parva Barracks was being held. During it the outgoing Colonel of The Regiment was presented with a silver tiger by the officers of the Regiment, and a warm welcome was extended to his successor in post, Major General D A ('Joe') Kendrew CB CBE DSO, who a few months later was to be knighted on appointment as Governor of Western Australia. How fortunate the Regiment was to have such a magnificent fighting soldier (and former international rugby player) as its Colonel[3]. During Kendrew's time abroad, the Regimental Secretary, Lieutenant Colonel Peter Upcher, was appointed as his Deputy.

Meanwhile, in Hong Kong, each of the 1st Battalion's three rifle companies entered a twelve-man team in the prestigious annual Round-the-Colony Race, thirty teams competing in a test of physical stamina and personal endurance over three days in mid-May. The course comprised three separate feats of endurance, with teams being divided into three sections, each section being responsible for one stage of the course. A Company's team, led by Lieutenant A T (Tony) Amos, Sergeant E ('Chris') Christopher and Corporal R ('Alpine') Johnson, finished in seventh place, the second highest non-Gurkha team. After just two months to acclimatize in the challenging climate, that was an immensely creditable and satisfying achievement by those Tigers.

At the end of the month, Exercise *Tiger Cub* was held, a joint live-firing exercise in which a seaborne landing took place at a bay on the east side of the New Territories, the Battalion's water-borne assault troops being supported by HMS *Brighton*, 1 Bty 4 Regt RA, 20 Bty RA, 20 Recce Flt AAC and the RAF. The RN, Gunners and RAF Hawker Hunters demonstrated their firepower to good effect. HMS *Brighton* was affiliated to the Battalion for her visit to the Colony, a relationship that was not confined solely to exercises – several sports fixtures were arranged and visits were made between the various messes. The RASC also most helpfully assisted in Battalion training by providing LCMs for seaborne movement and mules for supply of platoons in the mountainous terrain.

On 8 June, the Battalion was warned for deployment on operations in Brunei and North Borneo in September, for a five-month tour – which was to be the longest so far undertaken by any unit in that operational theatre. Since the unsuccessful Indonesian-inspired revolt in Brunei the previous December, the reinforcing British Forces there had spent several months seeking to eliminate all those rebels who had taken part in the revolt.

To see where Brunei and North Borneo fitted into the politico-strategic picture, for centuries the large island of Indonesian Borneo – also known as Kalimantan – had been administered by the Dutch and had formed an important part of the Dutch East Indies until Indonesia achieved independence in 1949. Sukarno, Indonesia's first President, had since 1945, dreamed of bringing the Malay Peninsula, Singapore, Sarawak, North Borneo and Brunei under the domination of a Greater Indonesia. In contrast, Tunku Abdul Rahman, Prime Minister of the Malayan Federation since the country gained its independence from Britain in 1957, had at an early stage realized that the only way to live with Indonesia, his giant neighbour to the south, was to create a large and, in his view, a more viable political unit consisting of the Federation of Malaya, and those other four British Colonies. He first

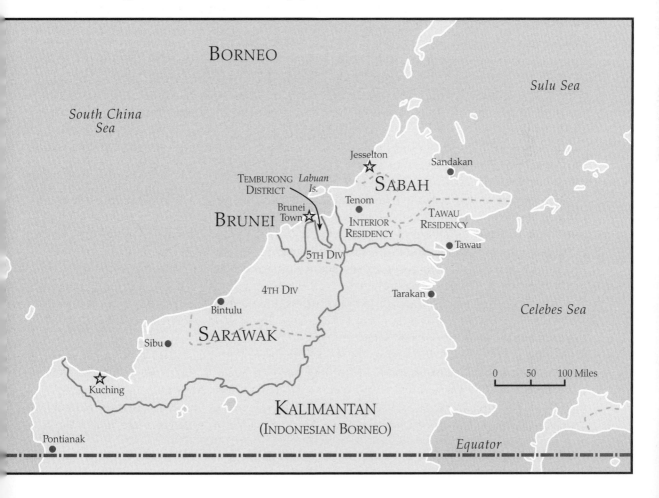

made public reference to this concept in 1961 and it soon gathered momentum, with only the Sultan of Brunei hesitating.

Whilst British troops were dealing with the last spasms of the 1962 Brunei revolt, Jakarta Radio broadcast a series of inflammatory statements designed to increase tension in Borneo. The Indonesian Foreign Minister announced a policy of 'confrontation' towards Malaya 'because at present they represent themselves as accomplices of neo-colonialist and neo-imperialist forces pursuing a policy hostile towards Indonesia'. The war of words dragged on, interspersed with various attempts at reaching political understanding. In parallel, groups of Indonesian 'volunteers' began, in April 1963, to infiltrate across the border into Sarawak and North Borneo where they engaged in raids, sabotage and attempted subversion. In July, President Sukarno stated, 'To crush Malaysia we must launch a confrontation in all fields. We cannot talk sweetly to the imperialists.' Then, in mid-August, the Gurkhas clashed with a group of about fifty Indonesian-based terrorists on the Sarawak border.

It was against the backdrop of this developing situation, which colloquially was known as the 'Indonesian Confrontation' and was to last until 1966, that between June and September 1963, 1st Battalion The Royal Leicestershire Regiment focused its training for the forthcoming deployment. A number of rifle company officers and SNCOs were dispatched at various times for courses at the Jungle Warfare School in Johore, and a group of six tracker-dog handlers went to Singapore to be trained. It was a challenge to get the Battalion, with many very young soldiers, prepared for jungle operations in Hong Kong, which contained no jungle! So the JEWT became the training medium of the day (Jungle Exercise Without Trees)! The Signals Platoon and Company signallers became proficient in HF Skywave communications, using the high-powered WS62 and Morse code. As the sets needed a minimum distance of some 30 miles, it was hard to do any useful communicating within the geographical confines of Hong Kong, but some training was carried out by sending detachments to the more distant islands. Company commanders displayed great imagination and air supply techniques were practised by giving rifle sections locations to get to in the most difficult country, where they would receive an airdrop at a specific time – hungry were those who missed the RV! The Commanding Officer opined that the greatest challenge was psychological: what would be the mental reaction of the typical young soldier when he was first deployed straight into some of the most inhospitable jungle in the world in detached bases where he could expect to remain for five months, completely out of touch with the outside world apart from a weekly air supply drop and an occasional visit by a helicopter? Leadership, preparation and training were tackled with a sense of purpose over the three hottest months of the year, and the men became very fit.

In addition to training, Garrison duties continued and on 12 June the Battalion assumed responsibility for Force Guards from 4 Regt RA, which involved A Company mounting guards at Government House, Flagstaff House and HQ BFHK on Hong Kong Island, making a pleasant break from life in the New Territories. Although on 17 June enough rain had fallen to allow the water restrictions to be lifted in the Battalion's camps, the situation in Kowloon and on Hong Kong Island remained grave. By the end of the month, due to the continuing water shortage in the Colony, all social parties were suspended, severely affecting Royal Tigers' Day festivities, which were only able to comprise a fine supper, beer and film shows. On 9 July, an Officers' Day was held at Sai Kung Camp, which, among other senior officers, was attended by HRH The Duke of Kent. A week later the monsoon broke and it poured with rain all day, 36" falling in twenty-four hours – water restrictions were lifted!

Despite the rigours of training, much time and effort was expended on competitive sport, albeit the various seasons being different from England's. There had been no serious athletics since the departure of the National Servicemen the year before so it was important to find some new gladiators from amongst the newly joined Regulars, and to train a team to compete in the very hot and sticky climate of Hong Kong. On 3 April, at the Battalion Athletics Meeting, HQ Company was Champion Company, Lieutenant A J G (Tony) Pollard going on to become the Far East discus champion. Although the Battalion Team won the Mile Medley at the 34 Fd Regt meeting two days later and had five men in the Army Team against the Civilians (during which Drummer C (Clive) Mallett won the Javelin with a throw of 157'), at the Garrison Meeting in mid-April, and again in the Hong Kong Inter-Unit Championships the following month, the Battalion came second to 1 Queens Surreys each time. The activities of the Hockey Team were confined to a series of friendly matches at the tail end of the season, as were the Football Team's, which played in a series of friendlies, including against the Sai Kung District League champions. Competitive swimming, golf, basketball and rugby were also played; in the latter, the team played in the Hong Kong Sevens very soon after arrival, but suffered a very early exit.

Early in August, notification was received that deployment to Brunei and Borneo in mid-September would be on the Commando Carrier HMS *Albion*, and the Battalion would be augmented by a platoon of one officer and forty soldiers of 4 Regt RA. A week later the prospective destination changed to Sarawak and interest grew markedly over the following days, with reports from 2/6th Gurkhas of attacks and ambushes against the Indonesians in the border area. Meanwhile in Hong Kong, on 15 August, Exercise *Marco Polo* took place, a signals and movement exercise involving Bn HQ and elements down to platoon HQs, to be followed by a week of training out of camp: A and HQ Companies at Stonecutter's and San Wai Ranges, B and C Companies at Gordon's Hard on watermanship training – in preparation for movement in Sarawak and North Borneo which would be mostly by river.

As the planned date of deployment neared, the method of transport to Sarawak changed to RAF transport or charter aircraft. HE The Governor and the Commander British Forces dined with the officers. The former then wrote to the Commanding Officer: 'I should like to take the opportunity, in thanking you for your hospitality, to include my thanks for the period of service here by the Regiment as part of the Garrison in Hong Kong and to send to you and to all ranks of the Regiment my best wishes for your tour of service in Borneo.' Other senior officers visited to wish the Battalion 'God speed', and a farewell cocktail party was held to repay the hospitality of numerous people in the Colony.

And then the deployment destination changed again, to Brunei and North Borneo, and for the next few days, while the Movements Staff sought to gather in Hong Kong sufficient RAF Hastings aircraft (which carried thirty-eight passengers) and civilian Britannias (which carried ninety), there were numerous examples of the Adjutant, Captain P N (Peter) Graham, and the Orderly Room staff having to rejig the movement staff tables. If that was not enough to test the patience and flexibility of the eager soldiers, a Storm Warning Flag 3 was hoisted in anticipation of Typhoon 'Carmen', the epicentre of which mercifully passed by 100 miles to the south. Nevertheless, all tents had to be struck before winds gusting to 50mph hit, the damage being confined to broken windows and doors blown off hinges.

The Band duly returned to UK from Hong Kong. At last, the first Main Body flight took off en route to Labuan Island in a Hastings on 12 September, but not before the thirty-eighth passenger was left off as the pilot wanted to take more fuel. When he heard the news, the offended soldier retorted, 'They'd go broke in civvy street'! On one of the chalks flying by chartered Britannia, the passengers were served breakfast in camp in Hong Kong, were served a second as soon as they had emplaned, were marched off for their third breakfast of the day on arrival at Labuan, and it was still only 0730 hours – the epitome of 'marching on their stomach', an activity which was to be constantly practised for the next five months!

Borneo Territories: September 1963 to February 1964

The total population of the Borneo Territories – Sarawak, Brunei and Sabah (as North Borneo was renamed in September 1963) – was 1.5 million, of whom half were indigenous. In Sarawak, 31 per cent were Chinese and 19 per cent Malay; in Brunei 28 per cent were Chinese and 54 per cent Malay, and in Sabah 21 per cent were Chinese and 7 per cent Malay. Most of the Chinese population – the dominant, industrious and ambitious – had settled in or near the towns, at trading posts or on farms beside the major rivers. The border regions were inhabited by the indigenous tribes – Dayaks, Ibans, Kedeyans, Muruts and Kelabits – who were for the most part unsophisticated, agricultural people living in tribal longhouses or kampongs. They were the famed tribes of 'head-hunters'.

Charged with 'supporting the civil power in defending its area from all hostilities mounted, supported, directed and inspired from outside Malaysia', the Battalion area of responsibility consisted of the Fifth Division of Sarawak, the Temburong District of Brunei, and the Interior and Tawau Residencies of Sabah – in all an area of about the size of Wales except that it was not grassy mountain slopes but infrequent cultivated areas dispersed with jungle-covered ridges. The Battalion's border with Indonesian Borneo ran for some 200 miles, partly along the top of the major watershed range that at its southernmost point rose to a height of almost 8,000 feet. For much of its length it was unmarked and in considerable dispute. Located just north of the Equator in a hot and humid climate, the area contains some of the toughest jungle in the world, as daunting as anything that British troops had met in the Malayan Emergency or the war in Burma, and interspersed with valleys and plateaus all of which are covered by tropical rain forest. The hillsides are sometimes almost vertical. Most of the hinterland is primary jungle with a treetop canopy as much as 200 feet from the ground, dense secondary jungle where the virgin growth had been felled, streams infested with leeches, and wide belts of virtually impenetrable mangrove swamp along the coast. There were few roads in the immediate neighbourhood of the towns: the real highways were rivers, which could quickly turn from peaceful waterways into raging torrents with complete tree trunks floating downstream at up to 15 knots. It was always humid and often raining.

By 19 September, the whole of 1st Battalion The Royal Leicestershire Regiment was in its new operational theatre on what was to be its last active service deployment. Its strength was twenty-five officers and 505 men. Senior appointments were held as follows:

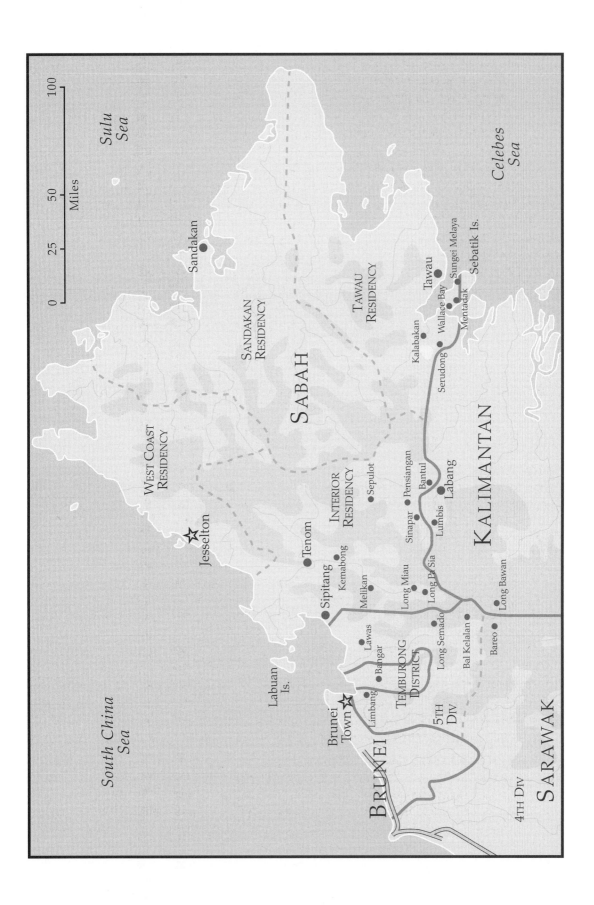

CO:	Lieutenant Colonel P E B Badger	OC B Coy:	Captain J C D Heggs
		CSM B Coy:	CSgt A Hill
2IC:	Major A J Parsons MBE	OC C Coy:	Captain C T Marshall
Adjt:	Captain P N Graham	CSM C Coy:	WO2 J Pearce
RSM:	WO1 H D Benham	OC HQ Coy:	Major A E R Ross
QM:	Lieutenant E P Kelly DCM[4]	CSM HQ Coy:	WO2 W Bradburn
RQMS:	WO2 C Murray	Air Supply Offr:	Major R H D Graveston
OC A Coy:	Major T Holloway	OC Rear Party UK:	Major J L Blackburn-Kane
CSM A Coy:	WO2 K Colclough	Adjt Rear Party UK:	Captain A S Moore

To relieve 2/6th Gurkhas in a variety of locations, the onward move from Labuan was not at all straightforward, and – depending on the destination – comprised a variety of means, including Beverley and Twin Pioneer aircraft, helicopter and boat. The takeover from the Gurkhas in many cases consisted of the incoming platoon rushing out of Whirlwind helicopters whilst the outgoing garrison emplaned, a problem further complicated as there was no common language between the two elements. Platoons and detachments were on their own from the start, some nearly 100 miles from any major base. They were entirely dependent on their own resourcefulness, the skill of their signaller for contact with the outside world and for supplies, on the planning of Major Dick Graveston for resupply by airdrop or helicopter, and on the QM, Lieutenant Ted Kelly, for getting the supplies to the airhead or quayside. The Battalion operated sixteen Land Rovers, six 3-ton lorries, and also sixteen outboard motor boats of various sizes and seaworthiness, driven by those normally employed as MT drivers and by members of the Assault Pioneer Platoon.

Bn HQ was located in the half-finished Chung Wha Chinese School in Brunei Town, and the various elements of the Battalion were initially deployed as follows:

Element	Location (Country)	Miles from Bn HQ
A Coy HQ and two platoons	Tawau (Sabah)	200
Sp Pl	Wallace Bay, Sebatik Island (Sabah)	180
B Coy HQ	Limbang (Sarawak)	20
5 Pl	Ba Kelalan (Sarawak)	80
6 Pl and Drums Pl	Bangar (Brunei)	20
C Coy HQ and 11 Pl(det 4 Regt RA)	Lawas (Sarawak)	30
9 Pl	Long Pa Sia (Sabah)	70
10 Pl	Pensiangan (Sabah)	100

1st Royal Leicesters was one of only five battalions in the Borneo Territories (which from 16 September 1963 were also known as East Malaysia). For the first month the Battalion was under command of HQ 99 Gurkha Infantry Brigade in Brunei Town, and in mid-October came directly under HQ Central Brigade (under Brigadier J B A Glennie CBE DSO). That in turn was subordinate to Commander British Forces Borneo Territories

(COMBRITBOR) at Labuan, the inspiring and dynamic Major General W C (Walter) Walker CBE DSO, who had established a considerable reputation as an expert in jungle warfare during the Malayan Emergency. From 6 December, Walter Walker was also Director of Operations in Sarawak and Sabah in East Malaysia, answerable to the Malaysian Government.

The Battalion had arrived a few days either side of the Federation of Malaysia formally coming into being, the trigger for Indonesia promptly to break off diplomatic relations with Malaysia. On Malaysia's formation both Sarawak and Sabah (as the former North Borneo was renamed) ceased being British Colonies, though Brunei finally opted out of the Federation and consequently remained a British Protectorate under its Sultan. Not that the British soldiers on the ground noticed it, but the Indonesian Confrontation then changed from being a British colonial war (run from GHQ at Singapore) to one in which the British were supporting a Commonwealth ally (with the Malaysian National Defence Council 'running the war' from Kuala Lumpur). With the formation of Malaysia, elements of the Malaysian Armed Forces were soon deployed to join the fray in East Malaysia, thus appreciably increasing the available force levels.

As Sukarno continued to make life difficult for the fledgling new country and his troops intruded into central Sarawak, the Battalion's main operational task from the outset was to hunt for small groups of the TNKU (*Tentera Nasional Kalimanta Utara*: North Kalimantan National Army) rebels either left over from the December rebellion in Brunei or who had subsequently infiltrated from Indonesian Borneo. Over the following five months this threat grew into an 'undeclared' border war with a number of incursions by progressively well-armed and well-led raiding parties, initially comprising Indonesian Border Terrorists (IBTs)[5] trained by TNI (*Tentera Nasional Indonesia*: National Army of Indonesia) regular forces (some leaders of which had been successful students at the British Jungle Warfare School at Kota Tinggi in Malaya). Later armed incursions included larger TNI elements.

The radio issued to platoons and sections was the Australian A510 set. It was an excellent small portable HF set for which a series of crystals were issued to provide exactly the right frequency – so no great netting skills were needed, only the correct crystal! The problem was a shortage of crystals and getting everyone using the right one. By and large, communications went well because of the excellence of the A510 (and of those who operated it so determinedly), which patrols could take out and platoons could use from their bases. It required considerable 'know-how' and expertise to make contact by day, and especially at night. Experienced signallers were therefore sent out to run the communications at most outposts. When using the HF WS62, it was not uncommon for US aircraft and units on operations in Vietnam to overlap or break into the Battalion radio net, which caused confusion, frustration, anger and amusement on both sides.

The Operations Room at Bn HQ in Brunei Town was manned by signallers and clerks, led by Captain G H (Humphrey) Bradshaw, the Intelligence Officer, and Captain Tony Pollard, the RSO. All operational radio traffic analysis and written and oral orders were processed there, including the preparation of the nightly operational Situation Reports (SITREPs), to be passed up and down the chain of command, and requests for resupply. The rifle platoons were airdrop-resupplied in response to a standard format listing the supplies required for the following week. There was a separate 'box' on the resupply demand form for 'other items'. The most unusual 'other item' demanded was 'birthday cards – love to mother – one'! Pollard and Bradshaw, aided by the Orderly Room Colour Sergeant, M J (Mick) Rigley, and his clerks even found time to compile and edit *Tiger Rag*, the Battalion newspaper that had first seen the light of day in Hong Kong. Someone unkindly described it as 'a monthly magazine which comes out seven times a year'!

Under Major Terry Holloway, A Company Group's area of responsibility comprised the Tawau Residency, the south-east portion of Sabah. It was based at Tawau, a prosperous centre for many rural industries and where three-fifths of the population consisted of Indonesian migrant workers and their families (making it potentially ripe for insurrection). The port stood on the northern shore of Cowie Harbour and the coastline was a maze of creeks and rivers that ran through the mangrove swamps along the coastline. South across the bay lay Sebatik Island, some 20 miles long and covered in jungle, of which the northern half belonged to Malaysia and the southern to Indonesia, the non-defined border being a straight west-east line drawn on a map by British and Dutch colonists in 1891. The Company Group (Coy Gp) was hard put to cover its large operational area with its vast river complex. Within two months a whole battalion was to deploy there, and in the meantime the Coy Gp gradually grew into a sizeable task force, with an RN inshore assault flotilla, a Special Boat Section RM, a troop of scout cars, an Auster reconnaissance aircraft and RN/RAF helicopters, all in direct support or under command.

Initially its tasks were to keep under review likely targets for raids, secure them by patrolling, practise their relief, show the flag throughout the area, liaise with HM Ships deployed in Tawau waters (usually a frigate or destroyer), secure the airfield against sabotage and practise its defence. Coy HQ and two platoons were based at the sawmill at Tawau, with one platoon on Sebatik Island at Wallace Bay, a logging centre some 15 sea miles from Tawau. The initial period saw work on the camp defences and familiarization patrols by land and sea. They also fitted in football matches against the Tawau Police and HMS *Barossa*, an RN destroyer, one of a series of such ships acting as Guardship and patrolling the local waters. As much of the deployment and resupply was by sea, the Coy Gp had four assault boats with outboard motors, and the RASC 50' launch 'Bob Sawyer'.

As a result of raids on villages by small parties of IBTs and piracy raids on civilian craft, it soon became necessary to position two platoons on Sebatik Island (one on the west side at Wallace Bay and later Mentadak, and one on the east side as a garrison at Sungei Melayu, a tiny hamlet at the head of a small tidal river). These deployments were to reassure and protect the villagers and to lay ambushes to catch insurgents crossing over onto the Malaysian part of the island. The situation was made the more dangerous and complicated because several thousand Indonesians worked on plantations on the Malaysian side of the border and there was only a small element of the Police Field Force. Therefore, to reinforce the Coy Gp further, an ad hoc platoon (3 Platoon) was initially deployed from 28 September to 11 October, and then again continuously from 19 October. Its manpower came from HQ Company in Brunei Town and it was commanded by Major Ted Ross – the erstwhile OC HQ Company. This enabled up to three platoons to be deployed onto Sebatik Island, with at least one and Coy HQ at Tawau.

On 1 October, an AAC Auster aircraft was attached to the Coy Gp, followed a fortnight later by a detachment of sixteen men of No. 2 Section RN Special Boat Service (SBS). The SBS's task was to patrol the sea and rivers to the west of Tawau and to seek to identify the

River patrol. *M R Charles*

incursions by the Indonesian Regular Marines, the *Korps Komando Operasi* (KKO), who had set up a training camp for IBTs on the southern part of Sebatik Island. The first Indonesian regular forces member, a KKO officer, was killed by a police ambush on Sebatik Island on 17 October, and it was believed that several KKO companies were based near the border. With Sabah's new Emergency Regulations being announced the next day, a new Police/Military/Navy operations room was set up at Tawau and the Royal Leicesters'

Commanding Officer was appointed Commander Task Force Tawau, with day-to-day command lying with Major Terry Holloway.

On 21 October, authority was issued for the Security Forces to return fire if engaged from Indonesian Borneo. Four days later Tawau and A Company were visited by a very senior group comprising Dato Ismail (the Malaysian Minister of Internal Security) and Mr Claude Fenner (the Inspector-General of Malaysian Police). On 27 October, a group of ten Indonesians walked into 3 Platoon's ambush near Sungei Melayu on Sebatik Island. Having been captured and despite initially claiming to be illegal timber extractors escaping the KKO, on further questioning they admitted to being part of a gang responsible for armed robberies on Malaysian Sebatik. That day a platoon of 1st Battalion The Green Jackets (1 Green Jackets) further reinforced A Company, and were initially deployed east of Tawau. The next day a party of Royal Malaysian Navy arrived for duty, and on 2 November two RAF Whirlwind helicopters were stationed at Tawau for use to deploy troops. This was followed three days later by a troop of scout cars of A Squadron The Queen's Royal Irish Hussars to patrol the timber plantation roads, and a platoon of 3rd Battalion The Royal Malay Regiment (3 R Malay). By then the Coy Gp's strength was about 250 all ranks, Services and Nations.

Over the next week or so, preparations were in full swing for the arrival of the remainder of 3 R Malay. The Royal Leicesters' A Coy Gp's platoons on Sebatik Island lived under some tension, knowing that there were considerably superior enemy forces just on the other side of the border, and ambushes were laid continuously. Indications of more aggression by elements from across the border included the sighting of a KKO armed motor launch and some assault craft on 6 November off Sebatik, and Indonesian Naval vessels off the east coast of Borneo. The Security Forces also arrested a number of the Sabah People's Revolutionary Front. Patrols were mounted to visit Serudong and Kalabakan, situated on rivers to the west of Cowie Harbour. On 14 November, flying at 1,400 feet, the Auster conveying Major Terry Holloway to take aerial photographs of the KKO camp just over the border on the western side of Sebatik was fired at by LMGs. The following day an SBS boat came under fire in the same sector. On 17 November, an Indonesian Air Force B25 Mitchell bomber and two Mustang fighters entered Sabah airspace over Wallace Bay, flying at 2,000 feet and 500 feet respectively – A Coy Gp's request to open fire was, however, refused on the political grounds that, as Malaysia was not at war with Indonesia, such an act might have been seen as aggressive. Tawau was clearly becoming the centre of attraction as a key potential 'enemy target', as prestigious as Kuching in western Sarawak. At the end of the month, HE The Governor of Sabah visited Tawau and the two platoons on Sebatik Island. In a letter of thanks, he 'was pleased to visit your men on the ground, who appear to be putting up well with difficult conditions and whose presence is undoubtedly very much appreciated by the villagers. I would like to pass my thanks especially to Mr Charles and Mr Davenport[6], who so kindly explained their dispositions.' Four days later, HE Viscount Head PC GCMG CBE MC, the British High Commissioner for Malaysia, paid a similar visit, after which the local newspaper reported him saying that 'everything was peaceful and cheerful in Tawau and along the east coast and that he found the people and authorities there fully prepared for any contingency that might arise out of Indonesian confrontation against Malaysia'. At least the area remained peaceful and cheerful until after the departure of A Company, which on 5 December handed over the area to 3 R Malay –

a Battalion 900 strong. Having infiltrated Sabah by sea to the west of Tawau, on 29 December a force of a 100 IBTs (stiffened by thirty regular KKOs) was to attack the Malaysian Battalion's company base at Kalabakan, killing eight and wounding seventeen.

At the conclusion of this unusual detached company three-month deployment, A Company left Tawau on 8 December to rejoin the Battalion 200 miles further west, flying by Beverley to Brunei airport, and thence by river to Lawas in north-east Sarawak. Major Terry Holloway, who stayed behind for ten days to draft a new local defence scheme, received a letter from the Hon H George, Resident of Tawau, which said, 'We shall be sorry to see the Leicesters leave. The troops under your command have rendered immense assistance to the people of this Residency. Their behaviour and bearing has been excellent at all times and they have created a very high reputation for themselves among members of the public and have set a high example of military efficiency.'

While A Coy Gp was thus occupied, B Company under Captain John Heggs had, since arrival in Brunei in September, quite a different task. Its area, on the approaches to Brunei Town, contained some of the most rugged jungle in the whole of Borneo. Company HQ and two platoons were based at Bangar, while 5 Platoon (under 2nd Lieutenant A E (Alan) Thompson) at Ba Kelalan was very close to the border and opposite a comparatively large Indonesian TNI military base at Long Bawan. The Coy was supported by a troop of Gurkha Engineers. In the jungle were a few small parties from the December Revolution which had to be hunted down. Week after week of sheer jungle-slogging, in which patrols were often out for several weeks at a time (being resupplied by air), produced little visible result but a number of important arrests were made. Food-denial patrols were mounted extensively to prevent invaders from acquiring supplies from the villagers. The whole area was kept thoroughly quiet, which involved a sustained effort of constant patrolling. On occasion, sections and even platoons were detached to be under the command of A Sqn 22 SAS, operating close to the border. B Company's turn to fight was to come, as will be seen later.

C Company under Captain Colin Marshall had yet again a different task. It was initially deployed with Coy HQ and 11 Platoon (manned by 4 Regt RA and commanded by Lieutenant P W (Peter) Barker RA) at Lawas, with 9 and 10 Platoons at Long Pa Sia and Pensiangan respectively, guarding the most likely approaches into Brunei from Indonesian Borneo, and patrolling the steep jungle-covered ridges, rugged tracks, rivers and streams flowing south across the border. It must be remembered that Malaysia was not at war with Indonesia and every effort was made by her Security Forces to prevent armed incursion through the rugged terrain and subversion of the inhabitants of villages and towns. Constant patrolling up to the border always carried a certain amount of tension as it was always possible for the enemy to slip across a much larger party as an ambush. The alertness of the patrols, however, prevented this. Among other tasks, patrols hacked their way through jungle and cleared helicopter landing sites (HLSs) near the border to enable other patrols to be easily deployed, particularly to cut off intruders along known trails. One HLS-clearing patrol, under Corporal R E (Roger) Jones, was away from base for over six weeks. It set out without a radio, which a week later was lowered to it by helicopter, the patrol's location being marked by a fluorescent helium-filled balloon floating above the jungle canopy. Colour Sergeant G A B (George) Davis was based at Pensiangan in charge of thirty men of the local Border Scouts, an invaluable 'eyes and ears' resource with knowledge of the local area and villages.

Jungle patrol. *M R Charles*

On 21 October C Company HQ and 11 Platoon moved from Lawas in Sarawak to Tenom in Sabah. Such was the terrain that a journey of 50 miles as the crow flies was 190 miles as the infantryman endured – but luckily not on foot, transportation being by Ramp Powered Lighter from Lawas to Labuan, by Landing Ship Tank (LST) to Jesselton, and thence by rail to Tenom. As with A Company at Tawau, C Company set up a new Police/Military operations room at Tenom for the coordination of operations in the Interior Residency. 11 Platoon was deployed forward to garrison a riverside village at Kemabong. Every opportunity was taken to reassure the locals in their kampongs and longhouses, and the 'hearts and minds' psychological operations (psyops) campaign was waged vigorously, with, for example, Company medical personnel tending to the indigenous population's sick and lame (and probably also to the lazy!).

It was opposite 10 Platoon in Pensiangan that the first major Indonesian incursion was attempted. To counter it Operation *Inglenook* was mounted. The next four paragraphs describe the tactical and terrain challenges.

The country to the south of Pensiangan was exceptionally rugged apart from the two obvious approaches, Lumbis to Sinapar and Bantul up to the Logungan River. There were a very few known tracks but many others were known only to local hunters. Most of the area consisted of very steep ridges heavily forested with primary jungle. All the main rivers in the area flow south into Indonesian Borneo, and there was also considerable doubt as to where the border in the Bantul area actually ran. The only HLSs were either alongside or on sandbanks in the rivers. Reports of Indonesian troop movement on the border south of Pensiangan built up during November, and Bantul was visited by a TNI officer and twenty men on the 20th, who indicated they were going to Pensiangan. The enemy might have chosen this time as it was leading up to the anniversary of the Brunei rebellion on 8 December 1962. Consequently, that village which routinely had a British garrison of a platoon of Royal Leicesters, supported by Colour Sergeant Davis' Border Scouts, was immediately reinforced by three other platoons to lay ambushes in the surrounding area, and later by three more platoons to be poised to cut off escape routes. These included one platoon from 1st Battalion The King's Own Yorkshire Light Infantry (1 KOYLI), the Brigade Reserve, and two from 1 Green Jackets on their 'last outing' as that latter Battalion returned to Singapore on 18 December.

In the event of the enemy making a reasonably large incursion, the concept was to lure him sufficiently far into Sabah territory that he could be attacked when he had no easy escape back over the border. To effect this, on this occasion the garrison at Pensiangan was the bait, kept largely out of sight and its size deliberately played down. The subsequent reactive operations would then be conducted from the nearest available airstrip 15 miles north at Sepulot, where four Whirlwind helicopters for troop lift and a Beaver for air recce were forward-based, and where Bn Tac HQ and the RAP also deployed for this operation.

On 5 December, two Border Scouts who had been captured by three armed Indonesians saw about eighty enemy at Kampong Pungut, armed with an array of infantry assault weapons and led by a TNI officer. Ambush patrols were deployed. On 9 December, a British helicopter en route to pick up an escaped Border Scout started to land near a longhouse in which there were forty Indonesian soldiers being observed by a C Company patrol under Lieutenant Peter Barker, which was about to attack them; four enemy ran out, the helicopter flew off and some of the enemy then proceeded towards Pensiangan. At that stage it was decided to close the outer ring round Pensiangan, as secretly as possible. The next day a patrol relocated the enemy and tracked them into a river valley but then lost them. Searches over the next two days failed to discover them. Reinforced ambushes were maintained and Border Scout patrols tried to make contact, further patrols being held in readiness to close the inner ring around Pensiangan the moment it was attacked. On 13 December, a strong patrol was dispatched as a backstop at the last HLS before Bantul on the border. This patrol found tracks later in the day of some thirty to forty men leading south, and also an amount of ammunition and equipment. Over the next day or so, the search continued in order to fix and destroy the enemy invaders, but breaks in radio communication confounded the operation. On 15 December, two helicopters set out from Long Semado to drop off a strong A Company patrol under 2nd Lieutenant Brian Davenport as a cut-off close to the border. Both were badly hit by ground fire as they began to land, inadvertently, on top of the enemy. Despite numerous bullet holes in the floor and two rounds passing through the map pocket and map of Sergeant 'Chris' Christopher, the aircraft and passengers were otherwise unscathed and the patrol alighted safely elsewhere. Because over the next few days no further contact was made with the enemy, it was assumed that a recce party of about twelve enemy had reached Pensiangan, and that the main party supporting them had given up the idea of an attack and turned south back to their side of the border.

In conclusion, although the major part of this operation cannot be said to have been a great success, neither was it a complete failure. The enemy did not achieve its probable aim of attacking Pensiangan. The main party was dispersed, harried and departed back 'over the border' in some haste, leaving behind a quantity of ammunition, equipment and documents. The lesson was learnt again that there could never be too many or even enough helicopters.

At the same time, to the west in B Company's Ba Kelalan area there were reports of TNI and TNKU activity over the border in the Lumbis/Labang areas, so the Battalion became very stretched. An extensive pattern of patrols, in conjunction with the SAS, sought to identify any cross-border incursions. To enable the majority of B Company (now under command of Major Ted Ross) to celebrate New Year and a belated Christmas, A Company's Tac HQ and two platoons were heli-lifted into Long Semado on 30 December. There they replaced B Company's Tac HQ and 7 and 8 Platoons, which all moved to Bangar to become the Brigade Reserve, in turn replacing a 1 KOYLI company which deployed to Tawau in the aftermath of the attack on 3 R Malay at Kalabakan. Major Terry Holloway was posted to become Brigade Major of the embryonic Tawau Force, a Brigade-sized Tri-Service formation created in early January to destroy the Indonesian intruders and control the land, sea and air of the Tawau Residency. He only returned to A Company at the end of the tour.

Without moving, 5 Platoon at Ba Kelalan came under command of A Company, now led by Captain W J G (Bill) Brown, its erstwhile 2IC. 5 Platoon's and its commander Alan Thompson's finest hour was soon to come. From mid-September he had commanded the garrison of that frontier base, with Sergeant H (Harry) Rankin as Platoon Sergeant. The village comprised a longhouse (the communal living area for all the villagers), a number of outhouses and animal enclosures, a couple of paddy fields and a short, grass landing strip. The hut occupied by 5 Platoon was of bamboo on stilts. Slit trenches (accessible vertically from the hut) were located around the base of it, and a barbed-wire double-apron fence surrounded the area. The defensive arrangements were improved when thousands of needle-sharp panji stakes were interposed in the wire, and the trenches were made deeper as the average Royal Leicester was somewhat taller than the Gurkhas who had dug the prototype! Thompson built up such a remarkable intelligence system that not only did he supply much of the information for the whole Battalion area, but he even exchanged letters with an Indonesian Intelligence Sergeant on the other side of the border through the medium of the local 'district nurse'. The enemy made several attempts to attack his position. On 20 November, a force of four to eight men opened fire on the OP sited on a hill covering the airstrip, one bullet grazing the head of a Tiger. The OP party withdrew back to the main position, from where the original target was engaged with light mortar fire. No enemy casualties were caused, but it later transpired that the villagers and the local policeman had fled the village some time before the attack. It is presumed that they had been subverted and so had not forewarned the Platoon.

In mid-December there had been several reports that the enemy had moved an MMG into the border area for the purpose of firing at British resupply aircraft, an eventuality Thompson sought to prevent. Whilst on a recce patrol of the area on 29 December 1963, he discovered a recently used enemy OP on the Sarawak side of the border. On 1 January 1964, he set out in a seven-man patrol to find the MMG and discovered it near the OP. Leaving five men at a firm base, he and Lance Corporal W ('Danny') Dance crept forward and sought to capture the crew, who were in a basha nearby. When called upon to surrender, the four enemy came out fighting and were shot dead. Coming

Lt Alan Thompson MC. *A E Thompson*

under LMG fire Thompson and Dance withdrew, having rendered unserviceable the MMG. Rejoining their covering party, all successfully returned to Ba Kelalan. A description of this encounter was found in the diary of an enemy soldier killed in a later operation as 'the furious action of the British Imperialists on 1 January 1964'. The Imperialists in question consisted only of Thompson and Dance!

Thompson was later awarded the MC for his performance during the tour, and Dance an MID for this action. The citation in the *London Gazette* dated 21 April 1964 relates Thompson's 'relentless determination to remain master of his area of responsibility and his example of personal leadership ... Displaying outstanding zeal and intelligence he has produced an exceptional flow of intelligence from the area and his platoon remains as alert and confident as when it was first deployed.' In describing the incident on 1 January it concludes by saying: 'He displayed leadership and courage of a high order and a calmness and maturity beyond his years and experience.'

From being a 'section commander's war' with the constant patrolling by JNCO-led patrols, the campaign now elevated more to a 'platoon commander's war', and even higher. There were indications that the Indonesians were 'upping the ante' right along the Battalion's front line, and more widely in East Malaysia. On 7 January, an Indonesian aircraft flew along the border parallel to an RAF Beverley carrying out its weekly supply drop to 5 Platoon at Ba Kelalan. The next day a cordon and search operation by B

Company near Brunei Town discovered TNKU uniforms and ammunition. Information was received that seventy Indonesian parachutists had dropped into Long Bawan and headed north, towards A Company's Long Semado and C Company's Long Pa Sia. An enemy radio listening station was located near Bantul. Company foot patrols and the Border Scouts patrolled endlessly to identify incursions and bring the enemy to battle as in Operation *Inglefoot*. Outpost platoons were reinforced, additional trooplift helicopters were allocated to the Battalion and backstop parties to cut off escape routes were heli-lifted into positions near the border.

Early on 23 January, a Border Scout patrol returned with stories of an enemy camp of some 80-100 near Long Miau, a few miles north-east of Long Pa Sia. In what was called Operation *Arrant*, 2nd Lieutenant M J (Mike) Peele was flown into Long Pa Sia from Long Semado with ten men of his own 6 Platoon of B Company. They were joined by a further eight men from 9 Platoon of C Company and two Border Scout trackers, and the patrol was ordered to find the enemy tracks, follow them up with all speed, and attack. Leaving that evening, they basha'd up near Long Miau village, the inhabitants clearly knowing something was afoot as the women and children had left. Setting out at first light on 24 January, they reached the empty enemy camp at 0900 hours and found tracks leading east. At full speed in pursuit, and later abandoning their packs in order to be able to move faster, they found another camp at 1100 hours that they estimated to have held about eighty, with further tracks leading from it. The patrol pressed on and at about 1300 hours heard three shots. A little further on, it sighted two bashas which appeared to be the start of an enemy camp spread along the side of a stream and which might have contained eighty men.

Peele planned to attack and sent a strong cut-off party under Corporal A ('Wally') Walton round to the rear of the camp before launching his assault. Detected by an unarmed enemy soldier but with still an element of surprise, Peele's assault group had to attack earlier than he had intended. Charging some 200 yards through the camp, they killed seven of the enemy, the remainder – probably about forty – fleeing into the jungle, having been caught completely unawares whilst preparing camp and the midday meal. Some forty men's worth of personal equipment, small arms, ammunition and documents were captured. Peele's patrol then rendered all the weapons unserviceable and hid the ammunition. As it had unfortunately been out of communications since leaving Long Pa Sia, it set out to return to base, spending a further night in the jungle en route before reaching Long Pa Sia on the morning of 25 January. Later that day Lieutenant David Michael's C Company patrol engaged three enemy near Long Miau.

On 26 January, Peele led his patrol back to the enemy camp where they blew down trees with explosives to create an HLS, via which a helicopter lifted out the half-ton weight of captured weapons and ammunition. These were subsequently conveyed to Brunei Town where on 30 January the Sultan inspected the haul. Meanwhile an SAS patrol following up from the 24 January battle found tracks of about twenty others, probably the balance of the sixty listed on the captured nominal roll, and made fleeting contacts.

For this action Peele was awarded the MC, which was the last gallantry medal to be won by a man serving in The Royal Leicestershire Regiment. The *London Gazette* citation[7] describes the action in a similar way as above, and concludes: 'The important success achieved by 2nd Lieutenant Peele and his patrol was largely due to his courageous and

Weapons haul from Operation *Arrant*, 24 January 1964. *Trustees R Leicestershire Regt*

aggressive leadership.' The other members of his patrol were later awarded a Regimental lanyard as a mark of distinction for their contribution.

The 24 January action had actually taken place after a ceasefire had been declared on 23 January to take effect on 25 January. Peele's patrol was out of communication with its base and doubtless the Indonesian incursors were with theirs. That President Sukarno of Indonesia, in response to the UN Secretary-General's appeal that the governments of Indonesia and Malaysia should agree to meet for peace talks, was ready to agree a ceasefire, by implication contradicted his claim that his regular TNI and KKO were not involved in the fighting. The Malaysian National Operations Council ordered Major General Walker to ease the pressure and, while trying to prevent further infiltration from Indonesian Borneo, to allow infiltrators already north of the border to return peacefully – in operations already in progress, they were to try to capture rather than kill the enemy. Yet violations of the border continued while ministerial delegations met in mid-February. Amid much high-level posturing, the talks never looked like

2Lt Mike Peele MC.
Trustees R Anglian Regt

succeeding as no agenda had been set. In East Malaysia nothing seemed to have changed and Indonesian crossings of the frontier continued on land and in the air.

It was against this political background that the Royal Leicesters played out their two final weeks on operations. While continuing to secure their bases against attack, patrols searched for the remnants of Peele's opponents and any other intruders, and a company of 1 KOYLI were flown in to block the area north of Long Pa Sia. To encourage the intruders to cease operations, an RAF Twin Pioneer flew over possible enemy locations on 29 January, broadcasting details of the ceasefire. On 31 January, an Indonesian Mitchell bomber flew over Melikan (30 miles inside Sabah) and a C130 Hercules dropped leaflets telling their men not to surrender but to 'hold weapons and fight'; and more leaflets were dropped there before dawn four days later. On 1 February, seven enemy surrendered near Long Pa Sia to the SAS and the garrison. Then on 4 February, a company of 1/10 GR took over the Interior Residency commitment from C Company of the Royal Leicesters, thus enabling the Royal Leicesters, with five rifle companies under command, both to commit more troops to track down intruders and also to be tactically better balanced at the time of handover.

The leading elements of 2/7 GR began arriving that day and were immediately moved to subunit bases to begin the process of familiarization. Meanwhile, those soon to depart confined their operations to local patrols and began to be withdrawn platoon by platoon to company bases in Brunei, hoping against hope that, despite information that the TNI were in some strength south of the border at Lumbis, they would not be committed forward again before their scheduled departure. The Main Body of 2/7 GR arrived from 12 February. The relief of the platoon bases was effected by a complex air movement plan. An equal number of Gurkha soldiers were flown from Labuan by fixed-wing aircraft to the nearest airstrip in the hinterland. From there a helicopter shuttle lifted them forward and recovered the Royal Leicester contingents, which were returned by reciprocal mode to the company bases. By 12 February, C Company was complete at Brunei Town. B Company was complete at Bangar by the next day, followed a day later by A Company at Lawas.

Much of the content of the preceding fourteen pages relates to operational matters. But more mundane non-operational duties occupied the days of those furthest from the forward bases; of necessity and as might be expected these were carried out with the same military efficiency. On 23 September 1963, the Adjutant, Peter Graham, RSM David Benham and thirty soldiers took part in the Birthday Parade of the Sultan of Brunei, where they acquitted themselves well – with all the parade words of command being in Malay! On Remembrance Sunday, a contingent of twenty men of HQ Company and two buglers attended a service in St Andrew's Church in Brunei Town. HQ Company occasionally provided the guard at Muara Lodge, the residence of COMBRITBOR which was the Sultan's beach house on the coast 30 miles west of Brunei Town. On 5 January, B Company provided a detachment at a ceremonial parade at Bangar at which was unveiled a commemorative stone to those Bruneians who had been killed in the rebellion in December 1962.

The visits of numerous VIPs were planned and executed. They invariably entailed a briefing at Bn HQ and almost always flights to visit the forward platoon bases. Visitors from outside East Malaysia included the Director of Infantry (Major General P Gleadell CB CBE DSO) on 7 November, and on 19 November COMBRITBOR accompanied correspondents from the *Observer*, the *Guardian* and the *Sunday Telegraph* over four days at Tawau and Ba Kelalan. Admiral Sir Varyl Begg KCB DSO DSC, C-in-C British Forces Far East, visited on 21 December. The Secretary of State for Defence, the Rt Hon Peter Thorneycroft MP, visited for two days in early January and had the opportunity to meet Alan Thompson and his men at Long Semado, just a week or so after their successful New Year's Day action on the border. It is recorded that before the Minister's briefing at Bn HQ an officer had surreptitiously placed a coloured patrol pin on the map deep inside

Peter Thorneycroft MP **with Capt Bill Brown, Lt Alan Thompson and 2Lt Brian Davenport at Long Semado.** *Trustees R Leicestershire Regt*

Indonesian Borneo, but only the Commanding Officer noticed and the pin was gone before the Minister viewed the map! In early February, the *News of the World* published an article of an interview with men of Peele's Operation *Arrant* patrol, headlined 'Life and Death on the Forgotten Front'. The final outside visitor a month later was Brigadier (Retd) W F K Thompson, Defence Correspondent of the *Daily Telegraph*.

Throughout the period of operations the administration of the Battalion was in the capable hands of the 2IC, Major John Parsons. After the formation of the HQ Company rifle platoon under Major Ted Ross in October, Parsons also became OC HQ Company. Every effort was made to keep the rifle companies' fighting platoons properly supplied with all their needs, and that included the weekly delivery of the *Leicester Mercury*, many copies of which were airlifted to Brunei each week and then onwards. Meanwhile, to keep the citizens of Leicestershire in the picture as what its Regiment was up to, numerous articles appeared in their local newspapers.

In order to brighten up the lives of the men far away from home, in November a Regimental caravan toured various locations in Leicestershire where parents and wives could record a personalized Christmas message onto a tape, which was then edited and sent to Brunei where the Padre, Revd T W (Tom) Metcalfe, arranged that the messages were played back with due discretion to the men over the Christmas period. Reciprocal arrangements were made for tape-recorded messages from the men in the jungle to be sent back to England.

Christmas was spent as traditionally as possible. Many soldiers of Bn HQ and HQ Coy were allowed the day off, and after gunfire, a church service and Christmas dinner, Lieutenant Humphrey Bradshaw laid on a Christmas show. The local people of Brunei displayed great kindness and collected $1,700 (equivalent to some £4,500 at 2008 prices) towards gifts for all and entertained forty soldiers in their homes. The people of the City of Leicester also donated gifts. The Commanding Officer accompanied by the Padre delivered the gifts by two helicopters to all the bases, together with turkey, plum pudding and mince pies. That day Private P G (Peter) Southin tragically died of injuries sustained two days before as a result of a fall from the Big Wheel at a circus in Brunei Town. His was the only fatal casualty throughout the tour, during which no soldier was harmed by enemy action.

The formal handover of command of the Battalion area to 2/7 GR was at midnight 14/15 February. A few days later companies moved by river to Brunei Town, handed in their kit and travelled by LST to Labuan Island, before flying home by Britannia charter aircraft to England. The soldiers on one flight landed at Stansted and, seeing an enormous and vociferous crowd, assumed they were being greeted as returning heroes. The following day they read in the national newspapers that the Beatles had arrived from their first triumphant tour in New York an hour later!

As the 1st Battalion was leaving Brunei a signal was received from Major General Walker, Director of Operations, which read:

> The prolonged and strenuous efforts of your Battalion have recently been crowned with notable success. I want to thank you all for the splendid example you have set of patience and dogged determination. Take pride in a job well done and, for a while, enjoy a well-earned rest. Bon Voyage, Good Luck and a happy reunion with your families from whom you have been separated for so long. They, like us all, have every reason to be very proud of you.

Seen off by Brigadier Glennie, the Brigade Commander, the last flight left Brunei on 21 February, arriving in England the following day at Stansted. Five weeks' leave followed. And so, after a twelve-month unaccompanied tour in the Far East, the men were reunited with their families.

It needs to be recorded that during the whole tour the Battalion received outstanding support from helicopter units of both the RN and the RAF. Its soldiers became expert in helicopter operations and relied on that support for resupply, troop movement, rapid reinforcement, liaison, casevac, visitor movement and air recce. At a tactical level and especially in jungle operations these helicopters were invaluable force-multipliers.

Almost the last word is left to the Commanding Officer, who in *The Green Tiger* wrote:

> Many memories will remain for a long time. The wonderful freshness of early morning at Long Pa Sia, 3,000 feet up, after the sweaty, humid heat of Brunei. The comradeship and tension amongst those who spent long nights in the trenches of the outposts when an attack was expected when – even to the most experienced – the fireflies appeared to be the flashing torch signals of the enemy. The spirit to 'get after them' when there

Roping from an RAF Sycamore. *M R Charles*

was any report of the enemy being about. The endless hours spent in aircraft of all types and the even more endless hours spent waiting for them.

One memory above all else remains. That of the remarkable flexibility, resourcefulness, endurance and cheerfulness of the British soldier when confronted with a really difficult task.

*   *   *

Peter Badger later used to boast that he had enough helicopter hours under his belt in Borneo to qualify as a pilot!

It was most fitting that on its last operational deployment (for which the new General Service Medal 1962 was awarded with the clasp 'Borneo') 1st Battalion The Royal Leicestershire Regiment had made a significant contribution to stemming the early tide and setting the conditions for the campaign's success. It had performed in keeping with the highest traditions of the Regiment, had earned the fulsome praise of its superiors, and numbers of officers and men were decorated for their professionalism and martial qualities. The young soldiers too had overcome the predicted challenges of living in jungle bases for five months in isolation. Clearly, they had been well trained, and then well led and cared for.

It was with considerable pleasure that the Battalion learned from the *London Gazette* on 13 June 1964 that, in addition to the decorations mentioned in the above pages, in the Queen's Birthday Honours List, Colour Sergeant George Davis had been awarded the British Empire Medal (BEM) for his work with the Border Scouts, and on 16 August that MIDs had been awarded to Lieutenant Colonel Peter Badger, the Commanding Officer, Major Terry Holloway, OC A Company, Lance Corporal T J (Tom) Reece and to Captain Peter Barker RA, the commander of 11 Platoon provided by 14 Regt RA. Reece had been a member of the Signal Platoon who at Pensiangan had single-handedly manned a radio on the Battalion net for five months, never failing to contact Bn HQ morning and evening with SITREPs and other messages.

While the 1st Battalion was serving with such distinction in Hong Kong and the Borneo Territories, other officers and SNCOs of the Regiment were soldiering elsewhere on secondment around the British Commonwealth, with Barbados Local Forces, the King's African Rifles, and the Sultan of Muscat's Armed Forces. Additionally six of its officers had at various times been serving with The Royal Warwickshire Fusiliers and at Depot The East Anglian Brigade.

The 'Indonesian Confrontation' (alias the 'Borneo Campaign') continued for a further two and a half years. Elements of the TNI and KKO regularly crossed the border from Indonesian Borneo, and invariably returned with a bloody nose. Indonesian bases near the border were also attacked, which kept their troops off balance. President Sukarno's position in Indonesia became critically undermined after his flirtation with the Communist Party, reducing him to a puppet president, while General Suharto took over effective leadership of the nation in March 1966. Peace feelers were put out, leading to the signing of a Peace Agreement in Jakarta on 11 August 1966. Since that date Malaysia and Indonesia have lived in harmony side by side. Brunei became fully independent from Britain in 1984 and still supports a British Gurkha Battalion.

In terms of overall casualties, the Borneo Campaign was a very minor war, but for both the Malaysians and the British too much was at stake not to engage the enemy in a forthright and wholehearted manner. Its success ranks as one of the British Army's tidiest post-war achievements, as it could easily have developed into an endless entanglement in a frustrating jungle war. In the event, a brave, if poorly led, enemy was soundly defeated without bravado and self-congratulation in less than four years. Rt Hon Denis Healey MP, the then Secretary of State for Defence, declared in the House of Commons in 1966 that the Borneo Campaign would be recorded 'in the history books ... as one of the most efficient uses of military force in the history of the world'.

In 2005, the Malaysian Government approached the British Government to seek approval to present their new Pingat Jasa Malaysia medal (commemorating forty years since the end of Confrontation with Indonesia) to British veterans and others who had served in operations in Malaya/Malaysia between August 1957 and August 1966. Of course, all those serving in 1st Battalion The Royal Leicestershire Regiment on its 1963-4 tour in the Borneo Territories qualified. The presentation of those medals in Leicester in 2007 is described in Chapter 14.

Notes

1 Peter Upcher, who had been awarded the DSO for his leadership commanding D Coy 1st Leicesters at Merxplas (east of Antwerp) in Belgium on 30 September 1944, had commanded 1st R Leicesters in Germany in 1947 and 5th R Leicesters (TA) in 1950-53, and was appointed a DL for Leicestershire in 1962.

2 John Morris had been awarded the MM as a Corporal section commander in 1st R Leicesters in Korea in 1951.

3 See Appendix N.

4 Ted Kelly had been awarded the DCM as a sniper in 1st Northamptons at Kohima in Burma in May 1944.

5 The IBTs were members of the TNKU and/or the Clandestine Communist Organisation (CCO).

6 2Lts Brian Davenport and Mike Charles were commanding 1 and Support Platoons respectively.

7 Confusingly, the *London Gazette* dated 17 November 1964 (published after the formation of The Royal Anglian Regiment in September that year) describes Peele's unit as 4th (Leicestershire) Battalion The Royal Anglian Regiment, which of course did not exist in January 1964.

Chapter 4

The Depot: Leicester, Bury St Edmunds and Bassingbourn 1955-75

❧

Leicester 1955-63

The connection between the 17th Regiment of Foot and the County of Leicestershire began in August 1782. In July 1881, Glen Parva Barracks in South Wigston became the HQ of the Regimental District, a name changed in 1928 to the Regimental Depot, whence its role was to train the recruits for the two Regular battalions, assist the Territorial Army (TA) and despatch reservists following mobilization. During the Second World War it was initially an Infantry Training Centre, and from 1941 was occupied by the Auxiliary Transport Service; a small Depot was maintained to guard regimental interests. From 1946 to 1948 it was 17 Primary Training Centre, training all who joined the Army and lived in Leicestershire, whereafter for a year it housed 1st Battalion The Royal Leicestershire Regiment.

After persistent pressure was exerted, at last, in late 1951, regimental county depots were given the privilege of training recruits for their own regiment. Major I W (Ian) Kennedy MBE[1] was CO Depot The Royal Leicestershire Regiment. The recruits were initially trained for six weeks at Glen Parva Barracks and then passed on to Depot The Royal Warwickshire Regiment at Warwick for the final four weeks. Much later it was decided that recruits should do the whole ten weeks' basic training at one location, in The Royal Leicesters' case at Glen Parva Barracks. Thus the Regimental Depot, which had lost its status as a unit of the Regiment since 1939, was at last restored. The career of the National Serviceman through the Regimental Depot to the 1st Battalion, back at the end of his service for demobilization and ending in the 5th Battalion (TA) formed a thread which drew the three units close together.

The Regimental Depot thus became very much the firm base and home of the Regiment, and it hosted Royal Tigers' Week annually in June. New recruits – both Regular and National Service – were trained there, and officers and men passed through regularly during their careers, either on posting or just calling in. The Depot was the focal point of the liaison between the Regiment and the City and County of Leicester, and their subordinate local authorities, and also with the principal sporting entities of the County – Leicester City Football Club, Leicester Football Club ('Leicester Tigers') and Leicestershire County Cricket Club. The sporting liaison ensured that the Leicester City footballers conveniently

Gates of Glen Parva Barracks. *Leicester Mercury*

spent their National Service at the Depot rather than being posted to the 1st Battalion. As a by-product there were season tickets in the Directors' Box at Filbert Street for the Officers' and WOs' & Sgts' Messes.

In 1956 senior appointments were held as follows:

CO:	Major D S Carden	QM:	Captain G H Greaves
Adjt:	Captain C P K Challen	OC Trg Coy:	Captain A J Parsons MBE
RSM:	WO1 H Brown	CSM Trg Coy:	WO2 G Seagrave
Admin Offr:	Lieutenant Colonel (Retd) S D Field	OC HQ Coy:	Captain C P K Challen

Early that year the Colonel of The Regiment appointed a Regimental Honours Committee, the task of which – meeting at the Depot – was to make recommendations to him about what Battle Honours should be requested for the Second World War (each infantry regiment being allowed ten battle honours for emblazoning on the Queen's Colour and appointments). The committee was chaired by Major General J M K (John) Spurling CBE DSO, and comprised Brigadier D A ('Joe') Kendrew CBE DSO, Lieutenant Colonel M (Mike) Moore MC, Lieutenant Colonel (Retd) S D (Stephen) Field, Major D S (Donald) Carden, and Captain R H D (Dick) Graveston. The resultant new battle honours are included in the list at Page 11. It was gratifying that, as in the First World War, many of them were won by actions of the TA Battalions.[2]

Two years later, a similar committee made recommendations for battle honours for the Korean War, as a result of which 'Maryang-San' and 'Korea 1951–52' were awarded, with the latter to be borne on the Regimental Colour and appointments. In the event, both were borne on the Regimental Colour, presumably to balance the design.

In addition to its primary function of training recruits, with the resultant passing-out parades at which the salute was taken by senior military and civic dignitaries, much inter-unit competitive sport was played within the Army's North Midland District and Northern Command, and in local county competitions and leagues. The Depot sports teams comprised permanent staff and talented recruits, reinforced by holdees who were passing through. There was also the bi-annual recruits' boxing match between the Depot and Depot The Sherwood Foresters, always keenly contested.

Leadership was from the top. On 15 March 1956, the Depot was called upon by the Police to help with the despatch of a wild, maddened bull which had been roaming the Oadby Racecourse area for two days, and RSM H ('Topper') Brown killed it with a single round from a .303" rifle; and in April 1957, Major D S (Donald) Carden refereed the Army Rugby Cup Final. His time in command ended with the Depot winning the Maxse Cup for the first time since its inception in 1921, awarded annually to the infantry depot within Northern Command which achieved the best shooting and recruiting figures.

With the July 1957 announcement of the reorganization of the infantry (which is covered in Chapter 1), Glen Parva Barracks was selected as the future Depot of The Midland Brigade. This was deeply gratifying for the Royal Leicesters who set about ensuring that it would be a fitting and happy home for all three regiments of the Brigade. Inevitably Field Marshal Viscount Montgomery, Colonel The Royal Warwickshire Regiment, was one of the several senior officers who visited to vet the new home. Colonel G E P (Teddy) Hutchins DSO[3] was the first Brigade Colonel and Major W G St J (Bill) Brogan the Brigade Major, with their HQ in Glen Parva Barracks.

It was about this time that recruits began to be trained on the new Belgian-designed FN 7.62mm self-loading rifle (SLR). This replaced the elderly bolt-action .303" Lee-Enfield, and it was to be the Army's rifle for the next thirty years.

November 1957 saw Depot Royal Leicesters defeat Depot Foresters in the Inter-Depot Boxing for the fifth consecutive time. In April 1958, the Lord Mayor of Leicester, Alderman F Jackson, held a dinner to welcome to the City the Regiments of The Midlands Brigade.

In 1958 senior appointments were held as follows:

CO:	Major P E B Badger	QM:	Captain G H Greaves
Adjt:	Captain M L Barclay	OC Trg Coy:	Major P G Bligh
RSM:	WO1 L Russell	CSM Trg Coy:	WO2 H D Benham
Admin Offr:	Lieutenant Colonel (Retd) P G Upcher DSO	OC HQ Coy:	Captain J L Wilson

Training continued apace, and much emphasis was placed upon recruiting so that the Regiment would be strongly placed when National Service was phased out. As part of the Regimental recruiting campaign, the Band and Drums of the 1st Battalion were based at the Depot in June and July and, in addition to performances at Glen Parva Barracks, they Beat Retreat at twelve venues round the county. On 9 May, the Regiment provided a Guard of Honour to mark the official entry into the City of Leicester by HM The Queen. Of the 103 all ranks on parade, the majority were recruits under training at the Depot, who had been

Presentation to the Lord Mayor of Leicester. *Leicester Mercury*

in the Army only eight weeks and were loaned No. 1 Dress (Blues) by the 1st Battalion. The balance was made up by members of the 5th Battalion and of permanent staff of the Depot – a true Regimental performance. During Royal Tigers' Weekend in June, the Colonel of The Regiment presented a silver tiger centrepiece to the Lord Mayor of Leicester, a gift from the Regiment to the Corporation of the City of Leicester in appreciation of the goodwill that has always existed between the County Regiment and the citizens of the City.

As a perfect example of the 'family Regiment', that summer Lieutenant R J M (John) Mosse, a third-generation Royal Leicester and recently a training subaltern at the Depot, was married at Woodhouse Eaves to Josephine Nutt. John's grandfather and father were both distinguished officers in the Regiment[4] and had each commanded the Depot at Glen Parva. Josephine Nutt was the third of her sibling sisters to marry into the Regiment, her elder sisters Jane and Mary having previously married John Marshall and Richard Everard respectively,[5] while the fourth, Norah ('Pug'), married Reg Charles of The Leicestershire Yeomanry.

As covered in Chapter 2, in July 1958 the Colonel of The Regiment made an announcement of further organizational change and the formation of The Forester Brigade, a title better reflecting the ancient roots of the three regiments comprising the Brigade. The Royal Warwickshire Regiment had been founded in 1674, The Royal Leicestershire

Regiment in 1688, and The Sherwood Foresters had their origin in The Nottinghamshire Regiment founded in 1741.

It was not long before the original plan to have Glen Parva Barracks, Leicester, as the Brigade Depot was finalized. The Barracks were chosen because, despite their eighty-year age, they had superior training facilities, sports grounds, married quarters, availability and accessibility of amenities outside barracks, and a central position in the Brigade area. Explicit in this choice of location were the plans to build a fine new barracks, incorporating the North Camp site as well as the Depot's existing footprint, but this rebuild was not expected to be completed until 1963. Meanwhile, using the existing estate, the provisional date for the formation of The Forester Brigade was August 1960, when the new capbadge would come into use, or earlier because both Regular and National Service recruits were soon being trained at all three regimental depots.

2nd Leicesters silver centrepiece.
M Abbs

Among the other aspects of the reorganization finalized over the ensuing months were: a green backing (a Sherwood Foresters tradition) would be worn to the Brigade capbadge and rank badges; the Brigade Flag (comprising the Brigade badge on a green background) would be flown at the Depot; the Royal Leicesters' Regimental Headquarters would remain at Glen Parva Barracks; and each regiment would loan its best 'Depot Silver' to the new Depot. Included among it was the old 2nd Leicesters' Officers' Mess handsome 20" long centrepiece. This is now (2008) on loan to 2nd Battalion The Royal Anglian Regiment.

It was rapidly evident that the City of Leicester was determined to show the same kindness and warmth of welcome to The Forester Brigade as it had showed to The Royal Leicestershire Regiment and The Midland Brigade. When it was confirmed that the Forester Brigade Depot was to be at Glen Parva, the Lord Mayor hosted a dinner to which senior representatives of all three regiments were invited, and it provided vivid assurance to them of a welcome to Leicester when the Brigade Depot formed. In March that year the Lord Mayor, Alderman Sidney Brown TD, attended the Annual General Meeting of the Royal Tigers' Association.

In February 1959, Private H (Bert) Godwin[6] enlisted as a National Serviceman at the Depot on a Thursday, played rugby for his club Coventry on the Saturday, and gained his first England cap against France a week later. On completion of recruit training in May (by which time he had gained a second England cap), he was posted to the 1st Battalion in Germany, where he strengthened its team immensely – see Chapter 2. It seems strange that more effort was not made by the Rugby Football Union to ask that he be retained in England – as were most of the professional football players.

In mid-1959, senior appointments were held as follows:

CO:	Major K P P Goldschmidt	OC Trg Coy:	Captain R H J Oliver MC Foresters
Adjt:	Captain J L Wilson		
RSM:	WO1 L Russell	CSM Trg Coy:	WO2 H D Benham
Admin Offr:	Lieutenant Colonel (Retd) P G Upcher DSO	OC HQ Coy:	Lieutenant P N Graham
		CSM HQ Coy:	Sergeant Brown
QM:	Captain S H Price Foresters		

Two passing-out parades were held during the summer; in May the salute was taken by Colonel Teddy Hutchins, Colonel The Midland Brigade, all the recruits being posted to 1st Royal Leicesters, and in August by Colonel G J (Guy) German DSO TD, the new Honorary Colonel of the 5th Battalion (TA), the recruits being posted equally to the three regiments of the Brigade. Permanent Staff members carried out Proficiency Tests for the Combined Cadet Force (CCF) contingents at Ratcliffe College, Uppingham School, and Loughborough Grammar School. This was an annual occurrence with each of the four affiliated CCFs, as is described in Chapter 13.

Athletics took up the early summer months. Despite some outstanding individual performances (particularly by Private B (Brian) Punter, a Lincoln City football professional), the Depot Team only managed sixth place out of eleven units at the Area Athletics Meeting. Cricket then tried to take centre stage as the major sport of the summer, but the Depot team was undistinguished. During Royal Tigers' Week, as was traditional, the Regimental Cricket Team played three matches on the beautiful ground, against the Gentlemen of Leicestershire, the Brigade Colonel's XI and the GOC's XI. Expertly prepared as ever by groundsman Mr Jack Woodward, the cricket pitch was generally considered by everyone (including the County players, MCC and other touring teams) to be much better than the one at the county ground at Grace Road! Jack Woodward also looked after the two splendid grass tennis courts outside the Officers' Mess.

The Band and Drums of the 1st Battalion over from West Germany were based at the Depot for six weeks. Their busy itinerary included a performance of Beating Retreat in seven towns, at a CCF camp, and at the Leicester and Market Bosworth Shows, and three weeks in Plymouth and Brighton. More engagements followed in Leicester including at two City football matches at Filbert Street. The tour in Leicestershire was a great success; their playing and execution of drill was of a very high order, and everywhere they were received most generously.

Passing-out parades were taken in August 1959 by Brigadier J H Prendergast DSO MC, Comd 147 Inf Bde (TA), and in January 1960 by Colonel B L (Basil) Gunnell OBE MC[7], late Royal Warwicks and the new Brigade Colonel The Forester Brigade.

In December, six pairs from the Depot competed in the *News of the World* 'March of the Century', 100 miles from Birmingham to London. Additionally, in another great example of the cooperation between the Regular and TA elements of the Regiment, Lieutenant Tom Hiney of the Depot and Corporal John Sinclair of the 5th Battalion won the event, foot-slogging in atrocious weather conditions – a feat which is covered in Chapter 7.

In that and the previous month the 'Cadet Season' was in full swing with three visits to the Depot by the Leicestershire and Rutland ACF, and one by Oakham School CCF. The Depot staff again conducted the annual Proficiency Tests at Uppingham School, Ratcliffe College and Oakham School, further forging links between the Regiment and those famous affiliated schools.

On the sporting front, the Depot Rugby Team reached the final of the North Midlands Area Minor Units, a match which they might have won had Private Bert Godwin, over from the 1st Battalion for a few days to play for the Army, been deemed eligible! The Football Team, which included four professionals (Privates Colin Appleton, Howard Riley,[8] and John Currie of Leicester City, and Brian Punter of Lincoln City), won twenty-one out of twenty-four matches, winning the local Thursday League and Thursday Knock-Out competitions. The Cross-Country Team, reinforced by the very fit professional footballers, lost but twice in the season. The Basketball Team, led by Colour Sergeant D G (David) Grove, won the Northern Command Minor Units Competition and was runner-up in the Major Units.

Planning continued apace for the significant changes in August 1960, when the Regimental Depot was to close and the Royal Tiger capbadge would no longer be worn by the Regular soldiers of the Regiment. Although many outward and visible things would alter, it became increasingly obvious that what really mattered in the Regiment would not. HQ The Forester Brigade and the Brigade Depot would be welcomed to Glen Parva Barracks. By then, all training at the Depot at Warwick was to have ceased. Depot Foresters at Derby was to remain on its present establishment and in its present role until the end of National Service training in April 1961. After that date it would become an outstation of the main Depot and be part of its establishment. The reason for keeping an outstation going was purely one of accommodation and it was to remain as such until the new building project at Glen Parva was completed. The main division of training would be: for the main Depot, regular recruit training and holdees; and for the outstation at Normanton Barracks in Derby, Junior Bandsman/ Drummer training, holdees and Regular recruit training, as the occasion demanded. The Junior Bandsman/Drummer Unit, under Bandmaster D K (Desmond) Walker (who had been Bandmaster of 1st Royal Leicesters from 1952 to 1959)[9], moved from Warwick to Derby in August 1960.

Detailed planning was put in place to create a very fine home for the new Brigade. It required a large rebuilding project at Glen Parva which over four years was to encompass the demolition of the old married quarters, the erection of new REME and RAOC Records Offices, the demolition of old Records Offices in North Camp, and finally the erection of new barracks in North Camp. However, the key to the long-term future of The Forester Brigade and its regiments was to be their ability to recruit in the Midlands area of high employment sufficient soldiers to man the Regular battalions in the post-National Service era. In the end, only the demolition of the old married quarters and the erection of new ones to the north of the old barracks were ever completed.

Life at Depot Royal Leicesters continued as usual through the spring and summer. Major General D A Kendrew CB DSO took the penultimate Passing-Out Parade in April. The cricket team was unable to achieve its target of leaving its mark in the cricket world, but the pitch – wonderfully cared for over many years by Mr Jack Woodward – was better than ever. The ground looked splendid with the planting of new rose bushes on the bank, making the cricket ground the showpiece of the Depot. Royal Tigers' Weekend – the last to be held at Depot Royal Leicesters – was as good as ever, blessed by beautiful weather, and supported by the Band and Drums of the 1st Battalion, which was on a six-week tour of the county. The gardens and grounds at the Depot were in colourful glory, in memory of the degree of Regimental effort put in over many years, planting trees and shrubs, levelling playing fields, and overcoming the challenges of clay and sandy soil. During the weekend the WOs' & Sgts' Mess fêted the retiring Mr 'Cis' Whitehead, its friend and Steward for forty-four years. At the Royal Tigers' Association Dinner, 2nd Lieutenant G M (Malcolm) Stonestreet, on behalf of the many National Service officers who supported his appeal,

Major General Kendrew inspects the penultimate Passing Out Parade. *Trustees R Leicestershire Regt*

presented to the Colonel of The Regiment a replica silver tiger statue to show that they had enjoyed their service with the Regiment. The Regiment would always be grateful to them for their excellent work, but a shade disappointed that, feeling as they did, not more of them became Regular officers.

As the date of the creation of The Forester Brigade neared, on 6 August, the Colonel of The Regiment took the final Passing Out Parade at the Depot Royal Leicesters, a unit which had occupied that barracks since 1881. Four days later, Colonel Basil Gunnell took the salute at the Brigade Depot Inauguration Parade. The parade was commanded by the Depot Adjutant, Captain J L (John) Wilson. The Revd Neil Robinson, Depot Officiating Chaplain and vicar of St Thomas's Church, South Wigston, dedicated the new badge. The new capbadges were then handed to three Lance Corporals (J (John) Hancocks representing The Royal Leicestershire Regiment) who symbolically changed their regimental capbadges for that of The Forester Brigade, the other parade troops already wearing the new capbadge when they marched on. In his

Major Ken Goldschmidt, the last CO Depot Royal Leicesters. *Mrs R T W Mellotte*

123

address to the Parade, Colonel Gunnell said, 'The reorganization of the regiments did not mean an amalgamation. Its main purpose is to centralize training … we must move with the times, and it is our sincere Brigade policy to preserve the best traditions and customs of the three regiments. I am confident that the new badge containing the emblems of glories of the past will not only retain them but add to them in the years to come.'

In recognition of the increased size and importance of the new Depot, the post of Commanding Officer was elevated to that of a lieutenant colonel. The permanent staff were increasingly made up of officers and SNCOs from all three regiments. At about that time, senior appointments at the Depot Forester Brigade were held as follows:

CO:	Lieutenant Colonel J W Tomes OBE R Warwick	QM:	Captain S H Price Foresters
Adjt:	Captain J L Wilson	OC Trg Coy:	Captain R H J Oliver MC Foresters
RSM:	WO1 L Russell	CSM Trg Coy:	WO2 H D Benham
Admin Offr:	Captain (Retd) G E W Harvey MBE[10]	OC HQ Coy:	Major R H D Graveston
		CSM HQ Coy:	WO2 R E Sprason

Field Marshal Viscount Montgomery, Colonel The Royal Warwickshire Regiment, was Representative Colonel The Forester Brigade. Brigade Colonel was Colonel Basil Gunnell, and Brigade Adjutant Major J A (John) Castle Foresters.

RHQ Royal Leicesters appointments were:

OIC Regtl Recruiting:	Colonel (Retd) D Shaw DSO MC
Regtl Secretary:	Colonel (Retd) P G Upcher DSO
Asst Regtl Secretary:	Captain (Retd) W Knight

The 32-ton Sherman tank, which had been used by the then General Montgomery while commanding Eighth Army from the Battle of El Alamein in Egypt in October 1942 to the River Sangro in Italy in December 1943, had stood for twelve years at Depot Royal Warwick at Budbrooke Barracks. It was also unique in that it had diesel engines, which being quieter than petrol ones, had made it less likely to be heard and spotted in the forward battle areas. Appropriately called 'Monty', it was moved to Depot The Forester Brigade at Glen Parva Barracks on 21 September 1960, where it was placed on a concrete plinth facing the main entrance and almost outside the CO's house. Royal Leicesters were not pleased that several of their commemorative trees had to be removed to make way for the plinth!

In early November, Field Marshal Montgomery visited Leicester to attend a reception to mark the formation of The Forester Brigade, given by the Lord Mayor of Leicester, Councillor Mrs Dorothy Russell. When at the Depot to see his tank in its new location, he said to the Press:

It would be a great mistake for the people of Leicester to think that The Royal Leicestershire Regiment does not now exist. It does exist the same as ever – just as my Regiment (the Royal Warwicks) does. The formation of The Forester Brigade just means that its three regiments are sharing one depot instead of having three small depots. The Army found it uneconomic to have little training depots all over the country. It is more economic to have one depot serving several regiments. This is what has happened, Leicester becoming the headquarters of the Brigade because it offered better facilities.

Speaking about his hopes for the future, in a mildly prophetic way he went on to say:

I look forward to the day when, for example, my Regiment will be known as the '1st Battalion Forester Brigade (Royal Warwickshire Regiment)' and when we have the '2nd Battalion (Royal Leicestershire Regiment)' and '3rd Battalion (Sherwood Foresters)'. In the process of evolution it will work out like that. Such a move would have no effect on recruiting. That is dependent on the economic position of the country – on wage packets offered outside the Army.

During a Defence Debate in the House of Lords fifteen months later in March 1962, Field Marshal Montgomery again publicly outlined his ideas for the three Forester Brigade regiments to become one regiment of three Regular battalions.

The final National Service intake passed out of Depot The Forester Brigade on 12 November 1960, with 147 recruits on parade, the salute being taken by Brigadier M S K Halford DSO OBE, Comd 147 Inf Bde (TA). Subsequently all recruits were on Regular terms of service, and on occasion it took up to several weeks for sufficient numbers to enlist to form a viable training intake. Each squad then spent a week's field training at Proteus Camp, near Ollerton. That month recruits and Permanent Staff from the Depot were deployed to three Leicestershire farms to dig up and thus save £4,000 (£4,000 was worth £60,000 at 2008 prices) of potato crops which had not been able to be harvested due to weeks of bad weather – another example of MACC (Military Aid to the Civil Community). Similarly, the Royal Leicesters established a special display of its museum items in the Army Recruiting Office in Granby Street.

That month too, the old married quarters at Glen Parva Barracks began to be demolished, and in the New Year a start was made on new buildings for REME and RAOC Records Offices. That proved a helpful diversion on the occasion of the Annual Administrative Inspection as the Inspecting Officer, Major General T H Birbeck CBE DSO, and his staff, seemed more interested than anything else in operating a mechanical crane which swung a large iron ball to demolish the eighty-year-old buildings!

During the 1960/61 sports season, the Basketball Team, led by CSMI Wootton APTC, won the Area Minor Units and the Northern Command Open competitions. Private 'Nobby' Clarke won the Area middleweight boxing championship. The Football Team, now denuded of National Service professionals, and the Hockey Team had undistinguished seasons. In Small-Bore Shooting, the Depot Team, led by QMSI W Collingwood SASC, won the Northern Command League, about which *The Green Tiger* quaintly recorded that 'Cpl Leffler never scored less than 97 and is to be congratulated on averaging 93.1'! That nucleus went on to bigger things with great success in the summer. In May, at the Northern Command Meeting, the Depot Team won the Minor Units' Rifle, LMG and Pistol Matches, and Corporal G A Wainwright and Lance Corporal Swannock were the LMG Champions. The following month at the Army Meeting at Bisley it came fourth in the Minor Units' Championship.

In the spring of 1961, senior appointments were held as follows:

CO:	Lieutenant Colonel J W Tomes OBE R Warwick	RQMS:	WO2 T Sunman R Warwick
		OC Trg Coy:	Major R H J Oliver MC Foresters
Adjt:	Captain B S Burditt R Warwick		
RSM:	WO1 D B Selby R Warwick	CSM Trg Coy:	WO2 R E Sprason
Admin Offr:	Captain (Retd) G E W Harvey MBE	OC HQ Coy:	Major R H D Graveston
		CSM HQ Coy:	WO2 G H Sprayson R Warwick
QM:	Captain S H Price Foresters		

Besides their core task of training recruits, Training Company ran a CCF Leadership Course in April. In March, an Open Weekend was held at the Depot, attended by sixty-eight 6th Form youngsters who spent two days sampling life in the Army, shooting, living in barracks, meals in the cookhouse and a social night. As the advertising indicated: 'If you think the Tigers are too fierce, you can opt to join the Warwicks or Foresters'! Four attendees directly enlisted into the Tigers.

The highlight of the summer was the first Forester Brigade 'At Home', held on 1 July. Some 480 attended the Garden Party on the lawns of the Officers' Mess, and nearly 900 old comrades, parents and friends attended the gathering on the spacious cricket field. The event ended with Beating Retreat by the Band and Drums of 1st Foresters and the Brigade Junior Bandsmen's Unit.

The Band and Drums of the 1st Royal Leicesters stayed at the Depot during their summer in the county and provided music for drill parades and passing-out parades. The Cricket Team carried out a full fixture list, the home matches being played as usual on the wonderful Depot ground. Despite some 200 recruits passing through the Depot during the summer, none were good enough to be selected for that team.

Elsewhere in the County, during its development and expansion, the village of Countesthorpe honoured one of its bravest former sons, Private W E Buckingham VC[11], by

The drummers of 1st R Leicesters at Loughborough. *B Ward*

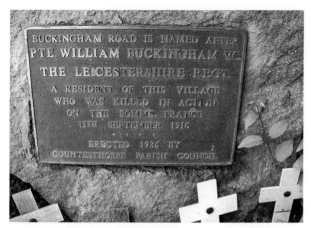

Memorial Plaque in Countesthorpe. *M K Goldschmidt*

Private W E Buckingham VC.
Trustees R Leicestershire Regt

naming a road after him. Later, in 1986, after adding his name to the village War Memorial from which it had inexplicitly been omitted sixty years before and no one had noticed, the Parish Council further honoured his memory by erecting a bronze memorial plaque on a granite plinth in Buckingham Road.

In late June 1961, the Recruiting Team from the 1st Battalion arrived at Leicester. Led by Captain B N (Neil) Crumbie, and comprising WO2 'Jimmy' Jenks MM, Sergeant Barlow and five men, and assisted in its first few weeks by the Band and Drums, it had a target to recruit 100 men from Leicestershire by Christmas. Until the Recruiting Team was formed, the 1st Battalion was receiving five or six Regular private soldiers a month, vastly insufficient to balance the outflow of the National Service drafts. The Team eagerly approached an area which – due to high employment – was previously considered barren from a Regular recruiting point of view. One of its messages to would-be recruits was: 'Get out of that rut into a life full of adventure'. In very close coordination with Colonel David Shaw at RHQ, the Recruiting Team met with kindness, help and encouragement wherever they went, and also great support and publicity from the county's Press, among which the *Leicester Mercury* lent them a shop in Coalville, which for five weeks was turned into a recruiting office. Through hard work and maximizing the availability of the Band and Drums, its mobile recruiting van operated on housing estates, prominent City landmarks and in the county towns and villages every evening, and there were stands at the City and County Shows, including the Ideal Home Exhibition. It met with great success, with the numbers rising steadily, to twelve recruits in each of July and August, and thirty-four in September, to the extent that it was soon decided that the Team would remain in Leicester until further notice. The 100th recruit signed on in mid-November, six weeks ahead of the Christmas target deadline. Captain J C D (John) Heggs took over command of the Recruiting Team in December. By April, a total of 203 recruits had joined, 180 on a nine-year engagement.

The Annual Administrative Inspection took place in October during which, after a ceremonial parade, the whole Depot was required to parade in battle order, ready to move off in Aid to the Civil Power. HQ Company was subsequently required to concentrate on Civil Defence Training, assisted by the County's Civil Defence Corps.

At the Depot recruit training continued to take centre stage, and with an upturn in recruiting – notably for the Royal Leicesters – passing-out parades took place every two or three weeks. The Lord Mayor of Leicester, Alderman Miss May Godwin, took the salute at one in November and the Colonel of The Regiment at one in March.

Sport continued to feature strongly. The Hockey Team, anchored by Orderly Room Colour Sergeant M J (Mike) Kinson, won the Northern Command Minor Units' Competition, while the Basketball Team – a founder member of the new Leicestershire Amateur Basketball Association – and the Football Team made many friends in competitive local leagues.

In the spring of 1962, senior appointments were held as follows:

CO:	Lieutenant Colonel J W Tomes OBE R Warwick	RQMS:	WO2 D L Lee R Warwick
		OC Trg Coy:	Major R H J Oliver MC Foresters
Adjt:	Captain B S Burditt R Warwick		
RSM:	WO1 D B Selby R Warwick	CSM Trg Coy:	WO2 R E Sprason
Admin Offr:	Captain (Retd) G E W Harvey MBE	OC HQ Coy:	Major R H D Graveston
		CSM HQ Coy:	WO2 W Reynolds
QM:	Major E H Scanlon		

As an example of the continuing connection between the Regiment and the county's sporting activities, on 29 March 1962, on behalf of the Regiment, Lieutenant Colonel A L Novis MC[12] presented a tiger's head to Leicester Football Club. Additionally, local links with the Garrison Church of St Thomas, South Wigston, were further cemented that month. There had been a very close connection since it was built in 1893, and its vicar was always Officiating Chaplain to the Depot. Over the years several plaques had been erected in memory of former commanding officers of the Depot, to which on 18 March 1962 was added one to Major J W E Mosse MC, placed alongside the one to his father, Lieutenant Colonel J Mosse. Two sets of Colours of 3rd (Militia) Battalion The Leicestershire Regiment were for many years laid up there (and with many others, they are now preserved in a casket under the altar in the Regimental Chapel in Leicester Cathedral). Outside the church, the war memorial lists among others from South Wigston the names of many men of the nineteen battalions of The Leicestershire Regiment killed in the First World War. It had been unveiled on 11 November 1923 by Major General Sir Edward Woodward KCMG CB, Colonel of The Regiment.

In May 1962, Colonel J D W (Dennis) Millar (late Foresters) assumed the appointment of Colonel The Forester Brigade, and in August, Lieutenant Colonel A L W (Alec) Moore MBE

War Memorial at St Thomas's Church, South Wigston. *M K Goldschmidt*

of the same Regiment took over as Commanding Officer of the Depot. Summer at Glen Parva Barracks continued at a cracking pace with 500 recruits being trained in the first nine months of the year. Drill parades and passing-out parades were enhanced by the presence of the Band and Drums of 1st Royal Warwicks and 1st Royal Leicesters, based there during recruiting tours of their counties. A very enjoyable 'At Home' was held on 30 June, combining relatives and friends of the serving soldiers with coach loads of Old Comrades of the three regiments.

On the Competition Shooting front, the Depot Team had a very successful season. It won the Northern Command Small-Bore League and was runner-up in the Command Central Rifle Meeting, with Corporal G A Wainwright winning the Class 'B' LMG pairs, SMG and Pistol, and RSM Selby winning the Class 'A' SMG. The season culminated at the Army Meeting at Bisley with an even higher place in the Minor Units Championship than the previous year, this time coming third out of eighteen teams. Meanwhile the Cricket Team, under Lieutenant B D (David) Hickman, had an enjoyable season, losing but two matches out of eleven. Yet again the groundsman Jack Woodward maintained a very high standard of pitches in that, his final summer; he retired at Christmas after seventeen years.

In the autumn of 1962, senior appointments at the Depot were held as follows:

CO:	Lieutenant Colonel A L W Moore	RQMS:	WO2 D L Lee R Warwick
	MBE Foresters	OC Trg Coy:	Major C J C Humphrey
Adjt:	Captain B S Burditt R Warwick		R Warwick
RSM:	WO1 S R Twort Foresters	CSM Trg Coy:	WO2 R E Sprason
Admin Offr:	Captain (Retd) G E W Harvey	OC HQ Coy:	Major J T Dudley
	MBE	CSM HQ Coy:	WO2 W Reynolds
QM:	Captain S H Price Foresters		

By October, after sixteen months of considerable effort and success, the 1st Battalion's Recruiting Team, by now under the leadership of Lieutenant J R E (Berty) Bowes and still with WO2 'Jimmy' Jenks, had recruited 378 Regular recruits for the Regiment. This was a record for an English line regiment over that period.

The next bombshell to greet the Depot was the announcement in Parliament on 14 November that The Forester Brigade was to disband and its component regiments would join other brigades to make them four-regiment ones. The Royal Warwickshire Regiment was to join The Fusilier Brigade and become The Royal Warwickshire Fusiliers, and The Sherwood Foresters was to join The Mercian Brigade (and in 1970 to amalgamate with The Worcestershire Regiment to form The Worcestershire & Sherwood Foresters Regiment (WFR)). The Royal Leicestershire Regiment was to join The East Anglian Brigade. Depot The Forester Brigade at Glen Parva Barracks was to close in May 1963, recruits for the Royal Leicesters thereafter being trained at Depot The East Anglian Brigade at Bury St Edmunds in Suffolk. This move was a particular blow as it brought Regular Infantry representation in Leicestershire to an end.

Despite its impending closure, every effort was made to end its time 'if not with a bang, then certainly without any whimpers'. Many very senior officers visited, all of whom expressed their sympathy and regret. They included the GOC Northern Command, Lieutenant General Sir Charles Jones, who also toured the REME and RAOC Records Offices in the Barracks. The prospect of disbandment failed to upset Christmas festivities, and the traditional round of social and family events were organized. The last recruit platoon began training on 28 January 1963, with the final Passing-Out Parade on 11 April, at which appropriately the salute was taken by the Lord Mayor of Leicester, Alderman Harold Heard. By that time some 1,100 recruits had passed through the Brigade Depot since its formation in August 1960. HQ The Forester Brigade closed on 1 May and the final event to be held there was Royal Tigers' Weekend on 13 May. RHQ R Leicesters moved to Ulverscroft Road during the summer, and the 'last men out of the gates', so to speak, were Major J T (John) Dudley, the Quartermaster Harold Scanlon, ORQMS Mike Kinson and Colour Sergeant 'Jet' Pearce in August 1963. And so, after eighty-two years Glen Parva Barracks ceased to be the home for the Royal Leicesters for whom it was to continue to evoke happy memories.

As a tailpiece, on Glen Parva Barracks, the sites of the REME and RAOC Records Offices and of the training area and playing fields at the west end have been built over, creating a Young Offenders Institution in 1974. Much of the remainder of the site of the former Depot has disappeared under concrete, either as car parking or a business park. What used to be the wonderful cricket ground is now totally unkempt. The former Officers' Mess/CO's House has been retained by the Ministry of Defence and accommodates B

(Leicestershire & Derbyshire) Squadron The Royal Yeomanry and Home Headquarters 9th/12th Lancers (Prince of Wales's).

Bury St Edmunds 1963-69

On 8 February 1963, the first Royal Leicester recruit started training at Bury St Edmunds at Depot The East Anglian Brigade (Lieutenant Colonel B J Palmer MBE 3rd E Anglian), the first person from the Regiment to be issued with the East Anglian Brigade capbadge. At the same time, Lieutenant F L B (Freddie) Vigers and five SNCOs also transferred there from Depot The Forester Brigade. A message from Bury St Edmunds in the Spring edition of *The Green Tiger* was well received by Tigers: 'It is a real pleasure and honour to welcome The Royal Leicestershire Regiment to The East Anglian Brigade. Their unqualified reputation is well-known and we are proud to take over the responsibilities from the Depot at Glen Parva Barracks.'

Blenheim Barracks at Bury St Edmunds had been Depot The East Anglian Brigade since the formation of that three-regiment Brigade in 1959. It was an old wooden-hutted camp built during the Second World War, and as far as the accommodation went was well past its 'sell-by' date. The addition of a fourth regiment to The East Anglian Brigade meant that the permanent barracks, which were being rebuilt in the former Depot The Suffolk Regiment at Gibraltar Barracks just across the road, were going to be too small for the new needs, and there was a clear prospect of a delay of three years before Depot The East Anglian Brigade could move to its permanent location.

In autumn 1963, the Royal Leicesters' WO1 'Jimmy' Jenks became RSM at Bury St Edmunds, an inspired choice to bring to bear his Regiment's ethos at the home of its new Brigade. He also worked wonders with the Depot Basketball Team. In parallel, several more Tiger officers and NCOs were posted in, just as would have occurred at Leicester. *The Green Tiger* records that 'the Rugby Team played games with local clubs most weeks, largely due to the Leicestershire element of the Depot.' Major P P (Paul) Young became OC Training Company in 1964 and Freddie Vigers the Adjutant in 1966. All the Tigers brought their various expertise, familiarized themselves with the East Anglian accents and vocabulary, and made friends with a new cross-section of the Infantry.

Life at Blenheim Barracks was not dissimilar to what it had been at Glen Parva: training adult recruits (and now also junior soldiers), accompanied by regular passing-out parades at which the inspecting officers were a range of military and civic figures. The Brigade Weekend was held in mid-July 1964, and the Beating Retreat for the first time comprised four bands: that of the Depot and of those to be renamed six weeks later, the 2nd, 3rd and 4th Battalions. On 1 September, a parade was held to celebrate the formation of The Royal Anglian Regiment, at which the salute was taken by Colonel J C (Jack) Denny OBE MC (late Northamptons), the first Regimental Colonel. All ranks exchanged their East Anglian Brigade capbadges for those of The Royal Anglian Regiment. Lieutenant Colonel H W Clarke assumed command of the Depot, and the Lord Mayor of Leicester, Alderman Archibald Kimberlin OBE, took the salute at a Passing-Out Parade that year.

The various officers and other ranks from the Royal Leicesters who filled appointments at the Depot all helped with their Regiment's transfer, first into The East Anglian Brigade in 1963 and then into The Royal Anglian Regiment in 1964. As some Tigers' WOs and SNCOs also began to be posted to other battalions of the Regiment and thus came to know them more widely, it eased the trauma – for some at least – to transfer from the disbanding 4th Battalion in 1970, a prospect which in 1964 was far from people's minds. Colonel P E B (Peter) Badger[13] became the second – and last – Regimental Colonel in 1966.

In 1964, a decision was made to move the Depot The Royal Anglian Regiment to RAF Barnham, no longer needed by the RAF.[14] The people of Bury St Edmunds were sad at the prospect of losing the status of a garrison town after eighty-seven years, although it was not expected that the move would take place until 1968 as Barnham Camp needed to be extended to meet the Infantry's needs. But that plan was to change too, largely because of the formation of The Queen's Division in late 1968 which brought with it the need to establish a very large Depot, centrally based, at which to train the recruits, junior soldiers and bandsmen of its three Large Regiments. The rationale for the establishment of The Queen's Division is described in Chapter 6. The site of the former RAF Bassingbourn, near Cambridge, was chosen for the location of HQ and Depot The Queen's Division.

One of the major Regimental events held in the latter years of Depot The Royal Anglian Regiment was the ceremony of Beating Retreat performed by the Massed Bands and Corps of Drums of the Regiment on 13 July 1968, in the presence of the Colonel-in-Chief, HM Queen Elizabeth The Queen Mother.

On being vacated by Depot The Royal Anglian Regiment, the majority of Blenheim Barracks was sold off to create a civilian industrial estate. A small proportion was retained on which was built a TA Centre for 6th (Volunteer) Battalion of the Regiment.

Bassingbourn 1970 onwards

On 29 August 1969, the RAF flag at Bassingbourn was lowered for the last time and thirty years of continuous RAF flying from there came to an end.[15] The Barracks was handed over to The Queen's Division represented by Major P W Worthy of The Royal Anglian Regiment and sometime Tiger, who was one of Queen's Div HQ's staff officers.

The newly acquired 'Barracks' covered a large area and, as would be expected from a 1938-build air station, was particularly well provided for in terms of married quarters, messes, stores, offices, sheds, playing fields, hardstanding and hangars (two of which were used as a huge gymnasium and an indoor parade ground). The area of ground interspersed with the elaborate concrete runways and perimeter track made an ideal training area and location for assault courses and rifle ranges, and a nine-hole golf course. The runways were also used for go-karting and land yachting.

Depot The Queen's Division began training recruits at Bassingbourn in January 1970 with permanent staff drawn from the regiments' former depots at Canterbury, Sutton Coldfield and Bury St Edmunds. The first Commanding Officer was Lieutenant Colonel W C Deller who had previously been the third and last CO of Depot The Royal Anglian Regiment at Bury St Edmunds. The Depot was envisaged at the outset as a fully integrated unit in whose staff all three regiments were represented and with no particular appointments tied to any one regiment. Geordies, Lancastrians, Poachers, Tigers, Brummies, Vikings, Swedes, Pompadours, Cockneys, Men of Kent and Kentish Men, and all the others that went to make up the Division, settled down together very quickly – without the need for interpreters! All proudly wore their own Regimental capbadges (to which were added RAChD, RAMC, REME, RAPC, SASC, RAEC, RADC, APTC, ACC, QARANC and WRAC), upheld their own traditions, and rapidly built up a remarkable corporate spirit at this the first of the new infantry divisional depots. Many former Tigers served with distinction on the permanent staff at the Depot and in the collocated HQ The Queen's Division, which was headed by the Divisional Brigadier.

The first adult recruit intake formed up at Bassingbourn on 22 January 1970. The Depot was responsible for training recruits undergoing their fourteen-week basic training before joining a Regular battalion of The Queen's Regiment, The Royal Regiment of Fusiliers or The Royal Anglian Regiment. It also trained recruits for the RAVC. This increased to fifteen weeks in 1973 and eighteen weeks in 1974. In addition, the Depot trained Junior Bandsmen, Junior Drummers and Junior Infantrymen on two-year and eighteen-month courses respectively, and ran two-week recruit and JNCO cadres for the TAVR battalions. It was also for many years the location for the Royal Anglian Regimental Weekend and, when in 1974 the Colonel-in-Chief also visited the Depot, it led to the Royal Anglian recruits (many of whom came from Leicestershire) to rate themselves as 'the greatest living experts in tent and marquee erection'. The Regiment's Sergeants' Mess Past and Present Dinner was also held there for many years.

It did not take long before 'Monty', the wartime Sherman tank of Field Marshal Montgomery, appeared as one of the gate guardians at Bassingbourn. As mentioned earlier in this chapter, it had arrived at Glen Parva Barracks in Leicester in 1960. On the closure of Depot The Forester Brigade in 1963, it was transferred to Depot RRF at Sutton Coldfield, whence it moved to Bassingbourn. In 1985, it was removed for refurbishment and now stands in the Land Warfare Centre of the Imperial War Museum at Duxford.

In September 1972, a small opened-sided shelter with a tiled roof, supported by dark timber uprights and wooden seats along two sides, was erected outside Depot HQ. It had originally been made by prisoners of war of the Japanese belonging to the 18th Division, who erected it at the entrance to the cemetery at Changi Prison in Singapore in 1942, where they were to bury nearly 600 of their dead. When the cemetery was cleared after the Second World War and the dead interred elsewhere, the 'Changi Lychgates' were removed and re-erected outside St George's Garrison Church in Tanglin, Singapore. In April 1971, during the rundown of the British Garrison in Singapore, the lychgates were dismantled and shipped back to East Anglia, to Bassingbourn. They are one of the few surviving relics of a remarkable upsurge of Christian faith that took place among the men who were imprisoned in Singapore during the Japanese occupation. They continue to serve as a

The Changi Lychgate at Bassingbourn Barracks.
Trustees R Anglian Regt

memorial to the men of East Anglia who comprised the 18th Division,[16] in particular to those who died in Changi, and as a reminder of the power of faith in God during those dark years of the Second World War in the Far East. Some deceased men of 1st Battalion The Leicestershire Regiment may well have been carried through these gates at Changi Prison in 1942. The Changi Lychgates at Bassingbourn were for many years the venue for the Far East Prisoners of War (FEPOW) annual Service of Remembrance, until they were moved to the National Memorial Arboretum at Alrewas in Staffordshire in 2003.

In 1975, the final year covered by this History, over 800 adult recruits successfully completed training at Bassingbourn and 230 junior soldiers passed into adult training.

As a tailpiece, in 1985, RAVC recruits ceased being trained there and in their place came those destined for the Royal Pioneer Corps. In 1993, Depot The Queen's Division at Bassingbourn changed its name to Army Training Regiment Bassingbourn, and became responsible for the basic training of recruits for regiments of The Queen's Division, and for the Royal Engineers and Royal Signals.

Notes

1   A company commander in 1st Leicesters in Malaya, Ian Kennedy was subsequently appointed MBE in 1946 for his conduct while a PoW of the Japanese.
2   The actions of 1/5th Leicesters had earned the battle honour 'Norway 1940' and of 2/5th Leicesters the two battle honours awarded for North Africa in 1943 and six for the Italian Campaign 1943-45.
3   See Chapter 1, Note 16.
4   Lieutenant Colonel J Mosse served 1879-1904 and 1914-16. Major J W E Mosse served 1910-39 and was awarded the MC as a company commander in 1st Leicesters on the Somme in September 1916.
5   Lieutenant Colonel J W B Marshall OBE served 1935-60, and Major R E Everard 1937-44.
6   See Chapter 2, Note 14.
7   See Chapter 2, Note 10.
8   Appleton and Riley played regularly for the Army and were subsequently to play for Leicester City in the FA Cup Final at Wembley in 1961.
9   See Chapter 2, Note 7.
10 'Len' Harvey had been awarded the MBE in 1946 for service as Lt QM of 1st Bn The Nigeria Regiment in the Arakan, Burma, in the spring of 1945.
11 William Buckingham had been awarded the VC while serving in 2nd Leicesters at Neuve Chapelle in March 1915. He was killed in action while serving in 1st Leicesters at the Battle of the Somme on 15 September 1916. His name is among 843 of The Leicesters inscribed on the Thiepval Memorial in France (to those who died in the Somme Sector and have no known grave). His medal and some personal effects are displayed in the Regimental Museum.
12 Tony Novis had been capped at Rugby for the Army fourteen times over the period 1929-35, had been a British Lion in 1930, and had played seven times for England, which he captained in 1933. He had been awarded the MC as a company commander in 2nd Leicesters at Sidi Barrani in Egypt in 1940, and commanded 1st Leicesters in France in 1944 and in Germany 1945-47, and 2nd Leicesters in India 1947-48.
13 Peter Badger had been CO 1st R Leicesters 1961-64 – see Chapters 3 and 4.
14 RAF Barnham (94 Maintenance Unit) was a Second World War mustard gas weapons storage depot. In the mid-1950s it became a storage and maintenance facility for nuclear freefall bombs. By 1963, the storage and maintenance of the replacement nuclear air-launched missiles moved to the V-bomber airfields.
15 Constructed in 1938, RAF Bassingbourn was used as a bomber base by the RAF until 1942 and then by the USAAF's Flying Fortresses. After the Second World War, the RAF used it as an Operational Conversion Unit for Canberra bombers. The station was vacated in 1969 when all Canberra flying training was moved elsewhere in Cambridgeshire.
16 18th Div's 53, 54 and 55 Inf Bdes comprised three R Norfolk battalions, two Suffolk, two Cambridgeshire, one Beds & Herts and one Foresters. 53 Inf Bde's battalions fought alongside 1st Leicesters (The British Battalion) in Johore in southern Malaya in January 1942. Of the 42,610 British soldiers who were captured by the Japanese in the Far East, 10,298 (24 per cent) were killed or died in captivity. Most of the survivors suffered terrible ill-health for the rest of their lives.

Chapter 5

1st Battalion/4th R Anglian: Watchet and Aden 1964-65

~~~

Watchet: March 1964 to February 1965

The commanding officers of the four Regular battalions had been closely involved in the next evolution of the East Anglian Infantry from very shortly after the Royal Leicesters had joined that Brigade nine months before. It nevertheless came as something of a shock when, on 24 February, during block leave, the War Office formally announced that in six months' time the four regiments of The East Anglian Brigade were to form the first Large Regiment, and become four battalions of The Royal Anglian Regiment. So it was against the background of that impending change that at the end of March, following five weeks' block leave after its eleven-month unaccompanied tour in the Far East, the 1st Royal Leicesters reassembled at Doniford Camp.

On 6 April, Lieutenant Colonel Peter Badger handed over command, and a fond farewell was extended to him and his wife Joan. He was presented with a silver tiger from all the officers who had served under his command. His successor was Lieutenant Colonel J A C (Alan) Cowan MBE[1], formerly of The Rifle Brigade. It was already clear that he was to be the last Commanding Officer of 1st Battalion The Royal Leicestershire Regiment. A warm welcome was extended to him and his wife Jennifer, and they both quickly settled into the Tiger family. A short while later, when asked at a cocktail party 'how things were done in your Regiment', he immediately responded that The Royal Leicestershire Regiment was his Regiment. It was not long too before his wife was seen sporting a large diamond Tiger brooch.

In the Second World War the 2/5th Leicesters had started the custom of awarding the Regimental lanyard, which at that time had only been worn by officers, to soldiers who gave outstanding service on active service. These lanyards were worn on the right shoulder to differentiate from the SNCOs who wore theirs on the left. They had subsequently been awarded in the 1st Battalion after the Korean War. On return from the Borneo Territories the custom was continued, and Regimental lanyards were awarded to: Corporals W Durant, A Hughes, T J Reece, A Walton, J S J Rourke, Lance Corporals W Dance, B R Henson, L Lock, F Rothery, and Privates V Berry, J Blasdale, P Bond, D J Foran, Grant, J Gray, M Gribbons, C Halford, N Hickling, Holder, Jones, M Mann, A Marsden, Roberts, Smith, P Tinsley and Wallace. Many of these men had been with Alan Thompson or Mike Peele in the actions for which they were awarded their MCs.

It was about this time that the policy of cross-posting field officers and SNCOs of The East Anglian Brigade to other than their parent Battalion came into full swing. As a consequence, over the following years many new faces appeared as 'Tigers', to the benefit of their own careers and of the 4th Battalion. The vast majority of the field officers posted in in this way had been decorated in previous appointments, as the following pages indicate. In mid-April twenty-one Other Ranks were cross-posted to 1/3rd E Anglian in Belfast to bring them up to strength for their tour in Berlin. The 4th Battalion remained bottom of the list of priority for manpower in The East Anglian Brigade – being the only UK Battalion in the Brigade.

In April 1964 senior appointments in the Battalion were held as follows:

CO:	Lieutenant Colonel J A C Cowan MBE	OC B Coy:	Major P L Philcox MC[2]
		CSM B Coy:	WO2 C Murray
2IC:	Major A J Parsons MBE	OC C Coy:	Major R M Seton-Browne
Adjt:	Captain P N Graham		
RSM:	WO1 H D Benham	CSM C Coy:	WO2 J Pearce
QM:	Captain N McColl	OC HQ Coy:	Major R H D Graveston
RQMS:	WO2 G E Veitch	CSM HQ Coy:	WO2 S Bryant
OC A Coy:	Major T Holloway	Bandmaster:	WO1 J E Battye ARCM
CSM A Coy:	WO2 K Colclough	Drum Major:	Sgt T Roberts

The Battalion's organization reverted to the same as before departure for Hong Kong: three rifle companies, each comprising two rifle and one support platoon. There was also a new element in HQ Company, namely the Reconnaissance Platoon (Recce Platoon). After shake-down exercises acting as enemy to the Staffordshire Yeomanry and Cheshire Yeomanry, the thirty-seven all ranks who began the Recce Platoon selection process were whittled down to twelve, mounted in four ½-ton Land Rovers, commanded by Lieutenant F L B (Freddie) Vigers and Sergeant R (Bob) Swain. At a similar time, as part of a new Army-wide initiative to bring *la vie militaire* into the minds of the youth of the country, Army Youth Teams (AYTs) were established. Captain A J G (Tony) Pollard was appointed the first OC 17 AYT in Leicester, with a further four men from the Battalion in his team. Its role, working in conjunction with the Army Information Office, was to get to know all the youth organizations in the county, offer advice and help, and provide some equipment and transport to youth and boys' clubs … and attract young men into the Army.

The Battalion was again part of the Strategic Reserve. For operations the Battalion was under command of HQ 19 Infantry Brigade Group (19 Inf Bde Gp) (Brigadier D W Fraser OBE) at Colchester; for training and A matters under HQ 5 Inf Bde Gp (Brigadier D H Davies MC) at Tidworth – both brigades being part of 3rd Infantry Division (Major General R M P Carver CB CBE DSO MC); and for local administration under HQ 43 (Wessex) Div/Dist at Taunton (Major General J R Holden CBE DSO). It had been hoped that it might be left alone for a few months to repair the 'administrative damage' caused by the Far East tour, before being required to take part in formal training at formation level. Its four main training requirements were: IS drills, counter-insurgency operations, all phases of conventional war, and to become proficient in the drills, procedures and techniques involved in 'airportability', the name given to tactical airlift by helicopter and strategic airlift by larger aircraft. Leaving behind memories of jungle and leeches, all companies vigorously embarked on conventional war and airportability training. The families made the best of 'being at home together' again, not that the busy summer programme allowed much of that. If individuals were not involved in driving, signals and support weapons cadres, then the companies were frequently out of barracks on a variety of training and shooting events, laying on study days for the Battalion, or practising pack-ups for air moves.

The MT Platoon, which had eighty vehicles on charge and initially only forty-three drivers, ran a driving cadre under Sergeant Stewart that ended in a convoy to Plymouth. There the Land Rovers and trailers embarked over the beach onto HMS *Rampart*, an LCT that conveyed them round to Carlyon Bay, where they then disembarked and drove back to Watchet.

The Ministry of Defence (MOD)'s Public Relations Department visited to take photographs of the men training to use in a national press recruiting campaign. The men also starred in three TV recruiting films: range work, canoeing and helicopters in the Army. The last-mentioned was filmed at RN Air Station Culdrose, where B Company engaged in company group assault by helicopter, including the MOBAT anti-tank guns underslung from Wessex helicopters. Then a Rank film scriptwriter came to pick the brains of the Borneo warriors as he planned a training film about jungle fighting. The product, loosely based on 2nd Lieutenant Mike Peele's Operation *Arrant* 'camp attack' action (see Chapter 3), eventually saw the light of day as an AKC training film, with the tailpiece credit of 'This film is based on the actual events of 1st R Leicesters in Borneo.'

In late June the Battalion embarked on three weeks' training on Salisbury Plain. The move there simulated an air move on light scales. It included processing through the Movement Control Check Point (MCCP) at Devizes, whereafter the convoys drove on to the Plain. There, in various dispersed locations, everyone operated on light scales for four days until B Echelon – simulating the result of heavy airlift – arrived with the heavier stores, including tentage. The first week was spent on basic platoon and company training. The second week involved infantry/tank training with C Sqn 5th Royal Inniskilling Dragoon Guards (5 Innis DG – 'The Skins'), and culminated with twenty-five all ranks travelling to Leicester for Royal Tigers' Weekend. The final week involved the Battalion operating as an additional unit on a short FTX with 4 Para Bde, and then as a Battalion Group (including 'The Skins' C Sqn, L (Nery) Bty 2 Regt RA, 1 Tp 20 Fd Sqn RE, 19 Recce Flt AAC, and 1 Sect 19 Fd Amb RAMC) on Exercise *Closed Fist* set by 19 Inf Bde. Over thirty-six hours, during an advance to contact, there were three company group attacks and a battalion night attack. During the three-week deployment the Battalion was visited by the GOC-in-C Southern Command, Lieutenant General Sir Kenneth Darling KCB CBE DSO, and by its two brigade commanders.

Shortly after the Battalion's return to barracks at Watchet, A Company set out to Okehampton to act as sponsor unit to the CCF Central Camp for a fortnight. C Company deployed to Salisbury Plain to act as enemy in an IS setting to the Kent & County of London Yeomanry on Exercise *High Noon*. Reinforcing ties with Leicestershire, the Chairman of the County Council, Lieutenant Colonel P H Lloyd TD DL, accompanied by the Deputy Colonel, visited the Battalion for two days at the end of July.

At the end of that month, 2nd Lieutenant A C (Tony) Taylor became the last officer to

2Lt Tony Taylor. *A C Taylor*

Cpl Geoffrey Booth with the boy he saved.
Trustees R Leicestershire Regt

be granted a Regular Commission in The Royal Leicestershire Regiment, joining the Battalion a month later. Told before commissioning that he should purchase a Royal Leicester mess kit to wear for the foreseeable future, he was none too happy to be told a few months after arrival that all officers needed to convert their pearl-grey faced jackets and waistcoats into Royal Anglian dark-blue faced ones, along with tight trousers and Mess Wellingtons – at their own expense!

The Battalion was on block leave for most of August, during which month the *London Gazette* published the award to Corporal G (Geoffrey) Booth of the Queen's Commendation for Brave Conduct for jumping into the treacherous swirling waters of Watchet harbour and saving the life of a boy on 10 June.

The day of amalgamation duly arrived. On 1 September 1964, The East Anglian Brigade disbanded and The Royal Anglian Regiment was formed, comprising four Regular battalions, with the Regimental HQ and Depot at Bury St Edmunds, Suffolk. 1st Battalion The Royal Leicestershire Regiment became 4th (Leicestershire) Battalion The Royal Anglian Regiment. The other Regular battalions of the new Regiment were:

1st (Norfolk and Suffolk) Battalion – formed from 1st Bn 1st East Anglian Regiment (Royal Norfolk and Suffolk)

2nd (Lincolnshire and Northamptonshire) Battalion – formed from 1st Bn 2nd East Anglian Regiment (Duchess of Gloucester's Own Royal Lincolnshire and Northamptonshire)

3rd (16th/44th Foot) Battalion – formed from 1st Bn 3rd East Anglian Regiment (16th/44th Foot)

Within the Infantry, The Royal Anglian Regiment was relatively senior as it took its precedence from The Royal Norfolk Regiment (9th Foot), immediately below The King's Regiment (8th Foot).

At Doniford Camp, the renamed 4th (Leicestershire) Battalion held a Formation Parade, during which the new Royal Anglian capbadge replaced the East Anglian Brigade one (see plate section). The new badge was similar to its predecessor: the Castle and Key of Gibraltar placed above a 'Royal Anglian' scroll, set upon an eight-pointed star – the Other Ranks' capbadge was much smaller than the previous East Anglian Brigade one. For the first time the new Regimental Quick March (the Royal Norfolk 'Rule Britannia' and the Suffolk 'Speed the Plough') and Slow March ('The Northamptonshire') were played on a Tigers' parade. The Commanding Officer read out a Special Order of the Day from the new Colonel of The Regiment, Lieutenant General Sir Reginald Denning KBE CB DL, and a special message from Major General Sir Douglas Kendrew, now a Deputy Colonel of The Regiment. Their contents are at Appendix I. He also read out a special message from the Minister of Defence (Army), who had written:

> On the occasion of the formation of the Royal Anglian Regiment I wish to send you and all ranks my most sincere good wishes for the success of this new venture. The magnificent history of service to Queen and Country of all the former Regiments is a guarantee of success and I am confident that the Royal Anglian Regiment, building on their splendid traditions, will go from strength to strength.

A telegram was received from the new Colonel-in-Chief, HM Queen Elizabeth The Queen Mother, which read:

> As Colonel-in-Chief I am proud to welcome your Battalion into The Royal Anglian Regiment. I am confident that you will bring to this new Regiment the tradition of loyalty and service of which you are justly proud and that the high reputation of your Battalion will be most worthily maintained. I send you my sincere good wishes for your new role in The Royal Anglian Regiment and I assure you that your interest will be my constant concern.

The Commanding Officer replied:

> With respectful duty to Queen Elizabeth The Queen Mother, I express to Her Majesty on behalf of All Ranks of the Battalion under my command our consciousness of the honour of serving in a Regiment of which Her Majesty is Colonel-in-Chief. The gracious message of Her Majesty is an inspiration to us all and we tender our devoted and loyal greeting to our Colonel-in-Chief.

HM Queen Elizabeth The Queen Mother's connection with the Regiment dated from her Colonelcy-in-Chief of The Bedfordshire & Hertfordshire Regiment since 1949. Of her new Deputies, HRH The Princess Margaret, Countess of Snowden CI GCVO, had been Colonel-in-Chief of The Suffolk Regiment since 1953, and HRH The Duchess of Gloucester GCB CI GCVO GBE had been Colonel-in-Chief of The Northamptonshire Regiment since 1937. The Princess Margaret was to adopt a special relationship with the 1st and 3rd Battalions, and The Duchess of Gloucester with the 2nd and 4th.

In addition to the afore-mentioned Colonel of The Regiment, there were four Deputy

Colonels, one for each of the former Regiments. In the case of the Royal Leicesters it was Major General Sir Douglas Kendrew. Brigadier R H L Oulton CBE, originally a Royal Lincoln and who now represented the former 2nd East Anglian Regiment, had commanded 1st Royal Leicesters in Germany for five months in 1947.

The determination of the Regiment to be a forward-looking entity did not preclude the preservation of time-honoured insignia, traditions and customs of the former regiments. With regard to orders of dress, in the 4th Battalion, apart from the new capbadge (which on the beret was worn with the Tigers' green backing), Royal Leicester badges continued to be worn as collar badges, and the red/pearl grey/black braided lanyard was retained. Similar accoutrements from former regiments were retained in the other three battalions, including – until a new one could be designed agreed, manufactured and issued – stable belts. All ranks of the Regiment wore a new 'Star and Castle' brass button on parade uniform, and anodized shoulder titles 'ROYAL ANGLIAN' were worn on several forms of dress.

In addition to the new Regimental Day (1 September) and Regimental Marches, the respective battalions were to continue to celebrate their previous Regimental Days and play their Marches – in the 4th (Leicestershire) Battalion's case, Royal Tigers' Day on 25 June, the Quick Marches 'Romaika', '1772' and 'The Hunting Call' (the three together also being known as 'The Royal Leicestershire Regiment'), the Slow March 'General Monkton 1762', and 'Wolfe's Dirge'[3].

All the battle honours granted to the former regiments over the years, from Namur 1695 to Korea 1951-52 (both of which happened to be Royal Leicester honours), were inherited by the new Regiment. They amounted to 299 battle honours: sixty-nine for the years up to 1914; 102 for the First World War; 126 for the Second World War; and two for the Korean War. The Regimental Council set up a Colours Committee to advise on battle honours and other insignia which should be included on the facings of the Colours to be presented to the Regiment in due course.

There was much discussion between the Colonels of the Former Regiments whose battle honours the Royal Anglian Regiment had inherited and who very naturally wished to retain as many of their 'own' honours on the new Colours as could be allowed. Sensible compromise enabled all main battle honours to be included in the total of forty-one honours allowed to be embroidered on the Queen's Colour and forty-five on the Regimental Colour. Of the eighty-six selected, twenty-seven were Royal Leicesters' honours. Indeed, only two Royal Leicesters' battle honours from before 1914, two from the First World War and two from the Second World War were not displayed on the new Regiment's colours.

Each former regiment was to be represented on the Regimental Colour by an 'Honorary Distinction'. In the case of The Royal Leicestershire Regiment, the Royal Tiger superscribed 'Hindoostan', granted in 1825 for service in India from 1804 to 1823, was to be in the lower hoist. The battle honours and honorary distinctions are shown on The Royal Anglian Regiment's Colours (see plate section). Therefore, 'when marching with the Colours, soldiers of The Royal Anglian Regiment will be properly and appropriately inspired by the record of the deeds of their forbears in The Royal Leicestershire Regiment, as well as the other Former Regiments'.

Although becoming part of The Royal Anglian Regiment, all the TA battalions of the former regiments retained their original titles. So, a unit bearing the name of The Royal Leicestershire Regiment lived on for a number of years in 4/5th Bn The Royal Leicestershire Regiment and The Royal Leicestershire Regiment (Territorial), of which the history is covered in Chapters 7 and 10 respectively.

Each of the former regiments retained an outstation HQ. Thus HQ R Anglian Leicester came into being, which was also RHQ R Leicesters, with Lieutenant Colonel (Retd) P G Upcher DSO DL as the dual-hatted Regimental Secretary there. Although *The Green Tiger* Regimental Magazine was published for the last time in autumn 1964, a *Green Tiger* Newsletter was published for many years – and is still going strong in 2008!

RHQ R Anglian at Bury St Edmunds was under Colonel J C (Jack) Denny OBE MC, the first Regimental Colonel, whose efforts to get the new Regiment to pull together were immense and successful. His exhortatory words in the Editorial of the March 1965 first volume of the new Regimental Journal, *Castle*, seemed to be followed to the letter: 'There is no doubt we have started to set an example of the ability of the British Army officers and soldiers to adapt themselves to new conditions, to sink differences, should there be any, and to show to the world a pride and affection for both the "old and the new".'

Back at Watchet, on 3 September, the Battalion was visited by its new Divisional Commander, Major General C H Blacker OBE MC. Two days later a Beating Retreat was held on Doniford Barracks Square, followed by cocktail parties in the Officers' and WOs' & Sgts' Messes, celebrating the new 4th (Leicestershire) Battalion The Royal Anglian Regiment. Thereafter it was full steam ahead in preparation for Exercise *Storm King*, which was preceded by a practice air move through the MCCP Devizes.

Storm King was a 19 Inf Bde FTX spread over three weeks, practising its Strategic Reserve role in all phases of war in a non-nuclear environment. Having driven by road to Salisbury Plain for a week, the Battalion were then flown from three airfields to RAF Ouston in Northumberland and on by helicopter to Otterburn training area. After a week there, it travelled by train to Stanford in Norfolk, where at the conclusion of that third week the Army Commander reviewed all the participating units.

On 12 October, Major Terry Holloway's A Company Group (which included the Recce Platoon, Band and Drums and elements of HQ Company) set out on a fortnight's KAPE tour. Accommodated in the old Glen Parva Barracks, it gave displays around Leicestershire and Rutland, introducing the newly titled Battalion to its counties and drumming up recruits.

At the end of October for one month the Battalion became the *Spearhead* Battalion of the Strategic Reserve, with Tac HQ and one company (the 'Leading Element' of 146 all ranks) at twenty-four hours NTM, and the remainder of the Battalion at seventy-two hours. The Leading Element kept its freight and vehicles loaded, while all companies continued training (including the Mortar Platoon live firing at Larkhill). Visits were received from various Formation Commanders who sought to satisfy themselves that the Battalion was on the ball.

November began well when it was announced that all ranks who had spent thirty days or more in the Borneo Territories since December 1962, were eligible for the new General Service Medal (GSM 1962) with the clasp 'Borneo'. Most of those serving in the now 4th Battalion qualified. When the award of Lieutenant Mike Peele's MC appeared in the *London*

Gazette on 17 November (see Chapter 3), B Company had the most unusual distinction of having three officers holding that decoration, the others being Major Peter Philcox and Lieutenant Alan Thompson. Within HQ Company, the new post of Technical Quartermaster (Tech QM) was introduced, and the first appointee was Lieutenant Ted Kelly, the erstwhile Motor Transport Officer (MTO). The Battalion provided G and Q lower controls for the 5 Inf Bde CPX *Autumn Trot* in the week ending 25 November, on which day most of the officers attended an inaugural Regimental Reception at St James's Palace, hosted by the Colonel of The Regiment. The Regiment felt honoured that its Colonel-in-Chief and two Deputy Colonels-in-Chief consented to be present, and for the first time had the opportunity to meet many of the officers and their wives. A week later at Watchet the Colonel of The Regiment paid his first visit to the Battalion, during which he reviewed companies training, and presented the BEM to Colour Sergeant G A B Davis for his work in Borneo training Border Scouts. The following day the Battalion paid a fond farewell to Major John Bromhead as he retired after forty years in the Army – twenty-two serving as a Tiger, fourteen as a combat officer and the final eight as Paymaster.

Mention must now be made of sport. On arrival back from Borneo in the spring, team building for football and hockey began in earnest, identifying new talent and improving skills. By good fortune and building on the many years' links with Leicester City Football Club, the offer by its Chairman and Directors to train the footballers at Filbert Street for a week in June was gratefully accepted and, under Captain B N (Neil) Crumbie, sixteen men learnt a great deal and 'in particular a lot about what they already thought they knew'! The Hockey Team likewise began to get engaged with local Somerset teams. Unfortunately, the busy military programme in the summer and up to Christmas precluded any meaningful participation in military or civilian competitions, though on an individual basis 2nd Lieutenant Mike Charles played Rugby for the Army, and Lieutenants Brian Davenport and D W (David) James had an Army Hockey Trial.

The Band, which had not been on the Borneo leg of the Far East deployment, had nevertheless had a busy time in England. The tempo quickened further when the Drums again became 'seriously musical' in April. Another full summer and autumn season under the baton of Bandmaster Edgar Battye culminated with the Band and Drums performing in Trafalgar Square in London on 11 December at the Lighting Up ceremony of the Christmas Tree donated annually by the people of Norway. This was a particularly fitting honour as it had been the 1/5th Battalion The Leicestershire Regiment that had fought so gallantly in Norway in 1940. The Colonel of The Royal Anglian Regiment wrote a very nice congratulatory letter afterwards.

The period of *Spearhead* duty successfully completed, military training refocused on to the upcoming Battalion overseas training period Exercise *Spring Canter*, to take place in Libya in January, for a week's reconnaissance of which the CO and QM set out on 6 December. Among other things the Exercise was designed to practise a full-scale air move of men, vehicles and equipment. Meanwhile, the traditional round of Christmas events took place and the Battalion proceeded on block leave for twelve days on 18 December.

On 2 January 1965, the Advance Party of eighteen all ranks set out for Libya. Five days later – and just nine months after the Battalion's return from eleven months unaccompanied in the Far East – the Commanding Officer found himself in the rather unusual position of having to announce that the Battalion was to deploy in February to Aden on a six-month unaccompanied Emergency Tour. Frantic preparation then ensued, several new and returning officers, and a new RSM, were posted in, and the Advance Party of forty-one all ranks under the Commanding Officer, 2IC and Adjutant, departed on 22 January. Major Dick Graveston commanded the Rear Party. Some explanation follows as to 'Where and why Aden, and why the hurry?'

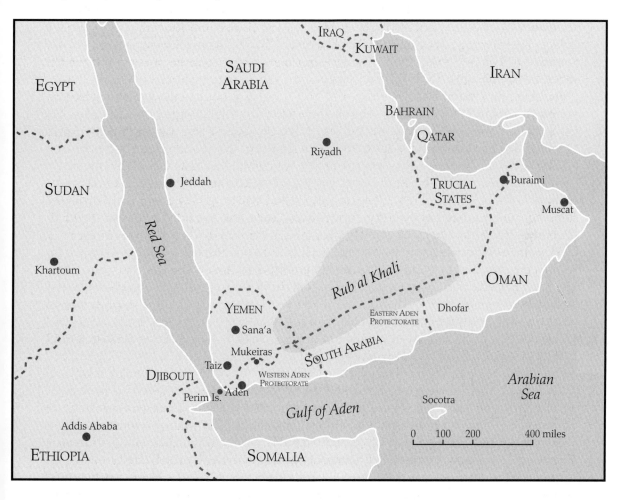

Aden: February to August 1965

Lying 100 miles to the east of the entrance to the Red Sea, Aden is a peninsula covering an area of 20 square miles. There are large bays on each side, dominated by Jebel Shamsan, a towering volcanic hill feature rising to 1,700'. On the eastern side of the peninsula lies the old town and main commercial centre, built within the bowl of an extinct volcano and aptly named Crater. On the western side lie Ma'alla (an Arab township with a large port area, and also containing many Service married quarters), Tawahi (the main business and shopping centre) and Steamer Point. This was effectively 'Big Aden'. Three miles to the west is the promontory of Little Aden. This, together with a strip of mainland including the township of Sheikh Othman and the airfield at Khormaksar, combined with Big Aden to form the Crown Colony of Aden, covering 70 square miles. The surrounding hinterland –

143

known as the Protectorates – covered 112,000 square miles (about the size of England and Scotland), stretching some 700 miles along the south coast of South Arabia.

The Protectorates were a disparate collection of emirates, sheikhdoms and sultanates. The Western Aden Protectorate (WAP) comprised eighteen tribal territories immediately adjacent to and to the north-east of Aden, and the Eastern Aden Protectorate (EAP) consisted of three larger territories much farther to the east. Over the previous century these territories' local rulers accepted British 'protection'. Britain became responsible for the defence and foreign relations of the Protectorates, yet the internal administration of the various parts of the territory was entirely a matter for the indigenous rulers. Aden, on the other hand, had, since 1937, enjoyed the full status of a Crown Colony.

In 1959, the Federation of South Arabia had been set up. It had its own new capital at Al Ittihad and its own Security Forces. The four rifle battalions of the former Aden Protectorate Levies (APL) had become the Federal Regular Army (FRA) of some 4,000 men, whose role was to be the defence of the Federation's frontiers, to support the Federal National Guard, and to assist the civil power in maintaining law and order among the tribes in the hinterland. By 1965, all but five of the Protectorates had joined the Federation, as had Aden in 1963. In its 1964 Defence White Paper, the British Government had declared that it would retain a military base in Aden but that South Arabia would be granted independence not later than 1968.

In response, both indigenous and regional Arab nationalism had become increasingly opposed to the Federation and to the enduring British presence. Much of the pressure for change had come from Yemen, the Federation's northern neighbour. Yemen, with very strong political and military backing from President Nasser's Egypt (fresh from its success over the British in the Suez Crisis of 1956), sought both to subvert the traditionalist tribesmen of the hinterland (especially astride the road in the Radfan) and to foment rebellion in Aden itself. Thus, from the early 1960s it had proved necessary to increase British military force levels, both in Aden and also in the Radfan mountains, where the tribesmen had been incited to begin a guerilla war, interdicting the main road from Aden to Dhala by ambushes and by laying mines. To that end the National Liberation Front (NLF) had been set up in 1963 whose aim was to drive the British out of South Arabia by the use of violence. In December 1963, the Federal Government had closed the frontier with Yemen and declared a State of Emergency throughout the Protectorates. Other new organizations such as the South Arabia League pursued a more political agenda with broadly the same aim. And the 80,000 Yemenis working in Aden had not needed much encouragement to make life as difficult as possible for the British.

Aden, the location of the tri-service HQ Middle East Command (MEC), was a major part of the UK's system of strategic bases, the other two being the UK itself and Singapore. In addition to MEC's responsibility for Aden and South Arabia, its forces had roles elsewhere in a wide region. They were charged with defending other parts of the Gulf such as Oman and Kuwait if this became necessary, and there was a battalion in Swaziland. Britain's capability of reinforcing Aden if needed was constrained by Cold War requirements in Europe; there were also concerns that Confrontation with Indonesia might escalate; and there was a clear possibility that problems with Southern Rhodesia might increase (as they did, leading to UDI in September 1965).

In 1964 in Aden, the NLF had begun its urban terrorist campaign which reached a crescendo in November and December. In response to that and to continuing unrest in the Radfan, the Ministry of Defence agreed to continue the deployment in Aden of an Emergency Tour battalion. To that end, in January 1965, 4 R Anglian was selected as it was able to fit in a six-month unaccompanied tour before its posting to Malta at the end of that year.

In January 1965 Sir Richard Turnbull KCMG had taken over as British High Commissioner in Aden, a man with a successful track record against the Mau Mau in Kenya and latterly in Tanganyika, where his establishment of good relations with the nationalists had ensured a peaceful transition of power. His task in South Arabia was to be his greatest challenge.

And so, some 124 years after The 17th (Leicestershire) Regiment had been stationed there from 1841 to 1845, and seventy-six years after the 2nd Leicesters had spent 1889 there en route from Burma to England, with little warning and scant specific training, 4th Battalion The Royal Anglian Regiment set out to play its part in operations in support of the civil power in South Arabia. On arrival in Aden in February 1965, senior appointments were held as follows:

CO:	Lieutenant Colonel J A C Cowan MBE	OC B Coy:	Captain J C D Heggs
		CSM B Coy:	WO2 C Murray
2IC:	Major T Holloway	OC C Coy:	Captain R H Robinson
Adjt:	Captain B N Crumbie	CSM C Coy:	WO2 J Pearce
RSM:	WO1 N H P Jenks MM	OC HQ Coy:	Captain W J G Brown
QM:	Lt E P Kelly DCM	CSM HQ Coy:	WO2 L Grant
RQMS:	WO2 G E Veitch	OC Rear Party:	Major R H G Graveston
OC A Coy:	Captain F B L Vigers	QM Rear Party:	Capt N McColl
CSM A Coy:	WO2 S Bryant		

The Battalion was organized similarly to when at Watchet: HQ Company, and three rifle companies of two rifle platoons and a support platoon of two 3" mortars and two 120mm MOBAT recoilless towed anti-tank guns. Except when deployed 'up country', the Support Platoons acted as rifle platoons. Two new weapon systems entered the inventory. The Bren LMG was replaced by the 7.62mm belt-fed General Purpose Machine Gun (GPMG), which had a range out to 800m in the light role, and out to 1,800m in the Sustained Fire (SF) role on a tripod (and using the same indirect-fire sight as the soon-to-be-issued new 81mm mortar). During the tour the historically ineffective 360-yard ranged 3.5" rocket launcher was replaced by the recoilless 84mm Carl Gustav medium anti-armour (MAW) weapon which had significantly greater punch and range.

The rifle platoons' other weapons were the 7.62mm self-loading rifle (SLR), the 9mm Sterling SMG, the 2" mortar, the No. 36 anti-personnel grenade and the No. 83 coloured smoke grenade. Communication was provided by C42, A41, A40 (all VHF) and the WS62 (HF) radio sets. Mechanical transport comprised ½-ton Land Rover 'jeeps', and 1-ton and 3-ton trucks.

From 23 January, the Battalion began to move into Radfan Camp near Khormaksar, the RAF station and civilian airport. The rather grandly named Radfan Camp had until recently been the Aden Transit Camp and was occupied by 1st Battalion The Royal Scots

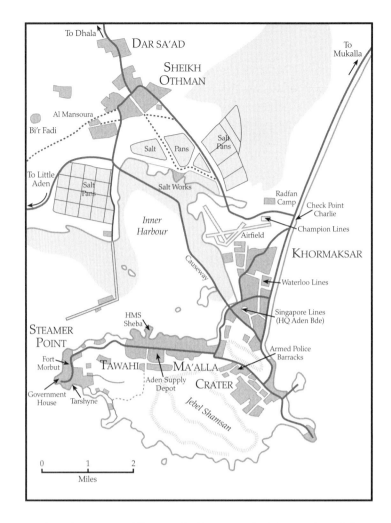

(1 RS), the outgoing Emergency Tour unit. It was primitive and mainly tented, with seven Twynham huts (some air-conditioned) as offices and accommodation, and was situated not far from the Indian Ocean. Bathing there was, however, forbidden because of the threat from sharks. Each tent had an overhead fan and a mosquito net protected each bed. It was in these early days that the Colonel of The Regiment met members of the Advance Party while in Aden to visit 1st (Norfolk and Suffolk) Battalion The Royal Anglian Regiment (1 R Anglian), based in Waterloo Lines.

The Main Body of the 4th Battalion began to arrive by Britannia charter aircraft on 7 February, and in some cases platoons deployed almost at once onto operational IS duties. For the majority, the first few days were spent in acclimatization and familiarization of the ground and the role, and improving the protection of the tents in the camp by erecting sandbag walls around them. On 9 February, B Coy took over standby duties in support of Check Point Charlie, a permanent Vehicle Check Point (VCP) near Radfan Camp that controlled entry into Aden from the north.

At 0600 hours 13 February, the 4th Battalion assumed responsibility for all of 1 RS's tasks in Big Aden. It was part of Aden Brigade (Brigadier R L Hargroves), the other manoeuvre unit being its sister battalion 1 R Anglian, a Resident Battalion eighteen months into an accompanied two-year tour. Within Aden those two battalions were simply known as 'the 1st Battalion' and 'the 4th Battalion' with no further qualification. The other British formation in the Federation of South Arabia was 24 Inf Bde, based at Little Aden and responsible for that peninsula, the Federal Government complex at Al Ittihad and security 'up country'. Force troops comprised 10th Royal Hussars, an armoured car regiment (with Saladin, Ferret and Saracen), 19 Fd Regt RA, a field engineer regiment RE, and Beaver and Sioux aircraft of the AAC. RN Wessex helicopters and RAF squadrons of Hawker Hunter FGA, Belvedere, Beverley and Twin Pioneer provided further air support. Both the Army brigades reported to Major General J H Cubbon CBE[4], GOC Middle East Land Forces (MELF), whose HQ was at Steamer Point, along with HQ MEC (Lieutenant General Sir Charles Harrington KCB CBE DSO MC) and the British High Commission (Sir Richard Turnbull).

Showing commendable foresight, Private G (Graham) Eustace[5] of A Coy brought with him to Aden a cine-camera with which he recorded over an hour's film of the Battalion's various activities, and copies are now held by The Imperial War Museum, The National Army Museum and the Regimental Museums at Leicester and Duxford.

Despite the fact that in the last months of 1964 there had been over thirty terrorist incidents and a similar number of casualties in Aden, there was little direct evidence of terrorism during the Battalion's first week in the Colony in February 1965. The NLF had embarked on a campaign of assassination of police Special Branch officers, and on the political front the Aden Legislature, which notionally represented Aden State and whose franchise included only those born in the Colony, was increasingly veering to the side of the People's Socialist Party (PSP). Nevertheless the terrorist threat was increasing and the IS situation deteriorating. It was clear that a high standard of alertness and watchfulness would be required of all ranks – seven days a week, on and off duty, in and out of camp; and a premium was placed on the competence of junior leaders.

For the next six months in Aden, the 4th Battalion was to experience the whole panoply of IS tasks (curfew control, cordon and searches, formal and snap roadblocks and personnel checks, snap searches of limited areas, foot and vehicle security patrols,

Radfan Camp: the lines of 4th R Anglian are the right half. *A E Fisher*

ambushes, OPs, static KP guards, VIP escort, checks and sweeps for explosive devices in camp and at KPs) with the exception of crowd dispersal. While deployed 'up country', it was to undertake counter-insurgency operations in mountainous terrain. Throughout the tour the soldiers were operating under arduous climatic conditions, living in unfavourable living conditions and were under the inevitable strain of being a potential target whenever an individual or vehicle left camp.

Fourteen hours after becoming operational and assuming the role of IS Battalion, men of the 4th Battalion experienced their first incident when a grenade was thrown into the Aden Supply Depot where B Coy's Corporal A C (Tony) Sprason's section was the guard force. His elder brother WO2 R E (Ron) Sprason, also a career Tiger, was at the time serving with the 2nd (Lincolnshire and Northamptonshire) Battalion The Royal Anglian Regiment (2 R Anglian) in Cyprus, an early example of the cross-posting of SNCOs within the Large Regiment. That regimental family was completed by their stepbrother, Corporal George Boss, serving in the 4th Battalion. Among other families, Colour Sergeant 'Doc' Hobday and his son, a REME craftsman, were also in the Battalion.

In the opening three weeks the Battalion, along with the 1st Battalion, were deployed in Big Aden wherever its platoons and companies were needed. The tasks they undertook and the incidents to which they reacted were many and various. On 15 February, at about 1900 hrs on the Ma'alla Strait, a grenade was thrown at a Land Rover in which a C Coy section was escorting Brigadier R C Gibbs DSO MC[6], Comd 16 Para Bde and out from the UK visiting one of his battalions. The following day the GOC commended the 4th Battalion on their actions at the time of the incident. A good start! Of significance, many of the families of other resident units of all three Services lived in blocks of flats among the civilian population in Ma'alla.

The very next day the Arab bakers working in the Aden Supply Depot refused to enter the compound, on the grounds that 'there were tigers guarding the Depot'. News had travelled fast and was easily corruptible! The bakers were finally persuaded to go in and work. On 17 February, the GOC came to address the Battalion at 0720. Comd Aden Bde visited the Battalion two days later.

Following an incident on 18 February when a terrorist grenade killed a policeman and injured three soldiers in a vehicle in Crater, B and A Coys 'flooded' the areas of Ma'alla and Crater respectively from 1900 to 2300. A Coy had one shot fired at it. During the evening of the 19th, reinforced by a composite platoon from HQ Coy based on the Recce Platoon and under command of the IS Coy of 1 R Anglian, B Coy again patrolled Crater, Ma'alla and Tawahi. The following evening, C Coy provided foot patrols in Crater, Ma'alla and Tawahi. On 20 February, following a grenade being thrown at a 1 R Anglian mobile patrol in Sheikh Othman, C Coy from Check Point Charlie cordoned an area at the Caltex Roundabout and arrested a number of Yemenis.

On 22 February, the Battalion received a Warning Order to deploy (less B Coy) to the Radfan on 3 March. The purpose of this deployment was to relieve 24 Inf Bde's battalions of the task for a short while and to experience a completely different form of operations from the tedious IS in Aden. A and C Coys conducted preparatory training at Little Aden and on Jebel Shamsan, and generally set their minds for mountain warfare. B Coy went under command 1 R Anglian for IS duties in Aden, and provided a mobile patrol in Al Mansura and a cordon party in Crater. It was subsequently decreed that B Coy would after

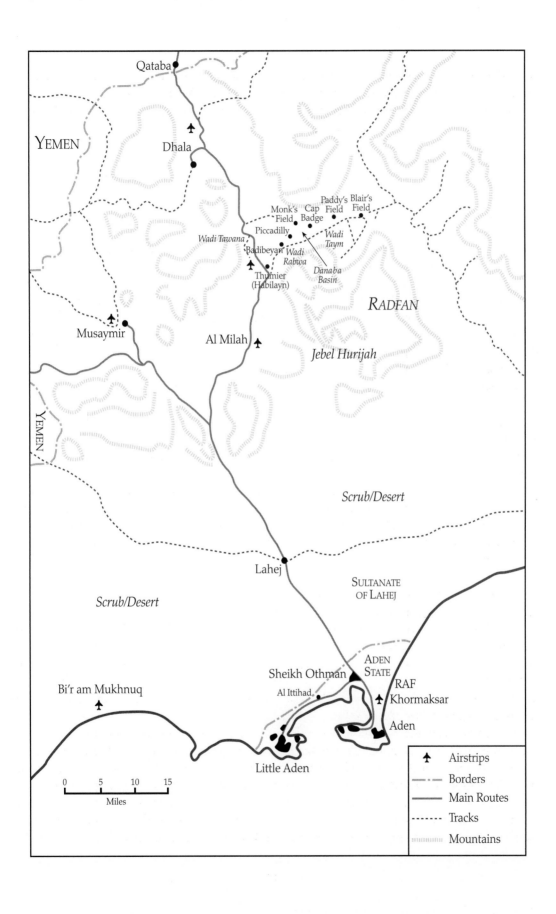

Qataba

YEMEN

Dhala

Monk's Cap Paddy's Blair's
Field Badge Field Field

Piccadilly

Wadi Tawana Wadi Taym

Badibeyan Wadi Rabwa

Thumier Danaba
(Habilayn) Basin

RADFAN

Musaymir

Al Milah

Jebel Hurijah

YEMEN

Scrub/Desert

Lahej

SULTANATE
OF LAHEJ

Scrub/Desert

Bi'r am Mukhnuq

Sheikh Othman

ADEN
STATE

RAF
Khormaksar

Al Ittihad

Aden

Little Aden

✈	Airstrips
—·—·	Borders
———	Main Routes
-------	Tracks
▨▨▨	Mountains

0   5   10   15
Miles

all deploy with the Battalion to the Radfan, and it reverted to under command 4th Battalion on 27 February.

On 1 March, the Advance Party moved by road convoy the 70 miles to Thumier, the Commanding Officer wisely travelling by air to the airstrip there. On 3 March, leaving a small rear party in Radfan Camp, the Main Body deployed before dawn by road convoy, a journey of five and a half hours in open-topped Land Rovers and 3-ton lorries, arriving in time to take over the area of responsibility from 45 Cdo RM at noon and under command of HQ 24 Inf Bde (Brigadier R M Bremner MBE).

The Radfan was the mountainous area in the Amirate of Dhala, with the steep-sided hill features intersected by wadis along which wound various grades of track or road. The flat bottoms of the wadis contained areas of cultivation and dispersed small clusters of mud huts and villages. In an area where some of the mountain tops reached well over 3,000 feet, the dry air was a pleasant change from the humidity of Aden. It was in the Radfan that the tribesmen, supported by the Yemenis, regularly interdicted the military convoys supplying the garrison at Dhala. In April the previous year, a British-led brigade-sized force had taken the fight to the local tribesmen in an area where few white men had ever previously ventured, in a militarily successful two-month campaign which had temporarily denuded Aden of British troops. 45 Cdo RM, 1/1 E Anglian (as 1 R Anglian had previously been titled, and commanded by Lieutenant Colonel J B Dye MC[7]) and 2nd Battalion The Federal Regular Army (2 FRA), with artillery and air support, had put to flight the 'Red Wolves of the Radfan' in a large-scale operation for which the General Service Medal with clasp 'Radfan' had been awarded. After a subsequent period of 'air control' of the region by the RAF, in December, 45 Cdo RM moved back to the Radfan to carry out further minor operations by dominating the Thumier, Dhala and Wadi Rabwa area. These enterprises required the approval of the Commander FRA and could only be carried out in conjunction with the local Political Officer. It was to 'continue that movement' that 4 R Anglian embarked in early March 1965, seeking to dominate the wadis and the mountains, prevent the tribesmen from attacking the bases and the Dhala Road road convoys, and through 'hearts and minds' to woo the local population away from any allegiance to the Yemen

The Radfan Mountains. *P Trowell*

Operations tent at Thumier Camp, Radfan, March 1965. *A E Fisher*

regime and the anti-British terrorist movements which had their logistic bases and safe havens in the Yemen. 'Tigers versus Wolves'! A much wider 'hearts and minds' campaign also included road-building up the Wadi Rabwa, the provision of new schools, and the installation of dams, wells and water pumps, in all a massive undertaking by the Royal Engineers and due reward to the loyal tribes' people.

On 3 March 1965, the Battalion's initial deployment in the Radfan was: Bn HQ, Echelon, and A and B Coys in a tented camp at Thumier beside an airstrip, and C Coy at Monk's Field. A Coy (now under command of Major K Burch MBE[8]) was responsible for the defence of the Thumier Camp area, which was the HQ and supply base for Radfan operations; B Coy patrolled from that secure base, a feature of which was the pervasive smell of oil sprayed on the airstrip runway and the adjacent Dhala Road to keep down the dust. Eight miles to the north-east at Monk's Field, C Coy was responsible for dominating the Danaba Basin. While the inhabitants of that cultivated valley were permitted to work in the open by day, no one was allowed to move through it by night and transit was denied by vigorous fire plans. Platoon picquets at Cap Badge and Piccadilly, communicating with their Coy HQ by radio and field telephone, helped dominate and observe the whole area, and call down indirect fire.

The threat was essentially from sniper fire, ambush and mining of roads and tracks. The rifle companies, supported by 67 Bty 19 Fd Regt RA, set about dominating their surroundings by vigorous patrolling, night ambushes to protect the camps and roads and tracks, and engaging the armed tribesmen by shorter-range medium mortar and longer-range 105mm Pack Howitzer artillery fire whenever the fleeting opportunities arose. Additionally routes had to be picqueted when road convoys passed and when RE/Assault Pioneer Platoon mine-clearing parties had to be protected.

First into contact with the enemy was C Coy at Monk's Field and A Coy's 'F' Picquet

The Assault Pioneers clear a road in the Radfan. *Trustees R Anglian Regt*

east of Thumier on the night of 4/5 March when small-arms fire was exchanged and artillery Defensive Fire (DF) tasks were fired. On 6 March, a C Coy patrol led by 2nd Lieutenant A W C (Andrew) Dexter clashed with a small party of enemy near Monk's Field, wounding at least one. The following morning the 3-ton supply lorry following the mine-sweeping patrol from Thumier to Monk's Field was blown up on a British Mk V anti-tank mine, to be followed thirty hours later by a 10th Royal Hussars Ferret scout car being blown up near Paddy's Field, neither incident incurring casualties. In the early hours of 9 March, one of C Coy's ambush patrols near to where the three-ton truck had been blown up, engaged an enemy party, with no casualties. At first light a strong patrol led by 2nd Lieutenant David James searched Badibeyan with no result other than increasing the latent hostility of the villagers. On 8 March, elements of C Coy proceeded from Monk's Field to Blair's Field, escorting the Political Officer and the RMO, Captain K (Keith) Clapton RAMC, on a 'flag march' patrol. The local Halmaini Tribal Levies helpfully handed in a Mk V anti-tank mine and 4 FRA found another north-east of Dhala.

Meanwhile B Coy, supported by a troop of armoured cars of 10th Royal Hussars, an FOO and an FAC, set out up Wadi Tawana, north-west from Thumier, with the purpose of practising picquetting and deployment under local conditions, reporting on the terrain and dominating the area. A train of twenty-nine camels (carrying the medium mortars, ammunition, food, water, radio batteries and stretchers) formed its mobile echelon. How much a camel would carry depended on how much money the Arab handler received! Artillery and mortar DF and Harassing Fire (HF) tasks were registered each night and the FAC, Captain David Hickman, controlled two RAF Hunters practising air attacks. An RAF Belvedere helicopter resupplied the Coy during its two-day operation.

152

Adjusting a mortar DF task. *N Patrick*

During that first week some thirty patrols were sent out by the Battalion, which thoroughly covered the area and were probably instrumental in the marked decrease in attacks on Thumier Camp. Nevertheless, reports from the patrols and picquets indicated considerable night movement by the dissidents.

On 11 March, a strong platoon of C Coy cordoned the village of Badibeyan while 3 FRA searched it and the surrounding area. The artillery and mortars at Monk's Field fired in support of the Halmaini Tribal Levies as they were engaged by dissidents to the north of the Danaba Basin. That same day the Battalion was visited by the GOC, on 12 March by Comd 24 Inf Bde, and on 13 March the Assistant News Editor of the *Leicester Mercury*, David Partridge, and two men from Midlands TV arrived for a prolonged visit. This was the first of many visits that David Partridge was to make to the Battalion over the following

A foot patrol in the Radfan. *Trustees R Anglian Regt*

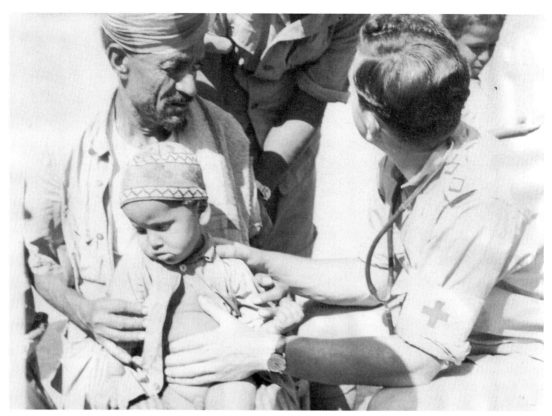

Capt Keith Clapton RAMC **treating a child in the Radfan.** *Trustees R Leicestershire Regt*

ten years, which invariably led to very informative and perceptive articles being published in that newspaper. He rapidly became a real and welcome friend to 'The Tigers'.

On 12 March, the Recce Platoon (under Lieutenant Mike Peele) was deployed south to Al Milah to carry out picquetting tasks on the Thumier–Aden Road, but not in time to prevent a 10-ton lorry of 24 Fd Sqn RE being blown up on a British Mk VII anti-tank mine on an unswept road near the airstrip the following day. On 13 March, in response to information that several men were hiding in bushes beside the Dhala Road 10 miles north of Thumier and might be waiting to plant a mine in the path of the down convoy from Dhala, B Coy was flown to the area by RAF Belvedere helicopter, and searched it without result. In parallel, the Mortar Section escorted by two Ferrets of 10th Royal Hussars deployed by road.

During that second week further patrols were carried out in the Battalion area, including a 36-hour one by a B Coy platoon west of Monk's Field. This level of operations probably accounted for no attacks on the Battalion's bases. Additionally, the RMO spent a great deal of time on 'hearts and minds' activities, providing medical treatment to local tribesmen and the villagers of Thumier.

After just a fortnight in the Radfan during which the Battalion had carried out fifty-nine night patrols/ambushes, it handed over to 2nd Battalion Coldstream Guards (2 Coldm Gds). On its penultimate night, at Thumier a B Coy patrol led by Sergeant Tony Sprason killed one dissident and injured another. C Coy returned to Aden by road on 16 March and to under command 1 R Anglian as its Reserve Company. The Battalion returned to Aden by road convoy on 17 March and re-established itself in Radfan Camp, reverting to under command Aden Brigade for IS duties in Aden. On 18 March, B Coy became the 1st Battalion's Reserve Company, and C Coy took over guards from 45 Cdo RM.

In the previous fortnight there had been a number of grenade-throwing incidents and minor explosions in Big Aden and Little Aden, including attacks on the oil pipelines. Almost coinciding with the Battalion's return to Radfan Camp, on the advice of ministers of the new Aden Government a significant change was made to the Security Forces' tactical posture, with foot patrols being withdrawn from the streets in an effort to stop them being the target for attack. This occurred two days before the 4th Battalion became Aden IS Battalion on 21 March, a role which it was on this occasion to hold for some four weeks. In outline, the Aden IS Battalion operated with four companies, rotating between tasks every three to five days. IS Company provided the IS Platoon at immediate notice and vehicle patrols (operating in pairs) based on the Aden Supply Depot, HMS *Sheba* (the RN shore base) and the Armed Police Barracks in Crater, and patrolling the Steamer Point, Ma'alla, Crater and Khormaksar areas. Guard Company provided the guards for Radfan Camp, Government House, Fort Morbut, HQ Aden Bde, the British Forces Broadcasting Service (BFBS) and the Aden Supply Depot. Reserve Company was at thirty minutes' notice in Radfan Camp, and on occasion had elements based at other locations. An Extra Reserve Company was provided by 1 R Anglian at four hours' notice in their barracks. The Bn CP was initially located at the Ma'alla Police Station. The Brigade Reserve Platoon was often based at the Aden Supply Depot. This otherwise tedious 1800 to midnight task was alleviated by the RAOC bakery there issuing steaming hot rolls at 2300 hours! HMS *Sheba* was also popular with the soldiers as they slept in proper beds there, had air-conditioning and were included in the rum ration.

On 22 March, the C-in-C MEC visited the Battalion. Later that week two off-duty soldiers of 2 Coldm Gds were injured by a grenade in Tawahi, a bazooka destroyed a Serviceman's car in the Ma'alla Straight, and there was an explosion in a transformer in RAF Khormaksar. The 4th Battalion's IS Coy deployed to the first incident. On 31 March, the Commissioner of Prisons was shot in Crater, and the Battalion assisted 1 R Anglian in imposing a curfew. Further grenade attacks occurred over the following days, including rockets fired at Servicemen's flats in the Ma'alla Straight, and grenades at the Tarshyne

Blocks of flats in the Ma'alla Straight. *N Patrick*

Officers' Mess and the Ma'alla Police Station (as a result of which the Bn CP was moved into HMS *Sheba* on 10 April). Reacting to these became the bread and butter of the IS Battalion.

Nevertheless, there was still time for some sport and socializing. Five-a side football was particularly popular. The Battalion Football Team was organized by the RSM, 'Jimmy' Jenks, captained by Orderly Room Colour Sergeant M J (Mick) Rigley and trained by Sergeant Instructor W Stoves APTC. In a friendly match, the team beat 1 R Anglian, the first sports encounter between two of the Regular battalions since the formation of the Regiment. Then, defeating 60 Coy RASC 7-1 and HQ 24 Inf Bde 4-0 en route, on 31 March, in 90° F and with armed guards patrolling the perimeter of the ground, it beat Command Ordnance Depot 4-1 in the final of the Army Middle East Football Cup. When off-duty, officers and soldiers made use of the beach facilities at Tarshyne, a secure area at Steamer Point, safe from the dissident threat and seawards caged-off from sharks. On 13 April, the officers held a cocktail party in the Officers' Mess in Singapore Lines, which was attended by some 130 guests, including the British High Commissioner. The Officers' Mess of the 1st Battalion was generous in its hospitality and various other resident units adopted elements of the 4th Battalion – for those few occasions when they had half a day off from operations. In addition, at the beginning of the tour, the Commanding Officer of the 1st Battalion had offered decent accommodation for one of the 4th Battalion's companies in his rather more amenable Waterloo Lines, a most generous gesture which was declined so as to keep the 4th Battalion unified in its desert Radfan Camp.

On 2 April, volunteers from the Territorial Army Emergency Reserve (TAER) – the 'Ever Readies' – joined the Battalion for a fortnight. Comprising one officer from 5/8 Foresters, nine soldiers from 4/5 R Leicesters and six from 4/5 Northamptons and 4/6 R Lincolns, they were attached to the rifle companies as individual reinforcements, and acquitted themselves very well.

Over the preceding months, the increasing level of terrorist threat in Aden was beginning to overstretch the available troops and to tie up the MEC Reserve Force, which needed to be reconstituted. Consequently, the Ministry of Defence agreed in March to reinforce Aden in April with a further infantry battalion. The two-company 1st Battalion The Royal Sussex Regiment (1 R Sussex), one of the two battalions stationed in Malta, was selected because it was available to complete a six-month unaccompanied tour before being posted from Malta at the end of the year. In early April, the 4th Battalion's Reserve Company had little rest as it was employed as a labour force to assist the Royal Engineers and the Assault Pioneer Platoon in doubling the size of Radfan Camp, in preparation for the arrival of the second Emergency Tour battalion.

It was about this time also that the operational posture of the Battalion changed in order to disrupt the movement of terrorists and weapons. Vehicle Checkpoints (VCPs) were set up at various key roundabouts and road junctions around the Battalion's area, and mobile patrols were more active in carrying out spot checks. For example, on 10 April, 314 vehicles and 1,004 people were searched at four VCPs, and forty-three vehicles and seventy people were searched by mobile patrols. During this period the VCP organization and methods continued to be developed. VCPs, of either a formal (i.e. semi-permanent) nature or 'snap' from vehicles, had become a major part of the Aden Brigade campaign against the terrorists. A number of good ideas and refinements to the Battalion's tactics came from those private soldiers whose job it was to man them night after night. In sharp contrast to the two or three coils of dannert wire that made a roadblock in Cyprus seven years before, lights, notices, fluorescent sleeves and battery operated aircraft handlers' wands were the standard equipment of a VCP in Aden. On one or two occasions, Arab soldiers from the FRA took over some of the VCPs from the Battalion and impressed everyone by their smartness and the way in which they carried out this, to them, strange task.

On 14 April, the Advance Party of 1 R Sussex arrived to share Radfan Camp. As it was only a month or so before that the 4th Battalion had been informed that on return to Watchet it would be posted to Malta on an accompanied tour of thirty months, it took the opportunity to glean much first-hand information about island life in the Central Mediterranean.

That same day – and somewhat disrupting the roster for IS Coy – C Coy (less one platoon) deployed by air to provide the infantry element for a fortnight at the garrison at Mukeiras. Some 50 miles east of Dhala on the Yemen Border in the Sultanate of Audhali, and at 7,000', the camp's garrison also included a field battery of 19 Fd Regt RA and a troop of 10th Royal Hussars Saladin armoured cars, a field troop RE and a platoon of the FRA. This important patrol base was a tented camp built by the Royal Engineers, who also spent much time keeping in serviceable shape the short airstrip, which could take a Beverley and helicopters. Its presence also provided support to the villagers of the town of Mukeiras, about 2 miles away. The Coy's role was to impede the movement of insurgents crossing the border from Yemen, to which successful end it patrolled vigorously and laid many night ambushes.

The other platoon of C Coy (10 Platoon under Lieutenant C P B (Chris) Keeble and Sergeant R E (Roger) Jones) and a mortar section, all under command of Captain Berty Bowes and the RQMS, WO2 George Veitch, was flown by an Aden Airways DC-3 the 200 miles west to Perim Island for a fortnight's tour of duty, reinforcing the small detachment

An RAF Belvedere landing at Mukeiras. *J R E Bowes*

of Aden Police. These 5 square miles of rocky and barren island rose to some 200 feet and had no natural water. Uninhabited until the nineteenth century when a desalinization plant was installed at what became a British coaling station, Perim Island was, in 1965, the site of a Diplomatic Wireless Service station, which beamed Western messages to the Arab world. The Platoon's task was to guard the station and prevent any hostile incursion onto the island, such as had occurred the previous week during another unit's guard duty when intruders burnt down a generator. Observation of the possible landing sites was somewhat easier to carry out with a few lookouts on the high ground by day, but by night it was hard work for everyone with constant patrolling of the shoreline. This commitment was also carried out over successive periods by 6 Platoon of B Coy (under Lieutenant A E (Andrew) Fisher and Sergeant A Benner), and A Coy's 2 Platoon (under 2nd Lieutenant Mike Charles and Sergeant S (Sam) Small) and 1 Platoon (under 2nd Lieutenant M E (Martin) Romilly and Sergeant A (Alex) Kerr).

On 21 April, HM The Queen's Birthday was celebrated by the Battalion with a short visit by the Bishop to the Forces, at which some 170 all ranks attended a short service. It was the first occasion on which was used the newly promulgated Regimental Collect (see Appendix D). That evening a Civil Police SB officer was shot dead in Crater and a rocket was fired into the married quarters' flats in Ma'alla. As a direct result, while the 1st Battalion was imposing a curfew in Crater, for four nights until 25 April, from 1830 to 2330 hours, 4th Battalion assisted the Police in imposing a curfew on part of Ma'alla. What was somewhat unnervingly reported by patrols on a number of occasions as incoming sniper fire, turned out to be the sound of small fire crackers which when left in the road detonated as a vehicle or foot passed over them. While these operations were in train, 1 R Sussex main body flew in from Malta and was complete in Radfan Camp on 23 April.

Meanwhile, in England, on 24 April the Deputy Colonel-in-Chief, HRH The Princess Margaret, Countess of Snowden, accompanied by the Earl of Snowden, paid a visit to the Rear Party and families at Watchet, where she was welcomed by the Acting Deputy Colonel, Lieutenant Colonel (Retd) Peter Upcher. The day was masterminded by Major Dick Graveston, OC Rear Party. The Deputy Colonel-in-Chief talked to many wives and children, and showed great interest in the Battalion's 1st Doniford Brownie and Cub packs, resplendent in the recently approved Tiger badges and led by the Mrs Colclough and Crutchley. It was members of Dick Graveston's team, supplemented by officers' and soldiers' wives who remained at Watchet, who visited, advised and generally looked after those families that needed help. The Battalion had good cause to remember with gratitude the efforts of so many of its wives during the three years disrupted by long unaccompanied postings.

Back in Aden, Big Aden was divided into three separate AORs: the 1st Battalion being allocated Crater, 1 R Sussex the area north of Radfan Camp, while the 4th Battalion's mission was to 'dominate Ma'alla and Tawahi'. These AORs were to remain until the end of the 4th Battalion's tour, though from time to time elements of each battalion reinforced the others. The 4th Battalion's standard deployment was along the following lines: one company less a platoon on guard duties; one company plus one or two platoons on IS operations; one company (sometimes less a platoon) away in one of the up-country stations; HQ Coy providing an ad hoc rifle platoon of about thirty men (mostly NCOs) at

Mrs N H P ('Jimmy') Jenks is presented to HRH The Princess Margaret. *Trustees R Leicestershire Regt*

about thirty minutes NTM. On the rare occasions that the third rifle company was wholly present, it was used either for IS operations or as a formal reserve.

Both the temperature and the operations hotted up. The Recce Platoon was used variously in some unconventional ways at the request of the Police Special Branch, and often dressed in civilian clothes. On occasion, overnight they patrolled the roofs of the Service married quarters' flats in Ma'alla, and by day strolled down the main thoroughfare in civilian clothes, carrying bathing trunks and towels in casually slung shoulder bags as if en route to the swimming pool at Steamer Point. The bags contained collapsed SMGs, which would be quickly assembled and put to use in the event of a daylight attack against the quarters or their occupants. Despite these and other undercover ruses, throughout the tour the Recce Platoon made no contact with any terrorist.

On 29 April, the GOC paid a short farewell visit to the Battalion in Radfan Camp and praised its activities, particularly the IS task in Ma'alla. On 3 May, three rockets were fired at the BFBS Building in Tawahi. That the attack was supported by small-arms fire, and white phosphorous grenades were thrown to cover the escape, indicated that the perpetrators were well trained and skilful. The following day a composite force of 1 Platoon A Coy and the Recce Platoons of the Battalion and 1 R Sussex, commanded by Captain F L B (Freddie) Vigers, swept the hillsides south of Ma'alla for possible hides and firing points. During that evening foot patrols were deployed on the streets for the first time for two months, and it was B Coy that provided them.

Mobile patrols and static guards remained the bread-and-butter operations. A 36 grenade was thrown at a mobile patrol of A Coy on 13 May in Ma'alla, which was followed by B Coy carrying out a cordon and search operation in the area two days later.

It may be wondered how the terrorists had such access to British munitions, notably hand grenades and anti-tank mines. The answer lay in the fact that when the British withdrew from Egypt in 1954 they left behind a large stockpile of munitions. With President Nasser actively supporting the communist cause in the Yemen, it was almost certain that Egypt was supplying Yemeni forces with the former-British resource, which was then used against the British in the Radfan and in Aden.

On 17 May, a 36 grenade was thrown at a C Coy mobile patrol in Tawahi. It bounced off the leg of Private K (Ken) Scotney who was lookout in the Land Rover, fell outside, and burst in the road, injuring an Arab. Scotney jumped out of the vehicle, and chased and captured his assailant, who was subsequently detained indefinitely under the Emergency Regulations. This particular act of alertness and initiative received the congratulations of the Bde Comd, and was cited as an example to all ranks in the Brigade. For this action, Scotney and the driver of the vehicle, Private D (David) Mogg, are among those listed later in this Chapter as being awarded a Regimental lanyard for their actions on the tour in Aden.

On 20 May, B Coy was detached to the Radfan, to be under command 2 Coldm Gds, whose HQ was at the newly named Habilayn. The inhabitants of Thumier village had objected to being associated with a British military base and so, in May, Thumier had been renamed Habilayn, after a nearby unoccupied hill. B Coy was replacing a Coldm Gds company which had been deployed in the MEC Reserve Force role to Mauritius to quell disturbances. Its role and conduct of operations was similar to that carried out by C Coy at Monk's Field in March, including manning permanent picquets on the hill tops at Cap Badge and Piccadilly. During its five weeks there, it carried out eighty-five night patrols/ambushes and over 100 day patrols. The Assault Pioneer Section under Corporal S (Stan) Barkby had to regularly check the route from Monk's Field to the waterhole and its surrounding area before the water bowser refilled. One of the most noteworthy events during B Coy's five weeks there was the incident in which Private K (Kenny) Ryder of Support Platoon was severely wounded. Shortly after 2200 hours on 11 June, an ambush led by Lieutenant Alan Thompson opened fire on four dissidents who were laying a mine. In the firefight that followed, Ryder was very severely wounded in the chest and abdomen by enemy grenade fragments. He was carried back under cover of mortar and artillery fire to Monk's Field, where he was kept alive through the night by the skill of the attached RAMC Lance Corporal. It was not until first light the next morning that a helicopter was able to reach Monk's Field and lift Ryder to hospital in Aden, where he survived; three weeks later he was evacuated to England and made a full recovery.

Back in Aden, on 22 May, a 36 grenade was thrown at an A Coy mobile patrol and exploded nearby injuring an Arab civilian. A week later, and four days after a short visit to the Battalion by the new GOC, Major General J E F Willoughby CB CBE, the Battalion Group carried out Operation *Icarus*, a large-scale cordon and search of all the local labour accommodation in the Steamer Point military area. This joint operation was commanded by the CO and involved a composite company of 4 R Anglian, two companies of 1 R Anglian, one company of 1 R Sussex, an RAF provost detachment, and six trooplift helicopters of the RN and RAF. The following day an RAF Dakota DC-7 was blown up by a bomb at RAF Khormaksar, and a day later a blindicide rocket was fired into the Service flats beside the Aden Supply Depot. Over the following days, in an effort to throw the NLF terrorists off balance, two further sizeable cordon-and-search operations were carried out. On 3 June, Operation *Straight Deal* sought out the blindicide rocket and its ammunition in the shanty town area of Ma'alla, with C Coy group providing the cordon and B Coy 1 R Sussex reinforced by two platoons of 1 R Anglian carrying out the search for over five hours. The physical temperature had risen also, with temperatures around 100° F, which made operations of that sort, with long periods standing in the sun, particularly unpleasant. On 4 June, with a similar aim and in a different part of Ma'alla, the 2IC commanded Operation *Butterfingers*, a night operation. The cordon was commanded by Major R E J (Dick) Gerrard-Wright[9], the new OC HQ Coy, and the search was carried out by a company of 1 R Sussex, while eight vehicle-mounted searchlights illuminated the area. Two grenades were thrown in Tawahi that night.

Meanwhile, a restructuring of nationalist forces was taking place that excluded the NLF. Initially the People's Socialist Party (PSP) and the South Arabian League formed a new movement called the Organisation for the Liberation of the Occupied South, a purely political entity. For its part, the NLF produced a charter dedicated to the expulsion of the British base in Aden, coupled with the destruction of the Federation of South Arabia and a merger with the Yemen Arab Republic. That, in conjunction with a continuance of violent terrorist activity, intimidation and strikes, led on 6 June to the High Commissioner declaring a State of Emergency in Aden State (for the internal security of which he had responsibility as it was a Crown Colony). The ensuing Emergency Regulations allowed the detention of suspects without trial for up to six months and the proscription of organizations believed to be engaged in subversion or terrorism. The NLF was duly proscribed. The previous day the GOC was appointed Security Commander, a new post designed to encourage greater cooperation between the two brigades, and also between government, the police, the intelligence community and all three Services.

Seemingly undeterred and unbowed, the NLF continued its attacks. Ten days later an explosion wrecked part of the dining room of the MEC Officers' Mess at Tarshyne, killing the bomber. On 20 June, the Battalion's IS Coy was closely involved in the follow-up search and arrest operations in the aftermath of an officer of 1 R Anglian chasing the car and catching the man who had thrown two grenades onto the patio of the Seamen's Club in Tawahi, which wounded seven people. This led to a complete enemy cell being rounded up and 'taken out of battle'.

B Coy returned to Aden from Monk's Field on 23 June and rejoined the IS Bn's roster. A platoon of the FRA was also attached to under command. Following two off-duty Servicemen being wounded by a grenade in Ma'alla the following day, on 26 June, in response to Police Special Branch information gained from a captured terrorist, B Coy took part in a very successful cordon and search of a house in Ma'alla. This resulted in the recovery of a pistol, ammunition, gelignite and other terrorist equipment. On 29 June, led by Captain Dick Robinson, a composite company executed Operation *Steel Helmet*, a dawn cordon and search in Ma'alla.

A week before, 1 Platoon A Coy deployed to the Yemen border at Mukeiras in a similar role to C Coy previously. Among other things while there, the Platoon engaged in that age-old 'soldierly' activity designed to build bridges with the locals: a football match against the team from Mukeiras village. That the Tigers' Platoon was leading 2-0 at half-time caused much consternation to the extent that some of the agitated local tribesmen began to fire their rifles into the air. A couple of diplomatic own goals led to the final score being 2-3, and the local supporters went away happy!

Also escaping the heat of Aden, for the whole of July, A Coy's Support Platoon (under Lieutenant B H M (Brian) Davenport and Sergeant R (Bob) Baker) was deployed to Al Milah, a tented camp occupied by a Field Squadron RE, two 105mm pack howitzers, a convoy escorting troop of 10th Royal Hussars Saracens, and a Sp Pl (provided on rotation by the brigades). The Platoon's role was to defend the Royal Engineers as they carried out road maintenance on the Dhala road. Each evening at Stand To, as elsewhere in the Radfan, a DF and HF 'fire plan' was fired, with the medium mortars firing HE and white phosphorous (WP) rounds and MOBATs firing HESH at the dissidents' likely avenues of approach. On one occasion the Platoon Commander's tent located beside the Command Post on top of the hill overlooking the main camp was demolished by a 'friendly' artillery shell, fired from a gun position in the main camp. The Gun Position Officer apologized that he hadn't quite got his crest clearance right!

July came, and with it the beginning of the last six weeks in Aden. As the temperature and humidity soared, so operations continued at a high pace, with platoons reacting to events with their customary verve and effectiveness. There was little time for recreation, yet some companies found time to climb Jebel Shamsan, not just to keep fit but because it was said that those who climb it would never return to Aden. A Coy climbed it three times during the tour, just to make sure! Presumably C Coy did not, as it was to return to Aden in early 1967 as is described in Chapter 6.

From the beginning of July, starting with the Advance Party that had left Aden on 29 June, as they were relieved by companies of 1 KOYLI, companies began to return to England and proceed on eight weeks' well-earned leave. Reflecting on the tour, as had been found in Borneo, the young soldiers and junior NCOs, in particular, grew up quickly. The days were very long and usually monotonous, but morale remained high. Everyone made the best of the not very good conditions in Radfan Camp, and learned to live with those restrictions on movement and life in general which IS operations always bring. 'Flexibility' had become the watchword. Platoons and companies learned to react to the unexpected (which had become the rule rather than the exception!) with great speed, energy and enthusiasm.

C Coy proved this perhaps as well as any on 16 August. The Commanding Officer had handed over operational command to 1 KOYLI, and 9 Platoon was in camp with no planned operational duties, and at no degree of notice. It was due to fly out to the UK the following day and therefore had packed all its uniforms. It had no weapons or equipment, these all having been handed over to 1 KOYLI. At 1930 hours, after a series of three incidents in Aden town, the Brigade Commander asked for this Platoon to be put at immediate notice. Within about forty-five minutes the whole Platoon was fully dressed in uniform, had drawn weapons, ammunition and radios, and was sitting in a vehicle ready to move. Everybody regarded this as a perfectly reasonable hazard of military life in the Battalion in Aden.

And so, on 17 August, the last elements of the Battalion left Aden after a very satisfactory tour. Moreover, it had been a pleasant experience to serve for six months in the same brigade as the 1st Battalion, the first such fruits of the Large Regiment and the operational comradeship (and rivalry) between its major components.

It is difficult to sum up the tour in any meaningful and objective way as to how successfully the Battalion took the fight to the enemy and at the same time sought to reassure locals by maintaining security. Some statistics give an indication of the level of activity. During the 117 days (21 April to 16 August) that the Battalion was responsible for Ma'alla and Tawahi, the level of violence did not increase. There were four rocket launcher and sixteen grenade attacks, six explosions caused by planted charges, one shooting and twelve occasions when arms and ammunition were recovered. For one eight-week stretch there were no incidents in Tawahi. Thirteen hundred half-platoon hours were spent on formal VCPs and over 550 platoon hours on foot patrol; nearly 10,000 vehicles and 37,000 persons were searched at formal VCPs, and over 4,000 vehicles and some 15,000 persons were searched at snap searches. The Battalion's vehicles' mileage was over 360,000 and petrol consumption was over 50,000 gallons.

Throughout, the men remained alert, self-confident, good-humoured and efficient. The junior leaders had great responsibility thrust at them daily – it was normal practice for a corporal (and sometimes even a lance corporal) to command a formal roadblock – and rose to the challenge. Overall the Battalion had grown in stature, gained in experience, and the youngsters had visibly matured. Its achievements are perhaps best summed up by the words of the Comd Aden Bde to the Commanding Officer: 'I have known The Tigers on and off for about a quarter of a century, but I have never known them in better form than they are at present.'

By their unstinting efforts, all ranks well earned the General Service Medal with clasp 'South Arabia' that was awarded to all who had spent thirty or more days in that theatre. Additionally, Regimental lanyards, in recognition of their work during the Aden tour, were awarded to Corporals Stan Barkby, C Brown and Riddle, Lance Corporals Barlow and V Moore, and Privates Conlon, David Mogg, Kenny Ryder and Ken Scotney. These were presented by the Deputy Colonel of The Regiment in November. After block leave the Battalion reassembled at Watchet on 12 October.

Notes

1 Alan Cowan had been awarded the MBE in 1956 as Military Assistant to VCIGS.
2 Peter Philcox had been awarded the MC while serving as a platoon commander in 1st Essex in Malaya in 1951.
3 'Romaika' is believed to be a Greek country dance tune and was authorized in 1882. '1772' was an adaptation from an old English air of that period. 'A Hunting Call' is an old Leicestershire hunting song, originally used by The Leicestershire Militia. 'General Monkton 1762' commemorates the seizure of Martinique that year, the British land force being commanded by Major General The Hon Robert Monkton, Colonel The 17th Regiment and of whose victorious force The 17th Regiment was part. 'Wolfe's Dirge' consists of a few bars as a lament to Major General James Wolfe; The 17th Regiment served in his Brigade at the siege of Louisburg in 1758 and its Grenadier Company was in his force when he was killed while seizing Quebec in 1759.
4 Of The Cheshire Regiment, John Cubbon had commanded 2/5th Leicesters in Italy and Greece from October 1944 to April 1945.
5 A true son of the Regiment, Graham Eustace's grandfather, Sergeant Harry Barratt, was wounded twice while serving in 2nd Leicesters in Mesopotamia in 1916, and his father Private Albert Eustace was killed while serving in 1st Leicesters in Normandy in 1944.
6 later Field Marshal Sir Roland Gibbs GCB CBE DSO MC, Chief of the General Staff 1976-79.
7 Jack Dye was awarded the OBE in January 1965 and the following year was promoted Brigadier to command the FRA until Independence in 1967, for which tour he was awarded the CBE. He and his successor in command of 1st R Anglian, Tim Creasey, were later successively to become Deputy Colonel and then Colonel The Royal Anglian Regiment.
8 Keith Burch had been awarded the MBE in January 1965 for his work as an SO2 in the War Office (MOD).
9 Dick Gerrard-Wright was awarded the MBE the following week for his previous work as BM of the East African Brigade in Kenya 1963-65.

Chapter 6

4th Battalion: Malta and Libya 1965-68

It was very early during the Aden tour in the summer of 1965 that the Battalion had received word that on return to Watchet it would be posted to Malta, on an accompanied tour of thirty months. This had been greeted with much joy and no little relief after the operational rigours and the disruption to family life caused by the two long unaccompanied tours in the previous three years. So, soon after reassembling at Doniford Camp in October after block leave, it was full steam ahead preparing for the move to Malta, to which the Advance Party under Major Terry Holloway set out on 2 November. Those weeks of preparation at Watchet were inevitably punctuated by a raft of senior visitors, but the Battalion was particularly pleased to welcome Major General J M K (John) Spurling CB CBE DSO[1]. Yet another distinguished Tiger officer, he had recently taken over the Leicesters' Deputy Colonelcy of The Royal Anglian Regiment from Major General Sir Douglas Kendrew, who since 1963 had been the Governor of Western Australia and, after two years abroad, considered that he could no longer carry out that Regimental duty effectively from so far away.

While the Battalion was in Aden, the Band had a busy time in England, among other things preparing for their inspection by the senior staff from the Royal Military College of Music. It played at the Suffolk Show and on 3 July played a fanfare and at lunch during the visit of the Colonel-in-Chief to Watford. Joined again with the Drums, it now prepared to display its considerable expertise to the people of Malta.

It was about this time that the new Royal Anglian Regiment stable belt was introduced, and the well-loved 3" wide red/pearl grey/black Royal Leicesters' one, with black leather side buckle, was confined to history in the Regular Battalion. The new belt – blue/red/yellow/red/blue striped – was 2¼" wide, and fastened with an unimposing 1938-style metal buckle at the front. Proud though the men may have been of its new colours, they never thought the same of the style.

A few words about Malta itself. It is 122 square miles in size and 17 miles from its north-west tip to the south-east corner. The capital is Valletta, with its impressive Grand Harbour built in the sixteenth century as the Knights of Malta's fortified base against the Ottoman Empire, and the population at the time was 98 per cent Roman Catholic. After a series of owners, Malta had become a British colony in 1814. In the Second World War the island was a crucial Allied base and was effectively besieged by the Axis Powers for three years, after which HM King George VI had awarded Malta the George Cross for its resilience, an accolade of which the population was justifiably immensely proud. After the granting – and rescinding – of various degrees of autonomy since 1887, Malta became autonomous again in 1947, and also became a key naval base for the British and US Mediterranean Fleets, and the location of HQ Allied Forces Southern Europe. Dominic 'Dom' Mintoff, head of the Maltese Labour Party, had been Prime Minister in the late 1950s, and in 1958 resigned over Britain's decision to cut aid. The Governor of Malta ruled directly until autonomy was restored in 1961, with Malta becoming fully independent in 1964, opting to remain in the British Commonwealth, and with a Governor-General as Head of State.

A year later 4th (Leicestershire) Battalion The Royal Anglian Regiment arrived to become part of the Garrison. This was The Tigers' third visit to the island. In 1855, four reserve companies of The 17th Regiment were stationed in Malta from where they passed men forward to the main body of the Regiment engaged in the Crimean War. They rejoined the main body as it put in to Malta in May 1856 en route to Canada. In 1919, 2nd Battalion The Leicestershire Regiment en route from England to India in TS *Moora* had an enforced stay of several months there after an outbreak of plague among the ship's Lascar crew.

The Main Body of the Battalion, together with the families, moved to Malta by air charter at the end of November, where it took over from 1st Battalion The Duke of Edinburgh's Royal Regiment. The Battalion was stationed in St Patrick's Barracks, near Ghargur (Victoria Lines) on the north side of the island. It was the northernmost of three barracks on that littoral, the others being St Andrew's (1st Battalion The Loyal Regiment (1 Loyals)) and St George's (Fortress Squadron RE). St Patrick's was dominated by its enormous four-storeyed, H-shaped main building (comprising accommodation, offices and stores) which faced north overlooking a terraced parade square and single sports pitch, and a series of rifle ranges whose range danger area extended several thousand yards out to sea. There were married quarters for officers and SNCOs nearby, though the majority of married personnel lived in hirings between the barracks and Sliema.

St Patrick's Barracks, Malta. *N Patrick*

The Battalion was organized similarly to that at Watchet, with an HQ Coy and three rifle companies (of two rifle platoons and a Support Platoon), plus, from the end of January, a small Training Company (T Coy) which conducted continuation training for new recruits, ran JNCO cadres and commanded the Recce Platoon. To reflect the increasing incidence of units being sent on unaccompanied tours, there was added to the Establishment of HQ Coy the new post of Unit Families Officer (UFO), the first incumbent being Major Peter Philcox. The Battalion's weapons were broadly the same. The anti-tank gun detachments were equipped with the 120mm WOMBAT, which were carried on ¾-ton Portee Land Rovers, and the mortar sections were equipped with the 81mm mortar. The rifle platoons were disappointed that their light machine gun was again the LMG Bren, though they retained the 84mm Carl Gustav anti-tank weapon which had been issued in Aden. Communication was provided by C42, A41, A40 (all VHF) and the WS62 and A13 (HF) radio sets. Vehicles were mainly Land Rovers and 3-ton lorries. As its command vehicle each HQ element had a 1-ton Humber armoured truck, nicknamed a 'Pig' on account of the shape of its bonnet.

The Battalion was part of Malta Garrison (under Brigadier Lord Grimthorpe OBE ADC), the other principal units being 1 Loyals, Fortress Squadron RE, 1st Regiment Royal Malta Artillery (1 RMA – which was partly a transport regiment) and 1st Battalion The King's Own Malta Regiment (1 KOMR), a TA battalion. Malta Garrison was in turn commanded by HQ Malta & Libya (under its GOC Major General J D Frost CB DSO MC), the other formations being HQ Cyrenaica Area and HQ Tripolitania Area, both in Libya. There was also a strong British RN and RAF presence in Malta.

On arrival in Malta, senior appointments were held as follows:

CO:	Lieutenant Colonel J A C Cowan MBE	CSM B Coy:	WO2 A W Buxton
		OC C Coy:	Major F A Godfrey MC[2]
2IC:	Major T Holloway	CSM C Coy:	WO2 J Pearce
Adjt:	Captain R H Robinson	OC T Coy:	Captain W H Morris
RSM:	WO1 N H P Jenks MM	CSM T Coy:	WO2 L MacDonald
QM:	Captain N McColl	OC HQ Coy:	Major R E J Gerrard-Wright MBE
Tech QM:	Captain E P Kelly DCM		
RQMS:	WO2 R E Sprason	CSM HQ Coy:	WO2 A Hill
OC A Coy:	Major K Burch MBE	FLO:	Major P L Philcox MC
CSM A Coy:	WO2 G Wood	Bandmaster:	WO1 J E Battye ARCM
OC B Coy:	Major P Worthy	Drum Major:	Sgt T R West

The Battalion expected to find life on Malta similar to that in a quiet military backwater where nothing much happened and where it could recharge its batteries after the rigours of the previous few years, in a gentle post-colonial setting in warm weather. The opportunity was to be grasped to refashion Regimental life, train the JNCOs (over fifty of whom had had no course training), close the gaps in the professional training of the private soldiers and train up men for the specialist platoons, play plenty of sport and engage in other extra-mural activity, and provide time for family life together. Part of the last-mentioned expectation changed as the Battalion settled in to celebrate Christmas, after the early visits by the GOC and by the Garrison Commander. As St Patrick's Barracks was in the throes of a year-long refurbishment of accommodation, it could not concurrently accommodate a full battalion. Therefore, one rifle company was deployed to a former Royal Marines training camp at Ghajn Tuffeiha some 8 miles further north-west up the coast. It was a stone-built, single-storeyed camp, with its own rifle range, and training and battle shooting area. The deployment of a company there (and first to bat was A Coy) further stretched the travelling distances and time for married soldiers on the PORPOD (Place of Residence Place of Duty) transport at opening and close of each working day; but the single soldiers were near some pleasant beaches and villages. Christmas came and went, accompanied by the traditional round of seasonal activities. This included the Officers vs Sergeants football match. Appropriately attired, the latter team arrived riding on two single-horsepowered karozzini, while the Officers were conveyed on a 'des car', a 3-ton lorry specially designed as a desert troop carrier. Sad to relate, Private Shuckford of HQ Coy died on 2 January from injuries sustained after falling out of a window.

The representational side of life also began in mid-January with the Officers' Mess holding its official welcoming cocktail party, to which some 260 guests were invited. It was

Officers on a three-ton Desert Car. *J E Tilley*

the largest and most lavish the Mess had held for many years, and the guests' enjoyment was apparent by their late departure.

That the Battalion expected to have many months' relative lack of domestic turbulence was further dispelled when it immediately proved necessary to deploy a rifle company unaccompanied to Libya.

Libya was a country of 680,000 square miles, the vast majority being uninhabited gravel plain and rolling sand. The population of almost four million was 97 per cent Muslim, the legacy of its rule by the Ottoman Empire from the sixteenth century. Libya had become an Italian protectorate in 1911, but it had not been until the mid-1930s that Fascist Italy annexed Tripolitania, Fezzan and Cyrenaica into a single entity. During the Second World War Libya had been the scene of much heavy and strategically important fighting between the Allies and the Axis powers until the latters' defeat there in 1943. After a short period of Franco-British administration, after a UN decision, Libya had become an independent monarchy in 1951, with the Sanussi leader ascending the throne under the name King Idris I. Oil had been found in Libya, and Britain and the USA used airfields as alternative staging posts to the East, in combination with small garrisons and the use of training areas. The King conducted a nationalist policy, which aimed at the evacuation of all foreign troops from Libya, a situation which pertained in 1966.

Before Christmas, 9 Platoon of C Coy deployed for three months to Benghazi (400 miles south-east of Malta) as part of the Garrison there. The balance of the Company deployed to Tripoli (200 miles south of Malta) at the end of January for two months. Accommodated

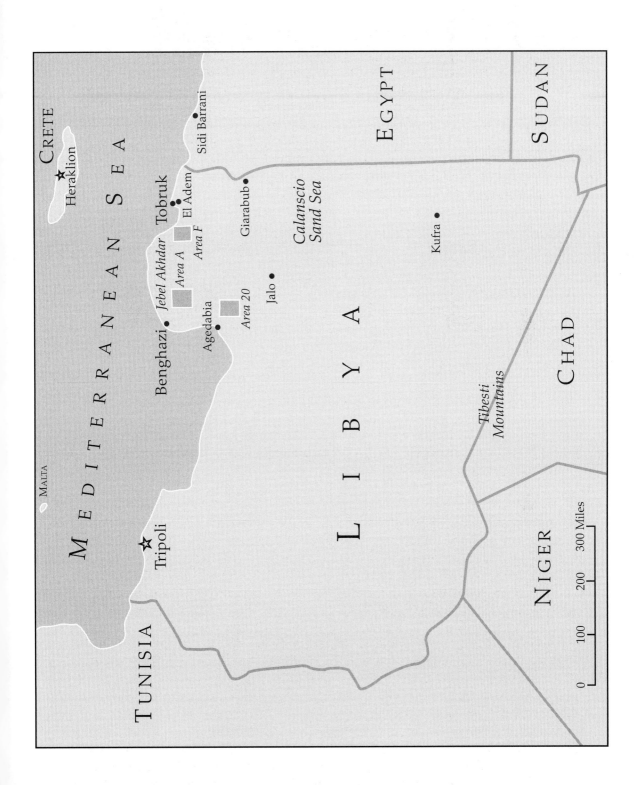

in the Ordnance Depot barracks, its role was to assist in the close-down of Tripoli Garrison. Apart from the occasional culture trip to see the remains of the ancient Roman ruins of Leptis Magna (now a UNESCO World Heritage Site), the soldiers provided guards and security, and worked like Pickfords to remove all stores and equipment out of the various offices and barracks into central locations, either loading them onto ships or making them ready for handover to the Libyan Army. Whatever, the routine was generally 'conducting an evacuation of the Empire'. The Company was stationed not far from the US Wheelus Airbase, where one of the USAF's disc jockeys went by the unlikely name of Herman T Shagnasty! The Tigers seemed to get on relatively well with their American cousins. There was no repeat of the politico-strategic falling out over the Suez Invasion ten years before, although things did get a little strained when a soldier purloined the Airbase Commander's Cadillac staff car, was saluted when he drove out of the gates and later abandoned the car!

That pattern of garrison duties in Libya, and companies carrying out exercises and Battalion-level training there once or twice a year, meant that on average the rifle companies were to be away from Malta unaccompanied for some four months a year.

At the end of March, British troops left Tripolitania, and C Coy returned to Malta. In tandem, the British military presence in Cyrenaica commensurately increased, and a rifle company from Malta was added to the Garrison at Benghazi. Its role was the protection of British and US civilians in the event of anti-Western hostilities. Under command of HQ Cyrenaica Area (Colonel A J S Martin OBE), the other teeth arm elements were the armoured car regiment, 5th Royal Inniskilling Dragoon Guards (5 Innis DG – 'the Skins') and an infantry company at El Adem – furnished by the Battalion from Gibraltar – which was collocated with the RAF staging post there. A Coy was sent there to D'Aosta Barracks[3] in Benghazi in March, as usual on a three-month tour of duty. At the entrance was a simple stone monument 'In glorious memory of the 1942 British Libyan Campaign conducted by the 8th British Army under General Sir Bernard Montgomery – the Dawn of Victory'. Such unaccompanied tours to Benghazi were to be a feature of Battalion life over the remaining

Entrance to D'Aosta Barracks, Benghazi. *M K Goldschmidt*

two years, that roster being shared between the two Malta battalions, 4 R Anglian and 1 Loyals. Immediately on its arrival in Benghazi, A Coy conducted a full IS turnout, drawing all its stores and first-line ammunition, and a recce of its operational tasks in the town, on Easter Saturday. This caused some consternation among the HQ Staff and the supply units – not least because all the vehicles were drawn up on the cricket ground – but it was a clear sign to all concerned that A Coy meant business in what otherwise might have been perceived a rather sleepy backwater.

Through those deployments to Benghazi a very good rapport was gained with 5 Innis DG, stationed nearby at Wavell Barracks; hospitality offered there was reciprocated in full when men of 'the Skins' visited Malta for Study Days, Skill-at-Arms Meetings, courses or leave. The other great advantage for the Company based in Benghazi was the easy access to be gained to the extensive training areas. Area 'A' was 80 miles away to the east, in the gravel plain and flattish 'desert' south of the Cyrenaican 'Jebel Akhdar' hills, and traversed by 'numerous small sebkhas' ('dried-up water courses', as the otherwise almost blank maps described part of the terrain). Moving by road from Benghazi to those areas was a much simpler activity than deploying the whole Battalion by sea and air from Malta.

Back in Malta, B Coy proceeded to march to Ghajn Tuffeiha to take over A Coy's former accommodation and caused quite a sensation as the Band and Drums led it through St Paul's Bay, the citizens of which were not used to such a display of pomp. The companies were conducting low-level military training, together with sport on which a great deal of emphasis was being placed after several years in the wilderness. At the end of January, a Command Post Exercise (CPX), *First Footing*, had been held, to test the Battalion and Company command structures on their respective radio nets. Captains Bill Morris and Anthony Swallow organized a Study Day, covering Malta's distinguished history and the Siege of 1565. Apart from being highly entertaining and informative for the officer and SNCO audience, it was very popular with those local people in Malta who were invited to participate, and it helped to build good relationships. Separately, several of the Battalion's officers were among the hundred or so from the Command who travelled by air and LSL to Gaeta in Italy, from where for two days they took part in a study of the Battle of Monte Cassino in 1943, and how it might have been fought with 1966's weapons and tactics.

Building on the accomplishments of those who had won the Middle East Land Forces Cup in Aden in March 1965, the Football Team, under the management of RSM 'Jimmy' Jenks, captained by Orderly Room Colour Sergeant Mick Rigley, and trained by Sergeant W (Bill) Stoves APTC, made a great impact. After success in the early rounds of the Army Cup while still at Watchet, the Team was permitted to remain in the competition if it played all subsequent matches in the UK and the players travelled to and from England at private expense. The RAF obliged by providing indulgence flights at £1-10s-0d per person – by Comet! In January the Team beat 1st Bn The Somerset & Cornwall Light Infantry 4-1 in the 3rd Round and 38 Regt RE 3-1 in the Quarter-Final. After a week back in Malta, they set out again for England. Having beaten the fancied 1st Bn The Lancashire Fusiliers 5-1 in the Semi-Final, on 2 March they were unlucky to meet a very proficient 24 Signal Regt in the Final and, playing below their form in previous matches, lost 0-3. To reach the UK Final was an outstanding achievement, the first such occasion since 1927 when 2nd Bn The Leicestershire Regiment won the Army Cup[4], having been Runners-Up in 1926. Tremendous support was given both in Malta and from many friends in the Regiment

UK Army Cup Finalists (see Appendix P for names). *Trustees R Anglian Regt*

whilst the Team was in England, including those at the Depot in Bury St Edmunds where the Team was based for a few days before each match. Thereafter, the Team discovered that the Maltese season had not quite finished and won the Services 6-a-Side Championship, in the Final beating the self-styled kings of Malta, RAF Luqa, a success which went some way to offset the disappointment of defeat in the UK Army Final.

Other Battalion sports teams made an early impact on the playing fields of Malta. The Rugby Team reached the final of the 7-a-Sides, and Lieutenant R (Roger) Howe, Lance Corporal A ('Waqa') Waqairoba and Private C (Charlie) Dutton played for the Army Malta and Combined Services teams. The Hockey Team, led by Lieutenant D W (David) James, who also captained the Army Malta XI, was one of the strongest teams on the island. The Cross-Country Team, led by Captain P B J (Peter) Carr RAPC, by the end of February provided the first two teams in the Malta Army Championships (in which Corporal N (Neil) Patrick won the individual event), provided six out of the eight in the Army Malta Team, and won the Malta AAA Championships against civilian and Service teams. In parallel with football, cross-country was the Maltese national sport. Go-karting began to take off and rapidly expanded to some fifteen drivers who, led by the MTO Captain J E (John) Tilley, with some success took part in the Inter-Services League. Improbably, one of the cooks serving with A Coy in Benghazi was flown back to Malta for an important table tennis match!

At the conclusion of his tenure as Commanding Officer, on 23 March 1966, Alan Cowan was presented with a silver tiger by the officers, warrant officers and sergeants as a token of appreciation for all that had been achieved by the Battalion while under his command. The contribution of Jennifer Cowan, particularly when the men were abroad on active service, had also been held in high esteem and was to be long remembered. On 6 April, Alan Cowan handed over command to Lieutenant Colonel D R C (David) Carter, most of whose previous career had been spent in the Bedfordshire & Hertfordshire part of the Regiment. A very warm welcome was extended to him and his wife Jean, and they both quickly settled into the Tiger family. His philosophy was simple: Malta is a peacetime posting; train as far as is possible on the island and make a greater effort when on deployment on exercise in Libya; combine these with maximizing the sporting and recreational facilities provided in Malta, with no sports team being expected to be successful unless it trains in Army time.

On 19 April, the Battalion was visited by the British High Commissioner, Sir John Martin KCMG CB CVO (for whom for a year the Battalion provided Captain D E A (David) Michael as ADC[5]). He watched many aspects of training, and appeared somewhat disconcerted when a company demonstration of riot control included the raising of a banner which declared in English and Maltese the time-honoured warning 'Disperse or we will fire'. He did not want the Maltese to know that that might be the Battalion's role so thereafter all such training was carried out with blank banners.

Lt Col Alan Cowan, last CO 1 R Leicesters and first CO 4 R Anglian. *Mrs J A C Cowan*

After a second CPX and a Study Day devoted to 'Advance and Attack in the Desert', the Battalion moved to Libya in early May for three weeks' field training. The aim of Exercise *Dry Fly* was to practise a sea-and-air move to North Africa and to operate in the desert. Using a Landing Ship Tank (LST) and RAF Transport Command's aircraft via Benghazi's sea and airports, the Battalion moved to a Concentration Area in the north-west of Area 'A', where it was joined by A Coy from Benghazi, which had recently conducted its first desert training when it acted as enemy to 1 Loyals on Exercise *Dust Cap*. Thereafter it prepared a defensive position for four days, which was followed by a week's company training, and concluded with a two-sided exercise controlled by the GOC. The exercise proved to be of great value as it was the first limited war training conducted by the Battalion for two years. It was also the first occasion when various elements had the opportunity to become skilled in the use of the sun compass. Area 'A', with the ruined Fort Msus near its centre, had been the scene of several armoured battles during the Second World War as the opposing forces had strived to outflank the other south of the Jebel Akhdar. Burnt-out vehicles, rusty jerry cans and other detritus of the battlefield were often found, but mercifully no unexploded mines – at least not in that part of Libya.

Meanwhile, back in England, Major General John Spurling, the Deputy Colonel, accompanied by Colonel G J German DSO TD, Honorary Colonel 4/5th Battalion The Royal Leicestershire Regiment (TA), presented to the Deputy Colonel-in-Chief, HRH The Duchess of Gloucester, a 'Tiger' brooch from all ranks of the 4th Battalion and of The Royal Leicestershire Regiment.

On return from Libya, the Battalion's training focus turned to athletics and to ceremonial drill in preparation for the Queen's Birthday Parade on 11 June. The Garrison Parade was held on the main square at St Patrick's Barracks, commanded by the Garrison Commander. Resplendent in No. 3 Dress, the Battalion provided the Colour Party, C Coy as No. 1 Guard, and the Band and Drums combined with those of 1 Loyals as a massed band. The GOC took the salute. In Benghazi, A Coy provided No. 4 Guard on the Queen's Birthday Parade of 5 Innis DG, where the salute was taken by Commander Cyrenaica Area.

The previous week the Battalion Inter-Company Athletics meeting was held – as were all major sports meetings – at the Marsa Stadium. HQ 1 was the Champion Company and Sergeant Instructor W (Bill) Stoves APTC was the outstanding athlete. On 14 June, at the Garrison Athletics Meeting, the Battalion Team won the team championship and its members won eight out of the fifteen events (SI Bill Stoves winning the Long Jump and Javelin) and took second place in all but one of the others.

David Partridge of the *Leicester Mercury* paid a two-week visit to the Battalion in June, including travelling to Benghazi and the training areas. He subsequently published a series of perceptive and interesting articles about life in the sun.

The water-ski boat, 'Tiger', was purchased for the Battalion by the Nuffield Trust. Having had four coxwains trained at the Garrison Club, it was ready for use from July. Every afternoon it could be seen speeding through St George's Bay towing one of the increasing number of expert mono-skiers, or weaving backwards and forwards picking up one of the beginners who had taken a tumble. Early morning (pre-First Parade) skiers also became increasingly apparent.

Following the Commanding Officer's ethos, the Battalion Rowing Team had been training for several months, with the fitness side being seen to by SI Bill Stoves and the technical rowing by Lieutenant A E (Andrew) Fisher. It crewed a clinker-built gig with fixed seats, six oarsmen and a cox. Being 'new boys' to the sport, the gig was borrowed. The annual Malta Command Boat Race was one of the sporting highlights of the year in Malta and taken very seriously by the Maltese. It was rowed over one nautical mile in Valletta's Grand Harbour on 12 July, and was watched by very large crowds lining the battlements. The Battalion Team was an unknown quantity and pitted itself against four other crews, including the much-fancied local favourites, 1 KOMR (TA). Rowing into a strong headwind the Tigers' strength was a telling factor; they moved into the lead at the three-quarters mark and held on to win a thrilling race by one length. This was a remarkable achievement and the first time a British infantry team had won since 1924. The triumphant team was: Sgt Tony Sprason (cox), Lieutenant Andrew Fisher (stroke), Sergeant Tim Elliott, Corporal Rick Whitcombe, Drum Major Ray West, Corporal Malcolm Tyler and SI Bill Stoves (bow). All were awarded the 'Green Tiger', probably the first ever for the sport of rowing.

After a third training exercise in the desert on Exercise *Second Thoughts*, at the end of June A Coy returned to Malta. The need for an infantry company in Benghazi having diminished, it was replaced by 6 Platoon of B Coy under Lieutenant Andrew Fisher. In mid-July, the three Support platoons, commanded by Lieutenants Mike Peele, David James and Chris Keeble, left Malta by LST for Benghazi to take part in the Command Support Weapons Concentration in Area 'A', and the following month C Coy went to Cyrenaica for two weeks' company training in the same place, while the Recce Platoon under Lieutenant

G A (Graham) Barrett went further east to Area 'F' for a fortnight. In July also, Lieutenant Andrew Dexter led a party of twelve men to Sicily. Travelling out from Malta by Army launch, they carried out canoeing and cross-country movement on foot, en route to climb the 11,000' active volcano, Mount Etna. They returned to Malta by US Navy aircraft as the sea was too rough for the launch to set sail.

With the whole Battalion (bar one platoon in Benghazi) unusually all at home in Malta, preparations were put in train for the visit at the end of August of the Lord Mayor of Leicester, and its attendant activities. The day before it, the Deputy Colonel arrived for a coincidental five-day visit. The Lord Mayor, Councillor Mrs Monica Trotter, arrived on 30 August and embarked on a busy programme, the centrepiece of which was a Battalion Parade on 1 September – Royal Anglian Day.

On that parade, with some 700 all ranks dressed in No. 3 Dress, the Lord Mayor paid the Battalion the very great honour of conferring on it the Freedom of the City of Leicester. To mark the occasion she presented it with the framed document of the Council's resolution[6] and with the City's magnificent gift of a new set of banners for the fanfare of seven trumpets originally donated to the Regiment by the City and County of Leicester in 1952. These new banners were embroidered with the badge of The Royal Anglian Regiment. In her moving and heartfelt address to the Battalion, she spoke of the very close ties between the City of Leicester, the County of Leicester and their County Regiment. Noting the links with The Royal Leicestershire Regiment which had received the Freedom in 1944, she stressed that:

> Those who felt that, as a consequence of amalgamation, the British Infantry Regiments would never be the same again must now know that there has been no severance of association: indeed, my presence here today is witness to that fact. I would assure all ranks of this Battalion that the people of Leicester and County still regard you all as their own Regiment, and look forward to even closer association with you in the coming years.

The March Past which followed showed in the excellence of its drill and dressing the pride the Battalion had in parading before its Lord Mayor.

That afternoon a popular fête was held on the Square which concluded with the Band and Drums performing Beating Retreat in magnificent style in front of a very large crowd of appreciative onlookers. The memorable day concluded with a Ladies' Guest Night in the Officers' Mess. Over the next couple of days the Lord Mayor toured the Battalion and watched various military activities, making the most of the opportunity of meeting all members of the Battalion and their families in a series of engagements which showed her all aspects of battalion life in Malta. On her departure, after a memorable visit, the Commanding Officer expressed to her the hope that the Battalion could exercise its newly granted Freedom at an early opportunity on its return to UK.

In early September, 5 Platoon (2nd Lieutenant S M (Shaun) Brogan) assumed the Garrison Security Platoon role in Benghazi, these tours of duty having been reduced to two months in order to reduce the length of unaccompanied absence from Malta. The Battalion deployed again to Libya, by LST and RAF air transport to Tobruk and El Adem respectively, for training in Area 'F'. The first phase of this exercise, *Desert Frost*, comprised the Battalion taking up a defensive position about a mile from the coast, to be attacked after a beach landing by 6th Bn 2nd Regt US Marine Corps (USMC) of the US Sixth Fleet. To widen the training value, C Coy 4 R Anglian swapped sides with H Coy of the Marines. After some familiarization training on the USS *Mountrail* in Grand Harbour, C Coy subsequently embarked on that ship off the Libyan coast. The US intelligence briefing indicated that the 4 R Anglian defending forces were 'a battalion of seasoned veterans', which in the light of its recent operational experience in Borneo and Aden it probably was, and it was gratifying to learn that the Americans recognized it.

During the dawn assault C Coy landed in the first wave of landing craft, preceded only by a USMC company in tracked amphibious vehicles. With the rifle platoons safely on dry land, C Coy then succeeded in getting all its vehicles ashore without one being 'drowned', a rather better success rate than the more experienced Marines. The US Battalion then advanced several miles inland, harried from the flanks by 4 R Anglian and an armoured car squadron of 5 Innis DG. That tactical phase was a good one and it was a change to hear Americans praising British equipment. Theirs was obviously not really suited to desert operations and the difference was noticeable. They also rather liked the British rations, tins of peaches going down particularly well.

The second phase of the exercise comprised companies carrying out platoon training deeper into the desert, and the USMC's support weapons were grouped with the Battalion's for live firing. In a subsequent combined British/American anti-tank gun shoot, Lance Corporal F (Frank) Ralph of A Coy's Support Platoon won the prize when his crew hit the target with his opening shot, before anyone else did.

The end of a memorable exercise was marked by a monumental deluge of which the Mean Point of Impact was Bn HQ and the Administrative Area. B and C Coys suffered too as flash floods flowed down some 'not so dried-up' sebkhas, while A Coy – the environmentally astute ones on the higher ground – looked on in some amusement. As the rain clouds threatened, the Americans had been advised by their hosts to move to higher ground, yet had ignored the warning. They too were flooded out and a certain amount of US 'loot' was readily bagged further down the sebkha.

On the Battalion's return to Malta, the sports teams embarked on their winter season. On 15 October, the Band and Drums performed a magnificent Beat Retreat under floodlights on the Palace Square in Valletta in front of a large and appreciative audience. In parallel, there was a concerted effort to train the Shooting Team for the Command Skill-at-Arms Meeting the following week. This paid off most handsomely as, led by 2nd Lieutenant Michael Goldschmidt, the Battalion was the Champion Major Unit and won the Rifle, LMG, SMG and Pistol team competitions, a distinguished performance. At the end of the month, 7 Platoon (2nd Lieutenant R H (Robert) Pepper) assumed the Garrison Security Platoon role in Benghazi.

As ever, Malta was a popular place for visits and visitors. Colonel P E B Badger[7], the new Regimental Colonel The Royal Anglian Regiment, visited the Battalion for four days, during which he addressed the officers about career structure within the Large Regiment. In November, the Battalion hosted a BBC (Midlands) Radio team for ten days as it compiled a programme featuring Service life in Malta and Libya. The Garrison Commander visited A Coy at Ghajn Tuffeiha. On 18 November, Monsignor Gonzi, the Metropolitan Archbishop of Malta and one of the shorter prelates, visited the Battalion where he was greeted by a Guard of Honour, inadvertently comprising the tallest men. Four days later seven members of a trade mission from the Leicester & County Chamber of Commerce dropped in during their important visit to explore Malta's potential.

Remembrance Sunday was commemorated at a Drumhead Service in St Patrick's Barracks, attended by large contingents from 4 R Anglian and 1 Loyals and smaller contingents from other Army units. The Band and Drums provided the music and the Commanding Officer commanded the parade, which marched past the Garrison Commander. In parallel, C Coy had been warned off for a two-month posting to Aden in January and embarked on special training for that, while the remainder of the Battalion got itself into good order for the GOC's Adminstrative Inspection, held on 6 December. The day's programme began with a full-blown parade during which all the companies marched past in slow and quick time, whereafter the GOC toured barracks and various activities laid on by the companies. In a letter the following day to the Commanding Officer, the GOC wrote, 'I was extremely pleased with the high standards pertaining everywhere, and I know that I and my successor have every reason to have great faith in your ability to meet all the calls that could be made upon you.' From those sentiments it was reasonably assumed that all had gone well!

Christmas passed and was again celebrated by the traditional round of seasonal activities. Just before New Year, 2 Platoon of A Coy (2nd Lieutenant R (Robin) Wright) assumed the Garrison Security Platoon role in Benghazi.

At the beginning of 1967, senior appointments were held as follows:

CO:	Lieutenant Colonel D R C Carter	OC C Coy:	Major F A Godfrey MC
2IC:	Major A F F H Robertson	CSM C Coy:	WO2 J Pearce
Adjt:	Captain A J G Pollard	OC Sp Coy:	Major C T Marshall
RSM:	WO1 N H P Jenks MM	CSM Sp Coy:	WO2 L MacDonald
QM:	Captain E P Kelly DCM	OC HQ Coy:	Major R E J Gerrard-
Tech QM:	Lieutenant J Eyeions		Wright MBE
RQMS:	WO2 R E Sprason	CSM HQ Coy:	WO2 A Hill
OC A Coy:	Major K Burch MBE	FLO:	Major P L Philcox MC
CSM A Coy:	WO2 I Marjoram	Bandmaster:	WO1 J E Battye ARCM
OC B Coy:	Major P Worthy	Drum Major:	Sgt T R West
CSM B Coy:	WO2 A W Buxton		

On 14 January, C Company deployed to Aden for two months to assist in the security of the airfield and installations at RAF Khormaksar, in the face of the increasing level of terrorist activity in what was to be the final year of British rule. By January 1967, two rival factions (the National Liberation Front (NLF) and the Front for the Liberation of South Yemen (FLOSY)) were as much fighting each other, to establish positions of power when the British departed at the end of November, as they were fighting British troops.

The cynics said that this second Aden stint was a punishment for C Coy for not having climbed Jebel Shansam on the 1965 tour! Whatever, the Coy knuckled down to all the various tasks required of it. Working in conjunction with the RAF Regiment, its men guarded married quarters, and carried out snap cordon and searches and VCPs on the Causeway; patrolling by helicopter they swooped down and searched unsuspecting Arabs' motor cars, guarded the numerous aircraft and acted as guards for aircraft flying upcountry. At that time, the most-requested tune on BFBS Radio was Tom Jones's 'Green, green grass of home', which well summed up the mood of all the Service personnel in the final year of their presence in Aden and South Arabia. On 16 March, on one of the very few occasions on which the Company was required to support the 3rd Battalion in Sheikh Othman, a grenade was thrown at its eight-man foot patrol, wounding Private Mileham in the nose and much more seriously Private Michael Smith in the leg and arm, as a result of which he was subsequently invalided out of the Army. C Company returned to Malta on 25 March.

The previous year, a company of 2 R Anglian from Cyprus had also carried out the similar Khormaksar role. From October 1966 to June 1967, 3 R Anglian were at Radfan Camp in Aden for eight months on an arduous tour, with responsibility for the lawless town of Sheikh Othman (not nearly as 'cushy' as the Khormaksar security role). Thus, in the course of two years all four Regular battalions of the Regiment had served with distinction in Aden, had endured their baptisms of fire under their new name and by their conduct had displayed the time-honoured pride in their Regiment.

As a tailpiece to Aden, in fulfillment of its promise to hand over Aden by 1968, British Forces finally withdrew at the end of November 1967. In response to 'Western' involvement in the Arab/Israeli War of June 1967, the Armed Police in Aden had mutinied. The NLF had already gained control of the former Aden Protectorates soon after the last British troops had withdrawn to Aden at the end of June. The Federal Government singularly failed to reconcile the differences between the 'upcountry' tribal Protectorates and the political forces in Aden, and proved themselves unable (and unwilling) to form a post-Independence government. In early November, the South Arabian Army (as the Federal Regular Army had been renamed) declared its support for the NLF, and on 13 November, the British Government agreed to negotiate with the NLF for the handover. At midnight on 29 November, South Arabia became independent.

The rival factions in the NLF ruled South Arabia for three years and in 1970 the fledgling state was renamed the People's Democratic Republic of Yemen (PDRY). In 1990, the PDRY united with its northern neighbour, the Yemen Arab Republic, to form the Yemen Republic.

Back in Malta, on 10 January 1967, B Coy left Malta by LSL and air for Benghazi for a three-week training period, Exercise *Fresh View*, in Area 'A' in Cyrenaica. On 20 January, Private A Kirton, a new recruit who had only arrived in Malta the day before, died from injuries sustained falling 80 feet down a wall in Valletta Harbour. He was subsequently buried with full military honours in the Pembroke Military Cemetery.

On 24 January, WO1 R E (Ron) Sprason assumed the appointment of RSM. He was to be the last of a long line of distinguished Royal Leicesters to hold that appointment. On the same day, the British Government announced its proposals for the rundown of British Forces in Malta, which caused much dismay, particularly over the future of the 8,000 Locally Employed Civilians who would lose their jobs. The Battalion began preparation for any emergency and A Coy selected a Standby Platoon. In retaliation for the British Government's intentions, on 29 January, the Maltese Government withdrew the 'duty free' supplies to British Forces – as a direct result of which the cost of a bottle of wine consumed in the various messes increased from 11d to a shilling and thrupence! Maltese dock workers refused to handle any stores or property of Service personnel and two days later the General Workers Union stated that strikes would take place without warning. In response, plans were put in place for troops to replace civilian labour, and 14,000 composite rations, together with quantities of water-filled jerry cans and petrol, were stockpiled in St Patrick's Barracks, all of which required guarding. Restrictions were then placed on the use of military transport. This 'Crisis' continued until 13 March, when the military restrictions were lifted and life returned to normal. It should be stressed that relations between servicemen and the Maltese population were unimpaired throughout, an enduring state of affairs which is well summed up by an extract from the 4th Battalion's notes in the Spring 1967 Royal Tigers' Association Newsletter, which read:

> We and our families are fortunate in being here in Malta, for nowhere else does the British soldier enjoy the friendliness and hospitality of the local population as we do with the Maltese. So that whilst it is refreshing to get away into the desert at frequent intervals, it is always pleasant returning to this civilised island. Eighteen local marriages to Maltese girls to date is testimony of their popularity!

On 26 January, on the arrival of Major General A R Leakey DSO MC as the new GOC Malta & Libya, the Guard of Honour at the Castile was provided by A Coy and commanded by Major Keith Burch.

On 13 February, A and T Coys moved to Benghazi by LST for field training in Area 'A'. They returned on 2 March, leaving behind 1 Platoon (Lieutenant M K (Michael) Goldschmidt) to take over the Garrison Security Platoon role in Benghazi.

Despite all the other military activities, sport continued to thrive. A Coy having won the Inter-Company Cross-Country at the beginning of the month, a particularly-talented Battalion Team travelled to Cyprus in mid-January where they were narrowly defeated by 2 R Anglian in the Near East Championships. Back in Malta, at the end of the month the sixteen runners in its two teams filled the first sixteen places in the Garrison Championships and Corporal Neil Patrick won the Individual Event. Four days later the Battalion provided seven of the Army Team which won the Malta Inter-Services Championships, and Private Kennerley won the individual event. On 11 February, the Battalion Team won the Malta National Road Running Competition, a remarkable achievement as road running is a national sport in Malta, and a fortnight later it won the Malta Cross-Country Championships. On the rugby scene, the Battalion provided eight members of the victorious Army Malta XV. The Hockey Team, led by Lieutenant David James, won three major tournaments and was runner up in the fourth.

The move from Malta to Libya for Exercise *Banbury Chase* began on 11 April with the departure of the first LST to Benghazi. Two separate training areas in Cyrenaica were used. T Coy Group, under Major Marshall and including the Recce Platoon, the Support Platoons, the Assault Pioneers, the Intelligence Section and the NCO Cadre, went south via Agedabia to Area '20'. In this desert area for ten days and despite sandstorms, all infantry weapons were fired, by day and by night, providing valuable experience. Meanwhile the rifle companies were doing section and platoon training in Area 'A', this phase culminating in an Inter-Platoon Patrol Competition. Each company carried out its own tests and training and one platoon from each company competed in the actual competition, a 36-hour patrol which tested both the leadership and endurance of the patrol. The competition was won by 1 Platoon of A Coy, under Lieutenant Michael Goldschmidt and Sergeant K (Ken) Wilson.

A CQMS' truck 'somewhere in Libya'. *E Christopher*

Navigated by Captain Terry Hutley, the Bn IO, T Coy Group's twenty-five vehicles completed the 125-mile journey cross-desert (rather than using the longer coast road via Benghazi) to join up with the remainder of the Battalion in Area 'A'. There then took place a Battalion test exercise set by the GOC over the now familiar ground. Over three days, the Battalion was exercised in defence, the advance, more defence, and withdrawal to the main defensive position.

The move back to Malta was punctuated by the never-unexpected delays to the Hastings aircraft of RAF Transport Command. The last chalk finally reached Malta on 10 May to bring to a close an enjoyable and thoroughly rewarding exercise. 4 Platoon (Lieutenant Tony Taylor) took over the Garrison Security Platoon role in Benghazi. Almost immediately a proportion of the Battalion's officers were among 200 or so from the Command who travelled by air and LSL to El Adem and Tobruk in Libya. For two days, they took part in a study of the several of the Second World War armoured battles: Gazala, Crusader, Knightsbridge and Bir Hacheim. 2nd Lieutenant Robert Pepper acted as translator to two senior German officers who had fought on the other side at the time. An unscripted visit was made by several Tigers to the wartime defences of Tobruk, where 2nd Battalion The Leicestershire Regiment had defended the eastern perimeter during the siege in late 1941, and to the beautifully kept military cemetery to honour the graves of some of their fallen.

Back in Malta normal relaxed summer routine began. In early spring the Inter-Company Athletics Meeting had been held. Then, on 23 May, the Battalion Team won the Garrison Inter-Unit Athletics Meeting, providing the individual winners of fourteen of the fifteen events, eleven second places and eleven third places. Lance Corporal Leslie Holman broke records each time in winning the High Jump and Triple Jump, and Private F (Fred) Tomlin won the 440 and 880. The Battalion's athletes then filled twenty-nine of the thirty-two places in the victorious Army Malta team, and in the Malta AAA Championships in early June carried off six firsts, six seconds and eight thirds. This included Corporal Rod Sarson's victory in the 100 yds and 120 yds Hurdles, and Holman's in the High Jump, when he set a Malta All-Comers Record of 5' 10". Holman went on to come fourth in the Army Individual Championships at Aldershot.

For most of the Western world (which included Malta), Monday, 5 June 1967 was the start of a normal working week. But, most importantly, it heralded the start of the Arab/Israeli 'Seven Day' War.

The morning also started peacefully in Benghazi. Then several thousand rioters went first to the American Consulate where they destroyed cars and entered the ground floor, and next to the British Embassy where they broke windows and set fire to the Residency flats. They also burnt premises owned by Jews. By 1000 hrs, 4 Platoon had been alerted to go to the assistance of the British Embassy and American Consulate. With its commander lying on his sick bed, Sergeant 'Chris' Christopher led the platoon that day, and successfully executed the operational plan which they had previously reconnoitred and practised. 4 Platoon reached the British Embassy at about 1230 hrs where their presence deterred further attacks; they recovered property from the burnt Residency flats, and even cooked a composite ration meal for the diplomatic staff on its No. 1 Burner dug in to the Embassy lawn. Working in conjunction with elements of 5 Innis DG, who had suffered several burn casualties from rioters near the American Consulate, together they assisted in the evacuation of the staffs of the British Embassy and American Consulate to the sanctuary of D'Aosta Barracks. At 0200 hrs on 6 June, 4 Platoon were out again escorting families from married quarters in Benghazi Town to sanctuary at Wavell and D'Aosta Barracks. By 0600 hrs the latter contained over 2,000 British civilians and military families, and with traditional British good humour was soon renamed 'D'Aosta Holiday Camp'. At D'Aosta, 'Chris' Christopher assisted in the planning and execution of the defence of the barracks perimeter, deploying the 'cooks and bottle washers' of the Garrison and later providing training in riot drill for a company of 1 D and D. That Germany-based Battalion had been conducting mechanized training in Area 'F' in their tracked APCs, and two companies had sped 200 miles across the desert to Benghazi.

On 5 June, the Malta element of A Coy had been 'quietly minding its own business', carrying out its range classification on the local ranges. Stood by for a quick move to reinforce the Garrison in Benghazi, an RAF Comet and a Hastings landed at Benina Airport shortly after midday on 6 June and deposited the balance of A Coy (now under command of Major J G Jones MBE[8]) into a ramshackle disused hangar, to hide from the Algerian paratroopers on their way to Egypt in their Russian-built Cub aircraft. The British vehicle convoy, escorted by armed men of the Libyan Cyrenaica Defence Force in Land Rovers, then made its way to the Skins' Wavell Barracks, where it met up with a second company of 1 D and D. A Coy 4 R Anglian was immediately 'stood to' for riot control in Benghazi, having been stood down from which it sited its anti-tank weapons to supplement the protection of Wavell Barracks in the face of the anticipated arrival of a Libyan armoured column from Tripoli moving east to help its Egyptian neighbours – and the column presumably ground to a halt en route to Benghazi. The D and D companies left for El Adem in the early hours of 7 June. A Coy settled down to a prolonged stay, living on a vehicle hangar floor and sharing the barracks with the Skins and 500 dependants, and were rejoined by 4 Platoon a few days later. The discomfort of cramped quarters in the height of summer was greatly tempered by the unstinting hospitality of the hosts and the feeling that a worthwhile job was being done.

The political tension subsequently lessened, restrictions eased and plans for an indefinite stay by the Company were put in place. As families moved back into their original married quarters in the town, so A Coy was allocated four Twynham huts. Very close liaison was established with their Armoured Recce hosts, and each side learnt a lot from the other. In return for familiarization with the armoured vehicles and AFV recognition training, A Coy gave IS demonstrations and loaned Sergeants Ken Wilson and Tony Crane to teach platoon anti-riot drills to dismounted troops. And inter-company/squadron sports were played most days.

The political and security situation in Libya stabilized. Although the Anglo-Libyan Friendship Treaty was not revoked, as a token of support for Egypt and Pan-Arab aspirations, the Libyan Government asked the British to leave Benghazi and forbade further large concentrations of troops in their country for training. The situation subsequently eased and training was permitted for units under battalion strength. For several months it remained necessary for two infantry companies to be based in Benghazi as a protection force for the large expatriate British community in event of further hostilities, and that commitment was shared with 1 Loyals. In early July, B Coy 4 R Anglian from Malta replaced A Coy at Wavell Barracks, and in mid-August, C Coy from Malta (now under command of Major A H V Gillmore MC[9]) was dispatched in parallel to D'Aosta Barracks for six weeks, while A Coy went back to Wavell Barracks for six weeks.

Apart from the extensive coming and going of troops to reinforce the British presence in Libya, life for those in Malta continued much as before. On 10 June, the Garrison's Queen's Birthday Parade was held at St Patrick's Barracks, with the Battalion providing one guard and the Band and Drums, resplendent in No. 3 Dress. The GOC was the inspecting officer and the Garrison Commander was the parade commander. On 1 July, the Band and Drums Beat Retreat on the Palace Square in Valletta, before a vast and enthusiastic crowd who much enjoyed the impressive performance. Four days later, the newly appointed Garrison Commander, Brigadier R E J Price CBE DSO, visited the Battalion.

The Command Skill-at-Arms Meeting was held in mid-July. There were no major unit competitions because 5 Innis DG, 1 Loyals and 4 R Anglian were too heavily committed in Libya to compete in strength. This was unfortunate as the Battalion was the holder of all the major unit trophies from the previous year and had hoped to defend them. As a result, all competitions were on a minor unit level. Secondly, despite the unsettled times and the ensuing lack of continuity in practice, the standard produced by the Battalion's competitors was considerably higher than the previous year. The notable results were HQ Coy's Rifle Team coming second in the Open event and winning the Junior Ranks, and Corporal Terry Ashford coming third in the Young Soldiers shoot. On the LMG, WO2 Ivor Marjoram and Corporal Bill McKenzie came second in the Minor Unit Team and Individual competitions. C Coy came second in the SMG team event, while Corporal Swannack and Private Boothby came 2nd and 3rd respectively in the Individual Pistol. In a cricket season which was more than normally affected by the availability of men variously occupied in Libya, four members of the Battalion represented the Army Malta. Sergeant John Rourke, fresh from an instructors' course, ran several rock-climbing cadres. Captain John Tilley found time to become the NEARELF go-kart champion.

As holders and in a new gig, the Rowing Team had been in training for two months as it strove to continue the previous year's success which had upset half a century's domination by Maltese teams. With four new members in the boat, the technical expertise was provided again by Lieutenant Andrew Fisher, with the fitness regime masterminded by SI Bill Stoves. An extremely comprehensive and effective training programme brought the crew to their 'peak pulling power' on the day of the Command Boat Race. In a class of its own, the crew won by eight lengths and broke the record by over three seconds. This was an outstanding achievement for which it was acclaimed throughout the island. The triumphant crew was: SI Bill Stoves (bow), Corporal R (Robbie) Allen, Drum Major Ray West, Corporal Charlie Dutton, Lieutenant B R (Brian) Cornish, Lieutenant Andrew Fisher (stroke), Sergeant E (Eddie) Davies (cox).

The victorious 1967 Boat Race crew 'at ease'. *A E Fisher*

The victorious Boat Race crew 'flat out'. *A E Fisher*

At the beginning of August, the Battalion restructured and formed Support Company, under the command of Major Colin Marshall. Amalgamating the mortar and anti-tank sections from the three rifle companies, Support Company comprised the Mortar Platoon (Lieutenant David James), the Anti-Tank Platoon (Lieutenant Chris Keeble), the Reconnaissance Platoon (Captain P W (Pat) King), and the Assault Pioneer Platoon (Sergeant Albert Glover). The Intelligence Section (Captain Terry Hutley) and Training Wing transferred to HQ Company. The three rifle companies were accordingly reorganized with three rifle platoons.

Later that month, Support Company sailed by LST to Cyprus to carry out live firing of mortars and anti-tank guns, returning in mid-September. The Battalion was also pleased to welcome two senior Regimental officers on separate visits. First, Major General John Spurling, the Deputy Colonel, visited the Battalion and also gave tuition to officers in the Command in military history in a locally run Staff/Promotion course. He also had time to attend the much heralded and very impressive Hindoostan Ball in the WOs' & Sgts' Mess, to which some 300 guests from all units and services on the island had been invited. Then the Regimental Colonel, Colonel Peter Badger, spent five days with the Battalion, and addressed the officers, WOs and SNCOs about career planning in the Large Regiment.

At the end of September, A and C Coys returned from Benghazi, the latter being replaced by B Coy. From then on, the physical rundown of British Forces in Cyrenaica began to be put in train.

Back in Malta, garrison life continued much as usual and the winter sporting season was embarked upon with vigour. In mid-October, the Commanding Officer informed the Battalion that it would be moving in July 1968 to Gordon Barracks at Gillingham, to become part of the Army's Strategic Reserve – the initial reaction was that chilly Kent would be a far cry from the Mediterranean.

The Band and Drums were much in demand for their musical prowess and regularly performed before enthusiastic and grateful crowds. The Band played twice on board visiting cruise ships conveying Leicestershire schoolchildren through the Mediterranean. Two other events were marching at the Malta Independence Day Parade in September and parading at the Searchlight Tattoo at Floriana Stadium in mid-November, in which all three Services took part. In addition to the Battalion providing the musicians and a physical training display, Major A F F H (Angus) Robertson, the 2IC, devised the battle scene, using A Coy as the attacking force which carried out a 'dry' assault river-crossing, and commanded the Final Muster. Not content with using up a year's supply of training ammunition, A Coy attempted to neutralize the vociferous (and up till then appreciative) spectators with a simulated nuclear explosion! The Tattoo took place during the five-day visit to Malta by HM The Queen and HRH The Duke of Edinburgh, and they graced the event by their presence at a truncated (and quieter) programme on the first of its four evenings.

In early November, B Coy was replaced in Benghazi by C Coy for a three-week tour of duty, with 10 Platoon (Lieutenant Brian Cornish) staying on till just before Christmas when it was replaced by 6 Platoon (2nd Lieutenant Robert Pepper) as part of a composite company commanded by 1 Loyals. In parallel, Sp Coy left Malta for four weeks' dry training and live firing in Area 'F', and they were also available for security duties at El Adem. Its absence from Malta was extended by it being moved by air as a rifle company to Cyprus, where for a fortnight it helped to guard installations at Dhekelia in the face of a Turkish threat. Its support weapons were taken back to Malta by the JNCOs cadre, and Sp Coy returned to Malta in time for Christmas.

As force levels in Benghazi reduced, Wavell Barracks was handed over by 5 Innis DG to the infantry and thereafter to the Libyan Army on 19 January 1968; married quarters were emptied of families and furniture, and stores and ammunition were outloaded mainly by LSTs. In addition to guard duties and being on standby for IS tasks, most of the hard graft of humping and dumping fell on the 'PBI'. By the end of January, in a formal parade on which the 1 Loyals composite company represented the British, D'Aosta Barracks was finally handed over to the Libyan Army. Those still needed in Benghazi for the final days were accommodated on the LST *Empire Gull*.

The last military personnel to leave Benghazi (including part of 6 Platoon) arrived in Malta by LST on 5 February, where they were greeted at the dockside by the Band of 1 Loyals and a flypast of four Canberra bombers. A fortnight later the GOC NEARELF sent a signal that read:

> I attended the final closure of Cyrenaica Area and the withdrawal of the garrison from Benghazi on 3 February. I would be grateful if you would convey my sincere thanks, firstly to the Defence Lands Adviser, Movement Staff, and all other agencies, for all they have done to assist in the withdrawal, and secondly to the companies of 4 R Anglian and 1 Loyals. The latter have done sterling work since August and the withdrawal could not have been completed on time without them. Thank you for all their help.

Thus the end of the British military presence in Cyrenaica (as in Tripolitania in 1966 and the Sudan in 1955) had intimately involved The Tigers in another job well done.

Meanwhile, back in Malta the Battalion prepared for and underwent the Annual Administrative Inspection by the GOC on 20 December. After inspecting the Battalion on the Square at St Patrick's Barracks, the GOC required the companies to carry out various tasks: A Coy paraded in battle order, B Coy (now under command of Major E (Teddy) Turnill) carried out company training, C Coy turned out for IS operations, Sp Coy did weapon maintenance, and HQ Coy (now under command of Major R J M (John) Mosse) the PT test. In his report the GOC wrote, 'I judge this Unit to be very highly trained and most efficient in every department. In the field they are equally good and highly professional. The tasks that I gave them were performed in the most efficient manner. Physically it must be the fittest Battalion in the British Army.'

Christmas came and went, accompanied by the traditional round of seasonal activities. After return to duty on 28 December, a sports morning was held, involving all companies and platoons in four sports.

At the beginning of 1968, senior appointments were held as follows:

CO:	Lieutenant Colonel D R C Carter	CSM B Coy:	WO2 P M Collins
2IC:	Major A F F H Robertson	OC C Coy:	Major S A Green
Adjt:	Captain A J G Pollard	CSM C Coy:	WO2 J Pearce
RSM:	WO1 R E Sprason	OC Sp Coy:	Major C T Marshall
QM:	Captain E P Kelly DCM	CSM Sp Coy:	WO2 D R Edwards
Tech QM:	Lieutenant J Eyeions	OC HQ Coy:	Major R J M Mosse
RQMS:	WO2 C Ladley	CSM HQ Coy:	WO2 A Hill
OC A Coy:	Major J G Jones MBE	FLO:	Major C P Culbert
CSM A Coy:	WO2 I Marjoram	Bandmaster:	WO1 J E Battye ARCM
OC B Coy:	Major E Turnill	Drum Major:	Sgt T R West

Early in the New Year, all officers, WOs and SNCOs attended a Battalion Study Day on Internal Security. On 16 January, shortly after midnight, a small party was stood to to join the RN in mounting an operation to assist the inhabitants of Sicily, which had been severely affected by earthquakes. Having been given a casual payment from the takings from the WOs' & Sgts' Mess that night (!), Corporal P (Paul) Clements and five soldiers left Malta well before dawn by RN Minesweeper HMS *Stubbington*, in convoy with others of the flotilla, and arrived at Trapani near Palermo that evening. In conjunction with RN medical parties and local forces, over the next five days they unloaded and erected marquees, 160lb and two-man bivouac tents to provide cover for the displaced inhabitants of Partanna and Montevago, and they distributed medical goods, food and blankets. Apart from their sterling humanitarian work, they got to like the Naval rum ration and Italian Army spaghetti.

On the sporting front, the Football Team had been permitted to enter the Army UK competition after a gap of a year, and it had a reputation of being a better side than when it had reached the UK Final in 1966. The Team were beaten 2-3 by 2 Para in thick snow in Aldershot, where the temperature and pitch were a far cry from Malta's. In Malta it went on to have a very good season, which included winning the Inter-Services Championship, defeating HMS *St Angelo* 8-0 in the Final.

Despite the departure before Christmas of Captain Peter Carr, who for three years had been a most successful OIC Athletics and Cross-Country, the Cross-Country Team was beginning to look formidable, with the hard training done by a regular cadre of twenty-eight runners. In the Inter-Company event, A Coy were again the victors, and the first two individuals were Privates Adams and Kennerley of B Coy. In a match against RAF Malta, A Coy's team won and the HQ & Sp Coys' team came third. Led by 2nd Lieutenant C W (Chris) Hewitt INT CORPS, a 'weak' Battalion team went to Cyprus in January and won the NEARELF Team Championships, avenging its second place to 2 R Anglian the previous year, and Private Adams was the third best individual. Back in Malta, the 1st Team won a four-race league, with Sergeant Neil Patrick finishing consistently in the first four. In February, in the Malta Army Championships, the Battalion's three teams came first, second and fourth, with Private Adams leading the individuals home. In the Inter-Services, the Army Malta team was composed totally of Tigers, who filled finishing positions three to nine. Two days later this same team came second in the Malta National AAA Championship by one point – it would most probably have won the race had not one of its leading runners failed to catch the transport to the event!

In Rugby, eight members of the Battalion played for the Army Malta and four players for the Combined Services Malta team on 27 February. The Battalion Seven-a-Side Team reached the final of the Inter-Services championship, losing to Overseas 9-10. The Hockey players entered two teams in all the competitions in Malta. The fine progress of the B Team, led by the determined RQMS Colin Ladley, prevented Lieutenant David James's A Team from becoming complacent. The A Team narrowly defeated the B Team in the final of the Combined Services Inter-Unit Knockout Competition. The development of such a strong squad bode well for the slower pitches in England the following season.

On the withdrawal of British troops from Cyrenaica, the Libya bit of 'Malta & Libya Command' ceased to exist. Consequentially, the post of GOC was discontinued in early February, and command of new 'British Troops Malta' was assumed by the erstwhile

Exercise *Batchelor's Fling* at Kufra Oasis.

Garrison Commander. Whereas unit-level exercises continued not to be permitted in Libya, subunit exercises were allowed again. A Coy left Malta for three weeks' desert training in Area 'F' in February, to be followed by B Coy and a JNCOs' cadre in early March, and C and Sp Coys at the end of the month.

In parallel with the military field training, a series of adventure training exercises were carried out in Libya and elsewhere. The first of these, Exercise *Bachelor's Fling*, involved men of B Coy. Led by Captain A T (Tony) Amos and Lieutenant Shaun Brogan, a party of twenty-one men departed from El Adem on 17 March, in three Land Rovers and four 3-ton trucks, all 'specially modified for desert use'. Driving along the Cyrenaican coast road to Agedabia, they then drove south-east to Jalo, south to Kufra Oasis, and then south-west into the unknown, seeking to reach the Tibesti Mountains, 250 miles further on. They got to within 35 miles of their objective but had to turn back having run short of petrol and time to return to El Adem by 7 April. It was a demanding and arduous three weeks, during which they had travelled some 2,200 miles and had learnt a great deal about the techniques and methods of desert navigation, driving and vehicle maintenance. And much of it was over real sand, not the dust and gravel of the training areas to the north.

Exercise *Charles Street* was next. Led by Lieutenant A W C (Andrew) Dexter and Sergeant John Rourke, a party of fifteen men from C Coy set out from El Adem on 18 April in two Land Rovers and four 3-ton trucks, all 'specially modified for desert use'. Heading directly south into the desert, via Giarabub and Jalo, the group reached Kufra Oasis. It returned northwards via the site of 'Lady Be Good', a crashed US Liberator bomber from the Second World War, and across the Calanscio Sand Sea, reaching El Adem some 1,500 miles and thirty-four days later. Despite the improvisation by the resourceful REME vehicle mechanic, the party had to spend nineteen days awaiting the resupply of vehicle spares at different points along the journey. Nevertheless, this Exercise taught its participants many

Army Malta athletics team May 1968 (see Appendix P for names). *Trustees R Anglian Regt*

of the skills needed to survive in the desert, the techniques of moving and living in the harsh environment, and the ability to adapt to changing circumstances.

Operating in totally different terrain and climate, on 17 April, 2nd Lieutenant Robin Wright led an expedition of eleven men to carry out adventure training in the Troodos Mountains of Cyprus. Finally, on 24 April, Lieutenant Roger Howe took eight men of A Coy to Turkey on Exercise *High Water* to climb the 12,300 foot Mount Erciyas. Extremely adverse weather caused them to turn back just 800 feet from the summit.

The majority of the previous year's Athletics Team formed the basis of a forty-strong squad, which began daily training in March. The Battalion Meeting was held in late April, the Inter-Company Championship being won by HQ Coy 1, where the athletic wealth lay in the Signals Platoon. At the Garrison Meeting on 9 May, the Battalion retained the Inter-Unit Trophy, with its individuals winning twelve of the fourteen events, leaving 1 Loyals a long way back in second place and the Royal Engineers even further back in third. Outstanding performances were Corporal Rod Sarson's victories in the 100 yds, 120 yds Hurdles and Long Jump, and Corporal Charlie Dutton's in the Javelin and Discus. On 24 May, the Army Malta athletics team, all but one of whom were from the Battalion, retained the Inter-Services Challenge Cup, seeing off a strong RAF Team, with Battalion athletes gaining eleven first and nine second places.

While the Athletics season's successes were largely team ones, there were some outstanding individual performers. Corporal Rod Sarson won the Garrison, Inter-Service and Malta 100 yds and 120 yds Hurdles, breaking the Malta All-Comers Record with 15.3 secs in the latter. Corporal Charlie Dutton was Malta Champion in the Shot and Discus, and Corporal Leslie Holman won all the High Jump events on the island, breaking the Malta All-Comers Record with a jump of 6' 0". Five athletes went on to compete in the Army Individual Championships in UK. Corporals R (Rod) Crook and Charlie Dutton came fifth in the 220 yds and the Discus respectively, Corporal 'Waqa' Waqairoba came fourth in the 120 yds Hurdles, Corporal Rod Sarson qualified for the 100 yds Final but was injured in a Hurdles heat. Pride of place went to Leslie Holman who became Army High Jump Champion, again clearing 6' 0". It was in May that a fond farewell was made to SSI Bill Stoves APTC, who had trained and inspired the Battalion's sports teams for three years and had personally competed with distinction.

On a small matter of Officers' Mess Dress, from early in the year the starched shirts with butterfly collars were replaced by soft-fronted golf-ball woven patterned shirts, which made things much easier for the wearer and the launderer.

Meanwhile, two other significant organizational changes were being planned which would affect the Regiment. First, was the creation of Divisions of Infantry. In the case of The Royal Anglian Regiment, it was to join with The Queen's Regiment (Queens) and The Royal Regiment of Fusiliers (RRF) to form The Queen's Division, starting in late 1968. At that stage each of those three regiments had four Regular battalions. The aim of such Divisions was to establish a structure for the Infantry that would last. The Colonel of The Regiment, now Lieutenant General Sir Richard Goodwin KCB CBE DSO, said in an article in the Regimental Journal *Castle* in May 1968:

> Change has certainly not been sought for the sake of change. By organizing existing Brigades and Regiments into larger groupings it will be easier, in the future, to meet the requirements of individual battalions as well as lessening the blow of possible future reductions. In each Division a Headquarters will be formed superseding existing Regimental and Brigade Headquarters. Basic training will be carried out on a Divisional basis. RHQ The Royal Anglian Regiment will probably be disbanded about April 1969. The new system will meet the needs of the future while preserving the best features of the Regimental system inherited from the past, and it is emphasized that we shall be joining The Queen's Division as The Royal Anglian Regiment and all that it has come to mean to us. Regiments will continue to maintain their full identity and territorial connections within The Queen's Division of Infantry.

Unlike the previous three efforts of restructuring, these Divisions of Infantry have stood the test of time. Forty years on, The Queen's Division continues to comprise its same three Regiments, albeit in 1992 The Queen's Regiment, on amalgamation with The Royal Hampshire Regiment, had been renamed The Princess of Wales's Royal Regiment, and each of the three Regiments has only two Regular battalions.

Secondly, although the Government's announcement in 1967 of the disbandment or amalgamation of eight infantry regiments had not affected The Royal Anglian Regiment, more recent indications were that it would probably be necessary to make further reductions in the Services, with details to be announced in a Defence White Paper in July 1968. As the Council of Colonels of The Royal Anglian Regiment considered that the

A Company Royal Guard marches past HRH The Duchess of Gloucester. *D R C Carter*

Regiment would be ordered to reduce by at least one battalion, it decided that the Regiment would move to Phase II of a Large Regiment on 1 July. On that day, all four Regular battalions would lose their subsidiary titles and be called simply 1st, 2nd, 3rd and 4th Battalions The Royal Anglian Regiment. The matter of badges, collar badges and lanyards became the subject of much debate. To the loss of 'Leicestershire' from the 4th Battalion's title (a title which had been borne since 1782) was added a clear possibility that nowhere in the dress of the Regiment would a place be found for the 'Royal Tiger', a prospect which grated with both the serving and former members of the Royal Leicestershire community, including the City and County. By late May, HM The Queen had agreed to the changes in title. The Council of Colonels had decided that the existing capbadge would be worn as the collar badge – although in the event they would not be available in sufficient quantities for another year or so – and that existing lanyards would continue to be worn after 1 July as a means of identifying a particular Battalion of the Regiment, not as being representative of any particular former regiment.

Against that background, in the last months of the Malta tour, two sets of important people visited the Battalion. First, the Lord Mayor and Lady Mayoress of Leicester, Alderman Sir Mark and Lady Henig. At the end of April they spent five days in Malta during which they saw many of the military activities of the Battalion. The Lord Mayor also called upon several members of the State, Political, Diplomatic and Military hierarchy, and visited several Leicester families in their married quarters. Lady Henig presented the prizes at the Battalion Athletics Meeting. He issued an invitation to the Battalion to exercise the Freedom of the City in October. This was an important visit, which further cemented the ties between the City and County with their soldiers, at the time when those ties looked as if they might be weakened by the forthcoming changes in the Battalion's title.

A fortnight later in mid-May, HRH The Duchess of Gloucester paid her first visit to the Battalion since becoming a Deputy Colonel-in-Chief; the Deputy Colonel of The Regiment, accompanied by Mrs Spurling, was also present. The busy programme for HRH included inspecting a Royal Guard, provided by A Coy and commanded by Major John Jones, touring a display of Battalion weapons, and attending a Battalion Relay and Field Event Athletics Meeting. To ring the changes from the more traditional format that had been followed just two weeks before, this Meeting comprised a series of Company Team relays over various distances, plus an individual Field Throws competition (won by Corporal Charlie Dutton) and a Field Jumps competition (won by 2nd Lieutenant Chris Hewitt). The Deputy Colonel-in-Chief presented the prizes. She took the opportunity to speak with a great number of soldiers and their wives and to meet the Battalion Cub and Brownie Packs, so ably led by the Mrs Sybil Hobday and Maureen Hughes. Her visit was a great honour for the Battalion, and all ranks were very touched and grateful for the great interest that she took in everything she saw. She was much affected by hearing from many sources in the Battalion the angst, disappointment and sadness at the impending loss of the 'Leicestershire' from the Battalion's title, compounded by there being no planned Royal Tiger representation in the future dress of the Regiment – a message she took home to England.

And so the final weeks of the tour were played out, the first element of the Advance Party leaving Malta on the same day as the Deputy Colonel-in-Chief – albeit on a different aircraft! Before his own departure two days later, Major General John Spurling addressed the Officers, WOs and SNCOs in Malta as to what the future might hold. The future was looked on with considerable interest by all members of this 'family regiment'. In the 690 all ranks in the Battalion at that time, among the non-commissioned ranks were twenty-eight sets of brothers (including Benner, Freakley, Sprason, Ralph), a father and two sons (Hobday), a father and son (Atkins), and sundry uncles, nephews and cousins. There were six officers (Major John Mosse, Captain Tony Pollard, Lieutenant John Tilley, Lieutenant Brian Davenport, Lieutenant Michael Goldschmidt, Lieutenant Shaun Brogan), whose fathers had served in The Royal Leicesters and who are shown left to right in this photograph. Missing from that photograph is Lieutenant Martin Romilly, shortly to rejoin from the RMCS; his father, uncle, cousin and great-uncle[10] had similarly served.

In mid-May, the Band and Drums made a farewell appearance in Valletta, marching down Kingsway to Beat Retreat on Palace Square in front of a large number of invited guests. This was the final parade of WO1 Edgar Battye, who after nine years of outstanding service to the Battalion handed over as Bandmaster to WO1 T G (Tommy) Cooper. The Band and Drums (with a strength of fifty-two musicians) left Malta on 6 June to Beat Retreat at Royal Tigers' Weekend at Leicester, to be part of the Massed Bands of all four battalions of the Regiment at the Regimental Gathering at Bury St Edmunds in the presence of the Colonel-in-Chief on 13 July, to play at the Cardiff Tattoo, and also at the Colchester Tattoo where, as the Massed Bands of The Queen's Division, nine of the twelve battalions' Bands and Drums paraded 452-strong.

Six officers whose fathers had served in The Royal Leicesters. *Leicester Mercury*

In Malta at the end of May, over three gloriously sunny days, the Battalion Skill-at-Arms Meeting was held. Led by Major Teddy Turnill, B Coy won the Inter-Company Shield, 5 Platoon (Lieutenant Shaun Brogan) was Champion Platoon. A week later the Battalion was particularly pleased to learn that Lieutenant 'Jimmy' Jenks, the MTO and lately RSM, had been awarded the MBE in the Queen's Birthday Honours.

It will have been noticed that the Battalion had been extremely successful at sport and shooting. The prosperity in the various competitions did not come about because the Battalion was being packed with sportsmen and other protagonists, nor was it through luck. It was largely because the Commanding Officer, David Carter, had the vision to encourage every sportsman to make himself known to those in charge, who were in turn given the opportunity to train their teams to a high standard in which he himself showed great interest and support.

Meanwhile, back in Middle England, the prospect that 'Leicestershire' would be removed from the Battalion's title caused great consternation also in the counties of Leicestershire and Rutland. The newly installed Lord Mayor of Leicester, Alderman Kenneth Bowder OBE[11], wrote to the Deputy Colonel-in-Chief, just back from visiting the Battalion in Malta, expressing sentiments that there was no planned Royal Tiger representation in the future dress of the Regiment ('Where would be the Royal Tiger badge, granted by HM King George IV in 1825 to the 17th Regiment as a "lasting testimony of its exemplary conduct in India, from 1804 to 1823"?'). Tigers, serving and 'the old and bold', felt similarly. Additionally, in the move to Phase II of the Large Regiment none of the

Royal Leicesters' music was to be retained; physically and psychologically Leicester was detached miles from RHQ and the Depot in Suffolk; and, as 'Johnny come lately' to The East Anglian Brigade, the not-unreasonable aspirations of the Royal Leicesters for some future visual recognition were now being ignored. All this chimed with what HRH The Duchess of Gloucester had seen and heard in Malta, and – with the support of the Colonel-in-Chief – she in her turn met with the Colonel of The Regiment to lobby for some form of Royal Tiger representation in the future dress of the Regiment.

In parallel, additional military arguments were strongly put forward on the grounds that no other junior battalion of a Large Regiment had been left in such a position. The situation compared unfavourably with the dress codes adopted for The Queen's Regiment and The Royal Regiment of Fusiliers (which with The Royal Anglian Regiment were to form The Queen's Division), where some of the accoutrements of the junior Middlesex Regiment and Lancashire Fusiliers were worn by the whole of their new Large Regiments.

Common sense eventually prevailed in the nick of time. Just a fortnight before change in titles was to come into effect as Phase II was activated, the Council of Colonels decided in mid-June that the Royal Tiger within the unbroken laurel wreath would be borne on all buttons throughout the Regiment. The promulgation of this decision was seen by the Tigers family very much as a sense of honour being restored and that it was an important gesture. Until that change, the younger Tiger officers felt that their views were not adequately represented in the important decisions being made by the senior officers who no longer had a career at regimental duty ahead of them. At the same time, Battalion collar badges were replaced by a common one for all Battalions in the shape of the capbadge.

The new Tiger button did not, however, seem to be universally welcomed across the Regiment. As one Captain, who was 'commissioned into The Royal Anglian Regiment and not its forbears', was to observe in a letter published in the January 1973 edition of *Castle* Journal decrying the various ad hoc changes in dress since 1964: 'Tiger Buttons. Hardly rationalization … perhaps embarrassed sentimentality? And how many officers have still not changed from Mess Kit buttons of their former Regiments, let alone the Royal Anglian!'

In achieving this important Royal Tiger button, recognition must be given to the indefatigable work behind the scenes by the Royal Leicesters' Regimental Secretary, Lieutenant Colonel Peter Upcher, for his efforts in rallying support in the County, drawing upon those who were influential, sounding out officers, and briefing the Deputy Colonel for key meetings with the Royal Anglian Regimental hierarchy.

The Advance Party of 1st Battalion The Lancashire Regiment (PWV) arrived in Malta in early June to begin the takeover.

It was on 1 July 1968 that Phase II of the Large Regiment came into effect, a transition that was marked by a Special Order of the Day by the Colonel of The Regiment, which is at Appendix J. The decision both to move to Phase II in such haste and in tandem that 'All Battalions of the Regiment should henceforth be regarded as belonging to all eleven counties which form our Regimental area' was made at that stage so that any future disbandment of the 4th Battalion would not be seen as the demise of the Leicestershire Battalion. As is described in Chapter 14, just ten years later, the decision to drop county titles was reversed in 1978, because of the loss of the Regiment's identity in the counties and the consequent adverse effect on recruiting.

Starting on 1 July and spread over ten days, the 4th Battalion's Main Body left Malta for

England, after a highly successful tour during which fifty-six soldiers had married Maltese wives. It was during that Battalion move and as the men proceeded on leave that (as an early – if unintended – incidence of 'how best to bury bad news') on 11 July, in a Defence White Paper, the Government announced the reduction of the Regular Infantry during the next four years by a further six battalions[12], one of which was to be 4th Battalion The Royal Anglian Regiment. The actual form of words used was: 'The Royal Anglian Regiment is to reduce by one battalion, the Fourth Battalion, and is to reorganise to form three battalions.' That not-entirely-unexpected news was assuaged to a degree by the knowledge that the Royal Tiger would live on in the dress of the Regiment. Nevertheless, it was with heavy hearts that the members of the Battalion proceeded on block leave, to reassemble at Gillingham at the beginning of September.

The same White Paper also announced that the Territorial & Army Volunteer Reserve (TAVR) Category III units would be disbanded, and that included The Royal Leicestershire Regiment (Territorial), the details of which are described in Chapter 10. So, 11 July 1968 dealt a 'double whammy' to The Royal Leicesters.

Notes

1   See Appendix N.
2   'Bob' Godfrey had been awarded the MC as a 2nd Lieutenant platoon commander in 1st Suffolk in Malaya in 1951. He later was the author of *The History of the Suffolk Regiment 1946-1959* (1988) and *History of the Royal Norfolk Regiment 1951-1969* (1993).
3   It was said that one of the locally enlisted Mess Staff still serving in D'Aosta Barracks in 1966 had been similarly employed during the Second World War; one day in February 1941 he had served breakfast to the retreating Italians and lunch to the advancing British.
4   In 1927, 2nd Leicesters had been under the command of Lieutenant Colonel W T Bromfield, whose grandson Sergeant C T Bromfield was serving in 4 R Anglian in 1966.
5   In 1967, David Michael went on to be ADC to the Governor of Western Australia, Major General Sir Douglas Kendrew KCMG CB CBE DSO, who had been the last Colonel The Royal Leicestershire Regiment.
6   The resolution of the Council of the City of Leicester on 28 June 1966 also conferred the Freedom on 4/5th Battalion The Royal Leicestershire Regiment (TA), and their successors. A colour photograph of the Resolution is in the plate section.
7   Peter Badger had been CO 1st R Leicesters 1961-64 – see Chapters 3 and 4.
8   John Jones had been awarded the MBE while a Lieutenant platoon commander at Depot R Norfolk assisting in flood relief in Norfolk in January 1953.
9   Adrian Gillmore had been awarded the MC as a Lieutenant platoon commander in 1st Suffolk in Malaya in 1951.
10 Captain F H Romilly was awarded the DSO while commanding D Coy 2nd Leicesters at the Battle of Neuve Chapelle in France in May 1915; he was killed in action near La Bassée Canal on 24 September 1915 in which day's attack twenty officers and 430 men of the Battalion were killed or wounded. C G and his twin brother P F served in 7th Leicesters in the Second World War, and H M de B served in 1st R Leicesters, retiring in 1958.
11 Kenneth Bowder had served in The Leicestershire Regiment in the Second World War.
12 The reduction of the other five battalions were 2nd SG, 4th Queens, 1st A & SH, 3rd RGJ to disband, and 1st Glosters and 1st R Hamps to amalgamate.

Chapter 7

The Territorial Army Battalions 1955-67

4th Battalion/'Q' Battery 438th LAA Regiment RA

By way of background, in 1936, to combat the perceived threat from German air attack, many of the urban-based TA infantry battalions were converted into the searchlight or anti-aircraft role. One such was 4th Battalion The Leicestershire Regiment – a Territorial Army (TA) unit formed in the City of Leicester and recruiting from that area – which became the 44th (The Leicestershire Regiment) Anti-Aircraft Battalion Royal Engineers (TA), equipped with searchlights. In the immediate lead-up to the Second World War, it had deployed in the air defence of Lincolnshire in August 1939. In 1940, it retitled and rebadged to 44th Searchlight Regiment Royal Artillery (RA), and in 1942 it changed its role and title to 121st Light Anti-Aircraft (LAA) Regiment RA, equipped with Bofors guns. In June 1944, it subsequently landed in Normandy on D+19, supporting VIII Corps with whom it fought through France, Belgium and Germany until on VE-Day it was at Lübeck on the Baltic Sea. In 1946, it was placed in suspended animation but, on the reformation of the TA, was reconstituted the following year as 579th (The Royal Leicestershire Regiment) LAA Regiment RA (TA), part of 76 AA Brigade (TA).

Although the men were in the Royal Artillery, in view of the Regiment's antecedence all ranks wore an embroidered flash on the arm depicting a green tiger against a black background. On 3 October 1953, new infantry colours of the old 4th Battalion had been presented by HRH The Duchess of Kent, an almost unique occurrence because it is traditional in RA regiments for the guns to be the Colours. Later that day the Regiment paraded through the City with 'Colours flying and Bayonets fixed'. Equally unusually for an Artillery Regiment, but because of its strong infantry antecedent, it had its own Band (and later Drums). In 1955, Anti-Aircraft Command was disbanded and its TA component was reorganized. 579th Regiment was reduced in size and reconstituted as 'Q' (The Royal Leicestershire Regiment) LAA Battery (TA), part of 438th LAA Regiment RA (TA). At that time the very close liaison that existed between the Regiment and the City and County of Leicester was exemplified by nine ex-officers of the Regiment being Deputy Lieutenants (DLs) of the County, while a number of former officers had served the City as Aldermen and Lords Mayor. A list of those Lords Mayor who had served in the Regiment is included in Appendix G.

As the story is taken up, the new 'Q' Battery – formed on 14 May 1955 – was commanded by Major W F (Bill) Adams RA (TA). It was stationed at Ulverscroft Road, Leicester, alongside its Regimental Headquarters (RHQ) commanded by Lieutenant Colonel L H (Leslie) Smith TD RA, who had received the last commission in the 4th Battalion and was the last CO of the 579th. The Regiment's other gun batteries were 'P' based at Derby and 'R' based at Northampton, both with similar antecedents to 'Q' Battery. The Regiment was part of 42 Army Group RA (AGRA) Field Force, with its HQ at York; the role of the AGRA was the air defence of VPs (Vital Points) within the UK.

'Q' Battery was equipped with the 40mm Bofors LAA gun, which was hand-controlled and operated, and towed by a Bedford 3-ton lorry. As personal weapons, the soldiers had .303" Lee Enfield rifles and the officers .38" revolvers. Radio communication was provided by the WS19 (HF) and 88 (VHF) radio sets. Like their infantry brothers, field dress was battledress with 1938 pattern webbing. In July 1955, Annual Camp was held at Weybourne on the Norfolk coast and the new sister batteries trained together for the first time. With a reduced number of regiments at the AA Permanent Range, firing took place each day and in ideal camp weather. Quite apart from the military training value, inter-battery rivalry soon emerged, and 'Q' Battery won the Six-a-Side Football Tournament.

Training and social activities took up much of the intervening months before, in September 1956, 'Q' Battery went to Annual Camp with the rest of its Regiment at Towyn in North Wales. The weather was atrocious. This camp was memorable for the appearance of some sixty Z Reservists who had been called out for training as part of the mobilization for the Suez Crisis. It proved difficult to raise any enthusiasm among them for the enforced training period. Nevertheless, all ranks were pleased by the visit of the Lord Mayor of Leicester, Alderman Alfred Halkyard CB MC TD DL[1]. Late 1956 and early 1957 were devoted to obtaining more volunteers. Recruiting reach was extended by establishing a troop at Burbage, and an ACF platoon at Kibworth was affiliated to the Battery. The AGRA Commander's Annual Administrative Inspection was successfully negotiated in March,

'Q' Battery's Bofors firing at Weybourne. *R G Wilkes*

whereafter much individual training took place every week, leading up to Annual Camp held again at Weybourne in glorious weather. High standards of gunnery, drill and efficiency were evident. The only person who was not fully regimentally employed was the RMO who, with no one reporting sick, had no one on whom to train. However, he did prove to be a most competent and enthusiastic Officers' Mess caterer – the Mess ate well that year!

In October, Major R G (Richard) Wilkes assumed command of 'Q' Battery, of which Captain J F M Wilkes was Battery Captain and WO2 Johnson the Battery Sergeant Major (BSM). Preparations were soon put in train for Annual Camp at Weybourne in July. Before that, on 5 July, the Battery played its part in the parade of TA units through Leicester to celebrate the Golden Jubilee Year of the TA. Training in the months leading up to Annual Camp paid off well: the standard of anti-aircraft gunnery was of a high order, and a four-day deployment and manoeuvre exercise run by the Artillery Group, aptly named Exercise *Rockets Galore*, was rather more successful than had been foreseen.

Early in 1959, the Battery received a complete change of equipment: an electrically operated and controlled 40mm L70 LAA gun, with twice the rate of fire and manoeuvrability, and supported by a Mark 7 gun-control radar, towed by an AEC Matador truck. Because of its large size this equipment had great difficulty being parked in the TA Centre garages, and also needed a police escort when being towed through the City! It was a race against time to train the soldiers, and particularly new recruits, on the new equipment and range of new vehicles (which already included the Austin Champ jeep and ½-ton Land Rover), before moving with the Regiment, via staged deployments at various training areas, to Bude in Cornwall for Annual Camp in June 1959, where live firing of the new guns was carried out for the first time.

The months following Camp were largely devoted to preparing most successfully for November's Annual Administrative Inspection, carried out by Brigadier G E C Sykes DSO, Commander 42 AGRA. For the whole of December, the Drill Hall at Ulverscroft Road was used by the Post Office as a mail sorting office in the run-up to Christmas – an unusual form of MACA (Military Aid to the Civil Authorities)!

At the beginning of 1960, WO2 V C (Vic) Grooms became BSM of 'Q' Battery. Training began in earnest on the new and even bigger and better gun-control radar set, which – as accurately predicted – helped considerably in blocking Britain's roads when on the move. Preparation began too for Annual Camp, to be held in North Yorkshire. It was to be the first time since the reformation of the TA that the guns would not be fired. Before then, in late May, the whole Regiment took part in a National Air Defence Exercise, its task being to deploy to a VP on the Lincolnshire coast, where plenty of air activity kept all fully occupied. Disastrously, it was found that 'Q' Battery's HQ had been sited in a perilous position – a hundred yards from a deep open silage pit, the contents of which the farmer proceeded to turn. The wind then changed direction in the night and an involuntary reveille occurred an hour before the time ordered!

Successful though the weekend had been from the training point of view, it was marred by the tragic death in a traffic accident of WO2 Vic Grooms, while moving to Lincolnshire. He had been a member of the Battery and its predecessors since 1937.

Annual Camp at Bellerby was one of the wettest camps that anyone in the Battery could recall, borne out in the six rum issues that were made. The first week was spent on technical training and short deployment exercises. The second week involved a two-day Regimental Exercise, including a night occupation, and a three-day AGRA-run Field Training Exercise (FTX), *Black Widow*. This latter exercise involved a lot of road movement, some very speedy as on the occasion when the Regimental 'recce party' nearly met disaster as it arrived on an airfield just as dawn was breaking to find itself suddenly faced with four Vulcan jet bombers powering up at the far end of the runway. No prizes for guessing 'Who took off first?'! GOC-in-C Northern Command, Lieutenant General Sir Michael West KCB DSO, was a welcome visitor to the Exercise.

In the planned reorganization of the TA (which is covered more fully in the 5th Battalion section below), the members of 'Q' Battery were sad to learn that they were not to continue as Gunners. Having accepted that fact, they were very pleased and proud that after twenty-five years the successor to the 4th Battalion The Leicestershire Regiment was to return to Infantry upon the amalgamation with the 5th Battalion to form the 4/5th Battalion The Royal Leicestershire Regiment. The men soon got used to the idea and looked forward with enthusiasm to their new duties (even if the idea of having to march once more did not immediately sound very inviting).

The greater proportion of the Battery, together with RHQ soldiers, were to transfer to the new Battalion, and to stay together as a whole to become its Headquarter Company (absorbing the 5th Battalion's existing HQ Company) and remaining at the TA Centre at Ulverscroft Road in Leicester. The fate of the other two gun batteries in the Regiment was to be not dissimilar: 'R' Battery at Northampton, which had originally been the 4th Battalion The Northamptonshire Regiment, was to amalgamate with its 5th Battalion to form 4/5th Battalion The Northamptonshire Regiment; 'P' Battery at Derby was to form a Field Park Squadron in 140 Corps Regiment RE. Gunnery training ceased after Camp that summer, and from 1 January 1961, infantry training began under the auspices of 5 R Leicesters.

A gun of 438 Regt RA drives past for the last time. *Leicester Mercury*

Over the following three months a series of farewell parties and events took place, in the various messes. On 18 March, the Farewell Parade of 438 LAA Regt was held on the Victoria Park in Leicester. The guns of the Regiment were paraded for the last time, and in slow time to the tune of the Royal Artillery March, 'The British Grenadiers', were driven past the Honorary Colonel, The Earl Spencer TD, and other distinguished guests of the Regiment from Derby, Northampton and Leicester. Buses brought in families of the members of the Regiment living at Derby and Northampton, but it was extremely disappointing that the day was cold and marred by a heavy shower during the drive-past. The drive-past proceeded through the streets of Leicester to Ulverscroft Road, where the guns were placed in their gun sheds for the last time.

So ended a period of almost twenty-five years in which 4th Battalion The Leicestershire Regiment served first as Royal Engineers and then Royal Artillery. In 1 April 1961, it returned to the infantry fold, its members having mixed feelings – sad to be leaving the Royal Regiment with whom they had been extremely proud to serve, and happy to be reverting to their original Regiment where they already had many friends, and with whom they had kept in close touch during the intervening years.

At about that time, inspired by Lieutenant Colonel (Retd) C D (Claude) Oliver OBE TD DL[2], Chairman of the Territorial & Auxiliary Forces Association (TAFA) for Leicestershire & Rutland, together with his brother Major F E (Ernest) Oliver CBE TD[3], a former Lord Mayor of Leicester, the officers who had served in 4th Battalion The Leicestershire Regiment presented to the City of Leicester a 26" high silver piece – the 'Oliver Cup'. It had previously been presented to the 4th Battalion by Claude and Frederick Oliver's father, Lieutenant Colonel C F (later Sir Frederick) Oliver, when the latter had handed over command in 1913. It was then used for 'any purpose that the officers might think fit'. For many years it had been the trophy for a shooting competition, which had since lapsed. This latest presentation was a mark of the close association of the City Battalion with the City of Leicester.

To mark the time that the 4th Battalion (and the other two batteries with infantry antecedents) spent as Gunners, the officers of 438 LAA Regt commissioned three silver Bofors guns from Garrards, the London silversmiths. Never having before made a model of a Bofors, Garrards sent two of their craftsmen to Ulverscroft Road where they spent two days dismantling a gun and measuring all the parts in order to make an accurate model. When completed, each battery presented to its successor battalion one of the silver guns as a memento of the time served in the Gunner role. The inscription on 'Q' Battery's silver gun was:

Presented to
4/5 Bn The Royal Leicestershire Regiment (TA)
by past and present members
of the 4th Battalion and its successors
on the occasion of the amalgamation of
5th Bn The Royal Leicestershire Regiment (TA)
with
Q/438 (The Royal Leicestershire Regiment)
LAA Battery RA (TA) 1st April 1961

Silver model of a Bofors LAA gun. *Trustees R Leicestershire Regt*

5th and 4/5th Battalion

The story is taken up in mid-1955. Commanded by Lieutenant Colonel M (Mike) Moore MC TD[4], a TA officer, 5th Battalion The Royal Leicestershire Regiment (TA) comprised Headquarter Company, four rifle companies, and Support Company, with Battalion Headquarters (Bn HQ) at The Magazine in Leicester. The rifle companies were based at Leicester (A), Oakham (B), Hinkley (C) and Loughborough (D). Rifle platoons weapons were the Lee Enfield .303" rifle and similar calibre Bren LMG, the 9mm Sten gun and the 2" mortar; the 3.5" rocket launcher was usually left in the armoury; the .38" revolver was also carried by officers. In Support Company, the Mortar Platoon was equipped with six 3" mortars, four 17-pdr anti-tank guns (towed by the M3 half-track), and six Vickers .303" medium machine guns (MMGs). Communication was provided by the WS19, 62 (both HF), 31, and 88 (both VHF) radio sets, and dispatch riders on motorcycles. Mechanical transport comprised ½-ton Land Rover and Austin Champ 'jeeps', 1-ton and 3-ton Bedford trucks. For training, all ranks wore worsted battledress (BD), with 1938 Pattern webbing belt and pouches, and on occasion a steel helmet. Officers wore Service Dress and peaked caps for parades, and Blues for ceremonial parades.

The Battalion was part of 147 Lorried Infantry Brigade, the other units being 7th Royal Warwicks, 4/6th Royal Lincolns and 5th Foresters. The Brigade was part of 49th Infantry Division, whose HQ was at Nottingham.

The summer of 1955 was to be the last when National Servicemen were obliged to attend

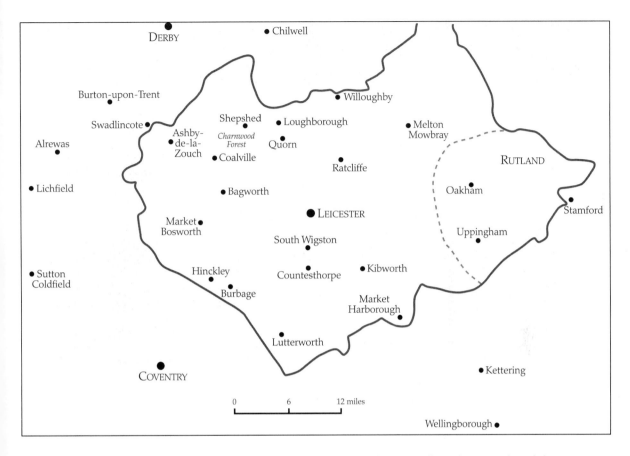

TA Annual Camp, and the 5th Battalion's was attended by 900 all ranks, at Fylingdales on the Yorkshire Moors north of Scarborough. Training was devoted to minor tactics and field firing up to platoon level. Annual Camp also witnessed the Band and Drums Beat Retreat for the first time since the Second World War, a ceremony that was repeated in Scarborough. The Battalion won the Brigade Championship-at-Arms for the third consecutive year. After three years in post, WO1 S E (Sidney) Clarke handed over as RSM to WO1 J R ('Dixie') Dean.

The National Service Act 1948 was modified in 1956 and from then on the part-time National Servicemen had to attend only one Annual Camp. The accent was, once more, on the true volunteer, and the spirit of the pre-war Territorials started to revive.

In August 1956, Lieutenant Colonel Mike Moore handed over to Lieutenant Colonel P McH (Peter) Preston MBE TD[5], a TA officer who had been commissioned into the 5th Battalion on his eighteenth birthday in 1938 and was to be the last CO who had been a pre-war Territorial. At Annual Camp, held at Wathgill in Yorkshire, the unit strength dropped away to 257 all ranks, of whom twenty-seven officers and 107 Other Ranks were Volunteers. The programme of work was devoted to individual training, and there was a valuable nucleus at all levels imbued with a spirit of the Regiment. All were ready and willing to do everything in their power to ensure that the 5th Battalion would play its part whatever the future should hold. In the Brigade Championship-at-Arms the Battalion was narrowly beaten into second place by 5th Foresters.

In May, a handsome memorial plaque was erected by the Regiment in the Nordsetter Hotel at Lillehammer in Norway. It was in memory of the succour which the owner Mr Haslev had bravely rendered to a group of officers and men of the 1/5th Battalion The Leicestershire Regiment in April 1940, thus enabling many to avoid capture by the Germans during the disastrous expedition to Norway.

In a separate commemoration in September, Major J (Jock) Cassie MC,[6] who had served there in the 2/5th Battalion The Leicestershire Regiment, represented the Regiment at the unveiling of the Cassino War Memorial in Italy. On it are inscribed the words:

> WITHIN THIS CEMETERY STAND PILLARS OF STONE WHICH BEAR
> THE NAMES OF SOLDIERS OF THE BRITISH COMMONWEALTH AND
> EMPIRE WHO FELL IN ASSAULTS UPON THE SHORES OF ITALY AND
> SICILY, OR IN LATER BATTLES TO FREE ITALIAN SOIL, AND TO
> WHOM THE FORTUNES OF WAR DENIED A KNOWN AND HONOURED
> GRAVE. AROUND THEM ARE THE GRAVES OF THEIR COMRADES
> WHO DIED FIGHTING IN THESE PARTS TO
> OPEN THE ROAD TO ROME AND THE NORTH

The names of nine men of the Regiment are listed on the pillars, and in the cemetery itself 4,200 Servicemen are commemorated by headstones on graves.

Meanwhile, back in Leicestershire, recruiting and training continued apace, and it was critically important that former National Service officers and soldiers should be encouraged to join this now Volunteer battalion. The Band and Drums, recently issued with No. 1 Dress (Blues), were providing a much-improved standard of music and drill that was favourably commented on at the important engagements they were undertaking in the County. The Battalion was very much involved in organizing and taking part in the Lord Mayor of Leicester's Remembrance Day Parade.

At the beginning of 1957, senior appointments were held as follows:

CO:	Lieutenant Colonel P McH Preston MBE TD	CSM B Coy:	WO2 N H S Parker
		OC C Coy:	Captain P A H Mockford
2IC:	Major A J Sudlow	CSM C Coy:	WO2 A J J Pryce-Howells
Trg Officer:	Major D R Dalglish MC	OC D Coy:	Captain D B Holyoake
Adjutant:	Captain R H D Graveston	CSM D Coy:	WO2 A Pervin
RSM:	WO1 J R Dean	OC Sp Coy:	Major A J Sudlow
QM:	Major L E Hollis MM[7]	CSM Sp Coy:	WO2 H Almen
RQMS:	WO2 F Monk	OC HQ Coy:	Major J Hartley
OC A Coy:	Major E H Tilley	CSM HQ Coy:	WO2 W H Heircock
CSM A Coy:	CSgt A S Harding	Bandmaster:	WO1 C I Carnall LRAM
OC B Coy:	Major J B Harrison	Drum Major:	WO2 T F Simpson

On 29 June, in Northern France, HM Queen Elizabeth The Queen Mother unveiled the Dunkirk Memorial. There are twenty names of the Leicestershire Regiment's Dunkirk fallen with no known graves, which are engraved on one of the walls of the main Memorial

The Dunkirk Memorial. *Commonwealth War Graves Commission*

Shrine. Lieutenant Colonel Sir Kenneth Ruddle TD DL[8] laid a wreath from the Colonel of The Regiment and all ranks.

That same month, back in England, the 5th Battalion's Rifle Meeting was held at Kibworth Range, and all attending camped out for the weekend. A new TA Centre was opened in Blackbird Road in Leicester, to be the home of Sp Coy. Annual Camp that year was held at the end of August for a fortnight, at Stanford Training Area in Norfolk, and for the first time no National Servicemen were there. Consequently, with only 140 all ranks volunteers attending, the scope of training was severely limited, but it was a useful and happy period. Captain A A J (Tony) Wilson of Sp Coy was the Brigade Champion Shot. Everyone came away satisfied, but fully realizing that it would be essential to recruit more Volunteers. A strong recruiting drive was launched in January 1958, with the incentive of imaginative and exciting training. For the first time a team entered the Nijmegen March in The Netherlands, an event with special appeal to the volunteer soldier because marching with full kit 24 miles a day for four days called for tough training, and an opportunity to go abroad and meet contingents from many nations. The team of seventeen, led by Lieutenant R E R (Dick) Buckingham, well earned their medals that year. It was particularly pleasing too that for his outstanding contribution to Battalion life, WO2 H ('Jack') Almen was awarded the MBE in the Queen's Birthday Honours List.

To mark the Golden Jubilee Year of the TA, a detachment from the Battalion was one of many that paraded before HM The Queen in London's Hyde Park on 22 June. A fortnight later, on 5 July, in Leicester, it formed part of the County's TA units' mechanised march past the Lord Lieutenant. Annual Camp was spent at Fylingdales in Yorkshire, numbers swelled by successful recruiting over the previous months, during which a number of former National Service officers and men had enlisted. In September, Colonel J C (John) Barrett VC

TD DL[9] handed over as Honorary Colonel to Colonel G J (Guy) German DSO TD[10]. A new Warrant Officers' & Sergeants' Mess (WOs' & Sgts' Mess) was opened at The Magazine in October. Recruiting continued to be buoyant.

With the announcement in July (see Chapter 2) that The Midland Brigade was to be renamed The Forester Brigade and that the Regular Army elements of the Regiment were to adopt a common Brigade capbadge in 1960, the TA element of The Royal Leicestershire Regiment were delighted to learn subsequently that they – and the affiliated Cadet units – would continue to wear the Regimental capbadge.

In early 1959, The Battalion's Shooting Team fared very well at the 49th Infantry Division Rifle Meeting, with Captain Tony Wilson winning the Individual Rifle Championship. This led to the Team competing at the National Meeting at Bisley for the first time in many years. In other sporting events the Battalion competed in the Divisional and Northern Command Cross-Country Championships, and Sp Coy also fielded an energetic football team, neither being normal TA Battalion activities. The Band and Drums, bolstered on occasion by individuals from 'Q' Battery of 438 LAA Regiment, took part in several passing-out parades at the Depot, and also appeared at various civic and local events within the county and at the Leicester Searchlight Tattoo in September. For the second year in July, a team successfully completed the Nijmegen March, that year led by Lieutenant S T (Stan) Pollard and Colour Sergeant R B (Roger) Curtis. On the military training front it was claimed that 'more weekends' training was carried out than there were weekends'! B Coy's team, led by WO2 N H S (Neville) Parker, won the Octathlon in April.

At the end of July, Annual Camp was held at Whitburn in County Durham. In the four-year training cycle it was an 'amenity' one, and local amenities there were aplenty. Although two small exercises were held at Otterburn in Northumberland, training was otherwise almost exclusively devoted to bringing recruits and the less-trained soldiers up to a good standard of basic infantry skills. At the Battalion's Annual Rifle Meeting, Sp Coy's team, led by Captain Tony Wilson, were worthy winners; and WO2 Neville Parker won the combined Rifle/LMG match. It was during Camp that Peter Preston, the last remaining pre-War TA officer, handed over command of the Battalion to Lieutenant Colonel J H (John) Marriott MC[11], a Regular officer. For the many years of his distinguished service in war and peace, Peter Preston had displayed a most ebullient and effervescent personality.

In early August 1959, senior appointments were held as follows:

CO:	Lieutenant Colonel J H Marriott MC	OC C Coy:	Major P A H Mockford
2IC:	Major A J Sudlow	OC D Coy:	Major D B Holyoake
Adjutant:	Captain G A Havilland MC[12]	CSM D Coy:	WO2 F Bentley
RSM:	WO1 J R Dean	OC Sp Coy:	Major J Hartley
QM:	Major L E Hollis MM	CSM Sp Coy:	WO2 H Almen MBE
RQMS:	WO2 F Monk	OC HQ Coy:	Captain M S Tuke
OC A Coy:	Major E H Tilley	CSM HQ Coy:	WO2 A A J Pryce-Howells
CSM A Coy:	WO2 W H Hiercock	Bandmaster:	WO1 C I Carnall LRAM
OC B Coy:	Major J B Harrison	Drum Major:	WO2 T F Simpson
CSM B Coy:	WO2 N H S Parker		

The Battalion was, as usual, very active during the winter months. It started with the

Leicester Tattoo, held during the last week of September. Sp Coy made a fine impression with their portrayal of a night attack, and the Band and Drums drew great applause despite the unfriendly attentions of a helicopter. The 49th Inf Div Rifle Meeting, unusually, did not provide the venue for much success for the Battalion's team in 1959, but the team was very much back on form at the Leicestershire & Rutland Meeting, where it swept the board in all matches, both team and individual.

The weeks before Christmas were spent preparing for the Annual Administrative Inspection. It was during this period that the new and gruelling sport of 'marching great distances at great speed' became popular. Corporal John Sinclair, a Hungarian-born machine gunner in Sp Coy, decided that he could outmarch most people. At his first attempt, in November, accompanied by twelve pacemakers, he marched the 110 miles from Leicester to Charing Cross in London and for a time held the unofficial record for this distance of 30 hours 40 minutes. He finished in grand style, with policemen escorting him down Regent Street in the early hours of a Sunday morning. At Charing Cross itself, he was welcomed by the Deputy Lord Mayor of Leicester, Alderman Sidney Brown TD[13], by his Honorary Colonel and Commanding Officer, all of whom had driven from Leicester overnight, and by the Press.

A month later, six pairs of marchers from the Depot, plus Sinclair and Lieutenant Tom Hiney, a Regular officer from the Depot, competed in the *News of the World* March of the Century, the 100 miles race from Birmingham to London. One hundred and nineteen pairs of service men (and some service women) started the race. Few of the competitors, and certainly not Hiney, had done any foot-hardening training, which made Hiney's feat all the more amazing. By dawn on the second day, after a night of appalling rain and cold, only twenty of the 228 starters were still on the road, and Hiney and Sinclair, closely pursued by the Royal Northumberland Fusiliers' pair, were leading. All other Royal Leicesters had been forced to abandon the struggle. Over the following twelve hours, in foul weather which never abated, all the remaining pairs, bar one from the RAF miles behind, succumbed to the pressure. The Royal Leicesters' leaders presented a weird picture, with torn 'pac macs' over their uniform, Hiney with a soaking cap comforter over one eye, a bandage round one knee, and a stick; Sinclair with a broad smile and a regimental beret on top. Finally, after a little over thirty-three hours' epic endurance, shortly after 2100 hrs (but too late to make the Sunday morning headlines – which could only report 'Looking every inch the winners'), Hiney and Sinclair walked in under the *News of the World* banner to victory, to be greeted by television arc lamps, reporters, curious bystanders, awkward questions, cold milk, an ambulance and nurses to massage their limbs.

Three weeks later, the *News of the World* gave a luncheon in Leicester, at which they presented to the Colonel of The Regiment a cheque for £500 for the Royal Tigers' Association, and £250 for the Unit PRI (£500 in 1959 would be worth about £7,500 in 2008). The winning pair themselves each received a silver cigarette case and a Philishave. General Callander in turn conferred on Hiney and Sinclair a unique honour for serving soldiers, by making both of them Honorary Life Members of the Royal Tigers' Association. Richly they deserved it, and grateful the Regiment was to them for the distinction and prize they brought in winning the contest.

Sinclair subsequently competed again, in the *Billy Butlin*'s John O'Groats to Land's End Walk, where, despite being dogged by septic blisters and a minor foot operation, he finished

Capt Tom Hiney MC **and Cpl John Sinclair.** *T B F Hiney*

thirtieth. Tom Hiney went with him by car, helped by carrying spare dry clothes and food, and arranging accommodation each night – and, when necessary, medical attention.

Meanwhile the disappointing news was received that Bn HQ and HQ Coy of the 5th Battalion would have to leave The Magazine, most of which was to be pulled down to make way for a new road system and a multi-storey car park. That would be a great loss, not only for sentimental reasons but because it was such a wonderful old building, and had for many years been the home of one or other of the TA battalions of the County and City. However, it was hoped that there would be advantages in new accommodation, wherever it was.

The Annual Administrative Inspection was carried out on 10 January 1960 by Brigadier J H Prendergast DSO MC, Comd 147 Inf Bde TA. Rather than review a Battalion Parade, he decided instead to hold a Guard Mounting competition in which each company entered a team. The standard of drill and turnout was very high, and before presenting the prizes, the Brigadier congratulated everyone on their efforts. The competition was deservedly won by HQ Coy, commanded by Captain M S (Michael) Tuke.

Early in the New Year a cocktail party was held in the Officers' Mess on the occasion of the unveiling of a wooden display board, recording the names of the Honorary Colonels, Commanding Officers, Training Majors and Adjutants of the 5th Battalion. The board was a very generous gift from Colonel John Barrett, the former Honorary Colonel of the Battalion. Everyone whose name appeared on it was invited to the party, and there were ten of the Commanding Officers present.

As well as long-distance marching with distinction, the main effort of the Battalion during the winter months was applied most successfully to recruiting, despite the grip of winter snow and ice, beating the drum, the Press, and almost anything else that would bring in recruits. A humorous brochure, depicting a tiger taking part in various TA activities, was devised and distributed in the County. A caravan, fitted out as a mobile recruiting stand, could be seen daily in the major towns of the area. With over 300 new volunteers signing on, one of the most pleasing aspects of the campaign was that a substantial number of the new men came from the Coalville area and, as a direct consequence, after a lapse of several years the drill hall there was reopened, a thriving element of D Coy.

The culmination of the Individual Training season was the Octathlon in May. The teams strode keenly through their tasks and tests of map reading, night patrols, forced marching, shooting, driving, weapon training, signalling and initiative. The B Coy team, under WO2 Neville Parker, triumphed for the third time, winning the cup outright. Sp Coy's Anti-Tank Platoon fired their 17-pdr gun on the RAF Bombing Range at Theddlethorpe on the Lincolnshire coast for the first and last time there – the bangs were loud enough to frighten the inhabitants out of their houses and their dogs into the fields, so once again it became necessary to find yet another place to fire the noisy weapon.

In the field of competition shooting, the Battalion Team did not reach top form. At Bisley, after a very promising start it came twenty-first in the China Cup, and, although the result was not as good as had been hoped for, it nevertheless bettered the other TA battalions of The Forester Brigade.

Annual Camp was at Redesdale, in the wilds of Northumberland. Accompanied almost throughout by Colonel Guy German, the Honorary Colonel, the Battalion spent many days deployed in the field in heavy mists and drizzling rain. At the Brigade Rifle Meeting at Ponteland, WO2 Neville Parker won the Offrs', WOs' and Sgts' Trophy and Private Smith of B Coy won the Young Soldiers' Championship.

The Band and Drums also went from strength to strength, and had many interesting and gainful engagements during the summer months. They acquitted themselves well in the massed Beating Retreat at Camp. WO1 S W (Sidney) Ord-Hume MBE[20], the new Bandmaster, was an inspiration to his musicians with his drive and enthusiasm.

Towards the end of the year the Battalion paid a fond farewell to WO1 'Dixie' Dean, who had been RSM for over five years, longer than any other RSM, having begun his Army career with the 5th Battalion in 1936. He was replaced by WO1 J A (John) Webb from 1 Foresters, an example of The Forester Brigade's planning to post the best throughout the Brigade's units.

In September, the Battalion Shooting Team departed in high spirits to the Divisional Rifle Meeting at Beckingham, but disappointingly could only finish fifth among the major units. The following month, the Leicestershire & Rutland Rifle Meeting was held. Since for many years this had been very much a 5th Battalion 'benefit' affair, it was decided that, as an experiment, the major units in the counties should enter company rather than unit teams, so that the small units would have more chance. This proved a great success, as there was a larger entry than for many years. B Coy, however, was somewhat ostentatious in that it won practically every trophy presented. As a further experiment, it was intended that the meeting the following year would be held in April, in the hope that it would be blessed by kinder weather and act as a more logical precursor to the summer shooting events.

The highlights of the many social activities were the Officers' Ball and the All Ranks' Ball, held on successive nights in December in The Magazine, and which were to be the final large events hosted within that famous building. And so, after some fourteen years, the Battalion finally left The Magazine, abandoning the sturdy walls of that near-fortress gateway and barracks. Only the thirteenth-century gateway and tower were to remain, later to become the Regimental Museum for thirty-three years – see Chapter 11.

The major item on which the Battalion then focused was the reorganization of the Territorial Army. The overall plan was to reduce the TA from 266 major units to 195, and to form it on an operational Brigade basis. In the reorganization there would disappear forty-six RA units, twelve of the RE, two of the Royal Signals, and eighteen infantry battalions. In Leicestershire there were three TA major units. On 1 January, the 5th Bn transferred to under command of 148 Inf Bde (147 Inf Bde at Leicester having been disbanded) – an early sign of TA reorganization – and the Annual Administrative Inspection was carried out by the new Brigade's Commander, Brigadier F A H Ling DSO.

Rumours had been rife that the strength of the TA was to be considerably reduced, and to be achieved by disbandment and amalgamation of units. LAA and Heavy AA units in particular were no longer needed in view of developments in rocketry. By very happy planning it was announced that not only was the 5th Battalion not to be axed, but that it was to absorb 'Q' Battery (The Royal Leicestershire Regiment), 438 LAA Regiment, RA (TA) – the successors of the old 4th (City) Battalion. Additionally 'R' Battery of that Regiment was to become a Field Park Squadron RE, the new Sapper unit designed to appeal to many young men in Leicester's engineering industry, and the 3rd (Northern Command) Casualty Clearing Station RAMC would be re-roled into a rather more active 148 Field Ambulance (148 Fd Amb). From the Leicestershire TA's point of view, these were excellent arrangements. The new infantry unit, which officially was to come into being on 1 April 1961 by amalgamation, was redesignated 4/5th Battalion The Royal Leicestershire Regiment (TA). Unusually it was to carry two sets of Colours, those of the former 4th and 5th Battalions. The amalgamation was easily effected, and the home of the former RA RHQ and 'Q' Battery, which was at the rather luxurious collection of buildings known as the TA Centre, Ulverscroft Road, became the location of Bn HQ and HQ Coy. Major Richard Wilkes RA moved from commanding 'Q' Battery to become OC HQ Coy 4/5th Battalion, and Other Ranks who elected to transfer to the 4/5th Battalion on the disbanding of their own unit were appropriately absorbed into the Battalion as its HQ Coy. The ex-Gunners rapidly began training hard as infantrymen.

Consequent upon the reorganization, the deployment of 4/5th Battalion was as follows:

2Lt J C Barrett VC, France, 24 September 1918. *Leicester Museums and Galleries*

2nd Leicesters, Crete, May 1941. *Leicester Museums and Galleries*

Chindits – Lake Indaw, Burma, March 1944. *Leicester Museums and Galleries*

LSgt Philip Smith VC, Sevastopol, June 1855. *Leicester Museums and Galleries*

Queen's Colour 1st Bn The Royal Leicestershire Regiment. *Newton Newton*

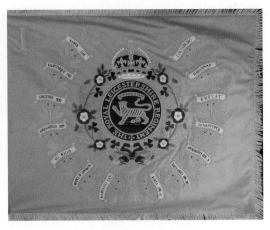

Regimental Colour 1st Bn The Royal Leicestershire Regiment. *Newton Newton*

Regimental Colour 1st Bn
The Royal Anglian Regiment.
Trustees R Anglian Regt

Queen's Colour 1st Bn
The Royal Anglian Regiment.
Trustees R Anglian Regt

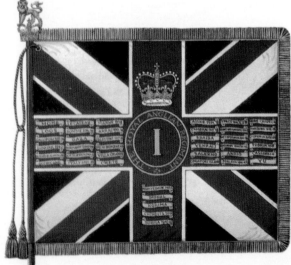

At a QUARTERLY MEETING OF THE COUNCIL OF THE CITY OF LEICESTER held at the TOWN HALL on the 27th day of June 1944: xxxxxxxx:–

CHARLES EDWARD GILLOT ESQ. LORD MAYOR, IN THE CHAIR. Moved by Alderman Wilford seconded by the Lord Mayor and carried unanimously:—

THAT in recognition of the very long and close association existing between the City and THE LEICESTERSHIRE REGIMENT WE, THE LORD MAYOR, ALDERMEN AND CITIZENS of the City of Leicester, being sensible of the great record and glorious tradition created by your most distinguished Regiment over many years of loyal and devoted service to King and Country, and in which so many of our Citizens have served, and are still serving, are desirous of still further cementing and fostering the goodwill and association which has so long been enjoyed. WE DO BY THESE PRESENTS express the desire that you will, on all ceremonial occasions, honour us, by marching through the streets of the City of Leicester with Bayonets fixed, Colours flying and Band playing.

IN WITNESS whereof we have caused our Corporate Common Seal to be hereunto affixed this twenty-seventh day of June One Thousand Nine Hundred and Forty-four.

Lord Mayor   Town Clerk

Freedom of the City of Leicester 1944. *Leicester Museums and Galleries*

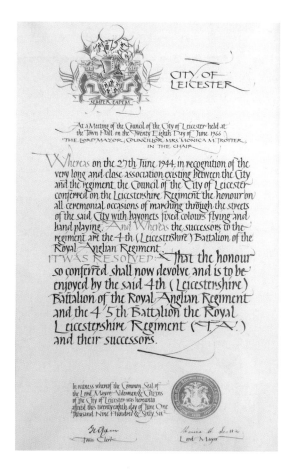

Freedom of the City of Leicester 1966. *Leicester Museums and Galleries*

Royal Leicestershire Regiment capbadge
Regular Officers 1947–60
TA Officers 1947–71. *Trustees R Leicestershire Regt*

Royal Leicestershire Regiment Service Dress
capbadge Regular Officers 1947–60
TA Officers 1947–71. *Trustees R Leicestershire Regt*

Forester Brigade capbadge
Regular Officers 1960–63.
Trustees R Leicestershire Regt

East Anglian Brigade capbadge
Regular Officers 1963–64.
Trustees R Leicestershire Regt

Royal Anglian Regiment capbadge
1964–date. *Trustees R Leicestershire Regt*

Royal Anglian 'Tiger' button
1970–date. *Trustees R Leicestershire Regt*

Regimental Flag. *M K Goldschmidt*

The Athens Memorial. *Commonwealth War Graves Commission*

Queen's Birthday parade in Hong Kong, 26 April 1963. *Trustees R Leicestershire Regt*

Overthrow on the War Memorial Gates at Victoria Park.
Trustees R Leicestershire Regt

Cover sleeve of 'Marching with the Tigers' 1970. *Mrs A E F Cowan*

2nd World War memorial window, Regimental Chapel.
R J Allen

Mosaic badge before the altar, Regimental Chapel. *M K Goldschmidt*

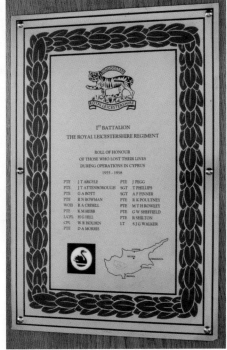

Cyrus memorial plaque, Regimental Chapel. *R J Allen*

Colours hanging in the Regimental Chapel.
R J Allen

A selection of kneelers, Regimental Chapel.
M K Goldschmidt

A display cabinet in the Regimental Museum.
Trustees R Leicestershire Regt

Planters of Royal Tigers' Wood (see Appendix P for names). *W G Dawson*

Figurine of Colonel Solomon Richards, and a pill box. *M K Goldschmidt*

The memorial stone at Royal Tigers' Wood.
M K Goldschmidt

Chindit Memorial at the National Memorial Arboretum. *National Memorial Arboretum*

Bn HQ and HQ Coy at Ulverscroft Road, Leicester; A Coy at Blackbird Road, Leicester; B Coy at Penn Street, Oakham, and at Asfordby Road, Melton Mowbray; C Coy at Station Road, Hinckley; and D Coy at Granby Street, Loughborough, and at Ashby Road, Coalville. Under new nomenclature drill halls were henceforth called TA Centres.

At the time of the formation of the 4/5th Battalion on 1 April 1961, senior appointments were held as follows:

CO:	Lieutenant Colonel J H Marriott MC	OC B Coy:	Major J B Harrison TD
		CSM B Coy:	WO2 N H S Parker
2IC:	Major J Hartley	OC C Coy:	Captain W G Dawson
Adjutant:	Captain R H Robinson	OC D Coy:	Major D B Holyoake TD
RSM:	WO1 J A Webb Foresters	CSM D Coy:	WO2 R B Curtis
QM:	Major L E Hollis MM	OC HQ Coy:	Major R G Wilkes TD
RQMS:	WO2 F Monk	CSM HQ Coy:	WO2 F J Botting
OC A Coy:	Major P A H Mockford	Bandmaster:	WO1 S W Ord-Hume MBE
CSM A Coy:	WO2 A Scarborough	Drum Major:	WO2 T F Simpson

It was shortly after this that the Battalion paid a sad and fond farewell to the Commanding Officer and his wife Pat, who together had done so much for the Battalion during his twenty months in command. Among other things John Marriott had arranged for a very smooth working amalgamation with 'Q' Battery, the move from The Magazine to Ulverscroft Road, the reopening of the Coalville Drill Hall, and the appointment of an outstanding new Bandmaster. He was followed as Commanding Officer by Lieutenant Colonel S A (Stuart) Smith MBE[14], a Regular officer who had been Adjutant of the 5th Battalion ten years before.

The next event of note was the Lord Mayor's Show on 27 May, reputed to have been the only show of its kind to be held outside the City of London. It was organized by the Leicester Junior Chamber of Commerce, one of whose council members was Major Richard Wilkes. Through his involvement members of the Battalion took part in the control of the Show and as participants. The latter comprised the Band and Drums, a 3" mortar and an MMG mounted on ¼-ton trailers, a 17-pdr anti-tank gun towed by a half-track, and a rifle platoon mounted in a 3-ton lorry, displaying a large and varied assortment of infantry weapons. Bringing up the rear was the recruiting caravan, towed by an Austin Champ.

The same contingent, vehicles and Band proceeded to Hinckley the following weekend, to head a similar procession through the Borough. As a direct result three young boys walked into the Hinckley TA Centre the following Monday and told the CO, who happened to be visiting, that having seen the display on Saturday, they wished to join the TA.

A Brigade Signal Exercise took place on Proteus Training Area in June. This was the first exercise of its kind in which the former members of 'Q' Battery had taken part, and when under pressure the following was occasionally heard: 'Hello 1, Target, Target, Target … correction, Hello 1…' That same month over a weekend four companies proceeded to Theddlethorpe, where they bivouacked and trained hard amongst the sand dunes. Virtually every weapon the Battalion possessed was fired – MMGs, 3" mortars, the 17-pdr anti-tank

An anti-tank detachment drives through the City. *Trustees R Leicestershire Regt*

gun and a selection of rifle company weapons – all at targets erected on the water's edge. The climax of that month was Royal Tigers' Weekend. The Band contributed a large part towards its success, playing at the Officers' Dinner at the Grand Hotel on Friday night, at the Garden Party at Glen Parva Barracks on Saturday, and escorting the contingents to and from the Cathedral on Sunday morning for the annual church service in the Regimental Chapel.

July was devoted to Annual Camp, held that year in the very different environment of the Army School of Civil Defence at Millom in Cumberland, as Home and Civil Defence had become one of the major roles of the TA at this time. Despite considerable apprehension of the TA soldiers, it turned out to be one of the most interesting in recent years, best explained by a chain of events that took place concerning a fairly new recruit. He had intended to remain for the first week only so, having completed his week's training, he proceeded to the station on the Saturday morning, but when he was about to board the train for Leicester he decided to return to Millom for a second week. Having completed his second week's training, he returned to Leicester and joined the Regular Army. The Battalion received an 'Excellent' report for their Camp at Millom.

A Battalion Church Parade was held on the middle Sunday morning, and the Honorary Colonel, who spent eight days at Camp, took the salute. On the last Wednesday at Camp, a dinner night was held, to which past commanding officers of both the 4th and the 5th Battalions were invited, and at which a silver tiger was presented to the Battalion by the Honorary Colonel and the brothers Oliver, the inscription on which read:

> Presented to the 4th/5th Battalion The Royal Leicestershire Regiment (TA)
> by Col. G. J. German DSO TD, Lt Col. C. D. Oliver OBE TD, and
> Maj. F. E. Oliver CBE TD, sons of Col Sir Frederick Oliver TD, and
> Col. George German DSO TD, to commemorate the service of
> these two friends who from 1908 to 1913 commanded the
> 4th and 5th Battalions The Leicestershire Regiment respectively
> and were later their Honorary Colonels. — 1961

That handsome and most apt piece of silver was the first to be presented to the new Battalion.

The silver tiger presented by Colonel Guy German and the brothers Oliver.
Trustees R Leicestershire Regt

The Band, unfortunately, was unable to spend the whole fortnight at Millom with the Battalion, arriving on the second Saturday. For their second week, they proceeded to the Army Outward Bound School at Towyn in North Wales, where they enjoyed a very hot week by the seaside.

211

For the third time, the Battalion entered a team for the Nijmegen March, led by Major John Hartley and, as on previous occasions, it completed the march without casualties.

A high-powered recruiting campaign was carried out in all the major towns of the County at various times throughout the year and resulted in a considerable increase in strength.

In late September, the Brigade Inter-Battalion Competition was held at Beckingham, the other units being 4/6th Lincolns, 4/5th Northamptons and 5th Foresters. It comprised Mortar and MMG Platoon competitions and Recruit Platoon weapon training, map-reading and drill. It was extremely gratifying that, in the first year of 148 Inf Bde, 4/5th Leicesters won the competition, albeit by a very small margin.

At the Officers' Dinner in October, Lieutenant Colonel Claude Oliver presented the silver Bofors LAA gun referred to above, marking the amalgamation of 'Q' Battery with the 5th Battalion in April.

On Remembrance Sunday the Battalion paraded in strength in various towns around the County, the only unexpected aspect being the appearance of a contingent of traffic wardens at the Leicester Parade, the problem being where to place them in the order of march. The traditional big events were held in the various messes in the lead-up to Christmas.

In the New Year of 1962, training again took centre stage, in parallel with preparations for the Annual Administrative Inspection, which was carried out in mid-February by Brigadier M J d'A Blackman OBE MC, Comd 148 Inf Bde. At the end of the month, two companies spent a training weekend at Theddlethorpe on the Lincolnshire coast and two at Leek. It was a matter of opinion whether a 60mph blizzard was colder on the coast or at 1,500 feet on the Derbyshire Dales. Recruiting was buoyant, and a new drill hall was opened at Lutterworth as an outstation of C Coy at Hinkley. As a result of a recruitment campaign, 'Stop a Tiger Jeep', young men interested in the TA were invited to stop a jeep as it toured various areas of the City and were taken to the TA Centre for a demonstration of what the TA could offer. By the autumn, 150 men had been enlisted, bringing the Battalion strength above the 500 mark, and rising.

The Battalion had a remarkably successful summer, the culminating highlight being winning the Brigade Skill-at-Arms Shield in the autumn, where it won every event by a fair margin: Mortar Platoon, MMG Platoon and Signals Platoon. A Battalion FTX was held in March, *March Hare*, a two-sided deployment exercise pitting Bn HQ and HQ Coy Gp against the rifle companies and the new Reconnaissance (Recce) Platoon in ¼-ton Land Rovers under Captain M A N (Mike) Clarke. The training was a very beneficial lead-in to the Brigade FTX, *Spring Fever*, in April. During the summer months, 2nd Lieutenant J F (John) Hampson enthused the volunteers by taking groups of fifty on adventure training to the Yorkshire Dales and the Lake District, a type of more rugged training that held great interest.

The Battalion Rifle Meeting was held concurrently with the Leicestershire & Rutland Meeting over a complete weekend in June. B Coy won the Inter-Company event and Battalion members won most of the Counties' matches. TA Battalions at this time were still armed with the .303" Lee-Enfield Rifle, were equipped with 38 Pattern web equipment and wore BD. Royal Tigers' Weekend for the Regiment was hosted mainly at Ulverscroft Road as opposed to at Glen Parva Barracks as in previous years. Annual Camp was held at St Martin's Plain Camp near Folkestone in Kent in July, where its local Hythe Ranges proved

The firing point at the Rifle Meeting, Kibworth, June 1962. *Trustees R Leicestershire Regt*

ideal for shooting training and for the numerous cadres around which the training period was based, and for which the 1st Battalion loaned fifteen instructors. That not only led directly to the overwhelming success in the Brigade Skill-at-Arms Competition, but life at Camp had so impressed the Volunteer soldiers that fifteen members immediately converted to Regular and reported to the Depot for training en route to the 1st Battalion – an excellent and unforeseen *quid pro quo* for the loan of instructors!

For the fourth consecutive year the 4/5th Battalion entered a team in the Nijmegen March, led by Lieutenant A J J (Albert) Price-Howells, where again it received a gold medal. B Coy also most creditably came sixth out of 357 teams in the TA Small-Bore Shooting Trophy. WO1 John Webb handed over as RSM to WO1 L E (Len) Loader from the 1st Battalion.

The Annual Administrative Inspection was carried out in November and an extremely favourable report was obtained – a highly satisfactory reward for the hard work put in by all ranks of the Battalion maintaining an astonishingly high level of activity, in training, administration and social events.

In early September, the Battalion took part in the 49th Infantry Division Rifle Meeting, and succeeded in winning the Young Soldiers' Cup, the very first year in which this match was included in the meeting. Participants had to be soldiers with less than one year's TA service, and without previous Regular or NS experience. The victory underlined the success of the recruit cadre at Annual Camp, and was a just reward for the keenness and enthusiasm which they, and all members of the team under Major D B (Brian) Holyoake, put into their preparation for the Meeting.

A Regimental Cocktail Party was held at Ulverscroft Road on 20 September to launch a month's recruiting drive in the County by the 1st Battalion, to which was invited a large number of distinguished guests from the City and County. During that month, A and B Company Groups of the 1st Battalion, having travelled up from Watchet, were billeted at

Ulverscroft Road, whence they toured the County, giving displays and demonstrations. The results in numbers of recruits, both for the 1st and 4/5th Battalions, were extremely pleasing.

The Officers' and Other Ranks' Balls were held in mid-December. The theme that year was the Wild West and depicted a Western saloon complete with swing doors and 'wanted' posters. The waiters were attired in cowboy uniform, the bar was installed inside the Corral, and the saloon sign read 'The Lazy Q', this latter innuendo giving the QM not a few ugly moments throughout the evening. The only item that seemed to be missing was the smell of gun smoke since enough corks 'popped' to satisfy even the most ardent Wild West fan.

Training throughout the winter period had been extensive and continuous. Companies travelled far and wide to satisfy their thirst for excitement and knowledge, despite arduous camping conditions and inclement weather. An example of training being fun, even when conditions were harsh, was a bitterly cold all-night exercise in mid-January to test the security of the Technical Stores Depot at Old Dalby. Some 150 members of the Battalion took part, assisted by guard dogs from the RAVC Depot at Melton Mowbray and by WD police. The greater part of the force was employed inside the depot to stop the infiltration of twenty saboteurs whose task was to blow up certain 'radar' equipments. Only one saboteur succeeded in using his flour bombs on the correct target. The guard dogs did sterling work, which resulted in the tailor being kept busy putting new seats in BD trousers!

One notable social event held in the WOs' & Sgts' Mess on 1 March was the Ladysmith Ball. In addition to senior officers as guests, the occasion was graced by the presence of two veterans who helped to earn the 1899/1900 'Defence of Ladysmith' Battle Honour, 87-year-old Mr Eato who was in the siege, and Mr J Howe who was in the relief column that raised the siege.

By the spring of 1963, the strength of the Battalion had reached 530, an indication that it had not only regained the large numbers lost to the 1st Battalion after Annual Camp in 1962 but had recruited even more. By the autumn, numbers had increased to 560. The Band and Drums slowly and surely increased in strength and efficiency, and began a new scheme for training Junior Bandsmen/Drummers for future enlistment. For the second year running the Battalion won all the Brigade Skill-at-Arms Competitions – the pattern of the competitions was now somewhat changed, the emphasis being on Young Soldiers, and included drill, inspection, weapon training and fieldcraft.

In preparation for an earlier-than-usual Annual Camp in June, plans were effected to ensure that the Battalion's command and communications reached a high standard of training early in the year – to which end the Signal Platoon, the Recce Platoon and the Battalion Command organization trained extremely hard, laying on numerous interesting exercises which were made most enjoyable for all by the imaginative deployment of the Recce Platoon, often as 'enemy'.

A Battalion Exercise was held towards the end of March at Proteus Training Area, followed in April by the Brigade Exercise, *Spring Fever II*, which entailed the deployment of three infantry battalions in defence, followed by an attack on the Sunday morning, an action which was filmed by TV cameras. In the subsequent broadcast, wives and mothers in Leicestershire, while being rewarded by seeing their sons and husbands on TV, probably could not recognize them in their 'war paint'.

Over Easter, some 250 soldiers proceeded on an 'interest' training exercise to Brecon Beacons in South Wales, made all the more 'interesting' by extreme weather conditions. Those deploying comprised 200 members of the Battalion, accompanied by cadets and Territorials of 148 Fd Amb and 566 Coy RASC. The training was based on the pursuit section of the Duke of Edinburgh Award Scheme. The Signals Platoon, with great ingenuity, maintained a radio net by establishing a relay station which seemed to be 'at 5,000 feet'! The challenge provided by terrain and weather (and the unknown) helped all participants realize just what they were capable of accomplishing when required.

Although tinged with sadness at the break-up of The Forester Brigade, the 4/5th Battalion entered The East Anglian Brigade on 1 May in a very positive frame of mind, helped no doubt by the retention of its title – and Royal Leicester capbadge. With the closing of the Depot at Glen Parva Barracks, a much bigger responsibility was assumed by the 4/5th Battalion's WOs' & Sgts' Mess to provide a place where former members of the Regiment could meet socially in Leicester, and keep in touch with each other. The Mess immediately (and characteristically generously) extended honorary membership to all members and Honorary Members of the Depot Mess. The response was overwhelming and social occasions at Ulverscroft Road were packed to capacity.

Royal Tigers' Weekend was held in mid-May, a month earlier than usual due to the imminent closure of the Depot at Glen Parva. The Dinner on Friday night was held at Ulverscroft Road, at which the Band and Drums of the Battalion played, as well as at the Garden Party at Glen Parva Barracks on Saturday and the Church Parade at the Cathedral on Sunday morning.

Annual Camp was held in the middle fortnight of June at Stanford Training Area in Norfolk, with accommodation in a tented camp in the centre of the training area. With a Battalion strength at Camp some 100 more than in 1962 (and a HQ Coy of 180), it was possible to carry out far more ambitious training. Although it was a Brigade Camp, it operated largely on individual Battalion training programmes. Recruit and specialist platoon cadres were carried out in the first week. A Battalion Exercise was held in the second week, practising company attacks, followed by a Brigade-run Company Test Exercise.

A Drumhead Service was held in the middle weekend, after which the Honorary Colonel made presentations of four TDs, three TEMs, and three clasps to TEMs. The parade ended with the whole Battalion marching past him. The Band and Drums also were very active at Camp, playing at the Church Parade, Officers' Mess functions, the Recruit Passing-Out Parade, and, most impressive of all, taking part in the Massed Band Beating Retreat Ceremony in Cambridge. They were equally extremely active throughout the year and their strength grew considerably. In place of the Brigade Band Competition that year, there was a Brigade Massed Band and Drums Concert and Beating Retreat ceremony in Lincoln, which proved overwhelmingly successful – and far more enjoyable for spectators and participants.

The Battalion Rifle Meeting took place at Kibworth in early July. B Coy was Champion Company and Captain Tony Wilson the Champion Shot. That same month, following on the successful arduous training in Wales at Easter, HQ Coy took forty men to the Glossop area of Derbyshire. That type of training – undertaken by other companies too – proved extremely popular with the TA Volunteers, and enhanced the soldiers' skills and confidence.

Later in the summer, a generous presentation was made to the Battalion by former members of the 4th Battalion. It took the form of a wooden display board – similar to that presented in 1960 to the 5th Battalion – on which had been recorded the names of the Honorary Colonels, Commanding Officers and Adjutants of the 4th Battalion, from 1908 to the date of the amalgamation. The splendid gift was proudly hung in the entrance to the Officers' Mess, opposite the board of the 5th Battalion.

In August 1963, senior appointments were held as follows:

CO:	Lieutenant Colonel S A Smith MBE	CSM B Coy:	WO2 N H S Parker
2IC:	Major J Hartley	OC C Coy:	Major W G Dawson
Adjt:	Captain R H Robinson	CSM C Coy:	WO2 J J Ward
RSM:	WO1 L E Loader	OC D Coy:	Major R D F Bream
QM:	Major L E Hollis MM	OC HQ Coy:	Major R G Wilkes TD
RQMS:	WO2 H Evans	CSM HQ Coy:	WO2 F J Botting
OC A Coy:	Captain W G Wallace	Bandmaster:	WO1 S W Ord-Hume MBE
CSM A Coy:	WO2 L W Grant	Drum Major:	WO2 T F Simpson
OC B Coy:	Major G W E Wootton		

In November, Lieutenant Colonel Stuart Smith handed over command to Lieutenant Colonel J P N (Pat) Creagh, a Regular officer who had been Adjutant of the 5th Battalion ten years before. It brought immense pleasure to the Battalion to learn six months later that Stuart Smith's most successful time in command had been recognized by the award of the OBE. The Regimental service of another 'old soldier' came to an end in the spring with the retirement of Major Les Hollis, who left after twelve distinguished years as the Battalion's QM.

The usual round of autumn reunions and Christmas social events took place at which many old soldiers travelled great distances to be present. The Battalion's own cooks prepared the food at the two Officers' Mess Dinners, and the results did tremendous credit to them and the PMC. More formally, for the Annual Administrative Inspection, the Battalion again received a most favourable report.

The Brigade Skill-at-Arms Competition took place in the spring 1964 and, as in the previous year, did not include support weapon platoons as in the past, but a rifle platoon only, consisting of first-year recruits who had had no previous military service. The Platoon had to undergo tests in drill and turnout, weapon training, fieldcraft and platoon tactics. The Battalion succeeded in winning every leg of the competition and so won the shield by a large margin, for the second year running. At the Divisional Rifle Meeting, while no trophies were won, numerous individuals were highly placed.

At Battalion level, there was a Signals Exercise, *Tiger Rag*, in March, followed by a Brigade Study Period and Brigade Signals Exercise. With the Battalion strength having reached 570 and a further effort to reach 600 by the time of Annual Camp in June, the enthusiasm of the new and the older soldiers was whetted by adventure training again at Easter, that year in the Lake District. The MT Platoon, under the direction of Sergeant Cook, busily trained for the Divisional Driving Competitions in April, spending numerous weekends on night-driving runs and negotiating cross-country courses.

Annual Camp, once again a Brigade Camp, was held at Otterburn in Northumberland.

Vickers MMG teams at Warcop. *Trustees R Leicestershire Regt*

Accommodation was completely hutted, and the training areas were far larger than at Stanford, but, being on moorland, it was rumoured that it was not unusual to see man or vehicle almost disappear in marsh. The weather was not unduly kind, but much useful recruit, platoon and company training was done, and the highlight was a Battalion Withdrawal Exercise, witnessed by the GOC-in-C Northern Command and the Divisional Commander. The Mortar, Anti-Tank and MMG Platoons had a very good three-days' live firing at Warcop, the last mentioned still equipped with the .303" Vickers MMG, long since disestablished from the Regular Battalion. The success of Camp could be partly attributed to the very considerable assistance provided by elements of the 1st Battalion, led by Lieutenant David Michael, and by 17 Army Youth Team, under Captain Tony Pollard. Whilst the Brigade was in camp, the Band and Drums as part of the Massed Bands of 148 Bde played a programme of music and Beating Retreat at Edinburgh Castle.

Very shortly after Camp there followed Royal Tigers' Weekend, which was held at Ulverscroft Road, and a good number came from the 1st Battalion, whose Band and Drums performed an excellent Beating Retreat.

Competition for the Coalville March was very keen, particularly in C Coy, which fielded three teams. Colonel Mike Moore MC TD DL, a former CO of the 5th Battalion, presented the cup to the winning team. Again a Battalion team entered the Nijmegen March, made up from members of A and D Companies. Led by Captain S (Stephen) Hartley, it was the fifth consecutive year in which the Battalion won a team medal in the event.

Since National Service had ended, that source of officers for the TA had dried up, and thus it became necessary for the Battalion to train its own junior officers. The process entailed a potential officer enlisting as a private soldier, and given the appointment of an Officer Cadet whereby he automatically became a member of the Officers' Mess. Training of officer cadets took place centrally at Battalion Headquarters. After that training period was completed, the individual was interviewed by the TA Association Chairman and Brigade Commander, and, if considered suitable, he went before a Command Selection Board. A successful candidate was then granted a TA commission.

The Battalion Rifle Meeting at Kibworth was held in glorious weather in May, and was enjoyed by both soldiers and families alike. The Falling Plate Competition was the most popular event. The Band, in their Blues and musketry order, though not winning the shooting prize, would surely have won one for the most colourfully dressed! D Coy won the Battalion Shooting Shield, and yet again Captain Tony Wilson was the Battalion Champion Shot.

In September, the TAFA HQ moved from London Road to Ulverscroft Road, so that there were even more old Tigers under the one roof. Collocated there were Bn HQ and HQ Coy 4/5th Battalion The Royal Leicestershire Regiment, RHQ The Royal Leicestershire Regiment, 17 Army Youth Team and HQ Leicestershire & Rutland TAFA. The TAFA Secretary was Lieutenant Colonel (Retd) D F (Donald) Coburn DL, a former Regular officer of the Regiment[15].

As the time approached when the 1st Battalion was to join The Royal Anglian Regiment and be renamed and rebadged, the Colonel of The Regiment, Major General Sir Douglas Kendrew KCMG CB CBE DSO, sent the following letter to the Honorary Colonel The 4/5th Battalion (TA), Colonel Guy German DSO TD:

> On this historic occasion, when the 1st Battalion of The Royal Leicestershire take the title of the 4th (Leicestershire) Battalion of a new Regiment, I know that you understand that your title as the 4/5th Battalion The Royal Leicestershire Regiment is not altered. However, you are now part of the Territorial organisation of The Royal Anglian Regiment.
>
> I know that you all will realize that our change of name will not in any way alter the close cooperation and ties between the Regular Battalion and our Territorial Battalion. The move that has taken place within the Regular Army is one for progress and greater efficiency.
>
> As I relinquish the Colonelcy of The Royal Leicestershire Regiment, I thank you for the close support and help you have all given me in the past. I also know that you will give that same loyalty and support to our new Royal Colonel-in-Chief, to our Royal Deputy Colonels-in-Chief and to the Colonel of our newly-formed Regiment – The Royal Anglian Regiment.
>
> May I wish you success in the future, and trust that the ties of the 4th (Leicestershire) Battalion of the newly-formed Regiment will always remain as solid and unshaken with the 4/5th Battalion of The Royal Leicestershire Regiment as they were in the past.

In his letter of reply Colonel German wrote:

> We appreciate the reason that has made necessary the change of title of our 1st Battalion and the formation of the new Big Regiment, but assure you that although we are fortunate enough to be allowed to retain our title and capbadge, we will strive continually to see that there is no weakening in the ties and cooperation that have for so long existed between the Regular and Territorial Battalion of The Royal Leicestershire Regiment.
>
> We feel deeply the responsibility that now rests upon us as being the only Battalion to bear the title of Royal Leicestershire and wear the Tiger Capbadge. This added responsibility will make us all the more determined to see that as far as lies in our

power the great traditions and successful records of our predecessors are maintained untarnished.

We welcome the news that, as Deputy Colonel, we shall retain your interest, help and advice. In thanking you for all you have done for us in the past, we assure you of our unbroken support in the future.

We would further ask you, as Deputy Colonel, to pass on to the Royal Colonel-in-Chief, to the Royal Deputy Colonels-in-Chief, and to the Colonel of The Royal Anglian Regiment, our loyal greetings.

The relative quiet of the winter months was soon replaced by the hurly-burly of the training season and preparation for Annual Camp. In 1965, the Battalion's training was directed towards the field of Home Defence. Cadres for First Aid were run, in preparation for the St John Ambulance Certificate.

In spring 1965, senior appointments were held as follows:

CO:	Lieutenant Colonel J P N Creagh	CSM B Coy:	WO2 N H S Parker
2IC:	Major R G Wilkes TD	OC C Coy:	Major W G Dawson
Adjt:	Captain A J G Pollard	CSM C Coy:	WO2 E Sowter MM[16]
RSM:	WO1 L E Loader	OC D Coy:	Major R D F Bream
QM:	Major J H F Leeson Northamptons	CSM D Coy:	WO2 J Brunskill
RQMS:	WO2 H Evans	OC HQ Coy:	Major G W E Wootton
OC A Coy:	Captain W G Wallace	CSM HQ Coy:	WO2 F J Botting
CSM A Coy:	WO2 R Rowlatt	Bandmaster:	WO1 G Williamson
OC B Coy:	Captain M A N Clarke	Drum Major:	WO2 T F Simpson

As part of their training, A Coy enjoyed a fruitful weekend's Initiative Exercise in January, during which members of the Company were despatched in pairs throughout the length and breadth of Britain on various tasks. These included such challenges as obtaining signatures from the team captains after the England-Wales Rugby International in Cardiff and obtaining the signature of comedian Arthur Askey at the London Palladium. All tasks were successfully completed and many far quicker than the Company Commander, Major Bill Wallace, had reckoned possible. It was later rumoured that he consequently actively tried to discourage members of his Company from using too much initiative!

WO1 Len Loader handed over as RSM to WO1 H D (David) Benham from 4th (Leicestershire) Battalion The Royal Anglian Regiment.

In April, nine TA Emergency Reserve volunteers of the Battalion (including Sergeants John Bloomfield and Stuart Copland) went to Aden for a fortnight and were attached to the 4th Battalion The Royal Anglian Regiment during its six-month Emergency Tour (described in Chapter 5). All benefited much from the experience of active service. In October, Lieutenant Trevor Holroyd went with twenty-four NCOs and men of the Battalion to West Germany, where they underwent a fortnight's training with 1st Battalion The Royal Northumberland Fusiliers, including taking part in a Divisional FTX.

Annual Camp was held at the Army Home Defence Centre at Devizes in June. The initial reserve with which that new type of training was greeted soon vanished as officers, NCOs and men found themselves involved in the intricacies of a new and interesting subject. Daily training was predictably hard work, with great emphasis on the physical practice of all subjects. In a rescue and first-aid competition held during the first week, the Battalion showed commendable skill in all the techniques they had been taught, and Sergeant T G Girvan's squad came first. The climax of the fortnight, after twenty-four hours of digging, was the Battalion going 'underground' to survive a simulated nuclear attack.

Prior to Camp, the Battalion won the 148 Inf Bde Support Weapons Shield at Warcop Ranges. All the men firing contributed to some very accurate shooting, none more so than Sergeant Stuart Copland, whose accuracy in controlling the Mortar Section astounded the School of Infantry representatives. For the MMG Platoon it was a rather sad occasion – when the Vickers machine guns had been cleaned and boxed, they were handed in for the last time.

The Band, under the direction of WO1 Gordon Williamson, and the Drums trained hard through the year and, with the massed Bands and Drums of 148 Inf Bde, Beat Retreat at Bath in June and later at Chilwell at the 50th Anniversary of the Battle for Hohenzollern Redoubt in France[17]. That anniversary was marked by a reception hosted by the Lord Mayor of Leicester, Alderman Sidney Bridges.

The Battalion Rifle Meeting was held at Kibworth in August. HQ Coy, as Champion Company, won the Burnaby Shield, and Corporal Burton, of A Coy, was Champion Shot. At the Divisional Rifle Meeting in September the greatly improved standard was evident when the Battalion Team came fourth. RSM David Benham trained the team well – Private Bozzoni, of HQ Coy, came second in the Young Soldiers' Competition, and WO2 J Brunskill of D Coy and Corporal Hall of HQ Coy were the highest scorers.

As a result of vigorous training conducted by Major Richard Wilkes, six of the Battalion's officer cadets were granted provisional commissions at the Northern Command Selection Board in September.

Before the training year ended, each company of the Battalion entered a team in the Northern Command Night March, for which much strenuous weekend training was evident among the highways of the County.

On 15 December, a most significant event occurred: a Government White Paper announced a future Reorganization of the Army's Reserves[18]. It foretold the disbandment of the Territorial Army and the Army Emergency Reserve, and that in their place would be created the Territorial & Army Volunteer Reserve (TAVR), to be effected by April 1967. The purpose of these changes would be to provide formed units as reinforcements for NATO and for major operations outside Europe, which would be more highly trained and better equipped than the TA. How these changes would affect the volunteers in Leicestershire and Rutland would be worked out over the succeeding sixteen months.

In December, also, the Battalion paid a sad and fond farewell to the Commanding Officer and his wife Rosemary who together had done so much for the Battalion during his thirty months in command. The departure of Pat Creagh ended a phase during which the Battalion had had a succession of three Regular commanding officers. The Tigers' Territorials were most grateful to John Marriott, Stuart Smith and Pat Creagh for the combined results they had achieved, and their names enter the Battalion history in much the same way as the triumvirate of post-1918 Adjutants – 'Tweaks' Weyman, 'Shargo' Sawyer and Jimmy Lowther. Those six in particular, amongst many others, exemplified the wonderful help, cooperation and encouragement the TA Battalions had always received from the Regular element of the Regiment.

Pat Creagh was succeeded in command by Lieutenant Colonel Richard Wilkes TD, a TA officer on promotion from Battalion 2IC. Richard Wilkes was to have a challenging time in command, spanning the introduction of the TAVR. Major A H V (Adrian) Gillmore MC[19] was posted in as Training Major, on a tour that was to last but a year. Senior appointments were held as follows:

CO:	Lieutenant Colonel R G Wilkes TD	CSM B Coy:	WO2 N H S Parker
Trg Major:	Major A H V Gillmore MC	OC C Coy:	Major W G Dawson
Adjt:	Captain A J G Pollard	CSM C Coy:	WO2 E Sowter MM
RSM:	WO1 H D Benham	OC D Coy:	Major R D F Bream
QM:	Major J H F Leeson Northamptons	CSM D Coy:	WO2 J Brunskill
RQMS:	WO2 H Evans	OC HQ Coy:	Major G W E Wootton
OC A Coy:	Captain W G Wallace	CSM HQ Coy:	WO2 F J Botting
CSM A Coy:	WO2 R Rowlatt	Bandmaster:	WO1 G Williamson
OC B Coy:	Captain M A N Clarke	Drum Major:	WO2 T F Simpson

Meanwhile the Battalion prepared for its Annual Administrative Inspection, which was carried out in February 1966 by Brigadier J A Spencer-Smith OBE MC, Comd 148 Inf Bde.

The training year was much the same as usual, carried out in parallel with the emerging plans for reorganization. In May, further details of the new TAVR as it would affect Leicestershire and Rutland TA were announced. One company of 115 all ranks from 4/5th R Leicesters would form a rifle company of a new Royal Anglian Regiment TAVR battalion, a Category II unit with Bn HQ at Peterborough and known as 'Volunteers'. That Battalion would be liable for callout to reinforce the Regular Army should Britain's military commitments demand it, would be equipped with the latest weapons and combat clothing, and would have a heavier training requirement. The remainder of the 4/5th Battalion would retain the title of the Regiment, be a Category III unit of some 270 all ranks in strength and be known as 'Territorials'. Its role would be Home Defence. The success of the new TAVR was predicated on its being built upon the foundations of the TA and it would depend upon the same enthusiasm and spirit of the part-time soldier who had existed before. TA units in the counties from other Arms would also be affected, and a number of TA centres would close in due course as the overall numbers of sub-units decreased. These changes were to be effective from 1 April 1967.

A Brigade Signals Exercise was held in South Lincolnshire in May. Keen training took place in preparation for the Battalion Rifle Meeting at Kibworth in June. Sergeant Alan Robey of D Coy was Champion Shot, and the Burnaby Shield was won by HQ Coy. Lieutenant G J Morgan went with sixteen NCOs and men of the Battalion to West Germany, where they underwent a fortnight's training with 1 DWR at Osnabrück and Soltau.

The Battalion was involved as usual in organizing and taking part in Royal Tigers' Weekend on 25-26 June. The Band played at the Reunion, and the Band and Drums led the March Past of the Old Comrades after the Sunday Parade Service in the Cathedral. In early September, the Band and Drums were part of the Beating Retreat by the Massed Bands and Drums of 148 Inf Bde at Lincoln.

On 28 June 1966, the resolution of the Council of the City of Leicester that conferred

Officers of 4/5th R Leicesters at Warcop (see Appendix P for names). *Trustees R Leicestershire Regt*

the Freedom of the City on 4th (Leicestershire) Battalion The Royal Anglian Regiment, also conferred the Freedom on 4/5th Battalion The Royal Leicestershire Regiment (TA) and their successors, an honour of which the TA Battalion was justly proud.

Annual Camp was held at Warcop in Northumberland for a fortnight from 30 July. Moving into camp was delayed by the desire of most to watch the Football World Cup Final on television, England's victory inspiring all ranks to put in creditable performances despite almost continuous torrential rain. The main training features of the fortnight were an exercise in which company teams had to complete different tasks at a number of different locations at various distances from Warcop, and a Section Test Exercise. The latter was won by an A Coy Section led by 2nd Lieutenant J A Kelly. Planning ahead, the Commanding Officer and Adjutant interviewed all volunteers individually to determine their wishes for the future in the forthcoming reorganization (whether to join TAVR II or TAVR III).

It was slightly disappointing that in this final year of the TA the Battalion team could only finish third overall in the Divisional Rifle Meeting at Beckingham. Nevertheless, Sergeant Smith and Corporal Dorman of C Coy won the LMG pairs, and Private Tidd of B Coy was the Young Soldiers' Champion Shot. The remainder of the year included a patrol exercise in Shropshire, a Battalion MT Rally (won by Privates Lauper and Bullock of HQ Coy), three officers' study periods devoted to the new roles, and the Brigade Commander's Annual Administrative Inspection.

The year began with the very pleasing news of the award of the MBE to WO2 D G (David) Grove. A Regular soldier, he had been based with 17 AYT at Ulverscroft Road for two years and he was well known for his outstanding work with teenagers throughout the county.

It having been decided that A Coy, commanded by Major Bill Wallace and based at Ulverscroft Road, would become the future (TAVR II) 4 Company of the new 5th (Volunteer) Battalion The Royal Anglian Regiment (5 (V) R Anglian), the Company held a shakedown weekend at Leek in mid-January. The following weekend the Battalion's Mortar Platoon carried out its last live firing of the well-loved 3" mortars, and in fine weather shot very accurately. That Platoon, as with the other specialist weapons platoons, would be disestablished from the future TAVR III Home Defence battalions, but fortunately it was to transfer in its entirety to 4 Coy 5 (V) R Anglian.

And so the final months of the TA drew to a close, and the Battalion prepared to play a full part in the new TAVR. A Battalion Reunion Dinner was held on 11 February and was attended by over 200 members past and present, including all former Regular COs, Training Officers and Adjutants of the 5th Battalion and the 4/5th Battalion since the Second World War, who were in the country that night. The occasion was marked by the presentation of a silver tiger statuette to Colonel Guy German in appreciation of his loyal and unswerving support to the Battalion during his nine years' tenure as Honorary Colonel. In late March, a final Officers' Mess Dinner was held, attended by the Lord Lieutenant and other senior guests. A statuette of a soldier in 17th Foot ceremonial dress was presented by the officers. It was a most fitting way to commemorate the end of fifty-nine years of the Regiment's distinguished contribution to the TA, which was formally to cease to exist on 1 April 1967.

The Royal Leicesters' part in the new TAVR is taken up in Chapter 10.

Notes

1   See Chapter 2, Note 12.
2   Claude Oliver had joined 4th Leicesters (TA) in 1922, and transferred in it to RE and RA. He had been awarded the OBE for his action when CO 122 Anti-Tank Regt RA in North Burma in February 1945. He was to be Chairman of that TAFA from 1957 to 1967.
3   Frederick Oliver, who served in 4th Leicesters (TA) and its successors for twenty-five years, had been Lord Mayor of Leicester 1950-51 and was to be knighted in 1962 for political and public service.
4   Mike Moore had been awarded the MC as a company commander in 2/5th Leicesters at Salerno in Italy on 12 September 1943.
5   Peter Preston had been awarded the MBE in 1945 for service with 69 Airfield Construction Gp RE in Italy.
6   Jock Cassie had been awarded the MC as a company commander in 2/5th Leicesters at Calabritto in Italy in December 1943. After the War he was a familiar figure on the streets of Leicester as an Inspector with the City police force.
7   Les Hollis had been awarded the MM as a platoon sergeant major in 2nd Leicesters at Sidi Barrani in Egypt in December 1940.
8   Ken Ruddle had commanded 2/5th Leicesters in France and Flanders in 1940. He was subsequently Chairman of Rutland County Council, for which he was knighted in 1957.
9   John Barrett had been awarded the VC at Pontruet in France on 24 September 1918 while a platoon commander in 1/5th Leicesters. One of the Regiment's Cuneo pictures shows that action (see Chapter 11 and plate section).
10 Guy German had been awarded the DSO for his conduct as CO 1/5th Leicesters in Norway in 1940 and as a Prisoner of War 1940-45, for part of which he was the Senior British Officer in Oflag 4C (Colditz Castle), the famous PoW camp for officers notorious for escaping. In 1945, his wife was awarded the MBE for her work for the Leicester Prisoner of War Fund which raised some £82,000 (which would be some £2,500,000 at 2008's values).
11 See Chapter 1, Note 8.
12 See Chapter 2, Note 3.
13 See Chapter 2, Note 1.
14 See Chapter 1, Note 5.
15 Donald Coburn had commanded 1/5th Leicesters in 1943 and 1944, and had been the last CO of 2nd R Leicesters in 1948.
16 Ernest Sowter had been awarded the MM as a Corporal in 2nd Foresters at Anzio in Italy in February 1944.
17 On 15 October 1915, the 4th and 5th Leicesters (TF) had fought with valour and distinction at Hohenzollern Redoubt during the Battle of Loos. Twenty officers and 453 men of the 4th Battalion died that day.
18 This Reorganization became disparagingly known as the 'Hack It and Carve Up' Reform, named after Generals Sir Shan Hackett and Sir Michael Carver, the plan's authors, who were at the time VCGS and CGS respectively.
19 See Chapter 6, Note 9.
20 Sidney Ord-Hume was awarded the MBE in 1955 as Bandmaster 1st Northamptons.

Chapter 8

4th Battalion: Gillingham and Bahrain 1968-70

Gillingham: May 1968 to August 1969

The Battalion Advance Party under Major J A (Jimmy) Hughes, the Second-in-Command, had left Malta in May 1968 and, after their leave, assembled at the new posting, Gordon Barracks, at Gillingham in Kent, a former Royal Engineers barracks that essentially comprised single-storey wooden huts and large corrugated-iron sheds. In poor condition, it certainly looked and felt as if it had been built before the Second World War. The Tigers were the first infantry battalion to be accommodated in it.

Reassembling in early September after block leave, members of the Battalion looked at an uncertain future as the Battalion was due to leave the Army's Order of Battle in about two years. Meanwhile the Regimental hierarchy (including the Royal Leicestershire element of it) set about finding the best way to organize the absorption of the men of the 4th Battalion into the other three battalions at that time.

In much the same way as earlier that summer he had masterminded the presentation of a silver tiger centrepiece from The Royal Leicestershire Regiment to the 5th (Volunteer) Battalion The Royal Anglian Regiment (see Chapter 10), Major General John Spurling, the Royal Leicesters' Deputy Colonel, also instigated the inspired plan for The Royal Leicestershire Regiment and the 4th Battalion to present silver tiger centrepieces to the Officers' and WOs' & Sgts' Messes of each of the other three Regular battalions. In addition, in the ensuing months, plans were made for, among other things, the disposal of silver on disbandment.

At Gillingham, the Battalion was part of 2 Infantry Brigade (2 Inf Bde) at Shorncliffe (Brigadier J M W Badcock MBE), which also included 1st Battalion The Light Infantry (1 LI) at Gravesend and 1 Loyals at Dover. 2 Inf Bde was part of 5th Division (Major General W B Thomas DSO MC) at Wrexham.

After two and a half years in which he and his Battalion had achieved notable success, David Carter handed over command on 6 September, and a fond farewell was extended to him and his wife Jean. His successor was Lieutenant Colonel Terry Holloway, who had last served with the Battalion as 2IC in Malta eighteen months before and had served in the previous four active service tours of the Battalion[1]. He inherited the unenviable position of having to preside over the dissolution of the 4th Battalion.

At that time, senior appointments were held as follows:

CO:	Lieutenant Colonel T Holloway	CSM B Coy:	WO2 P M Collins
2IC:	Major J A Hughes	OC C Coy:	Major S A Green
Adjt:	Captain J C Tyzack	CSM C Coy:	WO2 D E Ancliffe
RSM:	WO1 R E Sprason	OC Sp Coy:	Major C T Marshall
QM:	Captain E P Kelly DCM	CSM Sp Coy:	WO2 D R Edwards
Tech QM:	Lieutenant J Eyeions	OC HQ Coy:	Major R J M Mosse
RQMS:	WO2 C Ladley	CSM HQ Coy:	WO2 A Hill
OC A Coy:	Major J G Jones MBE	FLO:	Major C P Culbert
CSM A Coy:	WO2 R Swain	Bandmaster:	WO1 T G Cooper
OC B Coy:	Major R H Robinson	Drum Major:	CSgt T R West

The Battalion was an airportable battalion, organized similarly to in Malta, with an HQ Coy, three rifle companies and Support Company. In Support Company, the Anti-Tank Platoon reverted to the 120mm MOBAT, towed by ¾-ton Land Rovers, and the Mortar Platoon was equipped with the 81mm Mortar. The Rifle Platoons were equipped with the GPMG and the 84mm Carl Gustav anti-tank weapon. Communication was provided by C42, A41, A40 (all VHF) and the WS62 and A13 (HF) radio sets. Vehicles were mainly Land Rovers and 3-ton lorries.

In the next phase of the transition to The Queen's Division, on 11 September 1968, HQ Queens Div, based in Colchester, assumed responsibility for Other Ranks manning. It was to be a year later in August 1969 that Major Peter Worthy, the HQ's staff officer and sometime Tiger, took over RAF Bassingbourn in South Cambridgeshire from the RAF, and in July 1970 the HQ was to move to the renamed Bassingbourn Barracks, collocated with the new Depot The Queen's Division, which would 'open for business' there in January that year. In 1969, each Regiment lost its serving Regimental Colonel, whose function was superseded by that of the Queen's Division Brigadier, the first in post being Brigadier M W Holme CBE MC, late The Essex Regiment. His staff was drawn from across The Queen's Regiment, The Royal Regiment of Fusiliers and The Royal Anglian Regiment. RHQ R Anglian was thereafter led by the Regimental Secretary who supported the Colonel of The Regiment, and its staff worked to take an overview of the Regiment, develop policies, plan and manage events, dispense Regimental charity, edit *Castle* Journal and manage the recruitment of officers.

From September 1968, the 4th Battalion swiftly settled in to its new surroundings and to military life in England as part of the Strategic Reserve. While using rifle and field-firing ranges the men rather enjoyed the opportunity to rest their elbows on grassed firing points again. The other early excitement occurred in the early hours of 22 September, when a fire broke out in one of the large storage huts. Eight fire engines attended the scene but were unable to prevent the destruction of a lecture room and, more importantly, large quantities of families' property in packing cases. The Anti-Tank Platoon stores were destroyed, and the guns and training aids damaged. A fire-blackened scene therefore greeted Comd 2 Inf Bde on his first visit to the Battalion the following day. Some wag expressed the hope that the fire did not presage that the pace of soldiering in England would produce 'burn out'!

The start of October was unusual. First, the Commanding Officer informed the Battalion that in August 1969 it would start a nine-month unaccompanied tour in Bahrain, news which was greeted with a strange resignation to the course of fate for the final year of the

Battalion's projected existence. Secondly, later that week, complaints were received from the locals that blank rounds, thunderflashes and explosives were being used on the training area at night. It was pointed out that the barracks had previously been a RE stronghold when the training area had been used mainly for building bridges which made no noise; but that the Infantry had to practise night-fighting skills which inevitably made some noise. A compromise was made by limiting the noisy part of night exercises up to midnight. Thirdly, in culmination for what was to be a momentous week, the Battalion moved by coach to Leicestershire for overnight accommodation in various RAF stations in advance of the most important event of the year: the exercise of the Freedom of Leicester. A memorable day in the history of The Tigers, 12 October was long remembered by the serving and retired members of the Regiment.

The programme of events began with a short service in the Regimental Chapel in the Cathedral, where the Colours of 1st Battalion The Royal Leicestershire Regiment, which were still carried by 4th Battalion The Royal Anglian Regiment, were laid upon the altar and the Provost, the Very Revd J Hughes, gave an inspiring address to Tigers, old and current. The Colours were then marched onto parade from the Cathedral and the Battalion in four guards set off to exercise the Freedom of the City of Leicester, marching through the streets of the City, 'with Bayonets fixed, Colours flying and Band playing'. It was the first march since the Freedom had been granted to the Battalion in 1966, and the previous Freedom March had been fourteen years before, when 1st Royal Leicesters had returned from Korea in 1952.

In the pouring rain outside the Town Hall, the Lord Mayor of Leicester, Alderman Kenneth Bowder OBE, said in his address:

> When in July we heard that this Battalion was to be absorbed into the other three Battalions of The Royal Anglian Regiment by 1972, we formed the hope that the passage of time and the pressure of events before this date would be such that as may well be the case a regular Infantry Battalion will still continue to be recruited from the City of Leicester and the County of Leicestershire. Further we hope that this battalion will continue to call themselves 'Tigers' and that the identification of us here in the City and County with you will continue as cordially and effectively as before. The Tiger is still in excellent health. Long may he so continue.

Led by the Band and Drums, the Battalion then marched through the streets of the City, watched by hundreds of shoppers. As it reached Victoria Park the sun came out. The Lord Mayor took the salute and about 300 Old Comrades, commanded by Lieutenant General Sir Colin Callander, also marched past as the fifth guard. The parade formed hollow square at the War Memorial[2]. Preceded by the playing of 'Wolfe's Dirge', the Bishop of Leicester, Rt Revd R R Williams DD MA, read the Regimental Collect and blessed the parade, and wreaths were laid. The Deputy Colonel-in-Chief, HRH The Duchess of Gloucester, then inspected the Old Comrades.

The City entertained all ranks of the Battalion and sixty members of the Royal Tigers' Association to a magnificent Civic Lunch in the De Montfort Hall. In his speech in reply to the Lord Mayor's toast to the Battalion, the Deputy Colonel, Major General John Spurling, recalled the visit to Malta in May of the Deputy Colonel-in-Chief, 'During those two days we showed to Her Royal Highness that the Tiger was not only a fine fighting symbol of

The Colour Party near the War Memorial, Victoria Park. *Leicester Mercury*

past glory but a living example of the modern British infantryman at his best.' He expressed the Battalion's gratitude at the determination she had shown to ensure that the much-prized Tiger badge was perpetuated in the uniform of The Royal Anglian Regiment – to be worn by all ranks of all battalions.

> To emblazon a Royal Tiger on a button is not a trivial irrelevance. It is an outward and visible sign that all the best endeavours of The Royal Leicestershire Regiment are passed on to The Royal Anglian Regiment ... Perhaps it would be overoptimistic to think that some last moment stay of execution could save the 4th Battalion from disappearance in 1971 or our Territorial Battalion from disbandment.

Thereafter many of the Battalion attended the First Division football match between Leicester City and West Bromwich Albion at Filbert Street, where the Band and Drums played at half-time. The Chief Constable, whose men had most efficiently kept the streets clear and diverted traffic, subsequently instructed his officers not to stop and breathalyse any member of the Battalion that day!

An enormous amount of administrative assistance was rendered to the 4th Battalion that day by men of the Leicestershire TAVR units, both in the City and hosting a separate luncheon for the balance of the Old Comrades at Ulverscroft Road. Without their diligent hard work the events would not have run so smoothly. And so, as the Battalion set out to return to Gillingham and the Old Comrades also wended their way home, all looked back on a truly memorable day which had been enjoyed by so many and where, as ever, the hospitality of the Corporation of the City had been immense.

On 17 October, the Officers' Mess held its welcoming cocktail party, to which a number of local civilian and military dignitaries were invited, including the Mayor of Gillingham, who was not to pay his first formal visit to the Battalion until December.

On 21 October, WO1 P F (Paul) Garman, most of whose previous career had been spent in the Royal Norfolk part of the Regiment, assumed the appointment of RSM. It was at about this time that, in place of 'Jerseys Heavy Wool' in Barrack Dress, the officers and WOs started to wear dark blue pullovers with the Royal Anglian anodized shoulder titles. This experiment was relatively short-lived as the pullovers variously stretched or shrank when washed, and consequently soon became distinctly unsmart.

Thirty all ranks set out to provide some of the umpire party for the major FTX, *Swap*, in Northern Ireland. A joint exercise, it began with beach landings from HMS *Fearless* by 45 Cdo RM, supported by 2 RRF, RN helicopters and RAF FGA and transport aircraft. The opposition were 1 LI, the North Irish Militia and the Royal Ulster Constabulary. It was to be the last such exercise in the Province for about forty years, as 'The Troubles' broke out there during 1969 – for reasons totally unrelated to the exercise! The part that the Tigers played in Northern Ireland in 1971 and 1974 is covered in Chapter 9.

At the end of that month the Main Body of the Battalion left Gillingham by train for Otterburn for two weeks' field firing, where it was joined by the Exercise *Swap* umpire party. The training period was notable mainly because of the vile wet weather. Drying out nightly round the large coke fires in the barrack huts, the soldiers sat sipping mugs of hot tea and rum, and swapping stories as to who had swum the furthest before engaging the targets.

In preparation for its tour of duty as the *Spearhead* Battalion of the Strategic Reserve at the end of the month, on 11 December, the Battalion took part in an airportability exercise and C Coy conducted amphibious training at Marchwood. The traditional round of Christmas events took place before Christmas block leave. Tac HQ and C Coy (the 'Leading Element' of 146 all ranks) and the loading teams returned to barracks on 27 December to assume *Spearhead* duties, with their freight and vehicles loaded. The remainder of the Battalion returned three days later and came to seventy-two hours NTM.

The pace of life in the early months of 1969 was brisk. On New Year's Day, the Company loading teams took part in Exercise *Jigsaw 9* involving RAF aircraft at RAF Manston, and six weeks later sixty men and thirty vehicles went to Marchwood for a week's amphibious training. Meanwhile, in mid-January, a group of officers and soldiers took part in Exercise *Short Tack 4*, a Joint CPX with 19 Inf Bde and 38 Group RAF, whereafter the three rifle companies spent a week at a time conducting field training at Stanford. Thence C Coy marched back 60 miles to Chelmsford over three days before picking up its transport. Over the following months a series of cloth model exercises in barracks and TEWTs in the Kent countryside took place, studying Defence, Advance to Contact and Attack, and Withdrawal, as preparation for the Battalion training period at Sennybridge in June.

From the time of its arrival in Gillingham in the autumn of 1968, Battalion teams engaged with some success in a wide range of sports. Pride of place went to the Hockey

Team, led by Lieutenant David James. The Team was in its third year together but after the hard fast pitches of Malta it adjusted well to grass – and muddy – pitches, and to stiffer opposition in England. After eighteen matches it was unbeaten, including winning the South-East District Cup. Sadly it was beaten finalist in the Southern Command Cup, just two matches away from the Army Final. Captains Brian Davenport and David James, and Lance Corporal Leslie Holman represented the Infantry during the season.

The Football Team continued its Malta form and had an immensely successful season. Under the management of Lieutenant 'Jimmy' Jenks and captained by Corporal R (Robbie) Allen, it beat very strong sides in various competitions but also narrowly lost at key stages, including 0-3 to 1 RHF in the Army Cup, who went on to win the UK Section. Private L Northrop, QMSI W A (Bill) Robson APTC (an inspiring replacement in many sports for SSI Bill Stoves, he had played basketball for England in the mid-1960s and was a former BAOR Triathlon Champion), Private John Sorenson and Corporal John Farnham played for the Army XI; Farnham also played for an English FA XI (and for Gillingham Town on Saturdays!).

The Rugby Team made a promising start and had sufficient competent players to form two teams. Managed by Captain Roger Howe, the First XV was captained by Colour Sergeant Brian Newman. Twice in September teams sallied forth to Leicestershire, for the Stoneygate Sevens and a four-match tour. Much experience of English conditions was gained, but pressure of commitments prevented the full side being fielded together until *Spearhead* in January, when it lost 0-8 to 1st Battalion The Welch Regiment in the Army Cup.

For the relatively new sport of orienteering, a wood within reasonable distance of barracks was found which was big enough to confound the weaker brethren. Led by 2nd Lieutenant J M P (John) Walsh, the Battalion Team came fifth in the Southern Command championships and he came third in the South-East District championships.

At cross-country there were great hopes for the first season in England after three successful years in Malta. Over 5½ miles, with four hills of muddy farmland, Private Peacock was first home in the Inter-Company competition, won by his Sp Coy. In comparison, with the flat, fast road running of Malta, the Battalion Team lacked proper race fitness and confidence in their ability to run well in English conditions and could do no better than fifth in the South-East District championships. There was considerable enthusiasm for a full marathon race – perhaps the first ever organized by the Battalion. On 10 April, fifteen runners set out along the Pilgrim's Way to Harrietsham and back, supported by the Signal, MT and Medical Platoons. Of the three runners who completed the gruelling race, first home in 3 hours 46 minutes was Private Roger Cobbin, who on the strength of this feat was promoted Lance Corporal.

On the organizational side, in preparation for the Bahrain tour, Lieutenant D L H (David) Bulleid RRF joined the Battalion on 20 March to command the new Anti-Tank Guided Weapon (ATGW) Platoon, equipped with Vigilant. This wire-guided missile with a range of 1,500 metres was transported to the battlefield by ¾-ton Land Rover from which it was crew-portable into its firing position. The JNCO missile controllers needed to have a special aptitude. Selection for these and an intensive training course for the whole platoon was undertaken over two months at the Support Weapons Wing at Netheravon. At the same time the Anti-Tank Platoon (Lieutenant Michael Goldschmidt) converted from

MOBAT back to WOMBAT, as a weapon carried on a portee Land Rover had greater mobility in the terrain of the Persian Gulf than one towed behind a Land Rover.

As a further example of the manning policy within The Queen's Division, which posted manpower to where it was most needed, between April and July Lieutenant D J M (David) Daniels arrived from 1 RRF in April to command the Recce Platoon, to be followed a month later by seventy-two RRF soldiers posted in to bring the Battalion up to strength for the Bahrain tour: twenty-eight came from 1 RRF, nineteen from 2 RRF and twenty-five from 3 RRF. Finally, in August, Captain S R (Simon) Yates from 2 RRF took over Support Company. Of interest, not a few of those Fusiliers had volunteered to join the Battalion and to serve in Bahrain so that they could save enough money to 'buy themselves out' the following year!

At the end of March, the annual Fitness for Role (FFR) inspection was conducted by Comd 2 Inf Bde. A number of subunits were required to display IS techniques. After watching some sports events in the afternoon, the Brigade Commander seemed well pleased with all the standards he had witnessed that day. In his letter to the Commanding Officer he wrote:

> Thank you for a splendid day yesterday and I congratulate you upon nearly everything that you were able to show me. My general impression was one of confidence, competence in training and organization within your companies. It is backed by a sense of well-being and pride upon the part of the men and this is important when one considers that an impending separation of nine months for those that are married, is not altogether an enviable one.

The Battalion was required to provide a rifle company to reinforce 1st Battalion The Black Watch (1 BW) (Lieutenant Colonel A L Watson) for a six-week jungle training period in West Malaysia, Exercise *Safari*. As later that year it was to undergo a nine-month unaccompanied tour, it was decided to call for volunteers for what was called Safari Company. Based on Sp Coy's HQ, the ad hoc rifle platoons were manned by men from all the companies – there was no shortage of volunteers, including married men and those who sought to relive their Borneo jungle ventures. A trainers' Advance Party from 1 BW and the 4th Battalion's Safari Company had deployed in early March to do a five-week Jungle Warfare Instructors' Course, and were later to train all the companies in theatre. In early April, led by Major Colin Marshall, the balance of the 106 all ranks of Safari Company flew to Singapore. Based at the Jungle Warfare School at Kota Tinggi in Malaya, the 1 BW Bn Gp carried out section and platoon training in the jungle, culminating in a Bn-level FTX. The opportunity was taken by men of Safari Company to visit the Singapore Memorial at Changi where are recorded the names of 194 men of 1st Battalion The Leicestershire Regiment who died in that theatre of war in 1941-2.

Back in Europe, C Coy took part in April in the 2 Inf Bde four-day FTX *Nordic Night* on the Isle of Skye. Deploying by LCT *Abbeyville* and Andover aircraft, and RAF Wessex helicopters, it combined with elements of 1 Queens to oppose a light company of 1 Loyals. Unfortunately the exercise planners had failed to realize that it was the lambing season, so belatedly the use of blank ammunition and pyrotechnics were prohibited; the Exercise was renamed *Silent Night*!

On its return, the Battalion was visited by the Deputy Colonel, who was accompanied by Mr Bethel from Radio Leicester, who interviewed soldiers and recorded the Band playing The Royal Leicestershire Regiment marches. Previously, on 15 March, the Band and Drums had played at Twickenham for the England vs Scotland rugby international. After a subsequent musical audition at the BBC HQ, a letter was received on 9 May saying, 'This is to confirm that I have accepted the standard of the Band of 4th Battalion The Royal Anglian Regiment as being up to that required for broadcasting on the national network.' This was a fine achievement by all concerned.

It was about this time that the effect of posting into the Battalion of significant numbers of men from areas of 'Royal Anglia' other than Leicestershire (and Rutland) began to be felt in this once 'all-Leicestershire' Battalion. In *Castle* Journal an article appeared titled 'Parliamo Eastangliano'. It purported to be an extract from '4 R Anglian's East Anglian Phrasebook, published to assist those who were unfortunate enough to have been born west of the Ouse or south of the Deben'. Among the Do's and Don'ts was 'Don't overstay your welcome e.g. at sunset an East Anglian should take part in the sport of Dwile Flonking, so leave ten minutes before.'[3] With regard to pronunciation, the article said:

> Norfolk East Anglian is spoken slowly with a flat monotonous accent. Norwich East Anglian is jibbered rather than spoken, with a slight twang. Suffolk East Anglian has a sing-song accent. Fenland East Anglian is spoken with a heavy twang not uncommon in Australia. East Anglian Language Courses are now available at the Army School of Education, followed by a nine-month posting to Stratton Strawless or Dickleburgh.

On 30 May, the Battalion set out by road and rail for a week's FTX in Sennybridge, the first battalion-level training for two years. For various reasons all of the companies were somewhat light on numbers, not least because Safari Company was resting after its jungle rigours. The FTX began with a two-day work-up period, organized by the Commanding Officer. 2 Inf Bde then set and conducted a test exercise, with a company of 1 Loyals as live enemy. It began with a simulated air move through an MCCP, and 'deployment by air' (in 3-ton lorries) to a simulated island where the Battalion seized an airfield. This was followed by extensive OP work and patrolling, culminating in a successful search and destroy operation against a guerrilla force. Comd 2 Inf Bde's comments on the Battalion's performance included:

> Despite the fact that half of the Battalion was away, including some of the key figures, the organization worked like a charm ... if things creaked a bit at first, it was so refreshing to see the speed with which improvements occurred and by the end the Battalion's confidence was very obvious ... I feel that it has the confidence and organization to give a good account of itself when it arrives in the Gulf.

How right he was to prove to be!

On return to Gillingham, the Battalion's focus then turned to preparation for Bahrain. Fitness and the ability to operate in high temperatures and humidity were trained for, in among other places the gymnasium, which had all the doors and windows sealed and the central heating working full blast. Members of the Advance Party were the subjects of a series of Army Medical Services' experiments on renal stones, carried out before departure, and later in Bahrain.

As part of an Infantry-wide change of organization and establishment, HQ Company was disbanded in mid-June and Command Company and Administrative (Admin) Company were instituted in its stead. Command Company (under Captain Pat King) comprised: Bn HQ; the Orderly Room; Signals, Recce and Drums Platoons; Intelligence and Medical Sections; Regimental Police; Weapon Training staff; and APTC staff. Admin Company (under Major John Mosse) comprised: MT Platoon, Band, Offrs' and WOs' & Sgts' Messes, PRI, Padre, and REME, RAPC, RAEC and WVS personnel.

In the latter half of June forty members of B Coy took part in a KAPE tour, which comprised evening mini tattoos around Leicestershire (and Lincolnshire and Northamptonshire), culminating at Leicester with Royal Tigers' Weekend and the opening of the new Museum of The Royal Leicestershire Regiment in The Magazine (covered in Chapter 11).

4th Bn's Trumpeters at the Opening Ceremony, June 1969. *Leicester Mercury*

The Battalion set out on five weeks' block leave at the end of June, reaassembling at Gordon Barracks on 4 August. Meanwhile, the Advance Party of seventy-five all ranks, under Major M E (Mike) Duffie, left England by air for Bahrain on 28 July, where it moved to Hamala Camp. Almost as soon as it had arrived, several officers and SNCOs flew to Cyprus to act as umpires on a week-long FTX in the Eastern Sovereign Base Area that tested 1st Battalion The Green Howards.

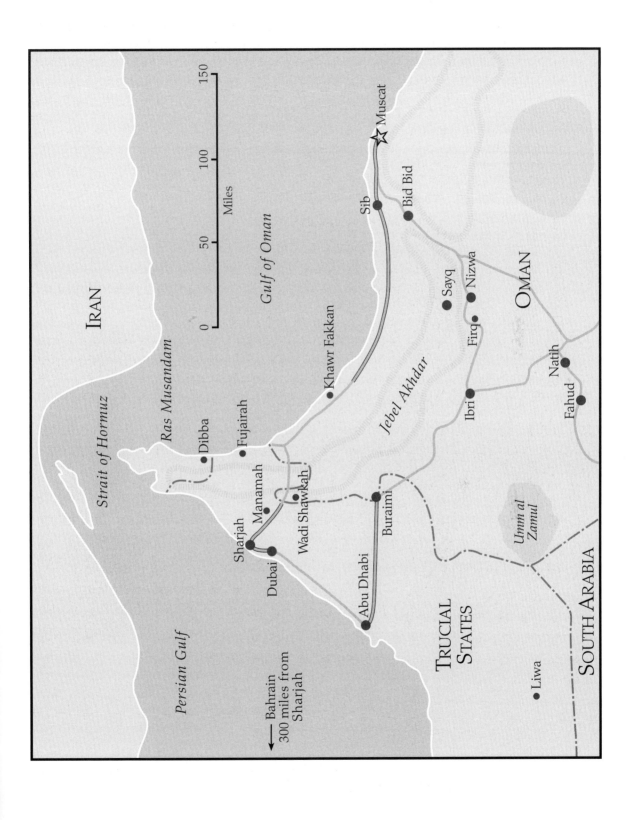

Bahrain: August 1969 to May 1970

Situated between Saudi Arabia and Qatar and 340 miles to the west of the entrance to the Persian Gulf, Bahrain is an island of 277 square miles, some 30 miles from north to south and 10 miles from west to east. Its terrain is mostly low-lying desert plain, rising to 400 feet in the central south. It is extremely hot and humid in the summer months. A Muslim country, from 1861 it was virtually a British Protectorate. In 1913, the British and Ottoman governments had signed a treaty recognizing Bahrain's independence whilst it remained under British administration. Originally renowned for its pearl trade, Bahrain had benefited from the discovery of oil in 1932, and developed one of the first oil refineries in the region. From 1956, as a result of anti-British riots in the wake of the Suez Invasion that year, various elements of British Armed Forces were stationed there, usually in battalion strength with elements of the RN and RAF. In 1961, when the Iraqis had threatened to invade Kuwait, a British garrison and new RAF station were established in Bahrain, the garrison initially including a Parachute Battalion Group. In 1967, after the British withdrawal from Aden, Bahrain became an even more important base, especially for the RN in the region, and it provided a secure place from which Britain could help to shore up the security of the developing Gulf States. Infantry battalions were then stationed in Bahrain and at Sharjah, 300 miles to the east on the Arabian mainland. After the British Government announced in 1968 that it would close its bases east of Suez by 1971, Bahrain's status as a protectorate ended when its agreement with Britain was cancelled by mutual consent. British Forces

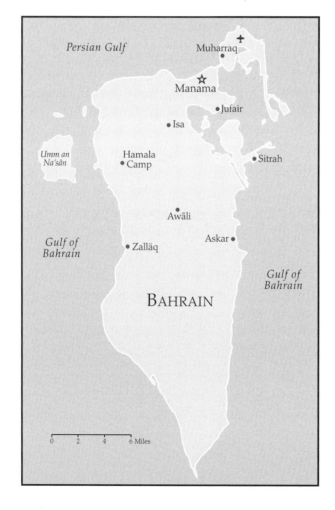

Hamala Camp, Bahrain, looking west. *M K Goldschmidt*

were to remain there for a further three years, and the Resident Battalion, while having a regional reserve role, retained an IS capability should Bahrain's Ruler need such help. This was politico-strategic situation in which the 4th Battalion found itself.

The Main Body began arriving in Bahrain on 10 August 1969, and four days later the Battalion formally took over from 1st Battalion The Cheshire Regiment, at Hamala Camp. The camp had been constructed in 1963 on a bare desert ridge, somewhat isolated from the outside world, being 15 miles from the nearest town and capital, Manamah. In effect it was a village of Twynham huts, made largely of aluminium and air-conditioned, and included a wide range of sports facilities, an outdoor cinema and covered swimming pool, a church and messes.

On arrival, senior appointments were held as follows:

CO:	Lieutenant Colonel T Holloway	OC C Coy:	Major S A Green
2IC:	Major M E Duffie	CSM C Coy:	WO2 J T Morris MM
Adjt:	Captain C P B Keeble	OC Sp Coy:	Captain M E Romilly
RSM:	WO1 P F Garman	CSM Sp Coy:	WO2 R B Freakley
QM:	Captain E A Holben	OC Comd Coy:	Captain P W King
Tech QM:	Lieutenant J Eyeions	CSM Comd Coy:	WO2 L MacDonald
RQMS:	WO2 C Ladley	OC Admin Coy:	Major R J M Mosse
OC A Coy:	Major J Robinette	CSM Admin Coy:	WO2 P Jones
CSM A Coy:	CSgt E Christopher	Bandmaster:	WO1 T G Cooper
OC B Coy:	Major R H Robinson	Drum Major:	CSgt T R West
CSM B Coy:	WO2 P M Collins	Rear Party/UFO:	Major M K D Gunton

The Battalion's strength in Bahrain was thirty officers and 554 soldiers, including the Band. The Rear Party in UK was some sixty-five all ranks. The Battalion shared its camp with both a Recce Flight of three Sioux helicopters (detached from 668 Avn Sqn AAC and

235

commanded by Captain D V (David) Fortune BW), and No. 3 Air Control Centre/Air Defence Centre RAF (a radar and communications unit). It was under command of HQ Land Forces Gulf (Brigadier A J Archer OBE)[4], whose other infantry battalion and artillery regiment was based at Sharjah. HQ British Forces Gulf (Major General R C Gibbs CBE DSO MC[5]) was also stationed in Bahrain (alongside the UK Foreign Office's Political Resident Persian Gulf (PRPG)), as were some RN ships at HMS *Jufair* and a number of RAF aircraft of various shapes and sizes at RAF Muharraq.

The Battalion spent its first three weeks acclimatizing in 120° F heat, and settling in to the new surroundings. Many briefings and study periods on the politico-strategic importance of the Gulf took place. At a lower level, the Commanding Officer reinforced the diktat which he promulgated before the Battalion left England: that all his men should treat the local population at every level with the greatest respect, and the use of any time-honoured pejorative phrases for men from the East was strictly forbidden. Among various contingency plans, the Battalion had an IS role in Bahrain, practice for which was called Exercise *Quick Silver* and preparations for which were rehearsed and tested. At all times there had to be one company, the Alert Company, confined to camp and at short NTM.

As there was very limited opportunity to train outside camp in Bahrain, there were regular training periods at company and battalion level on the mainland in the Trucial States.[6] Few, if any, men were to spend less than three months away from the island by the end of the nine-month tour; and it was said that 'they became as used to catching ships and aircraft of many types as most people were to catching buses.' When in Hamala Camp, the daily routine began with an early morning run, followed by breakfast; training until lunchtime and then 'into the cool' air-conditioning or swimming pool until 1600 hours; followed by sport and training. In mid-summer, when the Battalion arrived, such was the high temperature and humidity that the Medical Centre each day flew a series of coloured flags to depict the relative danger as the various gauges climbed. Green changed to Orange and then Red; when the Black with White skull and crossbones was raised, all soldiers had to move indoors or into the swimming pool. In contrast, during the winter months the weather could be very chilly, with the winds blowing down from southern Russia. By then the swimming pool was long closed, and on occasions the Medical Centre flew a green flag with white dots (signifying falling snow)! In the hottest months particularly, the task least looked forward to was the daily guard at the RAF Muharraq bomb dump, which most right-thinking infantrymen believed was the role of the RAF Regiment!

Part of the entertainment in camp was listening to the local area network radio station, 'Radio 17', led by Sergeant T (Terry) Fleming, the REME Telecommunications Technician. The Signals Platoon also provided the disc jockeys, prominent among whom were Private M (Mick) Platt and Sergeant S ('Stu') Pollitt, an RRF reinforcement and former Lancashire Fusilier – with an unusual sense of humour. Analogous to the 1944-54 popular Kenneth Horne's BBC Radio programme about a fictitious air station 'somewhere in England', Hamala Camp was referred to as 'Much-Binding-in-the-Sand'. Each morning those on the network were woken to the sounds of 'Good morning, Starshine', and each evening were sent to sleep by the recording of '*Je t'aime*', which did not leave much to the imagination. One particular morning the DJ played the wake-up record an hour early. After less than a minute he realized his mistake and switched off – but not before one very keen Colour Sergeant was out of bed, footwear and shorts on, and was running the perimeter of the camp wondering where everyone else was! During the tour there were also four CSE shows, which performed before enthusiastic audiences in the camp's open-air cinema and starred such artists as Hope and Keen, Joe Brown and Julie Rogers.

Due to the recently announced policy of the British Government to 'withdraw from east of Suez by 1971', British troops in the Gulf (and the Battalion in Bahrain) received an unusually large number of senior political and military visitors. Among them were: six British MPs, the Imperial Defence College and the C-in-C of the Bahrain National Guard (the son of the Ruler of Bahrain) in September; the Comd BFG in October; the Director of Infantry/Colonel Commandant Queen's Div in November; the Rt Hon George Brown MP, the Foreign Secretary, in December; Mr Ivor Richards MP, the US of S for Defence, and his Conservative opposite number, the Rt Hon James Ramsden, separately in January; and the Quartermaster-General in April.

On 1 September, the fifth anniversary of the formation of The Royal Anglian Regiment was celebrated, with a day's leave combined with many sporting activities including inter-company hockey, swimming and football. On a wider Royal Leicestershire Regiment scene, discussions began about the final disbandment date, and a disbandment parade in Leicester which would combine a 'Farewell to The Tigers', the dedication of a memorial plaque and the laying up of the Colours of 1st and 2nd R Leicesters. It was also necessary to plan the start of a campaign in Leicestershire and Rutland to accept/welcome/recruit for its County Regiment, The Royal Anglian Regiment.

On 17 September, the Officers' Mess held its welcoming party for the hierarchy of Bahrain, and it included cocktails, a BBQ supper, band concert and dancing. Five days later the first Bahrain edition of *Tiger Rag* was published, of which the Editor was Major Mike Duffie, with the publishing in the capable hands of Lance Corporal Coleman, his Bn HQ clerk. Eight 8-page editions were published, on the 22nd of each month, and were read with much mirth.

Leaving Sp Coy (now commanded by Captain S R (Simon) Yates RRF) behind in Bahrain as Alert Company, for ten days in October, the Battalion took part in its first FTX, *Milk Shake*, in the Trucial States, with the aim of introducing the Battalion to rugged jebel and wadi terrain, further acclimatizing soldiers, learning to cooperate with helicopter support, and generally to shake down. As was to be its frequent form of transport of the following months, the LSL *Sir Bedivere* ferried the sea party to Dibba in the State of Fujairah. The first phase comprised company-level training based in camps along the Dibba coastline, whereafter the Battalion conducted Advance to Contact, tasking aircraft for troop movement and resupply. Helicopter support was provided by the Scouts and Sioux of 13 Sqn AAC and Wessex helicopters from an RAF squadron whose emblem was a tiger. Consequently air tasking messages indicated the need for 'Tigers to support Tigers'. After the successful deployment, the Battalion recovered to Bahrain by Andover aircraft from Manamah and by sea from Dibba.

Over the next two months there were a series of company deployments to the mainland. Leading that series, Sp Coy sailed on LSL *Sir Bedivere* to Dubai in mid-October and drove 150 miles to Buraimi for a fortnight's training, including live firing at Jebel Ali. Then for three weeks each, B Coy, followed by A and C (now under Captain A E (Alan) Thompson MC), conducted field training, including live firing in Wadi Shawkah – the 'wadi of thorns'. While there with B Coy in early November, the action of the MT Platoon's Corporal John

Cpl Paul Clements' men train for an Omex Patrol. *P Clements*

Cross in extinguishing a burning Land Rover near a POL point earned him a GOC's Commendation for Bravery.

Setting out from Abu Dhabi, from 5 to 19 November, the Recce Platoon drove in their Land Rovers over a hundred miles to Liwa Oasis, which is situated on the edge of the Rub al Khali – the 'Empty Quarter' of north-east Saudi Arabia. They practised navigation by sun compass and driving on sand (the Liwa Hollows contain some of the highest sand dunes in the world), were resupplied by the RAF and generally 'showed the flag' en route.

Another part of the activity away from Bahrain was the provision of patrols to Oman, known as Omex Patrols. A subaltern and fourteen men would deploy for a fortnight, flying by RAF Argosy to Firq Oasis or Nizwa, thence either on foot with pack donkeys, or by RAF helicopter, or by Sultan's Armed Forces (SAF) Skyvan, up on to the Jebel Akhdar at Fort Sayq. Those who flew from Firq to Fort Sayq became entitled to wear the 'Firq-Sayq' tie! From this military outpost at 6,400 feet, the platoons patrolled through most of the villages in the surrounding area, received unending tribal hospitality, dispensed low-level medical treatment, and occasionally gave small-arms firepower demonstrations. The patrols also sought to bolster the economy in an unobtrusive way. Some patrol commanders were given quantities of Dinars and told to 'distribute' them generously. While visiting the villages, eating meals and drinking coffee, the patrols hired local guides, bought local food and the headmen were 'slipped' fistfuls of grubby notes. They also played sport with subunits of the SAF, including donkey polo. Four successive patrols were carried out by the Battalion's rifle platoons in September/October and a further three in March/April 1970. These patrols were important flag-showing undertakings, as it had been British troops who in 1958 had assisted the SAF to defeat a local rebellion centred on that area. It was helpful to show the tribesmen that Britain was still engaged in the region, thereby bolstering the waning authority of the old Sultan Said bin Taimur (who was subsequently deposed by his son Qaboos bin Said in July 1970). It was also useful training for the British patrols as it improved the soldiers' self-sufficiency and confidence whilst operating independently from the chain of command, and provided very pleasant interludes from the constrained facilities in Bahrain.

Flag-showing visits by RN ships round the Persian Gulf were also important and more often than not welcomed by the ship's company and the community on land. RN frigates and minesweepers often invited small groups from the Battalion to join their ship's company, the opportunity grasped with gusto to take passage and spend several days on board visiting ports of the Trucial States and Kuwait. One soldier even travelled as far as Karachi which he described as 'just like Birmingham'.

Troops deplaning from a Wessex near Manamah. *Trustees R Anglian Regt*

As the final major deployment of the year, the ship-borne party left on LSL *Sir Bedivere* in mid-December for Dubai to link up with A and Sp Coys and Tac HQ for an air tasking exercise, *Hawking Tiger*, in the Manamah area, in which AAC Scout and Sioux helicopters, and RAF Wessex helicopters and Argosys were called upon for troop and equipment-lift and resupply, and Hawker Hunters for ground attack. All the Battalion's participants returned to Bahrain in time for Christmas.

Apart from those fortunate enough to be able to fly to England for a few days' leave, the Christmas programme at Hamala Camp for the remainder was traditional and full, and, as might be expected, kept the Chaplain, Revd R A (Robin) McDowall[7], extremely busy. On 21 December, there was a carol service; on 23 December, the JNCOs held a Tramps' Ball in the NAAFI. On Christmas Eve, at the All Ranks Draw, the first prize – a free ticket to UK for Christmas – was won by Band Sergeant Cooper. This was followed by Midnight Mass. On Christmas Day 'Gunfire' was served to the soldiers by the officers, WOs and sergeants, and after another carol service they served their Christmas lunch to the junior ranks. On Boxing Day, an Inter-Platoon sports competition and the Offrs vs Sgts football match were held, and on 28 December in the cinema the officers, sergeants and attached RAF personnel staged a review, 'Stalag Follies'.

The festive season came to an abrupt halt on 30 December when the Inter-Coy cross-country race was held over 7 miles. First home was Lance Corporal Roger Cobbin, and Admin Coy was the winning company. The Battalion subsequently provided most of the Army Gulf Cross-Country Team that won the Inter-Services event. Lance Corporal K (Ken) McLavin won the Army Gulf Championships, and he and Lance Corporal Roger Cobbin represented the Services Bahrain in Cyprus. Admin Coy also won the Bahrain Minor Units title.

Many sports events were held during the tour, sport generally keeping the soldiers occupied and fit. There were numerous competitions including between other Army, RN and RAF teams. Due to the range of commitments which led to much movement of individuals/companies around the Gulf on military training, almost all competitions were Minor Unit rather than Inter-Unit. Within the Battalion there was a tour-long Inter-Coy basketball, cross-country, football, hockey, swimming and water polo competition, which was finally won by Admin Coy, under the command of Major Stuart Green.

Hockey was one of the main sports and the Battalion Team was led by Captain Brian Davenport. It had several teams in a league, was narrowly beaten in the final of the Bahrain Knockout Competition, and won the Gulf Joint Services Six-a-Side Festival. At eleven-a-side it won twenty-three out of thirty matches. Brian Davenport and Lance Corporal Leslie Holman represented the Army Gulf Team. At football, seven of the Battalion (QMSI Bill Robson, Corporals Robbie Allen and John Farnham, Lance Corporals John Sorenson and Nevil Jephcote, and Privates John Spiers and A W (Freddie) Dymond) were in the Army Gulf Team. Command Coy won the Inter-Services League, and Admin Coy won the Bahrain Knockout Competition. Led by the experienced boxer Sergeant Terry Fleming, who also masterminded a rigorous training programme, in the Army Gulf Individual/Team Championships the Boxing Team won five of nine bouts and the team prize by a wide margin.

At the Battalion Athletics Meeting in February, Admin Coy were the Team winners. Outstanding individuals were Lance Corporal Leslie Holman who won the 100, High Jump and Triple Jump, and Private John Spiers who won the 220, 440 and Long Jump. At the

Army Gulf individual championships in March, the Battalion provided five winners (Lance Corporal Ken McLavin the 1 and 3 Miles, 2nd Lieutenant P W (Peter) Field the Discus, Lance Corporal Leslie Holman the High Jump, and Corporal A ('Waqa') Waqairoba the Shot), two runners-up and six third places. The Basketball 'A' Team won the Inter-Services League and were unbeaten, and the Rugby, Cricket and Tennis Teams also gave good account of themselves during the Bahrain tour. A number of men enjoyed riding the horses at the Sultan's stables a few miles down the road, and sea fishing was also a popular weekend activity.

No competition shooting took place during the tour, but just a small amount of rifle and GPMG range classification. Way back in August, Staff Sergeant P O'Brien REME won second place in the ARA Non-Central .22" Individual Pistol Slow Fire Match.

There was, meanwhile, a great opportunity for soldiers to go on courses in Hamala Camp to upgrade their formal education qualifications. The Battalion was fortunate in having an RAEC subaltern on its strength for this training: 2nd Lieutenant M V A (Mike) Wilkinson, who made a significant contribution in the classroom and more widely.

In January 1970, at the beginning of the final year of the 4th Battalion's existence, senior appointments, which were to remain until the disbandment of the Battalion in September, were held as follows:

CO:	Lieutenant Colonel T Holloway	OC C Coy:	Captain A E Thompson MC
2IC:	Major M E Duffie	CSM C Coy:	WO2 J T Morris MM
Adjt:	Captain C P B Keeble	OC Sp Coy:	Captain S R Yates RRF
RSM:	WO1 P F Garman	CSM Sp Coy:	WO2 R B Freakley
QM:	Captain E A Holben	OC Comd Coy:	Major P W King
Tech QM:	Captain J Eyeions	CSM Comd Coy:	WO2 L MacDonald
RQMS:	WO2 A I James Queens	OC Admin Coy:	Major S A Green
OC A Coy:	Major J Robinette	CSM Admin Coy:	WO2 P Jones
CSM A Coy:	WO2 C J Philips	Bandmaster:	WO1 T G Cooper
OC B Coy:	Major R H Robinson	Drum Major:	CSgt T R West
CSM B Coy:	WO2 P M Collins	Rear Party/UFO:	Major M K D Gunton

Preparations began in earnest for the visit of the Lord Mayor of Leicester, and an Inter-Company Drill Competition was held in mid-January, being won by Support Company. In the week before the visit (while not unreasonably the RSM sought to have the Battalion on the parade square), B Coy and an Umpire Team deployed on FTX *Straight Flush* in the Trucial States where B Coy provided the energetic and controlled enemy in the wadis and on the jebel against 1st Battalion The Queen's Own Highlanders.

From 13 to 19 January, the Battalion hosted a visit by the Lord Mayor of Leicester, Alderman Edward Marston, and his Deputy, Alderman K Bowder OBE, to both of whom (amongst the plethora of other visitors during the tour) a warm welcome was extended. The visit was doubly welcome as not only did it renew the Battalion's ties with the City of Leicester, but the Deputy Colonel was present throughout. The very full programme included a Battalion Parade, many opportunities to watch training and sport, and to meet soldiers, a large number of whom were Leicester men, formal dinners in the Officers' and WOs' & Sgts' Messes, and a constant round of visits to people of importance and places of

The Band and Drums march onto parade. *Trustees R Anglian Regt*

interest. The Lord Mayor also called upon the Ruler of Bahrain, Sheikh Isa bin Sulman al Khalifa, to whom he presented a full-size Stilton cheese – and in return received a solid gold Omega Seamaster wristwatch!

In his speech at the Battalion Parade, he said:

> How disappointed the City of Leicester was to learn that the Tigers were to disband by April 1971. We are glad, however, that, unlike some disbanding units, most of the officers and men will be absorbed into the three remaining battalions of The Royal Anglian Regiment. I know that you have many friends in the other battalions, and this absorption will help considerably to cushion the effect of disbandment. The City will again extend its traditional welcome when the Battalion once more marches through the streets of the City on 12 September this year, on the occasion of the Farewell Parade and the Laying Up of Colours.

At a dinner which he hosted for the Battalion's officers and for British political and senior military officers in the Delman Hotel, Manamah, in proposing a toast to the Battalion, the Lord Mayor said:

> The Royal Anglian Regiment is now one of the youngest regiments in the British Army but it must embody the Regimental Spirit of all the regiments from which it has been formed. It will undoubtedly create its own history and in time it too will look back with the same pride upon its story. The new Regiment will blend its own traditions upon the past and I am certain that it will give our Nation the same devoted service that has characterized The Royal Leicesters and of course the other regiments which gave it birth.

The Lord Mayor also spent a day in Sharjah on a visit to 17 Fd Regt RA, another unit which recruited in Leicestershire. The whole of the Lord Mayor's visit to the Gulf was covered by David Partridge, military correspondent of the *Leicester Mercury,* and his reports were covered extensively in that newspaper.

Before the Lord Mayor's visit, much thought had been given to the way to approach the City of Leicester with the proposal that, when the 4th Battalion exercised the Freedom of Leicester on 12 September, the City Fathers should consider conferring that day the

Freedom on The Royal Anglian Regiment. That would enable large crowds to witness the parade, the last occasion Leicestershire's Battalion would be seen in the City. It would be right and proper that the Battalion representing The Royal Anglian Regiment that day should be the 4th Battalion, but would not have the local appeal if this were to be done at some later stage and another battalion was taking part. The Deputy Colonel and the Commanding Officer duly broached this matter with the Lord Mayor during his visit. A couple of months later it became clear that the City's Fathers were not minded to grant the Freedom of Leicester to The Royal Anglian Regiment for a number of years yet. In the event, as a clear indication that, as it had taken them 162 years (1782-1944) to grant its Freedom to The Leicestershire Regiment, they were in no mood to 'give it lightly' to their successors – that Freedom was not granted to The Royal Anglian Regiment for another thirty years, in 1996.

The next series of company training exercises then took place in the Trucial States over a period of two months. Sp Coy trained at Manamah in Sharjah, and its two anti-tank platoons live-fired at Jebajib near Dubai. That was also the occasion when the ATGW Platoon fired its Vigilant missiles. The Mortar Platoon (Captain Martin Romilly) live-fired near Buraimi. While there, a group of scruffy and heavily-laden men strayed into the danger area, which when accosted turned out to be a troop of G Sqn 22 SAS, carrying two medium mortars but with no ammunition. They were immediately offered hospitality, training and ammunition, and then live-fired beside Romilly's men. It was also during this period that the Mortar Platoon was placed at short notice to fly to Salalah in the Dhofar Province of Oman to protect the RAF airfield there which was coming under fire from insurgents at the beginning of the Dhofar War. Next, the 4th Battalion's rifle companies, in the sequence C, A and B, spent two-three weeks on Exercises *Tidy Tiger I-III*, dry training, live firing and clearing the accumulation of detritus from the training areas. Meanwhile, the Assault Pioneer Platoon (under Sergeant Stan Barkby) carried out a two-month attachment to 32 Fd Sqn RE in Sharjah. Previously WO2 L ('Mac') MacDonald had been attached to the Kuwait Liaison Team as a trainer for two months, and Lieutenant Robert Pepper was attached to the SAF Training Centre in Muscat for four weeks to assist in training Arab and Baluchi soldiers in SAF.

In early February, personnel officers from HQ Queen's Div began a four-day visit to interview all officers and soldiers with postings problems as a result of the impending disbandment. Not unnaturally, this was one of the two most important things on everyone's mind. Moreover, due consideration needed to be given to the wishes of the twenty or more sets of brothers and other 'family units'. As a planning guideline, it had been decided regimentally that soldiers would be posted where their military skills and qualifications were most needed and that specific battalions would not be packed with sporting gladiators.

The other important thing on the soldiers' minds was the new Military Salary. Details of it were promulgated on 27 February and it came into effect on 1 April. In return for a higher salary aligned to jobs of similar rank and importance in civilian life, among other changes marriage allowance was discontinued, and food and accommodation were paid for (except when on exercise or operations).

Among other unusual events was the Inter-Company gardening competition at the end of February. It was won by the Mortar Platoon, whom the losers rightly claimed already

RSM Paul Garman watches the tiger's teeth treatment. *T Holloway*

had greenery cascading up the side of the Twynham hut they had been allocated on arrival in August. Captain Alan Thompson won the Officers' Prize, purely for being seen to make an effort – in the rock hard and dusty ground outside his billet he had placed on a stick a coloured seed-packet that had arrived from his wife that morning! Also that month, the opportunity was taken to get the jaw of the tiger's skin from the WOs' & Sgts' Mess repaired, by courtesy of a dentist at the RAF Hospital Muharraq.

Throughout the tour in Bahrain, the services of the Band (the only one on the island) were much in demand. Under the baton of Bandmaster Tommy Cooper, among other things it provided the music for the full-blown musical *South Pacific* by the Jufair players, and played at the Queen's Birthday Reception at the British Residency (Political Resident Persian Gulf). With the Drums it paraded for the Lord Mayor's visit, and twice performed Beating Retreat by torchlight at HMS *Jufair*. Perhaps the most lasting legacy of the Band and Drums was the cutting of the Royal Leicesters/4 R Anglian's only 12" long-playing gramophone record, 'Marching with the "Tigers"'. A photograph of its cover sleeve is in the plate section. The first side contained old and new Regimental music: Royal Leicesters marches (the Quick March 'The Royal Leicestershire Regiment', the Slow March 'General Monkton 1762', and 'Wolfe's Dirge')[8] and Royal Anglian ones, together with a special fanfare 'The Green Tiger' composed by Bandmaster Tommy Cooper. The flip side, titled 'Beating Retreat', contained traditional infantry marching music. The record was very popular and sold very well. Audio cassette tapes of the record are still (in 2008) available from The Royal Tigers' Association in Leicester.

Back to field soldiering, in the first half of March, the Recce Platoon again successfully negotiated its way by Land Rover to Liwa Oasis and back, and again importantly met up with the RAF resupply helicopter.

On 20 March, the FFR Inspection was carried out by Comd LFG, Brigadier P J N Ward OBE. He witnessed the final stages of a drill competition (a training theme in the build-up to the Freedom March in September), and visited various companies and departments. B Coy were given the task of defending the adjacent RAF radar station and he witnessed the Football Team beat Combined Services Bahrain 4-1. A letter from him to the Commanding Officer indicated 'a very good inspection and you have every reason to be proud of your Battalion, its standards, performance in Bahrain and high morale in spite of the impending disbandment'. In an earlier letter he had said: 'You and your Battalion have made a fine name for themselves out here and but for you the Army's critics among the civilian community would have gained many recruits. I am very grateful to you for what you've done and what you are doing in this line.' In early May, a letter from the Colonel of The Regiment read: 'I have read with great interest your Brigadier's Annual Report on your Battalion's fitness to carry out its role. I congratulate you on this report which reflects great credit on the Battalion, and on yourself in particular … with the future reorganization looming ahead it is clear that you have not permitted this to influence your Battalion's spirit and efficiency.'

The following week the whole Battalion (less B Coy, in camp as the Alert Company) took part in Exercise *Tramping Tiger*. The two rifle coys embarked in RPLs of 73 Mar Sqn RCT, sailed to the south of the island and carried out an assault landing. They then advanced to defensive positions, advanced again, and night marched for a dawn attack. Thereafter the Battalion marched back to camp. This spirited exercise was followed by a five-day Easter stand-down.

It is important to recognize the immense contribution made to the sustenance of the Battalion in Bahrain by the Catering Team, led by SQMS J Drake ACC. Throughout the tour his men literally slaved under very hot roofs beside hot ovens in a very poorly found cookhouse, which was eventually radically refurbished just in time for the Battalion's successors to benefit from. At the end of March, working in rather more salubrious surroundings, three cooks under Sergeant Mortimer won the Army Gulf Cookery Competition.

In the first half of April, Exercise *Tigers Standard* took place in the Trucial States and Oman. A Company Group was based on A Coy HQ, one platoon from each rifle company (Lieutenants Kevin Ryan, Roland Thompson and John Walsh), the Recce Platoon, signallers and cooks, clerks from Comd and Admin Coys, detachments from 255 Sig Sqn and 668 Avn Sqn AAC, drivers and vehicles of 90 Sqn RCT, and a repair team from 1 Inf Wksp: in all 162 men with ten Land Rovers, eleven 3-ton lorries, one light recovery vehicle, a large water tanker and one Sioux helicopter. The Group married up in Sharjah on 31 March and departed on 1 April, to provide a military presence in northern Oman while two of the Sultan's regiments were involved in a unit rotation by road to and from the Dhofar Province. Its route took it on an arduous 'hearts and minds' journey through Oman as far as Muscat, and thence south of the Jebel Akhdar to Buraimi, Abu Dhabi and Dubai. The Group completed a thousand 'road' miles in a fortnight along some interesting roads and wadi tracks in some seldom-visited parts of the region where the rule of law and life itself was primitive. On paper it might not have seemed a tight schedule but over that terrain, which took a toll on the vehicles, it was a demanding undertaking that was successfully executed. The Group returned to Bahrain by LSL *Sir Bedivere*.

The Ruler of Bahrain presents a sword to Lt Col Terry Holloway. *Trustees R Anglian Regt*

On 15 April, the Ruler of Bahrain, accompanied by his elder son, Sheikh Hamid (the C-in-C of the Bahrain Defence Force), paid a short visit to Hamala Camp. He seemed genuinely grateful for the Battalion's contribution to security in Bahrain and very generously presented a gold ceremonial scimitar, which now hangs in the Regimental Museum in Leicester.

Over the following two evenings, the Officers' and WOs' & Sgts' Messes held their farewell parties, the former attended by senior political and military figures and their wives. They were held just in time to avoid the fierce sandstorm that struck Hamala Camp on 19 April. Despite the Regimental Digest (under)stating, 'The storm disrupted cinema shows in both the Officers' and Sergeants' Messes', it caused considerable damage to living accommodation.

Later that month, the ATGW Platoon gave a live-firing demonstration of the Vigilant missile to the Ruler of Bahrain on a Police rifle range. Some of the missiles hit their targets. The Assault Pioneer Platoon was tasked to prepare some bangs at the target end just in case, and they detonated them anyway! It is not known whether Vigilant was subsequently procured by the BDF.

No. 1 Coy 1st Battalion Scots Guards (1 SG) took over the Battalion's Bahrain Alert Company task at the end of April in advance of Exercise *Entrold*. This was an important week-long joint FTX to practise and demonstrate the UK's force projection capability in the era leading up to the UK withdrawing its garrisons east of Suez in 1970. For this exercise, on 27 April, the Battalion embarked in Bahrain in the LPD HMS *Fearless*, LSL *Sir Bedivere* and two minesweepers, and transited into the Indian Ocean, in conjunction with HMS *Andromeda*, a Fleet Diving Team (which defended *Fearless* from underwater attack by the SBS), and G Sqn SAS. Confronted by a controlled enemy provided by 1 SG, the Battalion carried out an amphibious beach landing in Fujairah, whereafter for three days it conducted operations in the hinterland, supported by RAF helicopters embarked in *Fearless*, before recovering to the amphibious shipping and returning to Bahrain. Lieutenant Brian Cornish, the newly appointed Anti-Tank Platoon Commander, was somewhat disappointed that his Platoon was required to deploy equipped with the hand-held 84mm Carl Gustav rather than the vehicle-carried 120mm WOMBAT. But he was not nearly as annoyed as the GOC was when confronted by the RN ratings protecting the beachhead as he and his ADC sought to replenish their water supplies. They were refused access and then arrested because they did not know the current password!

This vigorous exercise, conducted over inhospitable terrain and in a taxing climate, was a fitting end to a challenging and immensely satisfying tour in the Gulf, and proved that The Tigers could successfully complete whatever tasks they were given, and with considerable efficiency and expertise. Significantly, it was the last occasion that 4th Battalion The Royal Anglian Regiment deployed in full into the field anywhere. Well led by its officers and senior ranks, it prepared to march off proudly into history.

On return to Bahrain on 4 May, all eyes focussed on the return to England. The Advance Party of thirty all ranks under Major Mike Duffie left for UK by air on 8 May, and that of 2nd Battalion The Royal Irish Rangers arrived at Hamala Camp. The end was in sight – the fulfilment of one sober-note pessimist as he had arrived on the Advance Party in Bahrain in July 1969: 'All we've got to do now is get back!' And on Radio 17, one of the more popular requests was John Denver's 'Leaving on a Jet Plane'.

Troops advancing up a wadi in Fujairah, May 1970. *Trustees R Anglian Regt*

Officers of 4th R Anglian, May 1970. (See Appendix P for names) *Trustees R Anglian Regt*

WOs and Sgts of 4th R Anglian, May 1970. (See Appendix P for names) *Trustees R Anglian Regt*

Sport continued. On 9 May, the Battalion Team won the 14-mile Manamah-Hamala Road Relay Race, each of nine men running 1.6 miles. The officers attended a dinner given by the Ruler of Bahrain at the Rifa'a Palace, and the Commanding Officer presented him with a former silver menu holder in the shape of a tiger.

As thoughts turned to what lay in store on return to England, it was surely more than coincidence that, in the May 1970 edition of *Castle* Journal, Colonel M K Wardle DSO MC[9], in writing the obituary for Lieutenant Colonel A Weyman MC, summed up so very well what all Tigers were feeling. Mark Wardle had written:

Napier said that a British regiment had this much in common with the gods, 'immortality and perpetual youth'. And now, on the eve of the dissolution of our particular stream of youth and immortality, the passing of so true a Tiger as 'Tweaks' Weyman has for his oldest friends a special poignancy. We say Hail and Farewell not only to him but to the entity, until now undying, whether the 17th Foot, The Leicestershire Regiment, The Royal Leicestershire Regiment, or the 4th Battalion of The Royal Anglian Regiment.

It should not go without mention that, during the Bahrain Tour, the families back at Gillingham were extremely well cared for by Major Mike Gunton and a team of senior wives led by Bronwen Holloway, whose husband was the Commanding Officer. The members of the Wives' Club kept themselves busy and occupied by making a very large patchwork quilt, among other things. The product of that centuries-old craft contained material from Aden, China, Hong Kong, Kenya and Malta, and its sale raised funds for the Club.

Gillingham: June to December 1970

The first flight of the Main Body left Bahrain on 22 May, and the last on 31 May. Everyone then immediately proceeded on five weeks' leave. The Advance Party resumed duty at Gordon Barracks on 15 June, and the Battalion was complete at duty there on 6 July, on which day the new Comd 2 Inf Bde, Brigadier A F Findlay, paid his first visit.

Tailors were immensely busy as the new Tiger button became available and was worn by all ranks across the Regiment in all forms of dress with effect from 1 July. It had previously been announced that from 1 July, as the result of rationalization of dress within the Army, there would be standardization within The Queen's Division of certain items. As and when they could afford new ones, all officers were to wear the pattern and cloth (barathea) for their Service Dress as worn by the RRF.

However, a much more important and significant event took place while Battalion block leave had been taking place: the Conservative Party had won the General Election in mid-June. On 19 June, the day after the Conservative Party had been returned to power, the Colonel of The Royal Anglian Regiment wrote to Mr Eldon Griffiths, MP for Bury St Edmunds (where RHQ was), asking him to help 'save The Tigers'. All MPs for the counties of Leicestershire and Rutland, and of the City of Leicester, agreed to support such a move, and a joint motion was tabled by three of them in The House of Commons, which read: 'That this House believes that the order to disband the 4th Battalion The Royal Anglian Regiment, formerly 1st Battalion The Royal Leicestershire Regiment, should be rescinded', and the Rt Hon T G Boardman MP tabled the Question, 'To ask the Minister of State for Defence, if he will delay implementing the decision to disband 4th Battalion The Royal Anglian Regiment, formerly 1st Battalion The Royal Leicestershire Regiment, until there has been a further review of the strategy and requirements for defence.' Regimentally, it was properly decided that, unlike The Argyll and Sutherland Highlanders' 'Save the Argylls' campaign, The Royal Anglian Regiment would not sponsor a public campaign to 'save The Tigers'. Their more subtle political approach helped to influence opinion, and within a week there seemed to be 'a possibility of saving The Tigers'.

In early August the Army Board, while recommending to Ministers that Phase II of the rundown of the Army should proceed, sought important changes, one of which being that the six infantry battalions which were due for disbandment, or to be placed in suspended animation, would be given the opportunity of staying on, at company strength.[10] After due and speedy consideration and consultation with the respective two Colonels of Regiments, the Colonel Commandant The Queen's Division accepted the option for 4 Queens and 4 R Anglian (which had been due to leave the Order of Battle in December and September 1970 respectively) to remain at company strength. Each was to be a rifle company with no support weapons, and an as-yet-unidentified 'worthwhile role'. There was just time to cancel the planned Regimental programme for 12 September in Leicester to mark the disbandment of the 4th Battalion. In particular it would not have been appropriate to signify a full disbandment by laying up the Colours of the 1st and 2nd Battalions The Royal Leicestershire Regiment, because the Representative Company would have the 1st Battalion's Colours in its care, and none of The Royal Leicestershire Regiment's Colours should be laid up until new Colours were presented to battalions of The Royal Anglian Regiment, expected to be in the next few years. These sentiments were notified to Tigers, serving and retired, in a letter from Major General John Spurling, the Deputy Colonel. Also cancelled were the dedication of a plaque at the Victoria Park War Memorial and the arrangement for Terence Cuneo to paint his fifth picture for the Royal Leicesters, which was to have been of the laying up of the Colours in the Cathedral. As soon as the Lord Mayor of Leicester, Alderman George Baldwin, heard that the Regimental programme would be cancelled, he decided to hold a dinner for about thirty-five in his rooms, to include senior officers of The Royal Anglian and The Royal Leicestershire Regiments.

Meanwhile, it was business as usual in the Battalion. In mid-July, most of the RRF reinforcements for the Bahrain tour returned whence they had come, and the focus was on the final planning for the disbandment, with among other things the issue of posting orders for all ranks as they prepared for new postings – or life as civilians – from mid-September. Officers began to be posted out from mid-July.

The Battalion was now back as part of the Army's Strategic Reserve, and was to continue for the next two months to fulfil a number of tasks in the planned Regular Army Assistance Table, including providing seventy all ranks from C Coy putting on a patrol programme for the Dover Tattoo on 22 July. A farewell dinner was organized to be held on 17 July at Ulverscroft Road at Leicester. However, in the event, the Commanding Officer, 2IC and others invited were unable to attend as – unexpectedly – the Battalion was placed at twelve hours' NTM to Southampton to help during the National Dock Strike. A recce of accommodation there and of possible tasks was carried out, but in the end troops were required to neither deploy nor intervene.

As if there was not enough for all ranks to do in effecting the Battalion's rundown, senior officers continued to make farewell (and in some cases 'hail and farewell') visits, including, on 14 July, Brigadier A W Wise DSO MBE, The Queen's Division Brigadier, a week later Major General M James MBE, GOC 5 Div, and on 30 July the Colonel of The Regiment. Lieutenant General Sir Richard Goodwin inspected a Guard of Honour and then addressed the whole Battalion before meeting many members at their places of work.

On 1 August, the 4th Battalion's Band and Drums performed for the last time, on the occasion of the first Bassingbourn Open Day at Depot The Queen's Division, alongside the Band of 3 Queens, the Drums of 3 R Anglian, and the Division's Junior Band and Drums.

Armed with the knowledge that the Tigers might live on in some way in the Regular

Army Order of Battle, and with a consequential renewed spring in their step, on 6 August at Leicester, in front of international TV cameras and in a steady drizzle, eighty soldiers of the Battalion carried the national flags and name boards of the thirty-eight competing countries at the World Cycling Championships. These were opened by the Prime Minister, The Rt Hon Edward Heath MBE MP. It was on that occasion of his visit to Leicester that the Lord Major took the opportunity to lobby him over the future of The Tigers.

For the Edinburgh Tattoo, Lieutenant J T (John) Towns led a party which re-enacted the role played in 1714 when Wightman's Regiment (17th Foot) had provided the Castle Garrison during the installation of the Governor. And in mid-August, A and B Companies took part in Exercise *Kon Tiki* in the Hereford area where, alongside the SAS and the West Mercian Police, they hunted for the 'escape and evading' students from the Platoon Commanders' Course, very few of whom were intercepted as most completely disregarded the boundaries of the designated manoeuvre area!

The final confirmation that a Representative Company of the 4th Battalion would be retained came on 2 September, a matter which brought joy to the hearts of all Tigers, serving and retired. That day John Spurling sent a telegram to the Commanding Officer that read: 'Welcome and many happy returns to the Young Tigers', to which Terry Holloway replied: 'Thank you. We hope to make the next 282 years as successful as the last and to grow up soon.' In the meantime, many volunteers had requested either not to be posted to other units or not to leave the Army, but rather to join 'T' Company (as the Representative Company of the 4th Battalion was initially called). Having been selected from what turned out to be a surfeit of volunteers, they formed T Company at Gillingham under the command of Captain Martin Romilly on 9 September. The remainder of the Battalion came under command of HQ Coy, of which the role was to administer the planned postings and the other reduction administration. It was in the most capable hands of the Adjutant, Captain Chris Keeble, that the detailed planning and sensitive handling of the postings lay. He created a circular disc for every person in the Battalion and these were hung on his office wall. On the day the soldier was posted, the respective disc was moved to the receiving unit's column. There were no reports of anyone going astray!

Two significant events occurred on 12 September in Leicester: the presentation of silver tigers, and a Lord Mayor's Dinner. When, in 1968, it had been thought that the 4th Battalion was to be disbanded, and as most of its officers, WOs, sergeants and men would be posted to the remaining Regular battalions, it was decided to give a silver tiger to each of the Officers' and WOs' & Sgts' Messes of the 1st, 2nd and 3rd Battalions of The Royal Anglian Regiment. At 1900 hours, at a simple ceremony at the TAVR Centre, Ulverscroft Road, in the presence of the Lords Lieutenant of Leicestershire and Rutland, the Lord Bishop, the Lord Mayor of Leicester, the Colonel of The Regiment, the Provost, civic dignitaries and members of both the Officers' and WOs' & Sgts' Messes, Major General John Spurling presented these silver tigers. All Regular and TAVR commanding officers and RSMs of The Royal Anglian Regiment were present except the Commanding Officer of the 1st Battalion serving in Londonderry, who was unable to get away, but his Brigade Commander, Brigadier Alan Cowan, a former Tigers' CO, received it for him. The WOs and sergeants then had a dinner at Ulverscroft Road, presided over by RSM Paul Garman of the 4th Battalion.

Meanwhile, the officers and other distinguished guests moved to the Lord Mayor's

The silver tigers to be presented to the 1st, 2nd and 3rd R Anglian. *Leicester Mercury*

rooms where the Lord Mayor of Leicester gave a most enjoyable dinner to celebrate the 4th Battalion's partial reprieve and at the same time honour The Royal Anglian Regiment. He read a message from the Deputy Colonel-in-Chief, HRH The Duchess of Gloucester, in which she said that she had heard the news with great relief. He said it was necessary now to forge ahead and work hard at the promotion of a similar relationship between the City and County, and The Royal Anglian Regiment, as was enjoyed between the City and County and The Royal Leicestershire Regiment over a long number of years. It was very appropriate that the 4th Battalion Band should play at the Lord Mayor's Dinner for the last time prior to its disbandment. Both the Band and Drums had given most distinguished service to the Regiment, City and County over so many years.

As it had been perceived that the Royal Tigers' Association would no longer benefit from financial donations from a full battalion's worth of men of the 4th Battalion through the Day's Pay Scheme, the Lords Lieutenant of Leicestershire and Rutland (Colonel R A St G Martin OBE JP, and Captain T C S Haywood OBE) had launched appeals for funds for the Association, the closing date for which was extended until Armistice Day in November. Large sums of money were raised for that important benevolent cause, thus enabling the Association to fulfil its charitable objects for the foreseeable future.

Lieutenant Colonel Terry Holloway left the Battalion on 14 September, formally handing over command to Major Mike Duffie, the erstwhile 2IC. It was with considerable pride and satisfaction that he departed, safe in the knowledge that the 4th Battalion had remained a very competent, well-trained and well-led unit throughout the uncertain months of impending disbandment and while stationed abroad unaccompanied; and content that a small but significantly important 'rump' was for the time being to continue in the Regular Army's Order of Battle.

Most of the departing officers were posted out the following week, and in late September drafts of twenty-eight all ranks were posted to 1 R Anglian in Londonderry, seventy-two all ranks to 2 R Anglian in Colchester and eighty-two all ranks to 3 R Anglian in Aldershot (including Captain 'Jimmy' Jenks and most of the Football Team, which went on to win the Infantry Cup several times over the following years). Suitably reinforced by Tigers, over the following few years the 2nd Battalion came sixth in the Army Athletics in 1974, the 1st Battalion won the Army Athletics in 1977, and the 3rd Battalion became Army Cricket Champions in 1980. Given the quality of so many of those who had recently served, it is of no surprise that many Tigers made significant contributions by their service in other battalions and more widely in the Army. A gauge of those achievements can be gleaned from the list of Honours and Awards (Appendix A), the list of those who commanded other units/formations/organizations (Appendix C), the list of Late Entry Officers (Appendix E), and from those who served on the staff at the Royal Military Academy (RMA) Sandhurst (Appendix G).

Gordon Barracks became a strange and rather melancholy place with the barracks (which had been assigned for total closure) being emptied of stores, equipment and soldiers, except for T Company which by 7 October had a strength of three officers and 100 men. To the general gloom was added the burning down of a vacated H-shaped accommodation block. Gradually most of the old equipment was despatched to Army Depots to be replaced by new equipment to new schedules for the new independent company-size T Coy. When the MT petrol tank was finally drained, it was found that there were about 90 gallons of fuel short; the investigation discovered that the dipstick, which was over 2 yards long and made of steel ¾" by ¼" had, over the years, made a dent in the base of the tank causing a higher reading to be taken. Also during this time, the Government suspected that there would be a miners' strike, and so the unused and enormous equipment sheds in Gordon Barracks began to be filled to the brim with stockpiled coal and coke.

While the rest of the Battalion (in HQ Coy) quietly went about the final disbanding, command of it devolved to Major Pat King and then Major Mike Gunton, who was effectively the 'last man out of the gate' in December. Despite the 4th Battalion completely running down and emptying Gordon Barracks in anticipation of closure, 1 D and D actually moved into it in late 1971, to be followed by 2 R Anglian on their return from Münster in 1976.

Meanwhile, T Coy carried out garrison routine duties as an independent subunit in Kent, and began to take part in sports competitions as a Minor Unit. It was soon known that early in the New Year the Company would move to Hampshire and Surrey, and take over duties of Demonstration Company at Mons Officer Cadet School (OCS) and RMA Sandhurst in the spring, a prospect to which members of the new Company looked forward with relish. This led to a period of intense training, with emphasis on the basics of fitness, shooting and platoon level tactics. The soldiers also walked the Pilgrims' Way to Canterbury and canoed on local canals. The RQMS of the Battalion, Tony James, was commissioned and became Admin Officer. On 3 December, the Army Board approved the title for the erstwhile T Coy as '4th Battalion The Royal Anglian Regiment Tiger Company'. The official abbreviation was '4 R Anglian Coy'. Within the Regiment and colloquially it was referred to as 'Tiger Company'.

The silver fanfare trumpets that had been presented by the City and County of Leicestershire in 1952 were then loaned to RMA Sandhurst, to remain there and be played at all the Sovereign's Parades and other ceremonial occasions, until the 4th Battalion reformed at full strength. They were handed over into Sandhurst's safekeeping at the Sovereign's Parade on 17 December, a notable event in the Regiment's history. It was certainly the first, and probably the only occasion on which the Academy's officer cadets marched past to the Quick March of The Royal Leicestershire Regiment. After the parade, in the presence of the Lord Mayor and Lady Mayoress of Leicester, Major General John Spurling handed the fanfare trumpets to the Commandant and Director of Music. Field Marshal Sir Gerald Templer, representing HM The Queen at the parade, said how much he hoped that the reformation of the 4th Battalion would not be long delayed. Meanwhile, he knew how delighted The Queen and the Regiment's Royal Ladies would be to know that the Tigers' trumpets continued to sound loud and clear at Sandhurst, all the more appropriate now that Tiger Company was to become the Demonstration Company there.

The RMA trumpeters were soon using the fanfare trumpets: at the lighting of the Christmas trees in Trafalgar Square; and in March 1971, when The Queen unveiled a plaque at Twickenham at the RFU centenary match. The latter occasion was most apposite as the Tigers had provided two England captains, Tony Novis[11] and 'Joe' Kendrew,[12] in the 1930s when 2nd Leicesters' Team had been one of the best in the Army.[13]

At the end of December 1970, Major J C D (John) Heggs took over command of Tiger Company from Captain Martin Romilly. In his hands now lay the leadership of what remained of the Regular element of the former Royal Leicestershire Regiment. The further events in Tiger Company's life are covered in Chapter 9. The final years of the TAVR element of The Royal Leicestershire Regiment are covered in Chapter 10.

Notes

1   1st R Leicesters in Korea, Cyprus and Borneo, and 4 R Anglian in Aden.
2   The War Memorial, designed by Sir Edwin Lutyens, had been unveiled in July 1925. It commemorates the 9,348 Servicemen of all ranks from Leicester and Leicestershire who died in the First World War.
3   Dwile Flonking is an ancient sport found in the upper reaches of the River Waveney. A dwile is a rag soaked in beer, which is thrown by a flonker.
4   later Gen Sir John Archer KCB OBE, C-in-C UKLF 1978-79.
5   See Chapter 5, Note 6.
6   The Trucial States (Abu Dhabi, Ajman, Dubai, Fujairah, Ras al-Khaimah, Sharjah, and Umm al-Quwain) were a group of semi-independent Arab sheikhdoms located on the eastern edge of the Persian Gulf whose military defence and foreign policies were controlled by the UK. Following full independence in 1971, they were to become the United Arab Emirates (UAE).
7   Robin McDowall composed the unofficial Regimental Collect of the 4th Battalion which is recorded in Appendix D.
8   See Chapter 5, Note 2.
9   Mark Wardle had been awarded the DSO and MC in the First World War and commanded 2nd Leicesters in Palestine 1937-40.
10 In 1968's announcements, 2nd SG, 4th Queens (Albuhera Coy), 4th R Anglian (Tiger Coy), 1st A & SH (Balaclava Coy) and 3rd RGJ (Peninsular Coy) were ordered to disband, and 1st Glosters and 1st R Hamps (Minden Coy) to amalgamate. In August 1970, all six battalions were offered – and accepted – the opportunity to reduce to company strength, and took on the titles shown above in brackets.
11 See Chapter 4, Note 12.
12 See Appendix N.
13 See Chapter 1, Note 12.

Chapter 9

Tiger Company: Aldershot, Gibraltar, Canterbury and Northern Ireland 1971-75

Aldershot: January to December 1971

As 1971 dawned, Tiger Company began its move from Canterbury to take up its new role as Demonstration Company at Mons OCS and RMA Sandhurst, and was firm there by 15 January with a strength of 105 all ranks. Organized as a rifle company of an Airportable Battalion (Limited Scales), its third platoon was Admin Platoon, a mini-HQ Coy. Coy HQ, Admin Platoon and B Platoon were based at Mons Barracks, Aldershot, and A Platoon at RMA Sandhurst. Senior appointments were held as follows:

CO[1]:	Major J C D Heggs	CSM:	WO2 D W Spalding
2IC:	Captain P J S Child[2]	A Platoon:	Lieutenant P C Shalders
Admin Offr:	Lieutenant A I James	B Platoon:	2nd Lieutenant P W Field

As it was not needed to assume its role as Demonstration Platoon at Mons until April, B Platoon (2nd Lieutenant Peter Field) was sent to Northern Ireland for a month's operational experience. It was attached to 2 R Anglian in Belfast for ten days in early February at the end of its four-month roulement tour, and thence to 1 R Anglian, a Resident Battalion in Londonderry. 1 R Anglian was part of 8 Inf Bde, then commanded by Brigadier Alan Cowan, who had been the last Commanding Officer of 1 R Leicesters and the first of 4 R Anglian. While in Belfast, B Platoon was involved in riots and in Londonderry it carried out rural border patrols, and urban duties manning OPs. This was the first time elements of The Tigers had been in Londonderry since the 2nd Leicesters left in 1936, at which time Peter Field's father was serving in it[3]. On that occasion, when that Battalion had arrived in Londonderry in 1931, the locals had gently teased them at their failure in 1688 to raise the Siege, with the words to the effect, 'We are so glad that you have at last been able to make it.' It is unlikely that the locals in 1971 recognized the provenance of B Platoon Tiger Company!

As the men of B Platoon had served in the Province for only twenty-seven days, they missed by one day being eligible for the General Service Medal (GSM) with clasp 'Northern Ireland'. Ironically, it was about this time that Tiger Company received some young soldiers from 1 R Anglian who, despite having already served six months in the Province, were sent away until they reached eighteen years of age.

Back at home at Mons, having initially been temporarily accommodated in offices 400 yards from the nearest telephone, it was difficult to convince the local military authorities that the Company actually existed. It soon moved into splendid freshly painted buildings much to the envy of the permanent elements in the barracks. Relieving elements of 1st Battalion The Duke of Edinburgh's Royal Regiment (1 DERR), A Platoon had started work almost immediately as Demonstration Platoon at RMA Sandhurst (Major General P T Tower CB DSO MBE), and B Platoon took up its task at Mons OCS in mid-March (Brigadier Sir Jeffery Darrell Bt MC). Over the following months both platoons were involved in assisting the training of officer cadets in barracks and acting as enemy on exercises in Cyprus, Dartmoor, Germany, Sennybridge and Stanford, as well as providing a demonstration section at Depot The Queen's Division at Bassingbourn, and Platoon Battle Drill demonstrations for CCF and ACF Camps at Shorncliffe.

In March 1971, it was learned that Lieutenant Colonel Teddy Turnill, who had served in 4 R Anglian 1967-68, had been awarded the Sultan of Oman's Bravery Medal (the equivalent of the DSO) for his performance on Loan Service as Commanding Officer of The Desert Regiment. The citation for his award read that he 'had commanded The Desert Regiment Group in Dhofar for ten months from April 1970 to January 1971. The responsibilities which he has borne, and the demands on his personal qualities of leadership, robustness, judgement and courage have been exceptionally high. His achievements during the past year have been of a very high order: they reflect above all his unwilting devotion to his officers and soldiers and to the good of the Sultanate.' The words 'to the good of the Sultanate' are probably an allusion to the

Lt Col Teddy Turnill, The Desert Regiment. *Dr A Turnill*

overthrow of the aged Sultan Said bin Taimur by his son Qaboos bin Said in July 1970. In such high regard was Turnill held that Sultan Said insisted on surrendering to Turnill personally.

Despite the rigorous and tightly drawn programmes of officer cadet training, life for the two Demonstration Platoons was not all work, and time was found to play sport. 'The Tigers' Den' canteen was established at Mons, principally for the Company. However, its use was extended at weekends to include all the Permanent Staff as the NAAFI discontinued its service on those two days. It rapidly became an important feature of life at Mons, and disco and games evenings, social evenings, and wedding receptions were held there.

The Company provided many soldiers to assist invaluably on the administrative side of Royal Tigers' Weekend at Leicester at the beginning of July. On the Saturday, at the Granby Halls, items of regimental silver were handed over on loan to the City and County for safekeeping until such time as the Regular Battalion was reformed. It was forty-one years to the day, in 1930, that the silver drums and bugles had been presented to the Regiment into the care of 2nd Battalion The Leicestershire Regiment at Catterick. Now, in July 1971, the Lord Mayor of Leicester, Alderman Percy Watts[4], and the Chairman of the County

Chairman of Leicestershire County Council and the Lord Mayor examine the silver.
Leicester Mercury

Council, Colonel P H Lloyd CBE TD DL JP, received the items on behalf of their constituents. The incoming Deputy Colonel for Leicestershire, Colonel M St G (Mike) Pallot[5], said that the loan was a token of the high esteem which the Regiment held for the City and County, and the wonderful support the Tigers had received since the Regiment and County were first linked. The silver drums were passed to the City, and other pieces of silver candelabra and claret jugs were also loaned to the City and County.

Also that weekend, items of inscribed Regimental silver were presented to Major General John Spurling and Lieutenant Colonel Peter Upcher in appreciation for their service to the Regiment. The former had been Deputy Colonel for six years. The latter, also a DL and Commandant of the Leicestershire & Rutland ACF, had been Regimental Secretary for fourteen years. In the last seven years of his tenure, in particular, he had done so much to keep the Tigers' tail up in the unavailing battle against bureaucracy to preserve The Royal Leicestershire Regiment's identity. He was succeeded by Major John

Major John Dudley and Lt Col Peter Upcher. *Leicester Mercury*

Dudley, who had already been Assistant Regimental Secretary for seven years.

On 23 July, the Deputy Colonel, Colonel Mike Pallot, paid his first formal visit to Tiger Company, at the conclusion of which a Regimental Cocktail Party was held at Mons Officers' Mess. As Tiger Company was the custodian of the Colours of 1st Battalion The Royal Leicestershire Regiment, the Colours were on display.

During the officer cadets' long summer leave, some JNCOs supported 4 (Leicestershire) Company 5 (V) R Anglian at Annual Camp at Okehampton, while others supported 7 (V) R Anglian's first Annual Camp at Stanford. A Platoon spent three weeks in August on a KAPE tour in Leicestershire, during which it appeared at the Rutland County Show, the Leicester City Show, the Hinckley Steam Fair and a Royal British Legion Festival. The demonstrations of section level operations in a mixed humorous and serious setting, exaggerated by clouds of coloured smoke, were much appreciated by the crowds. The Platoon also provided some mutual publicity at the opening of the Everards Brewery's new public house, The Leicester Tiger, in South Leicester – which sold Tiger Best Bitter. But did any of this aid recruiting, so important for a successful resurgence of the 4th Battalion?

In September, Mons and Sandhurst reopened for the business of training officer cadets, and the Demonstration Platoons were again heavily committed to a variety of tasks, including being masters of the Platoon Attack (provided it was at Grid Reference 782983) and Section Battle Drills (so long as a football pitch was available). In early October, the Sandhurst Exercise *Pegasus* was held, in which cadets were led by Tiger Company JNCOs.

Lt Peter Shalders' KAPE Team outside 'The Leicester Tiger' public house. *Trustees R Anglian Regt*

So full of praise was the Commandant about the Company's performance that he directed that in future the Exercise would be known as Exercise *Tiger*.

Preparations were then put in hand for the visit of the Deputy Colonel-in-Chief, HRH The Duchess of Gloucester, on 14 October. Ill-fortuitously, it was the day after the Government's announcement that four Representative Companies[6] would be restored to battalion strength – but not Tiger Company (nor 4 Queens Albuhera Company). This was a bitter pill for all of the Tiger family. Nevertheless, Tiger Company rose to the occasion on the day of Her Royal Highness' visit. She met most of the members of the Company, watched platoon demonstrations at Mons and at Sandhurst, and also met Royal Anglian officer cadets and other permanent staff at both units. Her visit provided a great boost to morale and was an unforgettable day in Tiger Company's short life to date.

It was about this time that the Company was called upon to provide members of the firing parties at the funerals of some of the 1st Battalion's men killed in Northern Ireland.

On 3 November, Tiger Company was visited by the Colonel of The Regiment, just a few days before the announcement that it would go to Gibraltar for six months from January 1972, a prospect that was greeted with much enthusiasm.

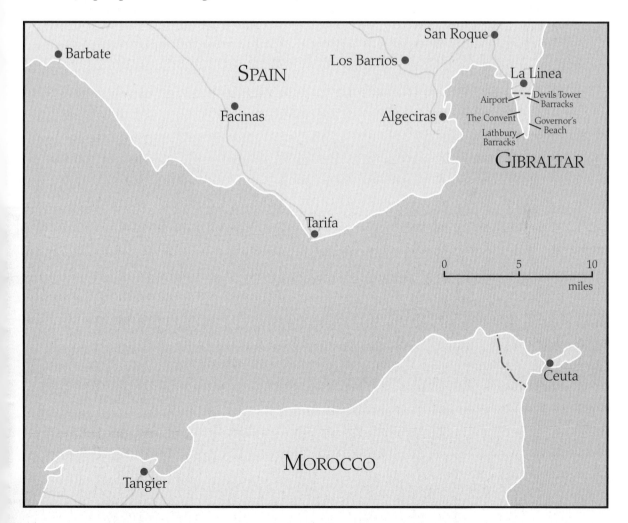

A few words about Gibraltar. Situated at the toe of Spain, it comprises 5.8 square miles, most of which is a granite ridge rising to 1,400 feet, with a population of some 21,000 in 1971. For several centuries, Gibraltar had been an important strategic base controlling the entry to and exit from the Mediterranean Sea via the only gateway to the Atlantic Ocean through the Straits of Gibraltar. In 1704, Admiral Rooke had taken 'the Rock' for England when he led an Anglo-Dutch force in the Spanish War of Succession. The Treaty of Utrecht of 1713 ceded Gibraltar to the British Crown in perpetuity and it is on the basis of that treaty that Gibraltar remains British to this day.

It was a key naval base, refuelling place and dockyard, and since 1934 had had an airfield, with a solid surface from 1939 and in 1955 the runway was extended to its current length of 6,000 ft. From 1939 to 1941 the Governor and C-in-C had been General Sir Clive Liddell KCB CMG CBE DSO, who was instrumental in putting the garrison on a war footing. One junction of the myriad of tunnels which honeycomb the Rock is named Liddell's Union. He was to be Colonel The Royal Leicestershire Regiment from 1943 to 1948. British Forces there controlled the Straits of Gibraltar, and it was the jumping-off point for the First Army's invasion of North Africa in 1942, subsequently remaining a staging post to North and West Africa, with its airfield capable of taking large transport aircraft, maritime recce, and bombers and fighters. It remains an operational deployment and staging facility, and a strategically important Forward Operating Base (FOB) from which aircraft, personnel and equipment can be deployed as required.

After the Second World War, Spain renewed its claims to sovereignty over Gibraltar, which as a British strategic air and naval base, continued to be a major source of friction between Britain and Spain, both of which were members of NATO. In 1967, the residents affirmed their ties with Britain in a UN-supervised referendum, voting overwhelmingly by 12,138 to 44 to remain British. In May 1969, a new constitution for Gibraltar was introduced by the UK Parliament, under which Gibraltar attained full internal self-government. The preamble to the Constitution stated that 'Her Majesty's Government will never enter into arrangements under which the people of Gibraltar would pass under the sovereignty of another state against their freely and democratically expressed wishes.' In response, Spain closed the land border with Gibraltar and severed all communication links. It closed its gates at the land frontier, while the Gibraltarians assiduously continued daily to open their gates from dawn to dusk. The closure of the border affected the people on both sides. Gibraltarians with families in Spain had to travel 35 miles by ferry to Tangier in Morocco, and from there 33 miles back to the Spanish port of Algeciras, while many Spanish workers (by then about 4,800) lost their jobs in Gibraltar. The only access to Gibraltar by air was from countries other than Spain, with no overflight of Spanish airspace permitted. This stand-off was to last thirteen years – until 1982. And it was not until 1985 that Spain would permit vehicles again to cross the border.

This was to be the third time The Tigers had been posted there. The first visit had begun in 1726 when a company of the 17th Foot arrived in transit but remained for four years – so perhaps there was subsequently something to be said for modern-day air trooping after all! The second was in 1854 when The Leicestershire Regiment had spent seven months there en route to the Crimean War. In 1968, HM The Queen had approved a formal alliance between The Royal Anglian Regiment and The Gibraltar Regiment, thus cementing associations which had existed for many years. Of note, units of the former regiments had spent no less than 110 years of service on the Rock, to which was added the nine months that 2 R Anglian had spent there as reinforcement in 1968-9. During that tour the picture of a Royal Anglian soldier had appeared on a commemorative stamp, issued by the Gibraltar Post Office. And The Suffolk, The Essex, and The Northamptonshire Regiments all played a distinguished role there during the Great Siege of 1779-83, as a consequence of which each had the castle of Gibraltar in their cap badges, which The East Anglian Regiments and The Royal Anglian Regiment inherited.

For many years Gibraltar had been garrisoned by a Regular battalion on a two-year accompanied tour, supported by the volunteer Gibraltar Regiment and other small Army units, commanded by the Deputy Force Commander. The RN component, principally the dockyard and visiting warships, was commanded by a Rear Admiral (Flag Officer Gibraltar), and the RAF component by an Air Commodore. All three elements came under the Governor and C-in-C (and Fortress Commander), who in 1972 was Admiral of the Fleet Sir Varyl Begg GCB DSO DSC. Gibraltar also housed a NATO command and control HQ, with assorted communications. The stand-off in turn led to the British increasing its force levels, which by 1971 included an additional rifle company to assist in frontier guard duties and three Hawker Hunter fighter-bombers as a deterrent to Spanish aggression. Tiger Company was to be that additional rifle company, on what was to be its last overseas tour.

In preparation for the Gibraltar tour, it was operationally necessary to create a Support Platoon of two 81mm mortars, two 120mm WOMBAT anti-tank weapons and three GPMG (SF) detachments. Reinforcements, and especially support weapons men, were transferred from the other Regular battalions (many men volunteering to serve again as Tigers), and the Support Weapons sections were given concentrated training by the SASC, plus live firing at Netheravon and Aldershot. For ceremonial purposes it was decided to reform a Corps of Drums, part of the redesignated 1 Platoon, commanded by Lieutenant Peter Shalders. No. 1 Dress (Blues) uniform was hastily acquired, the silver drums and bugles were 'loaned back' from the City of Leicester, and musical training began in earnest.

The Company's daily focus changed to preparation for Gibraltar. Handing over to a Company of 1/7 GR before Christmas, the JNCOs of the Company were nevertheless required to lead the Sandhurst cadets on the renamed Exercise *Tiger* at the beginning of the New Year. It was a fitting finale for the cheerfulness and flexibility in all circumstances which they had invariably displayed.

Early 1972 saw changes in Royal Anglian Regiment officers' dress regulations. First, for the officers the khaki beret with black patch behind the badge replaced the blue beret. This widened the tradition started by 1st Battalion The Royal Norfolk Regiment after the Second World War, and in some small measure compensated for the fact that the 9th Foot badges and accoutrements did not appear in the Royal Anglian dress to date. Secondly, the Service Dress hat was taken out of use, being replaced by the side hat. The use of the khaki beret applied equally to the TAVR battalions, though their officers also continued to wear the Service Dress hat.

In view of the poor recruiting figures for The Royal Anglian Regiment, the Colonel of The Regiment directed that each of the Regular battalions were to produce a recruiting team to recruit in their respective Battalion areas. Tiger Company produced a three-man team led by Sergeant D (David) Bausor, which became operational in Leicester in January 1972 and quickly got down to work. If that team and those of the other battalions were successful (and in the first three months there was an increase in recruits of 50 per cent over the previous year), it could not but be helpful for the prospects of the reforming of the 4th Battalion in due time.

In the context of 'indirect recruiting', it is important to cover the work and the role of 17 Army Youth Team (17 AYT), which is first mentioned in Chapter 5. As part of an Army-wide initiative to bring *la vie militaire* into the minds of the youth of the country, AYTs had been established in 1964. Their initial role was, working in conjunction with the Army Information Office, to get to know all the youth organisations in the county, offer advice and help, and provide some equipment and transport to youth and boys' clubs ... and to attract young men into the Army. 17 AYT was always commanded by a Tigers officer or WO. Based at Ulverscroft Road in Leicester, over time its role expanded and its strength evolved to an OC, Colour Sergeant and three soldiers. 17 AYT worked with cadets, Scouts, boys' clubs, school parties and other youth groups, doing canoeing, rock-climbing, fell walking and camping, in such places as Snowdonia and the Pennines, River Severn, Leek Camp in Staffordshire, the Dukeries in Nottinghamshire and Penhale in Cornwall. Initially much of the work was mainly at weekends. Progressively – and especially when in 1972 the raising of the school leaving age to sixteen meant that there were masses of youths in inner city schools and elsewhere, who were obliged by law to stay at school an extra year (much to the consternation of headmasters!) – the balance of activities was switched to weekdays, taking groups of these fifteen year olds for a week's adventure training.

Over the period covered by this and the preceding chapter, 17 AYT's OCs were Captain J E Tilley 1968-70, Lieutenant J M P Walsh 1970-71, Lieutenant P M L Ferrary 1971-73, WO2 R J Jackson 1973-74, and WO2 R E Jones 1975-76. And fine work they and their team did, though it is not possible to quantify how many men it attracted to (or distracted from) the Regiment.

Gibraltar: January to July 1972

The Advance Party of Tiger Company arrived in Gibraltar on 20 January 1972 and with the Main Body in place a week later, the Company took over from the 'other Tigers', Minden Coy 1 R Hamps, which returned to England to reform as a full battalion, as did their predecessors in Gibraltar, Balaclava Coy 1 A & SH. 'Would it be third time lucky?' wondered the Tigers.

On arrival in Gibraltar, Tiger Company's senior appointments were held as follows:

CO:	Major J C D Heggs	1 Platoon:	Lieutenant P C Shalders
2IC:	Captain M K Goldschmidt[7]	2 Platoon:	Lieutenant P W Field
Admin Offr:	Captain A I James	Sp Platoon:	Lieutenant R H Pepper
CSM:	WO2 D W Spalding		

The Company was accommodated near the border at RAF North Front, which the soldiers preferred to call by its other name, Devil's Tower Barracks. They also referred to the Rock as the 'High Ground'. The routine for Tiger Company was to provide the frontier guard force for three weeks in every four, the task in each fourth week being fulfilled by the

Resident Battalion (1 RRF), which was stationed at Lathbury Barracks, to the south of the Peninsula. Each of the platoons (the Frontier Security Platoon) fulfilled the duty for a week at a time, starting on 4 February. Operating from Four Corners Guardroom at the frontier gates, the Platoon manned the OPs along the 1,300-yard frontier across the isthmus and conducted mobile patrols. The task was tedious in the extreme, made all the more so when the temperatures increased as the Mediterranean summer approached and because there was scarcely anything of any significance for the OPs to see and report, other than their Spanish opposite numbers watching them and changing over, and the citizens of La Linea waving at relations in Gibraltar! On 24 April, Private G F (Glenn) Richard spotted an illegal immigrant landing by canoe at East Side, who was duly arrested. The Spanish Navy did have an old coal-fired minesweeper nicknamed 'Smokey Joe' that from time to time sailed into the disputed waters off the north-east and north-west coast of Gibraltar. One observant sentry wrote in the log: 'One enemy minesweiper travelling North to South, smoking like a good 'un'!

So serious was the danger to the constricted built-up areas of Gibraltar of fire breaking out in the scrub on the Upper Rock, that contingency plans were regularly practised to counter an Upper Rock Fire. During one such exercise, Private 'Snoopy' Goddard in a 4-ton lorry performed a 43-point turn on a narrow mountain ridge road!

For those platoons not on frontier security, low-level training took place on the Upper Rock ('secondary jungle' on a rock-infested incline) and the very small manoeuvre area (on foot only) and a rifle range at the southern end of the Peninsula. Maximum opportunity was taken to keep fit and play sport, including water sports, to take passage on RN warships and on occasion to conduct undemanding adventure training in Morocco, mainly driving by Land Rover and camping. Named *Barbary Tiger, Tiger Lily, Tiger Tim, Tiger Balm* and *Tigers Nuts*, and on which overall sixty-six members of the Company took part, these exercises were a nice gentle break from the confines of the Rock.

Ceremonial duties were also part of the routine, and each Thursday a Changing the Guard took place at the Four Corners Guardroom, abutting the border gates. It was mainly to support this event that Tiger Company had formed a Corps of Drums, which paraded with silver drums and tiger skins – eight drummers and eight buglers. The first such weekly event took place on 10 February. Another major event, the Ceremony of the Keys, was held three times a year, re-enacting the daily occurrence from the Great Siege of 1779-83. On 29 April, Tiger Company provided the Outpost Platoon (Lieutenant Peter Field and 2 Platoon) and the Escort to the Keys, the event being watched by large crowds. Men of the Company also on occasion provided the guard at The Convent, the residence of the Governor and C-in-C, and on 10 June provided thirty-three ground keepers at the Queen's Birthday Parade performed by 1 RRF.

On 11 February, the CQMS R E (Roger) Jones took over as CSM, an appointment he held for seven weeks until the arrival of WO2 C A (Chris) Aldridge, who came from the Norfolk and Suffolk part of the Regiment. A week later the officers held a welcoming cocktail party at the RAF Gibraltar Officers' Mess, to which 270 people were invited, and a fortnight afterwards the WOs and Sergeants held theirs. The Corps of Drums, which gave an impressive display at both events, was much in demand during the tour, performing at various small units' FFR inspections and at a Charity Variety Show 'It's in the Air'. Cementing local contacts, a public house, the Gibraltar Arms, generously allowed the

Changing The Guard at Four Corners Guardroom, 10 February 1972. *Trustees R Anglian Regt*

Company to inaugurate the 'Tigers' Den Bar' on its premises. Good liaison was established with the allied Gibraltar Regiment, who were most hospitable and whose Training Officer, Captain Tony Taylor, had been the 4th Battalion's last Signals Officer. With Lieutenant Colonel Jimmy Hughes and Major Stuart Green, Fortress HQ's staff had strong 'former Tiger' representation. For the Gibraltar Fair Procession in July the Company provided a float, a mock-up of a border OP carried by a 4-ton lorry.

The highlight of April was the visit by the Lord Mayor of Leicester, Alderman Percy Watts. Alighting from his aeroplane he inspected the Company drawn up on the South Dispersal (which Tiger Company irreverently described as an enormous drill square) and took the salute as it marched past. Over the following four days he watched Tiger Company at work and play, carried out a tour of The Rock, called on the Governor and C-in-C, the Mayor of Gibraltar, the Chief Minister and The Gibraltar Regiment. He spent a day in Tangier and hosted a civic dinner in Gibraltar. Throughout the visit he was accompanied by David Partridge of the *Leicester Mercury*, David Kirkwood of Radio Leicester and Peter Clawson of the *Melton & Rutland Journal*. This was an important visit and further cemented the links between the Regiment and the City of Leicester. Other visitors to the Company during its tour were the Bishop to Her Majesty's Forces in March, the Deputy Force Commander (Brigadier N H Birbeck) in April, and the Governor and C-in-C and, separately, the Director of Infantry in June.

In early May, Captain Robert Pepper and his Support Platoon embarked on HMS *Cavalier* for two days' live firing into the waters off Morocco. The ship was the fastest – at 35 knots – and oldest – at twenty-eight years – in the RN Fleet. 81mm mortar firing was conducted from midships and GPMG(SF) firing from the quarterdeck, facilities for the

Tiger Company's Mortar Section about to fire from HMS *Cavalier*. *Trustees R Anglian Regt*

former not being available on Gibraltar. Drummer Marsh spent a week on board, sounding the bugle at sunrise and sunset and whenever the ship left or entered harbour. A month later, he played three fanfares at the Queen's Birthday Reception held by the British Consul-General in Tangier. Lance Corporal B Cripps was one of three who played at sunset at the

265

frontier guardroom each evening. He was also called upon to play the Last Post at a wedding(!), as well as in front of American CBS TV cameras which were filming a documentary on British imperialism.

Later in May, the Company was involved in what might loosely be referred to as MACC (Military Aid to the Civilian Community), when it made a concerted effort to tidy up Royal Anglian Way. This was a half-mile pathway, with vantage points affording magnificent views, along the edge of the natural escarpment 700 feet up the west side of the Rock, which 2 R Anglian had originally created in 1969 and which was well-used by the public.

On 12 June, the Company set out on the five-day Exercise *Sandy Tiger*, which took place on Governor's Beach on the eastern side of the 'High Ground'. The majority of the Company marched to and from the beach carrying first-line scales of ammunition, while heavy stores were transported by Inter-Service cooperation: a Wasp helicopter from HMS *Juno* brought in ten loads and the underslung WOMBATs direct to the beach, and an RAF marine launch assisted by RE assault craft brought in loads of rations and tentage. The remainder of the stores were passed down the 425 steps by human chain. During the week's training, live firing of the platoon weapons was carried out, as was the annual 10-mile march of the Battle Efficiency Test. Midway through the exercise the officers held a curry lunch on the beach and the soldiers continued the party spirit through to the early morning, to celebrate – some eleven days early – the 147th anniversary of King George IV granting the 'Royal Tiger' badge to the 17th Regiment in 1825 as a 'lasting testimony of its exemplary conduct in India, from 1804 to 1823'.

On 19 June, the Director of Infantry in person announced to the Company that on return from Gibraltar in July it would be posted to Howe Barracks in Canterbury, there to provide about half of the Permanent Staff – leaders, instructors and administrators – of the new Junior Infantrymen's Wing (JIW) Canterbury.

Lt Peter Field throwing the discus.
Trustees R Anglian Regt

The final weeks in Gibraltar were spent in making the most of what the posting had to offer, which had included good opportunities for sport. Competing as a Minor Unit, Tiger Company throughout its tour fielded teams in most sports, including football, hockey, cricket and squash. Corporals A (Tony) Fuller and R W (Bob) Potter and Private Farrell played football for the Army Gibraltar.

At road running, Privates Tebbutt, Gaytor and John Man were in the Combined Services Team competing against the Gibraltarians for the Poachers' Cup, donated by 2 R Anglian in 1969. The Company's athletes performed most creditably in the Gibraltar AAA Track League, being rather better than the 1 RRF Battalion. In the Minor Units Individual Athletics Meeting, they gained seven 1st places, eleven 2nd and six 3rd; sixteen men of the Company were in the Minor Units Team which won the Command Inter-Services Meeting. It had two very good sprinters in Privates Farrell and David Parris, and its 4x100m relay team was the fastest in Gibraltar that season in 47.1 seconds. Lieutenant Peter Field was outstanding in the discus, four times breaking the Gibraltar Services' and Gibraltar AAA records, eventually throwing 144' 5½" to become the Gibraltar national champion.

Preceded a fortnight earlier by the Company 2IC, who went to the Junior Infantrymen's Battalion (JIB) Shorncliffe to help organize the manpower and the new training programmes, the Advance Party left Gibraltar on 18 July. The frontier security duties were handed over to 1 RRF on 20 July, and the officers held their farewell party on 29 July. The Main Body left Gibraltar for England on 31 July by Britannia aircraft. So good had become the relationship between the Company and the RAF with whom it had lived for six months, that the RAF did the Company the honour of escorting its Britannia out of friendly airspace with three Hawker Hunters. The Company proceeded on four weeks' block leave, the officers, SNCOs and corporals attending a three-day cadre in Shorncliffe as an introduction to their new role in Canterbury.

In the meantime, while preparations had been made for all aspects of the move to Canterbury (including stores and families from Aldershot), the saddest feature was the posting of all but six officers and sixteen soldiers back to the Regular battalions. That was a considerable downside from Tiger Company's point of view as the new role required 'chiefs' with very few 'Indians'. Consequently, the very robust and efficient Company, which under the ebullient leadership of Major John Heggs had had such a successful tour in Gibraltar, was scattered to the four winds. The many junior ranks in particular were not amused at the prospect of again having to be posted away from the Tigers (only six Privates remained on Tiger Company's Establishment), and many were immediately lost to the Army.

A tailpiece on Gibraltar. Despite the death in 1975 of the Spanish dictator General Franco, Spain's stance with regard to Gibraltar remained unchanged. In the lead-up to Spain seeking to join the European Community, the reopening of the border was delayed in the wake of the 1982 war between UK and Argentina over the Falkland Islands, during which Gibraltar was used by Britain as an FOB. The subsequent reopening of the border in 1982 was only partial, as Spain allowed only pedestrians, resident in Gibraltar or Spanish nationals, to cross the border, only one crossing each way per day. In 1983, all Gibraltarians became eligible for full British citizenship. Spain fully reopened the border in 1985.

In 1991, regular troops of the British Army effectively withdrew from Gibraltar, leaving the locally recruited Gibraltar Regiment as the Resident Battalion. The RN and RAF maintained an FOB, which was later used for Gulf War deployments. Gibraltar remained a Dependent Territory. Tension between Spain and Gibraltar continued through the 1990s, because Spain continuously accused Gibraltar of being 'a hotbed of drug trafficking, tobacco smuggling, and tax evasion'. The decade ended with HM The Queen granting The Gibraltar Regiment the prefix 'Royal'. In 2002, twelve months' negotiation between the British and Spanish Governments led to the proposed principle that Britain and Spain should share sovereignty over Gibraltar. In a referendum organized by the Government of Gibraltar and overseen by international observers, Gibraltar's citizens overwhelmingly rejected the proposal by 17,900 votes to 187. That same year, the British Overseas Territories Act 2002 changed the status of Gibraltar from a Dependent Territory to an

Overseas Territory. This act granted to the residents of all British Overseas Territories full British citizenship, which had already been available to Gibraltarians for nineteen years.

In 2004 Gibraltar celebrated 300 years of British rule (which Spanish officials labelled the celebration of 300 years of British occupation), and the Freedom of the City was granted to the Royal Navy. Spanish/Gibraltar negotiations are currently in abeyance.

Canterbury: August 1972 to February 1974

And so Tiger Company formed up in Canterbury. In 1972, the Army was seeking to maximize the last chance to recruit fifteen-year-olds before the raising of the school leaving age to sixteen. Accordingly, its capacity to train Junior Soldiers was expanded for one year and among other units the Junior Infantrymen's Wing (JIW) Canterbury was born. JIW Canterbury was housed at Howe Barracks (the home of Depot The Queen's Regiment until 1970, and still that of RHQ PWRR). It was a well-appointed and fairly modern facility, with copious playing fields and 450 acres of training area (180 acres worth of golf course being particularly useful). Commanded by Major P L Cutler RRW, it was a satellite of JIB Shorncliffe (Lieutenant Colonel K M Koe RGJ), and consisted of two Junior Soldiers (JS) Companies, Admin Company, an Education Wing, and several training departments. The second JS Company was manned by Albuhera Company 4 Queens whose members, like Tiger Company's, retained their individual identity within the Wing framework, working under the Drill, Weapon Training (WT) or Tactics Wings. Wing HQ and Admin Company were manned by men from a number of infantry regiments, and a number of RAEC officers ran the large Education Wing.

On arrival at Canterbury, senior appointments in Tiger Company were held as follows:

CO:	Major J C D Heggs	1 Platoon:	Lieutenant P J W Black
2IC/Wing Asst CI:	Captain M K Goldschmidt	2 Platoon:	Lieutenant P Barnes
Wing Asst Adjt:	Captain A I James	3 Platoon:	Lieutenant P W Field
CSM:	WO2 C A Aldridge	4 Platoon:	Lieutenant H Bradbury RRF

For the first three weeks the Permanent Staff bedded in and discovered their roles in the new JIW Canterbury. On 19 September 1972, 393 fifteen-year-old JSs arrived at Howe Barracks, to be trained there in Tiger and Albuhera Companies for just one year. One hundred were Royal Anglians, ninety Queens and sixty RRF, so it behoved the Wing to train well in particular these 250 for the future benefit of The Queen's Division. One hundred and ninety-six were in Tiger Company. More widely, Tiger Company's Recruiting Team, now six strong and led by Corporal Tony Fuller, continued busily in Leicester and was particularly successful in recruiting junior soldiers. Army-wide, there were 493 Royal Anglian junior soldiers in training in September 1972, which boded well for the Regiment as a whole.

Of the training the Junior Soldiers underwent during their year at Canterbury, one half was education (as if they were still at school), map reading and first aid; the other half was military: drill, WT, tactics, PT and sport. The short notice at which the Army had formed these new JS units severely challenged its logistic capability. This led among other things to a shortage of much equipment, stores, weaponry and vehicles. Apart from there being no 4x4 (4-ton) lorries (only road-bound 2x4s) issued at Canterbury, the most significant deficiency was that there was only one cleaning kit per ten rifles. This stretched the ingenuity of the Weapon Training Instructors teaching Lesson 1 on the SLR, and keeping all the weapons clean subsequently!

Over the following ten months the training staff were fully engaged in turning these middle-teenagers into persons much more robust and well on to their way to becoming competent infantrymen. There were three twelve-week terms, with generous breaks at Christmas and Easter. While most of the training took place in barracks and on nearby rifle ranges, some important developmental exercises were held at Stanford, Crowborough, Okehampton and Salisbury Plain. Due to its relative novelty, JIW Canterbury was visited by a number of senior officers. These included, on consecutive days in October, the Director of Infantry and Lieutenant General Sir Ian Freeland GBE KCB DSO, the Colonel of The Regiment, the latter in particular greatly encouraging the men of Tiger Company in their new role. In March, GOC SEDIST (Lieutenant General Sir Terence McMeekin KCB OBE) conducted the FFR Inspection and was well pleased with what he saw.

LCpl Nevil Jephcote MM.
Mrs N Jephcote

In early 1973, the announcement was made of the award of the Military Medal to Lance Corporal Nevil Jephcote, who had served in 4 R Anglian from 1967 to 1970. The award was made for his outstanding display of courage, leadership and initiative while a Section Commander in 3 R Anglian in Belfast in June 1972. Over three days and nights in the Clonard area, Jephcote and his Section shot and captured a gunman while under sniper fire, and he personally, while under fire, extracted a young girl from the danger of a gun battle. He then found a weapons arsenal and arrested a further terrorist in possession of ammunition.

On 23 January, it was announced in Parliament that, at the conclusion of its JIW training role in August, Tiger Company would be reformed at full Representative Company strength, and that its future was assured until 1975, with the position to be reviewed in the light of recruiting in The Queen's Division. In contrast, Albuhera Company 4 Queens was to disband at the end of 1973. This news was greeted with great elation by all Tigers, and the challenge was again laid down to The Queen's Division as a whole, and to The Royal Anglian Regiment in particular, to improve further its recruiting and retention. At that time the three Regular battalions of The Royal Anglian Regiment were at 'Minimum Manning Strength'. Planning soon began for later in the year when Tiger Company's strength would radically increase from five officers and forty men to six and 120. The following month, in its pamphlet 'In Defence of Peace' the Conservative Parliamentary Defence Committee recommended that Tiger Company should be expanded to Battalion strength whenever recruiting allowed.

Buoyed up by news of its future, in March 1973 the Company was honoured by a visit from the Lord Mayor of Leicester, Alderman Stanley Thompson, who toured the barracks, meeting the permanent staff of Tiger Company and some Junior Soldiers from Leicestershire. He later hosted a civic dinner.

On 6 April, Major John Heggs handed over command of Tiger Company to Major J A (John) Bacon, whose career to date had been in the Bedfordshire & Hertfordshire part of the Regiment. 'Peterborough' in the *Daily Telegraph* alluded to 'Bacon and (H)eggs'! John Bacon was to lead the Company during its final term of training JSs and into its early months as a full company.

The final passing-out parade of Junior Soldiers was held at JIB Shorncliffe on 4 July. The men of Tiger Company and all the others involved could be well pleased and proud of the way they had effectively trained so many young soldiers, who in due course would go on to fill the ranks of Regular battalions. JIW Canterbury then began to disband, along with Albuhera Company 4 Queens, whose demise was solely to help the recruited strength of The Queen's Division. Meanwhile Tiger Company prepared for its future and in August went on block leave.

Capt Roger Howe MBE*, **in disguise in Belfast.** *Mrs R Howe*

It was about this time that the announcement was made of the award of the MBE for Gallantry to Captain Roger Howe, who had served in 1 R Leicesters/4 R Anglian from 1963 to 1968. The award was made for his outstanding performance while Battalion Intelligence Officer of 2 R Anglian in Belfast in late 1972. He was fearless and courageous on the ground as well as completely ruthless in his pursuit of every conceivable lead in hunting down

Tiger Company, January 1974 (see Appendix P for names). *F A H Swallow*

terrorists. He frequently carried out covert operations in hostile territory, bravely putting himself in positions of danger as he sought very successfully to identify terrorists who were consequently dealt with by the Security Forces. His personal efforts enabled the Battalion to dominate its area so comprehensively.

News was also received of the award of the Military Medal to Corporal J ('Judd') Laker, who had served in 1 R Leicesters/4 R Anglian 1962-65. The award was made for bravery as a Section Commander while serving in 3 RRF in County Armagh in 1972.

In early September 1973, Tiger Company reformed at Canterbury at full Company strength to assume its operational role as an independent infantry company under command HQ 2 Inf Bde at Folkestone (Brigadier B N Fletcher). There were many new faces, including WO2 E (Eddie) Davies, who had joined 1 R Leicesters in the 1950s and was to be Tiger Company's last CSM. With many junior ranks recently posted in from the three Regular battalions,

Cpl J Laker MM. *J Laker*

the Company set about training for its new fairly general role, both locally, at Sennybridge, and for four days in December on FTX *Tiger Rag* at Stanford. In October, the Colonel of The Regiment visited, and a few days later it was announced that Tiger Company would deploy to Northern Ireland in March on a four-month unaccompanied Operation *Banner* tour as a subunit of 7 Para RHA in the South Armagh area.

On 28 November, the Lord Mayor of Leicester, Councillor Arnold Wakefield, visited the Company at Canterbury. In an address he said, 'Tiger Company will always take pride of place in Leicester, not only because of our longstanding association and friendship with the

County Regiment, but because it is the only Company in the Army that holds the Freedom of the City of Leicester, an honour which I know you value very much.' And how right he was. Plans to exercise that Freedom the following summer began to be formulated.

At about this time news was received of the award of the Military Cross to Captain S M (Shaun) Brogan, who had served in the 4th Battalion from 1966 to 1969. The award was made for his conduct over a year of sustained operations while serving in 22 SAS as Operations Officer and field commander in Oman 1971-72. In October 1971, Operation *Jaguar* had been launched to get Omani Government forces back on to the jebel in Dhofar Province and establish a permanent base there. A force of five firqat (local militia), led by teams from a squadron of the SAS and supported by a battalion of the Sultan's Armed Forces, set out to seize the

Capt Shaun Brogan MC.
S M Brogan

initiative from rebel tribesmen from the Yemen. During the several weeks of that operation, Brogan was in charge of one of the firqat and was involved in fierce fighting. The citation for the MC mentions three particular encounters with the enemy. On one day he called for air support on seven occasions and Strikemaster close air support jets bombed and strafed the attacking tribesman to prevent his firqat being overrun. On another occasion, with a troop of twelve SAS men leading the 100-man firqat, he was deploying to surround a village by dawn and was ambushed in the early light. Ignoring an order to pull back, though badly wounded in the leg he led his men to close with the enemy and seize their firing points. Yet again, he led an operation on 17 January 1972 to secure a firm base in enemy-controlled territory. At dawn his force landed on an unmanned LZ and moved swiftly through difficult country towards its objective. Shortly afterwards the force came under heavy fire, his local militia men took cover and would not continue. On two occasions during a seven-hour engagement he went forward under fire and by a display of energy, bravery, determination and personality persuaded them to advance again, and the objective was seized.

On 17 December, Major John Bacon handed over Tiger Company to Major F A H (Anthony) Swallow, a long-serving Tigers' officer. Early in the New Year 1974, the Company embarked on training for Northern Ireland (NI). An important feature of the preparation was ten days' special-to-theatre Counter Insurgency training under the tutelage of the NI Training & Advisory Team at Lydd. There, among other things, were included some new rifle ranges on which to practise close-range shooting in urban areas and house-clearing, a very realistic, necessary and exciting development in infantry training

Northern Ireland: February to June 1974

By way of background, 'the Troubles' in the Province of NI had been ongoing since 1969 and were a significant development from the initial Civil Rights marches of that year, which had been hijacked by the Irish Republican Army (IRA) for a much more radical agenda: many of the Catholic 'Nationalist' minority sought unification with Eire. Opposing them, the Protestant 'Loyalist' majority sought to remain in the United Kingdom. The Nationalist Extremists, with the Provisional IRA in the lead, were on the warpath against the Security Forces (especially the soft targets in the off-duty Royal Ulster Constabulary (RUC) and The

Ulster Defence Regiment (UDR)) and occasionally against soft Protestant targets, in the urban and rural areas. The 'Loyalist' Protestant Extremist paramilitaries (principally the Ulster Defence Association, the Ulster Volunteer Force (UVF) and the Red Hand Commando – in ascending order of violence) were on the warpath against the nationalist extremists and soft-target Catholics. The Security Forces were endeavouring to hold the ring, including defeating the Provisional IRA and preventing their members crossing into the Province with arms and explosives from their safe havens in Eire. On the political front, Direct Rule from Westminster, which the Conservative Government had imposed in March 1972 after the disbandment of the Assembly, had ended on 31 December 1973, with the implementation of the Sunningdale Agreement which produced a power-sharing formula that involved representatives of all sections of the community in a new NI Executive, replacing the old Assembly. The Agreement also set out the parameters for the 'Irish Dimension' in the government of Northern Ireland. The first public test of opinion came with the Westminster General Election on 28 February 1974 which was viewed in NI as a referendum on power-sharing and the Sunningdale Agreement. Those opposed to Sunningdale fought the election under the umbrella of the United Ulster Unionist Council. They won 51 per cent of the votes cast and took eleven of the twelve Westminster seats in a Parliament in which the Labour Party came to power. Those results showed the increasing Loyalist opposition to power-sharing and the Council of Ireland, and generally added to the deep sense of alienation that had grown in the Protestant community during the previous five years.

In contrast to just two resident battalions stationed in NI in 1969, during the worst period of 'the Troubles' between 1972 and 1973 some 28,000 military personnel had been stationed in Northern Ireland, the majority of them Army and including 5,300 of the UDR (which eventually expanded to eleven battalions of mainly part-timers). It was about that time that its counter-insurgency posture evolved into a counter-terrorist one. In addition to four resident battalions, there were six other roulement battalions (including Regular RAC and RA units in the dismounted infantry role). This was the military and political situation into which Tiger Company was about to move.

Following six previous and successful tours by the other three Regular battalions of the Regiment since 'the Troubles' began in 1969, at the beginning of March 1974 Tiger Company deployed to NI. Senior appointments at the time were:

CO:	Major F A H Swallow	2 Platoon:	Sgt R C McDonald
2IC:	Captain S R H Underwood	3 Platoon:	2nd Lieutenant C J B Groom
CSM:	WO2 E Davies	OC Rear Party:	Lieutenant J R Bass Queens
1 Platoon:	Lieutenant D Morris		

Although they had trained with 7 Para RHA Group, Tiger Company was sent to Mahon Road Barracks in Portadown where it took over from a company of 1 DERR, a resident battalion based at Ballykinler. Tiger Company was under the operational command of 3 RRF whose Bn HQ was in Armagh City. 3 Platoon (2Lt Chris Groom) was in parallel detached to under command a 3 RRF company at Dungannon. Throughout the tour one of Tiger Company's platoons was permanently based there, in rotation. Whilst its

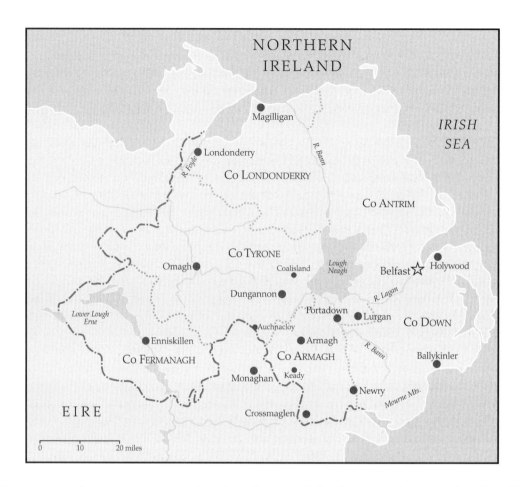

Dungannon platoon saw more action than the rest of the Company, it meant that Coy HQ never deployed with all three platoons under its own command, except for one night in May. 3 RRF (Lieutenant Colonel I R Cartwright MBE) was under command HQ 3 Inf Bde at Lurgan (Brigadier C S Wallis-King MBE).

Special IS equipment was issued for the tour, including flak jackets which were worn for all operations and by static sentries. Although officers and warrant officers would normally have worn the new brown beret, so as not to stand out as obvious targets for snipers during this tour, they wore instead the familiar blue berets with a green patch as backing to the blackened capbadge, the same as the more junior members. Life in Portadown was quiet but fairly full as the Company initially had a large area of operations (AOR) of 80 square miles.

In support of the Royal Ulster Constabulary (RUC) and in whose J Division HQ Corporal J (Jack) Weaver helped man telephones and radios in Portadown, the Company was involved in a range of operational activities, including foot and mobile patrols, and searches of houses and hedgerows, in urban and rural areas. The town of Portadown itself had yet to be subjected to the ravages of terrorism, but soon fire-bombing attacks became a prominent threat. By mounting foot patrols in its business areas, Tiger Company assisted in preventing firebombs (usually pocket-sized IEDs) being placed in the shopping premises. Foot patrols, while reassuring to the general population, were generally unexciting, although the soldiers were welcomed by cups of tea in the Protestant estates. In Portadown only one round was fired at a patrol, as it tabbed through a Catholic housing estate. On 13

March, for several days, and again from 5 to 9 April, as part of Operation *Lever*, Tiger Company's men manned VCPs from 0400 to 2100 at all the bridges over the River Bann, designed to intercept arms and explosives being moved into the urban areas. Foot patrols in the rural areas, designed to chat up and reassure the locals of either faction, were known as 'Farmers' Daughters'!

2 Platoon (Sergeant Bob McDonald) rotated to Dungannon vice 1 Platoon on 28 March, on which day Coy Tac HQ with 1 and 3 Platoons deployed for four days to the border near Omagh on Operation *Longstop*. 1 Platoon (Lt David Morris) had been reinforced by 2nd Lieutenant T R (Tim) Wilkes, the last officer to be posted into Tiger Company on commissioning. Among other activities, 1 Platoon provided OPs and a protection force in support of the Royal Engineers as they blew a large crater in the road to block an unauthorized border crossing point. On 3 April, in a joint operation with the RUC the Company helped to recover seven rifles, two shotguns, five pistols and a quantity of ammunition 3 miles south of Portadown. A fortnight later, a member of the Protestant Extremist UVF was killed when a bomb he was making exploded in his house in Portadown. It was subsequently discovered that this terrorist, Ronald Joseph Neill, had served in 4 R Anglian a few years before.

Ever since the formation of The Royal Anglian Regiment in 1964, the Lord Mayor of Leicester has held a civic dinner annually in honour of its Colonel, to which other senior officers of the Regiment are invited. It was at such a dinner on 16 March 1974 that in his speech the Colonel of The Regiment gave warning that Tiger Company was in danger of extinction unless there was marked improvement in recruiting. Fewer than thirty men had been recruited into the Regiment from Leicestershire in 1973, but 400 were needed and quickly. 'You give us more support for The Royal Anglian Regiment than in any other where we recruit.' He also praised the Lord Mayor for making the first of what he hoped would be many visits to the 1st and 2nd Battalions, as an indication that the Lord Mayoralty clearly understood that all of the Regular battalions took forward the traditions of all the Former Regiments. He also warmly thanked Leicester City Football Club for allowing the Regiment to show its flag at Filbert Street that afternoon, in an attempt to drum up more recruits. The tenor of the remarks by the Colonel of The Regiment nevertheless placed an unwanted cloud over Tiger Company's future – it was clearly fighting for its very existence, and all its subsequent activities that year were carried out in the shadow of disbandment. As an aside, the Lord Mayor of Leicester is the only one of about ninety civic heads in the Regimental area who hosts an annual dinner for the Regiment, a tradition which still continues to today (2008). Leicestershire County Council also holds annual dinners, to which representatives of all three Services associated with the County are invited.

Meanwhile, back in NI, Tiger Company had known that being based in Portadown would be short-lived as Mahon Road Barracks was being rapidly expanded to accommodate a roulement Battalion HQ and its associated elements, and a rifle company. The Protestant locals very generously provided for the expanding barracks, which also housed the part-time 11 UDR, at the time commanded by Lieutenant Colonel Paul Young, a former Royal Leicester and the first Royal Anglian to command a UDR Battalion. They became less well disposed when a Tiger Company patrol, tasked with removing a Nationalist tricolour flag of Eire, inadvertently took down a Loyalist 'Red Hand of Ulster' one.

Lt Col Paul Young, Major Anthony Swallow and CSM Eddie Davies. *F A H Swallow*

At the beginning of May, 1st Battalion The Green Howards arrived in Portadown, and Tiger Company moved to the Worcester Valve Factory just north of Armagh City. There it came under command of The Life Guards (LG) (Lieutenant Colonel S C Cooper) and assumed a rather active Brigade Reserve role. It was promptly given a large AOR near the border to look after for two weeks until an LG Squadron relieved it. To assist, it took under command four troops from Ajax Squadron 2 RTR and, from time to time, a platoon from 3 PARA. It was an interesting fortnight in an area that included the town of Keady where the police station had been badly damaged by a car bomb earlier in the year, and had also been subjected to a well-organized machine-gun attack. Among other activities, the platoons mounted night ambushes on the border at unauthorized crossing points.

The only incident of note occurred on 13 May when a bullock was killed when it triggered a suspected booby-trapped Improvised Explosive Device (IED) on the grass verge about 300 yards from the border south-west of Keady. The Company mounted a clearance operation, but nothing more of significance was discovered. The following day 2 Platoon rotated to Dungannon vice 1 Platoon. During the latter's three weeks there, at the Coalisland base (Coalisland being a nationalist stronghold where the IRA had first formed), its sentry sangar was fired at on three consecutive nights; fire was returned each time, amounting to sixty rounds, killing two canaries and a dog, as well as ventilating a passing bread van! The Platoon had also been involved in several operations, two to clear culvert bombs and one a car bomb. On one such operation, when three practice rounds from the Platoon's 84mm Carl Gustav had failed to detonate a 350lb device, the RAOC's Ammunition Technical Officer was called in and dealt with it more conventionally.

Meanwhile, the political situation which had prevailed since the General Election in February had continued to deteriorate until on 15 May the Ulster Workers' Council (UWC) called a General Strike with the purpose of forcing the British Government to shelve the Sunningdale Agreement and the power-sharing Executive. This led to roads being blocked by hijacked vehicles, buses being hijacked in Belfast, and electricity supplies being disrupted with rotating four-hourly power cuts occurring across the Province. The next day the effect of the strike deepened with the engineering sector of the economy being the hardest hit; the use of intimidation (or 'persuasion' as the Loyalist paramilitaries preferred to call it) had a significant impact on the number of people who managed to get to work. The strike then began to affect the farming sector with uncollected, or unprocessed, milk having to be dumped and fresh food not reaching shops. By Day 3, reductions in the supply of electricity continued to have serious consequences for industry, commerce and the domestic sector, including petrol distribution and postal deliveries following intimidation of Royal Mail employees. Car bombs in Dublin and Monaghan planted by Loyalist paramilitaries killed thirty-three people, one of the highest death tolls to occur during any single day of 'the Troubles'.

Against that background, on 17 May, Tiger Company moved to Auchnacloy where, based in the UDR Centre, it took over a small AOR on the tip of the Monaghan Salient, and its main task to man the permanent VCP at the border, supported by sixteen members of the RMP. On 21 May, due to the deteriorating situation of the UWC strike (by 20 May, many roads in NI were closed because of barricades, and electricity generation dropped to about one-third of normal levels), Tiger Company was relieved by a squadron of 1 RTR and regrouped at Worcester Valve Factory as Brigade Reserve.

There followed a few fairly hectic days operating in the Portadown area, protecting petrol stations and escorting essential supplies. On 27 May, Protestant Loyalists erected barriers throughout the Province, an illegal action which severely stretched the loyalty of the mainly Protestant RUC. Tiger Company helped to remove barricades in Portadown, and at affected power stations and petrol depots nearby. For everyone in the Province there were power cuts, and for the Army, tilley lamps and generators provided light. The following day, as with many other units across the Province manning the twenty-one Government-run petrol stations, 3 Platoon manned one in Portadown which supplied petrol to those essential users who could obtain a permit from the Ministry of Commerce. On 30 May, Tiger Company (including 2 Platoon from Dungannon) moved to Lurgan to cover a Protestant march, the only occasion during the tour when it operated as a whole company.

The sense of alienation meant that a large section of the Protestant community was prepared to give active or, at least tacit, support to the UWC Strike. Thus supported, the strike proved chillingly effective and demonstrated clearly that, without the support of the majority, the power-sharing NI Executive could not succeed. It brought down the Executive, and on 30 May responsibility for the government of NI then reverted to the British Parliament at Westminster under the arrangements for 'Direct Rule'.

Yet again, as in many other parts of the world in earlier colonial days, the Security Forces had operated in an even-handed way and had merely done their duty, successfully endeavouring – without fear or favour – to maintain essential services in the face of considerable opposition.

The trouble created by the strike died down again fairly quickly. As it was felt, however, that the situation remained volatile, Tiger Company remained in Brigade Reserve for the rest of its tour. This left a slight feeling of anti-climax because by the end of the tour, with the sole exception of one evening in Lurgan in May, no trouble had materialized for the Company as a whole to deal with. However, the platoons were quite frequently lent to other subunits to assist in specific operations. Opportunity was found to celebrate Royal Tigers' Day on 22 June, on which the operational rule of two cans of beer per man per day was relaxed – slightly!

All ranks who had served for four weeks in the Province earned the GSM with clasp 'Northern Ireland'. On 2 July, Tiger Company's Op *Banner* tour came to an end when, mercifully having sustained no casualties as a result of hostile action, it embarked at Belfast on the overnight ferry. It had successfully completed what was to be its last operational tour, coincidentally on the same island on which Colonel Solomon Richard's Regiment (later The 17th (Leicestershire) Regiment) had been deployed on operations in 1688 in the first year of its existence.

It was about this time that information was received that Captain David Daniels RRF, who had served in 4 R Anglian in Bahrain in 1969-70, had been awarded Oman's Distinguished Service Medal 'for Gallantry' – the Omani equivalent of the British MC. The citation covers his work on Loan Service with The Jebel Regiment in 1972-3. During the period he trained a newly formed Mortar Platoon, and was involved on Operation *Simba* near Sarfait in the long-running Dhofar Campaign. There he was a company operations officer, and later commanded 2 Company. The results achieved by his men reflected much of his aggressive outlook, great physical energy and determined leadership, as he took the fight to the enemy during a four-month deployment during which his company positions were under daily bombardment and regular close-range attack.

Capt David Daniels.
Trustees R Anglian Regt

A tailpiece on 'the Troubles' in Northern Ireland. Over the period 1969-2007, 763 servicemen and women were killed as a direct result of terrorism, including fifty-one military personnel murdered outside Northern Ireland. Over that period, 6,116 members of the Army and Royal Marines were wounded. Among the dead were two men who had previously served in the Tigers: Private R (Robert) Benner who, while serving in 3 Queens at Ballykinler in 1971, was murdered while on leave in Eire, and Private R M (Robert) Mason who was killed while serving in 2 R Anglian in Belfast in 1972. Along with all the others who have given their lives while on duty and those killed by terrorist action while serving in the Armed Forces since 1948, their names are recorded on the Armed Forces Memorial at the National Memorial Arboretum in Staffordshire. Benner and Mason (and each of those who were killed in NI) are individually commemorated by a named plaque beside an ash tree in their respective Regiment's plot in the Ulster Ash Grove. Mason is also recorded in the Royal Anglian Memorial Book in the Regimental Museum at Duxford.

Benner is recorded in the Regimental (Queens & PWRR) Book of Remembrance in the Warrior's Chapel in Canterbury Cathedral, and in a duplicate book on permanent display at RHQ PWRR at Howe Barracks in Canterbury. His name is also on a memorial at the barracks' entrance, commemorating all those from The Queen's Regiment who were killed in NI.

For the Infantry, 'the Troubles' were essentially 'a junior commanders' War'. Young and relatively inexperienced leaders bore the brunt of often violent confrontations including gun battles and riots, yet they proved that they could apply military force with restraint even in the face of serious provocation. It is well summed up by a sometime Tiger who commanded 2 R Anglian in Belfast[8]. He wrote in his battalion magazine in 1972:

> I want here to direct the highest praise towards those who most deserve it – the platoon commanders, platoon sergeants, section commanders and private soldiers. *They* are the people who have achieved the results. It is they who have worked almost impossible hours in a very dangerous environment, who have been constantly abused, insulted, assaulted and shot at. *They* are the people who have borne the brunt and have once again proved how incomparable the British soldier, and in particular the Royal Anglian soldier, is.

On the streets of Belfast and Londonderry and in the fields of South Armagh, Tyrone and Fermanagh, the Army pioneered and perfected the tactics that later proved invaluable in the Balkans, Afghanistan and Iraq. The civilian surgeons in Belfast's Musgrave Park Hospital became the world's leading exponents in treating gunshot wounds. Yet this well-equipped and trained Army did struggle against irregular forces, using a range of unusual weapons, in particular the ingenious IEDs. When the Provisional IRA eventually realized that it could not break the will of the British Government, 'win the war' and bring about a unification of Ireland by force of arms, it called its first ceasefire in September 1994, greeted with relief by a government which knew that it could not defeat the IRA militarily. It was to take over a decade to thrash out a political compromise, a period marked by repeated crises, including violent incidents, political upheavals and long periods of apparent stalemate. With the Good Friday Agreement of April 1998 an important milestone, reaching an endgame with the reinstitution of the NI Assembly proved that even the most intractable of conflicts could eventually be settled. It was the Army's steadfast actions over almost four decades which helped to create the situation where it could be brought about.

At one stage there were 106 military bases or locations in the Province. The number of troops and bases were gradually reduced in number until Operation *Banner* was superseded on 1 August 2007 by Operation *Helvetic*. The garrison was 5,000 military personnel in ten locations, trained and ready for deployment worldwide instead of being stationed in the Province specifically to provide military support to the Police (which in 2001 had been renamed the Police Service of Northern Ireland (PSNI)). Gone are HQ NI and the HQs of 3, 8 and 39 Inf Bdes, all four replaced by HQ 38 (Irish) Bde, which in turn is subordinate to HQ 2 Div in Edinburgh.

Operation *Banner* delivered continuous support to the police and civil authorities in NI for thirty-eight years, the longest continuous deployment of UK Armed Forces in their history. Thereafter the Armed Services have retained some limited but specific responsibilities with the capability to deploy in situations of extreme public disorder in support of the PSNI under Operation *Helvetic*. As across the UK the Armed Forces provide support to the civil authorities during emergencies under normal MACA, those arrangements have continued also in NI.

Those thirty-eight years of counter-terrorist operations in the Province covered about one and a half times the length of a soldier's normal 22-year career. Battalions of The Royal Anglian Regiment carried out twenty-eight tours in NI, a combination of two-year residential and four-month (later six-month) roulement tours. So often did many Service men and women deploy on operations in NI with only one GSM and one clasp to show for it, that in 1994 the Accumulated Campaign Service Medal was introduced, awarded for aggregated service of 1,080 days (three years) in those theatres for which the GSM is issued.

Many former Tigers had performed with great distinction as is shown in Appendix A detailing Honours & Awards, and in Appendix C which lists officers who commanded other units and formations, including UDR battalions and infantry brigades in the Province. Men of Tiger Company had played their small part in 1971 and 1974, just as their forbears had, across the globe and in Ireland. 2nd Battalion The Leicestershire Regiment had experienced a peaceful tour in Londonderry from 1931 to 1936. Previously, the 1st Battalion had served with distinction in County Roscommon (90 miles west of Dublin) from 1919 to 1922 during 'the Uprising' which led to the Partition of Ireland. This had created the Republic of Eire while six of the former nine counties of Ulster remained part of the United Kingdom of Great Britain and Northern Ireland. At the conclusion of that tour, the Commanding Officer, Lieutenant Colonel E L Challenor CB CMG DSO[9], was awarded the CBE, an award higher than the OBE, which many commanding officers received during 'the Troubles' of 1969-2007.

On 10 September 2008, in the presence of TRH The Prince of Wales and The Duchess of Cornwall, politicians and Service Chiefs, an Operation *Banner* Commemoration Service was held at St Paul's Cathedral in London to honour nationally the sacrifice made by so many. The immense contribution of the Armed Forces (and their families) had made a real difference to the lives of the citizens of Northern Ireland who previously had had conflicting aspirations and contrasting religious traditions.

Canterbury: July 1974 to July 1975

During their two weeks' leave, many of Tiger Company attended the Colour Presentation by the Colonel-in-Chief to the 1st, 2nd, 3rd and 5th (Volunteer) Battalions The Royal Anglian Regiment at Tidworth on 12 July 1974. Although none of the Company were on parade, several were presented to the Colonel-in-Chief, and Major Anthony Swallow, as Company Commander, was included in the formal photograph of the Colonel-in-Chief with the Colour Ensigns and all the commanding officers. The event is described in greater detail in Chapter 10, and the new Colours are shown in the plate section.

Tiger Company then reassembled at Howe Barracks in Canterbury. There, after watching the pageantry at Tidworth, it was to be no spectator for the march through the City of Leicester on 25 July, for which preparation and practice became the order of the day.

The last occasion on which the Colours of 1st Battalion The Royal Leicestershire Regiment were to be paraded through the City was on 25 July 1974 when Tiger Company exercised its right of the Freedom of the City of Leicester, marching 'with bayonets fixed,

Tiger Company marches through Leicester, 25 June 1974. *Leicester Mercury*

Colours flying, and band playing'. The plan that on this important occasion the Bands of 1st, 2nd and 3rd Battalions were to accompany the parade was not as straightforward as might have seemed. The coaches which were to have brought 140 musicians from Colchester were suddenly retasked to take 3 RRF to airfields to fly to Cyprus, which had just been invaded by Turkey. Much to the relief of the Leicester parade organizers, the Band of the 2nd Battalion arrived on time and after a short postponement they were joined by that of the 3rd. The 1st Battalion's Band was later still and only joined the proceedings at the end in Victoria Park – what might be described as 'incremental music'! Outside the Town Hall, Tiger Company was addressed by the Lord Mayor of Leicester, Councillor Mrs Irene Pollard[10], and then on a warm and dry afternoon it marched up Granby Street and London Road into Victoria Park where the Lord Mayor, accompanied by the Deputy Colonel, took the salute. It was very heartening to see the genuine pleasure that the people of Leicester felt as they turned out in large numbers to line the route and watch the march. Led by the senior Drum Major of the Regiment, WO2 Ray West, who had been the last Drum Major of the 4th Battalion, the Massed Bands then Beat Retreat before an appreciative audience, whereafter the Bands and the members of Tiger Company were treated to a wonderful tea in the De Montfort Hall, suitably decked out in Regimentalia. In her speech (the second of the day because the loudspeakers had not been working earlier at the Town Hall), the Lord Mayor congratulated Tiger Company on the exemplary way it had carried out its duties in Northern Ireland and went on to say, 'Let me assure you that the people of Leicester have remained affectionately and steadfastly proud of you over the years. It is our fervent hope that we shall long enjoy this association. Tiger Company's continued existence as part of The Royal Anglian Regiment – a Regiment with whom we now have close links of cooperation and friendship – is very dear to our hearts.' So ended a most enjoyable and memorable day.

Back to an anticipated 'normal routine' at Canterbury (whatever 'normal' might mean to Tiger Company!), half the Company moved to Catterick on 28 July to provide enemy for an RMA Sandhurst exercise for a week. The balance moved to Camberley and after a break of seven months took up Demonstration Company duties, expecting to relieve 10 GR for just three weeks. In the event, this task lasted three months because 10 GR was flown out to Cyprus as reinforcements. That unplanned extension at Sandhurst put paid to plans for an overseas exercise to Bermuda.

On 22 August, Major Anthony Swallow handed over Tiger Company to Major J P (John) Growse, who originated in the Northamptonshire part of the Regiment. John Growse, who was to be the last CO of Tiger Company, found that he just had time to settle his family in Canterbury before the prolongation of the tour at Sandhurst was announced. Thereafter he and CSM Eddie Davies developed almost magical ways of conjuring up men out of nowhere to demonstrate the 'Platoon in Attack' and other well-known scenarios. The tenth anniversary of The Royal Anglian Regiment (and its 4th Battalion) was duly celebrated on 1 September.

It was an interesting three months at Sandhurst during which the members of the Company put in their usual wholehearted performance in the demonstration role. Despite the inconvenience of the families being at Canterbury, it was enjoyable. A Company 1 D and D took over from Tiger Company at the end of October, which allowed a two-month break, during which time could be spent with the families. Important visitors to Canterbury during that period were the Lord Mayor of Leicester on 19 November and the Colonel of The Regiment on 3 December.

The final occasion on which a Tigers' regular unit drank a toast to 'The British Battalion' was on 20 December. That commemorated the amalgamation of 1st Battalion The Leicestershire Regiment and 2nd Battalion The East Surrey Regiment on that day in 1941 at Ipoh, Malaya after both battalions had suffered very heavy losses in battle against the advancing Japanese. The British Battalion had fought on until the surrender of Singapore two months later, and it stayed in existence right 'through the three and a half years of captivity, forming a real and permanent friendship. The spirit of comradeship between the officers and men of the two Regiments who served together in that Battalion was forged in battle and enriched by hardship and suffering shared.'

As 1975 dawned, Tiger Company again returned to Sandhurst as Demonstration Company for what was to be the last time. The not-entirely-unexpected announcement that Tiger Company was to be disbanded four months later came on 27 January. The reason for the decision was that there was an unsatisfactory level of recruiting in The Royal Anglian Regiment, and that Tiger Company's men would be better used as reinforcements for other Regular battalions. This sad news for The Tigers was in no way alleviated by the many valedictory messages received. In a letter to the Colonel of The Regiment, the Chief of the General Staff said:

> It is with deep regret that the Army Board has decided that Tiger Company 4 Royal Anglian is to disband. The Army Board has taken this decision in view of the overall manning situation only after very careful consideration and with great reluctance. Although the Company carried the nickname of the former Royal Leicestershire

Regiment, I know that the splendid traditions of that Regiment and of the County of Leicestershire will not cease on the disbanding of Tiger Company, because they are well established in the three battalions of The Royal Anglian Regiment. It is for good reason that the Royal Leicestershire Tiger is emblazoned on the button of the Regimental uniform.

Since Tiger Company came into being on the reduction of the 4th Battalion in 1970, it has given outstanding service in Gibraltar, in Canterbury as a wing of the Junior Infantrymen's Battalion, in an operational role in Northern Ireland and as demonstration company at RMA Sandhurst. These varied and challenging tasks have all been carried out in the finest traditions of your Regiment. The Company has served the Army well and those who have served in it can be justly proud of having done so. The Army Board is very grateful for the excellent work and wishes all members of Tiger Company every good fortune in the future.

And so plans were made for the disbandment. As could well be imagined, there was no way that Tiger Company, the embodiment of Leicestershire's Regiment, would fade away with a whimper. First, a fond farewell was paid to RMA Sandhurst on 11 April, where over the previous four years Tiger Company had acted as Demonstration Company on and off for a total of seventeen months. The Company then proceeded on two weeks' leave, and single soldiers reported to their new units shortly afterwards. On 14 June, everyone was delighted to learn that Colour Sergeant M E Taylor, who had been its CQMS for eighteen months, had been awarded the BEM in the Queen's Birthday Honours. These last weeks also saw the appropriate disposal of the Regimental silver and funds.

Tiger Company's final chapter was played out in Leicester during Royal Tiger's Weekend. It began on Saturday afternoon, 21 June 1975, with the dedication of a memorial overthrow on the War Memorial Gates at Victoria Park to 'The Service and Sacrifice of All Ranks The Royal Leicestershire Regiment (1688-1964)'.[11] A picture of the overthrow is in the plate section. This was followed by tea at the De Montfort Hall and later the annual dinner for Old Comrades was held at the TAVR Centre, Ulverscroft Road, which was attended by over 300 Old Comrades; as another milestone it was the 50th Annual Dinner. At the dinner Colonel Mike Pallot, Deputy Colonel The Royal Anglian Regiment (Leicestershire) and President of The Royal Tigers' Association, read a message from Lieutenant General Sir Ian Freeland GBE KCB DSO JP DL, Colonel The Royal Anglian Regiment, in which he said, 'The laying up of the Colours of the 1st and 2nd Battalions of the 17th Foot closes the chapter on one of the Infantry's finest Line Regiments, the traditions of which I am proud The Royal Anglian Regiment has inherited.'

This part of the long history of The Royal Leicestershire Regiment closed on Sunday, 22 June 1975, when the Colours of the 1st and 2nd Battalions The Royal Leicestershire Regiment (which had been presented in 1954 and 1927 respectively) were laid up. Prior to the Cathedral ceremony the Colours were paraded for the last time when they were marched from the Town Hall Square to Leicester Cathedral. The Colour Ensigns were Lieutenants A J T Wells, C R Groom, P M L Ferrary and T R Wilkes, the Senior Escorts were Colour Sergeant R C McDonald and Corporal A Grant, and the accompanying Warrant Officers were WOs2 E Davies, R B Freakley and R E Jones.

The Cathedral was filled to capacity. The Colour Parties standing in the centre aisle

The Very Rev J Hughes blesses the 1st R Leicesters' Colours held by Colonel Mike Pallot. *Trustees R Leicestershire Regt*

presented arms to the Lord Lieutenant of Leicestershire, Colonel R A St G Martin OBE JP, as he took his seat. The ceremony was conducted by the Provost of Leicester, the Very Revd J Hughes. In an outstanding and very moving address he made reference to the long history of the Regiment, its service to the nation and its many battle honours. The address concluded, and then processing to the Slow March of The Royal Leicestershire Regiment, the Colour ensigns and the escorts bore the Colours to the steps of the high altar where Colonel Mike Pallot received them and handed them to the Provost for their final blessing. The 1st Battalion Colours were laid up in the Regimental Chapel of the Cathedral and those of the 2nd Battalion placed in the Regimental Museum in The Magazine in the Newark.[12]

After the ceremony, the Old Comrades formed up outside the Cathedral and marched past the Lord Lieutenant of Leicestershire. A lunch was then held at the TAVR Centre, Ulverscroft Road, which was attended by many distinguished guests, principal among whom were the Lord Lieutenant and the Lord Mayor of Leicester, Councillor Mrs Lily Marriott JP. Lieutenant General Sir Colin Callander, the penultimate Colonel The Royal Leicestershire Regiment, spoke at the lunch and expressed the debt of gratitude which the Regiment owed to the City and County of Leicester. He reminded those present of the many thousands of men who had been trained at the former Regimental Depot at Glen Parva and the everlasting links in the Regimental Chapel and Museum.

Tiger Company left the Order of Battle of the Army on 1 July 1975, and marched proudly into history. How the legacy of The Royal Leicestershire Regiment lived on is covered in Chapter 11 (The Museum), Chapter 12 (The Regimental Chapel) and Chapter 14 (And onwards … post 1975).

Notes

1 John Heggs always maintained that the person in command of Tiger Company was a Commanding Officer because 'CGS told me so.'

2 John Child was the first of very few officers to serve in all four Regular battalions of the Regiment.

3 Peter Field was a fourth-generation 'Field' to serve as a Tiger. His great-grandfather G L served in the Regiment 1865-86, his grandfather Revd G H had been Chaplain in 4th and 5th Leicesters during the First World War, and his father G W H had served 1934-56.

4 Percy Watts had served in 4th Leicesters in the First World War.

5 Mike Pallot had commanded 1st R Leicesters 1958-61 – see Chapters 2 and 3.

6 2nd SG Coy, 1st R Hamps (Minden Coy), 1st A & SH (Balaclava Coy) and 3rd RGJ (Peninsular Coy).

7 Michael Goldschmidt had just rejoined after a tour as ADC to Major General Sir Douglas Kendrew KCMG CB CBE DSO, the Governor of Western Australia and the last Colonel The Royal Leicestershire Regiment.

8 Lieutenant Colonel R E J Gerrard-Wright OBE. Later Major General R E J Gerrard-Wright CB CBE, a Deputy Colonel The Royal Anglian Regiment.

9 See Chapter 13, Note 7.

10 Mrs Irene Pollard was the mother of the then Major A J G (Tony) Pollard, a former Royal Leicesters officer and at the time 2IC 1 R Anglian. He later became a Deputy Colonel The Royal Anglian Regiment.

11 Although 1964 saw the end of the Regular Battalion of The Royal Leicestershire Regiment, the Regiment had actually lived on in the TA until 1971, when Cadre The Royal Leicestershire Regiment (Territorial) became B (Royal Leicestershire) Company of the new 7th (Volunteer) Battalion The Royal Anglian Regiment – see Chapter 10.

12 The 2nd Battalion Colours were subsequently laid up in the Regimental Chapel in 2000 – see Chapter 12.

Chapter 10

The Territorial & Army Volunteer Reserve Battalions 1967-75

❧

On 1 April 1967, the Territorial Army was disbanded and replaced by the Territorial & Army Volunteer Reserve (TAVR). In a Special Order of the Day, the Colonel of The Royal Anglian Regiment, Lieutenant General Sir Richard Goodwin KCB CBE DSO, wrote:

In accordance with the gracious pleasure of the Queen, the Territorial & Army Volunteer Reserve has today formed and I have submitted to Her Majesty a message of loyalty and devotion.

The reorganisation of the Territorial Army is made necessary by the conditions of modern war and it is in realisation of this need that within the Corps of The Royal Anglian Regiment there are now one Volunteer and seven Territorial Battalions. The new Regiments formed today are steeped in the volunteer spirit and the traditions of the former Regiments. I have entire confidence that all Battalions will maintain the reputations which our former Volunteer Battalions gained by their devoted and distinguished service to the Crown and Country.

The six TA Battalions of the former regiments were disbanded that day and concurrently were reconstituted as Territorial Regiments[1] within the Corps of The Royal Anglian Regiment. They were all TAVR Category III units, with a Home Defence role. The entirely new unit was 5th (Volunteer) Battalion The Royal Anglian Regiment (5 (V) R Anglian). This TAVR Category II unit had five companies from the former six TA Battalions, and its role was to support the Regular Army in times of national emergency. The former 4/5th Royal Leicesters provided a rifle company, 4 (Leicestershire) Company, based at Ulverscroft Road in Leicester and commanded by Major W G (Bill) Wallace TD. How that Company proceeded and the part it played in 5 (V) R Anglian is described later in this Chapter.

The Royal Leicestershire Regiment (Territorial)
On 1 April 1967, the major part of 4/5th Battalion The Royal Leicestershire Regiment was redesignated The Royal Leicestershire Regiment (Territorial). It absorbed 115 (Leicestershire) Field Park Squadron RE[2] and some members of the disbanding 85 (Leicester & Northampton) Company WRAC (TA). Senior appointments were held as follows:

CO:	Lieutenant Colonel R G Wilkes TD	CSM A Coy:	WO2 R Rowlatt
2IC:	Major J T Dudley	OC B Coy:	Major R D F Bream
PSO:	Major (Retd) L T Hunt MBE[3]	CSM B Coy:	WO2 N H S Parker
RSM:	WO1 H D Benham	OC C Coy:	Major W G Dawson TD
RQMS:	WO2 H Evans	CSM C Coy:	WO2 E Sowter MM
OC A Coy:	Major B Pickford		

Bn HQ and A Coy were based at Ulverscroft Road, B Coy at Loughborough and C Coy at Hinckley. A new post was established in Bn HQ, the Permanent Staff Officer (PSO), combining the duties of Adjutant, Quartermaster and Training Officer. Lieutenant Colonel C D (Claude) Oliver OBE TD DL[4] was appointed Honorary Colonel of The Regiment. All ranks continued to wear Royal Leicesters' dress, including the Tiger capbadge.

It was largely due to the untiring efforts of Claude Oliver as Chairman of the Leicestershire & Rutland TAFA that his counties were able to keep about two-thirds of their previous TA strength, which was now to be some 750 vice 1,100. The other TAVR III units in Leicestershire and Rutland were The Leicestershire & Derbyshire Yeomanry and 933 Signal Troop Royal Signals, while 222 (Leicestershire) Field Dressing Station RAMC was a TAVR II unit.

The Royal Leicestershire Regiment (Territorial)'s Home Defence role was to provide support to the civil authorities in the maintenance of law and order, and to act generally in support of them in the event of nuclear attack or in time of great national emergency. As an indication of the Government's lack of real conviction in forming the TAVR III, this force of some 28,000 consisted of a number of units without any formation headquarters and it was paid for from the Home Office Vote. The required training commitment was less arduous and thus reduced, with the men being paid only for eight days' Annual Camp, four days out-of-camp training, and twenty-seven drill nights. The Training Bounty disappeared and equipment was of inferior standard compared to that with which the 4/5th Battalion had been issued.

The problem of recruiting people to be Territorials on less attractive terms of engagement, in order to bring the 'Territorial Tigers' up to strength, had been further aggravated by having to transfer eighty-five men to create the TAVR II 4 (Leicestershire) Company of 5 (V) R Anglian. Nevertheless, it was crucial to get a steady flow of recruits of the right type over the ensuing twelve months, otherwise the future of the Territorial side of the TAVR could be in jeopardy. However, the Commanding Officer was determined that as far as was possible it should be 'business as usual, with a different slant': providing an attractive and varied training programme with time for social activities. As the NCO posts within the three-company Regiment were not as numerous as in the five-company Battalion, a colour sergeant and four sergeants volunteered to drop a rank so that they could continue to serve as Territorials.

From 1 April, there was no formal place for the Band and Drums in the renamed Regiment's establishment, and so there would be no military band in the county. However, the members of the 4/5th Battalion's Band were persuaded to continue to serve voluntarily, being paid an honorarium and available to fulfil engagements within the county where a military band would enhance proceedings. An approach was then made to the City and County Councils which both agreed to support the Band with grants in exchange for its availability to both bodies for suitable functions. The Band played for HM The Queen when she visited Rutland in May. However, by mid-summer keeping the Band operational became no longer possible as the Bandmaster, WO1 G (Gordon) Williamson, an enthusiast of the scheme and whose continuance was vital, decided that he could not carry on for business reasons. That said, he had given outstanding service to the Battalion for two years and was largely instrumental in achieving the high standard of musical prowess. However short-lived this initiative had proved to be, the fact that it got off the ground at all was an indication of the high standing that the Regiment and Band had in the eyes of the local authorities.

Annual Camp was held at Strensall for a week in June, where in excellent weather the Regiment carried out exercises to train them for their new role.

In January 1968, there was a sudden and unexpected announcement that all TAVR III units were to disband, The Royal Leicestershire Regiment (Territorial) being one of them. Subsequently, the Government announced a 'stay of execution' until the publication of a Defence White Paper in the summer. Meanwhile, members of TAVR units would get no pay; there would be no Annual Camp in 1968 unless a camp at no cost to public funds could be arranged; and the Tiger Territorials would lose RSM Benham immediately (thus removing the last Regular serving permanent staff). Even medical fees for the examination of potential recruits had to be found by the units themselves. The consequential reaction of the Tiger Territorials filled all other Tigers with admiration for the stoic way they carried on despite so much frustration and uncertainty. Obviously disappointed at this turn of events, the Tiger Territorials were, however, immensely cheered at the offer extended by 4 R Anglian for them to spend a week with it at Gillingham at the end of August. There was thus a possibility for a number of them to have some form of camp, albeit without pay.

On 1 April, the East Midlands Territorial, Auxiliary & Volunteer Reserve Association (TAVRA) was created, with its HQ at Nottingham, to oversee reserve and cadet matters in that region. As such, among others it subsumed the Leicestershire & Rutland TAFA, of which Lieutenant Colonel (Retd) D F Coburn[5], the Secretary (alias Chief Executive) moved to become the powerful East Midlands TAVRA Secretary, to his former Counties' considerable pleasure and benefit.

The Tiger Territorials' training was designed to promote maximum interest in order to hold the support of its existing members. As described in Chapter 6, the Defence White Paper published in July 1968 announced not only the removal from the Regular Army's Order of Battle the 4th Battalion The Royal Anglian Regiment, but also confirmed the disbandment of all TAVR III units. There was therefore a clear prospect that with the demise of The Royal Leicestershire Regiment (Territorial), if and when the Regular 4th Battalion disbanded, only 4 (Leicestershire) Company 5 (V) R Anglian could call themselves 'Tigers'.

Undaunted, the Tiger Territorials, well led by Lieutenant Colonel Richard Wilkes, refused to have their spirit broken. The fact remained that Tigers everywhere found it as hard to bear the loss of the Territorial element of the Regiment as it did the prospective loss of their Regular Battalion.

Throughout the spring and summer several enjoyable exercises were held, and the Rifle Meeting was successful and well attended. The training year culminated in a fulfilling week of 'in camp' training, carried out with 4 R Anglian at Gordon Barracks, Gillingham, in the

2Lt Simon Tong, Major Basil Pickford, Lt Col Richard Wilkes and Major Len Hunt at Camp.
Trustees R Leicestershire Regt

last week of August. This was hosted by its Advance Party as the majority of the 4th Battalion was on disembarkation leave from Malta. Largely through its generosity in supplying instructors, weapons, wireless sets and other aids, the detachment of over fifty Territorial officers and men were given the opportunity of using equipment not normally available to them. Its WRAC members operated an efficient MT Section, though some Land Rovers had a tendency at times to roll, which was probably due to the ladies' association with the WRNS at HMS *Pembroke* with whom they were accommodated! Because the 4th Battalion's Band was on leave during Camp Week, arrangements were made for the Regiment's band members to join the Band of 1st Battalion The Light Infantry during their practice sessions at Gravesend. That was yet another example of the cooperation afforded to the Territorials by the Regulars.

Without the help of the Regular Battalion, the task of holding a week's 'in camp' training on a 'no cost to the public' basis would have been difficult. It was not generally realized in all quarters that each TAVR III unit had to bear all training costs. Petrol, rations, hire of additional transport, purchase of some types of ammunition, use of blankets, and many other items all had to be paid for from unit or personal funds. While the Regiment's bill for Annual Camp was large, it would have been much greater without the help of the 4th Battalion. Whatever the final cost, it was worth every penny.

Back in Leicester, 17 AYT, now under WO2 G A B Davis BEM, relocated to Glen Parva

289

Barracks, where – in contrast to the previous method of operation when the Team went out to the youth of Leicester and Leicestershire – they made the 'likely lads' come to them. It was pleasing that the old Depot facilities were being used once more to develop potential soldiers.

As the year 1968 drew to a close, the Tiger Territorials were able to repay the hospitality and assistance that had been extended to them in August. They did this by providing administrative assistance to 4 R Anglian when it exercised its rights to the Freedom of the City of Leicester on 12 October, an event which is described in Chapter 8.

So, after two long and depressing years, the time came for the disbandment of the Territorial regiments. On 31 March 1969, in a Special Order of the Day, the Colonel of The Regiment said that it was his sad duty to say farewell to those Territorial regiments, who were the natural successors to the TA battalions, had served Queen and Country for so long and had been the cornerstone of the military presence in the counties from which The Royal Anglian Regiment was so proud to recruit.

> Whatever the future may hold, you may rest assured that your County and your Regular Army partners in arms, both those who like you have suffered disbandment or amalgamation and those who serve in The Royal Anglian Regiment, are proud to have served alongside you. In your Cadres you will retain your names and traditions. The Royal Anglian Regiment will always cherish and preserve those traditions which you have built, both in peace and in war.

Accordingly, on 1 April 1969, The Royal Leicestershire Regiment (Territorial) was reduced to a Cadre at Leicester, sponsored by 5th (Volunteer) Battalion The Royal Anglian Regiment and administered by 4 (Leicestershire) Company. It had an establishment of eight all ranks, and comprised Major Bill Dawson as OC, a captain, a subaltern, a WO2, a colour sergeant, a sergeant, a corporal and a private. The Cadre sought to keep alive in its County the spirit of part-time soldiering. It was the custodian of the Colours of the 4th and 5th Battalions The Royal Leicestershire Regiment (TA), the regimental silver and funds of those former battalions. It had a reduced training commitment under the aegis of 4 Coy 5 (V) R Anglian, whose TA Centre at Ulverscroft Road it continued to share (along with RHQ Royal Leicesters/HQ R Anglian (Leicestershire), and 17 AYT). It was the nucleus from which the unit could be rebuilt if and when it was needed. Importantly, apart from cadet units, the Cadre was the only 'Tigers' unit that had the honour of still being able to wear the capbadge of The Royal Leicestershire Regiment. Some former members of the Territorials transferred to become Volunteers in 4 Coy 5 (V) R Anglian.

In June, the whole Regiment was delighted to learn that the last Commanding Officer, Richard Wilkes, had been awarded the OBE for his time in command. He worked indefatigably for the good of the Regiment, and was always very well supported by his wife Wendy. He was subsequently promoted to the rank of Colonel TAVR for the East Midlands.[6]

In late 1970, the Government announced that in April 1971 the TAVR would expand from 50,000 to 60,000. This entailed raising new units, among which were to be the new 6th (Volunteer) and 7th (Volunteer) Battalions The Royal Anglian Regiment, formed from the expansion of the cadres of Territorial regiments. Preparations were made to recruit men for these new battalions. The 6th, with its Bn HQ in Bury St Edmunds, was to recruit in East Anglia. Recruiting in the East Midlands, 7th Battalion was to have its Bn HQ at

Northampton and to include B (Royal Leicestershire) Company and the Leicestershire & Derbyshire Yeomanry (LDY) Squadron. How B Company proceeded and the part it played in 7 (V) R Anglian is described later in this Chapter.

4 (Leicestershire) Company, 5th (Volunteer) Battalion The Royal Anglian Regiment

On 1 April 1967, 4 (Leicestershire) Company, based at Ulverscroft Road in Leicester, became a rifle company in 5th (Volunteer) Battalion The Royal Anglian Regiment. The Battalion's HQ and HQ Coy was at Peterborough (based on the former 4/5 Northamptons), 1 Coy at Lowestoft (based on the former 4 R Norfolk), 2 Coy at Lincoln (based on the former 4/6 R Lincolns) and 3 Coy at Chelmsford (based on the former 4/5 Essex).

Led by Major Bill Wallace, Captain W G (Bill) Lewis, and WO2 L (Les) Coles, 4 Coy was organized on the basis of a Coy HQ, three rifle platoons, and a Mortar Platoon which was equipped with six 3" mortars. It had an establishment of five officers and 110 men, and on formation was some eighty-five all ranks strong. It included twenty-five TAVR I members, the new equivalent of the former TAER 'Ever Readies', who had a liability for call out at any time for a period not exceeding six months as individual reinforcements in Regular infantry units. In order to fulfil its new operational role of supporting the Regular Army, the Battalion was issued with combat kit (in place of the 'second BD'), and modern vehicles and weapons, including the GPMG and 84mm Carl Gustav medium anti-armour weapon. There was a more exacting training programme than for the previous TA, and for which the men were to receive an increased bounty of £80 per annum. The training requirement was of one night per week, one weekend per month and fifteen days' annual camp. Men were paid Regular rates of pay for time spent on active training. All ranks in the Battalion wore the Royal Anglian Regiment capbadge. 4 Coy retained the Royal Tiger in the laurel wreath as the collar badge, as well as having the same subsidiary title as the Leicestershire Regular Battalion to which it was affiliated. Indeed, amongst its war roles it was to provide the fourth rifle company for the Regular 4th (Leicestershire) Battalion The Royal Anglian Regiment, at that time stationed in Malta.

The Company paid its full part in the life of the 5th Battalion, including at Annual Camp at Otterburn in April, where the companies began to build a corporate spirit. With companies as widespread as Lincoln to Chelmsford, there was great inter-company rivalry, accentuated by each company being trained as an independent subunit. But this was not the old TA with a new name. The 5th Battalion began to weld together a new unit from the best fragments of many old ones.

In September, 4 Coy won the East Midlands District Volunteers' Shooting Cup at Beckingham, against nine other Volunteer units; the following February it won the Inter-Company Mortar Competition (thanks largely to the enthusiasm and experience of Sergeant Stuart Copland) and reached the Final of the East Midlands TAVRA Football Competition.

As only one of the Battalion's companies was authorized to train overseas in 1968 and 3 Coy was selected, it was not after all possible for 4 Coy to join the 4th Battalion in Malta as had been earlier forecast. Instead 4 Coy's Annual Camp was held at Rollestone Camp on Salisbury Plain in April, concentrating on ensuring the rifle and support platoons were fully conversant with section and platoon battle drills.

The Volunteers of 4 Coy – and the 5th Battalion as a whole – were not at all affected by the drastic cuts to the Territorials, and recruiting was buoyant. This Leicestershire Company was very proud that at the Battalion Skill-at-Arms weekend on 20 July a silver tiger centrepiece was presented to their Battalion from The Royal Leicestershire Regiment by Major General John Spurling, Deputy Colonel The Royal Anglian Regiment (Leicestershire). Members of the Company provided invaluable administrative assistance to the 4th Battalion during its Freedom March in Leicester in October.

Early in 1969, a fifth rifle company was formed in 5 (V) R Anglian, 5 (Hertfordshire) Company, transferring in from The Bedfordshire & Hertfordshire Regiment (Territorial), a TAVR III unit. On 22 March, fifteen men of 4 Coy formed part of the Battalion's Guard on parade to receive the Freedom of Peterborough on behalf of the Regiment, and to march through the City.

Recruiting continued to be buoyant and by the spring, 4 Coy was well over establishment, thanks partly to absorbing some of the TAVR III soldiers not required by Cadre The Royal Leicestershire Regiment (Territorial) and who wished to 'soldier on'. Among those who transferred was Captain C J (Chris) Lowe from TAVR III, who became 4 Coy's Support Platoon Commander.

Some 110 men of 4 Coy underwent Annual Camp in Haltern in Germany in late April, nominally sponsored by 2nd Battalion The Royal Green Jackets (2 RGJ). Despite having amongst its war roles to provide a fourth rifle company to a battalion in BAOR, it was disappointing that the Company was virtually left to its own devices miles from 2 RGJ, whose only commitment was to run a Support Platoon cadre for 4 Coy. Not only that, but given the two days at each end of the Camp taken by moving to and from Germany, it could be argued that better use of the time available might have been made had the Camp been

Major Bill Wallace at Sennelager. *Trustees R Leicestershire Regt*

held on home soil. That said, the logistic challenge of such a training period, the Company having to do all its own administration in the tented camp and having only limited training facilities, was good training in itself. The Company was very pleased to be visited by the Lord Lieutenant of Leicestershire and overall this first overseas training deployment by 4 Coy was deemed a great success.

On 9 June, again fifteen men of 4 Coy formed part of the Battalion's Guard on parade to receive the Freedom of Hertford on behalf of The Royal Anglian Regiment in the presence of the Colonel-in-Chief, HM Queen Elizabeth The Queen Mother, and to march through the City.

The Company was not among the prizewinners at the Battalion Skill-at-Arms Meeting at Stanford, but the Company Families Day at Kibworth in August was attended by many past members of 4/5th R Leicesters (TA) and of The Royal Leicestershire Regiment (Territorial). A team from the old Melton Mowbray Company (TA) won the Falling Plate competition. Later that year a new platoon was established at Loughborough under Lieutenant J R (John) Ward.

During that winter, 1969/70, 4 Coy and Cadre The Royal Leicestershire Regiment (Territorial) happily carried out training and social occasions together. There was the usual evening training and also successful weekends at Beckingham, Proteus, Stanford and Warcop. The traditional round of social occasions continued, almost as if there was a full Battalion at Leicester. After nearly three years in post, WO2 Les Coles handed over to WO2 A (Arthur) Hurst on promotion.

Battalion Annual Camp took place at Otterburn in the first fortnight of June 1970, in glorious weather. 4 Coy HQ's task in the first week was to train forty-five JNCOs from across the Battalion, while its own men were variously employed in a spectrum of other specialist cadres. The second week comprised an inter-platoon competition and a Battalion FTX.

The Company Families Day was again held at Kibworth in August. The Loughborough Platoon team won the Falling Plate competition. At the Eastern District Skill-at-Arms Meeting at Colchester in September, 4 Coy's team won the Falling Plate Competition.

With the posting and promotion of Bill Wallace to command the new 7th (V) Battalion in April 1971, Major Chris Lowe TD was appointed OC 4 Coy of the 5th Battalion, with Captain John Ward as 2IC. The creation of B (Royal Leicestershire) Company of the 7th Battalion (which is covered later in this chapter) meant that at a stroke the Volunteer 'Tigers' doubled in strength, there now being two companies at Ulverscroft Road, albeit in different battalions of The Royal Anglian Regiment. Consequently there was a greater level of activity at Ulverscroft Road, and the rivalry, comradeship and cooperation were a joy to behold, with many joint social enterprises being undertaken. For example, in December 1971 4 Coy's officers organized the joint annual Officers' Ball, and B Coy organized the All Ranks' Ball the following evening.

5 (V) R Anglian's Annual Camp was held at Okehampton in June. Of it was said, 'Never has so much rain fallen on so few people for so long.' 4 Coy was pleased to host a visit by the Lord Mayor of Leicester, Alderman Percy Watts, himself a former Tiger. The fortnight concluded with a large FTX, conducted through rain, mud and mist. Even the Commanding Officer got lost. In parallel, 4 Coy's mortars took part in a concentration at Warcop, with some very accurate live firing. The Company's Senior Ranks' Shooting Team came first at the Company Families Day at Kibworth in August.

4 Company's mortarmen LCpls Reeve, Revington, Ptes Asby and Rowden live firing at Warcop.
Trustees R Anglian Regt

In line with the rest of the Regiment, early 1972 saw changes in Dress Regulations for Officers, who were pleased to adopt the khaki beret with black patch behind the badge in lieu of the blue beret.

4 Coy went to Stanford on 22 January for the second year running on Exercise *Tiger Patrol II*. The following month saw it at Proteus on Exercise *Tiger Shovel I*, digging in on a hill and being attacked by a large and live enemy. As the last of the Battalion's series of exercises, in May the Company deployed to Stanford and dramatically created a finale by unintentionally setting fire to a fairly large part of the training area, which necessitated the men helping the local fire brigade to extinguish the blaze. The whole Battalion deployed there again in July.

In orienteering, Lance Corporal Johnson won the Southern Command Competition and came fourth in both the Army and the TAVR East Midlands District competition. The Company Football Team, led by Lieutenant F (Fred) Honnor, reached the final of the East Midland District cup. He was soon promoted to be Coy 2IC, and Captain John Ward became OC. The year also saw the retirement of WO2 Arthur Hurst after twenty-six years' service, during which he had participated in eleven successive years in the Nijmegen Marches. He was replaced as CSM in August by WO2 J (John) Bloomfield.

For Annual Camp, the Mortar Platoon and 12 Platoon reinforced 3 (Essex) Company and spent a busy fortnight in Cyprus, where they were hosted by Support Company 1 R Anglian. 4 Coy ran a Families Day at Kibworth Ranges in August, before the following month taking part in the Battalion Annual Camp at Sennybridge. The first week was devoted to individual training through to section and platoon level live firing. Everyone had the opportunity to practice emplaning drills with an RAF Puma helicopter, and Sergeant M (Mel) Gould came second in the Battalion Orienteering Competition. During the second week's FTX, 4 Coy provided the enemy in a wide-ranging series of manoeuvres and phases of war.

In the autumn, training began for Individual Test Exercises and the Mortar Competition. The Company's recruiting campaign was such a great success that early in 1973, with its strength at 110 per cent of establishment and being the strongest in the Battalion, it won the Recruiting Cup. Major A A J (Tony) Wilson TD became the OC.

On the sporting front, its Football Team won the East Midlands District Cup and was runner-up in the Eastern District Cup. Sergeant 'Mel' Gould won the East Midlands District Orienteering Competition. The Company took part in the CO's test exercise weekend at Stanford. It began with Counter Revolutionary Warfare, and culminated with a 12-mile penetration manoeuvre to attack a base area.

With the exception of the Mortar Platoon (Lieutenant A B Carr), which went with the Battalion to Warcop in November, 4 Coy's Annual Camp was held in Gibraltar at the end of May 1973. Most unusually for such a venture, 4 Coy took over the role of a company of the Resident Battalion (1 RRF) and spent the fortnight guarding the Spanish border, the same task which Tiger Company 4th Battalion had performed for six months in 1972. The task comprised mobile and foot patrols, manning OPs and providing a ceremonial guard at Four Corners Guardroom at the frontier gates, with the soldiers smartly dressed in No. 6 Dress with white belts and rifle slings. The platoons not on duty on the border carried out normal infantry training. The various messes of The Gibraltar Regiment cemented the Regiments' alliance with their hospitality. This Annual Camp was regarded as a 'hit'.

Reporting from a forward trench at Sennybridge. *Trustees R Anglian Regt*

Back in England, several members of the Company were on parade on 14 July at Depot The Queen's Division at Bassingbourn where the Colonel-in-Chief visited elements of all three TAVR battalions. 4 Coy put on a training display of the A13, C42 and A41 radio sets.

Families Day was again held at Kibworth Ranges in August. Twenty-four teams, military and civilian, entered the Falling Plate Competition and 12 Platoon from Loughborough were the winners. That month too, 4 Coy hosted fifty members of The Gibraltar Regiment, who were in England for their Annual Camp.

On the training side all was quiet up until Christmas, whereafter a long-term programme began in 1974, aimed at a Battalion Annual Camp in BAOR in 1975. 4 Coy's Football Team were again runners-up in the Eastern District Cup. That summer, the Deputy Colonel-in-Chief, HRH The Princess Alice Duchess of Gloucester, adopted a special relationship with the 5th and 7th Battalions, having done the same in 1964 with the 2nd and 4th.

Members of 4 Coy were particularly pleased when its first Company Commander, Bill Wallace, was awarded the OBE for his work as CO 7th Battalion.[7]

The most memorable event in 1974 was the Presentation of Colours to the 1st, 2nd, 3rd Regular and 5th (Volunteer) Battalions at Tidworth on 12 July by the Colonel-in-Chief, HM Queen Elizabeth The Queen Mother.

By way of background, as mentioned in Chapter 5, the Regiment's Colours Committee in 1968 had produced recommendations for the Battle Honours and 'honorary distinctions' to be carried on the Colours. After HM The Queen had approved the Colours' designs, on 10 June 1969 the Ministry of Defence had placed the contract for four sets of Colours, one each for the 1st, 2nd, 3rd and 5th Battalions. It would take five years for the four sets of Colours to be completed. Because in 1969 the 4th Battalion had already been earmarked to leave the Army's Order of Battle, and the 6th and 7th (Volunteer) Battalions were not formed until 1971, Colours for them were not part of this exercise.

In July 1973, detailed planning began for the Colour Presentation Parade. By mid-1974 the 1st Battalion was stationed at Tidworth. It hosted the Regimental event and provided the administrative back-up. For the parade, it provided the four guards, and the other three Battalions receiving Colours provided colour parties only. All three Regular battalions provided the Bands and Drums. Among those on parade at the Tattoo Ground at Tidworth were many Regular former Tigers.

Shortly before noon on 12 July, the Colonel-in-Chief was greeted by the Colonel of The Regiment as she alighted from the Royal helicopter. The ensuing ceremony on the Tattoo Ground was held in front of 3,000 spectators, including six Lord Lieutenants, two Lords Mayor, the mayors and mayoresses of sixteen boroughs, the chairmen of thirteen district councils, the commanding officers of three of the eleven allied regiments, and over 300 Old Comrades. In her speech to the Parade, the Colonel-in-Chief said:

> Although Colours are no longer carried in action, they are still the rallying point which embodies the spirit of the Regiment and they are the symbol of chivalry and an emblem of loyalty to your Queen, your Country and your Regiment. I entrust these new Colours to your safe keeping, and I am certain you will carry them with honour and pride, and guard them with courage and devotion.

Lt Tony Carr about to receive the 5th Bn's Regimental Colour. *Trustees R Anglian Regt*

The 5th Battalion's Colour Party contained three men from 4 Coy: Captain P V B (Philip) George receiving the Queen's Colour, Lieutenant A B (Tony) Carr the Regimental Colour, and Colour Sergeant B C (Brian) Lee being an escort. The many weeks of rehearsals made them equal to their task alongside the Regulars and they merged seamlessly into the large parade, where precision was the order of the day. The troops on parade, commanded by Lieutenant Colonel D C Thorne of the 1st Battalion, were superb – perhaps their rendering of the 'Three Cheers' after the 'Advance in Review Order' and 'Royal Salute' has been particularly remembered. The cheers echoed round the hills and so obviously showed the affection held for the Colonel-in-Chief and the pride of every man on parade in their new Colours, which were then marched past Her Majesty in slow and quick time.

The weather forecast had not been encouraging, but it remained dry and warm. At the very moment that the Chaplain General, The Venerable Archdeacon P Mallett QHC, laid his hand on the 1st Battalion Colours at the Consecration Ceremony, the sun shone and remained out until late in the afternoon.

After lunch, the Massed Bands of the 1st, 2nd and 3rd Battalions provided a well-executed display for forty minutes. Before departing, Her Majesty spent over half an hour walking amongst the Regimental members and their guests. As precisely as everything else had gone throughout the day, amidst the cheers and waves of the spectators, the Royal car drove off to the waiting helicopter which then circled the Tattoo Ground before finally heading north-east for Windsor. And then down came the rain!

Many of those Volunteers who took part or were able to be present were asked if they would have preferred to have had the 5th Battalion's Colours presented on a separate Volunteers' parade. The unanimous reply was that there could have been no finer way for the Volunteer Battalion to have received its Colours than with its sister Regular battalions. The Colour Presentation on 12 July was a significant demonstration that there was but one Royal Anglian Regiment, and that its Regular and Volunteer components stood side by side.[8]

Battalion Annual Camp was held at Otterburn in September, by which time Captain Philip George had become 4 Coy's 2IC and WO2 G (Geoff) Taylor the CSM. Much of the time was devoted to specialist cadres, with a separate exercise of fifty force-on-force patrols in atrocious weather and company field firing. All ranks were able to see the Colours for the first time at the middle weekend's Drumhead Service, and the Colonel of The Regiment was among the visitors. Despite the poor weather, with the sound foundations that the cadres had laid, the Battalion as a whole – and 4 Coy in particular – was in good shape in strength and morale, and was determined to build on that in anticipation of the greater demands of Annual Camp in BAOR the following year. Recruiting had gone well and by year end the 5th Battalion's strength was 95 per cent of establishment with 709 all ranks.

In spring 1975, 4 Coy's Football Team was runner-up in the Eastern District Cup for the third successive year. On the social side its WOs & Sergeants held the Ladysmith Ball in February. That was followed by a weekend in April at Stanford practising mobilization procedures, an essential precursor to Annual Camp. Held in late October, it was the first occasion that the Battalion had served overseas as a complete unit. It mobilized together with many other TAVR units as part of the UK-wide FTX *Inside Right* and then proceeded by sea and air to Soltau in West Germany, where it was sponsored by 2 RRF. Thus, the Battalion practised mobilization and deployment, in support of its affiliated 20 Armd Bde, grouped throughout with a section of 250 Fd Amb. The training was particularly enjoyable, encompassing the all-arms aspects of warfare, with support from Chieftain tanks, APCs, field and armoured engineers, and RAF Puma helicopters. The Company was pleased to be visited by Colonel G L (Gerry) Aspell TD DL[9], Deputy Honorary Colonel The Royal Anglian Regiment (Leicestershire).

The description of that successful training period concludes this phase of the history of 4 (Leicestershire) Company. These Tiger Volunteers were in very good shape. What occurred in the following years is touched upon in Chapter 14.

B (Royal Leicestershire) Company, 7th (Volunteer) Battalion The Royal Anglian Regiment

On 1 April 1971, Cadre The Royal Leicestershire Regiment (Territorial) was reconstituted and became B (Royal Leicestershire) Company of the new 7th (Volunteer) Battalion The Royal Anglian Regiment. Its members wore the Royal Leicestershire Regiment lanyard. The Battalion was commanded by Lieutenant Colonel Bill Wallace, the erstwhile OC 4 Coy 5 (V) R Anglian. Its Bn HQ, HQ Coy and D Coy were at Northampton, A Coy at Scunthorpe, C Coy at Wellingborough and the Leicestershire & Derbyshire Yeomanry (LDY) Sqn at Melton Mowbray (which wore the LDY capbadge and had RAC PSIs). The 7th Battalion was formed as a Home Defence battalion, for which somewhat vague role it was provided only with rifles and LMGs, and no support weapons.

B Coy was based at Ulverscroft Road in Leicester. Major W G (Bill) Dawson TD was OC and WO2 W (Wally) Moore the CSM. Captain G G (Geoff) Simpson became the first Coy 2IC five months later. Everyone who had served in Cadre The Royal Leicestershire Regiment continued to serve either in the new Company or at Bn HQ at Northampton.

The first few months were interesting and challenging, during which time the Company's strength was built up from seven to fifty-two. The new members were a healthy balance of trained NCOs or soldiers, and recruits, which was very helpful from a training point of view. The TAVR Centre at Hinkley reopened, and about 50 per cent of the Company were members of that detachment.

Annual Camp was held in September at Stanford. Training consisted mainly of cadres for NCOs, trained soldiers and recruits. On return, recruiting became a high priority for B Coy, with the aim of increasing the Company strength to 100 by 1972's Annual Camp. Meanwhile, the Company embarked on its winter training programme. The highlight was the Mobilization Weekend organized by East Midlands District in late November. Despite it being the coldest weekend of the winter, with assistance of the rum ration, the mission was accomplished and the new recruits seemed undaunted by the harsh conditions.

Early 1972 saw the retirement of WO2 Wally Moore after thirty-five years' TA service, having joined 4th Leicesters in 1937 and served with them throughout the Second World War. As B Coy's first CSM, he had been invaluable in getting the Company 'off the ground'. He was succeeded by WO2 D (David) Smith. Captain C H (Howard) Cole became Coy 2IC.

Battalion Annual Camp was held in late May at Warcop, where the training concentrated on live firing of platoon weapons and section and platoon field firing. It culminated in a Battalion FTX, *Springboard*. B Coy entered a team in the TAVR Football Championship.

The 7th Battalion held its first Rifle Meeting at the end of July. It was clear from the results that much more shooting practice was needed in order for the new recruits in particular to achieve a satisfactory infantry standard. By mid-year B Coy's strength was approaching 100, and it was expected that the full establishment would be reached within a few months. Most of the new equipment had been issued, and No. 2 Dress was also authorized for issue. At the end of 1972, after five years' sterling support from the inception of B Coy in the 7th Battalion, Colonel Claude Oliver handed over as Deputy Honorary Colonel to Colonel Gerry Aspell.

On being appointed Bn 2IC in 1973, Bill Dawson handed over B Coy to Major G G (Geoff) Simpson. It was 106 strong, with a steady inflow of recruits, especially to the Hinckley detachment, and there was a hard kernel of regular attendees.

Battalion Annual Camp, held in May at Sennybridge, was very successful. Full use was made of the field-firing ranges, and emphasis was given to IS training, culminating in a three-day exercise in the second week. In addition to the energetic training, members of B Coy had sufficient reserves of stamina to win both the Battalion's Sports Cup and Football Competition. In the following months a concerted effort was made to interest and recruit young men through displays around the county, which led to an historical high strength for the Company of 115 all ranks. The Company renewed a tradition by parading as a whole at Hinckley on Remembrance Sunday, where the TAVR presence was much appreciated.

Training continued apace in 1974. By 1 April, the Battalion's third anniversary, B Coy led the Battalion Champion Company Competition, in which points were awarded for recruiting, attendance, shooting and general training results.

Battalion Annual Camp was held in the middle of May, in three parts and three successive locations. The first four days were spent on the ranges at Altcar in Lancashire, during which the Colonel of The Regiment and the Lord Mayor of Leicester, Councillor Mrs Irene Pollard, made a visit. Then a week in the Lake District rock climbing, canoeing and fell-walking; and a concluding IS exercise in Staffordshire when the troops operated in support of the Civil Police. Movement between those venues was carried out by train, which ensured the efficiency of the Company's Railway Transport Officers.

During the rest of the summer the Company put on displays, took part in many local events and conducted weekend training in Wales and Lincolnshire. A successful Recruiting Week was held in September. In October, Lieutenant Colonel Bill Dawson took over command of the Battalion from Bill Wallace, whose OBE for his work as CO was particularly pleasing to all members of B Coy. In November, B Coy presented a piece of regimental silver to the Borough of Hinckley and Bosworth to mark the close association between the Town and the Territorials since 1908. The year concluded with the Company winning the Battalion's inaugural Champion Company Competition, and an increase in Establishment led to the need for more recruits.

In March 1975, the Lord Mayor of Leicester again visited B Coy, just before the fourth anniversary of the Battalion, which coincided with B Coy winning the Inter-Platoon Trophy. Both platoons (Lieutenants M (Mike) Dowling and P (Patrick) Wild) made a great effort on the Bn FTX, *Eightsome Reel*, held around Northampton and comprising tests in patrolling, map reading, assault course and a forced march.

Annual Camp was unusually late and held in October to enable the Battalion to take part in the National FTX, *Inside Right*, in which all TAVR Home Defence Battalions took part. During the exercise, B Coy deployed around Eastern England, ending up at Stanford Training Area where it had the opportunity to train with RAF Wessex helicopters.

Concluding this phase of the Royal Leicesters' History, at year end the role of 7 (V) R Anglian changed from Home Defence to that of a General Reserve Battalion, with the addition of Support Weapons Platoons. And, after four years, the LDY Squadron came fully on board – so to speak – by adopting the Royal Anglian Regiment capbadge. As a final act for this TAVR Chapter, Major Geoff Simpson TD retired after three distinguished years as OC B (Royal Leicestershire) Company. What occurred in the following years is touched upon in Chapter 14.

Notes

1 The Royal Norfolk Regiment (Territorial), The Suffolk & Cambridgeshire Regiment (Territorial), The Royal Lincolnshire Regiment (Territorial), The Northamptonshire Regiment (Territorial), The Bedfordshire & Hertfordshire Regiment (Territorial), The Essex Regiment (Territorial), and The Royal Leicestershire Regiment (Territorial).

2 This unit was the successor of 1st Leicestershire Battery RHA (TF), formed in 1908. It later became 115 Fd Regt RA (TA) serving in action with distinction in France and Belgium in 1940 and in Burma in 1945. In 1961 it became 115 Field Park Squadron of 140 Engr Regt RE (TA).

3 Len Hunt was awarded the MBE in 1967 for his service as PSO of 49 Div/Dist Provost Coy RMP (TA) based in Leicester.

4 Claude Oliver's father, Colonel Sir Frederick Oliver TD DL, had been Honorary Colonel 4th Leicesters (TA) before the Second World War.

5 See Chapter 7, Note 15.

6 In 1972 Richard Wilkes became an ADC TAVR to HM The Queen, in which appointment he served for five years.

7 Bill Wallace was appointed Colonel TAVR in 1975.

8 Colours were presented to the 6th Battalion in 1979 and to the 7th Battalion in 1980.

9 Gerry Aspell had joined 4th Leicesters (TA) in 1933 and in 1947 became the first CO of 579th (The Royal Leicestershire Regiment) LAA Regt RA (TA). In 1984 he was appointed Vice Lord Lieutenant of Leicestershire.

Chapter 11

The Regimental Museum

A long with the Regimental Chapel in Leicester Cathedral (see Chapter 12) and Royal Tigers' Wood (see Chapter 14), The Royal Leicestershire Regiment's Museum is the third of the key legacies of the Regiment.

Up until 1960, the Museum was housed in very ordinary premises beside the HQ at Depot Royal Leicesters at Glen Parva Barracks, South Wigston, Leicester. Many of the Regiment's collection of artefacts, acquired over the years were stored there, some of which were displayed. When Glen Parva became Depot The Forester Brigade in 1960, plans were made by the Regimental Secretary, Lieutenant Colonel P G Upcher DSO, for the Regimental Museum to be housed, displayed and cared for at another site within the City or County of Leicester. In 1961, a formal agreement was drawn up whereby the City authorities undertook to 'display the Regiment's artefacts in perpetuity', though the ownership of those artefacts remained (and still remains) with the Regimental Trustees.

The City made available a small amount of space at the Newarke Houses Museum, which was primarily (and still is today – 2008) a museum of the social history of the City and County. Amongst items displayed, there was a German machine gun captured by 2nd Leicesters in 1914 near Richebourg-L'Avoue in France.

In 1961, adding to the many artefacts in the Regimental collection, the Victoria Cross awarded to Lance Sergeant Philip Smith for his conduct at the Battle of Sevastopol on 18 June 1855 (a week before the thirtieth Royal Tigers' Day!) was purchased. The following year the medals of QMS John Emmett DCM (whose DCM was awarded in the Crimean War) were presented to the Regimental Museum by his son.

Col John Barrett VC, Aldm Harold Heard, Lt Gen Callander and Col P H Lloyd view a gun. *Trustees R Leicestershire Regt*

The Magazine. *Leicester Mercury*

But the major element of the 1961 Agreement with the City Council was effected when it made available the Magazine Gateway, which had been built in the early fifteenth century as the entrance to Leicester Castle. The gate having no portcullis, its main purpose was to impress visitors rather than be defensive. In 1894, a barracks and a drill hall had been built alongside it for The Leicestershire Militia. These were used before the Second World War by 4th Leicesters (TA) and from 1947 by 5th Royal Leicesters (TA) until the barracks were demolished in the 1960s to make room for the west inner ring road round the city. There were also plans to demolish the Magazine Gateway itself but local protests saved the building for future generations.

Thus, most appropriately, many of the Regiment's historical treasures were moved to The Magazine and displayed there. A weathervane showing the Tiger capbadge was installed atop the tower and is still there today (2008). The transition, preparation and funding of this new location for the Museum were overseen by Alderman Monica Trotter, the Lord Mayor of Leicester who had presided over the grant of Freedom in 1966 and who had acted as Chairman of the Museums, Libraries and Publicity Committee since 1960. In September 1966, during her visit to the 4th (Leicestershire) Battalion The Royal Anglian Regiment in Malta, she had announced:

As further expression of the relationship between the Regiment and the City, I am able to say to you as the Chairman of the City of Leicester Museums Committee, that my Committee have come to an arrangement with the Regiment regarding the Regimental Museum arising from the loss of the Museum's former home at Glen Parva Barracks. The Museum, I am pleased to say, is to have its permanent home in the Magazine Tower which, as you know, is the last remaining building of the Regiment's former home in The Newarke. I am sure that all of you would agree that this is a very happy solution, and that it will give future generations the rightful opportunity of looking at the proud history of one of the most famous County Regiments of England.

The Regiment was indeed extremely grateful for the City's generosity towards the establishment of this new Museum. It was formally opened in June 1969, literally to a fanfare of trumpets – the very silver trumpets which the City and County of Leicester had originally donated to the Regiment in 1952, resplendent with their Royal Anglian banners given by the City in 1966. Many artefacts were most strikingly displayed in the Museum there on several floors and, being close to the City centre, it was easily accessible to the public.

In 1972, the medals of the late Lieutenant Colonel P E Bent VC DSO[1] were permanently loaned to the Regiment by the Headmaster of Ashby-de-la-Zouch Grammar School, where Bent had been a pupil from 1904 to 1907. In March the following year, HRH The Duchess of Gloucester, Deputy Colonel-in-Chief The Royal Anglian Regiment, visited the Museum, which continued to have a good number of visitors. In that year, due to a reorganization of local government, ownership of The Magazine with the Museum was transferred to the County Council.

In 1996, due to the careful and detailed work of Lieutenant Colonel John Wilson, the Regimental Secretary, with the County's museum authorities, the Magazine Museum was

VIPs viewing the new Museum at The Magazine, June 1969. *Leicester Mercury*

granted a Heritage Lottery award of £64,500. It was the largest such award in the county to date, being the maximum 75 per cent of the cost of refurbishing and redisplaying the Museum. Implementation of the plans was started, the Museum closed and was stripped of its contents, which were stored. It then became apparent that further conservation work on the building would be required and, whilst plans were being redrawn, the Government decided to make Leicester City Council a unitary authority. As a result The Magazine, and the staff supervising the work, were transferred back in April 1997 from Leicestershire County Council to Leicester City Council, causing further delays and reappraisal. In due course it was deduced that the high cost of the restoration and refurbishment did not merit the use of anyone's money, allied to the fact that visitor numbers had fallen in the years prior to closure because the site itself had become isolated due to the new ring road system.

There followed a period in which the Regimental Trustees had discussions with both the City and County authorities about possible sites for the relocation of the Museum.

As an interim solution, space was provided at the City's New Walk Museum, where a gallery was made available, after the Trustees had invoked the 1961 Agreement with the City. Lieutenant Colonel John Wilson and his support team worked tirelessly to produce a worthy exhibit. Regrettably, the area was wholly inadequate as it did not enable an appropriate display of sufficient material to do justice to the Regiment's history, but at least some of the Regimental collection was on display again. The two Sevastopol cannons (which had been outside The Magazine from 1971 to 1996) stood guard at the New Walk entrance, where they had been first positioned in 1862. The new gallery was formally opened on St George's Day 1999 by the Colonel The Royal Anglian Regiment, General Sir Michael Walker KCB CMG CBE ADC Gen.

In December 2000, the Victoria Cross and other medals of the late Colonel J C Barrett VC TD DL FRCS[2] were donated to the Regiment on the death of his wife. This was another most important acquisition for the Regiment's collection.

Members of The Royal Tigers' Association bombarded the Lord Mayor, councillors and the Museum staff with their complaints about the most unsatisfactory gallery in New Walk. Responding to these complaints, the Trustees decided to propose to the City that some of the Regiment's funds be used to finance a bid to the Heritage Lottery Fund (HLF) for a grant to enable the construction of a new Museum. The City responded positively and after a review agreed to allocate the upper floor of Newarke Houses Museum (a Grade II listed building formed from three houses but in need of modernization) to the Regimental Museum whilst the ground floor would continue with the City's social history displays. As part of this arrangement the City would enter into an agreement with the Regiment to manage the Museum for a period of twenty-five years. Under the agreement, the City Museums would provide the accommodation, its maintenance and all the staffing needed. In return, the Regiment agreed to loan its collections for display.

Having set up these arrangements, the City and the Regiment engaged consultants, to prepare a joint bid for a Lottery Grant of £1 million. The bid included the condition that, if the grant was made, the City and the Regiment would each provide a further £250,000 in 'matched' funding to finance the £1.5 million project which would be run as a 'partnership' between the City and the Regiment during both the construction and subsequent management of the Museum.

It was with great joy and satisfaction to both the Regiment and the City that the news was received early in 2003 that the bid had been successful. The gamble of using the Regimental funds to finance the preparation of the bid had paid off! One of the significant factors in that success was the combination of the social history of the City and County with the Regimental story and its strong connections to and service in the Indian sub-continent. This fitted well with the story told in the social history section of the large immigration into the City in recent years from that sub-continent.

The Regiment established an Appeal to raise its £250,000 share of the funds required. This was launched on 20 June 2003 by the Lord Mayor of Leicester, Councillor Ramnik Kavia, and the President of the Royal Tigers' Association. The Trustees appointed Lieutenant Colonel T D A (Trevor) Veitch (a retired Royal Anglian officer with fundraising experience) to help raise money from the business community and the general public, and his input was invaluable.

Money began to accrue at a satisfactory rate to enable the planning to be put fully into effect. The numerous letters accompanying the donations proved the affection in which the Regiment was still held in people's hearts. Many Association members, families and friends of the Regiment contributed, arranged fundraising events and persuaded other people to donate to the appeal. However, the target of £250,000 increased almost inevitably, as it was discovered that an additional £30,000 was needed to cater for previously unforeseen (because of the listed status of the building) and unbudgeted costs, such as disabled access.

The interim Royal Tigers' Gallery in the New Walk Museum was closed in February 2004, so that preparations could start on the displays for the new Regimental Museum. The Newarke Houses Social History Museum closed four months later, to enable all its items in the existing display to be stored safely before the builders arrived. At that stage it was envisaged that the new museum would open in September 2005. Haley Sharpe, a Leicester company, was appointed as the lead 'Design and Construct' consultants for the exhibition displays in the whole museum, both Regimental and Social History. They busied themselves checking the plans for the displays made by Graham Black (a museum-design expert) and the Regimental team, led by Colonels Bill Dawson and Bill Morris, not least to assess space requirements and ensure that the likely costs were within the budget. As an outward sign of the Regiment's intent, the Sevastopol cannons were moved from New Walk to the Newarke Houses Museum as gatekeepers, thanks to the efforts of the Loughborough-based 203 Squadron 158 (Royal Anglian) Transport Regiment RLC (V).

Meanwhile the Fundraising Appeal, orchestrated by Lieutenant Colonel F A H (Anthony) Swallow, continued apace and with great success. Masterminded by Colonel R H (Richard) Robinson and his team, three concerts in Leicester's De Montfort Hall were performed by the Minden Band of The Queen's Division in the spring of the years 2004, 2005 and 2006. The third concert was an exciting evening of military music and included a performance by some wonderful musicians with the Corps of Drums of 2nd Battalion The Princess of Wales's Royal Regiment. The programme also comprised an organ recital and a singalong of some old favourites. Playing to full houses of some 1,500 people, each concert netted over £6,000. A Grand Prize Draw was extremely successful, principally because of the wonderful quality of the prizes, many donated by members of the Regiment. And so the revised fundraising target was met, causing the Trustees to express immense gratitude to all those who had helped to make the appeal such a success and, incidentally, to provide excellent publicity for the new Museum.

Sevastopol Cannon outside Newarke Houses Museum. *M K Goldschmidt*

Special mention must also be made of the marvellous support given to the Regimental fundraising campaign by the *Leicester Mercury*, which produced many articles and photos to assist so much in the huge task. The Editor, Nick Carter, and his staff were tireless in championing the Regiment's cause so forcefully and giving immense help and advice, which made such a huge difference to the success of the campaign.

In addition, as part of the Appeal, a donation of £100,000 was received from Leicestershire County Council, which was put into a separate Acquisitions & Development Fund. This fund is to be used to purchase important artefacts that come up for auction and to provide money to refresh and enhance the displays in the Regimental Museum in the coming years. It was soon put to good use. In 2005 it funded the purchase of five lots of important medals: the (very rare) Albert Medal won by Private W H Foster[3] in India in 1931, the Military Medal won by Lance Corporal S Markham of 2nd Leicesters in Crete in 1941, the Military Medal and Bar won by Lance Sergeant N French of 2/5th Leicesters in Tunisia in February 1943 and in Italy in 1945 respectively, the French Legion of Honour (one of only about ninety awarded in that campaign) in a group of five medals won by

Sergeant J Plant in the Crimea, and the Indian General Service Medal 1908-35 with the clasp 'Mohmand 1933' (a most unusual clasp) of Private C W Hodgkinson of the 1st Leicesters.

Various factors led to the date of the opening being postponed several times. In the end, following the 'soft' opening of the Regimental Museum by the Lord Lieutenant of Leicestershire, Jennifer, Lady Gretton JP, together with the Lord Mayor of Leicester, Councillor Gary Hunt, in June 2007, it was officially opened on 13 November that year by General The Lord Walker of Aldringham GCB CMG CBE, a former Colonel The Royal Anglian Regiment and lately Chief of Defence Staff, to a fanfare of trumpets by the trumpeters of the Minden Band of The Queen's Division. The fanfare was composed especially for the occasion and incorporated the Hunting Call from the Royal Leicesters' Regimental March at the end. It was followed by a moment of silence and a prayer for Remembrance by the Bishop of Leicester, the Rt Revd Tim Stevens. Major donors to the Museum Appeal were invited, together with a wide representation from the Regiment, Leicester City Council and the counties of Leicestershire and Rutland.

The Regimental Museum is in six upstairs rooms of the Newarke Houses Museum. The first room describes the lives of people who served in the Regiment, including recruiting, uniforms, drill and weapon training, discipline, sport and education; this leads into 'The Regimental Room' telling the story of the Regiment from 1688 to 1964, including campaigns throughout the world to expand and defend what became the largest empire in the world. There is a spectacular display of the Colours, Silver Drums, major silver items and many medals awarded to members of the Regiment over the years (see plate section). The next two rooms cover the two World Wars, with a reconstruction of Trench 47 at Ypres, Belgium (Flanders), facing the Hohenzollern Redoubt in October 1915 (where many men of the Regiment lost their lives in the First World War). The last room covers the Home Front and the huge impact that the wars had on those left at home.

On the walls hang the four oil paintings by Terence Cuneo, listed here in the chronological order in which they were painted. *Barrett VC*, painted in early 1958, depicts 2nd Lieutenant J C Barrett of 1/5th Leicesters winning his VC at Pontruet in France on 24 September 1918. *Crete*, painted in October 1958, depicts men of A Coy 2nd Leicesters in hand-to-hand fighting with German paratroopers in Buttercup Field south of Heraklion in Crete in May 1941; in the background are two hills named 'The Charlies' – steel wire was hastily strung between these by Australian troops in the hope of bringing down the gliders carrying German troops. *Chindits*, painted in March 1961, shows 2nd Leicesters in action against the Japanese at Lake Indaw in Burma in 1944, on the Second Chindit Expedition. *Smith VC*, painted in the summer of 1962, shows Lance Sergeant Philip Smith winning his VC and carrying a wounded man at Sevastopol 1855. All four are shown in the plate section.

Among the other medals on display are those of Major M A L (Tony) Cripps DSO[4], donated in 2006, and on loan are the decorations and medals of Major General Sir Douglas Kendrew KCMG CB CBE DSO, the last Colonel The Royal Leicestershire Regiment[5].

It is also worthy of note that, to mark the opening of the new Museum, Leicestershire County Council have set up permanent displays of a selection of artefacts, photographs and other memorabilia of the Regiment in the members' lobby at County Hall in Glenfield, recording the County's long association with its County Regiment.

The successful completion of the Museum would not have been possible without the generosity of many organizations, trusts and individuals who donated to the project, all of whose names are recorded in a Donors' Book in the Regimental Room. In addition major donors and others who provided significant help are listed on a Donors' Board on the staircase. The Regiment remains extremely grateful to them and to the team of Regimental guides who take turns to man the Museum to help visitors and answer their questions about the exhibits and the history of the Regiment in general.

In the short time since the Regimental Museum has been open, it has proved hugely popular with visitors, whose numbers have far exceeded one of the conditions of the HLF that the Museum should achieve at least 40,000 visitors a year. TRH The Prince of Wales and The Duchess of Cornwall visited in February 2008, accompanied by the Lord Lieutenant of Leicestershire, who has been such a wonderful supporter of the Regiment.

The Regiment is extremely proud that its collection is displayed in such an appropriate, poignant and dynamic manner, and gratified that, with the twenty-five year Agreement with the City in place, the Regimental Museum in Newarke Houses is assured for the foreseeable future.

The mutual and enduring benefit of that site is best summed up by quoting a letter which Sarah Levitt, Head of the Arts and Museums Service, wrote in 2007 to the President of The Royal Tigers' Association:

> Now that the Newarke Houses project is well and truly launched, this is to say thank you on behalf of Leicester City Council to all of The Royal Leicestershire Regimental Association members who have put so much hard work and effort into making it happen in different ways over the years.
>
> These include all the members of the project team; everyone involved in the fundraising campaign; the members supporting events; and all of the people over the years who have donated items to the collection and provided information. It has been a long and complex process, but we feel that the end results are outstanding, and I would like to thank you and your members for your tremendous contribution to the success of the project.
>
> It has been a unique and successful partnership, and we feel proud to have played a role in creating this lasting memorial to the Regiment and its members.

Notes

1 Philip Bent was awarded the DSO in June 1917 while in command of 9th Leicesters. He was awarded a posthumous VC for his action in command of the same battalion at Polygon Wood in Belgium on 1 October 1917. His body not having been found, he is commemorated on the walls of the Memorial to the Missing at Tyne Cot, Passchendaele, Belgium. In the 1970s, his sword hung in St Helen's Church, Ashby-de-la-Zouch, for a few years, until stolen.

2 See Chapter 7, Note 9.

3 Private William Foster was awarded the Albert Medal (the then equivalent of the later George Cross) for gallantry when saving the life of a comrade in 1st Leicesters in a forest fire near Sabathu in the Simla Hills in the Punjab, India, on 11 June 1931.

4 Tony Cripps had been awarded the DSO as a Major company commander in 2/5th Leicesters at Montaigne Farm in Tunisia in March 1943.

5 See Appendix N.

Chapter 12

The Regimental Chapel

A long with the Regimental Museum (see Chapter 11) and Royal Tigers' Wood (see Chapter 14), the Regimental Chapel of The Royal Leicestershire Regiment in Leicester Cathedral is the third (and oldest) of the enduring legacies of the Regiment.

The Regimental Chapel, situated in the Cathedral Church of St Martin, Leicester, was instituted in 1897. After consultation with officers commanding the 1st and 2nd Battalions, Colonel W M Rolph, commanding the 17th Regimental District, Leicester, asked the Revd Canon Sanders MA LLD, Vicar of St Martin's Church, for a 'Regimental Corner' in which the Colours and monuments which had been placed in various parts of the church might be collected together and where future monuments might be accumulated. Canon Sanders readily agreed and appropriately gave to the Regiment the Chapel dedicated to Saint George, the Warrior Patron Saint of England. It is a revered place, containing many memorials to campaigns in which The Royal Leicestershire Regiment served and also to individual members of the Regiment. A number of the Regiment's Colours hang there. These and other memorabilia are described in this chapter. On Armistice Day 1921 (St Martin's Day, 11 November), the Bishop of Peterborough dedicated the Chapel of St George 'restored by The Leicestershire Regiment as a thank-offering to Almighty God, and a memorial to all ranks of the Regiment who fell in the Great War 1914-19'. St Martin's Church became the Cathedral Church of St Martin in 1927.

On the west side of the Regimental Chapel there is a large stained-glass window, called the Ladysmith Window, which refers to the services and sacrifices of 1st Battalion The Leicestershire Regiment in the South African War. There are five lights, with numerous tracery openings of the fourteenth-century or 'decorated' character. The lights are of equal dimensions. In the centre light is a figure of Our Lord in Resurrection as the Victor Mortis, bearing the banner of Triumph. In a small panel beneath, the two angels of the Sepulchre are represented bearing tablets inscribed with the words: 'He is not here He is risen as He said.' Within the other four lights are represented military characters: Joshua and David as warriors of the Old Testament, followed by the Centurion as referring to the early Christian Church, and St George symbolic of later times and after whom the chapel has been named since mediaeval times. Beneath the figure of Joshua is the scene of his command to the sun to 'stand still'. Under that of David is the incident of his victory over Goliath. In connection with the figure of Cornelius is the incident of his baptism, while St George's triumph over the Dragon completes the series.

In the opening at the vertex of the window is displayed the badge of the Regiment.

Immediately contiguous are introduced angels bearing olive branches and palms. At a lower level, within four openings, are the words – borne by angels – 'Thanks be to God which giveth us the victory'. Then follows the names of the engagements of the South African Campaign 1899-1902 in which the Regiment fought with such distinction: Talana, Defence of Ladysmith, Laing's Nek, Belfast, Cape Colony, Orange Free State, Transvaal, Natal. Within the canopies above the principal figures, angels bear scrolls bearing the words 'Watch ye', 'Stand fast in the faith', 'Be strong'.

The window, which was designed and erected by Clayton and Bell, of Regent Street, London, was unveiled by Major General A H Utterson CB on 12 November 1903.

There are two large stained-glass windows on the south side. The first is in memory of Lieutenant Colonel F W Reader, who died at Pietermaritzburg, Natal, in November 1898. It was 'presented by officers and men of 2nd Bn The Leicestershire Regiment and by officers who served with him in the 3rd and 1st Volunteer Battalions'. While Adjutant of the Volunteers, it was he, probably in conjunction with the above-named Colonel Rolph, who first brought forward the idea of collecting all the Regimental memorials into one corner of the church.

The second window on that wall is in memory of those who died in the Second World War (see plate section). Its dedication by the Bishop of Leicester, Rt Revd R R Williams DD MA, was movingly described in *The Green Tiger* in 1949:

Sunday 26 June 1949 was a memorable day for the Regiment, for on that day, before a vast congregation that packed Leicester Cathedral, the Regimental War Memorial was dedicated. In addition to the many members and ex-members of the Regiment and their wives, there were large numbers of next-of-kin of those who had died, who had travelled from all over the Kingdom to be present at this service. Many were still in mourning and, as poignant memories stirred, some were in tears. Many were wearing the medals of their fallen sons.

The window was designed and executed by Mr F Spear ARCA FRSA (of Stanmore, Middlesex) and is a most beautiful piece of craftsmanship. The sidelights contain the names of the theatres of war in which the Regiment fought during the Second World War.

The whole idea of the design for the stained glass was that it was chiefly a memorial for the Regiment, linked up with the idea of Christian sacrifice and that to defeat Evil one must do Good. So, above the Regiment's badge and their past Battle Honours, and surrounded in the two outer lights by their newly added Honours, is the figure of St George of England, Patron Saint of Soldiers. He is depicted defeating the Dragon which symbolizes Evil, whilst he is armed and defended by the Cross – the symbol of Goodness and Sacrifice. This Sacrifice is taken further in the tracery lights to a higher plane, for on shields heraldically treated so as to harmonize artistically with the design generally, are the Emblems of the Passion of Christ. In the left-hand shield are the Scourge and Crown of Thorns on a purple ground – this is the Mocking. The two centre shields symbolize the Crucifixion: the Cross on which is shown in initials of Christ, I.H.S. ('*in hoc signo*' tr: 'in this sign'), and the crossed Spear which pierced His side and the Rod with the sponge on which drink was offered to Him. Surrounded by the three nails and in the right-hand shield are the ladder and the pincers emblematic of the descent from the Cross. Above everything are the rays of glory descending from above, suggesting the Risen Christ and the Life Everlasting, which is reached through Sacrifice that combines Love and Justice.

The Roll of Honour was prepared and executed by Messrs E A Roberts and J Mason of the College of Arts, Leicester, under the supervision of Mr A E Christopherson ARCA, Head of the School of Industrial Design at the College. It is a perfect example of craftwork, and is bound in morocco, inlaid and gold tooled, hand-written on vellum. The names of the Fallen are arranged in Theatres of War, thirty to a page.

Also dedicated that day were the altar cross, candlesticks and vases. A glass-topped desk at the west side (the back) of the Chapel houses the Roll of Honour of the Second World War, and three others listing those who died in the First World War, on active service in the years between the World Wars, and those who have served as Tigers but died in peacetime (now three volumes). In the desk there is also a 6" silver crucifix 'saved from the burning Ypres Cathedral during the Battle of Ypres in September 1917 by Pte H Orton'. The desk is flanked by panelling engraved with the battle honours awarded in the First World War. On the north wall are engraved the battle honours awarded before 1914.

Of group memorials, on the west wall there are four stone monuments, in memory of: officers and soldiers of 1st Battalion The Leicestershire Regiment who lost their lives in Afghanistan 1878-79; officers, NCOs and men of 2nd Battalion The Leicestershire Regiment killed in action and died in Burma 1888-9; officers, NCOs and men of The Leicestershire Regiment who were killed in action, died of wounds or disease in South Africa 1899-1902; and officers, NCOs and men of 2nd Battalion The Leicestershire Regiment who died while serving in Egypt 1900-02. A large stone monument on the south wall commemorates those who died in the Crimean Campaign 1854-56. There are three brass plaques. The oldest commemorates officers and men of 1st Battalion The Leicestershire Regiment who died in Bermuda and at Halifax of enteric fever and other causes 1888-91. The newer ones, to the right of the altar, commemorate more recent conflicts: one lists those who lost their lives during the campaign in Korea 1951-52, and the other lists the seventeen Tigers who lost their lives during operations in Cyprus 1955-58 (see plate section). They were dedicated in 1999 and 2003 respectively.

Of memorials to individuals, there are currently (2008) forty-three memorial plaques to individual officers, and they hang on the north, west and south walls of the Chapel. The older plaques are made of bronze and the more modern ones of brass. In 1905, it was ruled by the officers of the Regiment that the only memorials, in future, to be erected in the Regimental Chapel were to be to officers who had been killed or died on active service, or from wounds received in action. In recent years, the criterion for being eligible to have a plaque erected is that the officer should have been the Colonel of The Regiment, have commanded one of its battalions, or have been a Deputy Colonel of The Royal Anglian Regiment. The plaques are paid for by family members of the deceased. The dedication of the plaques usually takes place during the Regimental Parade Service, held annually on Royal Tigers' Weekend. The alphabetical list of those officers so commemorated is at Appendix K.

In the floor before the altar is a mosaic badge of the Regiment (see plate section). Near to it stands the wooden Palestine lectern. The lectern was moved to the Chapel in 2000 having previously been in the Garrison Church of St Thomas in South Wigston for many years. It had been made by the carpenters of 2nd Leicesters in Acre in Palestine and, together with candlesticks and an altar cross, was presented to St John's Chapel there in December 1939. It commemorates the Battalion's service and its dead at Sarafand, Nablus,

Tiberias and Acre 1938/39 and at Megiddo, Sharon and Damascus in 1918.

Among the other memorabilia is a silver book rest which was dedicated in 1955 to the memory of the late Lieutenant Colonel A T le M Utterson DSO[1], for use on the altar, and a Holy Bible presented in memory of General Sir Clive Liddell KCB CMG CBE DSO[2]. There were also embroidered kneelers, worked by Lieutenant Colonel J H Marriott MC and family and by the family of Lieutenant Colonel M Moore MC TD DL. A selection are shown in the plate section.

But above all, literally and figuratively, hanging over the Regimental Chapel above the north wall are fourteen of the King's and Regimental Colours carried by the various battalions of The Royal Leicestershire Regiment over the decades. Originally dedicated and blessed in the solemn splendour of a Colours Presentation Parade, when through the passage of time the Colours are no longer required or are worn out and replaced by new Colours, the old Colours are laid up, usually in a church. In the case of The Royal Leicestershire Regiment, the majority were laid up in this Chapel. Those of the 3rd (Militia) Battalion were originally laid up in the Garrison Church of St Thomas, South Wigston, and were brought to the Cathedral in 2000. The first set of Colours was issued to The 17th Regiment in 1766, and the last set presented to 1st Battalion The Royal Leicestershire Regiment at Iserlohn in Germany in June 1954. As is described at the end of Chapter 9, on 22 June 1975 the King's and Regimental Colours of 1st and 2nd Battalions of the Regiment were laid up there. The final occasion when Colours were laid up was on 21 June 1981, when those of the 4th and 5th Battalions (TA) were brought there. They were then encased in the Officers' Mess at Ulverscroft Road until 2000 when they were hung in the Regimental Chapel. A picture of Colours hanging in the Chapel is shown in the plate section.

At Appendix L is a list of those Colours hanging in the Regimental Chapel. A further twenty-five of the very old Colours are laid up in a mahogany casket under the altar.

Among the most notable hanging in the Chapel is the King's Colour, which together with the Regimental Colour, was presented to 1st Battalion The Leicestershire Regiment by Lord Linlithgow, Viceroy of India, at Jubbulpore in 1938, the 250th Anniversary of the founding of the Regiment. In January 1941 the Battalion moved from India to Penang in Malaya. The deployment was classified as a normal peacetime change of station, and the Battalion, in accordance with orders, took with it the King's and Regimental Colours, a certain amount of the less valuable silver, and quite a lot of personal luggage. Thanks, however, to the foresight of the Commanding Officer, valuable regimental property was stored in Bombay. In June 1941, when the Battalion took up battle positions on the northern frontier of Malaya to face the Japanese, the Colours (and the balance of the Officers' Mess silver) were deposited in a bank in Penang. At the end of the war against the Japanese, on release from PoW camp in 1945, Major R G G Harvey DSO, the Bn 2IC, went back to Penang to search for the Colours. At the time nothing was found as the bank had been looted. Subsequently the Police carried out searches and the King's Colour was found, minus the pole and the tassels, thrown on a rubbish heap. It was in remarkably good condition, save for lots of tiny holes made by insects. It was laid up in the Regimental Chapel in 1949. The Regimental Colour was never found.

Every Saturday in the Regimental Chapel, when the Dean gives prayer biddings, the following Regimental Collect is used: 'Strengthen O Lord Jesus the hearts of those who have served in The Royal Leicestershire Regiment, that all that is best in them may rise to meet the challenge of each coming day, and that they may worthily maintain the traditions of those who lived, fought and died under the Colours which surround these walls, for thy tender mercies' sake.'

There is also a First World War memorial window on the east wall of the Sanctuary of the Cathedral, which dates from 1920. Its words of dedication are: 'This window is erected by the parishioners and worshippers of St Martin's Leicester to the Glory of God and in grateful memory of those connected with the Church and Parish who fell in the Great War 1914-1919.'

The Regiment will always be most grateful to the Dean and Chapter of Leicester Cathedral for the assistance they provide and the interest they take in the Chapel of St George, the Regimental Chapel. A tangible mark of that gratitude was the donation it made in 2000 towards the £1,250,000 raised in the Cathedral's Millennium Appeal, which paid for the Cathedral Centre and the Visitor Centre.

It has been the greatest privilege to read and rerecord the happenings of the men of the Regiment. The feelings aroused by those stories were never stronger than when, on 12 September 2008 (almost 320 years to the day since the raising of The 17th Regiment by Colonel Solomon Richards in 1688)[3], I sat in the Chapel, quite alone, enveloped in history. I could sense all about me the presence of so many people: the builders of the Chapel; the artisans who raised the Cathedral; the countless thousands who had worshipped there; the many, many unknown and unsung soldiers in red and khaki who had fought and fallen in military service in the Regiment since 1688. Above my head were some of the old Colours, worn and threadbare, all proudly borne in the past by generations of soldiers. Many others were in the casket beneath the altar. In one of the stained-glass windows I could see the badge of the Bengal Tiger, 'Hindoostan', and the unbroken laurel wreath, an honour awarded after the Battle of Princeton 1777 – emblems as they were before 1946, the year in which the Regiment was honoured with the prefix 'Royal' in recognition of its battalions' contribution in almost every major theatre of the Second World War. On the walls of the Chapel, brass panels commemorate many campaigns, all of them bearing the names of members of the Regiment.

To sit in the Chapel alone, surrounded by a silence, a stillness far removed from a battlefield, was a very moving, emotional experience from one who had seen and had served with those marvellous and modest men of Leicestershire. I remembered above all the men, the individual personalities about whom I had read, whom I had met, and with whom it had been my privilege to serve. In that quiet place I reflected on two recurrent impressions gained from the numerous accounts in this volume. First, the variety of places round the world in which these men had served their Monarch and their Country; and, secondly, the willingness, enthusiasm, skill and efficiency with which they performed every task given to them.

May this Regimental Chapel remain one of the key legacies of The Royal Leicestershire Regiment.

Notes

1   Archie Utterson joined The Leicesters in 1906. He was awarded the DSO as 2IC 1st LF during the Battle of the Somme in 1916. He commanded 8th Leicesters 1917-19, and 2nd Leicesters 1933-37.
2   Clive Liddell was Colonel The Royal Leicestershire Regiment 1943-48. See Appendix N.
3   There is a statue of Solomon Richards in Westminster Abbey.

Chapter 13

Alliances and Affiliations

The City of Essendon Regiment (Melbourne, Australia)

The origin of the link between the 32nd Infantry Battalion (the predecessor of The City of Essendon Regiment) and The Leicestershire Regiment dates from the Boer War 1899-1902, when both had battalions engaged in operations in South Africa. Colonel C S Davies CMG DSO, who was commissioned into The Leicestershire Regiment in 1900 and later served as an instructor at the Royal Military College Duntroon in Melbourne, commanded the 32nd Battalion Australian Imperial Force (AIF) in Flanders in 1917-18[1]. A letter from the Governor-General of Australia in September 1925 to the Secretary of State for Dominion Affairs reads: 'With reference to correspondence on the subject of alliances between Australian and British Army Regiments, I have the honour, on behalf of my Prime Minister, to ask that approval may be given for an alliance to be formed between The Leicestershire Regiment and the 32nd Battalion Australian Military Forces. My Ministers understand that the desire for affiliation is mutual between the regiments mentioned.' Consequently, an alliance between 32nd Battalion (The Footscray Regiment) and The Leicestershire Regiment was granted Royal Approval in February 1926.

A letter to the Editor of *The Green Tiger* in 1926 expressed the aim to accomplish a long and lasting friendship, in the truest sense of the word, between all ranks of the two regiments. All ranks of The Leicesters then subscribed to present to the 32nd Battalion a sterling silver rose bowl valued then at about £120 (£6,000 at 2008 prices), to be known as the 'Tigers' Cup' for annual competition within the unit.

With the dispersal of the 32nd Battalion in 1943, The City of Footscray Regiment, as such, virtually came to an end. A third Citizens Military Force (CMF) Battalion was raised in the Melbourne area in 1948, being based predominantly in the western and north-western suburbs. Initially encompassing Footscray, and known as The West Melbourne Regiment and then in 1955 as The Melbourne Rifles, the Battalion eventually expanded to be 58th Battalion, The City of Essendon Regiment. It had one surviving VC holder from the First World War, Lieutenant V R Moon. The Regiment established its Headquarters at Pascoe Vale Road, Moonee Ponds, and had companies at Footscray and Brunswick. It gained many new members through National Service, but lost many when the scheme ceased. Members of the Battalion were involved in the organization of the Melbourne Olympic Games in 1956.

In July 1958, Captain H Schuldt MM ED paid a visit to The Royal Leicestershire

Presentation of the Essendon Regiment clock, Glen Parva Barracks (see Appendix P for names).
Leicester Mercury

Regiment's HQ, and on behalf of old comrades of the 32nd Battalion, presented a clock, which was installed on the cricket pavilion at the Regimental Depot.

The Green Tiger records that in summer 1960, at the Annual Camp of 5th Battalion The

Royal Leicestershire Regiment (TA) at Redesdale in Northumberland, 'Another very refreshing visitor this year has been Lieutenant Bill Hocking of The City of Essendon Regiment, our affiliated Australian unit. He kept us all most amused with histories of "down under", long-faced horse breeders, and his spirited singing of 'Waltzing Matilda'. We will always remember him with affection, and it is rumoured, so will the inhabitants of Edinburgh!'

When the reorganization of the CMF occurred in 1960, the 58th Battalion, The City of Essendon Regiment was absorbed into 1st Battalion The Royal Victoria Regiment. It has not since reappeared in the Australian Army's Order of Battle, yet strong links were maintained by the 58th/32nd Battalion Association. The Moonee Ponds Depot remained the location for their annual ANZAC Day service.

The alliance between The Royal Leicestershire Regiment and The City of Essendon Regiment ceased when the Australian unit disbanded. The 58th Battalion's Colours were laid up on 10 May 1970 at the Essendon Town Hall. The 32nd Battalion's Colours were laid up in August 1970 at St John's Anglican Church in Footscray, Melbourne.

The Sherbrooke Regiment (Quebec, Canada)

The history of The Sherbrooke Regiment, with which The Leicestershire Regiment formed an alliance on 5 July 1934, dated from 1803. The circumstances which led to the formation of the alliance are described in a 1934 letter from the Colonel The Leicestershire Regiment, Major General Sir Edward Woodward KCMG CB, of which a précis follows.

> In the early 1930s, economic conditions overseas were considered unfavourable to emigration, and it was unwise at that time to encourage people in the UK to emigrate except in those cases where the emigrant had definite prospects awaiting him overseas. In those conditions, the flow of emigrants to the Dominions considerably reduced, and consequently the opportunities for maintaining personal touch between the peoples of the Old and New Countries were correspondingly lessened.
>
> Much good could, however, be achieved by forming alliances between regiments of the Dominions and British Regiments. Such alliances created an interesting link with the Old Country and establish that personal touch which is so valuable in promoting friendship and goodwill between the Dominions and the Home Country.
>
> In January 1934, on my behalf Major General C G Liddell CMG CBE DSO[2] wrote to the Canadian Military Authorities inviting their good offices in arranging an alliance between The Leicestershire Regiment and a regiment of the Canadian Forces. This request met with an immediate response from Canada to the effect that the officers of The Sherbrooke Regiment (an Infantry regiment of the Non-Permanent Active Militia of Canada) would be very happy and grateful to start an alliance, noting that it would be a particularly fitting regimental relationship in so far as the Leicesters' previous history in Canada is concerned. After the 17th Foot had been involved in the capture of Louisburg in 1758[3], it was transferred to Crown Point on Lake Champlain.[4] Later, after the fall of Quebec in 1759, the 17th Foot marched to Montreal to take the surrender of the survivors of Montcalm's French/Canadian army. In those years it must therefore have marched throughout the whole area in which The Sherbrooke Regiment recruits.[5]

A further coincidence was that 1st Battalion The Sherbrooke Regiment was the descendent of the 117th (Eastern Townships) Battalion of the Canadian Expeditionary Force in the First World War. It also had a 2nd (Reserve) Battalion.

The Sherbrooke Regiment's view, expressed in a letter between the Regiments' Colonels in August 1934 indicated that the alliance would 'become an incentive to All Ranks to attain more of the soldierly spirit, broader views and closer ties with our famous comrades in Britain'. And so the alliance was born.

The Sherbrooke Regiment was presented with a silver tiger trophy when it was remobilized and came to England in 1941, by when elements had amalgamated with Les Fusiliers de Sherbrooke, to form The Sherbrooke Fusiliers Regiment (27th Canadian Armoured Regiment), an armoured regiment. It landed in France on D-Day (6 June 1944) and fought throughout the campaign, for which it was awarded many battle honours, including 'Scheldt', 'Antwerp-Tournout' and 'North-West Europe 1944-45'. These were also awarded to The Leicestershire Regiment, whose 1st Battalion had landed in Normandy on D+27 (3 July 1944). The balance of The Sherbrooke Regiment remained as infantry until in 1946 when the whole Regiment re-roled from infantry to armour, taking on the title 12th Armoured Regiment (Sherbrooke Regiment). In 1958 it was renamed as The Sherbrooke Regiment (RCAC).

In the intervening years at least two Royal Leicesters' officers visited The Sherbrooke Regiment: Lieutenant Colonel Duggie Dalglish MC in 1953 and Captain Bill Brown in 1963. In an article in *The Green Tiger* in 1963, the latter mentions receiving

> a friendly letter from the Sherbrooke Regiment's Adjutant, written on headed notepaper, under the crest of which was printed boldly: 'The Sherbrooke Regiment – allied to The Royal Leicestershire Regiment'... The Sherbrooke Regiment, in addition to its HQ Squadron and three Sabre Squadrons, also had a Band ... To say that, as a Tiger, I was feted by The Sherbrooke Regiment is no exaggeration. I was most impressed by everything I saw, and two main things stood out in my mind. Firstly, the fact that thousands of miles from Leicester there is a Regiment of first-class officers and men who are very aware of the fact that they are allied with The Royal Leicestershire Regiment, and who follow our movements and activities with great interest, through the pages of *The Green Tiger*. Secondly, I realised that we are allied with an active, virile Regiment who are not 'occasional week-end' soldiers, but a fighting Regiment with a history of loyal and efficient service to the Crown dating from the early 19th Century, through two World Wars to today. A symbol of this service is 'Bomb', which stands outside the Drill Hall in Sherbrooke. It is a Sherman tank, which landed in France on 'D-Day' and fought continuously with the Regiment until 'VE Day'.

There are two regimental plaques of The Sherbrooke Regiment on display at the TA Centre at Ulverscroft Road, Leicester, presented to the Officers' and the Sergeants' Messes of The Royal Leicestershire Regiment by their opposite numbers of 'The Sherbrooke Regiment, 12 Armd Regt (RCAC)'.

The Royal Leicestershire Regiment's alliance with The Sherbrooke Regiment was transferred to The Royal Anglian Regiment in 1964. In 1965, The Sherbrooke Regiment amalgamated with 7th/11th Hussars to form The Sherbrooke Hussars.

'Bomb', the Sherbooke Regiment's Second World War 'Sherman' tank. *Sherbrooke Hussars*

The Barbados Regiment

Throughout the colonial history of Barbados, Britain routinely stationed large segments of its West India regimental troops on the island of Barbados. The troops acted principally as a force to secure the island against any invasion by other European powers as well as to help protect other neighbouring British territories in the Eastern Caribbean from invasion. So successful were British colonial troop deployments to Barbados, it has been said that Barbados is the only country in the Caribbean region never to have changed hands since the British first landed and established the city of Jamestown (around the first quarter century of the 1600s) until independence.

The 17th Regiment staged at Barbados in late 1761 as part of a large British force en route to seize the French colony of Martinique in early 1762, for which it earned a battle honour. In early 1794, its Grenadier and Light companies were part of the British force which spent a month at Barbados en route to another seizure of Martinique.

Bn HQ and four companies of 1st Leicesters were stationed in Barbados from March 1893 to the end of 1895 (its other four (!) companies were in St Lucia and Jamaica). An obelisk was erected in the military cemetery at Garrison on Barbados in memory of certain members of the Regiment. There is also a memorial shield bearing the Regiment's crest in St Patrick's Cathedral in Bridgetown, indicating that 'among the Barbadians who served in the Regiment were Major-General E E Carter and Brigadier-General E L Challenor, the start of a close relationship.' Those two became prominent military figures: Major General Sir Evan E Carter KCMG CB MVO[6] and Brigadier General E L Challenor CB CMG CBE DSO[7]. Carter died in 1933. In the Regimental Chapel in Leicester Cathedral there is a commemorative plaque to Challenor, who died in 1935.

The Barbados Regiment was founded in 1902 as the Barbados Volunteer Force (BVF), a unit raised to provide for the local defence of the island following the withdrawal of the British garrison. Soldiers of the BVF were involved in the First World War serving in The British West Indies Regiment, and in the Second World War as part of the Barbados Battalion of The South Caribbean Force and The Caribbean Regiment.

In 1948, the BVF was re-established and renamed The Barbados Regiment. Lieutenant Colonel J Connell OBE ED, the Commanding Officer, approached Commander South Caribbean Area, Brigadier C E Morrison DSO MC (late R Leicesters)[8], to discuss a possible alliance between the two regiments. He cited Regimental and also personal links between the two regiments: the afore-mentioned Challenor family, the ancestors of Brigadier H S Pinder[9] (one of whom had founded the Theological College) and three Leicestershire Regiment retired officers who were resident in Barbados in 1948 (Major L G McKinstry, and Captains St J Hodson and E Evans). This approach was subsequently formalized, the alliance receiving Royal approval in 1949. That year, the Royal Leicesters presented to The Barbados Regiment 'The Royal Leicestershire Regiment Cup' for shooting, which for a number of years was keenly competed for by teams of twelve of the officers and sergeants.

The Barbados Regiment received its first stand of colours in 1953, presented by their new Honorary Colonel, HRH The Princess Royal. Between 1959 and 1962, Barbados was part of the Federation of the West Indies and thus contributed to the 3rd Battalion The West India Regiment, though The Barbados Regiment lived on. The sixtieth birthday of the Regiment was celebrated in 1962, commemorated on The Queen's Birthday Parade day by a re-enactment of a raid on Barbados by Cromwell's forces in 1652.

Two Royal Leicesters' officers held the appointment of Adjutant The Barbados Regiment/Staff Officer to Barbados Local Forces: Major A J (John) Parsons MBE 1958-61 and Major W J G (Bill) Brown 1961-63. They were preceded by Major H C W M Tulloch Foresters from 1955.

The Royal Leicestershire Regiment's alliance with The Barbados Regiment was transferred to The Royal Anglian Regiment in 1964. The 'old' Barbados Regiment was discontinued in 1979 when the Barbados Defence Force was formed, commanded by a Chief of Staff. The Barbados Defence Force comprises a 'new' Barbados Regiment (with a major in command) and the Barbados Coast Guard.

5th Battalion The Frontier Force Regiment (Pakistan)

The 3rd Sikhs were raised in Ferozepore in India in 1846 and were presented with Regimental Colours in August 1848. They were using flint muskets up until 1852, during which year they were issued with percussion muskets. They fought in the Second Afghan War 1878-80 and many other frontier battles (as did The Leicestershire Regiment, being awarded the battle honour 'Afghanistan 1878-79'). One of the 3rd Sikhs' more memorable exploits was in the storming of the heights at Dargai on 20 October 1897 during the Pathan Revolt of 1897-98. That was the same battle which brought The Gordon Highlanders into the limelight when Piper George Findlater, despite having been shot in both ankles, won the VC for continuing to play his bagpipes. The 3rd Sikhs were right behind the Gordons and shared the victory when the tribesmen were routed.

In the First World War, as 53rd Sikhs, it served in India, Aden, Egypt and Mesopotamia. The 2nd Battalion The Leicestershire Regiment joined 28 Infantry Brigade of the 7th Meerut Division in 1915. 53rd Sikhs were in the same Brigade and fought alongside the Regiment for two years in Mesopotamia. Both battalions moved to Palestine at the beginning of 1918 and ended the war together in the same infantry brigade.

In 1922, 53rd Sikhs became the 3rd Battalion 12th Frontier Force Regiment and were made a Royal battalion in the Silver Jubilee honours of 1935, becoming 3rd Royal (Sikhs) 12th Frontier Force Regiment. In the Second World War, it served in India, Italian East Africa, Egypt, Iraq, Cyprus, Sicily, Italy and Greece. After the Partition of India in 1947, it became the 5th Battalion The Frontier Force Regiment, in the Pakistan Army.

In view of the previous connections between the two Regiments, particularly during the First World War, the alliance between The Royal Leicestershire Regiment and 5th Battalion The Frontier Force Regiment was first brokered by the Adjutant-General in 1962. It was granted Royal Approval in July 1964, the year of the formation of The Royal Anglian Regiment, to which the alliance passed on 1 September that year.

HMS *Tiger*

The idea of starting a Regimental affiliation with HMS *Tiger* had been first broached by Captain J S Dalglish CVO RN, to his brother, Major Duggie Dalglish MC, when the ship was being completed in 1958.

With her famous name, the latest of a long line of men-o'-war dating back to the sixteenth century – this had seemed an excellent idea, particularly as the Regiment, with the crest of the same illustrious beast, could also boast of a fine tradition dating back 272 years. Work had started on building this HMS *Tiger* in 1944, but due to rapid progress in the development of electronic equipment, it had been shelved for a decade. By the time she was commissioned in 1959, she was the most modern cruiser in the world, the first of three 'Tiger' Class ships, the others being *Lion* and *Blake*. The two greatest developments in her design were the revolutionary gun turrets, with their very rapid rate of fire and electronic equipment, and her nuclear protective system by which the whole ship could be sealed off against nuclear fallout and radiation rays.

The original idea became a reality in late 1959. A month before the formal affiliation

HMS *Tiger*. *M P Gretton*

ceremony, on 26 October for four days, Captains Colin Marshall and Bill Brown, with Sergeants Brown and Kelly, joined HMS *Tiger* on her commissioning cruise from Kiel to Antwerp. Before leaving the ship, Sergeants Brown and Kelly presented a Regimental plaque to the President of the Chiefs & Petty Officers' Mess; in return they received a presentation pennant in the ship's colours with the ship's crest, for their Sergeants' Mess.

On 20 November, a small party of officers, both serving and retired, visited HMS *Tiger* alongside at Portsmouth, where – fresh out of final dockyard adjustments – she was preparing to leave to join the Mediterranean Fleet. The Colonel of The Regiment and serving officers were dressed in Mess Kit and Colonel L ('Shargo') Sawyer DSO[10] in white tie. The Ship's Captain, R E Hutchins RN, was regrettably absent. In his speech in reply to Commander J Templeton-Cotill RN (who had mentioned among other things that a former HMS *Tiger* had also been involved at the Battle of Martinique in 1762), the Colonel of The Regiment said how appreciative those Tigers were of the great honour it was to be on board and of the great debt they as soldiers owed to the Senior Service. He recalled those difficult days in the Mediterranean when the 2nd Battalion were carried to and from Crete, and later, up to Tobruk from Syria by HM ships and the fine showing they made. He finished by saying, 'I'll ask the members of the Regiment present to rise and drink to HMS *Tiger* and to wish good luck and "God Speed" to all who sail in her.'

The Regiment immediately became very proud of its new affiliation with HMS *Tiger*. A fine plaque from the Regiment was presented and the ship's crest mounted on a board was accepted in exchange. Thenceforth the ship's officers wore the Regiment's Mess Kit buttons and its Band played the Royal Leicesters' Regimental March. The Colonel of The Regiment was the only soldier allowed to wear the HMS *Tiger* tie and wore it with great pride when taking the chair at the AGM of The Royal Tigers' Association in March 1960.

On that November 1959 visit it was noted how youthful the ratings looked, but an old weather-beaten and bearded tar was seen here and there. Perhaps one of those youngsters might have been the son of yet another old sweat of whom the story was told: in a destroyer off Crete with Stukas black in the sky, bombs raining down like hail and not an RAF plane in sight, he was seen blowing up his Mae West life vest. On being asked why he did this so prematurely, he replied, with a blue eye cocked towards the sky, 'I reckon it's the only air support we'll get today.'

On 2 May 1961, the Colonel of The Regiment and two officers attended the recommissioning of the ship at Devonport when Captain P W W Graham DSC RN was in command, and in December that year two officers of HMS *Tiger* attended the Officers' Regimental Dinner in London.

In February 1962, HMS *Tiger* paid an official call to the port of Bremen, some 120 miles north of Münster where the Battalion was then stationed. Various visits by members of the Battalion to the ship were arranged. Captains John Wilson and Jeremy North, Colour Sergeant P M Collins, and Sergeants Perkins, D W Green and A Rollins spent two days on board, enjoying the considerable amount of entertainment organized by the Bremen civic authorities. This level of official activity, coupled with the hospitality of the ship's company, made the visit a most memorable one. In between the receptions, cocktail parties and visits to Bremen, the visiting 'pongos' were taken over and shown the workings of the ship. It gave the visitors tremendous pride, as members of the Regiment, to have so strong an affiliation with such a ship.

A second group of two officers and thirty-five Other Ranks paid a one-day visit to the ship. They were taken everywhere on board, from the galley to the bridge. Anti-tank gunners played with the 6" guns, admitting that the rate of fire that *Tiger* could produce would be a useful addition to the supporting fire of the Battalion. Signallers were even confused by the communications as they couldn't find any A41 or C42 sets, but only very complicated radar or rather pretty coloured flags! The Commanding Officer and Second-in-Command were also able to pay a short visit.

The only regret was that not enough was able to be seen of her and her crew, and little opportunity to reciprocate their excellent hospitality. The Colonel of The Regiment, accompanied by Lieutenant Colonels P D S (Philip) Palmer and Stuart Smith MBE, had a wonderful time when they visited the ship at Plymouth on 21 March, on which occasion the Colonel of The Regiment presented her with a silver Tiger.

HMS *Tiger* set off in April 1962 for a commission in the Far East, with the best wishes of all ranks of the 1st Battalion. Major General 'Joe' Kendrew, Head of UK Special Liaison Staff in Australia, visited the ship when it was in Sydney in September 1962. She returned to Plymouth in March 1963.

The next meeting was in Malta in November 1965. In the first week of the Battalion's tour there, a hundred men spent a day on the ship in Grand Harbour, which concluded with football and hockey matches, and the following day sixty soldiers went to sea as the ship's crew carried out an anti-aircraft practice shoot. The respective commanding officers (Lieutenant Colonel Alan Cowan MBE and Captain G J Kirkby DSC RN) exchanged plaques, and HMS *Tiger* produced some photographs of graves of men of the 2nd Leicesters who had been killed in Crete in 1941 and were buried there.

When the white minority Government of Rhodesia published its Unilateral Declaration of Independence (UDI) on 11 November 1965, the first response of the British Government was patient diplomacy. That included a meeting between Prime Minister Harold Wilson and Mr Ian Smith on HMS *Tiger* off Gibraltar in December 1966.

Subsequently, after an extensive four-year refit and conversion to a helicopter cruiser, HMS *Tiger* was recommissioned on 7 July 1972 at Plymouth. Her Captain and the ship's company were keen to renew the ties of friendship with The Royal Leicestershire Regiment, whose representative at the ceremony was Lieutenant Colonel Terry Holloway. He was very proud to hear Captain C T Goodhugh RN making complimentary references to the strong links with the Regiment. There was even a live tiger cub on parade! The close affiliation continued for another six years until HMS *Tiger* was paid off in April 1978. She was finally disposed of in 1980, and broken up by Desguaces Varela in Spain in 1986.

Cadet Forces

The Royal Leicesters' affiliation to cadet forces (at the time called Officer Training Corps (OTCs)) dates from around 1924.

By way of background, the first Volunteer Cadet Corps at schools were formed in 1860. At intervals thereafter various schools raised Cadet Corps. The Officer Training Corps (OTC) was formed in 1907, and the School Cadet Corps became the Junior Division thereof. Consequent to the decision that all candidates for commissions must pass through the ranks, the name was changed to Junior Training Corps (JTC). In about 1945, it was felt that the administration of contingents of the JTC and of the Sea Cadet Corps and the Air

Training Corps, which existed simultaneously at some schools, might be simplified if a Combined Force was formed. The Combined Cadet Force (CCF) therefore came into being in 1948. Its aim was to 'develop the character and powers of leadership, including the ability to instruct, produce good citizens, produce potential leaders for the fighting Services, to produce volunteers for the Regular Forces, and to produce for National Service, entrants who are already well-grounded in basic training.' The CCF contingents were not part of the Armed Forces of the Crown, and its members were volunteers. By 1952, about 70 per cent of all entrants to RMA Sandhurst for Regular Commissions and 60 per cent of all entrants into OCS for National Service commissions were ex-CCF cadets. So the Regiment regarded the affiliations with CCFs as an important medium through which to attract potential officers to the Regiment in particular, and to the Armed Forces in general. The counties' cadet contingents wore the Regiment's capbadge.

In parallel with the CCF (members of whose contingents trained during school hours and at weekends), the Army Cadet Force (ACF) catered for working lads who trained in the evenings and at weekends. In 1863 the formation of Cadet Corps by Volunteer battalions was authorized, and they wore the uniform of their parent Battalion. In 1910 the Cadet Force became the responsibility of the newly formed Territorial Force Associations. The British National Cadet Association was founded in 1930, and in turn in 1942 was superceded by the ACF Association, which worked in conjunction with the War Office to administer the ACF, administered by TAFAs. There was significant benefit of pre-Service training to cadets: apart from the inherent character-building value of such training, the ex-cadet normally got a flying start in the Army. By 1952, the ACF produced 10 per cent of all Regular and National Service officers in the Army, and 10 per cent of all volunteers for the Regular Army. Hence, the importance of the Regiment's link with the ACF. And the counties' ACF detachments wore the Regiment's capbadge.

The Regiment's affiliation with Oakham School OTC (whose contingent had originally formed in 1910) dated from 1924, with Uppingham School OTC from 1925, with Ratcliffe College CCF from 1955 and with Loughborough Grammar School CCF from 1957. The first three in particular produced many officers for the Regiment, both Regular and National Service, right up until the early 1960s, the leading provider being Uppingham. They also provided officers for the TA and TAVR elements.

The affiliation with these schools was mainly effected through the Depot Royal Leicesters at Glen Parva Barracks in South Wigston providing instructors and staff to carry the annual individual proficiency tests, and the training facilities at the Depot itself. To a lesser extent, the 5th Battalion (TA) also provided assistance. This interaction was of mutual benefit and especially appreciated by the schools. Some detail of what occurred follows.

With regard to Uppingham School, an obituary of R E Small DCM stated:

In the Great War in France he was RSM of the 5th Leicesters and won the DCM, under that great commander, Lieutenant Colonel C H Jones CMG TD. After the war they continued as CO and RSM together of Uppingham School OTC. They left no doubt in the minds of the boys as to which was the best Infantry Regiment in the Army and what an honour it was to wear the Tiger capbadge. RSM Small was at Uppingham from 1918 to 1929, and during that time sent at least eight officers to the Regiment.

It was no surprise then that Lieutenant Colonel J H (John) Marriott MC[11], an Old Uppinghamian who was to play Rugby for the Army and Blackheath, wrote in his unpublished autobiography about his last term at RMC Sandhurst in 1934:

I was joining the Army so that I could enjoy my youth and have an open air life with plenty of sport and congenial company. I did consider the Royal Sussex as my county regiment for they were keen on hockey which I enjoyed. The Leicesters however were an obvious choice; there were already 18 Old Uppinghamians of differing ages in it and they had Tony Novis[12] and Joe Kendrew[13], both captains of the England XV in turn.

Much later, in 1955, the Colonel of The Regiment carried out the Annual Inspection of the CCF at Uppingham, and there was a full-bore shooting match between the School and the Depot teams.

The Colonel of The Regiment also carried out the Annual Inspection of the CCF at Ratcliffe College that year and in 1960 presented the 'Callander Cup' for shooting. In 1956, Lieutenant Colonel C D (Cyril) Wain MBE TD DL[14] was appointed Commanding Officer of the new CCF Contingent. He had previously commanded 579th (The Royal Leicestershire Regiment) Light Anti-Aircraft Regiment, RA (TA), and so brought some useful Tiger influence to bear over many years in post at Ratcliffe. One of the areas of mutual assistance to the College was for the CCF's 'Bass and Tenor Drummers to attend at The Magazine during Sunday morning Band Practice of the 5th Battalion, to receive instruction in "stick swinging" from the Battalion's expert'.

Major General J M K Spurling CBE DSO[15], Chief of Staff HQ Northern Command, carried out the Annual Inspection of the CCF at Oakham School in 1957. In 1961, the contingent spent Annual Camp with 1st Royal Leicesters at Münster, Germany.

Little is recorded about the affiliation with Loughborough Grammar School, except that some of its cadets spent Annual Camp with 1st Royal Leicesters at Münster and when, in 1960, the school was asked if it wished to change its affiliation to another regiment or corps, it replied firmly, 'No'. With the transition of Depot Royal Leicesters to Depot The Forester Brigade in 1960, the main conduit for the provision of training support to these schools switched to 4/5th Royal Leicesters (TA). With the end of National Service, the importance of the cadet forces' Proficiency Tests diminished as they were not a prerequisite for a National Service Commission. The CCF's syllabus was widened to include arduous training, for which assistance was given in the two counties by 17 Army Youth Team and the requirement for Depot support reduced. In July 1968, four years after the formation of The Royal Anglian Regiment, all four schools' contingents decided to keep the Tiger capbadge – at their own expense if necessary. Uppingham School CCF is still wearing a Tiger capbadge in 2008.

With regard to the ACF, shortly after the Second World War, three cadet battalions were formed in Leicestershire and Rutland: the City of Leicester & District Cadet Battalion The Royal Leicestershire Regiment (with its HQ at The Magazine), 1st Leicestershire Cadet Battalion (with its HQ at Loughborough) and 2nd Leicester & Rutland Cadet Battalion (with its HQ at Melton Mowbray). The first-mentioned included detachments at various times at Brentwood Road, Linwood Lane, Maynard Road, Ulverscroft Road, Caldecote Road, City Boys' School, Wigston and Blackbird Road, and from 1946 to 1949 was commanded by Alderman Sidney Brown TD[16]. There were also cadet companies in such towns as Hinckley, Loughborough, Lutterworth, Market Harborough and Melton Mowbray. In 1953, a party from the 2nd Cadet Battalion visited 1st Royal Leicesters at Iserlohn in Germany.

In 1955, those three battalions were reorganized into The Leicestershire & Rutland ACF. The first County Commandant was Lieutenant Colonel S D Field[17], followed by Lieutenant Colonel P G Upcher DSO DL 1956-62[18], and Lieutenant Colonel M J B Farnsworth 1962-71. Previously the Commanding Officer of the 2nd Cadet Battalion, Major J (James) Clamp DCM MM[19] became Deputy County Commandant in 1955 and for his outstanding work was awarded the MBE in 1961. The County Adjutant for several years until 1956 was Captain J T Meredith DCM[20], He was succeeded by Major G W Killinger. In 1956, the two counties' ACF strength was 351 cadets and fourteen officers, and 200 of them went to Cadet Camp at Proteus. In 1956 its strength was 302.

The Regiment's affiliation with its two counties' ACF was not dissimilar to that with the CCFs, and Depot Royal Leicesters provided support and facilities.

In 1960, the centenary of the formation of the first cadet units in the country was celebrated. On 4 May, a large detachment of The Leicestershire & Rutland ACF marched through Leicester and Loughborough carrying the Duke of Edinburgh's Banner and escorted by the Band of 1st Royal Leicesters.

In that same year the Brentwood Road Detachment won the Montgomery of Alamein Trophy for shooting, a non-central competition, open to teams of four from cadet units of all three Services. It won again in 1961, with its B Team coming second in the national competition. That summer, twenty cadets went to Annual Camp with the 1st Battalion in Münster, Germany.

With the demise of Depot Royal Leicesters, The Leicestershire & Rutland ACF switched affiliation to 4/5th Royal Leicesters (TA) and to other sponsoring units whose capbadges some detachments began to wear. On the whole the two counties' ACF cadets continued to wear the Royal Leicestershire Regiment capbadge until 1971, when they rebadged to The Royal Anglian Regiment and amalgamated to form The Royal Anglian (Leicester, Northampton and Rutland) ACF.

Notes

1 Charles Davies was awarded the DSO in 1917 as CO 32nd Battalion AIF during the Battle of Polygon Wood near Ypres in September 1917, and the CMG in 1920. As he also commanded 1st Leicesters 1927-31, he therefore most unusually commanded both units in the alliance.
2 General Sir Clive Liddell KCB CMG CBE DSO was to be Colonel The Leicestershire Regiment 1943-48. See Appendix N.
3 Louisburg, one of the Regiment's battle honours, is on the east coast of Nova Scotia, Canada.
4 Crown Point was a town of strategic importance on Lake Champlain which straddles the current border between Canada and USA (New York State).
5 The town of Sherbrooke is 80 miles east of Montreal.
6 Evan Carter served in The Leicesters for eighteen months 1889-90, before transferring into the Army Service Corps, where he had a distinguished career, culminating as Director of Supplies of the British Army in France 1915-19, for which he was appointed KCMG. His career was akin to that of George Payne fifty years later who, after serving most of the 1930s in The Leicesters, transferred to the RAOC and eventually became Major General G L Payne CB CBE, Director-General Ordnance Services in 1965.
7 Neddy Challenor served in 1st Leicesters during the Siege of Ladysmith in 1899-1900, and was awarded the DSO

while CO 6th Leicesters at Guedecourt in the Battle of the Somme in France in September 1916. He commanded 63 Bde in France 1917-18, for which he was appointed CB and CMG, and commanded 1st Leicesters in Ireland 1919-23, for which he was appointed CBE. He played cricket for Leicestershire in 1906, for Aldershot Command 1910-12, and for the MCC in the late 1920s.

8   See Chapter 1, Note 9.

9   See Appendix N.

10 'Shargo' Sawyer had been awarded the DSO while serving as a company commander in 8th Y & L at Le Sars in France in 1916, aged twenty-two. He transferred to The Leicesters in 1921 and commanded 2/5th Leicesters in 1940.

11 See Chapter 1, Note 8.

12 See Chapter 4, Note 12.

13 See Appendix N.

14 Cyril Wain had been awarded the MBE in 1946 in recognition of his service as Adjutant of 133 LAA Regt RA in North-West Europe 1944-45.

15 See Appendix N.

16 See Chapter 2, Note 1.

17 Stephen Field had been CO 1st R Leicesters 1947-50 and Regimental Secretary 1952-7.

18 See Chapter 3, Note 1.

19 James Clamp had been awarded the DCM and MM while serving with The Queen's Westminster Rifles in the First World War, and commanded the Coalville Home Guard of The Leicestershire Regiment during the Second World War.

20 John Meredith was awarded the DCM as RSM 1st Leicesters and The British Battalion in Malaya 1941-2. He was also renowned as being a tower of strength while a PoW of the Japanese 1942-5.

Chapter 14

And onwards ... post 1975

This chapter, written in 2008, describes how the residual interests of The Royal Leicestershire Regiment have developed in the last thirty-three years. Because of the variety of topics covered which overlap timelines, it will of necessity be fragmented.

Orbats, or 'What's in a name?'

At the beginning of 1976, The Royal Anglian Regiment comprised 1st, 2nd and 3rd Regular Battalions and 5th, 6th and 7th (Volunteer) Battalions, all six of which wore Tiger buttons as their survivors do to this day. The evolution of the Regular and Volunteer battalions in so far as they affect Leicestershire is shown in the Family Tree on Page 12. The three Regular battalions were each taking forward the traditions of all the Former Regiments. In early 1977, the Colonel of The Royal Anglian Regiment decided that, as Leicestershire now had no Regular battalion, the 2nd Battalion would have special responsibility for recruiting and for looking after the Royal Anglian Regiment's affairs in Leicestershire. Moreover, after ten years since the removal of the county titles from the names of the Regular battalions in 1968, and despite the success of the Regiment in every field (and particularly on operations in Northern Ireland), it was felt that the 'county connection' had fallen away. This led to the Regimental image in the counties being weak which also had an adverse effect on recruiting. In order to redress this, in 1978 all three Regular battalions were retitled, initially informally. As the Regimental area covered nine counties, each battalion was given three county names in parenthesis. Accordingly, the Royal Leicesters' traditions were subsumed by 2nd Battalion (Lincolnshire, Leicestershire and Northamptonshire) The Royal Anglian Regiment.

In 1978, the District Council of Hinckley & Bosworth in Leicestershire granted its Freedom to The Royal Anglian Regiment, and on parade that day the 2nd Battalion accepted it on behalf of the Regiment. Hinckley's main claim to fame is that the Hansom Cab was invented there and it is also the home of Triumph Motorcycles Ltd, the last British motorbike manufacturer. Nearby, Market Bosworth has been an important market town since the Middle Ages. The City of Leicester granted its Freedom to the Regiment in 1996 (thirty years after granting it to the 4th Battalion), and in June 2007, the Borough of Loughborough granted its Freedom to the 2nd Battalion in thanks and recognition of its service in Iraq, Bosnia, Sierra Leone and Afghanistan.

In 1980, the 'three counties in parenthesis' was made official and, in addition to the longstanding Battalion lanyards, the former East Anglian Regiment's Battalion collar badges were also reintroduced. The 2nd Battalion The Royal Anglian Regiment ('The Poachers') wore (and still do) the Royal Lincolns' Sphinx, subscribed by the Northamptons' Talavera scroll.

This shape continued until 1992 when a further round of defence cuts led to the removal from the Army's Order of Battle of the Regiment's 3rd Battalion, as it was merged into the 1st and 2nd. Most of the other Large Regiments suffered a similar fate. As a result of the 3rd Battalion's disappearance, The Royal Anglian Regiment's Regular Battalions' county titles in parenthesis were dropped, and county titles were instead given to the companies of the remaining two Regular battalions. Hence appeared B (Leicestershire) Company in 2 R Anglian. The policy introduced in 1968 (with the adoption of Tiger buttons) of recognizing disappearing Former Regiments in enduring dress codes was continued. Tokens of the disbanding 3rd Battalion's former regiments were adopted as dress for the whole Regiment, namely the Essex Regiment 'Eagle' badge on the left upper arm of parade dress and the Beds & Herts' black & yellow lanyard. Furthermore, to compensate for the Regular battalions' loss of the 'three counties in parenthesis', the three TAVR battalions took those titles upon themselves, the 7th becoming 7th (Volunteer) Battalion (Lincolnshire, Leicestershire and Northamptonshire).

Not surprisingly and quite separate from unit titles, over time the role, size and shape of the Regiment's Volunteer battalions altered. In 1978, the 5th Battalion, which was already a NATO-roled unit, and the 7th Battalion, which discarded its General Reserve role, joined the reorganized NATO-roled 7 Field Force (the successor to the previously all-Regular 19 Inf Bde), whose HQ was at Colchester (Brigadier P M Davies OBE). Its war role was rear area security in BAOR. Under the evolving 'One Army' concept, Regular and Volunteer teeth arm units served alongside each other in the same formation. This change in role meant that these battalions were upgraded, with changes in weapons, vehicles and equipment. Training for the Volunteers became much more demanding and exciting, with plenty of helicopter support and testing exercises, while the higher priority and faster administrative back-up was most welcome. The Regulars benefited from the no-nonsense approach of business-minded Territorials who had no military career concerns to worry about.

A number of organizational and location adjustments were simultaneously carried out to rationalize the geographical areas covered by the 7th and 5th Battalions, the 7th Battalion's companies becoming concentrated in the East Midlands area. Accordingly, 4 (Leicestershire) Company 5 (V) R Anglian and B (Royal Leicestershire) Company 7 (V) R Anglian formed Bn HQ and HQ Company 7 (V) R Anglian, of which the Bn HQ moved from Northampton to Leicester. The Battalion's support weapons were under command of HQ Coy, although the platoons and detachments were located throughout the Battalion area, with for example some of the 120mm CONBATs being at Loughborough. So, after a break of nine years, a Tigers' Bn HQ was again located at Ulverscroft Road. At the same time the Hinckley detachment of B Coy 7 (V) R Anglian transferred to the LDY Coy, and the Lincoln Coy of 5 (V) R Anglian joined the 7th Battalion.

The City of Leicester was very pleased that once again a battalion nicknamed 'the Tigers' should have its HQ in Leicester. Successive Lord Mayors continue to hold annual dinners for senior officers of the Regiment, a level of hospitality which remains unique among the towns and cities of the Regimental area. Lord Mayors also visit the 2nd Battalion each year when the operational tempo permits.

In 1977, celebrating its first ten years, 4 Coy 5 (V) R Anglian, presented to the City of Leicester a mounted and inscribed bayonet.

Colours were presented to the 7th Battalion at Victoria Park, Leicester, in 1980. In 1982, the TAVR was disbanded and the Territorial Army reformed. The 7th Battalion left 7 Field Force and came under command the newly formed HQ 49 Inf Bde at Chilwell in Nottinghamshire under HQ 2 Inf Div at York. At the same time, an organization called the Home Service Force (HSF) came into being. Each TA unit was invited to form an HSF subunit, to be recruited from volunteers aged twenty to sixty with previous Army (TA or regular) experience and who were to have a training liability of ten days a year. Its role was to guard key points and installations likely to be the target of Russian 'special forces' and saboteurs, so releasing other units for mobile defence. There were, at its height, some 4,500 enlisted men in forty-eight companies all over Great Britain. 7 (V) R Anglian formed E (HSF) Company, with 13 and 14 Platoons at Leicester and 15 Platoon at Lincoln. Its first OC was Major A A J (Albert) Pryce-Howells MBE, with WO2 R (Dick) Rowlatt as CSM. When, in 1985, Lieutenant Colonel J C D (John) Heggs became the HSF OC, the Battalion unusually had three officers of that rank, the others being the Commanding Officer, G I G (Gordon) Brett, and the QM, D H (David) Greenfield MBE. With the end of the Cold War, the HSF disbanded in 1992. In its ten years it proved that once again the men of Leicestershire would 'respond to the call'.

Not part of Leicestershire's story but, as a further reorganization of the TA, 5 (V) R Anglian was re-roled from an Infantry battalion to a Transport Regiment in 1996, and became 158 (Royal Anglian) Transport Regiment Royal Logistic Corps (V). As a result the remaining two TA battalions lost the 'three counties in parenthesis' from their titles. That year, The Royal Anglian Regiment was honoured to be granted the Freedom of the City of Leicester at a parade commanded by the Commanding Officer of the 7th Battalion, Lieutenant Colonel J B C (Jeremy) Prescott, and in which four guards and the colour parties of the 2nd and 7th Battalions took part.

Now reverting to Leicestershire's infantry, the 7th Battalion disbanded in 1999. Its HQ Company at Leicester combined with C (Northampton) Company to form C (Leicestershire & Northamptonshire) Company at Leicester with a platoon at Northampton, part of The East of England Regiment (EER). This Battalion, which comprised four former Royal Anglian TA companies and one from The Worcestershire & Sherwood Forester Regiment (WFR) TA, was so called as a political initiative linked to the Government's aspiration to form an East of England Region. Bn HQ and HQ Coy was at Bury St Edmunds, based on the former 6 (V) R Anglian, whose Colours it carried; and no subunit was required to change capbadge or collar badge. It was a Light Role reserve battalion, which was soon called upon to support the Regular Army. Over the following few years, the EER sent three *ad hoc* companies to Iraq on six-month tours on Operation *Telic*, where they were involved mainly in force protection tasks.

In 2006, (re)organizational commonsense again prevailed. The WFR company left the EER, which was retitled 3 R Anglian (TA) and comprised four rifle companies and HQ Coy. C Coy transferred to the newly titled Battalion, and kept its same title and organization. That year the Lord Lieutenant of Leicestershire, Jennifer Lady Gretton JP, and the Colonel of The Royal Anglian Regiment, Lieutenant General J C McColl CBE DSO, presented Iraq medals to twelve members of C (Leicestershire & Northamptonshire) Company after the

Annual Regimental Service at Leicester Cathedral on Royal Tigers' Weekend. In 2007, one *ad hoc* platoon deployed to Afghanistan on Operation *Herrick*, where its men became an integral part of 1 R Anglian's successful tour. Also, in 2008, fourteen men of C Coy were attached to 2 R Anglian as individual reinforcements (one a fully qualified Arabic interpreter) for their tour on Operation *Telic* in Iraq.

The Royal Tigers' Association

The Royal Tigers' Association has continued in being, with several enduring roles. First, to continue to look after and administer the general affairs of Regiment, including its property (mainly the silver and the Regimental collection). Second, to provide for the welfare of all former Tigers and their families in need of support, financial or otherwise. Third, to organize Royal Tigers' Weekend, and other reunions and anniversary events. Many men of all ranks have served as General Committee Members of The Royal Tigers' Association.

In 1978, it was agreed that all ex-members of The Royal Anglian Regiment could automatically become members of The Royal Tigers' Association on application. There was already a thriving branch in Loughborough and another began to blossom at Ulverscroft Road. The following year The Royal Tigers' Association became formally affiliated to the Royal Anglian Regiment Association, and its Charitable Fund has subsequently received generous financial support.

From an office in Ulverscroft Road TA Centre, assisted by the long-serving Mrs Ladwa who took up post in 1990, and by many other volunteer Committee members, the Regimental Secretaries (their names are listed in Appendix B) have borne the brunt of the work of the Association. The work of Peter Upcher has already been described in Chapter 9. Preceded by his seven years as Assistant Regimental Secretary, John Dudley's ten-year tenure spanned the period when the Regular and Volunteer Tigers left the Army's Order of Battle. John Wilson presided over the move of the Regimental Museum from The Magazine, the setting up of Royal Tigers' Wood, and the 300th year anniversary, while Anthony Swallow was Regimental Secretary on four occasions, spread over eleven years. Anthony was heavily involved in Royal Tigers' Wood, two moves of the Regimental Museum and its fundraising appeal, and rationalizing the future of the Colours in the Regimental Chapel. The inability of the system to find a long-term replacement for him when he retired from his first formal spell as Secretary in 2003 left the Association with big gaps which he volunteered to fill on three occasions. Without his selfless contribution, the Association would not be the flourishing organization that it is in 2008. To these four men in particular, the Regiment owes an immense debt of gratitude.

The General Committee, invariably chaired by a former officer, is currently chaired by Captain R J (Bob) Allen. Since 2004 it has delegated work on benevolence cases to ex-WO1 R E (Roger) Jones, the Vice-Chairman. Some of the previous vice-chairmen were Mr M C Bush, Captain J H Jacques, Tommy Marston (twenty-five years) and John Sheppard who retired aged ninety-three in 2006 after twenty-nine years on the Committee.

In 2008, Colonel R G (Richard) Wilkes stood down after twenty years as Chairman of the Trustees, a long and distinguished tenure which he carried out with great skill and devotion, during a period which had seen many changes in Regimental affairs, including the establishment of Royal Tigers' Wood and the new Regimental Museum. Colonel R H (Richard) Robinson is currently Chairman of Trustees. Also in 2008, the Trustees of The

Royal Leicestershire Regiment, formerly all officers of the two regiments, appointed to their body some civilians with specialist skills to provide a balanced team for the long term.

In 1955, Lieutenant Colonel Peter Upcher DSO, the Regimental Secretary, had a beautiful Standard made in silk, pearl grey[1] and to Colour specifications. It was bought by subscriptions from members of the Association and units of the Regiment, to be present on all parades and occasions when the Association is represented. It differs from the Regimental Colours in these respects: it has no historical association with the battlefield and is not in any way a military emblem (and therefore is not saluted on parade, though it is often flanked by an escort). It was dedicated at Leicester Cathedral on 26 June by the Bishop of Leicester, the Rt Revd R R Williams DD MA.

The Standard has been successively carried over the years by John Meredith[2], Tommy Marston (for twenty-five years), Roger Jones and Denis Foran. However, after nearly fifty years' service and many loving repairs, the silk was tearing every time the Standard was used. Consequently, a high-quality replacement was made by Mr Clifford Newton of Newton Newton, and very generously donated to the Association. He had been a National Serviceman in the Regiment and since then built up a very successful family business making flags.

Royal Tigers' Wood

Along with The Royal Leicestershire Regiment's Museum (Chapter 11) and the Regimental Chapel in Leicester Cathedral (see Chapter 12), Royal Tigers' Wood is the third of the key legacies of the Regiment.

The idea of a new multi-purpose forest for the nation was first mooted in the Countryside Commission's 1987 policy document 'Forestry in the Countryside'. The aim would be to demonstrate in lowland Britain that a large-scale, attractive forest could be created, blending commercial forestry with ecological, landscape and public benefit. Economic regeneration would come from the restoration of mining sites and in the long term many other benefits would also be achieved. The future of agriculture would be supported through opportunities for rural diversification.

The site for The National Forest, linking the ancient forests of Needwood in Staffordshire and Charnwood in north-west Leicestershire, was selected from five alternatives and announced in October 1990. The choice was symbolically central to Great Britain, spanning three counties in the centre of England – Derbyshire, Leicestershire and Staffordshire. These were not the same three forests (Arden, Charnwood and Sherwood) which formed the basis of The Forester Brigade in 1960 (see Chapter 2).

The Trustees of the Regiment rapidly embraced the opportunity to establish a further lasting memorial to the Regiment during the transformation of 200 square miles in three counties of central England. The National Forest was a bold project, blending new and maturing woodland within a wide variety of landscapes, presenting opportunities for many to take part in its development, and transforming the landscape. Within its boundary are miles of rolling farmland and a former coalfield which was in desperate need of regeneration. Forest towns and villages include Burton upon Trent (famous for its brewing), Coalville and Swadlincote (formerly associated with the coal mining industry) and the historic town of Ashby-de-la-Zouch. Many individuals and organizations were involved in the creation of the forest – these being its communities, landowners, public and voluntary sector bodies, private businesses and people from all over the country.

The Woodland Trust and Wildlife Trusts developed many sites in The National Forest, with particular commitment to nature conservation and high-quality woodlands. The purchase of 85 acres for £44,000 and the establishment within it of the 36-acre Royal Tigers' Wood at Bagworth near Coalville was facilitated by the fact that a former Regimental officer, Colonel J C D (John) Heggs DL, was Director of the Leicestershire Rural Community Council. The Regiment's steering committee was set up under the enthusiastic and energetic chairmanship of Colonel W G (Bill) Dawson TD DL, and included the Regimental Secretary, Lieutenant Colonel J L (John) Wilson DL. It ensured that step-by-step development of the wood was maintained. Many friends of the Regiment were involved, and more than 450 people contributed towards it. Leicestershire County Council, Hinckley & Bosworth Council, the Woodland Trust and the National Forest also made sizeable donations.

The first trees – in the form of 3,000 whips – were planted on 29 January 1994, when a large number of people turned out to turn many sods. A picture taken that day is in the plate section. At about the same time a granite memorial stone was erected on the site, most generously donated by Hanson Aggregates of Shepshed, on which an engraved plaque was carved on slate by Collin Bros of Loughborough. The Countryside Commission, Leicestershire County Council and Hinckley & Bosworth District Council made generous donations towards its cost. The memorial stone is shown in the plate section.

As part of the development of the Wood, a small arboretum was planted. The trees represent countries in which the Regiment served and for which battle honours were awarded. The International Tree Foundation provided funding towards the cost of the trees, and researched and nominated the appropriate species – which had of course to be able to survive in the Midland environment.

Purchased from the Royal Botanical Gardens at Kew, the seventeen trees were planted on 23 February 1995 by individuals and representatives of those organizations who have been so supportive to this Regimental living memorial and by a number of members of the Regimental Association. The trees were: Black Poplar (Namur 1695), Snake Bark Maple (Louisburg 1758), Red Maple (Canada 1759), Stone Pine (Martinique 1762), Bhutan Pine (Khelat 1839), Scots Pine (Sevastapol 1855), Indian Chestnut (Ali Masjid 1878), Eucalyptus (South Africa 1899-1902), English Oak (Neuve Chapelle 1915), Turkey Oak (Mesopotamia 1915-18), Plane (Somme 1916), Judas Tree (Palestine 1918), Holm Oak (Sidi Barrani 1940), Hardy Cork Oak Pine (Crete 1941), Italian Alder (Italy 1943), Golden Poplar (Scheldt 1944), Dove Tree (Chindits 1944) and Korean Hill Cherry (Korea 1951-52). In addition, four seats with Regimental crests were later positioned with restful views of the open meadows within the wood.

It would seem that this tree planting had an important historical precedent as in 1848 The 17th Regiment, then stationed in the Infantry Barracks at Chatham (now Kitchener Barracks), planted a row of trees, seventeen on either side of the roadway in front of the officers' quarters. Although unable to identify them specifically, the current incumbents of Kitchener Barracks report that there are a row of now fifteen elderly oak trees along a road near a Grade II Listed quarters' building and, separately, a commemorative plaque and eleven young trees astride another road.

Maj Gen Pollard plants Mercer's Oak, Royal Tigers' Wood, June 1995. *Trustees R Anglian Regt*

Back to the twentieth century. Having visited the battlefield of Princeton in the USA, where in 1777, 240 men of the 17th Regiment defeated an American brigade, the President of The Royal Tigers' Association instigated the presentation of a 'Mercer's Oak' from the Princeton battlefield to be planted in Royal Tigers' Wood. In late March 1995, John Mills, the curator of the Princeton Battlefield State Park, despatched two White Oaks grown from acorns of the 'Mercer's Oak'[3] on the battlefield site under which American Brigadier General Mercer was bayoneted by soldiers of the 17th Regiment and later died. Dormant and boxed, the young oaks were transported to England in a USAF cargo plane under the personal care of a National Guard officer. Three months later, on the Sunday of Royal Tigers' Weekend, a dedication service of Royal Tigers' Wood was held at Bagworth. The Provost of Leicester, the Very Revd Derek Hole, officiated, and a memorable address was given by the Revd Malcolm Stonestreet, who had served as a National Service officer in 1st R Leicesters in Cyprus during the Emergency in 1955-6. After the Service, John Mills oversaw the planting of the Mercer's Oaks, fittingly in a prominent location next to the Memorial Stone.

The Annual Regimental Service on Royal Tigers' Weekend was held at Royal Tigers' Wood in 1998 and 2002, with the services being conducted by former officers of the Regiment, the Revd Ben Elliott and the Revd Tom Hiney MC in respective years. Another is planned for 2009. Additionally, at 1100 hours on 11 November each year, under the leadership of Colonel W G (Bill) Dawson, and attended by local organizations and clergy, a short remembrance service is held beside the memorial stone.

Over the succeeding years, most of the trees remained in good shape and grew well. The non-survivors were replaced as necessary. The site was developed to include culverts to ease access across, to and from the area of the special trees, and a spring-fed pond near the top of the wood to assist the wildlife and increase the visual diversity. In autumn 2005, the 'Forest of Flowers' project, organized by the Woodland Trust and the Landlife Trust, came to fruition with the sowing and planting of wildflowers in selected open spaces. The seeds germinated well and the following year there was a profusion of wild flowers, which have begun to spread further, thus improving the woodland biodiversity.

Willing assistance has continued to be given by the International Tree Foundation, the Woodland Trust, the Landlife Trust, and the Bluebell Arboretum in Smisby, thus helping to ensure that at Royal Tigers' Wood there is coherent development and an enduring feature on the County's landscape. In this way, it will be possible to maintain a lasting heritage and perpetuate a truly wonderful living memorial to The Royal Leicestershire Regiment.

Royal Tigers' Weekend and Reunions

The Reunions at Royal Tigers' Weekend, including the Annual Regimental Service in Leicester Cathedral or at Royal Tigers' Wood, continue to be well supported, including and especially by a contingent of ex-National Servicemen from the North-East from whose contribution in Korea with 1st Royal Leicesters much benefit and appreciated comradeship accrued. The AGM of the Association and Annual Dinner were for twenty-five years held at Ulverscroft Road, and since 2001 at Devonshire Place, London Road, Leicester.

The Officers' Dinner continued for many years to be held in October at the Army & Navy Club in Pall Mall, London. This later changed to a luncheon with the ladies as guests, held at the same venue on the first Saturday in December – a popular arrangement as it can be combined with Christmas shopping in London!

The Royal Tigers' Association is usually well represented at the Annual Reunion of The Royal Anglian Regiment, originally held in July at Depot The Queen's Division at Bassingbourn. In recent years it has been held at the Imperial War Museum at Duxford in September (close to the date of the Regiment's formation), and where the Royal Anglian Regiment Museum is also located. In that Museum, some scrapbooks and photographic archives of 4th (Leicestershire) Battalion are stored.

The Hindoostan Dinner Club was formed in 1966 with the aim of keeping alive the name of the Regiment and the traditions of the WOs' & Sgts' Mess by fostering the spirit of comradeship between all members. The qualification for membership is to have served as a mess member in 1st Battalion The Royal Leicestershire Regiment at any time from 1 January 1948 to 1 September 1964.

The idea for the club was formed in conversation at Tommy Marston's pub, 'The Three Horseshoes' at Willoughby on the Wold in Leicestershire, between former WOs, 'Mick' O'Sullivan, 'Sandy' Sanderson, John Sheppard and Tommy Marston, the latter becoming its first President. The first dinner, with fourteen members present, was held at The Saracen's Head, Leicester, on the first Saturday in November 1966. Initially it was a men-only dinner but in 1988 ladies and guests were made welcome.

The membership has fluctuated over the years and slowly dwindled. Before Tommy Marston died, he wrote a letter to the new President, Roger Jones, indicating that he wanted the Club to go out 'with a bang and not a whimper'. With that in mind, and whilst members are still fit and able, the final dinner is planned to be held on 7 November 2009, and so will end a proud chapter of the Regiment that will have lasted forty-three years.

The Cyprus Veterans Association (CVA) was set up by ex-Sergeant R (Bob) Freeman in 1997. The CVA has its own badge incorporating the 'Dirty Duck' emblem of 51 Indep Inf Bde, encircled by the words 'Cyprus Veterans Association' above the Roman Numeral XVII. It also has a standard which incorporates the emblem, and the Regiment's and the Association's names. It was dedicated at St Peter's Church, Braunstone, in October 2003, near to which the CVA's annual reunions are held in October. In May 2005, at the National Memorial Arboretum at Alrewas in Staffordshire, a service of thanksgiving was conducted by Revd A D Barlow (a former National Service officer in the Regiment). A plaque was dedicated and an oak sapling planted in remembrance of men of the Regiment who lost their lives during the Cyprus Emergency 1955-58.

Starting in 1947 under the guidance of Lieutenant Colonel Peter Upcher, an annual reunion was held of the 50th/8th/1st Battalion The Leicestershire Regiment. At the outset about 300 former members of the Battalion attended, many travelling from the London area and some from Manchester. Held in the autumn in Leicester, the reunion continued successfully until time began to take its toll and attendance figures dropped off markedly. By 2005, only four people attended. The last reunion was in 2006, with only three attending.

Memorials

In addition to all those in the Regimental Chapel (see Chapter 12), The Royal Leicestershire Regiment has been commemorated on a number of memorials which have been dedicated in recent years.

There are three that deal with the Malaya and Burma campaigns 1941-5. On 9 June 1982, at RMA Sandhurst, in the presence of Aileen, Viscountess Slim (widow of the Commander Fourteenth Army in Burma 1943-45), the Rt Revd Robin Woods KCVO dedicated The Indian Divisions Memorial 1939-45. On Burma teak wood panels are inscribed the names of units which formed the brigades and the sixteen Indian divisions which fought in that war. 1st Leicesters had been in the 15th Indian Infantry Brigade (15 Ind Inf Bde) of 11th Ind Div in Malaya in 1941-2; 2nd Leicesters had been in 16 Inf Bde and 7th Leicesters in 14 Inf Bde of 3rd Ind Div (The Chindits) in Burma in 1944.

The Chindit Memorial was unveiled on 16 October 1990 by HRH The Prince Philip, Duke of Edinburgh, on Victoria Embankment, London, situated next to the MOD Main Building. On it, among many other units, are recorded 2nd Battalion and 7th Battalion The Leicestershire Regiment. A second Chindit Memorial was unveiled on 10 June 2007 by Colonel The Viscount Slim OBE DL in the Burma Star section of the National Memorial Arboretum at Alrewas in Staffordshire. Its inscriptions are similar to those on the Embankment Memorial, and that below the Chinthe Badge reads: 'The multi-national Special Force which engaged the Japanese within enemy lines Burma in 1943 and 1944. Their motto reads "The boldest measures are the safest".' A picture of this memorial is in the plate section.

In 2000, the old memorial at Ladysmith in South Africa was refurbished in time for the centenary of the Relief of the Siege, an event which was attended by members of The Royal Tigers' Association. At a similar time, the Record Office for Leicestershire, Leicester & Rutland (ROLLR) held a mobile exhibition 'Tigers Caged' to commemorate the Defence of Ladysmith 1899-1900. This toured the county and was very popular, becoming the longest-running exhibition that the ROLLR could remember.

In April 2001, the Rats of Tobruk Association memorial was dedicated at the National Memorial Arboretum. The Regiment was represented by Capt R L (Richard) Lane and by Tommy Marston, who had fought at Tobruk in 2nd Leicesters in 1941.

A new memorial was dedicated at Le Havre on 10 September 2000, the 56th Anniversary of 1st Leicesters' assault on the city. It features a Churchill tank. A year later another ceremony took place to celebrate the completion of the project. A low memorial wall, orientated north-south, symbolizes the 'Atlantic Wall' (which was breached by the Allied

Chindit Memorial, Embankment, London. *M K Goldschmidt*

landings on 'D-Day 1944') with two wings representing the fortifications Montivilliers-Harfleur and Montivilliers-Octeville, near Le Havre. Regimental plaques, including a stainless steel one of The Royal Leicestershire Regiment, are mounted on those walls.

On 29 August 2003, at Asmarka in Norway, a plaque was unveiled by HM King Harald V of Norway to commemorate the actions of 20-21 April 1940 which took place in and

HM King Harald V of Norway at the Asmarka Memorial. *Trustees R Anglian Regt*

around Asmarka, when British and German land forces faced each other for the first time in Norway. This is in memory of those Norwegian and British personnel who were killed. From all the British regiments present in 1940, the only British veteran able to attend was John Sheppard DCM[4], Vice-Chairman of The Royal Tigers' Association, and he was accompanied by Captain R J (Bob) Allen, Chairman of the Association. After the ceremony attended by thirty Norwegian veterans, John and Bob presented to HM The King a recently published copy of *Fighting Tigers* in which the actions of the 1/5th Battalion in Norway are

338

chronicled. They also laid floral tributes in honour of other British regiments that could not be represented. Ten years before, the Lord Mayor of Leicester[5] hosted a reception for those who had taken part in the 1940 ill-fated Norway Campaign. It had been attended by members of 1/5th Leicesters, 5th Foresters, and the RN and RM.

On 21 September 2004, a Service of Dedication was held at the Ulster Ash Grove of the National Memorial Arboretum at Alrewas in Staffordshire in memory of the eighteen members of The Royal Anglian Regiment who had lost their lives in Northern Ireland over the period 1971-89. Among the dead to whom an individual memorial plaque and ash tree was dedicated was one man who had previously served in Tiger Company: Private R M (Robert) Mason, who was killed while serving in 2 R Anglian in Belfast in 1972.

Three years later, in October 2007, the Armed Forces Memorial was dedicated at Alrewas by His Grace The Archbishop of Canterbury, in the presence of HM The Queen, and TRH The Duke of Edinburgh, The Prince of Wales and The Duchess of Cornwall. It is the first national memorial dedicated to the men and women of the United Kingdom Armed Forces (Regular and Reserve) killed on duty or as a result of terrorist action since 1 January 1948, the day after the Commonwealth War Graves Commission (CWGC) ceased being responsible for new war graves and cemeteries. On that Memorial are engraved the names of those Royal Leicesters who died in Korea, Cyprus and elsewhere, including the above-mentioned Robert Mason.

The long-running and successfully concluded saga of the Hohenzollern Redoubt, the rubbish dump and the Memorial, merits being described in some detail.

In November 2004, a phone call from Capt Richard Lane sparked a major campaign by the *Leicester Mercury* to protect part of a First World War battlefield. He had been to visit the Hohenzollern Redoubt – once a German stronghold in northern France – and was horrified to see it was being turned into a dumping ground. The hill in a field near the town of Auchy les Mines had been fiercely fought over on 13 October 1915. On that day the 4th and 5th Leicesters had taken part in the attack by the 46th (North Midland) Division on the heavily fortified German position known as the Hohenzollern Redoubt in the closing days of the Battle of Loos. By the end of the day those two battalions had incurred 660 casualties with nearly 300 being killed. Every officer in the 4th Battalion who took part in the attack had either been killed or wounded in a few hours of fighting. Overall, the Division suffered 3,763 casualties, over 90 per cent of whom have no known grave.

The *Leicester Mercury* broke the story on 8 November 2004. There were first-hand reports and pictures from the site, with photos of soldiers and the battleground at the time. An editorial promised action. French officials faced a barrage of protest over the work to transform the historically important ground into a waste tip. Leicestershire politicians were united in their condemnation and two of its MPs pressed the Foreign Secretary to step in. In addition, the *Leicester Mercury* printed a letter in French protesting against the plans, and invited readers to cut it out, sign it and send it to the paper to forward to the Mayor of Auchy les Mines.

Three days later, the CWGC said it was investigating reports that remains were being disturbed in a French field. An open letter to President Jacques Chirac from editor Nick

Carter appeared on the front pages of the *Leicester Mercury*. It said, 'On behalf of the readers of the *Leicester Mercury*, I appeal to you, as leader of the French people, to stop this dumping until a proper inquiry can be held into what should happen to the site and the remains of the British dead buried there.'

On 13 November, Auchy's Mayor, Jean Clarisse, promised the British Consul that any remains found at the site would be treated with respect. By now, a thousand people had signed letters calling for action. Two days later, the landowner, Eugene Bernus, agreed to stop the work on the field. Within a week the Mayor signed a decree closing the landfill site to protect the whole area, and promised to turn the field into a historical site and erect a permanent memorial. The Regimental Association had every reason to be very grateful to the *Leicester Mercury*, and particularly the Editor, Mr Nick Carter, for its fervent campaign to halt the desecration of this important site and to thank Captain Richard Lane for bringing this matter to the attention of the public and the Press.

A team of historians in Lincoln enlisted the financial support of the Lincolnshire Cooperative Society, who undertook to manufacture, transport and erect the memorial on site as well as finance it. Consequently, on 13 October 2006, the elegant monument was dedicated, bearing the names of the eight regiments involved in the battle ninety-one years before to the day. Eight members of The Royal Tigers' Association and representatives of The Royal Lincolnshire Regiment, The Sherwood Foresters and the Royal Artillery were present at the unveiling of the memorial by HM's Consul-General.

John Sheppard DCM lays the Regimental Wreath at the Hohenzollern Redoubt Memorial, October 2006. *Trustees R Anglian Regiment*

Anniversaries

The 300th Anniversary of the raising of the 17th Regiment of Foot took place in 1988, but for obvious reasons it could not be celebrated as a Tercentenary of the Regiment because it no longer existed. A '1688 Committee' was formed in 1986 to plan the celebrations which centred around Royal Tigers' Weekend 1988. On 25 June, the Band and Drums of 2 R Anglian Beat Retreat in Victoria Park in front of some 3,000 spectators, and the Lord Mayor of Leicester, Councillor Guy Collis, took the salute. This was followed by the Annual Dinner of the Association at Ulverscroft Road which 450 members and their guests attended. On the Sunday, the Tercentenary Service was held at Leicester Cathedral in the form of a Sung Eucharist. After a most memorable service, some 600 members of the Association marched past the Lord Lieutenant of Leicestershire. Then the City of Leicester and the County of Leicestershire jointly hosted a reception in the City Rooms.

Other events took place during the year: the Hindoostan Club held a special dinner and an Officers' Ladies' Night was held in the School Hall at Uppingham School. It was a most apt venue, the place where so many Old Uppinghamian members of the Regiment would have taken their meals during their schooldays. The seven-course dinner was presided over by Major W G St S Brogan DL, the 1688 Committee Chairman. Various items of memorabilia were commissioned for sale during the year, including an 8" high china figurine of Colonel Solomon Richards, who raised the Regiment on 27 September 1688, and an enamel pill box (see plate section).

The only thing missing from the 250th Anniversary held in Leicestershire in July 1938 was that in 1988 there was no repeat of naming a train. In 1938, a 'Patriot' Class locomotive, 5503, had been named 'The Leicestershire Regiment'. It should be said, however, that in 1985, in honour of the 300th Anniversary of the raising of the 9th (Norfolk), 10th (Lincolnshire) and 12th (Suffolk) Regiments, an electric locomotive on the East of England Line was named 'The Royal Anglian Regiment'.

In May 1990, around seventy former members of 1/5th Leicesters, along with men of 5th Foresters, the other battalion in 148 Inf Bde, returned to Norway to commemorate the 50th Anniversary of that campaign. Two days were spent touring the battlefields near Lillehammer. On 17 May (Norwegian National Day), wreaths were laid at the Lillehammer War Cemetery, followed by a service at the Cathedral during which an altar cross from St Michael's and All Angels' Church in Leicester was given to the Cathedral in commemoration of the British soldiers who had died in defence of the town in 1940. Those travelling were of the clear opinion that the North Sea crossing on a Fred Olsen Line ferry was far more comfortable than the 1940's sea transport!

In May 1991, Tommy Marston, Vice-Chairman of The Royal Tigers' Association, and four other former members of 2nd Leicesters, returned to Crete fifty years after their gallant ten-day battle in defence of the island on 20 May to 1 June 1941. During the visit, ceremonies were held at several memorials, monuments and cemeteries. In the presence of HRH The Duke of Kent, on behalf of the Association, Lieutenant Colonel J E D (Derek) Watson DSO[6] laid a wreath at the Suda Bay CWGC cemetery at a special service. The UK Crete Veterans Association then presented a large cheque to the Greek Red Cross in appreciation of the bravery of the Crete people in succouring escaping British servicemen in 1941.

The 60th Anniversary of VJ Day was a poignant commemoration for the Regiment as 1st Leicesters had fought throughout the Malayan Campaign and in Singapore before captivity for three and a half years 1942-45, and 2nd and 7th Leicesters had taken part in the second Chindit Expedition in 1944. A parade in the form of a drumhead service was held on 20 August 1995 in Victoria Park in Leicester, at which the Regiment's silver drums were piled. Those drums had been presented in 1930 at a parade in Catterick commanded by Lieutenant Colonel P H Creagh DSO[7], commanding 2nd Leicesters. The Royal Tigers' Association contingent on 20 August 1995 was commanded by Lieutenant Colonel J P N (Pat) Creagh, his son.

On 20 October 1996, the 50th Anniversary of the opening of the Princeton (USA) Battlefield State Park was held. It was attended by the Chairman of The Royal Tigers' Association, and the 1777 Battle was re-enacted. It was at Princeton, on 3 January 1777, that the 17th Regiment, 240 strong, under Lieutenant Colonel Mawhood, was surrounded by superior numbers of General Washington's American Army. Fixing bayonets, it charged and broke through the American right wing, incurring 101 casualties in killed, wounded and missing, and continued its march to join up with General Cornwallis' British Force. While there is no surviving record of any formal accolade having been conferred on the Regiment to commemorate this gallant action[8], the Regiment was permitted the unique distinction of bearing an unbroken laurel wreath on its crest. This first manifested itself on officers' silver buttons before 1830, from which it could be surmised that it had been adopted on or about the 50th anniversary of that battle (1827), which was but two years after HM King George IV conferred on the Regiment the badge of the 'Royal Tiger' superscribed 'Hindoostan' in 1825. Now, at Princeton, in 1966, the authorities invited Colonel John Heggs to give a presentation on the battle from a British (or 17th Regiment) point of view. He titled it 'We don't think we lost'!

On 3 January 2002, the Chairman of the Association, Captain Bob Allen, represented the 17th Regiment at the 225th anniversary of the Battle of Princeton. A re-enactment, performed by some 1,200 people, took four hours. It was followed by a service at the Cenotaph on the battlefield, at which the Chairman laid a wreath to honour those of the 17th of Foot who fought and died on that day 225 years before, and also on behalf of all the Crown Forces who took part, and who are suitably commemorated. Finally, on behalf of the Regiment, a silver tiger, mounted on a slate block, and inscribed to commemorate the anniversary, was presented to John Mills, the curator of the battlefield and a good friend of the Regiment. It was he who had brought the Mercer's Oaks to Royal Tigers' Wood in 1995. The silver tiger was placed in the Museum in Thomas Clark's farmhouse and forms the basis of a section devoted to the 17th Regiment of Foot.

On 18 July 2002, at 1900 hours (to coincide with his name being read out at the Menin Gate at Ypres), a short ceremony was held at Leicester Football Club at Welford Road to remember Frank Tarr, a former member of the Club, an England International, and officer in 1/4th Leicesters, who had been killed in action in July 1915[9]. About thirty members of The Royal Tigers' Association and a dozen representatives of the Club listened to the Regimental Secretary's description of the ceremony at Ypres and Frank Tarr's life. This was followed by an extremely moving reading about Farr's death by the Chairman of the Regiment's Trustees (Colonel Richard Wilkes), before buglers of 2 R Anglian sounded the Last Post.

On the occasion of the commemoration of the 60th anniversary of the end of the Second World War on 10 July 2005, 'Dixie' Dean and John Sheppard DCM had the honour of lunching with HM The Queen and HRH The Duke of Edinburgh at Buckingham Palace. Major V W J Roussel MC[10] and Mr R P Savage[11] represented the Regiment at the special commemorative service in Westminster Abbey attended by 2,000 veterans. Captain P W Rogers MC[12], Mr L V Cheney, Mr T Sansome, Mr R Vincent and Mr D Foran represented the Regiment amongst the 10,000 veterans at the nostalgic, reflective and commemorative events on Horse Guards Parade during the afternoon. About 200,000 people packed the Mall to greet Her Majesty and The Duke of Edinburgh after they arrived back at the Palace from Horse Guards Parade where they had carried out a review of the many thousands of veterans. They had been preceded by 724 Standards, including the Royal Tigers' Association Standard carried by Mr Denis Foran, and a 150-strong Tri-Service Band.

Organized by ex-SQMS (RAPC) Cis Keightley MBE, a party of thirty-five associated with the Regiment attended the ceremonies in France to commemorate the 90th anniversary of the Battle of Loos in which a great number of the Regiment had died in 1915. On Saturday, 24 September 2005, the first visit was to the CWGC cemetery at 'Duds Corner' where so many members of The Leicestershire Regiment are listed on the panels as having 'no known grave'. The next stop was the cemetery at the Dressing Station 'St Mary's', where the people of Haines held a service of remembrance and the Association Standard, with the Standards of other regiments, was paraded alongside those of the French. This was followed by an exhibition of Great War articles and artefacts, and by a *vin d'honneur* while the pipers of the London Irish Rifles entertained the crowds. On Sunday morning there was a parade of all the military contingents for a service and wreath-laying ceremony at the cemetery at Loos, concluding with a march past led by the pipers of the London Scottish Regiment and the London Irish Rifles.

In 2005, the Malaysian Government approached the British Government to seek approval to present their new Pingat Jasa Malaysia medal (commemorating forty years since the end of Confrontation with Indonesia) to British veterans and others who had served in operations in Malaya/Malaysia between August 1957 and August 1966. Of course, all those serving in 1st Battalion The Royal Leicestershire Regiment on its 1963-4 tour in the Borneo Territories qualified. In February 2007, in Leicester, Colonel Tajri Alwi of the Malaysian Army presented medals posthumously to seventeen widows and then to 105 Royal Leicesters veterans at a ceremony at which he declared that it was 'a great pleasure to stand before all those who have served my beloved country'.

Books
A number of books which feature the Regiment have been published in recent years:

From Leicestershire to the Somme by Major Aubrey G de A Moore MC. Second volume of his memoirs, finished in 1992 just before he died aged ninety-eight years.

Recollections of his experiences when serving in 5th Leicesters for the whole of the First World War. ISBN 9780862990367.

Tigers Never Sleep by Charles R Pell (1994). Describes his experiences in 1st Leicesters in N W Europe 1944-47. ISBN 0-9524656-0-4.

The Korean War 1950-53: The West Confronts Communism by Michael Hickey (1999). Most regrettably it is inaccurate and disparaging about the part played by 1st R Leicesters in battle at Maryang San in November 1951. Ironically it is one of the Regiment's battle honours, and consequently the President of the Association challenged the author, who undertook to amend the text in a subsequent reprint.

The Tigers – 6th, 7th, 8th & 9th (Service) Battalions of The Leicestershire Regiment by Matthew Richardson (2000). Covers the actions of those battalions in The Leicestershire Brigade in the First World War. ISBN 0 85025 719-8.

A Tiger and a Fusilier by Derek Eaton (2001). Describes two Leicester VC holders, Private W H Buckingham VC, The Leicestershire Regiment, and Captain R Gee VC MC, The Royal Fusiliers. ISBN 0-9528948-2-3.

Fighting Tigers by Matthew Richardson (2002). Covers fourteen epic actions of battalions of the Regiment, from the Boer War in 1899 to Borneo in 1964. ISBN 0 85025 895-X.

No Need to Worry by Peter J de A Moore MC[14] (2nd Edition 2002). Recollections of service in the 2/5th Battalion in North Africa, Italy, Greece and Austria in the Second World War. ISBN: 9780947828950.

The British Battalion by Chye Kooi Loong (Revised in 2004)[13]. Covers the 1st Leicesters (and its incorporation with the 2nd East Surreys into The British Battalion) in the Malayan Campaign 1941-42 during the Second World War, the fall of Singapore and captivity by the Japanese. As a boy, the author had watched the Battle of Kampar take place around his home. ISBN 967 9935 18 3.

Tigers along the Tigris by E J Thompson (2007). A reprint of a book originally published in 1919, *Beyond Baghdad with The Leicesters*, about the 2nd Leicesters in Mesopotamia in 1917. ISBN 1846773660.

Single-handed: Letters from the Front by Michael Hickey (2008). It is about Kenneth Dalgleish, who lost an arm in 1915 while serving in 1/4th Leicesters in France and remained in the Army. ISBN 9781846242250.

To the Last Round: The Leicestershire and Rutland Home Guard 1940-1945 by Austin J Ruddy (2007). ISBN 978 1 85983 559 3.

8th King's Royal Irish Hussars' Korean War 1950-51, CD-ROM on the 2007 seminar on the campaign during which the Hussars' tanks supported 1st Royal Leicesters. Contains input from three Royal Leicesters: Geoff Havilland, Monty Cairns and David Grove.

Do Birds Still Sing in Hell? by Horace 'Jim' Greasley (2008). An autobiographical work about his time in 2/5th Leicesters and as a POW in Germany and Poland 1940–45. ISBN 1905988796.

Marching with The Tigers by Michael Goldschmidt (2009). Describes the actions and events of all elements of the Regiment from 1955 to 1975. ISBN 978 1 84884 035 5 (this book!).

Miscellany

After the disbandment of the 4th Battalion The Royal Anglian Regiment and Tiger Company, much of the best and most important silver belonging to The Royal Leicestershire Regiment was given to The Royal Anglian Regiment – some is held at its RHQ but most is used by the 2nd Battalion. On two occasions since 1975, the Regiment saw fit to sell off those of its smaller items of silver which were no longer in routine use. Most items were bought by their former respective Mess members, be they officers or WOs and sergeants. Of the silver still belonging to The Royal Leicestershire Regiment, some is held on long loan by the 3rd Battalion The Royal Anglian Regiment (TA), and some by the City and County authorities, where it can be seen on display in the Lord Mayor of Leicester's Rooms, the Judges' Chambers, and at County Hall.

In 2002, Denis Foran found the grave of Lance Sergeant Philip Smith VC in Glasnevin Cemetery, Dublin. Born at Lurgan in Ireland in 1825, after his military career he had lived in Dublin to the age of eighty-one years, and was buried unmarked in a family grave. Like many VC holders, he had risen from obscurity to win the highest award for valour and then returned to obscurity. Such a sequence was especially common with Irishmen who served in the British Army, whose relatives were reluctant to speak of the military connections. In December 2003, a Regimental party travelled to Dublin to hold a memorial service in that cemetery with fourteen descendants of Philip Smith who had come from England, Scotland and Ireland to attend the service. In torrential rain a memorial stone was put in place and wreaths laid by relatives. The President of The Royal Tigers' Association, Major General A J G (Tony) Pollard CB CBE DL, gave an address about Philip Smith and his gallant action at Sevastopol in 1855. In June 2004, twelve members of his family came to Royal Tigers' Weekend to attend the Annual Regimental Service in Leicester Cathedral and after lunch saw the Cuneo painting of Philip Smith winning his VC, at that time housed in the New Walk Museum.

The centenary of *The Green Tiger* took place in 2004. Its first edition was published at 3d a copy in October 1904 by Corporal Leslie Wadsworth of the 2nd Leicesters. It was such a success that the second issue was published on 30 November of that year at a reduced price of 2d; the journal was smaller containing twelve pages. Circumstances prevented its publication in December that year, but the third issue appeared in January 1905 and editions continued fairly regularly thereafter. Captain A H Buchanan-Dunlop then became the Editor, the paper being chiefly for the 2nd Battalion.

In April 1906, it became the Regimental Journal in the sense that it gave news of all battalions and the Depot. When the 2nd Battalion went to India in 1906 and the 1st Battalion returned to England, Major H Stoney Smith became Editor and acted as such for some years.

By January 1910, the Journal contained sixteen pages and by January 1913 twenty pages. But publication ceased in July 1914 – the August issue was in the press but never published as the 1st Battalion went to France with the British Expeditionary Force.

Publication started again in November 1917 with volume number XI and was produced every month until November 1918. It then settled down to be produced less frequently, but continued even throughout the Second World War. Throughout all its years *The Green Tiger* has been regarded as holding a very important position in the life of the Regiment. The 'Last Edition' was published in 1964, after which reports about Regimental activities appeared in *Castle*, the journal of The Royal Anglian Regiment. From 1966 The Royal Leicestershire Regiment/Royal Tigers' Association Newsletter continued to be published until 2003 when it was retitled *The Green Tiger*.

In August 2006 the Government announced that all 306 soldiers who had been shot at dawn for cowardice or desertion in the First World War were to be granted posthumous pardons. Among the pardoned were two members of The Leicestershire Regiment who had been found guilty of desertion: Private E A (Ernest) Beaumont of the 2nd Battalion, aged twenty-seven, shot at dawn on 24 June 1915 and buried at St Vaast Post British cemetery at Richebourg-L'Avoue near Béthune in France; and Private Joseph Nisbet, of the 1st Battalion, aged twenty-six, shot at dawn on 23 August 1918 and buried in the Nine Elms British cemetery near Poperinge, Flanders. May they and their families *'requiescant in pace'*.

And so 2008 finds The Tigers marching on. Despite no one having become Tigers in the original sense since the time of the disbandment of The Royal Leicestershire Regiment (Territorial) in 1971, or of Tiger Company 4th Battalion The Royal Anglian Regiment in 1975, the number of people who actively support The Royal Tigers' Association has held up. Royal Tigers' Weekend is still held annually in Leicester. The Association's members attend many private and public events, at which its Standard is often proudly paraded – and given almost similar honour as were the Colours of old. They have been prominent during the various activities linked to the TA's Centenary Year. In honour of that year, HRH The Duke of Gloucester, Colonel-in-Chief The Royal Anglian Regiment, was joined by TA soldiers from across the East Midlands on 8 November when at Quorn and Woodhouse Station, on the preserved Great Central Railway in Leicestershire, he renamed the Oliver Cromwell steam engine 'The Territorial Army 1908-2008'.

Men too from the counties of Leicestershire and Rutland – both Regulars and Volunteers – serving in namesake subunits of The Royal Anglian Regiment, have been on operational service abroad in 2008. Long may that tradition and way of life continue, wearing the Tiger button and serving under the Colours on which many of the Royal Leicesters' battle honours and the Royal Tiger are displayed.

It is now possible to understand how much the Tiger badge inspired and animated every unit of the Regiment. For the fighting qualities of the tiger continually sprang forth in the high temperatures of the sports field, the boxing ring and the battlefield. In those arenas, wherever special efforts were required, the battle cry 'Come on The Tigers' always achieved instant response.

In addition to all the activities of the residual members of The Tigers, the three legacies of the Regiment – the Regimental Chapel in Leicester Cathedral, the Museum in Newarke Houses and Royal Tigers' Wood at Bagworth – provide the enduring memory of the deeds of so many fine soldiers across the globe … 'ordinary men doing extraordinary things'.

Notes

1   The Regiment's original facing colour (used on uniforms and the Regimental Colours) had been white, for which reason one of the Regiment's earlier nicknames had been the 'Lilywhites'. From 1881 (when infantry regiments adopted County titles), white facings became the established colour for all English (except Royal) regiments. In 1931 The Leicesters' facing colour changed to pearl grey, which therefore still lives on whenever this Standard is on parade.
2   See Chapter 13, Note 20.
3   Sadly this historic tree has since fallen down, but has been replaced.
4   John Sheppard was awarded the DCM for his actions when he and the men of his Mortar Platoon of 1/5th Leicesters stoutly defended a vital position until all ammunition had been exhausted and when the woods and buildings around their position were on fire. During that fight John had the personal distinction of knocking out the first two German tanks in the Second World War – with a PIAT which, for lack of training ammunition, he had not fired before.
5   See Appendix G for Cllr Robert Wigglesworth.
6   Derek Watson was CO 1st R Leicesters 1953-56 – see Chapter 1.
7   See Chapter 2, Note 9.
8   The 2nd Battalion having disbanded in 1802, the official books of the 1st Battalion were lost in the wreck of the *Hannah*, the ship transporting the Regiment from Kurrachee to Bombay in March 1840, when all baggage, including the mess plate, had to be thrown overboard to lighten the ship.
9   See Appendix G.
10 He had been awarded an immediate MC for his actions commanding A Coy 1st Leicesters near Breda in Belgium on 21 October 1944.
11 Raymond Savage was the only officer to have served in the regiment in the ill-fated Norway and Malayan campaigns. Unlike many 1/5th Leicesters in Norway in 1940, he avoided captivity and escaped on foot into Sweden. Repatriated to England, he was immediately posted to 1st Leicesters in Penang, with whom he served and in The British Battalion until the surrender of Singapore. He was a Japanese PoW 1942-45.
12 Initially a 7th Leicester, Philip Rogers had been awarded the MC for his actions while serving with 9th Y & L in the Arakan, Burma, in 1945.
13 A great friend of the Regiment, he was awarded the MBE in 2008 in recognition of his efforts to preserve the Green Ridge battleground as part of the Battle of Kampar in Malaya in December 1941. Aged twelve, he had first met The British Battalion during the battle.
14 Peter Moore was awarded the MC for his action as Lt Platoon Commander in 2/5th Leicesters at Mondaino, Italy, on 30 August 1944.

Appendix A

Honours and Awards
1955-2008

This appendix contains details of those who served in The Royal Leicestershire Regiment, the 4th (Leicestershire) Battalion, and in the Leicestershire Companies of the 5th and 7th Battalions The Royal Anglian Regiment during the period 1955-75, who were decorated at that time or subsequently. **Those serving with the Royal Leicesters at the time of their award are shown in bold.** Ranks are as at the time of the award. Awards made before 1955 are not included.

1955	KCB	Lt Gen Sir Colin B Callander KBE MC	Military Secretary, War Office
	CBE (civil)	Maj (Retd) F E Oliver TD DL	Political and public service in Leicester
	MSM[1]	**WO1 (RSM) H Brown**	**Service to the Regiment**
	MSM	**WO2 G B Payne**	**Service to the Regiment**
1956	CB (civil)	Col (Retd) A Halkyard MC TD DL	Service to the TA
	OBE	Lt Col (Retd) H A G Havilland MBE	QM, RMA Sandhurst
	OBE (civil)	Lt Col (Retd) R G G Harvey DSO JP DL	Service to SSAFA in NI
1957	Knight Bachelor	Lt Col (Retd) K G F Ruddle TD DL	Political and public service to Rutland
	CB	Maj Gen J M K Spurling CBE DSO	COS, HQ Northern Command, York
	MC	Maj O J Mirylees	3rd Bn The Malay Regt, Malaya
	MC	Lt E M C D Taylor	Pl Comd, 1 R Lincolns, Malaya
	MID	**Pte T M Jervis**	**MT Dvr, 1 R Leicesters, Cyprus**
1958	CB	Maj Gen D A Kendrew CBE DSO	GOC and Director Ops, Cyprus
	OBE	**Lt Col A W D Nicholls MC**	**CO 1 R Leicesters, Cyprus**
	MBE	**WO1 T J Marston**	**RSM, 1 R Leicesters, Cyprus**
	MBE	**WO2 H Almen**	**CSM, 5 R Leicesters (TA)**
	MID	**Maj M St G Pallot**	**2IC, 1 R Leicesters, Cyprus**
	MID	**Maj P E B Badger**	**Coy Comd, 1 R Leicesters, Cyprus**
	MID	**2Lt A J G Pollard**	**Pl Comd, 1 R Leicesters, Cyprus**
	MID	**Cpl N James**	**Sect Comd, 1 R Leicesters, Cyprus**
1959	MBE	WO2 G B Payne	RQMS, 1 Foresters, Malaya
	MID	Capt G H Greaves	QM, 1 Foresters, Malaya
1960	OBE	Lt Col J W B Marshall	SO1, HQ Aldershot District
1961	MBE	Maj (Retd) J Clamp DCM MM	2IC, Leicestershire & Rutland ACF

	MC	Capt T B F Hiney	2nd Bn Ghana Regt, The Congo
1962	Knight Bachelor	Maj (Retd) F E Oliver CBE TD DL	For political service
	MSM	**WO1 J T Marston MBE**	**Service to the Regiment**
1963	KCMG	Maj Gen D A Kendrew CB CBE DSO	Governor of Western Australia
1964	OBE	**Lt Col S A Smith MBE**	**CO 4/5 R Leicesters (TA)**
	MC	**Lt A E Thompson**	**Pl Comd, 1 R Leicesters, Borneo**
	MC	**2Lt M J Peele**	**Pl Comd, 1 R Leicesters, Borneo**
	BEM	**CSgt G A B Davis**	**Det Comd, 1 R Leicesters, Borneo**
	MID	**Lt Col P E B Badger**	**CO 1 R Leicesters, Borneo**
	MID	**Maj T Holloway**	**Coy Comd, 1 R Leicesters, Borneo**
	MID	**Capt P W Barker RA**	**Pl Comd, 1 R Leicesters, Borneo**
	MID	**LCpl W Dance**	**Sect Comd, 1 R Leicesters, Borneo**
	MID	**LCpl T J Reece**	**Signals Pl, 1 R Leicesters, Borneo**
	Queen's Commendation	**Cpl G Booth**	**1 R Leicesters, Watchet**
1967	MBE	Capt A D Russell	QM 3 HQ & Sig Regt, Bulford
	MBE	**WO2 D G Grove**	**17 AYT, Leicester**
1968	Knight Bachelor	Lt Col (Retd) Hon H A P Fisher QC	High Court Judge
	MBE	**Lt N H P Jenks MM**	**RSM, 4 R Anglian, Aden/Malta**
1969	CBE	Col D S Carden	Defence Attaché Baghdad
	OBE	**Lt Col R G Wilkes TD DL**	**CO 4/5 R Leicesters (TA)**
1971	CBE (civil)	Maj (Retd) M A L Cripps DSO TD QC	For public service in the judiciary
	OBE	Lt Col R E J Gerrard-Wright MBE	CO 2 R Anglian, Belfast
	OBE	Lt Col E Turnill	CO Desert Regiment, Oman
	Bravery Medal[2]	Lt Col E Turnill OBE	CO Desert Regiment, Oman
1972	MBE	Maj R H Robinson	SO2, HQ Southern Command
	MC	Capt S M Brogan	Coy Offr, 22 SAS, Oman
	DSM[3]	Lt Col P Worthy	CO Jebel Regiment, Oman
	MM	LCpl N Jephcote	Sect Comd, 3 R Anglian, Belfast
	MID	Sgt D J Foran	Pl Sgt, 1 R Anglian, Londonderry
	MID	LCpl P L Ludbrook	Sect Comd, 1 R Anglian, Londonderry
	Commendation[4]	Capt R Wright	Coy Offr, Muscat Regt, Oman

1973	MBE (Gallantry)	Capt R Howe	Bn IO, 2 R Anglian, Belfast
	MBE	Capt A E Thompson MC	SO3 Int, HQ 39 Inf Bde, Belfast
	MM	Cpl J Laker	Sect Comd, 3 RRF, County Armagh
	MID	Maj P P Young	2IC 1 R Anglian, Londonderry
1974	CBE	Col T A Cave	Defence Attaché Prague
	OBE	**Lt Col W G Wallace** TD	**CO 7 (V) R Anglian**
	DSM (Gallantry)[3]	Capt D J M Daniels	Jebel Regiment, Oman
	DSM[3]	Lt Col S A Green	COS, HQ SAF, Oman
	MBE	Maj G H Bradshaw	MIO, HQ 39 Inf Bde, Belfast
	MBE	WO1 G E Veitch	WO Admin, Jungle Warfare Wing, Malaysia
	MID	Capt A E Thompson MBE MC	IO, 2 R Anglian, Londonderry
	MID	Lt Col R E J Gerrard-Wright OBE	CO 2 R Anglian, Belfast
1975	OBE	Lt Col S A Green	COS, HQ SAF, Oman
	BEM	**CSgt M E Taylor**	**CQMS, Tiger Coy 4 R Anglian**
	MID	CSgt C Mallett	Pl Comd, 3 R Anglian, Londonderry
	MID	Lt Col P P Young	CO 11 UDR, Portadown
1977	CBE	Brig R E J Gerrard-Wright OBE	Comd 39 Inf Bde, Belfast
	CBE	Col K Burch MBE	COS, HQ 2 Armd Div, Lübbecke
	OBE	Lt Col R H Robinson MBE	Comd Union Defence Force
1980	CBE	Brig A F F H Robertson	Comd British Forces Belize
	OBE	Lt Col F A H Swallow	CO 5 (V) R Anglian
	MBE	Maj A J J Pryce-Howells TD	OC 222 (V) Fd Amb
	MID	Lt Col A J G Pollard	CO 1 R Anglian, Belfast
	MID	Capt K M Ryan	IO, 1 R Anglian, Belfast
	MID	CSgt P A Cookson	Pl Comd, 1 R Anglian, Belfast
1981	MID	Capt K M Ryan	SO3, HQ 39 Inf Bde, Belfast
1982	DSO	Maj C P B Keeble	2IC, 2 Para, Falkland Islands
	OBE	Lt Col R Howe MBE	CO 2 R Anglian, Londonderry
	OBE (civil)	Maj (Retd) E J Townsend TD	Service to the Charity CARE
	BEM	Sgt R C Willmott ACC	Cook Sgt, 13 Sig Regt
	MID	WO2 R Travis	Asst IO, 10 UDR, Belfast
1983	BEM	CSgt J McBride	2IC COP, 3 RRF, Hollywood
1984	OBE	Lt Col D W James	CO 6 (V) R Anglian
1985	CB	Maj Gen R E J Gerrard-Wright CBE	Director TA & Cadets, MOD
	CB	Maj Gen K Burch CBE	Director Personnel, MOD
	CBE	Brig A J G Pollard	Comd British Forces Belize

	CBE (civil)	2Lt (Retd) D C Samworth DL	Service to food and meat marketing
1986	OBE	Lt Col M E Romilly	CO 2 UDR, Armagh
	MBE	Maj D W Spalding	QM 1 R Anglian, Londonderry
	MBE	WO2 T D Smith	COP Comd, 1 R Anglian, Londonderry
1987	MBE	Maj K M Ryan	Coy Comd, 1 R Anglian, Londonderry
	MBE	Lt P L Ludbrook	RSM 1 R Anglian, Londonderry
1988	Knight Bachelor	2Lt (Retd) P F Holmes MC	CEO, Shell Oil Company
1989	CBE (civil)	2Lt (Retd) P M North QC	Chairman of Road Traffic Law Review
	MBE	Maj R J Jackson	PSO, Recruit Selection Centre
	BEM	WO2 S Pollitt	Trg WO, Depot Queen's Div
	BEM	CSgt A Ali	Med Sgt, 2 R Anglian, Celle
1990	CBE (civil)	Col (Retd) R G Wilkes OBE TD DL	Service to the accountancy profession
	OBE	Lt Col M J Kinson	SO, Mil Sec's Dept, MOD
	MBE	WO1 S Dexter	Staff Asst, BMM to SANG, Riyadh
1992	CB	Maj Gen A J G Pollard CBE	GOC South West District
	CBE (civil)	Maj (Retd) C J Lowe TD	Service to education
	OBE	Lt Col P W Field	CO 7/10 UDR, Belfast
	MBE	Capt W Burford	QM, 3 R Anglian, Londonderry
1993	CBE (civil)	Brig (Retd) J A C Cowan MBE	Sec to Government Hospitality Fund
1994	MBE	Capt R W Potter	QM (Tech), 3 R Anglian, Londonderry
1995	OBE (civil)	Maj (Retd) W G St S Brogan DL	Service to the ABF
1996	MBE (civil)	Maj (Retd) P N Graham	Service to ICAC, Hong Kong
1998	Knight Bachelor	2Lt (Retd) P M North CBE QC[5]	Service to international law
2000	OBE (civil)	Lt (Retd) G N Corah DL	Service to the community in Leicestershire
	OBE (civil)	Lt Col (Retd) J L Wilson DL	Service to the community (esp St John Ambulance) in Leicestershire
2001	MBE (civil)	WO2 (Retd) R P Cunningham	Security Officer, BHC Islamabad
2005	MBE (civil)	Rev (2Lt (Retd)) G M Stonestreet	Service to the community in Cumbria
	Nawab	Capt (Retd) D E A Michael	Service to the Nizam of Hyderabad
2008	MBE (civil)	2Lt (Retd) R L Burnett	Service to music
2009	MBE	Major (Retd) A E R Peters	Service to the RBL in Somerset

The following awards were omitted from the Honours and Awards listed on Pages 274-7 in W E Underhill's *History of The Royal Leicestershire Regiment 1928-56*, published in 1958:

Albert Medal	Pte W H Foster, 1 Leicesters, Punjab, India 1931[6]
Military Cross	Maj I H Stock DLI, 1 Leicesters, the Netherlands 1945[7]
	Lt V S Boyd, 1 Leicesters, the Netherlands 1945[7]
Distinguished Conduct Medal	WO2 A Swinburn, Special Service Tps, Tobruk 1942
	Sgt D Poole, 1 Leicesters, Belgium 1944[8]
	Cpl T J Kearns, 1 Leicesters, the Netherlands 1945[7]
OBE	Lt Col G F H Stayner, HQ Tps Sudan/Eritrea, 1941
	Lt Col E A Wood, HQ Constantine Area, North Africa, 1943
	Lt Col C D Oliver, CO 122 ATk Regt RA, Burma 1945
MBE	Maj R Barratt, AFHQ Italy, 1945
	Capt M M Campbell RAMC, 7 Leicesters, Burma 1944
	Maj C S Hemsley, HQ 185 Inf Bde, NW Europe 1944-45
	Capt C E G Yates, Adv HQ 15 Army Group, North Africa/Sicily 1943
BEM	Sgt J Price, Training Unit in England, 1944
Bronze Star Medal (USA)	Brig G F H Stayner, HQ Fifth (US) Army, Italy 1944
Medal of Freedom with Bronze Palm (USA)	Lt Col R Barratt, HQ US Forces Mediterranean, 1943-46
Knight of the Order of Orange Nassau (with swords)	Capt J C Stevenson, the Netherlands 1945[9]
Croix de Guerre with Bronze Star (France)	Cpl R Smith, 1 Leicesters, France 1944
King Haakon VII Liberty Medal	Brig F W Sandars DLI, HQ 304 Inf Bde, Norway 1946

Efficiency Decoration (TD) 1955-75

Barnes, Maj T W	1963	Lowe, Maj C J	1971
Bream, Maj R D F	1970	McKenzie, Maj C L	1969
Clarke, Capt M A N	1967	Mockford, Maj P A H	1960
Coleman, Maj (Retd) R G	1966	Pickford, Maj B	1969
Cooper-Smith, Maj A R	1963	Pryce-Howells, Capt A J J	1969
Davies, Capt E N	1955	Simpson, Maj G G	1975
Dawson, Maj W G	1966	Wallace, Maj W G	1969
Harrison, Maj J B	1960	Ward, Capt J R	1974
Hartley, Maj J	1966	Wilkes, Maj J F M	1965
Holyoake, Maj D B	1961	Wilkes, Maj R G	1958
Lewis, Capt W G	1975	Wilson, Capt A A J	1963
Lodge, Capt G B	1966	Wootton, Maj G W E	1965

Efficiency Medal (Territorial) 1955-67

Bentley, WO2 F	1964	Horton, Sgt A R	1964
Broadbent, Pte R	1969	Hurst, Sgt A	1963
Clamp, Cpl C	1963	Parker, WO2 N H S	1963

Girvan, Sgt T G	1967	Simpson, WO2 T F	1968
Granger, Sgt J	1967	Tweedie, Cpl P S	1964
Harrogate, CSgt S	1959		

Efficiency Medal (TAVR) 1967-75

Collins, Pte D B P	1971	Pryor, Cpl G	1970
Copland, Sgt S	1969	Randall, LCpl M	1972
Cutting, Cpl E C	1969	Rowthorne, Sgt C	1971
Fox, Cpl J R RAPC	1972	Wainer, Pte W	1971
Hassell, Sgt K	1969	Welbourn, Cpl E R	1972
Haynes, Sgt J E L	1970	Whitehead, Sgt S RAPC	1970
Housby, Sgt H ACC	1970	Williamson, Cpl J	1972
Lee, Cpl A A	1974	Wood, WO2 D H	1970
Lee, CSgt B C	1975		

Long Service & Good Conduct Medal 1955-75

Battye, WO1 (BM) E	1964	Gilkes, CSgt J A	1958
Benham, WO1 (RSM) H D	1962	Jones, WO2 R E	1974
Blythe, Lt G	1957	Kinson, Lt M J	1972
Brothwell, Pte B	1956	Loader, WO1 (RSM) L E	1964
Burrell, Sgt T	1956	MacDonald, CSgt L	1964
Buxton, WO2 A W	1966	Marston, WO1 (RSM) J T	1956
Christopher, CSgt E	1967	Moorhouse, Sgt T	1956
Clark, WO2 A L	1961	Newbitt, CSgt G L	1956
Collins, SSgt P APTC	1960	Oates, WO2 H P	1963
Cook, WO2 K J	1966	Ross, WO2 (RQMS) R A MM	1955
Dean, WO1 (RSM) J R	1957	Russell, WO1 (GSM) L	1962
Emerton, Cpl P A	1959	Sanderson, WO2 C	1967
Evans, Sgt H	1955	Stevenson, CSgt J	1957
Farrell, Sgt T	1961	Walker, WO1 (BM) D K ARCM	1961
Garman, Lt P F	1972	Wallis, WO2 (AQMS) P J REME	1968
Gibbons, Sgt E G T	1960		

Notes

1   Award of the Meritorious Service Medal requires twenty years of good, faithful, valuable and meritorious service with conduct judged to be irreproachable throughout.
2   The Bravery Medal is the Omani equivalent of the British DSO.
3   The Distinguished Service Medal 'for Gallantry' is the Omani equivalent of the British MC. The DSM 'for meritorious service' is the equivalent of the OBE/MBE.
4   The Commendation Medal is the Omani equivalent of a British 'Mention in Despatches'.
5   Peter North, a National Service subaltern in 1955-56, was Principal of Jesus College, Oxford, 1984-2005 and Vice-Chancellor of Oxford University 1993-97.
6   See Chapter 11, Note 3.
7   For their conduct in the battle at Zetten in the Netherlands 18-20 Jan 1945, men of 1st Leicesters were awarded four MCs, three DCMs, and one MM. The names of the other five recipients and the account of the battle are covered in Underhill's *History of The Royal Leicestershire Regiment 1928-56*.
8   For their conduct in the battle at Merxplas in Belgium on 29-30 Oct 1944, men of 1st Leicesters were awarded one DSO, two MCs, one DCM, and five MMs. The names of the other eight recipients and the account of the battle are covered in the History mentioned in Note 7.
9   John Stevenson was Adjutant of 1st Leicesters throughout the campaign in NW Europe. The award was for meritorious service to the Dutch state, many of whose displaced persons he assisted.

Appendix B

Colonels, Deputy Colonels, Honorary Colonels (TA) and Commanding Officers 1955-75 and Presidents, Chairmen and Regimental Secretaries 1955-2008

Colonels The Royal Leicestershire Regiment
1954-63 Lt Gen Sir Colin Callander KCB KBE MC
1963-64 Maj Gen Sir Douglas Kendrew KCMG CB CBE DSO

Deputy Colonels The Royal Anglian Regiment (Leicestershire)
1964-65 Maj Gen Sir Douglas Kendrew KCMG CB CBE DSO
1964-65 Lt Col P G Upcher DSO DL (Acting)
1965-71 Maj Gen J M K Spurling CB CBE DSO
1971-77 Col M St G Pallot

Honorary Colonels 5th and 4/5th Bns The Royal Leicestershire Regiment (TA)
1953-58 Lt Col (Hon Col) J C Barrett VC TD DL
1958-67 Lt Col (Hon Col) G J German DSO TD
1967-71 Lt Col (Hon Col) C D Oliver OBE TD DL

Deputy Honorary Colonel 7th (Volunteer) Bn The Royal Anglian Regiment
1971-72 Lt Col (Hon Col) C D Oliver OBE TD DL

Deputy Honorary Colonels The Royal Anglian Regiment (Leicestershire)
1972-79 Lt Col (Hon Col) G L Aspell TD DL
1979-81 Lt Col (Hon Col) M Moore MC TD DL
1981-88 Col R G Wilkes OBE TD DL
1988-96 Lt Col (Hon Col) W G Dawson TD DL
1996-99 Lt Col (Hon Col) J C D Heggs DL
1999-date Lt Col (Hon Col) J B C Prescott

Commanding Officers 1st Bn The Royal Leicestershire Regiment
1953-56 Lt Col J E D Watson DSO
1956-58 Lt Col A W D Nicholls OBE MC
1958-61 Lt Col M St G Pallot
1961-64 Lt Col P E B Badger
1964 Lt Col J A C Cowan MBE

Commanding Officers 4th (Leicestershire) Bn The Royal Anglian Regiment
1964-66 Lt Col J A C Cowan MBE
1966-68 Lt Col D R C Carter
1968-70 Lt Col T Holloway

Commanding Officers Tiger Company 4th Bn The Royal Anglian Regiment

1970	Capt M E Romilly
1971-73	Maj J C D Heggs
1973	Maj J A Bacon
1973-74	Maj F A H Swallow
1974-75	Maj J P Growse

Battery Commanders 'Q' Battery/438 LAA Regiment RA (TA)

1955-58	Maj W F Adams TD
1958-61	Maj R G Wilkes TD

Commanding Officers 5th Bn The Royal Leicestershire Regiment (TA)

1952-56	Lt Col M Moore MC TD
1956-59	Lt Col P McH Preston MBE TD
1959-61	Lt Col J H Marriott MC

Commanding Officers 4/5th Bn The Royal Leicestershire Regiment (TA)

1961-63	Lt Col S A Smith OBE
1963-66	Lt Col J P N Creagh
1966-67	Lt Col R G Wilkes TD DL

Commanding Officers The Royal Leicestershire Regiment (Territorial)

1967-69	Lt Col R G Wilkes OBE TD DL
1969-71	Maj W G Dawson TD

Company Commanders 4 (Leicestershire) Company
5th (Volunteer) Bn The Royal Anglian Regiment

1967-70	Maj W G Wallace TD
1971-72	Maj C J Lowe TD
1972-73	Capt/Maj J R Ward
1973-76	Maj A A J Wilson TD

Commanding Officers 7th (Volunteer) Bn The Royal Anglian Regiment

1971-74	Lt Col W G Wallace OBE TD
1974-77	Lt Col W G Dawson TD DL

Company Commanders B (Royal Leicestershire) Company
7th (Volunteer) Bn The Royal Anglian Regiment

1971-73	Maj W G Dawson TD
1973-76	Maj G G Simpson TD

Commanding Officers Depots
Depot The Royal Leicestershire Regiment, Leicester

1955-57	Maj D S Carden
1957-59	Maj P E B Badger
1959-60	Maj K P P Goldschmidt

Depot The Forester Brigade, Leicester

1960-62	Lt Col J W Tomes OBE R Warwick
1962-63	Lt Col A L W Moore MBE Foresters

Depot The East Anglian Brigade/The Royal Anglian Regiment, Bury St Edmunds

1962-64	Lt Col B J Palmer MBE 3 E Anglian
1964-67	Lt Col H W Clarke R Anglian
1967-69	Lt Col J V Miseroy R Anglian
1969-	Lt Col W C Deller R Anglian

Depot The Queen's Division, Bassingbourn

1969-71	Lt Col W C Deller OBE R Anglian
1971-73	Lt Col M J Doyle MBE Queens
1973-76	Lt Col C D Piggins MBE RRF

Royal Tigers' Association

Presidents

1954-63	Lt Gen Sir Colin Callander KCB KBE MC
1963-65	Maj Gen Sir Douglas Kendrew KCMG CB CBE DSO
1965-70	Maj Gen J M K Spurling CB CBE DSO
1971-85	Col M St G Pallot
1985-93	Col T Holloway
1993-date	Maj Gen A J G Pollard CB CBE DL

Chairmen

1957-71	Lt Col P G Upcher DSO DL
1971-74	Lt Col P G Bligh
1974-84	Col M Moore MC TD DL
1984-85	(Acting) Mr T J Marston MBE MSM
1985-96	Lt Col W G Dawson TD DL
1996-99	Col J C D Heggs DL
1999-2001	Lt Col J L Wilson OBE DL
2001-date	Capt R J Allen

Regimental Secretaries

1952-57	Lt Col S D Field
1957-71	Lt Col P G Upcher DSO DL
1971-81	Maj J T Dudley
1981-96	Lt Col J L Wilson DL
1996-2003	Lt Col (Hon Col) F A H Swallow OBE
2003-04	Maj I R J Dexter
2004-05	Lt Col (Hon Col) F A H Swallow OBE
2005	Maj J A B Borthwick
2005-06	Lt Col (Hon Col) F A H Swallow OBE
2006-07	Maj J N Turquand TD
2007	Lt Col (Hon Col) F A H Swallow OBE
2007-date	Lt Col P J Long

Appendix C

Those of The Royal Leicestershire Regiment and those who served in 1 R Leicesters and 4 R Anglian 1955-75 who subsequently commanded other units/formation/organisations

Name	Lt Col's Command	Dates	Higher Command
C B Callander			Military Secretary 1954/5-57
D A Kendrew			GOC Cyprus District 1956-58; Director Infantry 1959-61
J M K Spurling			Chief of Staff West Africa 1953-55 Chief of Staff HQ Northern Command 1955-58
J W B Marshall	12 Para (TA)	1955-58	Comd (designate) 160 Inf Bde (TA) 1960
P Wills-Rust	1st Gold Coast Regiment	1955-57	
D S Carden	2nd Mobile Bn, Aden Levies	1958-60	
B W Briggs	1st Mobile Bn, Aden Levies	1958-60	
R G M Green	5 Foresters (TA)	1960-63	
K P P Goldschmidt	Military Prison Shepton Mallet	1961-65	
D R Dalglish	Northern Frontier Regt, SAF	1962-64	
J A C Cowan			8 Inf Bde, Londonderry 1969-71
T A Cave	Int & Sy Group (BAOR)	1966-68	
E Turnill	Desert Regt, SAF	1968-71	
A F F H Robertson	23 (V) SAS	1969-72	British Forces Belize 1978-80, Rhine Area 1980-83
P Worthy	Jebel Regt, SAF	1970-72	
M L Barclay	Dubai Defence Force	1974-76	
R H Robinson	Union Defence Force, UAE	1974-77	
B N Crumbie	Jebel Regt, SAF	1974-75	
D R C Carter			Deputy Fortress Commander Gibraltar 1978-80
K Burch	3 R Anglian	1969-71	Director Personnel, MOD 1983-85
R E J Gerrard-Wright	2 R Anglian	1970-73	39 Inf Bde, Belfast 1975-77; Eastern District 1980-82; DTA&C 1983-85
J L Wilson	Infantry Junior Leaders Bn, Oswestry	1972-74	

Name	Lt Col's Command	Dates	Higher Command
P P Young	11 UDR	1973-75	
J C D Heggs	8 UDR	1975-77	
A J G Pollard	1 R Anglian	1977-79	British Forces Belize 1983-84, School of Infantry 1984-87, BMM to Uganda 1985-86, South West District 1990-92
S A Green	Infantry Junior Leaders Bn, Shorncliffe	1977-79	
W H Morris	Training Bn and Depot ACC	1977-79	
F A H Swallow	5 (V) R Anglian	1977-80	
A E Fisher			Catering UKLF 1993, Log Sp UKLF 1993, Log Sp London District 1994, Director Catering (Army) 1994-95, Director Sp Svcs (Army) 1995-96
R Howe	2 R Anglian	1980-82	
A E Thompson	3 R Anglian	1981-83	
D W James	6 (V) R Anglian	1982-84	
C P B Keeble	2 Para	1982	
	15 (V) Para	1985-87	
M E Romilly	2 UDR	1984-86	
A C Taylor	6 (V) R Anglian	1986-88	
M K Goldschmidt	Depot The Queen's Division	1986-88	
P W Field	7/10 UDR	1989-91	
R H Pepper	Int & Sy Group (V)	1992-94	

Appendix D

Regimental Collects

The Royal Leicestershire Regiment

From the flysheet of the 1st Bn's Regimental Digest which had been started on 8 May 1945

Grant thy perpetual blessing, O Lord, to the officers and men of The Royal Leicestershire Regiment. Keep far from it all that would stain its honour and destroy its comradeship.

Let the consciousness of Thy presence be with its members wheresoever they may be, that in Thy light they may see light and come at last unto Thy everlasting Kingdom, through Jesus Christ our Lord. Amen

From an Order of Service dated 7 July 1957 in the above-mentioned 1st Bn's Regimental Digest

O God, who art slow to anger, and of great kindness, have mercy on thy servants of The Royal Leicestershire Regiment, who put on the boldness of a tiger in the day of battle, that we may never let the sun go down upon our wrath; and that, though victory be turned to mourning, we may remember that thou wilt wipe away our tears, for the love of Jesus Christ our Lord. Amen

The Royal Anglian Regiment

Used from 1 September 1964

O Lord God, who by the brightness of a star[1] didst lead men to the Saviour of mankind; give Thy grace to The Royal Anglian Regiment, that trusting in Thee as our strong rock and our castle,[2] we may in unity[3] with Thee and with one another so serve our Sovereign[4] and our native land[5] that at the last we may be led to Thy heavenly Kingdom, through Jesus Christ our Lord. Amen

The 4th Bn's unofficial Collect, composed by Revd R A McDowall RAChD, and used from September 1969

Lord Jesus, who commands us to watch and pray,[6] grant that we of the 4th Battalion The Royal Anglian Regiment may at all times be as alert as the tiger,[7] ceaselessly be on guard[8] to defend those things which are dear to us and to our country; and to attack those things which threaten our faith. Through Christ our Lord. Amen.

Notes

1 (a) Matthew Ch 2 verse 2, 'We have seen his star in the east and are come to worship Him.'
   (b) The badge of The Royal Anglian Regiment includes the Garter Star.

2 (a) Psalm 31, verse 4, 'Thou art my strong rock and my castle; be Thou also my guide.'
   (b) The badge of The Royal Anglian Regiment includes the Castle of Gibraltar.
3 (a) Ephesians Ch 4 verse 13, 'Till we all come in the unity of the faith, and the knowledge of the Son of God.'
   (b) The Royal Anglian Regiment has been formed from four former Regiments which, in their turn, came into being as the result of the union of many other regiments at earlier dates.
4 (a) 1 Peter Ch 2 verse 9, 'But ye are a chosen generation, a royal priesthood, an holy nation.'
   (b) Sovereign – compare the title 'Royal'.
5 (a) Isaiah Ch 57 verse 13, 'He that putteth his trust in me shall possess the land, and shall inherit my holy mountain.'
   (b) Native land - the Angles conquered and settled central and eastern England in the fifth and sixth centuries, and gave their name to the country. The Regiment recruits from the area of Angle settlement. This area includes eleven of our present counties.
6 Matthew Ch 26 verse 41.
7 The badge of The Royal Leicestershire Regiment.
8 The stance of the Tiger in the badge.

Appendix E

Late Entry Officers – Soldiers who served in the ranks in The Royal Leicestershire Regiment, 4 R Anglian, and the Leicestershire companies of 5 (V) and 7 (V) R Anglian 1955-75 and were subsequently commissioned

Rank/Name while last serving in 'Leicestershire' element 1955-75	Unit Name	Unit served in on commissioning	Date
Cpl R J M Mosse	Depot R Leicesters	1 R Leicesters	1954
Cpl C T Marshall	1 R Leicesters	1 R Leicesters	1955
Cpl W H Morris	Depot R Leicesters	1 R Leicesters	1956
WO2 (RQMS) R A Ross MM	1 R Leicesters	1 R Leicesters	1957
WO2 A J J Pryce-Howells	5 R Leicesters (TA)	5 R Leicesters (TA)	1960
Pte J E Tilley	5 R Leicesters (TA)	1 R Leicesters	1960
WO1 (BM) D K Walker ARCM	1 R Leicesters	RTR Band as DoM[1]	1962
WO2 A D Russell	1 R Leicesters	2 E Anglian	1962
WO1 (BM) J E Battye ARCM	4 R Anglian	1 R Anglian	1968
WO1 (RSM) N H P Jenks MM	4 R Anglian	4 R Anglian	1968
WO2 (RQMS) C Ladley	4 R Anglian	3 R Anglian	1969
WO1 (RSM) P F Garman	4 R Anglian	2 R Anglian	1970
CSgt (ORCS) M J Kinson	1 R Leicesters	1 R Anglian	1970
WO2 (RQMS) A I James	4 R Anglian	Tiger Coy 4 R Anglian	1970
WO2 (ORQMS) M J Rigley	4 R Anglian	Selection Centre Corsham	1971
CSGT A E Parker	4 R Anglian	2 R Anglian	1975
WO2 (ORQMS) R J Jackson	4 R Anglian	RSC Sutton Coldfield	1975
CSgt B Newman	4 R Anglian	2 R Anglian	1976
WO2 D W Spalding	Tiger Coy 4 R Anglian	1 R Anglian	1977
WO2 J Bloomfield	4 Coy 5 (V) R Anglian	7 (V) R Anglian	1978
WO2 D R Edwards	4 R Anglian	2 R Anglian	1978
WO2 (ORQMS) D G Ridgway	4 R Anglian	1 R Anglian	1978
CSgt J S J Rourke	4 R Anglian	1 R Anglian	1979
CSgt C T Bromfield	4 R Anglian	3 Queens	1980
Sgt A Ainsworth	4 R Anglian	3 Queens	1980
Pte W Burford	1 R Leicesters	3 R Anglian	1983
Sgt C Mallett	4 R Anglian	7 (V) R Anglian	1984
Sgt G W Meen	Tiger Coy 4 R Anglian	1 R Anglian	1984
WO2 G Taylor	4 Coy 5 (V) R Anglian	7 (V) R Anglian	1984

Rank/Name while last serving in 'Leicestershire' element 1955-75	Unit Name	Unit served in on commissioning	Date
CSgt T Ashford	4 R Anglian	10 GR	1985
Cpl P L Ludbrook	4 R Anglian	1 R Anglian	1986
Cpl L L Cook	4 R Anglian	6 Ord Bn RAOC	1987
CSgt R C McDonald	Tiger Coy 4 R Anglian	2 R Anglian	1987
WO2 (RQMS) B C Lee	HQ Coy 7 (V) R Anglian	7 (V) R Anglian	1988
LCpl J McBride	4 R Anglian	3 RRF	1988
Cpl R W Potter	4 R Anglian	3 R Anglian	1989
Cpl T Taylor	4 Coy 5 (V) R Anglian	7 (V) R Anglian	1989
Cpl P A Cookson	4 R Anglian	1 R Anglian	1989
LCpl S Dexter	Tiger Coy 4 R Anglian	3 R Anglian	1990
Sgt G G Smith	4 Coy 5 (V) R Anglian	7 (V) R Anglian	1990
Pte N J Richardson	Tiger Coy 4 R Anglian	2 RRF	1991
Pte R G H Bilner	Tiger Coy 4 R Anglian	Queens	1992
Cpl T D Smith	HQ Coy 7 (V) R Anglian	2 R Anglian	1994

Notes

1   later DoM RASC/RCT 1963, and DoM Welsh Guards 1969.

Appendix F

National Service Officers
1955-61

Those marked * later became Regular officers

R J Allen	1954-56	B Moloney	1956-57
A D Barlow	1955-56	C H Moore	1955-57
P G Beauchamp	1956-58	R J M Mosse*	1955-57
A J Bettles	1955-57	D M A Needham	1959-60
G H Bradshaw*	1953-55	P M North	1955-56
R E R Buckingham	1955-57	M W North	1955-56
R W Carpenter	1957-58	J M Osborne	1960
J H Chatterton	1956-57	C F D Palmer	1955-56
J O Church	1955-56	T F Parr	1956-57
T A J E Connor	1956-57	D T Plewman	1959-60
R S Copley-Smith	1960-61	A J G Pollard*	1956-57
B N Crumbie*	1954	C G O Reynolds	1954-55
I S Davidson	1959-60	J Riley	1959-60
M G A Day	1958-59	J B W Robbins	1954-55
M J Disney	1958-59	C J H Roberts	1955-57
W H V Elliott	1956-57	I G Runciman	1959-60
P L Fisher	1956-57	D C Samworth	1955-56
A W Garlick	1957-58	A G Sayer	1957-58
J E Gowler	1959-60	J D Spence	1955-56
J Hadfield	1958-59	P R Starkey	1956-57
W Hays	1958-59	G M Stonestreet	1957-58
N Héroys	1956-57	F A H Swallow*	1957-58
C J Howells	1955-57	G N L Stubbs	1955-56
P J W Humpidge	1955-56	M B P Tamlyn	1958-59
E C T Hugo	1957-58	R W Tarring	1955-57
D M Jackson	1958-60	R D Thomas	1954-56
R B James	1954-55	D R Trentham	1957-58
J A Liddiard	1958-59	C R Tustain	1955-57
E Malcolm	1954-55	R A Wessel	1957-59
J W Mansfield	1957-58	J R A Wilkes*	1953-55

Appendix G

Miscellaneous Groupings

Lords Mayor of Leicester who served in The (Royal) Leicestershire Regiment

Name	Year of Office	Years of Service in the Regiment
Councillor Herbert Simpson DL	1924	Leicesters (TF) and 2/4th Bn, 3/4th Bn 1914-15.
Alderman Ernest Oliver TD DL	1950	4th Leicesters (TA) 1922-39, and 1939-45.
Alderman Colonel Alfred Halkyard CB MC TD DL[1]	1956	4th Leicesters (TF) 1916-18, 1921-36 (TA).
Alderman Frederick Jackson	1957	1st Leicesters 1918.
Alderman Sidney Brown TD	1958	2/5th Leicesters 1938-45; CO City ACF Bn 1948-57.
Alderman Kenneth Bowder OBE	1968	Leicesters 1939 (then RAF).
Alderman Percy Watts	1971	4th Leicesters (TF) 1915-17 (then RFC).
Councillor Bernard Toft	1976	44th Searchlight Regt Royal Artillery 1939-45
Councillor Robert Wigglesworth	1992	1st R Leicesters 1950-52, 5th R Leicesters (TA) 1952-57

Members of the Regiment who served on the staff of RMA Sandhurst 1955 onwards

Lt Col H G G Havilland OBE	1946-56	Capt M E Romilly	1971-73
Major D P Carey	1954-55	Capt B R Cornish	1975-77
Capt M L Barclay	1961-63	CSgt R C McDonald	1975-77
CSgt L MacDonald	1962-64	CSgt P L Ludbrook	1977-79
CSgt E Christopher	1964-67	CSgt J McBride	1978-80
CSgt C T Bromfield[2]	1969-71		

Members of the Regiment who served on the staff of Officer Cadet Schools 1955 onwards

Capt R H D Graveston	1953-55	(Eaton Hall)	Sgt R Baker	1964-65	(Mons)
Lt Col J W B Marshall	1956-58	(Eaton Hall)	Sgt A C Sprason	1967-69	(Mons)
Lt Col D R Dalglish MC	1964-66	(Mons)			

Members of the Regiment who were international rugby players

Name	Country	No of caps	Years	Remarks	Christian Name(s)
W C Wilson[3]	England	2	1907	Richmond FC.	Walter Carandini
F N Tarr	England	4	1909-13	KIA 18 Jul 1915; 1/4th Leicesters; Leicester FC.	Francis Nathaniel
T M Moll	South Africa	1	1910	DOW 14 Jul 1916; 9th Leicesters; Transvaal/Western Province.	Tobias Mortimer
A L Novis[4]	England	7	1930-34	Captain 1933; Blackheath RC.	Anthony Leslie
D A Kendrew[5]	England	10	1930-36	Captain 1935; Leicester FC.	Douglas Anthony ('Joe')
H Godwin	England	11	1959-67	Coventry RFC.	(Her)'Bert'

Underhill's *History of the Royal Leicestershire Regiment 1928-56* (1958) at Page 49 covering 2nd Leicesters in the Battle of Crete 1941 states, '2nd Lieutenant Young, who had played rugby football for Scotland, was twice wounded, the second time fatally.' The Commonwealth War Graves Commission website shows 2nd Lieutenant Wilfred Greenfield Young of 2nd Leicesters died on 20 May 1941 and is buried in Suda Bay (Crete) War Cemetery. The Scottish Rugby Union have no record of Wilfred Greenfield Young having played rugby for Scotland.

Members of the Regiment who were subsequently ordained as ministers of the Church

Rank and Name	Unit/years	Ordained	Denomination
Lt Col S D Field	CO 1 R Leicesters 1947-50	1958	C of E
Capt A T Green	5 R Leicesters (TA) 1947-c1955	1964	C of E. Later RAChD(TA)
LCpl J Roe	1 R Leicesters 1948-53	1964	Anglican – NZ
2Lt A D Barlow	1 R Leicesters 1955-56	1962	C of E
2Lt W H V Elliott	1 R Leicesters 1956-57	1962	C of E
2Lt P R Starkey	1 R Leicesters 1956-57	1965	C of E
2Lt G M Stonestreet	1 R Leicesters 1957-58	1963	C of E
Capt T B F Hiney MC	1 R Leicesters/4 R Anglian 1957-68	1969	C of E. Later RAChD
Maj A R Cooper-Smith TD	4/5 R Leicesters (TA) 1960-67	1973	C of E
Lt D Morris	Tiger Coy 1973-74	1996	Methodist

Notes

1   See Chapter 2, Note 12.

2   Charles Bromfield's grandfather, W T Bromfield, as a Brevet Lt Col commanded 2nd Leicesters in Delhi 1920-21 and as a Lt Col commanded them at Colchester 1925-27. It was in 1927 that the Bn won the Army Soccer Cup, having been finalists the previous year.

3   later Gp Capt W C Wilson CBE DSO MC. He was awarded the DSO as a Captain commanding A Coy 2nd Leicesters near La Bassée Canal on 25 September 1915 and a bar as the BM 70 Inf Bde in France in 1917; he was also awarded the OBE and MC for his work during the First World War. He reached the rank of Gp Capt in the Second World War and was awarded the CBE as Senior Air Staff Officer at HQ 54 Gp, Flying Training Command.

4   later Lieutenant Colonel A L Novis MC. See Chapter 4, Note 12.

5   later Major General Sir Douglas Kendrew KCMG CB CBE DSO, Colonel Royal Leicesters 1963-64, Governor of Western Australia 1963-73. See Appendix N.

Appendix H

An Appreciation of the Regimental History

H.Q., 29 Infantry Brigade, Dover.

The Editor, THE GREEN TIGER.   4th June, 1958.

Sir,

Would it be out of order for me to say how enormously I have enjoyed reading the Regimental History edited by Brigadier Underhill? General Callander has been kind enough to send me a copy; and I have read it from cover to cover with real relish and enjoyment. I have read a good many other regimental histories, and some of them can have been of interest only to a very limited number of readers; but this one might be taken as a blueprint. It preserves the contemporary atmosphere of all the campaigns, in the same way as letters home might have done but for those beasts the censors.

Naturally it has been of particular interest to me as an old friend of the Regiment, which I first met in Aldershot when I was ADC to General Wavell. I met it next in the Tobruk siege in 1941, and dined with it at Qassassin the following January, soon after the siege was lifted. If on that occasion an Egyptian fortune-teller had told me that within two years I should be commanding it as part of my brigade, I would have asked for my money back; but such was my good luck. I shall be proud as long as I live of having had the 2nd Battalion under my command during a period when it added such distinction to its long history; and I shall never forget its performance at the Indaw Lake in March, 1944. John Marriott,[1] Alan Sheppard[2] and I had sinking hearts when we got Colonel Wilkinson's[3] signal: 'Withdrawing slowly owing to wounded', so soon after we had been able to offer no reassuring answer to his previous one: 'Any diversion would be of help'. In the eyes of the world, it was a minor, inconclusive and unsuccessful action; but technically and in terms of courage, so far as your 2nd Battalion was concerned, it was superb. I remember with what satisfaction we heard of Sgt. Chandler's DCM being granted. Awards were scarce in that theatre at that time, or there would have been many more; but none better earned than his.

I have had immense fun in the course of 27 years' service. When eventually I retire, I shall count among my battle honours and scars: Dining with the Royal Leicesters at Aldershot in 1936; Having Joe Kendrew[4] as one of my platoon commanders when I was a company commander at Sandhurst in 1939; Enduring both John Marriott and Spike Nicholls[5] as brigade majors; Obeying the orders of Alan Sheppard as Brigade Orderly Officer in 1943-4; Serving under General Callander[6] as my divisional commander in Germany in 1950. But I shall especially remember how the 2nd Battalion of your Regiment helped to stem the defiles in the thin, undermanned days of Crete and Tobruk, early in the war; and became thereafter the tip of the spearhead of victory in the east.

I am, Sir,

Yours truly,

Bernard Fergusson,   Brigadier

Notes:

1   Major J H Marriott MC, BM 16 Indep Inf Bde, 2nd Chindit Expedition, Burma 1944.
2   Captain A V C Shepherd, Orderly Officer HQ 16 Indep Inf Bde.
3   Lieutenant Colonel C J Wilkinson, R Norfolk, CO 2nd Leicesters and OC 17 Column. Awarded DSO in 1944.
4   Captain D A Kendrew. In June 1958 Major General D A Kendrew CB CBE DSO***, GOC Cyprus. Appendix N.
5   Major A W D Nicholls MC, BM 16 Indep Inf Bde.
6   Major General C B Callander CB MC, GOC 2nd Inf Div. In June 1958 Lieutenant General Sir Colin Callander KCB KBE MC, Colonel The Royal Leicestershire Regiment. Appendix N.

Appendix I

Special Order of the Day on 1 September 1964
by Lieutenant General Sir Reginald Denning KBE CB DL
Colonel The Royal Anglian Regiment

In accordance with the gracious pleasure of the Queen, The Royal Anglian Regiment has today been formed and I have submitted to Her Majesty a message of loyalty and devotion. The Queen has marked the occasion by conferring on the Regiment signal honour by appointing Her Majesty Queen Elizabeth The Queen Mother to be Colonel-in-Chief and Their Royal Highnesses The Princess Margaret and The Duchess of Gloucester to be Deputy Colonels-in-Chief.

We have all therefore today become members of a Regiment new in name but old in the spirit and in the traditions we inherit from our former Regiments.

The grouping of Infantry into larger Regiments is made necessary by the conditions of modern war and it is a realisation of this need that we have now become The Royal Anglian Regiment of four Regular Battalions and seven of the Territorial Army.

I have entire confidence that all units of the Regiment will maintain the high reputations which our former Regiments gained by their devoted and distinguished service to the Crown and Country.

Special Message of the Day on 1 September 1964 from
Major-General Sir Douglas Kendrew KCMG CB CBE DSO
Deputy Colonel The Royal Anglian Regiment

On this historic occasion of our Regiment forming a part of The Royal Anglian Regiment and, in future, taking the title of the 4th (Leicestershire) Battalion of this new Regiment, we fully understand that a chapter of our military history has been closed.

Changes take place in organisation, equipment and personnel, but the loyalty of those who serve Her Majesty accept change as a pattern of progress.

We are now part of a larger Regiment. We will be strengthened by this new amalgamation. Our loyalties to our County and our City remain untarnished, and the association will remain as strong as ever.

Today, as I relinquish the Colonelcy of The Royal Leicestershire Regiment, I thank you for the support you have given me in the past.

I know that you will give that same support and loyalty to our Royal Colonel-in-Chief and our new Deputy Colonels-in-Chief, and to the Colonel of our newly-formed Regiment – The Royal Anglian Regiment.

I wish you all success for the future as part of a bigger organisation within the Corps of Infantry.

The Royal Leicestershire Regiment lives on as a Battalion of a new Regiment.

Appendix J

Special Order of the Day on 1 July 1968
by Lieutenant General Sir Richard Goodwin KCB CBE DSO
Colonel The Royal Anglian Regiment

Today, the 1st July 1968, marks a further stage in the evolution of The Royal Anglian Regiment in that we move to Large Regiment status in all respects. This means we now discontinue the use of subsidiary Battalion titles which denoted affiliation to a former Regiment or County.

We are doing this not because of any weakening in our Regimental traditions and County connections but to ensure that, whatever reductions or changes may face us in the future, the spirit and traditions of all our present Battalions and the Regiments from which they stem will be safeguarded and perpetuated by The Royal Anglian Regiment within The Queen's Division.

As from today each Battalion becomes a component part of The Royal Anglian Regiment and takes to itself responsibility for safeguarding the former traditions and customs of all the original Regiments which formed The Royal Anglian Regiment. Thus the Regular components of The Royal Anglian Regiment, apart from the Depot, are the 1st, 2nd, 3rd and 4th Battalions, each equal within the Regiment. All Battalions of the Regiment should henceforth be regarded as belonging to all eleven counties which form our Regimental area and which give us such splendid support. For example, the 1st Battalion will no longer be connected solely with the counties of Norfolk and Suffolk but should be equally regarded in Lincolnshire, Leicestershire, or any of the other Counties.

I realise that the dropping of subsidiary titles may cause distress, particularly perhaps to the older and retired members of the various Regiments, but I feel it is inevitable and only by doing this can we ensure that our roots remain in the Regimental area.

Appendix K

Officers commemorated by individual plaques in the Regimental Chapel

Maj G G B Anderson killed in action 2nd Leicesters Crete 1941

Col J C Barrett VC TD DL FRCS 5th Leicesters 1916-39 Hon Col 5th Royal Leicesters 1953-58 born 1898 died 1977

Maj Gen C G Blackader CB DSO CO 2nd Leicesters 1912-14 born 1869 died 1921

Maj Gen G T Brice CB Col Leicesters 1903-05 died 1905

Lt Col G L Burnett CO 1st Leicesters died in command 1904

Lt Gen Sir Colin B Callander KCB KBE MC Col Royal Leicesters 1954-63 born 1897 died 1979

Brig Gen E L Challenor CB CMG CBE DSO CO 1st Leicesters 1919-23 born 1873 died 1935

Lt Col B Clarke served 1905-28 died 1940

Brig J A C Cowan CBE last CO 1st Royal Leicesters/first CO 4th R Anglian 1964-66 born 1923 died 1999

Maj Gen Sir Henry L Croker KCB CMG commanded Battalions 1910-15 (Maj Gen GOC 28 Div Macedonia/Mesopotamia 1916-20) died 1938

Col G German DSO TD DL Hon Col 5th Leicesters 1927-38 born 1870 died 1946

Col G J German DSO TD CO 1/5th Leicesters 1940-45 Hon Col 5th R Leicesters 1958-66 born 1902 died 1984

Maj R J German born 1906 killed in action September 1944

Col A Halkyard CB MC TD DL LLB 4th Leicesters 1914-36 Chairman TAFA 1948-57 born 1892 died 1964

Col J P W Jamie MC TD DL 5th Leicesters 1914-53 Hon Col 1949-53 born 1895 died 1972

Capt H S Logan died of wounds 1908 in The Sudan

Lt Col J H Marriott MC CO 5th Royal Leicesters 1959-61 born 1916 died 2007

Lt Col J W B Marshall OBE born 1916 died 1960

Lt Col Sir Robert E Martin CMG TD VL JP MA LLB 5th Leicesters 1908-15 CO 1915 born 1874 died 1961

Col M Moore MC TD DL CO 5th Royal Leicesters 1952-56 born 1916 died 1984

Brig C E Morrison DSO MC CO 1st Leicesters/British Battalion 1941-45 born 1893 died 1966

Lt Col A W D Nicholls OBE MC CO 1st Royal Leicesters 1956-59 born 1913 died 1996

Col Sir Charles F Oliver TD DL JP 4th Leicesters 1892-1913 born 1869 died 1939

Col M St G Pallot CO 1st Royal Leicesters 1958-61 born 1916 died 2004

Lt Col F E Parkinson 2nd Leicesters died 1902

Maj E H Peacock 1st Leicesters born 1856 died at St Helena 1897

Brig H S Pinder CBE MC CO 1st Leicesters 1936-39, Col Royal Leicesters 1948-54 born 1889 died 1974

Lt Col S A Rolfe-Smith OBE CO 4/5th Royal Leicesters 1961-63 born 1920 died 1989

Capt C C Rolph 2nd Leicesters killed in action October 1915 born 1888

Col W M Rolph CO 1st Leicesters 1890-94 CO 17th Regimental District 1896-99 born 1842 died 1918

Col J E Sarson CB OBE VD TD DL 4th Leicesters 1860-1937 born 1845 died 1940

Lt Col E R Scott CO 2nd Leicesters 1902-06 born 1857 died 1938

Maj D M Sergeantson OBE DL Leicesters 1891-1908 Secretary TAFA 1908-37 born 1871 died 1940

Lt Col H Stoney Smith DSO CO 1st Leicesters killed in action 1915 born 1868

Maj Gen J M K Spurling CB CBE DSO Dep Col Royal Anglian Regiment 1965-70 born 1906 died 1980

Col H W Tyler MC TD DL CO 4th Leicesters 1922-30 Hon Col 1939-54 died 1970

Brig W E Underhill OBE CO 7th Leicesters 1940-42 died 1968

Lt Col P G Upcher DSO DL Dep Col Royal Anglian Regt 1964-65 born 1909 died 1980

Maj Gen A H Utterson CB Col Leicesters 1905-12 born 1836 died 1912

Lt Col J E D Watson DSO CO 1st Royal Leicesters 1953-56 born 1910 died 2002

Maj A G P Withington 2/5th Leicesters killed in action Tunisia May 1943 born 1908

Maj Gen Sir Edward M Woodward KCMG CB Col Leicesters 1916-43 born 1861 died 1943

Appendix L

Regimental Colours

Hanging in the Regimental Chapel

Battalion, Colour	Presented	Retired	Laid Up	Remarks
1st Leicesters, King's	2 Mar 1938	Feb 1948	27 Jul 1954	Presented by Lord Linlithgow, Viceroy of India, at Jubbulpore. Rescued in Penang 1946.
1st R Leicesters, Regimental	25 Jul 1954	22 Jun 1975	22 Jun 1975	Presented by Lt Gen Sir Colin Callander, at Iserlohn, Germany. Later carried by 4th R Anglian and by Tiger Company.
1st R Leicesters, Queen's	25 Jul 1954	22 Jun 1975	22 Jun 1975	As above.
2nd Leicesters, Regimental	25 Mar 1927	25 Jul 1954	22 Jun 1975	Presented by FM Sir Claud Jacob, at Colchester. Carried by 1st R Leicesters 1948-54.
2nd Leicesters, King's	25 Mar 1927	25 Jul 1954	22 Jun 1975	As above.
4th Leicesters, Regimental	19 Jun 1909		15 Aug 1941	Presented by HM King Edward VII, at Windsor.
4th Leicesters, King's	19 Jun 1909		15 Aug 1941	As above.
4th R Leicesters, Regimental	3 Oct 1953	1 Apr 1971	21 Jun 1981	Presented by HRH The Duchess of Kent, at Leicester.
4th R Leicesters, King's	3 Oct 1953	1 Apr 1971	21 Jun 1981	As above
2/4th Leicesters, King's	10 Nov 1921		11 Nov 21	Presented by Cllr J W Heath, Mayor of Leicester, at Leicester. (Note 1)
5th Leicesters, Regimental	19 Jun 1909	1 Apr 1971	21 Jun 1981	Presented by HM King Edward VII, at Windsor.
5th Leicesters, King's	19 Jun 1909	1 Apr 1971	21 Jun 1981	As above.
7th Leicesters, King's	10 Nov 1921		11 Nov 1921	Presented by Mr H Simpson-Gee, High Sheriff of Rutland, at Leicester. (Note 1)
14th Leicesters, King's	10 Nov 1921		11 Nov 1921	Presented by Sir John Turner DL, at Leicester. (Note 1)

Note: 1. Because the Royal College of Needlework had not completed embroidering the King's Colours for the three battalions listed above (2/4th, 7th and 14th) and for the 2/5th, 6th , 8th , 9th, 11th, 51st and 52nd Battalions before the battalions were disbanded, those Colours were presented by county and military dignitaries to all ten battalions on the same day (10 November 1921) at Leicester Football Club's ground, and were laid up the following day, Armistice Day 1921. The seven Colours of that batch not hanging in the Chapel are among the twenty-five Colours laid up in a casket under the altar.

Appendix M

Colonels of The Regiment 1688-1964

1688.09.27	Col Solomon Richards
1689.05.01	Col Sir George St George
1695.05.01	Col John Courthorpe
1695.09.01	Col Sir Matthew Bridges
1703.08.26	Maj Gen Holcroft Blood
1707.08.20	Maj Gen Joseph Wightman
1722.09.28	Brig Gen Thomas Ferrers
1722.11.07	Lt Gen James Tyrrell
1742.08.31	Lt Gen John Wynyard
1752.03.14	Brig Gen Edward Richbell
1757.02.25	Brig Gen John Forbes
1759.10.24	Lt Gen The Hon Robert Monckton
1782.05.29	Lt Gen George Morrison
1792.08.08	Gen George Garth
1819.06.14	Gen Sir Josiah Champagné GCH
1840.02.17	Gen Sir Frederick Augustus Wetherall GCH
1843.01.02	Gen Sir Peregrine Maitland KCB
1854.05.31	Lt Gen Thomas James Wemyss CB
1860.07.20	Lt Gen Sir Richard Airey KCB
1868.05.01	Lt Gen John Grattan CB
1871.04.30	Gen William Raikes Faber CB
1879.06.25	Gen Richard William Penn Curzon-Howe CB, 3rd Earl Howe
1890.04.08	Lt Gen John Christopher Guise VC CB
1895.02.06	Gen Sir John Ross GCB
1903.07.29	Maj Gen George Tito Brice CB
1905.09.23	Maj Gen Archibald Hammond Utterson CB
1912.07.29	Maj Gen William Dalrymple Tompson CB
1916.12.07	Maj Gen Sir Edward Mabbott Woodward KCMG CB
1943.03.22	Gen Sir Clive Gerard Liddell KCB CMG CBE DSO
1948.05.01	Brig Harold Senhouse Pinder CBE MC
1954.04.22	Lt Gen Sir Colin Bishop Callander KCB KBE MC
1963.05.20	Maj Gen Sir Douglas Anthony Kendrew KCMG CB CBE DSO

Notes:

1. Ranks shown were the highest achieved during and decorations shown were acquired before or during the officer's tenure as Colonel.

2. Short biographical details of all these Colonels of The Regiment (less the last six) were published in Appendix 2 of Lieutenant Colonel E A H Webb's *A History of the Services of The 17th (The Leicestershire) Regiment 1688-1912* (revised 1912). Those of the last six, plus the first two Deputy Colonels (Leicestershire and Rutland) The Royal Anglian Regiment, are in Appendix N of this 2008 book.

Appendix N

Biographical details of the last eight Colonels of The Regiment

Major General William Dalrymple Tompson CB
1912-1916

William Tompson was commissioned into The 17th Regiment in October 1952 and, except for a few months in The 2nd (Queen's) Regiment, served all his regimental service in it. He fought in the Crimean War 1854-56, being present at the two assaults on the Redan at Sevastopol in 1855. Mentioned in Dispatches for the attack on 18 June (in which Lance Sergeant Philip Smith won his VC), he was seriously wounded in the second one on 8 September. He was awarded the British Crimean Medal with clasp 'Sevastopol', the Turkish Crimean Medal and the French Knight of the Legion of Honour. He commanded the 1st Battalion The Leicestershire Regiment from 1879 to 1884, during which it was engaged in the Second Afghan War 1878-79. He was involved in the attack and capture of Fort Ali Musjid, the action of Chenar, both expeditions to the Bazar Valley, the action on Kabul River and at Maidanak. He was Mentioned in Dispatches, awarded the Medal with clasp, and appointed CB in November 1879. Promoted Colonel in October 1881, he retired from the Army in 1884 with the honorary rank of Major General.

He was Colonel of The Regiment from 1912 to 1916, and died in post.

Major General Sir Edward Mabbott Woodward KCMG CB
1916-1943

Edward Woodward was born in July 1861. Brought up in Leicestershire and educated at Harrow School and the RMC Sandhurst, he was commissioned into The Leicestershire Regiment in 1882, serving initially in the 2nd Battalion in India. He was present at the Presentation of Colours at Lucknow in 1885 (and, as Colonel of The Regiment, at the presentation of the next Colours at Colchester in 1927).

He passed into the Staff College in 1891 whilst still a subaltern, and as a Captain was DAAG in Malta in 1893. In 1896 he took part in the British East African operations which followed the revolt of the Sudanese troops in Uganda, and was Mentioned in Dispatches. In 1900 he became a Staff Captain (modern-day SO3) in the Directorate of Intelligence at the War Office. As a Major in 1903, he was first Intelligence Officer with the Somaliland Field Force and then Base Commandant at the port of Berbera, and was again Mentioned in Dispatches. The experience gained during this period stood him in good stead during the Army's mobilization ten years later.

After serving as SO2 in the Directorate of Military Operations at the War Office, he rejoined the Regiment in 1905, but was back at the War Office the following year in the Directorate of Personal Services. He was promoted Lieutenant Colonel in 1907, and Colonel in 1912, serving as AAG at HQ Southern Command. In May 1913, he became Director of Mobilization, a key post from which he directed the speedy mobilization of the Army in 1914 which had such an important bearing on the course of the early operations of the First World War. From 1915 to 1917 he served as DAG to the Mediterranean Expeditionary Force. For these services he was rewarded by a CB in 1915, promotion to Major General in 1916, KCMG in 1917, and was four times Mentioned in Dispatches. He retired in 1920.

He was the longest-serving Colonel of The Regiment (from 1916 to 1943), and died in post.

General Sir Clive Gerard Liddell KCB CMG CBE DSO
1943-1948

Born in 1883 and educated at Uppingham School and the RMC Sandhurst, Clive Liddell was commissioned into The Leicestershire Regiment in 1902. He served initially in the 2nd Battalion. He was a fine Rugby player, playing for Blackheath. He was Adjutant of the 2nd Battalion in India for three years from 1908, and a member of the 1st Leicesters Rugby XV which won the Army Cup in 1912. Having been one of three officers responsible for the formation of the Army Rugby Union (ARU) in 1906, he became a member of its Executive Committee in 1911. After a spell as Staff Captain in HQ 6 District, he returned to Regimental duty in October 1914 in France. Shortly afterwards he became DAA & QMG in HQ I Corps, and was awarded the DSO in 1915 after the First Battle of Ypres. He was AA & QMG of HQ 55 (West Lancashire) Div (TF) in 1916 during the Battles of the Somme. In early 1917 he became an AAG in the Directorate of Organization at the War Office for two years, being appointed CMG in 1918 and CBE in 1919. He was also Mentioned in Dispatches six times.

From 1919 to 1922 he was an instructor at the Staff College, whereafter for two years he was Deputy Administrator of the British Empire Exhibition, earning Brevet Lieutenant Colonel. After serving with the 1st Battalion in Egypt in 1926, he spent 1927 as a student of the Imperial Defence College before spending three years as a Colonel in the Directorate of Military Operations and Intelligence. In 1931 he took over command of 8 Bde at Devonport, before being promoted Major General in 1933 and becoming GOC 47 (2nd London) Div (TA) in 1935. That year he was appointed CB and also GOC 4 Div. In 1937 he was recalled to the War Office to be Adjutant General to the Forces at the time when the Army was expanding. He was appointed KCB in January 1939 and in July became Governor and Commander-in-Chief of Gibraltar, putting the defences in a fine state of preparedness at the beginning of the Second World War. In 1941 he became Inspector-General of Forces training at home, and retired from the Army aged fifty-nine in 1942. He was President of the ARU from 1940 to 1943, and from 1943 to 1949 was Governor of the Royal Hospital Chelsea and Director of St John Ambulance.

He was Colonel of The Regiment from 1943-48, and died in 1956.

Brigadier Harold Senhouse Pinder CBE MC
1948-1954

Born in 1889 and educated at Wellington College and RMC Sandhurst, Harold Pinder was commissioned into The Leicestershire Regiment in 1908. After four years with 1st Battalion in Shorncliffe and Aldershot, he served in The King's African Rifles for the next seven years, in East Africa and mostly in its 4th Battalion. He was involved in campaigns in Turkhana and Uganda in 1913-14, and in British, German and Portuguese East Africa, Nyasaland and Northern Rhodesia from 1914 to 1918. He was awarded the MC in 1918 and Bar the following year, and

Mentioned in Dispatches in 1917 and 1919. From 1919 to 1923 he served in the Somaliland Camel Corps including the campaign against the Mad Mullah in 1920, and he commanded it for a time.

Returning to more conventional soldiering in 1924, he worked in the Directorate of Military Operations for a year, before being posted to 2nd Battalion and then becoming a student at the Staff College. Thereafter he was Staff Captain (modern-day SO3) in HQ 3 Div at Bulford and SO2 at HQ 50 (Northumbrian) Div (TA). In 1933 he became SO2 Jamaica, in which appointment he was able to visit Barbados, where an ancestor had been the founding father of the Theological College.

From there he was promoted and posted to command the 1st Battalion in India from 1935 to 1939. This period included the 250th anniversary celebrations of the founding of the Regiment and the presentation of new Colours at Jubbulpore in March 1938, and the first four months of the Battalion's year of active service on the North West Frontier in Waziristan 1938-39. He retired from the Army that year on reaching the age of fifty.

On the outbreak of the Second World War he rejoined for duty in the rank of Lieutenant Colonel and so began the second phase of his illustrious military career. He was a DA & QMG administering the BEF's affairs at Dieppe in France 1939/40 for which he was appointed OBE. A fortnight after the BEF's evacuation from Dunkirk, he was among the 5,000 escapees who embarked on the SS *Lancastria* at St Nazaire, which was sunk and half its passengers drowned. He was then successively DA & QMG HQ Eastern Command and then HQ 18 Div, which supported the Free French's abortive attempt to seize Dakar in Senegal in September 1940. He commanded 6th Leicesters in the Midlands in 1940-41 and then a battle school near Loch Lomond in Scotland. He was Commander of the Algiers Base for the First Army's landing and subsequent operations in North Africa for which he was appointed CBE in 1943. His logistics expertise was next utilized by his appointment as Commander of 8 Base Sub-Area of 21st Army Group in 1944, first at Ostend in Belgium, and later in Hamburg until September 1945. He was Mentioned in Dispatches. He then retired from the Army for the second time.

He was Colonel of The Regiment from 1948-54, and died in 1974.

Lieutenant General Sir Colin Bishop Callander KCB KBE MC
1954-1963

Born in 1897 and educated at West Buckland School, Somerset, and at the RMC Sandhurst, Colin Callander was commissioned in 1915 into The Royal Munster Fusiliers (RMF). He served in 1st RMF in Flanders, was Mentioned in Dispatches and awarded the MC in 1916. He was wounded three times. He became Adjt of 2nd RMF in Egypt in 1921 before, on the disbandment of the Southern Irish Regiments in 1922, transferring to The Leicestershire Regiment. He served with 2nd Leicesters in India, Khartoum, Colchester and Londonderry from 1922 to 1931, and was a student at the Staff College in 1932. He was a Brigade Major in India before becoming 2IC of 1st Leicesters during the Waziristan campaign 1938-39 on the North-West Frontier of India for which he was Mentioned in Dispatches.

He commanded and trained the reformed l/5th Leicesters in 1940-41 after its gallant fight in North Norway against superior German forces. From 1941 to 1943 he commanded 159 Inf Bde in England, and then spent a year in a major general's staff appointment. From 1944 to 1946 he commanded 4 Inf Div in Greece with the task of keeping internal law and order in a revolutionary situation. This he handled with political acumen and operational firmness, being appointed CB in 1945. Most satisfyingly in May that year he took the surrender of the 22,000 strong German Army garrisoning Crete, a small comfort for the heavy losses to 2nd Leicesters in the unsuccessful battle for Crete in May/June 1941.

In the post-war years he held a series of senior appointments: Director of Tactical Investigation 1946-48, Director-General of Military Training in 1948, GOC 2 Div in BAOR 1949-51, C-in-C British Army of the Rhine 1951, Director-General of Military Training again 1952-54, and finally Military Secretary 1954-56. Appointed KBE 1952 and KCB in 1955, he retired from the Army in 1957.

He was Colonel of The Regiment from 1954 to 1963. During the years of infantry reorganization, he was particularly keen to retain the Regiment's close ties with its City and County, whose interest and generosity it so much appreciated. He died in 1979.

Major General Sir Douglas Anthony Kendrew KCMG CB CBE DSO
1963-1965

Born in 1910 and educated at Uppingham School, Douglas ('Joe') Kendrew was commissioned into The Leicestershire Regiment in 1931, serving in the 2nd Battalion in Londonderry. He was a formidable Rugby front row forward, for Leicester and others. Aged twenty, in 1930 he was a member of the British Lions tour to Australia and New Zealand. He played for the Army 1932-36; and for England ten times (captain twice in 1935; in 1936 he played in the winning side vs. New Zealand in Obolensky's match).

In 1936-38 he was an instructor at the Tank Driving and Maintenance School at Bovington, and then at the Armoured Fighting Vehicle School. In 1939, in the rank of captain, he was a platoon commander at RMC Sandhurst, before becoming a company commander in the newly formed 7th Leicesters at Nottingham. He then joined the staff of HQ First Army, and in 1942 became Brigade Major of 36 Indep Inf Bde, with whom he landed in Algiers in early 1943.

Three days after becoming CO of 6th Y & L he was awarded the DSO at the Second Battle for Sedjanene (50 miles west of Tunis) on 30 March 1943. He was Mentioned in Dispatches at the conclusion of the North African campaign in September that year. He was awarded an immediate Bar to the DSO while commanding the same battalion just after the landings at Salerno in Italy on 9 September, and an immediate Second Bar for his leadership on 5 January 1944 at the River Peccia, south of Monte Cassino. Shortly afterwards he became Comd 128 (Hampshire) Brigade which he commanded in Italy and Greece, being appointed CBE in December 1944 for the manner in which he had transformed the fighting ability of the Brigade.

After the Second World War, he held a further five brigadier's appointments. From 1946 to 1948 he was Commandant School of Infantry, Rhine Army, and from 1948 to 1950 Commandant Army Apprentice School Harrogate, followed by two years as Chief of Staff, HQ Northern Ireland District. From 1952 to 1953 he was Comd 29 (British) Inf Bde in Korea, for which he was awarded a third bar to his DSO for his leadership during the Battles of the Hook in early 1953. He is one of only nine Army officers to be awarded the DSO four times.

After attending the Imperial Defence College in 1954, in 1955 he was Brigadier Administration, HQ Northern Command. Promoted Major General, from 1956 to 1958 he was GOC Cyprus District and Director of Operations during the EOKA campaign, and was appointed CB. He was Director of Infantry 1958-60 and then Head of British Defence Liaison Staff at Canberra, before retiring from the Army in 1963.

For the next ten years (1963-73) he was Governor of Western Australia, being appointed KCMG in 1963 and a Knight of St John the following year. From 1965 to 1973 he was Honorary Colonel of the SAS Regiment (Australia) and of The Royal West Australia Regiment. He was made an Honorary LLD of the University of Western Australia in 1969.

On return to England, from 1973 to 1983 he was President of the Knights of the Round Table and from 1974 to 1980 a Commissioner of The Royal Hospital Chelsea.

He was the last Colonel The Royal Leicestershire Regiment from 1963 to 1964 and a Deputy Colonel The Royal Anglian Regiment 1964-65. He curtailed his tenure of office as he considered that he could no longer carry out that Regimental duty effectively while living in Western Australia. He died in 1989.

Major General John Michael Kane Spurling CB CBE DSO
1965-1971

Born in 1906 and educated at Oundle School and the RMC Sandhurst, John Spurling was commissioned into The Leicestershire Regiment in 1927. He served initially in the 1st Battalion in India and then in the 2nd Battalion at Londonderry, Aldershot and in Palestine (being Adjutant 1938-39). After attending the Staff College, he was in turn an SO3, a Brigade Major and an SO 2 twice all within the period October 1939 to April 1942. He was appointed an SO1 in May 1942 serving twice in this capacity up until a period spent in Burma. For the campaign in North-West Europe, he was a reserve Commanding Officer waiting to replace a casualty. In June 1944, he duly took command of 2/5th Battalion The Lancashire Fusiliers (in 197 Bde of 59 Div), taking part in the fighting near Caen until the whole formation was disbanded in August 1944. He commanded 131 Lorried Infantry Brigade (of 7 Armd Div) from October 1944 until November 1945. During this period he was awarded an immediate DSO for his leadership in an action on 6-8 April 1945 on the Dortmund-Ems Canal at Ibbenburen, a few miles west of Osnabrück. On 3 May, he accepted the surrender of Hamburg and in June 1945 he led his Brigade into Berlin as the first British formation to enter the German capital. He was responsible for the organization and execution of the British Victory Parade in Berlin on 21 July where the salute was taken by the Prime Minister, Winston Churchill.

In December 1945, he was appointed Deputy Director of Military Training at the War Office and then commanded 4 Para Brigade (TA) from 1948 to 1950. In May 1950 he became Commandant of the Senior Officers' School, being appointed CBE in 1953. In November of that year he was appointed Chief of Staff HQ West African Coast. In June 1955, on promotion to Major General, he became Chief of Staff HQ Northern Command at York, being appointed CB in 1957. He retired from the Army in 1958.

In retirement he gained a great reputation for his success in coaching officers for their Promotion and Staff College exams. He also became a Governor of Milton Abbey School, Dorset.

He was Deputy Colonel The Royal Anglian Regiment (Leicestershire and Rutland) from 1965 to 1971, during which time he strongly fought The Tigers' corner over the period that its Regular and TA Battalions were disbanded. He died in 1980.

Colonel M St G Pallot
1971-1977

Born in 1914 and educated at Newton College, Devon, and at RMC Sandhurst, Mike Pallot, choosing a keen rugby regiment, was commissioned into The Leicestershire Regiment in 1937. He served initially in the 1st Battalion in India, including the Waziristan Campaign 1938-39 on the North-West Frontier of India.

He returned to England in 1940 and was posted to 1/5th Leicesters in Belfast. After Staff College in 1943, he came Brigade Major of 144 Inf Bde. In 1944, shortly after D-Day, he went to Normandy as 2IC of 2nd Bn The Essex Regiment, which was involved in the intense fighting around Falaise. After being wounded and convalescing in England, he took over a company of 6th Bn The King's Own Scottish Borderers in March 1945. While preparing for the crossing of the River Rhine, he had the unusual distinction of calling for fire of the entire divisional artillery, and some 600 field, medium and heavy shells rained down on the enemy position. At the end of the war in North-West Europe, he was Mentioned in Dispatches and moved to HQ 43 Div, before serving as an instructor at the Senior Officers' School at Dehra Dun in India 1945-48.

Back with 1st R Leicesters, he served as Adjutant in 1948 and as a company commander in Iserlohn, interspersed with three years in the Military Training Directorate at the War Office 1949-52. He was Commanding Officer of the Regimental Depot 1953-55, before being posted to HQ British Troops Egypt. He became 2IC of the 1st Battalion in Cyprus in September 1956 during the EOKA Campaign and was Mentioned in Dispatches in 1958. He took over command of the Battalion in Plymouth in 1958 and commanded it in Münster in Germany until July 1961. He then fulfilled a logistics post at NATO's HQ Land Forces Central Europe at Fontainebleau, France, on completion of which he was promoted and took up a three-year posting at the Ministry of Defence as Colonel Q (Maint). After two years as Colonel AQ at the District HQ at York, he retired from the Army in 1970.

On retirement, he became Secretary of Yorkshire TAVRA (1970-73) and Sports and Estates Officer at RMA Sandhurst (1974-82). He was Master and Joint Master of the Sandhurst Beagles for thirteen of the twenty years between 1974 and 1994.

He was Deputy Colonel The Royal Anglian Regiment (Leicestershire and Rutland) 1971-77, his tenure coinciding with the years of Tiger Company 4th Battalion and its disbandment in 1975. He died in 2004.

Appendix O

Commanding Officers of The Royal Leicestershire Regiment
1708-1971

XVII Regiment	From	To
Lt Col Bourguet	1708	
Lt Col W Congreve	20 Feb 1747	21 Sep 1756
Lt Col A Morris	21 Sep 1756	14 May 1759
Lt Col J Darby	14 May 1759	1 Feb 1762
Lt Col J Campbell	1 Feb 1762	26 Oct 1775
Lt Col C Mawhood	26 Oct 1775	4 Oct 1778
Lt Col H Johnson	4 Oct 1778	15 Jul 1794
Lt Col G Hallam	15 Jul 1794	14 Sep 1799
Lt Col J Burnet	14 Sep 1799	1801

1st Battalion		
Lt Col R Stovin	1801	4 Jun 1811
Lt Col F Hardyman CB	4 Jun 1811	Aug 1819
Lt Col W T Edwards	12 Aug 1819	4 Nov 1822
Lt Col A Maclaine CB	4 Nov 1822	30 Jul 1829
Lt Col J Austin	30 Jul 1829	13 Aug 1829
Lt Col H Despard	13 Aug 1829	4 Mar1836
Lt Col W Croker CB[1]	1 Apr 1836	5 Nov 1847
Lt Col J Pennycuick CB[1] KH[2]	5 Nov 1847	7 Apr 1848
Lt Col J Stoyte	7 Apr 1848	24 Mar 1853
Lt Col P McPherson CB	3 Dec 1852	1854
Lt Col A L Cole CB	9 Mar 1855	15 Jan 1861
Lt Col W Gordon	15 Jan 1861	23 Jan 1869
Lt Col D L Colhurst	23 Jan 1869	31 Jul 1869
Lt Col A H Cobbe[3]	31 Jul 1869	14 Oct 1878
Lt Col W D Tompson CB[4]	14 Oct 1878	14 Jul 1884
Lt Col A H Utterson CB[5]	14 Jul 1884	1 Jul 1887
Lt Col T Bradell	1 Jul 1887	5 Feb 1890
Lt Col W M Rolph	5 Feb 1890	5 Feb 1894
Lt Col C W Vulliamy	5 Feb 1894	10 Feb 1897
Lt Col W S D Liardet	10 Feb 1897	1 Jan 1898
Lt Col F W Reader	1 Jan 1898	10 Nov 1898
Lt Col G D Carleton	3 Dec 1898	14 Dec 1902
Lt Col J G L Burnett	24 Feb 1903	9 Sep 1904
Lt Col G H P Burne	10 Sep 1904	10 Sep 1908
Lt Col L C Sherer	10 Sep 1908	11 Nov 1910
Lt Col H L Croker[6]	12 Nov 1910	20 Mar 1915

Lt Col H Stoney Smith DSO	20 Mar 1915	20 Oct 1915
Lt Col A H Buchanan-Dunlop	25 Oct 1915	6 Feb 1916
Lt Col R H Gillespie DSO	7 Feb 1916	20 Sep 1916
Lt Col R S Dyer Bennet	21 Sep 1916	12 Dec 1916
Lt Col R H Gillespie DSO	13 Dec 1916	26 Mar 1917
Lt Col H B Brown DSO	27 Mar 1917	1 May 1917
Lt Col R H Gillespie DSO	2 May 1917	4 Jul 1917
Lt Col H B Brown DSO	5 Jul 1917	16 Jan 1918
Lt Col D L Weir DSO MC	17 Jan 1918	25 Feb 1918
Lt Col F Latham DSO	26 Feb 1918	29 Apr 1918
Lt Col S T Hartshorn MC	10 May 1918	20 May 1918
Lt Col D L Weir DSO MC	21 May 1918	25 Jul 1918
Lt Col F Latham DSO	26 Jul 1918	2 Nov 1918
Lt Col J H Martin DSO MC	3 Nov 1918	11 Nov 1918
Lt Col F Latham DSO	12 Nov 1918	3 Aug 1919
Lt Col E L Challenor CB CMG CBE DSO[7]	3 Aug 1919	3 Aug 1923
Lt Col F H Edwards DSO MC	3 Aug 1923	3 Aug 1927
Lt Col C S Davies CMG DSO	3 Aug 1927	3 Aug 1931
Lt Col F Latham DSO	3 Aug 1931	3 Aug 1935
Lt Col H S Pinder MC[8]	3 Aug 1935	27 Mar 1939
Lt Col E Lindsay-Young	27 Mar 1939	11 Nov 1941
Lt Col C E Morrison DSO MC	11 Nov 1941	15 Feb 1942
Lt Col C E Morrison DSO MC (during captivity)	15 Feb 1942	15 Aug 1945

8th Battalion (retitled 1st Battalion on 28 May 1942)

Lt Col P A B Wrixon	28 May 1942	7 Jan 1944
Lt Col A L Novis MC	7 Jan 1944	30 Jul 1944
Maj R J German	30 Jul 1944	Aug 1944
Maj I D M Liddell	Aug 1944	Sep 1944
Lt Col F W Sandars DSO DLI	Sep 1944	22 May 1945
Lt Col A L Novis MC	4 Jul 1945	8 Mar 1947
Lt Col R H L Oulton R Lincolns	Jul 1947	Nov 1947
Lt Col S D Field	Nov 1947	23 Jun 1950
Lt Col G E P Hutchins DSO	23 Jun 1950	28 Jun 1953
Lt Col J E D Watson DSO	28 Jun 1953	27 Jun 1956
Lt Col A W D Nicholls OBE MC	28 Jun 1956	28 Dec 1958
Lt Col M St G Pallot	29 Dec 1958	4 Jul 1961
Lt Col P E B Badger	4 Jul 1961	5 Apr 1964
Lt Col J A C Cowan MBE	6 Apr 1964	31 Aug 1964

1st Battalion retitled 4th Battalion The Royal Anglian Regiment on 1 September 1964

Lt Col J A C Cowan MBE	1 Sep 1964	6 Apr 1966
Lt Col D R C Carter	6 Apr 1966	6 Sep 1968
Lt Col T Holloway	6 Sep 1968	14 Sep 1970

2nd Battalion (formed for the second time in March 1858)

Lt Col H D Crofton	24 Mar 1858	16 Dec 1859
Lt Col G W Francklyn	16 Dec 1859	17 May 1861

Lt Col A W McKinstry	17 May 1861	14 Jan 1871
Lt Col G T Brice CB[9]	14 Jan 1871	6 Dec 1878
Lt Col J B H Boyd	7 Dec 1878	15 Oct 1880
Lt Col C G Grant	16 Oct 1880	14 Jul 1884
Lt Col C McPherson	14 Jul 1884	1 Jul 1887
Lt Col S Bradburne	1 Jul 1887	3 Dec 1890
Lt Col C W F Moir	3 Dec 1890	3 Dec 1894
Lt Col W Gregg	3 Dec 1894	3 Dec 1898
Lt Col A W McKinstry	3 Dec 1898	11 Nov 1902
Lt Col E R Scott	11 Nov 1902	11 Nov 1906
Lt Col V T Bunbury DSO[10]	11 Nov 1906	11 Nov 1910
Lt Col L C Sherer	12 Nov 1910	10 Sep 1912
Lt Col C G Blackader DSO[11]	10 Sep 1912	Jan 1915
Lt Col H Gordon DSO	Jan 1915	8 Nov 1915
Lt Col F Lewis DSO	8 Nov 1915	13 Jan 1916
Lt Col R N Knatchbull DSO	13 Jan 1916	24 Jul 1917
Lt Col A W S Brock DSO	24 Jul 1917	27 May 1919
Lt Col B C Dent CMG DSO	27 May 1919	10 Sep 1920
Lt Col C H Haig CBE DSO	25 Jul 1921	25 Jul 1925
Lt Col W T Bromfield	25 Jul 1925	25 Jul 1929
Lt Col P H Creagh DSO	25 Jul 1929	8 May 1933
Lt Col A T le M Utterson DSO	8 May 1933	8 May 1937
Lt Col M K Wardle DSO MC	9 May 1937	8 May 1940
Lt Col C H V Cox DSO MC	9 May 1940	23 Sep 1941
Lt Col O G A Phillips	23 Sep 1941	15 Mar 1943
Lt Col C J Wilkinson DSO R Norfolk[12]	16 Mar 1943	28 Aug 1944
Maj A W D Nicholls MC	29 Aug 1944	May 1945
Lt Col K S McGregor	26 May 1945	4 Jul 1945
Maj F R Wilford Northamptons	5 Jul 1945	12 Oct 1945
Maj G E P Hutchins	12 Dec 1945	2 Feb 1947
Lt Col J N Carter OBE R Warwick	Mar 1947	Jun 47
Lt Col A L Novis MC	Jun 1947	15 Jan 1948
Lt Col D F Coburn	16 Jan 1948	24 Feb 1948

In Feb 1948 the unit was merged with 1st Battalion The Royal Leicestershire Regiment.

4th Battalion (Territorial Force (TF) till 1922, then Territorial Army (TA))

Lt Col E C Atkins	1908	1909
Lt Col C F Oliver	1909	1913
Lt Col W A Harrison TD	1913	1914
Lt Col R E Martin	1914	1915
Lt Col J E Blackwall DSO TD	1915	1920
Lt Col J E Viccars DSO OBE TD[13]	1920	1922
Bt Col H W H Tyler MC	1922	1930
Bt Col A Halkyard MC TD[14]	1930	1936
Lt Col F M Mantle TD	1936	1941

In 1936 the 4th Battalion was rebadged and became **44th (The Leicestershire Regiment) Anti-Aircraft Battalion Royal Engineers (TA)**. In 1940 it was rebadged and became **44th Searchlight**

Regiment Royal Artillery (RA), and in 1942 it changed its role and title to **121st Light Anti-Aircraft Regiment RA**. In 1947 it became **579th (The Royal Leicestershire Regiment) Light Anti-Aircraft Regiment RA (TA)**.

Lt Col G L Aspell TD[15]	1947	1951
Lt Col C D Wain MBE TD DL[16]	1951	1954
Lt Col L H Smith TD	1954	1955

In 1955 the unit was retitled **Q/438 (The Royal Leicestershire Regiment) Light Anti-Aircraft Battery RA (TA)**.

Maj W F Adams	1955	1957
Maj R G Wilkes TD	1957	1961

In Apr 1961 the Battery amalgamated with 5th Battalion to form **4/5th Battalion** (see below).

5th Battalion (TF)

Lt Col G German TD DL	1908	1913
Lt Col C H Jones TD	1913	1914

1/5th Battalion (TF)

Bt Col C H Jones CMG TD	1914	1918

2/5th Battalion (TF)

Lt Col E C Atkins TD	1914	Jan 1917
Lt Col G B G Wood DSO LF[17]	Jan 1917	Sep 1917
Lt Col G German DSO	Sep 1917	Dec 1918

5th Battalion (TF till 1922, then TA)

Bt Col W S N Toler DSO TD	1920	1926
Bt Col J L Griffiths DSO TD	1926	1931
Bt Col J P W Jamie MC TD	1931	1937
Lt Col J C Barrett VC TD[18]	1937	1939

1/5th Battalion (TA)

Lt Col J C Barrett VC TD	30 Jun 1939	14 Oct 1939
Lt Col G J German DSO TD[19]	14 Oct 1939	27 Apr 1940
Lt Col C B Callander MC[20]	May 1940	Jun 1941
Lt Col E A Wood	Aug 1941	Jun 1942
Lt Col R E H Ward MC	5 Jun 1942	20 Jun 1943
Lt Col D F Coburn	26 Jun 1943	18 Aug 1944
Lt Col K F May OBE Essex	10 Sep 1944	12 Aug 1946

2/5th Battalion (TA)

Lt Col G J German TD	30 Jun 1939	13 Oct 1939
Lt Col G K F Ruddle TD	27 Oct 1939	Jun 1940
Lt Col L Sawyer DSO[21]	Jun 1940	Dec 1940
Lt Col R N Gale MC Worcesters[22]	Dec 1940	Aug 1941
Lt Col S E P Moran South Lancs	17 Sep 1941	5 Aug 1942

Lt Col G L Dolman Loyals	29 Aug 1942	4 Apr 1943
Lt Col C W B Orr OBE DWR	4 Apr 1943	16 Sep 1943
Lt Col E S Orpwood R Berks	16 Sep 1943	29 Sep 1943
Lt Col S Enderby DSO MC RNF	7 Nov 1943	Apr 1944
Lt Col F L Martin DSO South Staffords	19 Apr 1944	Jun 1944
Lt Col J H Cubbon OBE Cheshire	30 Oct 1944	22 Apr 1945
Lt Col D W S Price Dorset	22 Apr 1945	Nov 1945
Lt Col P G Upcher DSO	29 Nov 1945	May 1946

5th Battalion (TA)

Lt Col K W Symington TD	1947	1950
Lt Col P G Upcher DSO	1950	1 Aug 1952
Lt Col M Moore MC TD	2 Aug 1952	1 Aug 1956
Lt Col P McH Preston MBE TD	2 Aug 1956	Aug 1959
Lt Col J H Marriott MC	Aug 1959	May 1961

In Apr 1961 the unit amalgamated with Q/438 (The Royal Leicestershire Regiment) LAA Battery RA (TA) (whose antecedent until 1936 had been 4th Battalion The Leicestershire Regiment (see above)).

4/5th Battalion (TA)

Lt Col S A Smith OBE	May 1961	Nov 1963
Lt Col J P N Creagh	Nov 1963	Dec 1966
Lt Col R G Wilkes TD	Dec 1966	31 Mar 1967

The Royal Leicestershire Regiment (Territorial)

Lt Col R G Wilkes OBE TD	1 Apr 1967	31 Mar 1969
Maj W G Dawson TD (Cadre)	1 Apr 1969	31 Mar 1971

6th Battalion

Lt Col L Dexter Foresters	Nov 1939	16 Dec 1939
Lt Col L Wood MC	16 Dec 1939	Oct 1940
Lt Col H S Pinder OBE MC	Oct 1940	Jun 1941
Maj C H Emerson MC	Jun 1941	13 Oct 1941

7th Battalion

Lt Col W E Underhill	4 Jul 1940	27 Apr 1942
Lt Col P D S Palmer	4 May 1942	5 Oct 1943
Maj F R Wilford Northamptons	25 Nov 1943	1 Jun 1944

8th Battalion (which on 28 May 1942 was retitled 1st Battalion) (see above)

Lt Col P A B Wrixon	Oct 1940	28 May 1942

50th Battalion (which in October 1940 was retitled 8th Battalion)

Lt Col P A B Wrixon	28 May 1940	Oct 1940

Notes

1 Croker, the Lt Col commanding, and Major Pennycuick, were both appointed CB for their conduct at the capture of Khelat in Afghanistan in 1839.

2 Pennycuick's KH indicates that he was a Knight of the Royal Hanoverian Guelphic Order, an Order instituted in 1815 by The Prince Regent (later HM George IV) and discontinued in Britain in 1837, on the accession of Queen Victoria. Holders of that knighthood were not entitled to be called 'Sir'.

3 later Maj Gen Sir Alexander H Cobbe KCB.

4 later Maj Gen W D Tompson CB, Colonel The Leicestershire Regiment 1912-16. See Appendix N.

5 later Maj Gen A H Utterson CB, Colonel The Leicestershire Regiment 1905-12.

6 later Maj Gen Sir Henry L Croker KCB CMG, GOC 28 Div in Macedonia/Mesopotamia 1916-20.

7 See Chapter 13, Footnote 6.

8 later Brig H S Pinder CBE MC, Colonel The Royal Leicestershire Regiment 1948-54. See Appendix N.

9 later Maj Gen G T Brice CB, Colonel The Leicestershire Regiment 1903-05.

10 later Brig Gen V T Bunbury CB CMG DSO, Provost Marshal BEF in France 1914-6.

11 later Maj Gen C G Blackader CB DSO ADC, GOC 177 Bde 1915 and 38 (Welsh) Div 1916-18. Contemporary photographs indicate that he had a close likeness to the fictitious General Sir Anthony Hogmanay Melchett, played by Stephen Fry in the 1980s' First World War TV comedy series 'Blackadder'.

12 later Brig C J Wilkinson DSO, Colonel The Royal Norfolk Regiment 1951-59.

13 Awarded the DSO on 3 Jun 1918 for distinguished service in connection with military operations in France and Flanders.

14 See Chapter 2, Footnote 12.

15 See Chapter 10, Footnote 9.

16 See Chapter 13, Footnote 14.

17 Awarded the DSO as Adjt 5th LF at Gallipoli 1915.

18 See Chapter 7, Footnote 9.

19 See Chapter 7, Footnote 10.

20 later Lt Gen Sir Colin Callander KCB KBE MC. See Appendix N.

21 See Chapter 13, Footnote 10.

22 later Gen Sir Richard Gale KBE CB DSO MC, GOC 6 AB Div at Arnhem 1944, CinC BAOR 1953-57, DSACEUR 1958-60.

23 later Brig W E Underhill OBE, the author of *The History of The Royal Leicestershire Regiment 1928-56*. See Chapter 2, Footnote 4.

Appendix P

Key to names in group photographs

1st R Leicesters officers – July 1956 (Page 30)
Back Row: 2Lts R E R Buckingham, P M North, C H Moore, J C D Heggs, A S Bettles, A D Barlow, G N L Stubbs, A P G Brown.
Middle Row: Lts J R A Wilkes, C T Marshall, C W Byham, Capts T Holloway, A E R Ross, J T Dudley, A E R Peters, M W McD Cairns, 2Lts J O Church, D C Samworth, M W North.
Front Row: Capt J P N Creagh, Majs R J H Pacy, G E Smart, I G Jessop MC, K P P Goldschmidt, Lt Cols A W D Nicholls MC, J E D Watson DSO, Majs D P Carey, P E B Badger, A C V Sheppard, S A Smith MBE, P G Bligh, Capt (QM) E H Scanlon.

1st R Leicesters Connaught Trophy Pistol Team – 1957/58 (Page 41)
Back Row: SSgt Bidwell REME, Lt J C Wrighton, Lt W H Morris, 2Lt J C D Heggs.
Front Row: Lt J H Rees, Maj J L Bromhead RAPC (Captain), Lt Col A W D Nicholls MC, Maj D R Dalglish MC.

1st R Leicesters Rugby Team – 1957/58 (Page 46)
Back Row: Lt D R Nevile, WO2 N H P Jenks MM, Lt W H Morris, SSgt Bidwell REME, Cpl Stewart, Sgt Castleton, 2Lt R W Carpenter.
Sitting: Lt C J Wrighton, Lt J C D Heggs, Lt Col A W D Nicholls MC, 2Lt D R Trentham, Maj D R Dalglish MC, Lt J R A Wilkes (Captain), Lt J H Rees, 2Lt J W Mansfield.
Front Row: Pte Clark, Cpl Baldwin.

4th R Anglian Football Team – UK Army Finalists 1966 (Page 172)
Back Row: LCpl R Longland, Pte S Coley, Cpl R Allen, WO1 (RSM) N H P Jenks MM, Cpl J Rourke, LCpl A Williamson, Pte S Issacs.
Front Row: Pte J Collins, Cpl J Hinson, Pte K Wright, SSI W Stoves APTC, WO2 (ORQMS) M J Rigley (Captain).

4/5th R Leicesters (TA) officers – 1966 (Page 222)
Back Row: Mr R Dimblebee, 2Lts C H Cole, R C Lane, C W Hampton, W E Cronin, J A Kelly, P Frost.
Middle Row: 2Lt J R Ward, Lt T J Lant, Capt M A N Clarke, Rev A T Green RAChD, Capts M I M Joule, J F Hampson, W G Lewis, Lt J E Underwood.
Front Row: Majs A H V Gilmore MC, J T Dudley, A A J Wilson TD, W G Wallace, Col G J German DSO TD, Lt Col R G Wilkes TD, Capt A J G Pollard, Majs W G Dawson, R D F Bream, (QM) J H F Leeson.

4th R Anglian (Army Malta) Athletics Team – May 1968 (Page 188)
Standing: Ptes Moreau, Kennerley, N Jephcote, J Sorenson, Cpl T Fleming REME, Lt D W James, Lt M K Goldschmidt (Captain), Capt A J G Pollard, LCpl Bradley (1 Loyals), 2Lt C W Hewitt Int Corps, Maj J G Jones MBE (OIC Athletics).
Kneeling (centre): Sgt T Elliott, Cfn Hessel REME.
Kneeling (front): Cpl R Crook RAPC, LCpl L Holman, Cpls R Sarson, C Dutton, Pte J Spiers, Cpls A Waqairoba, Austin, Bdsm Ziska.

4th R Anglian officers – May 1970 (Page 248)

Back Row: Lts J A Darnley, J M P Walsh, D L H Bulleid, P C Shalders, 2Lt R Thompson, Lt B R Cornish, 2Lt M V A Wilkinson RAEC, Lt J T Towns, 2Lts P M L Ferrary, K M Ryan.

Middle Row: Capts A C Taylor, J E Findlow RAMC, B H M Davenport, N H P Jenks MBE MM, Rev R A McDowall RAChD, Capt M E Romilly, Lt D J M Daniels, 2Lt P W Field, Lt R Wright, Capts M J Peele MC, G H Taft RAPC, (QM) J Eyeions.

Front Row: Capts (QM) E A Holben, S R Yates, Majs J Robinette, S A Green, M E Duffie, Lt Col T Holloway, Capt C P B Keeble, Majs R H Robinson, P W King, Capt A E Thompson MC.

4th R Anglian WOs & SNCOs – May 1970 (Page 248)

Back Row: Sgts N Cooper, A Hurry, Reid R Signals, D Stewart, C Mallett, Brophy RAPC, M Tyler, J Pepper, Douse REME, V Moore, A J Pemberton, C Holyoak, P Hughes.

3rd Row: Sgts M Bradbury, B Collins, L Lock, T Bodenham, T Simpson, A Mackay, Mortimer ACC, Robinson, R Nesbitt, J Brown, P Dobson, K Delaney, P Cranfield, T Fleming REME, D Wells, D Bausor.

2nd Row: Sgts S Barkby, CSgts G Bould, K Pearce, E Davies, SSgt P O'Brien REME, CSgts C Roberts, E Christopher, R E Jones, SSgt R Cronie RAPC, CSgts A Rollins, A C Sprason, Sgts Thompson ACC, R Taylor RA (AAC).

Front Row: WO2s D W Spalding, J T Morris MM, P Jones, L MacDonald, (RQMS) A I James, WO1(RSM) P F Garman, Lt Col T Holloway, WO1(BM) T G Cooper, WO2s (SQMS) J Drake ACC, (QMSI) W A Robson APTC, K Atkins, R B Freakley, C J Phillips.

Tiger Company – February 1974 (Page 270 and 271)

Back Row: Ptes Scott, Chapman, D Horne, Cpl Heeley, LCpl M Lemmon, Ptes Theobald, Sanders, Randall, Howard, Johnson, LCpl O'Donnel, Ptes Batterbee, Carter 17, Eastabrook, Harper, LCpl P Coleman, Pts G Silver, Bell.

Fourth Row: Ptes Horton, Godfrey, Donnison, Chadwick, Townsend, Martin 23, LCpl Blyth, Ptes Bligh, LCpl Whitwell, Ptes Carter 34, Capper, Lloyd, Cpl J Winship, Ptes Sharpe, Hay, LCpl Edie, Cpl Smith, LCpl A Barley, Pte J McBride.

Middle Row: Ptes Payne, Fitzgerald, Larder, Boughen, Cpl T Stocks, Ptes Bishop, D Gregory, Cpl Robinson, Ptes Wood, Martin 48, M Dobbs, Decaux, LCpl Hazel, Cpl Houlden, LCpl Newberry, Cpls Wharton, Boswell, Ptes Cooper, Smith, LCpl Wilson.

Second Row: Ptes K Freeston, S Dexter, D Hawkins, Clarke, Beast, LCpl Smith, Pte Hampson, LCpls Swinn, Clayton, Tebbutt, Pte Barrett, Cpl E Dexter, LCpl Umney, Ptes Wesley, Harrison, Thomson, Champion, Dunkley, Moss.

Front Row: Cpls J Weaver, J Harrison, T Watson, P Venn, Sgts T Basham, S Parker, W Kerr, R C McDonald, Lt C J B Groom, WO2 E Davies, Maj F A H Swallow, Capt S R H Underwood, Lt D Morris, CSgt M E Taylor, Sgts D Madlin, R Mayes ACC, P Vowles RAPC, Cpls P Staples, P Ling, A Grant.

Presentation of the Essendon Regiment clock – July 1958 (Page 316)

Capt John Wilson, Lt Tony Palfreyman, Col Teddy Hutchins DSO, Capt Harold Schuldt MM ED, Aldm Sidney Brown TD, Maj Peter Bligh, Maj Peter Badger.

Planting of the first trees at Royal Tigers' Wood – 29 January 1994 (Plate Section)

Lt Col John Wilson, Lady Brooks, Sir Timothy Brooks KCVO JP (Lord Lieutenant of Leicestershire), Susan Bell (Chief Executive, National Forest), Maj Gen Tony Pollard CB CBE, Col Bill Dawson TD DL, Maj Berty Bowes.

Appendix Q

Key to Abbreviations used in the text

AA	Anti-Aircraft
AAC	Army Air Corps
AB	Airborne
ABF	Army Benevolent Fund
ACF	Army Cadet Force
ACV	Armoured Command Vehicle
ADC	Aide-de-Camp
Adjt	Adjutant
Admin	Administrative[/ion]
AGRA	Army Group Royal Artillery
AKC	Army Kinema Corporation
Aldm	Alderman
ANE	'*Valiant Youth of EOKA*'
AOR	Area of Responsibility
APC	Armoured Personnel Carrier
APL	The Aden Protectorate Levies
APTC	Army Physical Training Corps
ARA	Army Rifle Association
ARCM	Associate of the Royal College of Music
Armd	Armoured
ARU	Army Rugby Union
Asst	Assistant
ATAF	Allied Tactical Air Force
ATGW	Anti-Tank Guided Weapon
AYT	Army Youth Team
A & SH	The Argyll & Sutherland Highlanders
BAOR	British Army of the Rhine
BD	Battle Dress
BDF	Bahrain Defence Force
Bde	Brigade
Bdsm	Bandsman
BEF	British Expeditionary Force
BEM	British Empire Medal
BF	British Forces
BFG	British Forces Gulf
BFBS	British Forces Broadcasting Service
BFHK	British Forces Hong Kong
BM	Brigade Major (Major)/Bandmaster (WO1)
BHC	British High Commission
BMM	British Military Mission
Bn	Battalion

Br/BR	British
BSM	Battery Sergeant Major (WO2)
Bty	Battery
BVF	Barbados Volunteer Force
BW	The Black Watch
Capt	Captain
Casevac	Casualty evacuation
CB	Companion of the Order of the Bath
CBE	Commander of the Order of the British Empire
CBF	Commander British Forces
CCF	Combined Cadet Force
Cdo	Commando (Royal Marines)
CENTO	Central Treaty Organisation (Iran, Pakistan, Turkey, UK 1959-79)
CEO	Chief Executive Officer
Cfn	Craftsman
Cheshire	The Cheshire Regiment
CIGS	Chief of the Imperial General Staff
C-in-C	Commander-in-Chief
Cllr	Councillor
CMF	Citizens Military Force (Australian TA equivalent)
CMG	Companion of the Order of St Michael & St George
CO	Commanding Officer
Coldm Gds	Coldstream Guards
COS	Chief of Staff (principal staff officer in a formation HQ)
Comd	Commander
Comdt	Commandant
COP	Close Observation Platoon
Coy	Company
Cpl	Corporal
CPX	Command Post Exercise
CQMS	Company Quartermaster Sergeant (SSgt)
CSM	Company Sergeant Major (WO2)
CSE	Combined Services Entertainment
CSMI	Company Sergeant Major Instructor
CVA	Cyprus Veterans' Association
CVO	Commander of the Royal Victorian Order
CWGC	Commonwealth War Graves Commission
D	Deputy (in an appointment title)
DAAG	Deputy Assistant Adjutant General
DAA & QMG	Deputy Assistant Adjutant & Quartermaster General
DAG	Deputy Adjutant General
D and D	The Devonshire and Dorset Regiment
DCM	Distinguished Conduct Medal
DComd	Deputy Commander
DERR	The Duke of Edinburgh's Royal Regiment
Det	Detachment
DF	Defensive Fire (pre-planned artillery and/or mortar targets)
Dir-Gen Mil Trg	Director-General Military Training
Div	Division(al)

DL	Deputy Lieutenant
Dmr	Drummer
DoM	Director of Music
Dorset	The Dorsetshire Regiment
DQD	Depot The Queen's Division
DSACEUR	Deputy Supreme Allied Commander Europe (NATO)
DSM	Distinguished Service Medal (Oman)
DSO	Companion of Distinguished Service Order
DTA&C	Director Territorial Army & Cadets
DWR	The Duke of Wellington's Regiment
E Anglian	The East Anglian Regiment
EAP	Eastern Aden Protectorate
EER	The East of England Regiment
EOKA	*Ethniki Organosis Kypriou Agonistou* (Gr)
ERE	Extra-Regimental Employment
Essex	The Essex Regiment
FAC	Forward Air Controller
FARELF	Far East Land Forces
Fd	Field
Fd Amb	Field Ambulance RAMC
FEPOW	Far East Prisoners of War
FGA	Fighter Ground-Attack (aircraft)
FLO	Families Liaison Officer
Flt	Flight
FM	Field Marshal
FOB	Forward Operating Base
FOO	Forward Observation Officer
Foresters	The Sherwood Foresters
FNG	Federal National Guard (South Arabian paramilitary)
FRA	Federal Regular Army (South Arabia)
FRG	Federal Republic of Germany (West Germany)
FSMO	Field Service Marching Order
GCB	Knight Grand Cross of the Order of the Bath
GCH	Knight Grand Cross of the Royal Hanoverian Guelphic Order
GCMG	Knight Grand Cross of the Order of St Michael & St George
GCVO	Knight Grand Cross of the Royal Victorian Order
GHQ	General Headquarters
Glosters	The Gloucestershire Regiment
GOC	General Officer Commanding
Gp	Group
GPMG	General Purpose Machine Gun
GPMG (SF)	General Purpose Machine Gun in Sustained Fire role
GR	The Gurkha Rifles
GSM	General Service Medal; Garrison Sergeant Major
HF	High Frequency/Harassing Fire
HLF	Heritage Lottery Fund
HLS	Helicopter Landing Site
HMS	Her Majesty's Ship
HMT	Her Majesty's Trooper

HQ	Headquarters
HSF	Home Service Force
IA	Immediate Action
IBT	Indonesian Border Terrorist
ICAC	International Commission against Corruption
IED	Improvised Explosive Device
IJLB	Infantry Junior Leaders Battalion
Ind	Indian
Indep	Independent
Inf	Infantry
Int & Sy	Intelligence & Security
IO	Intelligence Officer
IRA	Irish Republican Army
IS	Internal Security
JEWT	Jungle Exercise Without Trees (see also TEWT)
JHQ	Joint Headquarters
JIB	Junior Infantrymen's Battalion
JIW	Junior Infantrymen's Wing
JNCO	Junior Non-Commissioned Officer (LCpl/Cpl)
JTC	Junior Training Corps
JS	Junior Soldiers
KAPE	Keep the Army in the Public Eye
KAR	The King's African Rifles
KCB	Knight Commander of the Order of the Bath
KCMG	Knight Commander of the Order of St Michael & St George
KCVO	Knight Commander of the Royal Victorian Order
KD	Khaki Drill (a cloth material)
KFS	Knife, Fork and Spoon
KH	Knight of the Royal Hanoverian Guelphic Order
KKO	*Korps Komando Operasi* (Indonesian Marines)
KOMR	The King's Own Malta Regiment
KOYLI	The King's Own Yorkshire Light Infantry
KP	Key Point
LAA	Light Anti-Aircraft
LCM	Landing Craft Marine
LCpl	Lance Corporal
LDY	The Leicestershire & Derbyshire Yeomanry
(R) Leicesters	The (Royal) Leicestershire Regiment
(R) Lincolns	The (Royal) Lincolnshire Regiment
LF	The Lancashire Fusiliers
LFG	Land Forces Gulf
LMG	Light Machine Gun
L of C	Line of Communications
Log Sp	Logistic Support
Loyals	The Loyal Regiment
LPD	Landing Platform Dock (HMSs *Fearless* and *Intrepid*)
LRAM	Licentiate of the Royal Academy of Music
Lt Col	Lieutenant Colonel
LSgt	Lance Sergeant

LSL	Landing Ship Logistic
LST	Landing Ship Tank
MACA	Military Aid to the Civil Authorities
MACC	Military Aid to the Civil Community
Maj	Major
Mar	Maritime
MBE	Member of the Order of the British Empire
MC	Military Cross
MCCP	Movement Control Check Point
MEC	Middle East Command
Med	Medical
MELF	Middle East Land Forces
MID	Mention in Dispatches
MIO	Military Intelligence Officer
MM	Military Medal
MMG	Medium Machine Gun
MOD	Ministry of Defence
MPSC	Military Provost Staff Corps
Mshl	Marshal
MSM	Meritorious Service Medal
MT	Motor Transport
MTO	Motor Transport Officer
NAAFI	Navy Army & Air Force Institute
NATO	North Atlantic Treaty Organisation
NCO	Non-Commissioned Officer
NI	Northern Ireland
NLF	National Liberation Front
NORTHAG	Northern Army Group
Northamptons	The Northamptonshire Regiment
NTM	Notice To Move
OBE	Officer of the Order of the British Empire
OC	Officer Commanding
OCTU	Officer Cadet Training Unit
OCS	Officer Cadet School
OG	Olive Green (a cloth material)
OP	Observation Post
OR	Other Rank
Orbat	Order of Battle
Ord	Ordnance
ORQMS	Orderly Room Quartermaster Sergeant
OTC	Officer Training Corps
OXI	"No" (Gk)
Para	The Parachute Regiment
pdr	pounder
PMC	President of the Mess Committee
POL	Petrol Oil Lubricant
PoW	Prisoner of War
PBI	Poor Bloody Infantry
PRI	President of the Regimental Institute

PRPG	Political Resident Persian Gulf
PSI	Permanent Staff Instructor
PSNI	Police Service of Northern Ireland (successor of the RUC)
PSO	Permanent Staff Officer/Personnel Selection Officer
(P)US of S	(Permanent) Under-Secretary of State
PWRR	The Princess of Wales's Royal Regiment
QM	Quartermaster
QMS	Quartermaster Sergeant
QOH	Queen's Own Hussars
Q O Hldrs	The Queen's Own Highlanders
Queens	The Queen's Regiment
Queens Div	The Queen's Division
RA	Royal Artillery
RAC	Royal Armoured Corps
RAChD	Royal Army Chaplains Department
RAMC	Royal Army Medical Corps
R Anglian	The Royal Anglian Regiment
RAOC	Royal Army Ordnance Corps
RAP	Regimental Aid Post
RAPC	Royal Army Pay Corps
RASC	Royal Army Service Corps
RAVC	Royal Army Veterinary Corps
R Berks	The Royal Berkshire Regiment
RBL	Royal British Legion
RCAC	Royal Canadian Armoured Corps
RCT	Royal Corps of Transport
RBL	Royal British Legion
RE	Royal Engineer(s)
REME	Royal Electrical and Mechanical Engineers
Regt	Regiment
RF	The Royal Fusiliers
RFC	Royal Flying Corps/Rugby Football Club
RGJ	The Royal Green Jackets
RHA	Royal Horse Artillery
R Hamps	The Royal Hampshire Regiment
RHF	The Royal Highland Fusiliers
RHQ	Regimental Headquarters
RIF	The Royal Inniskilling Fusiliers
RM	Royal Marine(s)
RMA	Royal Military Academy/Royal Malta Artillery
R Malay	The Royal Malay Regiment
RMC	Royal Military College
RMCS	Royal Military College of Science (Shrivenham)
RMF	The Royal Munster Fusiliers
RMO	Regimental Medical Officer
RMP	Royal Military Police(man)
RNF	The Royal Northumberland Fusiliers
ROLLR	Record Office for Leicestershire, Leicester & Rutland
RPL	Ramp Powered Lighter

RQMS	Regimental Quartermaster Sergeant (WO2)
RRF	The Royal Regiment of Fusiliers
RRW	The Royal Regiment of Wales
RS	The Royal Scots
RSM	Regimental Sergeant Major
RSO	Regimental Signals Officer
R Sussex	The Royal Sussex Regiment
Rt Hon	Right Honourable
RTR	Royal Tank Regiment
RUC	Royal Ulster Constabulary
RUR	The Royal Ulster Rifles
R Warwick	The Royal Warwickshire Regiment
SAF	Sultan (of Oman)'s Armed Forces
SANG	Saudi Arabian National Guard
SAS	Special Air Service
SASC	Small Arms School Corps
SBS	Special Boat Section (the RN's equivalent of the SAS)
Seaforths	The Seaforth Highlanders
Sec	Secretary
SITREP	Situation Report
SG	Scots Guards
SLR	Self-Loading Rifle
SMG	Sub Machine Gun
SNCO	Senior Non-Commissioned Officer (Sgt/CSgt/SSgt)
South Lancs	The South Lancashire Regiment
South Staffords	The South Staffordshire Regiment
SO1, SO2, SO3	Staff Officer Grade 1 (Lt Col), Grade 2 (Maj), Grade 3 (Capt)
Sp	Support
SQMS	Staff Quartermaster Sergeant (WO2)
SS	Steam Ship
SSAFA	Soldiers', Sailors', and Airmen's Families Association
SSgt	Staff Sergeant
SSI	Staff Sergeant Instructor
SWB	The South Wales Borderers
TA	Territorial Army
Tac	Tactical
TAER	Territorial Army Emergency Reserve
TAFA	Territorial & Auxiliary Forces Association
TAVR	Territorial & Army Volunteer Reserve
TAVRA	Territorial, Auxiliary & Volunteer Reserve Association
TD	Efficiency Decoration
Tech QM	Technical Quartermaster
TEM	Efficiency Medal
TEWT	Tactical Exercise Without Troops (see also JEWT)
TF	Territorial Force (forerunner of the TA)
TNKU	*Tentera Nasional Kalimanta Utara* (Indon tr: North Kalimantan National Army)
TNI	*Tentera Nasional Indonesia* (Indon tr: National Army of Indonesia)
Tpt	Transport

Trg	Training
TS	Transport Ship
TRH	Their Royal Highnesses
UAE	United Arab Emirates
UDR	The Ulster Defence Regiment
UKLF	United Kingdom Land Forces
UN	United Nations
USAF	United States Air Force
UVF	Ulster Volunteer Force
VC(I)GS	Vice Chief of the (Imperial) General Staff
VCP	Vehicle Check Point
VHF	Very High Frequency
VP	Vital Point
WAP	Western Aden Protectorate
WD	War Department
WFR	The Worcestershire & Sherwood Foresters Regiment
Worcesters	The Worcestershire Regiment
WO1	Warrant Officer Class 1
WO2	Warrant Officer Class 2
WRAC	Women's Royal Army Corps
WRMP	Women's Royal Military Police(woman)
WS	Wireless Set
WT	Weapon Training
WVS	Women's Voluntary Service
Y & L	The York & Lancaster Regiment
2IC	Second-in-Command
3IC	Third-in-Command
5 Innis DG	5th Royal Inniskilling Dragoon Guards

Index of Names and Places